Computer Animation Primer

Computer Animation Primer

David Fox and Mitchell Waite

McGraw-Hill Book Company

New York   St. Louis   San Francisco   Auckland
Bogotá   Hamburg   Johannesburg   London   Madrid
Mexico   Montreal   New Delhi   Panama   Paris
São Paulo   Singapore   Sydney   Tokyo   Toronto

Library of Congress Cataloging in Publication Data
Fox, David, date
    Computer animation primer.

    Includes index.
    1. Computer animation. I. Waite, Mitchell.
II. Title.
TR897.5.F68 1983   778.5'347'02854   83-7713
ISBN 0-07-021742-4

1234567890   DOC/DOC   8987654

ISBN 0-07-021742-4

ATARI is a registered trademark of Atari, Inc.
400, 800, 600XL, 800XL, 1200XL, and 825 are trademarks of
Atari, Inc. used by permission. BYTE/McGraw-Hill is not
affiliated with Atari, Inc., and Atari is not responsible for any
inaccuracies.

Editorial staff: Bruce Roberts, Peg Clement, Peg McCaulley, Stephen
    G. Guty, and Barbara B. Toniolo
Design staff: Ellen Klempner-Beguin and Mark Safran
Production staff: Ellen Klempner-Beguin, Jaymia Ryll, and Thomas G.
    Kowalczyk
Text set in Times Roman by LeWay Graphics
Printed and bound by R. R. Donnelley & Sons Company

The authors each dedicate this book, with love, to their parents.

David Fox
Mitchell Waite

Contents

Preface / xi

Preface

A squadron of spacecraft roaring through a star-filled void, a high speed chase through a canyon of eerie, snowcapped mountains, a man in a tuxedo juggling colorful geometric solids whose finale is a backflip into thin air . . . Are these segments from a George Lucas film or a Disney feature? No, they are scenes created entirely inside a computer using state-of-the-art advances in computer animation.

A small town, a man taking a brisk walk down the street, cars, trees, houses zooming by, a waterfall cascading into a valley, a bird flying across a blue sky, three dozen horses galloping in perfect unison, a forward dive into a channel of kaleidoscopic colors . . . Are these images from the same high tech computers? No, these startling effects actually take place on the screen of a low cost personal computer. They are programmed in BASIC (a popular computer language), and this book will show you how to create them.

Computer Animation Primer is actually two books in one. It is the first book to explain simply the details of the new high-tech computer animation as used in the film and television industry. It is also the first to show BASIC programmers how to create superior animation on a low-cost ATARI Home Computer (400, 800, 600XL, 800XL, 1200XL, and the rest of the XL models). Part I covers the theory and applications behind computer animation, including graphics hardware, software, and programming. Part II contains a tutorial describing animation capabilities of the ATARI Home Computers. In this way, the first half of the book will allow you to become familiar with what the computer animation professionals are doing and how they are doing it, while the second part will provide you with the necessary tools to try out some of these ideas at home.

We have also added special flip book movies to these pages. (Flip books are an old-fashioned way to do animation and are still fun to play with today.) When flipped, these pages will give you a taste of computer animation. You will find a sampling of animated segments from the best animation houses in the United States. They will provide you with a preview of the kinds of special effects that are in vogue today and the impact of computer animation. To see the animation in six films, flip right-hand pages from the back of the book to the front and left-hand pages from the front of the book to the back. The starting points of the films are as follows: Film 1, "Running Boy," page 393; Film 2, "Vol Libre," page 369; Film 3, "The Juggler," page 201; Film 4, "Panasonic Commercial — Paper Airplane," page 2; Film 5, "Times Square," page 218; Film 6, "Walking Man," page 316.

Throughout the text the illustrations are printed in black and white. Color renditions of most of the photos, Figures 5.20 and 5.21, and nine additional images appear in a 16-page insert located between pages **396** and **397**.

The chapters of Part I are organized as follows:

Chapter 1, "Animation Perspectives," discusses the theory behind basic animation, i.e., its mechanics and methods. We describe the general theory and psychology of animation — how the eye and brain may be fooled by the computer to perceive motion and how a computer program does the same thing by flipping frames. The chapter then describes the difference in approaches to animation between high tech and personal computers. We present a concise but intriguing history of animation, followed by a description of the computer applications that animation has made possible. Finally, we tell how YOU can get started in this amazing field.

Chapter 2, "Computer Animation Hardware," covers the computer hardware (the nuts and bolts) that makes computer animation possible. We discuss CRT's, stroke and raster graphics, pixels, gray scale, bit planes, frame buffers, and so on. This information will prepare you for understanding the next chapter and how the software tells the hardware to perform its graphic duties.

Chapter 3, "Computer Animation Software and Applications," covers the interesting secrets and tricks which the animation experts use today for creating their images. Included are descriptions of techniques used for defining objects with programs, transformations, achieving realism, removing hidden lines, shading, and various computer paint systems. We will preview some fancy animation equipment used in the film industry and contrast it with some low cost personal computer-based equipment developed by hobbyists. The making of a computer-animation-based movie *(TRON)* is highlighted to show you how the hardware and software fit together.

Chapter 4, "Personal Computer Animation Features," describes the 13 key capabilities available in many personal computers that make them suitable for animation. With this chapter, you can learn which features to look for when purchasing a personal computer for animation.

The second part of the book describes in detail how to do your own animation on the ATARI Home Computers. To accomplish this goal, we have included a number of impressive animation demo programs for the ATARI Computers that can be entered immediately into a computer and run, or just studied. In addition, there are a collection of special ''black box'' machine language routines that will give the reader the tools to harness some of the ATARI Computer's more advanced features. By black box, we mean that the programmer does not need to understand how the routines work to use them. Just plug a series of values into the routine from BASIC and watch the desired effect on the screen. We encourage people to use these routines in their own software, which they can then market. To make learning really easy and to avoid typing in the source code, all the software examples in the book are available on a diskette from Adventure International.

Here is a description of the chapters in Part II:

Chapter 5, ''Character Set Animation,'' covers the use of character set graphics in animation. We show you how to use the ATARI'S built-in character set for simple animation (such as birds flapping their wings), and how to create your own character sets for animation. This last technique allows us to create a man who gingerly walks across the computer screen. Next, we cover character set flipping, showing how to make 36 horses gallop on the screen at once. Finally, using a multi-colored character set (and a redefined display list), we show how to produce an arcade-like explosion on the screen, complete with sound effects.

Chapter 6, ''Color Register Animation,'' describes the use of ATARI'S color map. This color map is a high-tech feature which allows you to change the color on the screen almost instantly with one instruction and without redrawing the image. We first fill the screen with a hypnotic, ever-changing kaleidoscope of colors. A *Star Wars* type trench program is then created to demonstrate the effect of motion using color registers. This is followed by a program that displays a beautiful cascading water-fall in a peaceful valley.

In Chapter 7, ''Player-Missile Graphics,'' a distinctly ATARI feature, is covered. Players allow you to move animated objects on the screen without having to worry about erasing parts of the background. We'll provide you with a sample program of a bouncing ball to illustrate how Players work. True to cartoon reality, the ball even flattens when it strikes the floor!

Chapter 8, ''Using Machine Language Routines in BASIC Programs,'' uncovers the secrets of enhancing your animations with our black box machine language routines. These routines (which don't need to be understood to be used) are easy to enter from BASIC and bypass much of the tedious work that is required to animate Players. Players can be instantly moved anywhere on the screen, given a horizontal velocity, and automatically animated (using Vertical Blank Interrupts) with as many frames of information as you desire.

Finally, in Chapter 9, ''Creating a Scrolling Background,'' we will present the powerful techniques of fine scrolling and Display List Interrupts. The ATARI Display List will also be covered in depth. There is a demonstration program here which scrolls an entire suburban background across the screen at various speeds. In this chapter there is an impressive concluding animation demonstration program of a little man walking down the street, head bobbing, arms swinging. In the background, trees and houses with lawns and fences scroll by while numerous cars and trucks with roaring engines pass by in the foreground.

The pushing and shoving that goes on around an arcade game and the willingness of people to feed these machines a steady stream of silver, the millions of low-cost computer games sold for the home, and the popularity of special effects films all attest to the fact that a revolution in the video/graphics/film industry is upon us. It is our belief that graphics-oriented personal computers are forerunners of a new and exciting type of home entertainment. Film quality animation effects, perhaps created remotely and downloaded to your system via cable, will be combined with the arcade capability of your personal computer. The result will give you an interactive experience where you become the dominant player in a world of graphics figures and flashing colors.

This book is intended to inspire the development of high quality, graphics-oriented software for home computers, thus harnessing the animation potential of these marvelous machines and speeding us towards the future.

David Fox
Mitchell Waite

December 24, 1983

Acknowledgments

Saying that the creation of this book was a large project is a gross understatement. Not only did it require more than a year of work, but it also involved hundreds of hours of consultation, research, telephone calls all over the country, programming, programming, and more programming. In fact this book project had the creative support of more people than *all* our previous books combined. Therefore we would like to pause and express our sincere gratitude to everyone who contributed time and energy to this project.

First and foremost, we want to thank Annie Fox for her constant support and fantastic editing. Without her help, this book would not have been nearly so interesting and easy to read.

We would like to thank Steve Catechi, Adam Janin, Scot Kamins, Ph.D., Corey Kosak, Christopher L. Morgan, Alvy Ray Smith, Tandy Trower, and Lane Winner for their thoughtful, encouraging, and incredibly complete reviews of our manuscript.

We thank Clark Brown and Ted Richards of Atari for making their Dicomed film recorder available to us for our Atari screen photos, Jerry Jessop of Atari for keeping our equipment in good working order, and Chris Crawford of Atari for first turning us on to the animation power of the ATARI Home Computers.

We would like to thank the following people for their help in providing us with information and materials for the book:

Susan Anderson, Loren C. Carpenter, Pat Cole, Clark Higgins, K.C. Hodenfield, Andy Neddermeyer, Alvy Ray Smith, and Susan Trembly of Lucasfilm Ltd.

Richard Taylor, Arnie Sorenson, Bill Dungan, Art Durinski, and Lynn Wilkinson of Information International, Inc.

Bill Kovacs, Shirley Shackman, and Steve Cooney of Robert Abel and Associates

Ken Perlin of Magi (Mathematical Applications Group, Inc.)

Nelson Max of Lawrence Livermore National Laboratory

Wendall Mohler, Michael Bonifer, Mary Dill and Sue Muscarella of Walt Disney Productions

Judson Rosebush and Susan Bickford of Digital Effects

Peggy Allen, Ken Balthazar, Anne Bernstein, Harry Brown, Douglass Chorey, Paul Cubbage, Jerome Domurat, Ann Louise Gechman, Clyde Grossman, Bob Kahn, Ted Kahn, Peter Nelson, Jack Perron, Wanda Royce, Joe Steele, Larry Summers, Don Teiser, Marilyn Theurer, and Bonnie A. Umphreys of Atari, Inc.

Glen Entis and Carl Rosendahl of Pacific Data Images, Inc.

Dr. James F. Blinn and Charles E. Kohlhase of Jet Propulsion Laboratory

Philip Knopp of Gebelli Software, Inc.

John Williams, John Harris, and Gita Whelan of OnLine Systems

Bill Wilkinson of Optimized Systems Software

Jaime Cummins of The Solitaire Group

Joe Vierra, James Leatham,

Robin Ziegler and Bruce Merritt

Leo Christopherson

Nancy Bavor, Kate Kimelman, Anita Mosley, and Debbie Shepard of Stanford University Museum of Art

Roy Smith of Advanced Electronics Design, Inc. (AED)

Mike White of Valpar Corporation

Doug Carlston and Olaf Lubeck of Broderbund Software

John Loveless of Synapse Software

Patricia Glenn and Mary Lock of Penguin Software

Gary Kofler and Patrick Ketchum of Datasoft, Inc.

Cherie Bauman of Versa Computing, Inc.

Herman Towles and Patrick T. Garvey of Computer Creations

Allan Sadoski and Mary C. Whitton of IKONAS

Tom Gemighani of Spectacolor, Inc.

Colin Cantwell of Crystal Chip, Inc.

Jane Veeder and Phil Morton

Frank Dietrick of Real Time Design

Dick Shoup of Aurora Imaging

Louis Schure of New York Institute of Technology Computer Graphics Laboratory

Dave Eccles, Derek Lee, and Bruce Fox of Evans & Sutherland

Alice E. Ahlgren, Ph.D. and Mike Maldonado of Cromemco

Sharon H. Nelsen and Jody Peake of Tektronix, Inc.

Bill Kimberlin of W.A. Palmer Films, Inc.

Lynn Wedel and Sandy Vorheis of Apple Computer, Inc.

T. Barry Vincent of Commodore Computer Center

Sheri Correa of NorthStar Computers, Inc.

Ed Judd and Dennis Tanner of Tandy-Radio Shack

Jim Dugan of Texas Instruments

Grif Hamlin and Carolyn Robinson of The Los Alamos Scientific Laboratory

Everett S. Joline, Ph.D. of Aviation Simulations International

Robert Holzman and Guy M. Lohman of Jet Propulsion Laboratory

Stephen H. McDaniel of Hanna-Barbera Productions, Inc.

Bob Christanson of Quality Software

David Sosna of MGM

Allen A. Wall of IBM

Steve Sipe and David Luther of IMLAC Corporation

Jim Higgins of Colorgraphic Communications Corporation

Peggy Grim of Chromatics Inc.

Daniel Clark of Terak Corporation

Ted Dyer of Grinnell Systems Corporation

John Walker of Marinchip

Kim Hoeg of Strider Productions

Nadara A. Craun and Terry Hostek of Digital Engineering

Ray Slane of Aydin Controls

Frank Magalski of Industrial Data Terminals

Ed Dwyer of Matrox Electronics

Christel I. Kiefer, Jim Forbes, Don Lewis, and Rudann Clark of Hewlett Packard

James R. Smith of NASA — LBJ Space Center

Tom Crispin and Mark Nehamkin of Intek Manufacturing Company

Linda Buxbaum of Digital Equipment Corporation

We would also like to thank Peter Bloch, Larry Cuba, Thomas A. DeFanti, Louis Ewens, Godbout Computers, Allan Lundell, Tom Meeks, MicroPro, Mike Schmidt, Sean Turner, and J. T. Whitted.

And finally, we would like to thank the countless people who helped us but we failed to mention above.

Part I

Chapter 1

Animation Perspectives

Levon Klein knew very little about computer animation. He had heard that many recently produced television commercials and feature films were making use of computer-generated graphics, but he wasn't really sure what that meant. So computers could be programmed to draw pictures, so what? Being so uninformed on the subject, he couldn't figure out why his editor had sent *him* to cover the annual computer graphics conference meeting in his home town this year. He wondered about this as he walked up the auditorium's steep flight of steps, his press badge fluttering in the wind. In preparation for today's event, a film showcase of recent computer animation films, he had read everything he could get his hands on. Yet the written word hadn't been enough to enlighten him as to what all the excitement was about.

The guard at the door glanced at Levon's badge and with a disinterested nod, let him pass. Once inside the immense room, he began looking around for a place to sit. It was then that the enormity of the event began to sink in. Most of the auditorium's 10,000 seats were already filled with people. The air crackled with the electricity of excited anticipation. Someone with a staff badge walked up to the slightly stunned reporter and hustled him to a seat towards the front of the room.

Three movie screens occupied the stage. As he impatiently waited for the show to begin, he wondered once again what all the excitement was about. Even without a sense of the technology, the high tech jargon bandied about coupled with the tension in the room brought beads of sweat to Levon's forehead. At last the overhead lights dimmed, the projector rolled, and Levon took a deep breath as a brave new world unfolded on the screen.

His eyes stared at the screen, unsure about what to make of the images. The position of the camera placed the audience above a human figure standing on a grey checkerboard grid. As the camera floated down towards the ground, Levon noticed that the man on the screen, wearing a black tuxedo and top hat, was juggling three brightly colored objects — a red cone, a blue cube, and a green sphere. One thing that made this unlike any ordinary movie was the colors. They were all of an extraordinary intensity, brighter and purer than any Levon had ever seen on film. The

Film 4
"Panasonic Commercial —
Paper Airplane," Robert Abel and
Associates. To promote their new
stereoscopic television, Panasonic
commissioned Abel to produce a
computer generated film which really
showed it off. Their new television is
essentially a standard TV with a
connection for a pair of special glasses
which are synchronized with the
display. By flipping between the right
and left eye views every sixtieth of a
second, the viewer sees a full 3-D
scene. Directed by Randy Roberts.
*Courtesy of Robert Abel and
Associates.*

background sky showed a most beautiful sunset with a bright red tinge at
the horizon, blending upward into blue, then darker shades of blue, and
finally a star-studded black night. An eclipsed sun flared brightly in the
sky, lending an eerie quality to the images. The color was so intense, so
surreal, that he felt it was safe not to try to predict anything about what
would happen next.

Thus suspending the earth-bound laws of physics, Levon's gaze
returned to the juggler whose face was now coming into view. He saw
that this was not a man at all, and in that moment it became clear that
these computer people had done something revolutionary.

"What is going on?" Levon wondered out loud, not feeling prepared for what he was experiencing.

The juggler was not alive and yet he moved as if he were. As Levon
scrutinized him, he was hard pressed to explain the figure's origin. His
movements were too fluid for any robot, and every detail about him was
too flawless to have been hand painted. The man's face, for example,
possessed a manufactured quality, like a clothing store manikin, and
appeared android-like, totally devoid of expression, and too perfect to be
human.

Levon's puzzling over the figure was abruptly interrupted when
suddenly the scene shifted to a series of television commercials. Levon
recalled that he had watched these many times, but now he was amazed to
find that these images were all computer generated. Watching them at
home, he had just enjoyed their spectacular movements. Now he began to
appreciate the technology that had helped to create them.

The juggler appeared again, but this time the entire screen was
swimming with brilliantly colored geometric objects. One of them, a red
sphere, started flying towards the camera and Levon found himself
involuntarily ducking at the last moment. Never had he seen such realism
and such unlikely camera angles. He knew that what he was watching had
all been created by a computer, and that there was no live actor in a suit,
no real objects, no sun, no sky. All the objects and colors he was
witnessing were simply cold numbers, datapoints once nestled in the
vastness of a computer's memory banks, now converted to film images
for his entertainment. Levon was impressed in spite of, or because of this
fact, and the visual experience was absolutely compelling.

Another series of exceptional film segments flashed by, and then the
juggler's three geometric shapes reappeared on the screen. Rainbow
colors swirled through the objects as the camera moved to a point above
them. The scene suddenly changed, and the three objects became three
round dots sitting above three silver I's. The camera began to fly away
from the object, which gradually revealed itself to be a badge on one of
the juggler's lapels. Levon was stunned at the smoothness of motion as
the camera continued to retreat. The juggler just stood there blinking.
Suddenly yet casually, the juggler did something quite unexpected. The

Photo 1.1: This is the famous Triple I "Adam Powers Juggler" photo from the film "The Juggler." Created from a digitization of a human model in three dimensions, it is one of the first computer graphics images which comes close to passing the Turing Test for Realism. Except for the face (which looks some-what like a manikin), it is almost impossible to distinguish this juggler from a person on film! Triple I has created perhaps the most realistic images ever de-vised on computers. Because Triple I doesn't want the power of this film imag-ery to be lessened in any way, they are reluctant to allow it to be shown on video equipment. *(Courtesy of Information International, Inc. [Triple I], Culver City, CA.)*

figure in the tuxedo simply stretched out his arms, took one brave leap over his own head, and did a back flip, disappearing in a brilliant flash. All that was left above the grey checkerboard was his top hat which promptly tumbled to the ground, rolled around a few times, and came to a stop.[1]

The audience burst into spontaneous applause. Levon found himself wildly clapping along with everyone else, joining the roar of appreciation which now echoed across the vast hall. "So *this* is computer animation," he thought to himself. "How in the world did they do that?"

---

[1]To see the juggler do his disappearing act, flip the pages of the book. *(Courtesy of Information International, Inc.)*

1.1. WELCOME TO COMPUTER ANIMATION

Definition

an·i·ma·tion (an'ə ma'shən), n. 1. to breath artificial life into images for films or computer-generated displays. 2. a sequence of drawings, each slightly different from the preceding one so that, when filmed and run through a projector or when shown on the computer screen in rapid succession, the resulting figures seem to move, dance, or fly about. 3. a motion picture effect which can elevate otherwise mediocre films to financial success. 4. a technique, when combined with fast action and loud noise, which causes millions of people to drop billions of quarters into strange looking boxes.

This definition points out that we are a species of animation and special effects lovers. This has been the case since the days of the early cave dwellers, when flickering flames inspired a sense of wonder in young hearts. As children, we have always been fascinated with animation. Who cannot recall when hands held in front of lamp light created moving butterfly shadows and scary monsters on the wall?

Today the animation love affair has exploded with such intensity that the stars of movies are no longer actors and actresses, but rather behind-the-scenes complex computers and special effects technicians. To the new producers, the entertainment world has become a high-tech special effects race, with those having the best animation leading the pack. The producer with the fastest and highest performing computer will have the tool to make the flashiest special effects (although without a story to go with it, the film may barely break even). In fact, these days we can no longer go to a film and be sure that what we are seeing ever existed in physical space. As our juggler episode showed, it won't be long before discriminating between real actors and their computer-generated counterparts will be impossible. An entirely new chapter is being written in the film industry. It includes taking the finest aspects of the cliff-hanging adventure thrillers and science fiction films of old and remaking them using high technology's special effects. Likewise, the television industry is also utilizing the new products of computer animation. The best of today's animated television commercials are so well done that you can't even tell that a computer was involved!

1.2. OUR PREMISE

This is a book about computer animation. We have written it to fill a long existing void. For years, very few people could afford to do

computer animation. Skilled mathematicians and computer scientists were required to operate expensive, megalithic machines, and huge sums of money were needed to produce just a few seconds of animation. Consequently, the knowledge of computer animation remained cloistered, the exclusive domain of a small select body of professionals. This book is designed to change that because it was specifically written for the vast number of personal computer users across the country. Today, anyone who can afford to buy a good stereo system can afford to purchase a computer. With the advent of the microcomputer (a.k.a. personal computer, a.k.a. home computer), the rudiments of animation have suddenly become available to a vast body of consumers.

Therefore, a basic premise of this book is:

AS BIG COMPUTERS GOETH, SO DOTH THE SMALL.

In other words, some of what was being accomplished yesterday on expensive high-tech computers (i.e., highly technical, large, expensive, computers) can be accomplished today on low and moderately priced personal computers. To understand this transition from the few to the many, let's look at an example.

Today a high-tech computer suitable for animation of quality feature length films has a resolution of 1024 × 1024 pixels (dots) and a choice of over 16 million colors for each dot. Such a computer animation system might be based on a minicomputer like the DEC VAX 780, which alone costs more than $160,000.

A typical personal computer, on the other hand, has a resolution of 320 × 192 dots, can display as many as 16 colors and costs less than $800. Even though the cost ratio of these two systems is 200 to 1, the performance ratio, as we shall soon see, is much closer. The personal computer is generally much easier to control than the high-tech machine, particularly in the area of real time animation. Before we get too involved with the technical side of computer animation and explain how these two machines differ, we want to tell you how this book is organized and how to best use it.

1.3. ABOUT THE BOOK

We have organized this book into two main sections. Part I covers the theory and applications behind computer animation, including

graphics hardware, software, and programming. Part II contains a tutorial describing animation capabilities of the ATARI Home Computers (although some of the ideas can be implemented on computers which have features similar to the ATARI Home Computer). In this way, the first half of the book will allow you to become familiar with what the ''big boys'' are doing in the field of animation, while the second part will provide you with what you need to try out some of these ideas at home.

Flip Book

We have also added special flip book movies to the pages of this book. Flip books, an old-fashioned way to do animation, are still fun to play with today. On the upper page edges you will find an assembly of computer-animated sequences collected from the best animation houses in the United States. By rapidly flipping through the pages, you can preview the kinds of special effects that are in vogue today and get an idea of the vast power of computer animation. We have also put one of our ATARI animated figures in the flip book so you can see it work without the aid of an ATARI computer.

So now that you have an idea of what this book is about, it's time to plow forward, animated head first, into this exciting world of computer special effects and animation.

1.4. WHAT IS ANIMATION?

Animation is the process of creating images that appear to move. Motion pictures don't really move. Anyone that has looked at a piece of film knows that the medium is made up of many still images. From a strictly scientific standpoint, animation relies on the mechanics (and in a way imperfections) of the eye. When things move faster than a certain rate (between 18 and 24 times per second), a physiological phenomenon called *persistence of vision* comes into play and the motion tends to blur together. This happens because a single image flashed at the eye is retained by the brain longer than it is actually registered on the retina. Thus, if a second image is flashed within a certain minimum time (about 50 milliseconds), the brain still retains the last image and the two images may be combined. When a series of images is flashed in rapid succession, as is accomplished with a movie projector, the brain blends the images together. When these images are only slightly changed one to the next, the end effect is that of continuous motion. This very remarkable illusion is the perceptual foundation of film and television. (You can imagine that if the eye didn't have persistence of vision, the world would appear a strange place indeed.)

Animation can be created in several different ways, as we shall soon see. In each of these approaches, the number of images presented to the

eye in one second determines the "flicker rate" of the scene. Flicker occurs when the eye can detect the individual frames of the picture because the time between frames is too long or the degree of motion within consecutive frames is too great (e.g., a "pan" which moves too rapidly across a landscape). When this happens, the picture appears to strobe uncomfortably. Standard 35 mm film, the kind shown at movie theaters, uses a frame rate of 24 frames per second. This means that every second, 24 frames of information appear on the screen. At this rate, there is usually no visible flicker. In low-cost 8 mm camera film, on the other hand, the 18 frames-per-second rate makes the flicker of these films more noticeable. (A point of information: when a film is shown on television, there is a frame rate discrepancy. Television has a frame rate of 30 frames per second, however a film being broadcast usually was created with the 24 frame-per-second format. This conversion is accomplished by showing every fourth frame twice.)

The speed at which objects appear to move in an animation is a function of the number of drawings used to obtain a movement and the distance between the object's position in successive frames. For example, if we are animating a bouncing ball, the farther the ball has moved in each adjacent frame, the faster the ball will appear to travel across the screen. If there is too much distance between balls in successive frames, the ball will appear to jump from one spot on the screen to another, rather than move smoothly.

One can appreciate that a high frame rate can result in there being many frames. Consider a typical two-hour animated movie: 24 frames in 1 second is equivalent to 1440 frames in 1 minute. An hour's worth of animation, therefore, may have up to 86,400 individual frames. A two-hour animation would then need 172,800 individual frames! Before computers were put to work as animation machines, each of these frames had to be hand drawn, painted, and photographed. It is easy to see why animation is such a laborious task and how computers have opened the door to a whole realm of animation possibilities.[2]

[2]Even today's most popular animation computer (VAX from Digital Equipment Corp.) needs around 10 minutes to generate a single frame of animation for a high-resolution moderately complex scene. Thus five minutes of animation can take $5 \times 60 \times 24 = 7,200$ frames $\times 10$ min. $= 72,000$ min. $= 1,200$ hrs. $=$ fifty 24-hour days! Very complex scenes might take as much as four hours to generate each frame. By the way, a computer that could do this even faster and is now being used by a few of the really wealthy Hollywood studios is the Cray Research CRAY X-MP, which can do 100 to 200 million floating-point instructions per second and costs a mere $15 to $20 million.

What is an Animator?

Although some people consider an animator to be an individual who merely draws the individual frames of a film, giving some object the illusion of motion, nothing could be farther from the truth. An animator is actually an imparter of emotion (definition thanks to Alvy Ray Smith of Lucasfilm). The really great animators (Preston Blair and Frank Thomas, for example), are much more than great artists. Rather than just capturing the essence of a character in a static picture, they must also breathe life into two-dimensional images. The animator quickly sketches the different parts of the figure in motion using intuitive gifts. Assistants to the animators then convert sketches into final art. Although anyone can do a simple animation, the really great animations from studios such as Disney came from such highly gifted individuals. It is therefore unlikely that a computer will ever be able to automatically produce original animations which possess the depth of character of the classics. A human will probably always be needed to "start the ball rolling."

1.5. WHAT IS COMPUTER ANIMATION?

Computer animation is the process of creating visual movement through the use of a computer. There are two basic divisions of computer animation covered in this book. One is high-tech computer animation used for making films. The other is the low-cost computer animation used in the personal computer and video game area. The techniques and hardware involved in each of these areas differ greatly and consequently will be explained separately.

High-Tech Computer Animation for Film

Let's first take a look at how computer animation is used in producing effects on film. You know now that cartoon animation traditionally is done by hand-drawing or painting successive frames of an object, each slightly different than the preceding frame. In computer animation, although the computer may be the one to draw the different frames, in most cases the artist will draw the beginning and ending frames and the computer will produce the in-between drawings. (This is more generally referred to as *computer-assisted* animation, because the computer is more of a helper than an originator.)

High-Tech Computer Animation Programs

In full computer animation, complex mathematical formulas are used to produce the final picture. These formulas operate on extensive databases of numbers that define the objects as they exist in mathematical space. The database consists of endpoints, color and intensity informa-

tion, and so on. Highly trained professionals are needed to produce such effects, because animation that obtains high degrees of realism involves computer techniques for three-dimensional transformation, shading, curvatures, and so on. (This whole area of database animation will be covered in more detail in Chapter 3.)

High-tech computer animation for film involves very expensive computer systems along with special color "terminals" or "frame buffers." The frame buffer is nothing more than a giant image memory for viewing a single frame. It temporarily holds the image for display on the screen.

A camera can be used to film directly from the computer's display screen, but for the highest quality images possible, expensive film recorders are used. The computer computes the positions, colors, etc. for the figures in the picture and sends this information to the recorder which captures it on film. (Sometimes, though, the images are stored on a large magnetic disk before being sent to the recorder.) Once this process is completed, it is repeated for the next frame. When the entire sequence has been recorded on the film, the film must be developed before the animation can be viewed. If the entire sequence doesn't seem right, the motions must be corrected, recomputed, redisplayed and rerecorded. Obviously, this approach can be very time consuming and expensive. Often, computer animation companies first do motion tests with simple, computer-generated line drawings before setting their computers to the task of calculating the high-resolution, realistic looking images. These low resolution images can often be viewed in motion directly from the computer's screen. When these tests look right, the final scenes are computed with a much higher chance of success.

Personal Computer Animation

At the other end of the spectrum is animation done on personal computers. These may be for use in video games or educational programs. These low cost units (such as an Apple or an ATARI) have no frame buffer per se. Instead, their relatively small memory is used to temporarily store the image, and the television screen is used to display the animation.

The major difference between the animation generated on personal computers and that of most high-tech computers is that personal computer animation is presented in *real time*. This means that you see the animation as it is occurring on the screen as opposed to waiting for the filming process to capture all the frames. Real-time animation allows effects to be created and checked out almost instantly, which means that decisions about particular scenes can be made on the spot. On the negative side, since personal computers have fewer available colors and lower screen resolutions than the high tech machines, animations produced on them are lacking in these respects. Even if they had these

features, the lack of fast computing power would make the calculation of three-dimensional, shaded objects *highly* impractical. Most personal computer animations consist of two-dimensional, cartoon-like figures such as space ships, cars, and people and other simple objects running, bouncing, or flying across the screen. Occasionally, enterprising designers will create games on personal computers that have a third dimension, such as moving through a corridor or around a raceway, but this is the exception rather than the rule.

Personal Computer Animation Programs

The programs for doing computer animation on personal computers vary from very simple to extremely complex. A simple program could, for example, be written in BASIC. It might use a statement like DRAW 1 AT X,Y to draw a predefined object. The X and Y coordinates would be changed and the object redrawn at a series of new positions, moving the object across the screen. The next level of animation would be to animate the moving object itself (e.g., flapping a bird's wings or moving a figure's legs). This could be accomplished by substituting the object on the screen with a new, slightly different object (DRAW 2 AT X,Y), and then a third object is substituted (DRAW 3 AT X,Y), and so on. This is called real-time animation, and it is essentially the technique used in computer games and video arcades.

For microcomputers, non-real-time animation, the method used by the high-tech animators, is definitely a more complex and expensive approach to animation. As with the large systems, it involves drawing a detailed single frame, photographing it on film, or saving it on disk. This process is repeated until all the frames have been drawn. Ideally, the computer will control the camera so the operator doesn't need to do it manually over the many hours needed to shoot a short segment. In Chapter 3, we will show how an Apple computer is used for just such a process.

1.6.   A LITTLE HISTORY OF ANIMATION

Animation using machines has existed for over 150 years! The first animation device was called the Thaumatrope (pronounced THAW-ma-trope). See Figure 1.1. It was invented by an English doctor, John Paris, in the mid-1820's. The idea behind it involved using strings to twirl a disc with a different picture on each side. When the disc was twirled, you could see both pictures at the same time. The idea for the Thaumatrope probably originated from a spinning coin. When a coin is spun and viewed from the side, the eye's persistence of vision phenomenon makes the front and back images appear superimposed on each other. (Of course, if the inventors had an ATARI or Apple they could have filled the entire screen with Thaumatrope images.)

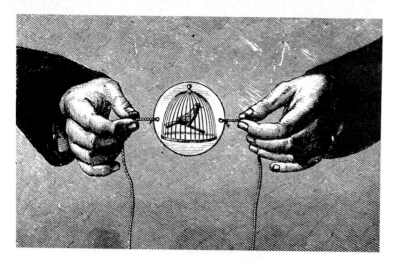

Figure 1.1: The first animation device — the Thaumatrope (circa 1826).
(Courtesy of Stanford University Museum of Art.)

The first device that actually produced animated pictures was the Phenakistoscope (fen-a-KEES-ti-scope, meaning motion shower), which dates back to 1832. (Its inventor, Joseph Plateau, was partially blind from staring at the sun for 20 minutes — he was testing persistence of vision!) This device consists of a notched spinning wheel attached to one end of a handle. The spinning disc contains a series of drawn images, each representing a frame of animation. To view the animations, you held the wheel in front of a mirror, peeked through the notches and spun the wheel. The notches acted like the shutter of a movie projector, letting you see each frame for only a fraction of a second rather than a continuous blur. See Figure 1.2.

Figure 1.2: The first animated picture — the Phenakistoscope (circa 1832).
(Courtesy of Stanford University Museum of Art.)

The next important animation tool, the Zoetrope, or Wheel of Life, was invented around 1834 by William G. Horner in England where people called it the wheel of the devil (much like some people today think video games are entertainment of the devil). It was redesigned in France by Pierre Desvignes in 1860. The Zoetrope is a revolving drum with images drawn inside. Like the Phenakistoscope, the Zoetrope too has equally spaced slits in the sides. When the drum is spun, the images can be seen when viewed through the slits. A record player can be substituted for the drum.

Figure 1.3: Zoetrope — the wheel of the devil. *(Courtesy of Stanford University Museum of Art.)*

Long before movie cameras were invented, a man named Eadweard Muybridge lined up a series of still cameras to photograph a horse as it ran down a racetrack. Muybridge had the camera shutters connected to strings across the track so that the horse's legs would trip each camera as it passed by. He was hoping to settle an argument between Governor Leland Stanford of California and another millionaire. Stanford claimed that when a horse is galloping it has all four feet off the ground at one time. As you can see in Figure 1.4, the Governor was right![3]

---

[3]In Chapter 5, we present an ATARI animation program that has three dozen horses galloping on the screen. The images for these horses were based on the original photographs by Muybridge. Imagine that . . . one-hundred-year-old data being used in a twentieth century computer program!

Figure 1.4: The horses of Eadweard Muybridge.

Photo 1.2: Muybridge's Zoopraxiscope. *(Courtesy of Kingston-upon-Thames Museum and Art Gallery, Stanford University of Art.)*

Figure 1.5: The Praxinoscope. *(Courtesy of Stanford University of Art.* [*Reproduced from Gaston Tissandier,* Popular Scientific Recreations, *N.Y., c. 1880, n.d.*] *)*

Later, Muybridge developed the Zoopraxiscope (zoo-o-PRAX-a-scope) to project his motion studies on a screen. He used glass wheels with his images running along the outer edge. The disk spun in a projector showing a repeating cycle of motion. A complete cycle, however, only lasted about half a second.

The Praxinoscope (prak-SIN-a-scope) was a device that replaced the Zoetrope's slits with mirrors. Inventor Emile Reynaud created a version of this device which projected images on a screen. Using long strips of translucent paper with frames drawn on them as film, he eventually went into commercial production and opened the world's first movie theater in Paris in 1892. The show lasted only a short time, but this didn't keep people from flocking to see it. In Chapter 9, we present a show of our own, the Great Movie Cartoon. Because it is programmed in BASIC and uses randomness to create figures, this show never repeats itself. Reynaud would have loved it.

Another popular way to produce animation in the old days was the flip book, technically called the Kineograph (KIN-e-o-graf). With this device you draw animated figures on individual cards, stack them up like a deck, and fasten them together. Flip through the stack with your thumb and watch the action. The flip book was patented in 1868 but was in use long before that. Today you can still find peep shows lined with Muto-scopes, Kinetoscopes, and Kinoras. You can cut out the animation frames in the pages of this book and assemble your own custom Kineo-graph to impress your friends.

Film animation cartoons were pioneered in 1908 by another Frenchman, Emile Cohl. He put black line drawings on sheets of white paper and photographed them. On the screen he used the negative to show white figures moving on a black background.

Animation techniques began to move forward as methods improved for producing movement and life-like motion. In the next few years a rush of new cartoons were produced, including Gertie the Trained Dinosaur (1909), and in 1917 the first really memorable cartoon character, Felix the Cat, was born.

The following techniques were devised and experimented with pri to the appearance of Felix the Cat:

- Silhouette films. Black cut-out figures were used on plain wl backgrounds to create the animation. These figures were easy to draw and move compared to line drawings.
- Phase animation. In this approach, sketches were superimposed on top of each other to save the repeated drawing of a background for different phases in the movement of foreground figures.
- Cel animation. This eliminated phase animation by using transparent celluloid for the foreground and simply superimposing them over an opaque background. Now foreground figures could be moved anywhere on the background and only one photograph was necessary.

In the early 1920s the work of drawing the backgrounds became separate from the main task of the animation movement. Specialists in backgrounds perfected the scenes that the animation people placed their figures upon. In a further division of labor, the time consuming task of taking the outlines of the figures and filling in the color on the transparency or cel was isolated. This separate job is referred to as opaquing or filling.

In 1928, Walt Disney Studios began turning out popular animated cartoons. From the early 1930s to the early 1960s, film animation produced a large number of notable and memorable cartoons that captured the imagination of the public. It became common to expect cartoons to appear at the beginning of every movie. Eventually these cartoons became a main part of television. Among the more popular were: Max Fleischer's Popeye (1933), Mickey Mouse, Snow White, Pinocchio, Fantasia, Dumbo, Donald Duck (all Walt Disney); Tom and Jerry (MGM); Woody Woodpecker (Walter Lantz); Bugs Bunny and Sylvester (Warner Brothers); Mr. Magoo (UPA).

In the 1960s two scientists from Bell Labs developed the world's first computer animations. Messrs. Zajac and Knowlton's achievements were in the area of abstract and texturized patterns. This set the early stages for later high-tech animations on computers by demonstrating that textures could in fact be modeled on a screen. Further research in the use

of computers for graphic output helped progress the field of computer animation. Some of the largest and best funded laboratories developed uses for computer animation including simulation of the flow of viscous fluids (Los Alamos), propagation of shock waves in a solid (Lawrence Livermore National Laboratory), vibration and landing of an aircraft (Boeing Aircraft).

Since the 1970s, computer animation has grown as computers improved and new techniques for manipulating pictures were discovered. Companies specializing in generation of computer animation have been founded across the country, including such names as MAGI, Information International Incorporated, Lucasfilm Ltd., Robert Abel and Associates, Digital Effects, etc. Television advertisers have become primary buyers of animation, using it to grab the viewer's attention and hopefully to get them to remember "the incredible commercial" they saw on the box. Whether they actually recall the name of the product is another story.

1.7.   HOW IS COMPUTER ANIMATION USED TODAY?

Today people are creating hundreds of applications for computer animation. Due to the popularity of the home computer, we are, in fact, in the middle of a revolution in computer animation applications. This low-cost device is driving manufacturers to pursue new techniques for the generation of visual effects. Since we are such a visual culture, the computer screen, the television screen, the photograph, and the movie screen are all blending together. In one study done by Sony Corp., it was discovered that people will more likely trust the validity of an image they see on television over one they see in a photograph or a book! Consequently, Sony is designing all its future products to output to the TV screen.

Applications in the Film Industry

Perhaps the fastest growing use of computer animation is in the film industry. Did you know, for example, that computer animation was used in filming the Death Star simulation at the pilot's briefing in the film, *Star Wars — A New Hope*? Although the rest of that movie's special effects utilized either hand-built models or conventional animation, these will not be the methods of choice for long. One very desirable but not yet fully realized approach is to use computer-generated animation to replace the hand-built models and hand-painted matte backgrounds. (See Photo 1.3 for an example of the kind of incredible realism that is possible today.) Since the resolution provided by computers can now exceed that of film and since a computer-simulated model destroyed by phaser never needs rebuilding, the computer approach promises to improve realism and lower production costs at the same time. Unfortunately, there is still an important drawback to all of this computer generated animation — it takes a long time to enter all the coordinate information for the model the first time. Luscasfilm, for example, finds that hand built models can be constructed, destroyed and reconstructed faster than a similarly complex model can be entered into the computer database. One potential answer to the database entering problem is to ''grow'' the model in the computer. If this were possible, we could let the computer create its own database, using brief guidelines set out by the designer of the model.

Photo 1.3: This X-Wing Fighter is based on those used in *Star Wars* films. The realism is so outstanding that the animated fighter can't be distinguished from a model of "the real thing." (*Courtesy of Information International, Inc.*)

One movie that used a large amount of computer animation (a full fifteen minutes worth) is *TRON* from Walt Disney Productions. Although Disney's Studio was the king of the mountain for many years, the rising labor costs of hand-painted cels made it too expensive to produce full-length feature animation cartoons. With *TRON*, Disney hoped for a major comeback. As shown in the figure below, *TRON* takes place inside a giant computer controlled by an evil master control program.

Photo 1.4: Light Cycles race through a simulated landscape of *TRON*. High-tech artist Syd Mead designed the vehicles. MAGI created the images. Notice the good shading effects. (*Courtesy of Walt Disney Production.* ©MCMLXXXII Walt Disney Production, World Rights Reserved.)

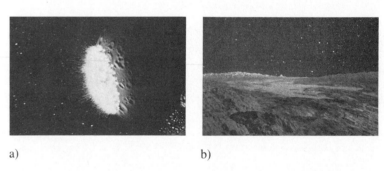

a)   b)

Photo 1.5: a) As we approach a dead, moon-like planet at 100,000 miles per hour, a wall of flames begins spreading over and melting its entire surface from the impact of the Genesis bomb. Four separate programs were used to generate this image. One produced a star field as seen from the star Epsilon Indi using an accurate database, another generated the planet and its texture mapped cratered surface, a third generated the fires, and a fourth composited all the elements together (with no matte lines). b) From the planet's molten surface has arisen *fractal mountains* (mountains developed from controlled randomness) and beautiful lakes and oceans. The faint blue atmosphere just beginning to form can be seen in the color insert. The once dead planet has turned into an earth-like planet because of the Genesis effect.

Even though *TRON* used the largest quantity of computer graphics to date, the most sophisticated computer graphics ever put on the big screen appeared in *Star Trek II — The Wrath of Khan*. The one minute segment showing the Genesis device simulation was produced in a five month period by the computer graphics wizards at Lucasfilm Ltd. Photo 1.5a) and b) show two scenes from this segment.

Although they are revolutionary in their own ways, *Star Wars*, *TRON*, and *Star Trek II* were not the first uses of computers in special effects movie making. Early science fiction used analog computers (called Scanimates) to produce weird bending and waving, mandala patterns, and other effects. These devices simply distorted the picture signal before it reached the screen.

The advent of the digital computer made it possible to have the picture exist completely inside the computer memory. Mathematical formulas could then be used to manipulate the scene and the result was some very realistic pictures with special qualities. The tradeoffs are that special formulas called transformations are needed (we'll describe these in Chapter 3) and that mathematically minded programmers must be enlisted. As we mentioned earlier, however, good animation requires artistic talent. As the computer software for doing these animations becomes more user oriented, it will become easier for non-computer oriented animators to create and control them. And who knows, after a while simple animations without much detail may become totally automated.

Applications of Animation in Space

In the area of space exploration, computer animation serves a most valuable function. The Pioneer and Voyager space probes launched by the National Aeronautics and Space Administration (NASA) were simulated by James Blinn (with Charles Kohlhase) at the Jet Propulsion Laboratory. (See Photo 1.6.) By putting physical laws of space and motion into the computer, NASA scientists could see what certain trajectories would look like and observe scenes as if they were riding on the vehicle itself! The computer also allows alterations in perspective which can place the observer behind the vehicle, thereby letting him view the entire scene with both vehicle and planet visible. These same simulation techniques were employed with the space shuttle to test its entry into the atmosphere. In addition, with the help of the computer, otherwise devastating errors could be dealt with safely. If, for example, a launch

Photo 1.6: NASA/JPL "Voyager-2 encounter with Uranus on 1-24-86." Computer simulation of the space probe as it approaches the planet Uranus in 1986. *(Courtesy of James Blinn with Charles Kohlhase of NASA/JPL.)*

orbit was mistakenly calculated, the worst that could happen was that all the dots in the picture turned fiery red as the probe crashed into the planet or shot off the edges of the frame buffer (i.e., into uncharted space).

Medical Research Applications

The use of animation in the medical sciences is becoming important in helping doctors and researchers to visualize the composition of a particular organ or bone structure. In Photo 1.7 we can see several views of the spine as modeled by a computer. The doctor can literally fly about the spine structure as if in a helicopter. Since it's formed like a wireframe model, this kind of visual examination actually permits the structure to be viewed more thoroughly. One day doctors might fly around inside our bodies, having first scanned them with whole body scanners to obtain cross sections. The computers would assemble these cross sections into a three-dimensional model, and physicians could then study the resulting computer images on the screen. By storing these images, patients could look at them too, and thereby better understand what the doctor had viewed. With this increased awareness of his body's disfunctioning, the patient might be better able to help in the healing process.

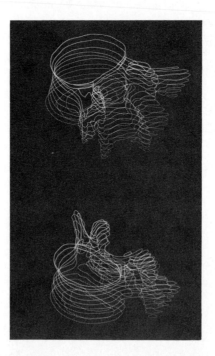

Photo 1.7: This high-resolution three-dimensional wire frame image of the spine shows two different views. (*Courtesy of Digital Effects — Rutgers Medical School, "Spine," 1981.*)

Sports Applications

Animation can be used in the sports world to help athletes improve their performance. Below, for example, we see four frames of a running man. It is possible to simulate a certain runner's motion, captured by computers and turned into images on the screen. Close examination could reveal imperfections in the runner's stride and suggest improvements that could make the difference between winning and losing. Similar ideas could apply to the swing of a tennis racquet, golf club, or baseball bat. The computer digitizes the swing or converts it into a form that the computer can manipulate, so it can transform it into a screen image. (We'll explain that in more detail later.) The trainer utilizing this technique could then modify the actual swing data base for a more ideal swing. The athlete would try to mimic the improved version of the swing while the computer monitored. Audio feedback would be provided to indicate the approximation of the athlete's swing to the ideal. The louder or higher pitch in the tone, the closer the approximation is getting to the ideal programmed case. The use of audio feedback removes the necessity of having to watch the screen at all times.

Photo 1.8: The Running Man shows the kind of detail possible in a frame buffer. Compare this with the Running Boy in the ATARI program in the second part of this book. *(Courtesy of Advanced Electronics Design, Inc. [AED].)*

Educational Applications

Computer animation has a promising future in the educational fields. Currently however, there hasn't been too much evidence of its use here. The main reason for this is that software companies with the ability to create impressive animation have not yet been willing to divert their programmers from the lucrative game market to the burgeoning educational market.

Computer animation will most likely be utilized to embellish teaching programs (courseware) on personal computers. To begin with, a classroom computer could be set up in an "attract" mode just like arcade games, presenting a beautiful visual stimulation that entices the student

to try a programmed lesson. Book covers are supposed to serve this function, and a computer screen could do it much better. See Photo 1.9.

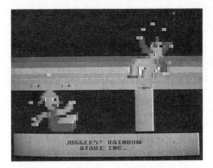

Photo 1.9: This is the opening screen from "Juggles' Rainbow," a program that teaches young children the difference between above and below, left and right. The balls are moving through space as music is played in the background. *(Courtesy of Atari, Inc. and The Learning Company.)*

Once the student has been lured by animation, more animation could be used to create an exciting lesson. For example, a program that might teach a student geography could simulate a spinning globe on the computer screen in real time, as shown in Photo 1.10. (This sequence was actually taken off the display of an ATARI Home Computer.)

Computer animation could also be used in the physical sciences. In physics, for example, it could effectively simulate motion on the screen. In this way we could plot the course of a comet as it passed by a planet, the flight of a bumblebee landing on a flower, or the path of a baseball as it flew towards the batter. All the vector arrows we see in physics books could be superimposed right on the computer screen, and as the object moved, these arrows would change, reflecting the object's changes in velocity, inertia, etc. Likewise, in the study of engineering, computer animation could be used to teach how robots walk, or in electronics, to show the flow of electricity in wire. The possibilities for using animation as a teaching tool are limitless.

a)   b)   (continued)

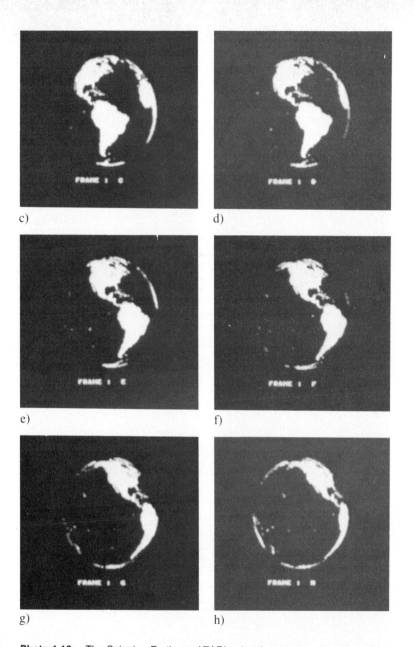

c)

d)

e)

f)

g)

h)

Photo 1.10: The Spinning Earth, an ATARI animation program, contains 24 frames worth of data (first eight frames shown here) showing the spinning earth. Each frame represents 15 degrees of rotation, so when the entire sequence is animated on the ATARI Home Computer, the effect of a spinning globe is produced. The original data base was on an IBM 370, had a 256 × 256 resolution, and occupied 196 K bytes of data. This program made a transition from the IBM 370 to a CP/M system to a Sorcerer and finally to an ATARI Home Computer. The resolution was lowered, and the pictures were compressed so they would all fit in the ATARI memory at once. Two screen pages were used. When one has been drawn, it is switched on and displayed while the other is being created by decoding the frame data. These photos illustrate the high-resolution effects possible on an ATARI Home Computer. *(Courtesy of Robin Ziegler. Created by Robin Ziegler and Bruce Merritt.)*

Engineering Applications

Engineering lends itself ideally to the capabilities offered in computer animation. Essentially, animation allows designers and engineers to visualize complex processes and to make better decisions regarding them. For example, animating a complex structure allows viewing from many angles and better understanding on all levels. Consider the three-dimensional wire frame photos below. Because of the transparency of a wire frame structure, the entire shape can be viewed at the same time. In addition, animation enables us to study structures in motion. Complex DNA strands, for example, are difficult to comprehend when viewed from a stationary position. When you see them rotating and spinning on the computer's screen, however, the underlying structure becomes clear.

In civil engineering, the ability to model a building before it is actually constructed can prevent enormous structural blunders from occurring. For example, a computer animation of the sun rising on an

Photo 1.11: The circular red and yellow wire frame structure (see color insert) is being rotated in three dimensions, showing a good variation of perspective. *(Romulus, "Merck Timoptol," 1981. Courtesy of Digital Effects.)*

office complex can be simulated. At the same time, an engineer could take a simulated drive down the road that was to be constructed as an entrance to the new building. The computer could display the precise angle of the sun as reflected off the building. If the subsequent reflection was found to be disturbing and potentially dangerous to oncoming drivers, the angles and position of the building could be adjusted accordingly before anything was committed to concrete and steel.

Air flight simulations on the computer are invaluable to the airframe engineer. (An airframe engineer designs the structural frames of aircraft.) Mathematical storms, wind shear, and icing effects are variables encountered in flight that can be simulated by computer. The airframe engineer can watch the flight path on the screen and judge the performance of the plane as the variables are manipulated.

The advantages of computer animation in engineering are limited only by your imagination and the power of the computer.

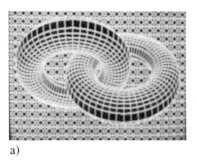

a)

b)

Photo 1.12: These two photos show the wire frame output of the NorthStar Advantage personal computer. This special computer has a built-in graphics BASIC (called GBASIC) and graphics calls in the operating system. *(Courtesy of NorthStar Computers.)*

Artistic Applications

The world of art is still a relatively unexplored territory for computer animation. For many years, artists in general shied away from computers as a medium of expression. Today, however, computers and artists are beginning to mix. Now with sophisticated paint systems that are more user-oriented, artists are discovering that a computer which offers a palette of 16 million color combinations opens new realms of visual delights. Once an artist becomes adept at using the new tools, the level of artistic productivity is greatly increased.

In Photo 1.13, an artist is using a computer system to change the appearance of a Victorian home. The house itself was entered into the computer from a photograph, and now that it is stored, the artist can play around with different elements that will alter its external structure. For example, the computer allows the artist to draw in different shrubs to see

how they enhance the house's image. Also, the computer makes experimenting with different color combinations child's play. In a matter of seconds, you can completely change the color of the house's entire facade.

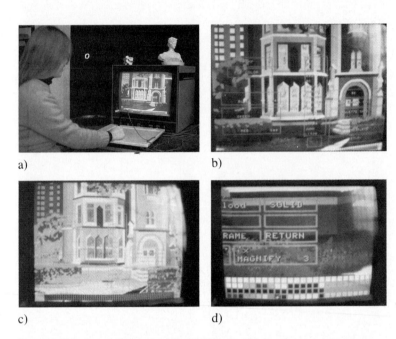

a)　　　　　　　　　　　　　b)

c)　　　　　　　　　　　　　d)

Photo 1.13:　Susan Bickford, of Digital Effects, NY, is using a paint system, Video Palette 3, a $125,000 system which includes a DEC 11/34 computer, graphics tablet, and paint software. Susan is using the system to paint a house that was digitized from a black and white photograph. She later added the color and the bushes in front (you can see the hand-drawn quality of the bushes). This system uses a palette of 256 colors, selected from 16 million. It allows you to vary the brush size and type, save images, and repaint these images in a different size and location on the screen. You can zoom in on an object or pan the scene to the right or the left. The menu for this paint system can be seen overlayed on the photo in b). In c) Susan instructed the computer to change the values in the color registers, producing a dramatic "digital effect on the final picture. This photo also shows the high quality of the characters on the screen's paint menu (see color insert). *(Courtesy of Digital Effects.)*

Another attractive art-oriented feature of computer animation and graphics is the degree of realism the computer offers over paint. Because the computer has higher resolution than film, visual effects can be produced which were never possible with the standard art media. Shades of color too subtle to be mixed by the unskilled hand can be created and recreated with ease by anyone. Blending of color can be controlled with incredible precision. Note the fantastic realism of the scene in Photo 1.14. Also note the wire frame structure of the paint tubes.

Photo 1.14: Triple I Oil Paint Tubes shows three oil paint tubes on a grid-like floor. From the tube in the foreground a luxurious flow of paint spills out into space. The first tube is represented as a wire frame image, revealing the underlying structure of the shapes used in computer graphics (see color insert). *(Courtesy of Information International, Inc.)*

Another example of what computer animation offers the artist is shown in Photo 1.15. These are two frames of a computer-generated film called "Carla's Island." In the film, the computer was able to simulate completely the sun setting and the water waves lapping at the shore. The light is absolutely perfect because each ray was traced from the viewer's eye to the object. At this time, the artist would need to have programmer assistance to help create a film of this complexity. In the future, using newly developed tools, however, the artist/animator will be able to create entire films without the aid of the computer programmers.

a)   b)

Photo 1.15: Illustrating reflectance and natural light, these two photos are part of the film "Carla's Island." The film shows a sun setting over ocean waves. The waves are playing on the beach, reflecting the sun's rays perfectly. For every pixel, a ray of light had to be traced from the viewer's eye out to the scene mathematically and further reflected from the water to another part of the scene. This was done using a vectorized ray-tracing algorithm on the extremely powerful Cray 1 computer. The clouds, waves, and islands were all created from mathematical formulas rather than from a data base. Different times of day were created from the same pixel data by changing the values in the color table as the picture was plotted on the Dicomed D-48. The sun was added as the picture was drawn. *(Courtesy of Nelson Max, Lawrence Livermore National Laboratory.)*

Computer animation may be used for other interesting artistic effects. It is possible to have the computer take one picture and convert it into another showing all the in-between stages as it's done. Frames from such a dissolve, or *object blend sequence,* are shown in Photo 1.16.

Not all artists need to be mathematically inclined to produce an effective animation on computers. The animation called Walking Man located on the page edges of this book was created for us by an artist who simply used cylinders of various sizes and forms to generate the shape of the mechanical man.

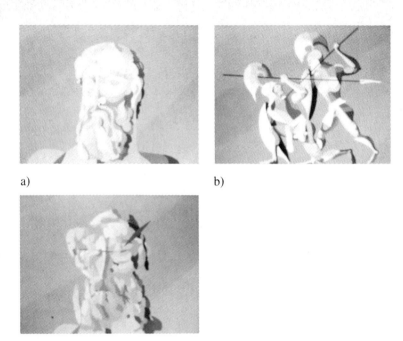

a)

b)

c)

Photo 1.16: These three key frames are from an object blend sequence and illustrate how the computer can merge one image into another. The sequence starts out as a detailed bust of a statue and goes through several frames to become two Grecian warriors fighting each other. This sequence is from the award-winning fully animated short entitled "Dilemma" (1981, Educational Film Centre, Great Britain and Computer Creations Inc., South Bend, Indiana). *(VideoCell™ animation courtesy of Computer Creations, South Bend, Indiana.)*

Animation in Advertising

Advertising is where the big money is being spent in computer animation today. This is probably because the special effects of computer animation are so novel that even people who don't like computers are attracted to them. Eventually computer animation may become so commonplace that advertisers will have to try something new to avoid the technocratic, overkill blues. Laser art and three-dimensional television may provide that novelty. Some computer graphics commercials, on the other hand, may not need anything new because they are already so slick; their computer influence is not readily detectable. It is possible that computer animation techniques will be used to produce exceptional graphics effects that would have otherwise required live action film.

One of the oldest uses for computer animation in advertising is the Times Square marquee display. This display is made up of thousands of light bulbs that are controlled by computers housed inside the building. In Photo 1.17 an artist prepares the display for a Timex watch ad.

a)

b)

c)

Photo 1.17: This three-frame sequence shows the famous Times Square display (by Spectacolor, Inc.) in New York. The 40 × 20 foot display has a resolution of 64 × 32 pixels. Each pixel is a four light bulb cluster (red-blue-green-white). The entire display consists of 8192 bulbs. A computer (a Mark 420 by World-Wide Sign and Indicator Corp.) is used to develop the individual frames that will be animated on the display. In photo a) animator Tom Gemighani is working on an ad for Timex watches. The screen of the computer simulates the resolution of the light bulb display. Tom is working from a storyboard (above the terminal) that tells what each frame of the animation should be like. He has control over each pixel in the display and uses the keyboard to fill in the colors he wants. The final squence will be displayed at 8 frames per second. Photo b) shows a "big apple" generated on the display, and photo c) is a close-up showing the individual bulbs that comprise the display. Note the "glitches" in the display where bulbs are burned out. *(Times Square display courtesy of Spectacolor, Inc.)*

The opening sequence of the popular television series, *Nova*, incorporated some fantastic animation from New York Institute of Technology. This group, located on Long Island, is one of the hotbeds of computer animation research. Photo 1.18 shows the section of the scene where the galaxy that had filled the screen a moment ago begins to shrink leaving the letter "O" (in the word NOVA) to grow and encompass the entire screen.

Photo 1.18: This is a frame from the NYIT-produced opening sequence of *Nova*, the popular PBS television program. *(Courtesy of New York Institute of Technology, Computer Graphics Lab. Graphics by David Geshwind.)*

An advertisement for a radio was completely produced with computer animation using a rather old-fashioned yet extremely effective approach (see Photo 1.19). A digital plotter (device for drawing lines on paper under control of a computer) was employed to plot each frame of the ad on paper. The paper images were then photographed through colored filters until the finished ad was created.

Photo 1.19: In this advertisement for a radio, a standard line plotter was used to draw each frame of this sequence with black ink on white paper. (A line plotter is a device that draws lines on a large paper surface in response to commands given to it by a computer.) Various color filters were then used to photograph the image onto film. The filters were placed in front of the line drawings, and then the photographs were overexposed, giving a candy apple neon effect to all the lines. (Separate drawings were created for each color.) The car's dashboard was painted with conventional techniques and matted in with the computer-generated drawings. What makes this sequence amazing is that the equipment used to create it, an HP Desktop Computer, is quite an affordable machine. *(Computer graphics by Colin Cantwell. Courtesy of Marks & Marks.)*

State-of-the-Art Computer Animation Center

One of the most prestigious computer graphics houses, where the first computer graphics paint system was developed (more on that soon) and from which many experts got their start, is the New York Institute of Technology (NYIT) Computer Graphics Lab. Manned by a team of over 60 employees, and housed in a pastoral setting, some of the most exciting and realistic computer graphics ever imagined have been created here. Privately funded, the founding fathers of the NYIT system were Ed Catmull, Alvy Ray Smith, Malcolm Blanchard, and David DeFrancisco, who all went on to work at Lucasfilm Ltd.

NYIT probably has the largest and most extensive graphics environment in the world. To display and hold their graphic images, it has over twenty *visible* frame buffers (frame buffers with a separate processor and video output) and more than fifteen *blind* frame buffers (large blocks of memory with no video output). NYIT also has an impressive array of large, medium, and small DEC computers. To store the completed images, they have three 2 inch video tape recorders. Connected with a private animation house and video production facility, NYIT is responsible for some of the best video animation yet to appear on a screen. In fact NYIT has produced several computer-animated commercials that are so good that it is impossible to deduce that a computer was on the production payroll. Examples of these are: VW Does It Again, Lincoln Center Live, Nova Opening, Walter Cronkite's Universe.

Whereas NYIT aims for high-quality video graphics suitable for television (525 line), other computer animation centers, such as Lucasfilm, are geared for super high resolution for film. Towards this end, Lucasfilm is developing a laser printer capable of directly drawing images on film, thereby eliminating the degradation caused by filming off a CRT screen (we'll explain what a CRT is in Chapter 2 — for now it's just like a television screen).

Biological Simulation Applications

One growing application of computer animation is in the simulation of how molecules are formed. In most cases, molecular structures are inferred from special x-ray techniques. By shining x-rays on the specimen, a shadow or flat imprint of the internal composition of the molecule is obtained. From this imprint, mathematical relationships between the various parts of the molecule can be generated and fed into a computer. Once the database for the molecule is inside the computer, animation and graphics can be used to draw it on the screen and rotate it to various viewing angles. Photo 1.20 shows a virus that was modeled in the computer. Note the fabulous detail and fine shading that the computer graphics were able to produce.

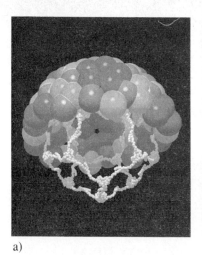
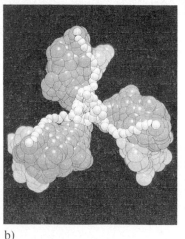

a)   b)

Photo 1.20: Photo a) is a computer photograph showing a hemisphere of 90 of the full 180 amino acid subunits contained in the protein coat of the tomato bushy stunt virus. X-ray crystallography was used to reveal the basic structure of the virus. Nelson Max then used this information to create the model. Hidden surface computations, which give the outlines of the visible parts of the spheres, were done on the CDC 7600 at the LLNL Computer Center. Color shading and highlights were calculated on a Sperry-Univac V75 minicomputer and then plotted on a Dicomed D-48 color film recorder, which uses a high-resolution black and white CRT tube. Color filters were used while transferring the image to film. A special program used to produce the visible surfaces called ATOMLLL was employed. ATOMLLL is adapted from a similar program called ATOMS developed at Bell Labs. Spheres are divided into trapezoids of vertical slices in the ATOMLLL algorithm. Nelson Max added code that allowed shading and light reflection. The shading took five minutes to compute (4096 × 4096 resolution). Photo b) shows three of the red protein subunits in greater detail. The big red spheres from a) are broken down into greater detail where each smaller sphere represents an individual amino acid. Although the yellow spheres appear in both pictures, it is now apparent that the yellow chains are wrapped around a three-fold helix. The pink regions of the protein extend beyond the shell of the virus and are not indicated in a). (See color insert.) *(Courtesy of Nelson Max, Lawrence Livermore National Laboratory.)*

Arcade Game Animation

Arcade games found at bars, pizza parlors, and shopping centers are among the most sophisticated examples of real-time animation you can find. Our earlier explanation of computer animation mentioned that personal computers take advantage of displaying action on the screen as it is occurring, rather than using the display and film approach of the high-tech computers. The arcade games utilize very sophisticated microprocessors and computer technology to achieve their effects. Anyone who has played some of the newer high-speed arcade games knows that the action can be so exciting as to actually cause dizziness and elevations in blood pressure.

One car-racing game has the player looking out the front window of a car, steering wheel clutched in sweating palms. While you are in the

driver's seat, you rapidly tear around the corners of the racetrack. Houses and trees zoom by the screen edges at incredible speeds, while other racing cars pass you and smash into your car causing it to careen off the road and crash in a screaming tangle of exploding light and sound. (This is definitely not a game for someone with a weak heart!) Other games have you piloting a jet over complex futuristic terrain while being showered with flack and attacking rockets. The perspective in these games is so engrossingly real that the playing time seems like seconds instead of minutes. Technically, these games are able to achieve real-time animation via custom high-speed circuits and non-standard programming techniques.

1.8. GETTING STARTED IN ANIMATION TODAY

Now that you have seen what can be done with animation you might well be wondering "How do I get started?" The answer depends on what kind of animation you want to explore. There are about four general areas to examine: personal computer animation at home for fun, personal computer animation for profit (i.e., writing games), arcade game animation, and high-tech animation for the film or advertising industry. Let's take a look at each of these.

Personal Computer Animation for Fun

If you wish to simply play with computer animation on your own computer for fun, your task is relatively simple. As we explain in Chapter 4, plenty of home computers will give impressive animation effects without much programming required. You will probably want to do real-time animation; home computers are set up for that. You will also probably want to start by learning a computer language such as BASIC, Pascal, or Logo, because these languages are relatively easy to learn and apply. (Of all three, Logo is the easiest, BASIC next, and then Pascal. However Pascal is probably the most powerful for animation.) Finally, you will want to take a close look at purchasing a computer that has good color capability, has a fast display, has a selection of powerful graphics-oriented languages, and allows custom character set graphics (see Chapter 4).

You could produce non-real-time animation at home on a personal computer too. This will require more investment in hardware (a camera, filters, special motors for turning them, etc. — see Chapter 3) and some knowledge of graphics transformations (which are really not too difficult to understand). Of course, you must have a fundamental knowledge of computer graphics. This book will aid in your understanding of graphics and the use of ATARI products. *Computer Graphics Primer* by Mitchell Waite (Howard Sams & Co., Indianapolis, IN) will help in your discovery of Apple Computer's graphics.

Personal Computer Animation for Profit

If you want to write computer games for personal computers that effectively use animation, your task will be a bit tougher. You need to know a high-level computer language such as BASIC or Pascal and probably assembly language (the programming language of the micro-processor). You need to know assembly because good animations must be *fast,* and BASIC (and sometimes even Pascal) lacks this high speed. You should also look at Forth and C, two high-speed languages that are now available for many personal computers. You will also need to play around with games already on the market and at arcades to get an idea of what people are looking for.

Arcade Game Animation

If you want to do animation on arcade games, you'll need to learn assembly language for several of the more popular microprocessors. In addition, you will need to be well versed in electronics because these games pull out all the technological stops to obtain an effect. You might also need to understand something called bit-slice microprocessors, as well as the Forth language. Forth is a tricky, powerful, exclusive (bordering on religious) language that is also extremely fast. If you don't intend to do all of this as an independent agent, it would help to get a position with a company that programs and sells arcade games. A job with an outfit like that might enable you to learn by osmosis.

High-Tech Animation for Film or Advertising

If you wish to get into high-tech computer graphics, such as the kind Lucasfilm uses, then you'll need to learn the language C and frame buffer technology. Most of the animation houses across the country use large, expensive Digital Equipment VAX or similar minicomputers hooked up to a commercial or custom frame buffer. Some universities have similar computers you could study on. Even if you had access to one of those, most of the software for doing animation on these machines are custom-made, one-of-a-kind products. One solution would be to go to work for a company that makes frame buffers or computer graphics terminals.

The Bottom Line

Obviously there is no right way to get started in computer anima-tion. The best approach is to absorb everything you can about it. You can attend the SIGGRAPH[4] conventions that occur each year around the end of July and rub shoulders with the computer graphics pros.

---

[4]SIGGRAPH Conference Office, 111 East Wacker Drive, Chicago, Illinois 60601, (312) 644-6610, Telex: 25-4073 SBA.

We'd like to see you get your own computer and start programming away in the haven of your home. In this way you can create a computer animation that may impress someone enough to give you a job or to buy your computer game. Who knows, one day your animations may be viewed across the country either on film or on a computer screen. If you study personal computers in depth, you will be in a position to write special effects that have never been seen before. For example, one student in a computer graphics class wrote an ATARI program that simulates three dimensions just like the old three-dimensional movies, using a pair of red/blue glasses! Good luck and happy animating!

Photo 1.21: Pyramid. *(Courtesy of Information International, Inc.)*

Chapter 2

Computer Animation Hardware

In the previous chapter we explained the theory of simple animation. We covered the techniques behind hand-drawn animation as used for years in the film industry and (briefly) the differences between high-tech and personal computer animation. Now we are ready to take the next step by examining the hardware (machinery) that is necessary to achieve these animated wonders.

Animation is the most complex and technically sophisticated of all possible computer graphics applications. This being the case, solid grounding in computer graphics hardware is the best way to get started in learning about computer animation. In this chapter we will answer the question "What are the devices that make animation on computers possible?"

Since computer graphics usually starts with a drawing on a computer screen, we will first learn how the hardware of the graphics machine draws on this screen. We will cover the different technologies found in computer graphics (stroke and raster), as well as bits and pixels. We will also be examining how the gray scale works, where color fits in, and how character graphics are done. Finally, we will be presenting material about the purpose and technology of digital frame buffers, the encoding of pictures, video mixing, color in a television, personal computer graphics hardware, and graphics peripherals.

2.1. THE CRT CANVAS

In computer graphics, the most popular "canvas" on which the computer does its painting is called a *CRT* (cathode ray tube). [1] Although we are no longer in the Flash Gordon Age of Rays, or the Edison Age of

---

[1]Computers may also draw on paper using special devices called digital plotters. These plotters are very slow devices and therefore less popular than CRTs. They are useful, however, when a hard (tangible) copy of the graphics is needed. (We'll be discussing them later.)

Tubes, this device persists because as of yet there is no better way to draw with a computer. (Solid-state flat panel displays are still a number of years away.)

As shown in Figure 2.1, the CRT (pronounced C-R-T) is a glass tube-like affair with one large flat end and a long neck. All air is removed, thus the inside of the tube is a vacuum. At the neck end of the CRT is a device that emits billions of electrons. The electrons, like tiny bullets, are shot out towards the flat face end of the tube in a narrow beam, much like squirting water from a hose. The interior side of the CRT's face is coated with special materials (phosphors) that emit light when struck by electrons at high velocity. (Although this special coating never wears out, too many electrons striking the same spot for a long time can burn the phosphors.) At the point at which the beam of electrons strikes the face of the tube, a tiny spot of light appears. This narrow beam of electrons is the brush with which all images are created on the screen.

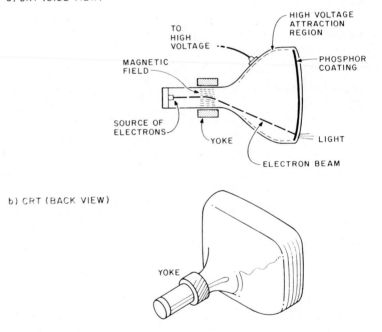

Figure 2.1: The CRT is revealed.

Controlling Our Beam "Brush"

Now that we have a brush (our electron beam) that will draw on the screen, we need a way to control its position. This can be done by putting an electronic field around the neck of the tube at the place where the beam starts its journey.

Just as a magnetic field pulls the needle of a compass, an electric field will bend the electron beam as it travels towards the screen. The goal is to deflect the beam in a predictable manner that can be controlled by external signals. (The problem associated with this is akin to trying to move a hose that is squirting colored water in such a fashion that it draws a picture on the grass.) There are two ways to accomplish the deflection. One is by using metal plates inside the neck of the tube and applying an electric voltage to them. The other involves using wire coils wrapped around the neck and applying electric current to them. The use of coils is the preferred method for televisions and computer graphics CRTs, whereas plates are employed more often for deflection in *oscilloscopes*. (Oscilloscopes are instruments used by technicians and engineers to study the images of electronic signals. We describe them in this section to help explain the evolution of the graphics computer.)

There are two sets of plates or coils on the tube, one vertical set and one horizontal set. In terms of plates, if we apply a positive voltage to the right horizontal plate, the beam will be pulled (deflected) to the right. Reversing the voltage (positive on left) pulls the beam to the left. A similar effect occurs with the vertical plates, and the beam is deflected up and down. See Figure 2.2.

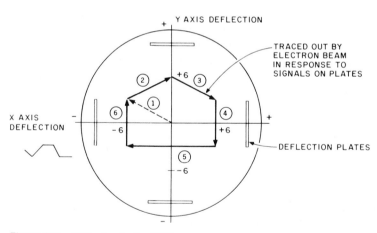

Figure 2.2: Deflection in the CRT.

As the beam moves across the face of the CRT, it also causes the spot of light to move, leaving a trace of light behind it. The trace of light then corresponds to the electric signals that are deflecting the beam. Basically, the position of the spot of light is proportional or analog to the signals controlling it, and consequently we call such signals analog voltages. For example, the greater the amplitude (strength) of the voltages applied to the vertical plates, the higher up the beam (and dot of light) moves on the screen. By applying repetitive voltages to the plates

of the CRT and by varying the amplitude and repetition rates (number of times the voltages change amplitude per second), it is possible to actually see these signals on the face of the CRT. This is the designed purpose of oscilloscopes as a service and research tool, although for many years underground artists used them to generate some beautiful effects by combining special signals on the face of the scope. See Photo 2.1 for an example of this.

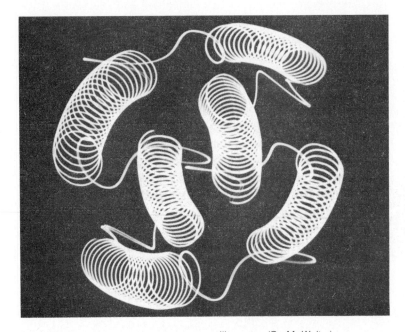

Photo 2.1: Lissajou art pattern on an oscilloscope. *(By M. Waite.)*

Drawing on Our CRT with Analog Circuits

Now that you have an idea of how the beam is deflected and moved about, let's see how we can capitalize on this method to draw an actual shape on the face of the CRT.

Take a look at Figure 2.3. It shows the face of the CRT, the horizontal and vertical deflection plates, and two signals applied to the two sets of plates. The two signals are called waveforms. Each waveform has been carefully produced by special analog signal generation circuits. The signals repeat over and over. One of the signals goes to the electron gun and can turn it on and off. When the signal is steady (indicated by a horizontal line on the waveform), the beam holds its position steady on the screen for that axis. When the signal is ramping (indicated by an angled line going up or down in the waveform), the beam moves from left

to right, or up and down depending on the plate receiving the ramp.[2] In essence, while one signal holds the beam steady on one axis of the screen, the other is moving it in a straight line. By properly coordinating these two signals, we can construct a box shape, the shape of a house as shown in the example, or any shape at all, for that matter. (If you follow the signals and the numbers on the figures you will see how the beam is traced out on the screen.)

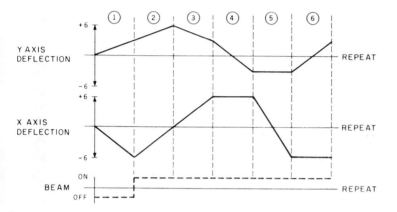

Figure 2.3: Drawing a house on the CRT with analog circuits.

As you can see from the figure, even drawing a shape as simple as a two-dimensional house requires fairly complex waveforms. As the shape we wish to display increases in complexity, so do the signals needed to create that shape. Although it is a simple matter in electronics to generate symmetrical, repetitive waveforms, the generation of irregular asymmetrical repetitive signals like the kind used in our example is costly and difficult. Sophisticated generation circuits are required, and herein lies the problem. Such circuits are complex, bulky, expensive and unreliable. Because they are analog, they require passive components (resistors, capacitors, etc.) and are sensitive to heat, therefore varying in value with the passage of time. Consequently the display image would be subject to change, requiring repeated trimming (adjusting) of the components. And yet, for many years, despite all of these inherent problems, analog circuits were the *only* approach in use for generating graphic displays. With the invention of the digital computer, however, a major shift occurred in computer graphics that doomed a lot of expensive analog equipment to the already cluttered closets of the research laboratory.

---

[2]For the purposes of the discussion, the waveforms in the figure are actually a distortion from what would be used in a real application.

2.2. STROKE GRAPHICS

Digital computers marked the next logical step in graphics evolution by replacing the analog circuits of the display with digital numbers. Digital numbers are special in that they are made up of several signals. Each signal is very simple and has only one of two possible states, ON or OFF. Since they do not cover the smooth range of values that the analog signals cover, they are not subject to the drift and reliability problems. To create a number with the digital values, several ON-OFF signals must be combined. This is done to represent numbers using the binary numbering system. (Binary is just another way to count. The decimal system counts to ten before creating a new digit; the binary system counts to two before creating a new digit.)

Imagine that each digit of a binary number is a switch. When the switch is ON the digit is called a 1 and when it is OFF, it's called a 0. The number of binary digits that are used controls the size of the binary value.

Below we show some values of a four-digit binary number. On the left are the switch settings, in the middle is the binary representation of these, and on the right are the decimal equivalents of the binary numbers.

Switches					Binary					Decimal
OFF	OFF	OFF	OFF	=	0	0	0	0	=	0
OFF	OFF	OFF	ON	=	0	0	0	1	=	1
OFF	OFF	ON	OFF	=	0	0	1	0	=	2
OFF	OFF	ON	ON	=	0	0	1	1	=	3
OFF	ON	OFF	OFF	=	0	1	0	0	=	4
		·								
		·								
		·								
ON	ON	OFF	ON	=	1	1	0	1	=	13
ON	ON	ON	OFF	=	1	1	1	0	=	14
ON	ON	ON	ON	=	1	1	1	1	=	15

Thus, instead of the analog circuits generating complex waveforms, the digital computer manipulates the binary ON-OFF values. The computer works directly with numbers instead of signals and uses mathematics in a more practical fashion. Unfortunately, the use of digital computers created a new problem: they produce binary voltages but the CRT requires analog voltages. Therefore, an additional device called a digital-to-analog convertor (DAC) was installed between the digital output of the computer and the analog input of the CRT. The DACs converted the binary ON-OFF language of the computer into the smooth analog signals needed to bend the electron beam.

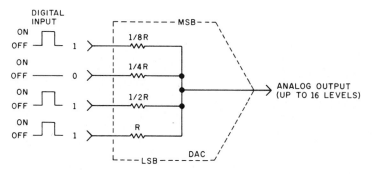

In Figure 2.4, we see that a DAC is nothing more than a series of resistors hooked together to sum the various binary values. Each resistor is chosen so that the binary digit attached to it contributes a certain amount of electricity that is proportional to its weight in the number. This means that the topmost significant digits of the binary value have a bigger effect on the final voltage than the lower, least significant digits.

Figure 2.4: How a digital-to-analog converter works.

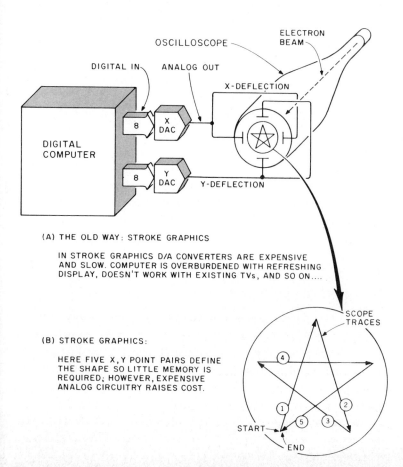

(A) THE OLD WAY: STROKE GRAPHICS

IN STROKE GRAPHICS D/A CONVERTERS ARE EXPENSIVE AND SLOW. COMPUTER IS OVERBURDENED WITH REFRESHING DISPLAY, DOESN'T WORK WITH EXISTING TVs, AND SO ON....

(B) STROKE GRAPHICS:

HERE FIVE X,Y POINT PAIRS DEFINE THE SHAPE SO LITTLE MEMORY IS REQUIRED; HOWEVER, EXPENSIVE ANALOG CIRCUITRY RAISES COST.

Figure 2.5: Stroke graphics using DACs.

Figure 2.5 shows the complete DAC-based graphics computer. Let's see how to draw with it. To begin with, pairs of numbers (in binary) representing the voltage values of the endpoints of the shape's lines are put in the computer's memory. For example, using our previous figure of the house which was painted with the analog circuits, we would set up the binary voltage pairs to correspond to the values in the figure, i.e., the first pair would be $-6 / +3$, the next $0 / +6$ (X values given first), and so on. (If you're interested in how to do negative binary, see *Microcomputer Primer* by Mitchell Waite and Michael Pardee, Howard W. Sams and Company, Indianapolis, IN.)

The computer feeds the binary endpoint pairs to the DACs, and they in turn convert the binary values to analog voltages that are sent to the deflection plates. This technique is referred to as stroke graphics because in a single stroke, the beam draws a line from the last point on the screen to the next point. The computer only has to deal with line segments. This stroke approach is also called vector graphics, a vector being a line defined by a start point and an endpoint. The shape drawn with the vector display consists of a list of endpoints defining the shape. To add a new piece to the display, the computer would generate new endpoints and insert them in the list. Moving the shape on the screen requires that some offset value be added or subtracted to all the values in the list. With the development of vector displays, life for the graphics computer user became much easier.

The vector approach ushered in a new era of capability. CRTs and computers began to be used for radar displays, for modeling mathematics, and for revealing the insides of molecules. Although the vector approach allowed dramatic displays and is still in use, it has a serious drawback. Like the analog circuits described earlier, high performance DACs suitable for good quality graphics contain analog circuits that must be adjusted, are temperature sensitive, and relatively unreliable. Therefore DAC-based graphic computers are expensive and utilized only when money is not a primary concern.

2.3. RASTER GRAPHICS

The most popular approach to computer graphics, known as raster graphics, is based on ideas similar to the weaving of rugs. In weaving, an image is created by many strands that all run in lines in one direction. By dividing individual lines into segments of color and coordinating them to coincide with adjacent lines above and below, or right and left, a very beautiful pattern can be formed.

In computer graphics, the CRT beam can be deflected in a similar weaving pattern for drawing on the screen. The weaving pattern is referred to as a raster. In raster scanning, the CRT beam is deflected in a weaving pattern that zig-zags across the screen and down, many times

per second (see Figure 2.6). A standard television also uses raster scanning. The actual lines are visible when you look at the screen at close proximity. For the purpose of the following discussion, when we talk about the raster display, consider that it applies to the television display. (The television has additional components that will be described later in more detail.)

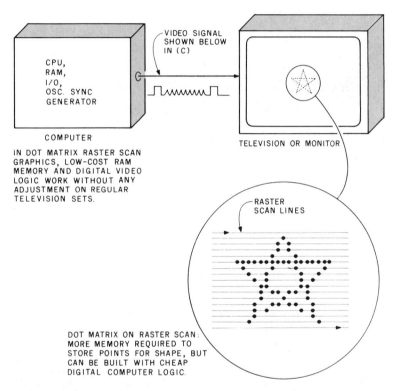

Figure 2.6: Raster scanning.

Basically, the graphics computer draws on a raster-scanned screen by keeping track at all times of where the beam is in its scanning field. If it can turn the beam on at the proper location on the raster, a picture can be formed. Because there are a limited number of lines in the display, a closely scrutinized picture will appear to be made up of a series of dots. If there are enough lines and you don't observe from too close a vantage point, however, the individual picture dots will blend together and a finely detailed image will result.

How does the computer know where to put the dots so as to create the image? And how does it get the raster on the screen in the first place? The answer to these questions is found in the sync circuits and sync pulses.

To get the beam to scan on the screen properly, the raster display contains special vertical and horizontal scanning generators. These are devices that produce a signal which is sent to the deflection plates. The signal is a sawtooth-shaped waveform that, like the signals we saw for driving the oscilloscope, cause the beam to move across the screen, from the top to the bottom and back. The horizontal transit is controlled by the ramping portion of the horizontal sawtooth. During this time the beam can be turned on to display a dot somewhere on the line. The trip back to the beginning of the line happens very quickly by the falling, straight line portion of the sawtooth. At the same time the beam is brought across the screen, a vertical sawtooth signal is driving it downwards.

In standard U.S. video, the beam traces out 525 horizontal lines (actually only 484 plus two half lines are visible). This is done at a rate of about 30 times per second. To decrease the amount of flicker this would produce, the picture is divided into two parts, called fields. Each field contains *every other* line of the 525 line display. The fields are thus interleaved so that the entire screen is filled with an image 60 times per second.[3] This is called video interlace. Since the weaving pattern is repeated at such a high rate, any dot that is illuminated will appear to the eye to be steady on the display (because of persistence of vision). The 60 cycle rate is called vertical refresh because an entirely new field is scanned (refreshed) 60 times per second.

The scanning generators inside the display device need some way to stay in coordination with the computer, or the computer will not know where the beam is. The solution is that special sync pulses are developed in the computer. These sync pulses are inserted into the main video output that is sent to the display (the information for turning on the beam is inbetween the pulses). These pulses tell the scan generators when to start scanning a line and when to return the beam to the top of the screen. Circuits in the display strip off and use the pulses to get in step with the computer's signal. (Without the sync pulses the picture would roll vertically or tear horizontally as you have probably seen it do when it is "out of sync.")

Horizontal sync pulses start the horizontal sweep of the beam, and vertical sync pulses start the vertical trace of the beam. In between these pulses is the video information, also in the form of pulses, that makes up a single horizontal line on the TV. The horizontal lines are like the threads

---

[3]The reason for scanning the picture 60 times per second and not 24 or some other value has to do with the way the United States distributes electricity. In the U.S., all electrical power is alternating at 60 cycles per second (AC). In Europe the rate is 50 Hz. If the vertical refresh rate was anything other than 60, any leakage or ripple from the power line would "beat" with the refresh rate. The result would be a picture that would roll on the screen. By using 60 cycles, we can lock the picture at the same rate as the power line and have a very steady display.

running through the rug, and the video information is like the intensity or color changes on each thread. The sync pulses are the beginnings and endings of the threads.

On a single one of the 525 lines, a large number of dots may be defined, but only a limited number may be displayed due to the mechanics of the display and the limitations of the electronic circuits. An upper limit of about 500 different dots on a line is possible on a black and white display, whereas about 200 are possible on a color display.

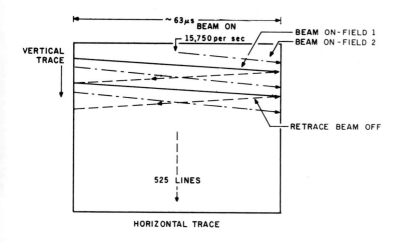

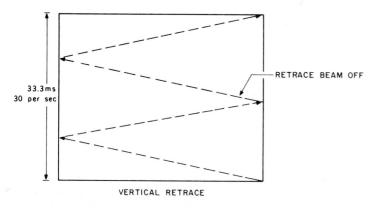

Figure 2.7: Details of the standard raster.

On a black and white display, video information on each line tells the beam of electrons how intense the dot of light is to be. The light can be controlled from very white to gray to black (no light). In the case of the simplest black and white graphics computers, the video information is represented as a single pulse that indicates whether a dot on a line should be white or black. More sophisticated graphics computers allow the dot

to be one of many shades and are referred to as having gray scale capability.

A computer that is properly synchronized can turn the beam on at any point in the display's X-Y plane, thus forming a dot there. The raster-scanned screen can thus be imagined as a super dense matrix of about 500 dots by 500 lines. If the beam is turned on at specific locations on the screen, we get a shape made of tiny points. This may seem quite a bit more complex than the stroke graphics, but, in fact, raster scanning graphics considerably reduces the cost of the circuits needed for displaying information and leads to a much less expensive computer. The main reason this is true is because the analog circuits of the vector display (the DACs) can be eliminated; also, because the circuitry for televisions is mass produced, it is quite inexpensive.

The negative aspect to the raster graphics approach is that unlike stroke graphics, it must store *all* the points for the shape being drawn rather than just the endpoints. All these points are stored in the computer's memory. This used to present more of a problem than it does today, since the costs of computer memory devices have been drastically decreased.

Now that you have an idea of what the screen of the computer is all about, let's take a look at how the computer takes its stored pictures from its memory and puts them onto the screen.

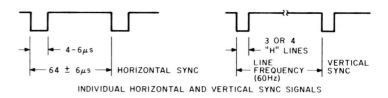

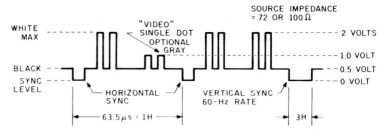

Figure 2.8: Sync signals.

2.4. THE GRAPHICS COMPUTER — A FIRST LOOK

Any graphics computer, whether it's a low cost $99 personal unit (like a Sinclair/Timex ZX-81) or a large expensive mainframe, contains several identically functioning components. (See Figure 2.9.) These are the central processing unit (CPU), the bus, read/write memory (RAM), read-only memory (ROM), keyboard, graphics input devices, the video I/O section (shown expanded in the figure), and mass storage devices.

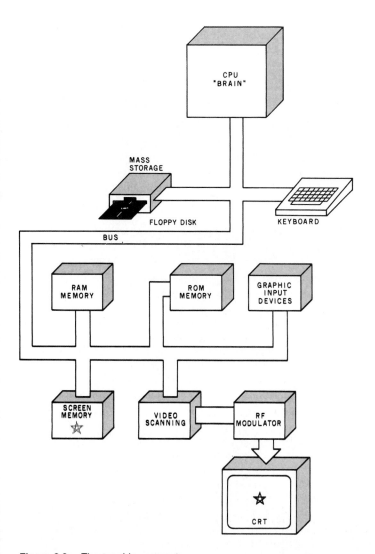

Figure 2.9: The graphics computer.

The CPU can be thought of as the thinking part of the computer's brain. It is the required intelligence that tells the rest of the computer what to do and how to do it, and is primarily used to interpret the instructions of the computer program. In personal computers the CPU is a micro-processor, a small, mass-produced device, the size of a stick of chewing gum, which contains thousands of transistors. In expensive mainframe

computers, the CPU is usually a complex arrangement of custom devices, each specially designed for the job.

The computer's bus is where information flows back and forth between the different devices. It is like a high-speed railroad on which signals carrying graphics information can travel. You don't really need to understand fully how the bus or microprocessor work to do graphics or animation. It is important, however, to be aware of their basic functions in the system.

Photo 2.2: A typical graphics computer. *(Courtesy of Tektronix.)*

Let's continue with our explanation of the standard components of the graphics computer. The computer's keyboard, which resembles a typewriter, is for entering alphanumeric (letters and numbers) information, such as instructions and programs, into the computer.

The RAM is where the instructions and data for the computer are temporarily stored while the computer is doing its processing. The RAM is also where the image of the picture that is on the screen is stored. Screen memory may be either a portion of the RAM memory or a separate RAM memory. Its purpose is to hold the image that will be displayed on the CRT.

The ROM is where special programs and data are kept. When the power is turned off, information in RAM is lost, but information in ROM stays. This special data is always instantly available to the computer.

The graphics input devices are the channel through which graphic information, such as picture and drawings, may be entered into the computer (more on these later). The video scanning circuits are used to take the image in the screen memory and put it on the CRT. You'll learn more about this soon.

Finally, every graphics computer needs a mass storage device. This device functions as a long-term storage of information that has been processed by the computer, i.e., computer programs that will be loaded into the memory, and other data. (Information from the computer can be stored on magnetic material in the same way music is stored on magnetic tape.)

2.5. THE BIT AND THE PIXEL

Earlier we described how pictures could be drawn on a raster-oriented computer screen by having the image composed of tiny dots of light. These dots, which have specific locations on the screen, are called pixels (or pels), which stands for picture element. Pixels become visible by turning on the electron beam at the proper location and proper moment on the screen line.

Where do these pixels come from, and (since timing is crucial to creating animation) what tells them to turn on? They are stored in a special area of the computer's memory called screen memory or the bit plane.[4] The dots are represented in screen memory as voltage levels using the same binary system we described earlier. A dot that is visible on the screen is stored in memory as an ON voltage, while all invisible dots are stored as OFF voltages. We can consider the ON and OFF voltages as switches that can be on or off. The locations that store these on and off

---

[4] The remaining portion of memory that is NOT devoted to holding the screen image also contains bits that are on or off. These bits, however, correspond to instructions for the microprocessor or special program data. The versatile computer actually has the ability to store data, pictures, and instructions all in the same memory.

voltages are called bits, an abbreviated way of saying binary digit. Figure 2.10 shows this relationship. In a typical graphics computer there are thousands of these bits devoted to holding our precious image. In our simple example, each bit in the computer's memory corresponds exactly to a certain pixel location on the screen.

Contained inside the computer are scanning circuits, called multiplexors, that fly through the screen memory synchronized with the scanning of the raster. They are digital devices that very quickly count all the addresses of the memory and read each memory location. The purpose of these scanning circuits is to look at every memory location in the screen memory and decide if a bit is on or off. If it is on, then the video information that is being sent to the display is given a pulse to cause the beam on the screen to turn on (and thus become white and visible). Otherwise, the beam is left off, and black is visible at the location.

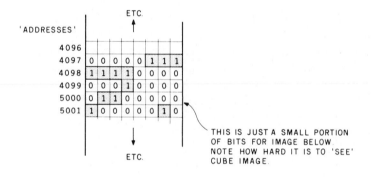

(a) HOW BITS LOOK IN 8-BIT WIDE MEMORY

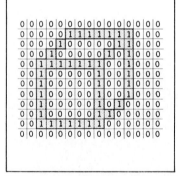

NOTE: 1's CORRESPOND TO DARK DOTS IN PICTURE ON RIGHT.

(b) TWO DIMENSIONAL REPRESENTATION

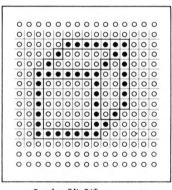

● = 1 = ON BIT
○ = 0 = OFF BIT

(c) PIXELS ON SCREEN

(continued)

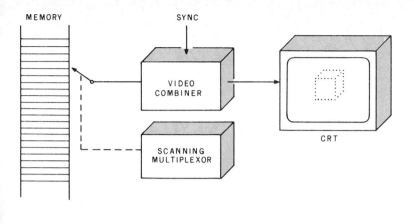

(d) SCANNING PIXEL MEMORY

Figure 2.10 Pixel memory and scanning it.

The correspondence between memory and dots on the screen can tell us the amount of memory bytes needed for a certain desired resolution. For example, suppose the computer is to have a black and white (or black and green) display and that each dot will take up one bit of memory. If the display is to have a resolution of 320 horizontal dots by 200 lines, the result is 320 × 200 or 64,000 pixels on the screen. This means that for our example of one bit per pixel, there must also be 64,000 bits in the memory. Since computers usually specify memory storage in terms of bytes (8 bits = 1 byte), we need 64,000/8 or 8,000 bytes for this particular display. Later we will see how adding color or extra shades to each pixel increases the number of bits per pixel and subsequently the number of bytes needed in memory to hold the image.

Bit Planes

Imagine the screen memory for the computer as a two-dimensional plane of bits, with each bit corresponding to a pixel on the screen. (Even though the screen memory is probably organized in bytes, looking at it as a bit plane simplifies our discussion.) Figure 2.11 shows a bit plane for our black and white 320 × 200 display.

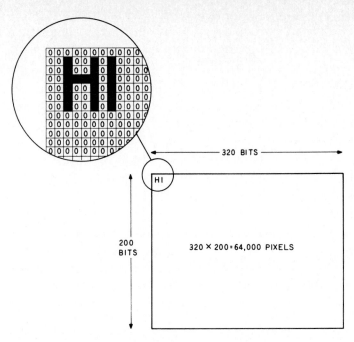

Figure 2.11   A 320 × 200 bit black and white bit plane.

2.6. ADDING GRAY SCALE

If we wanted to create a picture with some tonal gradations, how could we do it? In other words, how can we add shades of gray to our black and white display? The gray scale can be created by controlling the intensity of the electron beam as it goes through scanning each pixel on the screen. Recall that so far the beam has been either ON (resulting in white), or OFF (resulting in black). Now we are going to add several levels of intensity between white and black.

For example, if we wish eight levels of gray, then eight intensity levels of the beam are required. Where do these intensity levels come from? Simply by adding more bits for each pixel. Remember our binary switches? How many switches are necessary to offer eight different levels? Or, in other words, how many bits are needed to count from 0 to 7 (0 to 7 represents 8 different states)? Three bits are required, as shown in the following table:

Switches				Binary				Decimal
OFF	OFF	OFF	=	0	0	0	=	0
OFF	OFF	ON	=	0	0	1	=	1
OFF	ON	OFF	=	0	1	0	=	2
OFF	ON	ON	=	0	1	1	=	3
ON	OFF	OFF	=	1	0	0	=	4
ON	OFF	ON	=	1	0	1	=	5
ON	ON	OFF	=	1	1	0	=	6
ON	ON	ON	=	1	1	1	=	7

Another way to determine how many bits are required is to use the following formula: 2 raised to what power equals the desired number? In the example above, we want 2 raised to a power that equals 8. We know that 2 raised to the third power is 8. So how do we get the extra bits into our image? We simply stack two additional bit planes to our existing plane, as shown in Figure 2.12. Now each pixel on the screen has 3 bits of information. Since we are allowing the amplitude of our video information to take on one of eight different levels, we need to convert the 3 bits of digital pixel information to eight levels of analog information for controlling the beam's intensity. Again, the DAC comes to the rescue. In this case, we need a DAC with three inputs. The output on the DAC is mixed with the sync pulses and sent to the display. Now it will convert the 3 digital bits in each scanned memory location to the respective voltage level for the amplitude of the beam.

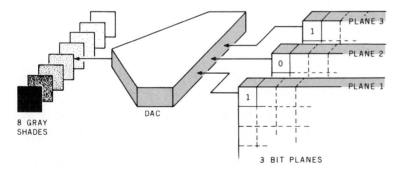

Figure 2.12 Adding gray scale with three bit planes.

Gray scale is one way that high-tech computers accomplish staggering realism. When the number of bits per pixel is increased beyond a certain number (about 8 bits or 256 levels of gray), it is almost impossible to tell the difference between the digital image of a computer and a photograph.

2.7. ADDING COLOR TO THE DISPLAY

Now that we have a gray scale, the next consideration is to add color. As it turns out, this is not as difficult as you might imagine. Before we explain the process, we first must digress a "bit" and see how color is put on the CRT display device in the first place.

The Famous Red Green Blue (RGB) Monitor

Color is obtained on today's high-tech graphics computers by using the Red Green Blue (RGB) direct drive monitor. This is a fairly expensive ($800 to $5,000) CRT that contains three separate electron beams, one for each of the three primary colors of light: red, green, and blue. In addition, this CRT has built-in scanning circuits for moving the beams on the screen. But, unlike the surface of the black and white CRT, which is coated with a smooth layer of white light-emitting phosphor, the surface of the color CRT is coated with three different phosphors arranged in a triad of dots. (See Figure 2.13.) (Note that instead of dot triads some CRTs use bands of the three color phosphors.) A special metal aperture mask is placed inside the CRT directly over the dots. The holes in the mask allow each of three beams to illuminate its corresponding color dots. The beam designed to produce the color red, for example, will only illuminate the red phosphors.

The computer sends a separate video signal to each of the three color guns, each signal representing an intensity of a screen color. The intensity of each beam then determines how much of that primary color is to be mixed at the pixel location. In other words, if the color at a particular location was to be pure blue, we would turn off the red and green guns and turn on the blue gun full force. If the desired color was purple, we would turn off the green gun and turn on the red and the blue. To produce white, we would turn on all three guns. We can fine tune the exact color that gets shown by controlling the amount of each of the primary colors that gets mixed in at each pixel. This is done precisely the same way as we did with shades of gray, i.e., each gun's intensity is controlled by the computer.

The intensity of each color is in turn set by the number of bits representing that color in the bit plane. For example, suppose we allocate 3 bits for each of the three primary colors, so as to get eight intensities (or shades for each color). This would make a total of 9 bits dedicated to each pixel on the display, and we would have 9 bit planes. The 3 bits per primary color means that we can have eight shades per color at each pixel location, for a total of $8 \times 8 \times 8$ or 512 possible colors! Believe it or not, the human eye can actually distinguish many more colors than this.

We now need three separate DACs in our graphics computer, one for each of the primary colors. The circuitry for driving these DACs increases the complexity and cost of the color display, as does the additional screen memory.

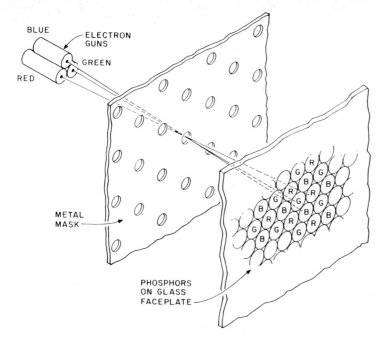

Figure 2.13: The RGB color CRT and aperture mask.

2.8. FRAME BUFFERS

Today most high-tech raster-scan displays are based on the use of a large digital memory called a frame buffer. The frame buffer (which we alluded to when we discussed bit planes) is nothing more than all the bit planes, stacked one upon the other and considered as a single entity. The name "frame buffer" comes from the fact that the device is a large memory designed to hold a single frame of a film, graphic picture, etc.

The number of bit planes being used sets the pixel depth of the frame buffer, which in turn sets the number of bits available for the color description of each pixel. The bit depth, in turn, sets the overall cost of the frame buffer. Obviously, the more bits used for each pixel, the greater the color capability of the buffer. Likewise, the number of horizontal and vertical bits in the frame buffer sets the resolution obtainable on the screen. State-of-the art animation houses, graphics designers, and others use frame buffers with dimensions of 1024 × 1024 pixels and a depth of up to 24 bits. (See Figure 2.14.) In a 24-bit deep frame buffer there are usually 8 bits devoted to each of the primary colors. (Later we'll be showing how there are other ways to organize the bit planes.) This results in 256 × 256 × 256 = 16,777,216 different colors. Although it is unlikely that any living creature could differentiate between two adjacent shades, it points out the range of color the high-tech frame buffer allows.

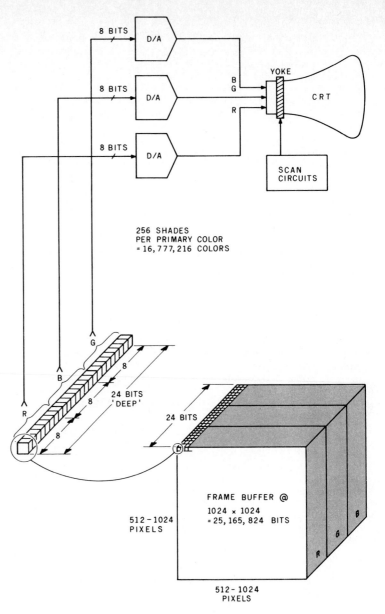

Figure 2.14: A hi-tech 24 bit per pixel frame buffer.

Let's do a little exercise to see what such a frame buffer might cost. The total number of bits used in the frame buffer is 1024 × 1024 × 24, which is 25,165,824 bits (24 Mbits for short, pronounced Megabits — one Mbit equals one million bits). Today, a 64 K-bit RAM chip costs (in quantity) about $8.50 (price obtained from the classified ads of BYTE magazine). We would need 24 Mbits ÷ 64 Kbits = 384 chips for our frame buffer. At $8.50 per RAM chip, this comes to $3,264 just for the memory portion of the frame buffer. This price does not include the expensive circuits for driving the DACs that are required for each gun.

In general, frame buffers on the market today represent each color gun's intensity with 1, 2, 4, 8 or more bits of memory. As we saw earlier, 1 bit is sufficient for simple graphics and leads to a low cost display; 2 and 4 bits are useful for solid colors or shades of gray, and 8 bits are required for finely detailed, shaded pictures.

2.9. GETTING THE FRAME BUFFER IMAGE ON FILM

The purpose of the frame buffer is to allow graphics designers to scan their latest work of art on the CRT. This doesn't, however, solve the problem of getting the image onto 35 mm film, which is the main concern of animation houses. The way this is done is interesting in that it points out the flaws in the color CRT. The most straightforward approach would be to simply display the frame buffer's image on a high-quality CRT and take a picture of it. This, however, is not the way they usually do it. Remember the dots and the aperture mask used to keep the guns from illuminating adjacent pixels? Well, because the mask and dots cannot be made smaller than a certain measurement, they end up determining the maximum resolution obtainable on the CRT. This is usually much less than what the frame buffer, the computer, or the film is capable of. Therefore, the film will never show a resolution greater than that mask.

The standard solution to the problem of photographing color is to use a device called a film recorder to photograph the images. It contains a very high-quality black and white monitor and three color filters. Since the black and white monitor contains no mask or color dot triads, it can resolve extremely high-resolution images. Here's how it's done.

Three color filters are employed, one at a time. The frame buffer is grouped into three primary colors, red, blue, and green, each having eight bits and planes of intensity information. When the red filter, for example, is placed in front of a black and white monitor, the output from the red planes are turned on and the green and blue planes are disabled. Thus the intensity information for the red part of the picture is now on the CRT and the red filter is in front of it. The frame of film is then exposed. Next the blue plane is enabled, the red and green are disabled, a blue filter is placed in front of the CRT, and the photo is taken again without advancing the film. This same process is then repeated for the green plane. The film automatically mixes the three colors for us. This will produce an image with the same resolution as the frame buffer.

Bypassing the Frame Buffer

It is possible, however, to bypass the frame buffer and send to the film recorder much higher resolution images, even higher than the best of today's film can resolve. This is accomplished by sending the film recorder a single scan line at a time. The computer displays this single

line on its CRT, exposes the film, and then accepts the next scan line, erasing the first from the screen. This is repeated for each scan line of each frame, producing resolutions as high as 6000 × 4000 pixels with 9 bits per color.

Unfortunately, even this approach has a major drawback. It can take as long as five to ten minutes to record each frame at high resolutions. To solve this and many other problems, Lucasfilm is developing the ultimate film animation system, called a Pixar. It is a general-purpose picture computer, complete with processors, plenty of memory, and lasers for I/O (input/output) devices. This hardware production instrument can ''suck'' pictures from film with its lasers, manipulate the images, and spew them back out with another set of lasers onto new film. Lasers are used because they are the most controllable light source available and produce extremely vivid colors. Future *Star Wars* films should be of an incomparable visual quality.

2.10. ENCODING THE PICTURE IN THE BUFFER

The process of encoding refers to the way the picture information is organized inside the buffer. There are several ways to accomplish this in the frame buffer. Often, bits are divided in some manner to represent the three primary colors. If the pixel depth is only 8 bits, for example, we might allocate 3 bits to red, 3 bits to green, and 2 bits to blue. The reason for the underrepresentation of blue is that the eye is less sensitive to the blue region of the color spectrum, because it has the smallest number of blue receptors. Thus we allocate fewer bits to blue because they would otherwise be wasted. These three components are then fed to the three guns of the color monitor.

2.11. COLOR MAPPING

The trouble with the simple, 8-bit color encoding scheme above is that the range of colors is limited. With 3 bits per primary color we can only have eight shades of that color. In our example of 3-3-2 bits, we can have up to 8 × 8 × 4 or 256 different shades. Although this may seem like a lot, the human eye is capable of resolving many more shades than this. Fortunately, there is a good way to obtain more color shades without utilizing more frame buffer memory. This method, called color mapping, is used by more high-tech frame buffer manufacturers today (and some personal computer manufacturers such as Atari).

With color mapping, the bit values that are normally stored in the frame buffer are interpreted as addresses or pointers into a table of colors, rather than directly as colors. This table may be an area in RAM or a collection of special color registers. This means, for example, that the

8-bit value at a certain pixel location would point to a table address which contained three individual color values, one for each of the primary colors. (See Figure 2.15.)

By using such an approach, an 8-bit per pixel frame buffer can address a color table with a maximum of 256 color values in it. This means that the screen could display 256 different colors at one time. In addition, each of these individual color components can be defined to a high degree of precision, because the bit length of the table can be much greater than the 8 bits per pixel we showed earlier. For example, the table could be 24 bits wide, therefore allowing 8 bits for *each primary color*, or 256 shades for each color, or a maximum of 16 million shades per pixel! Keep in mind, though, that only eight bits are required per pixel. (See the box that follows for another explanation of color mapping.)

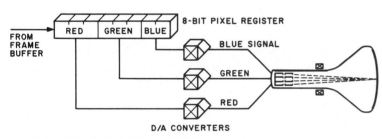

a) SIMPLE DECODING OF 8-BIT PIXELS

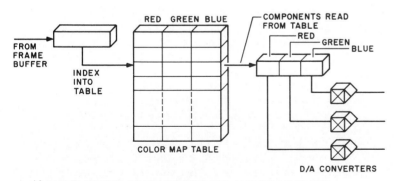

b) SAME 8-BIT PIXEL VALUES INDEXING INTO A 24-BIT COLOR MAP

Figure 2.15: Pixel values indexing into a color map (a & b).

Another, less apparent advantage of the color map is that changing any colors in the color map table changes all associated colors on the screen instantly! This is useful for painting on the screen and for color animation. For example, suppose there were several balloon shapes on the screen. Some are filled with green, some with magenta, and some with yellow. Suppose we wanted to change all the magenta balloons to pink. In a simple color encoding scheme, we would have to change all the magenta pixels to pink pixels. This would prove to be a time-consuming task. Color mapping, however, enables us to simply change the magenta value in the color map table to pink, and instantly all the magenta balloons turn pink. Frequently, the color map table is referred to as color registers, and the entire process is called color register encoding. We will talk more about color register animation in Chapter 6.

Color Mapping and the Magic Paint Store

Here is a simple analogy you can use to understand the idea of color mapping and color registers. Although we will be using an ATARI Home Computer in our example, with its maximum of 128 colors, the analogy holds true for other machines if you assume the appropriate number of available colors.

Imagine a paint store shelf filled with 128 cans of different color paint. In front of you there are nine magic, empty paint buckets, each one labeled with a number from 0 to 8. Each bucket has a brush in it with the same number (the buckets are the color registers and the paint cans are the colors you can put in the registers). A large canvas is before you, begging for a picture. Feeling artistically inspired, you begin by filling the first bucket with one of the 128 colors (a light blue color), pick up the brush, and paint the sky on your canvas. When you have finished with that color, you fill another bucket with your second color selection and paint some more. You continue this process with the remaining seven buckets. Since there are no empty buckets left, you decide to empty Bucket 0 and fill it with a new color, a deep orange, chosen from the paint cans.

This is where the magic comes into play. Lo and behold, as soon as you put the new color in Bucket 0, the sky in your picture, originally painted with Brush 0, immediately changes to orange! In fact, *everything* that was previously painted with Brush 0 now appears in the *new* color currently in Bucket 0! When you try this with Bucket 1, the same thing happens with everything previously painted with Brush 1. You have magically changed your painting from a cool mid-afternoon scene to a fiery sunset — and you didn't even have to use paint thinner to clean out the old color from the bucket before putting in the new. The new color has the property of completely expunging the old color.

The fact that all colors on the screen painted with a certain bucket change color together can be less than desirable at times. For example, if your sun was setting over a blue ocean, you probably wouldn't be thrilled by having the Caribbean looking like orangeade.

Another potential problem is that the ATARI Home Computer limits you to a maximum of nine different colors on your canvas when using its color registers. Of course, the machine costs only $200 to $800, so you can't really complain.

Photo 2.3 shows an example of color mapping being used to change the primary colors of a graphic display (see color insert).

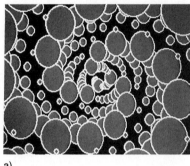

a)

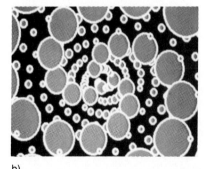

b)

Photo 2.3: These photos show the effects of color registers. In a) the circles are all red, while in b) they are blue (see color insert). This was done by changing only one byte in the color register. These graphics are done by Jane Veeder, who is using ZGRASS language on a Datamax UV-1 computer. ZGRASS, developed at the University of Chicago, is a very powerful language especially designed for graphics. *(Courtesy of Jane Veeder.)*

2.12. VIDEO MIXING VIA BIT PLANES

By treating the frame buffer as several bit planes rather than a single unit, each can be made to hold a *separate* image. For example, an 8-bit per pixel frame buffer can be divided into two images of 4 bits each, four images of 2 bits each, or eight individual black and white images. In

animation, this means several frames of the image can exist in the buffer at the same time. The video from each plane can be turned on and off, and thereby one image part can be faded out while another is merged in. So by having several bits per pixel, we can do more than just represent different colors and intensities. Using this technique, it is possible to have a static background image while another image transverses it. No special logic operations need to be performed for the movement since each bit plane is independent of the other.

2.13.   OTHER ENCODING TECHNIQUES

While the frame buffer is an extremely useful innovation, it does have its problems. For one, it does not offer the most compact way of storing graphic images, and therefore the large amount of memory required keeps costs high. Further, since every byte of the image must be changed if the image is to be shifted the smallest amount, the frame buffer is extremely slow in its response time for moving highly detailed images. Finally, when transferring the image in the frame buffer to the disk for permanent storage, much time is required and much space is used up on the disk itself. One solution to this last problem is based on the compacting of the image via encoding techniques.

Real-Time Scan Conversion

The viability of the frame buffer really deteriorates in terms of compactness of storage when we consider a simple line drawing such as a three-dimensional box. Compared to a stroke graphics display that stores endpoints, the box image could be stored in about 1 percent of the time and 0.2 percent of the memory space as the frame buffer. A solution to this problem is called scan conversion. In scan conversion, the image is stored as geometric descriptions rather than as pixel intensities of the frame buffer. Scan conversion relies on a special display file, which is simply another area of memory for holding endpoint values for an image. A special circuit looks at the display file several times per refresh cycle to generate the image and mathematically determines if a line segment intersects the current scan line being drawn. The image can be easily modified by changing the description in the display file. The problem with this approach is that special hardware is needed to perform the scan conversion at rates of 30 frames per second. Very expensive graphics systems, such as the Link Flight Simulator (a device that allows pilots to be trained in flying new aircraft) uses scan conversion hardware and achieves impressive degrees of realism.

Run-Length Encoding

Another approach to compact storage of images that works on both memory and disk is called run-length encoding. This technique works best for images involving solid gray or color areas. The approach has been applied even on personal computers such as the Apple and is based on the fact that a typical scan line has pixel values that remain at the same intensity or color for several pixels. This being the case, if we encode the length and intensity of each sequence of identical pixels, we will reduce the amount of memory and disk space required to store the image. Each encoded scan line will then consist of one or more instructions, each of which defines a run length and intensity.

Special hardware can be used in this approach to allow real-time run-length encoding and decoding of the image. It is also possible to design software that will encode and decode the image in non-real time for a savings in memory. Run-length encoding has been employed in some software for the Apple II, when many images need to be stored on the limited space of mini-floppy diskettes. The pictures of the spinning globe from Chapter 1 were encoded in this manner to allow all 24 frames to reside in ATARI's RAM at once.

Simulation of Resolution with Intensity — Block Pix

It is possible to simulate a much higher resolution than the X and Y coordinates would imply by using intensity modulation carefully. For example, if you correctly select the color in a single pixel, it is possible to trick the eye into thinking that the resolution is quite high, when, in fact, just the opposite is true.

The series of photographs in Photo 2.4 shows a block pix representation of President Lincoln.[5] Note the marvelous realism the first picture achieves despite the fact that the pixels are relatively large. Shading has greatly affected the way the image is perceived. Note also that when you stand back and squint, the three photos seem very similar. This demonstrates the role of shading and intensity over resolution. A continuing controversy exists among computer graphics experts pertaining to the primary importance of high display resolution versus copious color capability per pixel.

---

[5]The original block pix picture of Lincoln is a classic by Leon Harmon of Bell Labs done many years ago. These photos are a commercial derivative of the original image.

a)

b)

c)

Photo 2.4: This three frame set (a, b, c) shows a picture of Lincoln evolving through a block pix process where the picture is broken up into fewer and fewer blocks and lower and lower resolution. The intensity and shade of each block, however, is carefully chosen so that the original image can still be recognized, showing that intensity modulation can substitute for absolute resolution. *(Courtesy of Digital Effects/R. Greenberg Associates — Lincoln Bank, 1981.)*

2.14 ADVANCED GRAPHICS HARDWARE

Thus far, we have limited our discussion to the most fundamental of high-tech graphics hardware. There are much more advanced systems on the market, however, some of which cost in the millions of dollars! A complete understanding of the concepts behind these more advanced devices is not necessary, however, for you to proceed.

2.15. PERSONAL COMPUTER GRAPHICS HARDWARE

Now that you better understand the hardware of the high-tech graphics computer, you are in a good position to tackle the workings of the personal computer hardware used for graphics. We needed to introduce the high-tech hardware first, because, as strange as it may seem, the low-cost color graphics personal computers are actually a bit more complex than their big brothers. This is true for two primary reasons. First, they must work with a color television and consequently a constraint in operation is placed upon them (as you will learn). Second, they must be mass produced and made inexpensively, and this means special tricks are often needed to get the cost low (as you will also soon see).

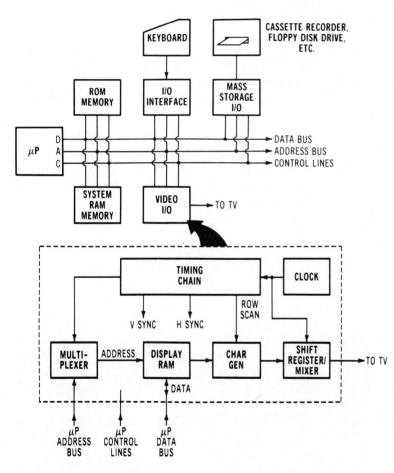

Figure 2.16: Personal graphics computer block diagram. This is the same as the previous graphics computer block diagram except for the addition of an RF modulator (as an option).

A block diagram of the personal graphics computer is shown on page 67. It is very similar to the block diagram we showed earlier, except for the inclusion of an RF modulator. The purpose of this is to convert the video information coming from the computer into a high-frequency signal that can be accepted by the television.

Televisions are set up to pull transmitted signals out of airwaves and operate in what is called the radio frequency (RF) spectrum. The RF modulator simply places the computer's video information on an RF wave so it can "ride" into the television. Once the video is inside the TV, usually entering through the antenna terminals, the television strips out the RF, discards it, and merely retains the video portion. From this point, the black and white television works almost identically to the raster-scanning CRT you already learned about. In fact, some of the newer TVs have jacks on the back that allow them to work as direct coupled CRTs!

Getting Color on the Television

When we add color to the personal computer and require it to operate with a standard color television, we have an entirely new ball game. To see how the color computer works, we must first understand how color televisions work.

When color TV was first proposed, it had a major stumbling block to overcome. It had to be compatible with the millions of black and white TVs already on the market. In other words, when a color signal was received it could not interfere with a TV that could only receive black and white. This reality put some real restraints in the design of the color signals. (Had the color television been designed first, things probably would have been much simpler. So much for hindsight.)

Basically like the RGB monitor, the color TV picture tube has three separate intensity-modulated color guns. It also has a shadow mask and a coating of color dot triads (or in some of the newer televisions, stripes) spread over the front interior surface of the tube.

At the transmitting end of television, there are three color signals, often derived live from a camera. The problem is how to get these color signals, which are mixed in with the black and white signal at the transmission end, separated from the black and white signal and finally use them to modulate the three corresponding color guns in a color television.

In 1953, after much head scratching, the television industry came up with the first monochrome (B&W) compatible color transmission method. It is called the National Television System Committee (NTSC) color standard, and it applies to all government-regulated broadcast television systems in the United States and several other countries. The basic underlying principle of the NTSC color standard is the merging of two separate image transmissions, a wide-band signal carrying luminance information and a narrower bandwidth signal containing chrominance information. (*Luminance* is the brightness or intensity of the three colors red, blue, and green. *Chrominance* represents the actual color or hue coming from the three guns.) These signals are derived from mixing the red, blue, and green color signals from the camera (or computer) in a very special way. This special mixing of the color signals and combining for transmission is called NTSC encoding.

After the colors have been mixed in their proper proportions by the encoder, they are used to modulate a high-frequency (3.58 MHz) subcarrier signal. The subcarrier is phase modulated, which means its delay can be varied in different increments. This permits the use of a simple, inexpensive circuit modulator that converts the color bits in the screen memory to phase changes. The carrier is, in turn, mixed in with the waveforms containing the sync signals and sent to the television.

At the television, an NTSC decoder circuit takes apart all the things done by the encoder, thereby separating the colors into their original chrominances. In addition to the color subcarrier signal, a special color burst signal is mixed in with the video signal. This burst contains reference information about the frequency of the color subcarrier and allows the television to "lock" with the original color oscillator.

Another restriction inherent to the functioning of a television is the bandwidth. The television's bandwidth is the maximum frequency that the television will allow to pass. It sets a limit on the maximum number of color changes possible on a particular line of the screen. Before anything can be received, color signals for the television must fit within the signal bandwidth (4 MHz) of the set. This breaks down the quality of the picture. In addition, all of the encoding and decoding that takes place adds noise to the color signal, further degrading it. At this point we can appreciate why the direct drive RGB monitor gives better quality color than the color television. In a RGB monitor, the bandwidth may be as high as 35 MHz, thus allowing many more color changes to be resolved.

Every personal computer that is designed to work with a color TV has an NTSC coior encoding circuit in it. Most personal computers, however, have only the chrominance information encoded. Since the luminance or brightness is fixed, this simplifies the encoding circuits by eliminating the need for a DAC.

2.16. COLOR IN THE PERSONAL COMPUTER

Given that personal computers must keep the cost down, their approach to getting color on the display is more constrained than that of the high-tech graphics machines. For one thing, even though the price of memory is dropping fast, its use must be kept to a minimum, or the computer will be too expensive. The designers of the early personal computers had to invent ways to get color graphics without using up much system RAM. Several methods were used. One was to share

graphics memory with the program memory. For example, in the Apple, ATARI, and in many of today's new computers, the RAM for the color display is part of the system RAM and is referred to as screen memory. If a program used on such machines is large enough to creep into the area occupied by the screen RAM, high-resolution graphics will not be obtainable. Given this constraint, programmers learned to keep their programs small enough to still use the graphics. (The alternative was forfeiting the graphics and using as much of the RAM as they needed.)

Another way to keep the use of graphics RAM to a minimum is with special encoding techniques that limit the color to certain pixels on the screen. This technique originated with the Apple II's high-resolution screen and caused programmers many hours of frustration until they finally learned to work around it. In a way, it was a brilliant maneuver by Steve Wozniak, the Apple's designer, because it allowed the Apple II to be advertised as a system that had 280 × 192 resolution in six colors while consuming only 8K bytes of RAM. A little calculating will show this is not possible, as 280 times 192 is 53,760 pixels. Six colors requires about 2½ bits. Two and one half times 53,760 is 134,400 bits. But the Apple's 8192 byte screen RAM has only 65,536 bits. There is a discrepancy here. The answer is that any color *cannot* appear in every pixel! Actually you can only have a resolution of 140 × 192 on the Apple and get the full 6 colors. To get 280 pixels on a row you have to be willing to accept that every seven pixels only be from one of two color sets. (This is explained in more detail in Chapter 4 in the section pertaining to the Apple II.) Our point here is not to discredit the Apple II, but to show the color limitations of all personal computers.

Newer personal computers, which are following the high-tech machines more closely in their use of graphics, still have some constraints. For example, the IBM Personal Computer has a full 16K bytes of RAM set aside for the graphics and is separate from the program RAM. The IBM PC allows up to 16 colors in a 320 × 200 resolution. In reality, however, there are only eight colors and two color sets, one brighter than the other, so that the 16K bytes can handle the full range. Otherwise, 32K bytes would be needed for the graphics RAM.

2.17. MEMORY-MAPPED VIDEO AND TEXT STORAGE

In both kinds of raster-scanned systems, the most popular way to display text is to encode the letters, numbers, and special symbols to be displayed into a unique 6- or 7-bit value called an ASCII (ass-key) character. (ASCII stands for American Standard Committee for Information Interchange and is a special set of rules determining what bit patterns are designated for what characters. Almost all computer manufacturers follow the standard.) The ASCII characters are then stored in the computer's memory.

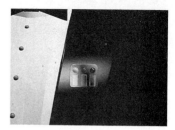

Photo 2.5: This Triple I "Computer Picture" advertisement shows the company's capability and illustrates the high quality and fine detail possible in computer graphics. *(Courtesy of Information International, Inc.)*

In order to display the characters, circuits are built that convert the bit patterns stored in the screen memory into dot images. These images are then mixed in with the video and sent to the screen. Usually, a character-generator ROM is used to hold the actual dot images that correspond to the ASCII values stored in memory. There are different kinds of these ROMs, each giving a different style of character on the screen for the ASCII code. The density of the dot matrix for each character that appears on the screen varies from computer to computer. It can have a density ranging from 5 × 7 (the most coarse and not allowing lowercase) to 9 × 12 (the most dense and allowing all symbols of the alphabet as well as special graphic symbols).

In some personal computers, the dot patterns for the characters can be defined in system RAM rather than in a character-generator ROM. This allows the characters to be redefined by the programmer to be whatever is desired. This can include graphics characters, special math symbols, and foreign fonts.

Since the ASCII code is a 7-bit code, there is 1 bit of an 8-bit byte left over. In fact, if only capital letters are used, 6 bits are needed and thus 2 bits are left over. Usually the extra bits of each byte are set up to contain color, intensity, reverse video, or blinking information. In this way, it is possible for each text character to have its own color. In some computers, like the IBM PC, 2 bytes are automatically set aside for each character. One stores the ASCII code and the other stores the attribute for the character, i.e., its foreground and background color, its blinking state, etc.

It should be noted that in many personal computers the screen RAM can simultaneously contain both text characters and graphics. The computer can interpret the byte of screen memory as containing either a ASCII character or several dots of color. In fact, by controlling how many bits make up a pixel and the way in which they are interpreted for color, it is possible to control the amount of color and resolution for several different graphics modes. This is also why you will find that the color graphics personal computers consume different amounts of memory depending on which mode is being used.

2.18. CHARACTER GRAPHICS

Another approach to graphics on personal computers is called character graphics. In this approach, the ASCII text character is replaced by a graphics character, which has been designed by the computer user. In some computers this graphics character may be of several colors and have a density of 8 × 8 or larger. By carefully designing several graphics characters, the user can define complex objects that are made up of several of these characters.

In the example below, there are eight distinct graphics characters. The box figure uses nine characters because one character is actually used twice. Had the box been larger, we would have been able to use several of the graphics characters more than once. This graphics character approach to animation is used in several of the sample programs presented in Chapter 5.

With character graphics, we use PRINT statements from BASIC to send the characters to the screen. We draw a figure by PRINTing several parts of it at distinct locations on the screen. We animate by redrawing the figure with new graphics characters that represent the next movement of the figure. One drawback to this technique is the fact that we are limited to the location on the screen where we can start the figure.

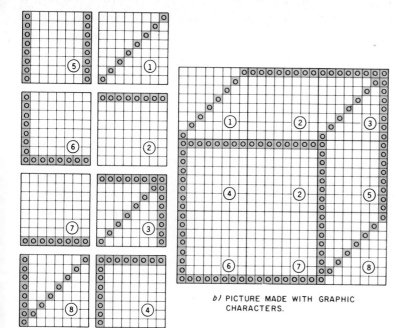

a) GRAPHIC CHARACTERS USED
TO CONSTRUCT PICTURE IN b)

b) PICTURE MADE WITH GRAPHIC
CHARACTERS.

Figure 2.17: Graphic characters for creating a box.

Now you know about the part of the graphics computer that creates the image on the screen. But how does one go about getting an original image into the computer to begin with? Unfortunately, the computer is not yet equipped to accept commands like ''Draw me a cloud.'' Getting objects into the computer is the function of graphics input devices, which we will cover next.

2.19. GRAPHICS PERIPHERALS

How are graphic drawings, paintings, lines, maps, and other images entered into the computer? The keyboard can be used, but it requires the laborious typing of the coordinates of every line, color, and pixel that makes up the image. Instead of entering coordinates, you could use the keyboard's cursor keys to move a cross-hair cursor on the graphics screen to point to the place where you wanted to draw lines or shapes. If software is set up to allow previously formed graphic objects to be ''dragged'' into place, the cursor will allow the user to position them anywhere on the screen. In other words, you can use the cross-hair to pick up an object, drag it to some location on the screen, and then paste it in place. Often this dragging is used with paint systems where a selection of preformed objects are displayed at the bottom of the screen.

For the easy manipulation of graphic images, the keyboard leaves much to be desired. There are several graphics peripherals in use today which make manipulation of graphics much easier. These include the joystick, mouse, light pen, and digitizing tablet.

Joystick

The joystick is a stick that protrudes out of a small box, like a miniature gearshift lever on an automobile with a standard transmission. The joystick can move in any direction (north-east-south-west), and there are usually two potentiometers connected to the joystick that convert its movements to changes in voltages. These changes, in turn, are converted to digital values for the computer (usually with an analog-to-digital convertor, or ADC, the opposite of the DAC). There are two values, one for the X position of the joystick and one for the Y position of the joystick. Software in the computer can then use the X-Y position information to move a cursor on the X-Y plane of the screen.

The problem with the joystick is that an expensive analog to digital convertor (ADC) is required for movement on high-resolution screens, and, if it is a poorly designed joystick, it will require good coordination to master. By this we mean that it can be tricky to physically relate the stick position to the cursor position on the screen. Joysticks, however, are quite popular for low-cost displays such as those found in personal computers. They are great for games where the user must maneuver a ship or fly an object through a maze.

Mouse

The mouse used with a computer is not a furry animal with a long tail. Instead, it is a small box resting on two small wheels whose axes are at right angles to each other. Two or three buttons are on the top of the mouse, and the whole device is rolled around on a flat surface thereby turning the wheels. Shaft encoders (devices that convert mechanical rotation to binary signals) connected to the wheels convert their turning to digital pulses that are sent to the computer. By counting the pulses, the computer can figure out the position of the mouse in the X-Y plane and then use the information to move a screen cursor, like the joystick did.

Mice are becoming quite popular and offer features joysticks lack. They are ideal for positioning objects and can also work well for pointing. (Stanford University did several studies that proved this.) The mouse need not be picked up (like the light pen — see below) to be used. In fact, when it is picked up, the cursor won't move at all.

Some users don't care for the mouse because they don't like having to search for it after using the keyboard in a dark room. Another, more important limitation has to do with the fact that the mouse can't be used to trace outlines from paper images since a small error in rotation will cause a cumulative mistake in the readings. Another is that the electronic shaft

encoders that are used to translate the information from the turning wheels are expensive. This last problem may be eliminated soon, as several companies are developing low-cost integrated circuits that do the encoding job. With the addition of a microprocessor to these new circuits, this very powerful graphics input device could possibly become more popular than the joystick.

Photo 2.6: The joystick.

Photo 2.7: The mouse.

Light Pen

The joystick and mouse discussed above are primarily used as positioning devices. They allow us to represent the current position of a cursor or object on the screen and to move it about. A light pen, on the other hand, is a pointing device. When it is pointed at an item right on the screen, its program can identify what item is being indicated.

The light pen is made of a hollow stylus that contains a small lens at one end and a photocell at the other. Whenever the pen is close to the screen, light from the screen enters the pen and falls on the photocell. A switch on the pen allows the user to alert the computer that this is the position to be selected. The output of the photocell goes to a storage device similar to one bit of memory (called a flip-flop). This flip-flop can be triggered when light strikes the pen. It is reset or untriggered when it is read by the computer.

The light pen does not have the X-Y tracking hardware described for the pen and mouse. Instead, it uses software for location of its position. There are two ways to do this: polling and interrupt. In the polling method, as the raster on the screen is being scanned, each individual pixel is being illuminated. In some cases a pair of counters in the computer are constantly updated with the current row and column number of the pixel that is being displayed. In other systems, it is sufficient to simply note that the address of the pixel in the display memory tells us its current location on the screen. Regardless, the computer can decipher where on the screen the pen is pointing at any time. The computer simply checks the flip-flop after displaying each point to see if it's been triggered. Since the counters contain the X-Y position of the current pixel, when it finds the flip-flop set, it knows exactly where the pen is pointing. This approach may place heavy constraints on the computer, however, since it doesn't have much time to check the flip-flop between plotting each pixel.

In the interrupt approach, as soon as the light pen's switch is pressed, the flip-flop sends a signal to the computer that interrupts whatever it is doing and says "I have a light pen point for you." The computer then simply notes the current X-Y position of the pixel being plotted (assuming the same counters are being used to keep track of the column and row or the address of the pixel in the display RAM), and this is where the pen must be pointing. This method also assumes that the interrupt occurs fast enough so that no more pixels get plotted.

Light pens are not used for drawing on the screen because it is hard to hold them steady on the glass surface of the CRT. They are better for pointing to on-screen menus. Also, there must be light coming from the screen for the light pen to receive. Thus, a cursor has to be sent to every OFF pixel, so that the pen will be noticed when it is pointing to a location that doesn't contain any ON pixels.

Tablets

A tablet (or digitizing table) is a flat surface, separate from the display, on which the user may draw with a special stylus or pointer. Using a tablet is much like drawing with pencil and paper, and this explains their popularity.

There are several ways to build a tablet. The most common approach simply embeds into the surface a matrix of tiny wires running at right angles to each other in the X-Y plane. One system, might, for example, contain $1024 * 1024$ wires. Each line carries a special digitally coded signal. The stylus contains a sensitive amplifier that picks up the signal and amplifies it. Special decoding circuitry figures out the X-Y position of the stylus. By pressing the pen down on the tablet, a switch inside of the pen allows the user to indicate a selected X-Y position.

Another approach puts a resistive plate on the tablet and applies voltages to it, first horizontally and then vertically. The X-Y position of the pen can be tracked by measuring the voltage of the pen during the times the sheet is being scanned. Still other approaches use strip microphones on the edges of the tablet and let the stylus generate a spark that is then heard by the microphones. Counters record the delay for the sound to reach the microphones and can then compute the position of the stylus.

The tablet is perhaps the most frequently used of the graphics input devices. By placing a sketch on its surface, the stylus can be traced over it

and the drawing will be transferred directly into the computer. A line drawing can be digitized on the tablet by touching the pen to the intersections of the various lines on the drawings. If three sides of a figure are drawn and digitized, it is possible for the computer to create a three-dimensional model of the figure. Transformation software can then manipulate this information to create three-dimensional movements and perspective drawings on the screen. We will learn more about how these images are manipulated in the next chapter on software and applications.

Photo 2.8: The light pen.

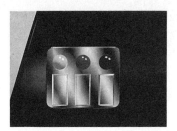

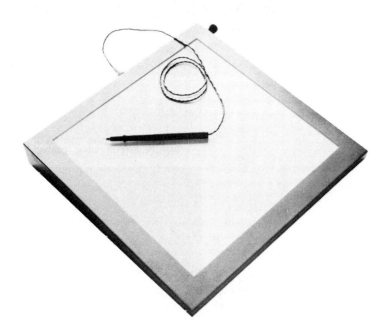

Photo 2.9: The digitizing table.

Photo 2.10: Artist using digitizing table. *(Courtesy of Aurora.)*

The hardware used today in computer animation is among the most sophisticated you can find. Yet as complex as it is, the computer revolution's trickle-down effect is making more and more of this sophistication available to the average personal computer user. It is truly remarkable to think that the devices that were once the exclusive domain of rich companies are now being studied and played with in homes across the country. Yet as advanced as the hardware is, hardware alone is not enough. Any computer, from the most expensive Cray-1 (a multimillion dollar computer being used in computer animation) to the almost throwaway $99 Sinclair, needs another half to be worth anything, to do anything useful. This other half is the software program, that marriage partner of the hardware that tells the hardware what to do. In the next chapter we will learn about the programs and software that make animation possible, and we will see how graphics software is a set of rules that tells the hardware what to do with itself. We will learn how the software can make the hardware perform incredible feats of animation and how, over the years, software has become a driving force in computer graphics.

Chapter 3

Computer Animation Software And Applications

To appreciate the full capability of the graphics hardware, we need to be aware of the hardware's nebulous marriage partner: the graphics software. This chapter introduces you to techniques for defining graphics objects that the computer hardware can understand and for moving those objects on the screen (transformation). We will also be explaining what clipping and windowing are, how three-dimensional visual realism is achieved with hidden line/surface removal, shading, color use, and more.

You will see how the software breathes life into the computer's complex circuitry. This will be revealed along with the ways in which software allows lines to be drawn, circles to be plotted, shadows to be cast, and surfaces to be colored, textured, and shaded. In addition, we will also give you insight as to how computer movies are made, revealing the techniques behind the Juggler film (described in Chapter 1), the making of Saturday morning cartoons, and inside production information about *TRON*, a recent film that relies heavily on computer animation.

3.1. GRAPHICS SOFTWARE — THE BASICS

In most high-powered graphics computers, the hardware will plot (turn ON) a point anywhere in the frame buffer or display memory when that point's X and Y coordinates are specified. In other words, if, for example, you wish the hardware to turn a pixel ON at X,Y location 100,200, then your program must pass the X coordinate of 100 and the Y coordinate of 200 to the frame buffer hardware. The hardware or software, depending on what machine you are using, will cause the bit in the frame buffer corresponding to the coordinate 100,200 to turn on, and consequently the screen will reflect this with a dot appearing at that location.

Some of the more sophisticated graphics machines have, besides just plotting hardware, built-in line-drawing circuits. With these machines you simply send the beginning and ending coordinates of the line you want on the screen, and presto — the computer draws it for you. If, however, line-drawing hardware is not included in your computer, you

may wonder where line drawing comes from. The answer lies in the software.

Software, as most know by now, is a sequence of computer instructions that creates some end effect. In a graphics computer, the instructions may be in one of several languages, including BASIC (popular with microcomputers), Pascal, or even the more fundamental language of the microprocessor that forms the heart of the computer. You don't really need to understand all these languages to appreciate that a higher, more complex level of control is operating in the graphics machine as the software steers the hardware to achieve certain effects on the screen. The software can be thought of as the soul of the machine, a higher force that can't easily be viewed but makes the computer tick, nonetheless. This higher level of control is the sequence of instructions that causes the hardware to plot in certain places and in certain ways.

Let's look at a simple example to make this clearer. Suppose that all your graphics computer can do is plot points. Say it has only the instructions HPLOT X,Y which plots a point at the location on the screen X,Y. (By the way, this is a graphics statement found in Applesoft BASIC; it is called PLOT in many other BASICs.) How can a line be drawn using just this HPLOT statement? The program in Figure 3.1 shows how. It's written in BASIC, but could be also written in Pascal, FORTRAN, machine language, or whatever language is at your disposal. In the industry, the program has a name that sort of describes what it does. It's called a Digital Differential Analyzer (DDA) because it generates lines from their differential equations, another way of saying it uses fancy "incremental" methods of plotting and replotting for drawing a line. It can be used to draw curves as well. If you have a personal computer, you might wish to type this program in and RUN it, otherwise you can follow it on paper, providing you know about BASIC, FOR/ NEXT loops, and so on. (If you don't know BASIC, then skip over it, and realize its purpose is to draw lines when line-drawing hardware is absent.)[1]

In the program in Figure 3.1, entering the endpoints of the line causes the line connecting those points to be drawn automatically. (This particular program is not complete; it will only draw lines with positive startpoints and endpoints.) There are even better algorithms than this one for drawing lines. Bresenham's Algorithm is one. It is better in the sense that the line will appear cleaner on the screen, and the program will run faster. (These algorithms can be found in *Fundamentals of Interactive Computer Graphics* by James D. Foley and Andries van Dam (Reading, M A.: Addison-Wesley, 1982) or *Principals of Interactive Computer Graphics* by William M. Newman and Robert F. Sproull (New York: McGraw-Hill, 1979).

[1]You can learn BASIC by reading *BASIC Programming Primer* by Mitchell Waite and Michael Pardee, Howard W. Sams & Co., Indianapolis, IN, or *Armchair BASIC* by Annie Fox and David Fox, Osborne/McGraw Hill, Berkeley, CA.

From the primitive capability of just plotting a pixel (HPLOT in Apple-soft), we can use software to develop more powerful features such as line drawing or curves, and from these we can draw circles, polygons, three-dimensional figures, and so on.

Figure 3.1: This DDA program in BASIC has rather simple instructions (Line 6: HCOLOR = 3) for setting the color of the line to be drawn. In a more sophisticated graphics frame buffer we might have to write additional programs that set the color or shade of the pixel as required.[2]

```
4    REM   SIMPLE DDA SIMULATION FOR APPLE II
5    HGR                    : REM puts
     Apple in the HI resolution mode
6    HCOLOR=3               : REM sets
     plotting color to white
100  INPUT "X1,Y1 ";X1,Y1   : REM input
     the beginning coordinates
110  INPUT "X2,Y2 ";X2,Y2   : REM input
     the ending coordinates
120  L = INT (ABS (X2 - X1)) : REM L is the
     "increment"
130  IF ABS (Y2 - Y1) > L THEN L =
     ABS (Y2 - Y1)
140  XI = (X2 - X1) / L : YI =
     (Y2 - Y1) / L
150  X = X1 + .5  : Y = Y1 + .5
160  REM LOOP AND PLOT LINE
170  FOR I = 1 TO L
180    X = X + XI : Y = Y + YI
190    HPLOT X,Y              : REM here's
     the actual plot
200  NEXT I
210  GOTO 100                : REM plot
     another line
```

Defining Graphics Objects

Once we can plot points and draw lines on the screen, we have all that is required for drawing simple to complex two- and three-dimensional shapes. This is done by storing the data points for the objects we want displayed (i.e., the X and Y coordinates of the object's

---

[2]In all fairness we should mention that the Apple II *does* have a line-drawing statement (called HPLOT X1,Y1 TO X2,Y2). However, the above algorithm actually draws a better line than the Apple's statement!

corners). These data points are fed to our line-plotting routines which then draw out the shape. It's all really quite simple! For example, a rectangle would require four pairs of coordinates, a triangle three pairs, and so on. For three-dimensional objects, a third coordinate describing the depth is needed for each corner. Each of the eight corners of a cube, for example, would contain three numbers, X, Y, and Z, each specifying the location of that corner in three-dimensional space.

3.2.   TRANSFORMATIONS

Once we have the capability to draw our shapes on the screen, we will want to move (translate), shrink or expand (scale), and rotate them. This can be accomplished by using the mathematics of transformations. A transformation is a mathematical formula that operates on the coordinate pairs that make up our shape. It takes the various coordinates and changes their values in distinct ways. There are three fundamental transforms in computer graphics, and they are not really as complex as their names imply.

Translation

This transform moves an object to a new location on the screen without affecting its overall shape. It works by simply adding a constant value to each coordinate pair. For example, if you have a shape made up of one point called X,Y (not much of a shape, but good for an example) and want to move it 100 units to the right and 50 units down, you would perform this transformation:

$$X' = X + 100 \qquad Y' = Y + (-50)$$

where X',Y' are the new coordinates of the point. If this formula is applied to every point in our shape, they will each shift the same distance. (Note that in many personal computers you would not need to put the −50 in parentheses because the Y axis begins at zero at the top of the screen and increases as it travels downward.)

Scaling

In computer graphics, scaling has nothing to do with fish. Rather, it is the graphics industry word for shrinking and expanding an image. Such a transformation is needed when we want to magnify some portion of our shape or to shrink it to allow more of the background to come into focus.

The scaling transform works by simply *multiplying* each coordinate point by a constant value, as follows:

$$X' = X * S1 \qquad Y' = Y * S2$$

(Note that in computers, the asterisk symbol * represents multiplication.) To expand a shape to twice its current size, all points would be multiplied by 2, as follows:

$$X' = X * 2 \qquad Y' = Y * 2$$

To contract or shrink a point, multiply all the coordinates by a fractional value. For example, to shrink our shape to one half its current size, we would multiply all coordinates by 0.5. (The same results would occur if we divided all coordinates by 2.)

If we change the size of S1 and S2 so they are not equal, then we will create distortion in the X or Y direction. To understand the visual effects of scaling, look at Figure 3.2. It shows the corners of a rectangle centered on the coordinate axis. Note that multiplying each coordinate by 2, moves each corner *outward* from the center of the axis. If we simply added or subtracted a value from the coordinates, the result would be that the corners would all shift in the same direction (up, down, left, or right). This would result in translation rather than expansion or contraction.

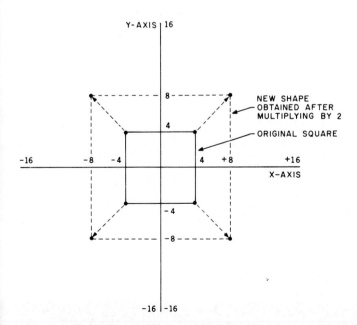

Figure 3.2: Example of scaling to magnify a shape.

Rotation

Rotation is the most complex transform because it uses the trigonometric functions sine (SIN) and cosine (COS). These are functions found in most of the high-level computer languages like BASIC and Pascal. When given an angle of a triangle, these functions produce a number that represents the ratio of two of the sides of that triangle. For example, when an angle of 45 degrees is fed to the SIN function, the result is the number .707. To rotate an object by an angle (A), we simply apply these formulas to all points:

$$X' = X * COS\ A + Y * SIN\ A \quad Y' = -X * SIN\ A + Y * COS\ A$$

The old points are X,Y, and the new points will be X',Y'. The angle used can be from 0 to 360 degrees of rotation. Note we only have to calculate the COS and SIN of the angle once, then it is simply multiplied as shown in the formula. Figure 3.3 was created by laying a piece of grid paper over a drawing and marking coordinates on the grid. These coordinates were then entered into DATA statements in BASIC. Finally, a simple line-drawing algorithm was used to draw the shape. It was rotated by recalculating the points with a certain angle using the above algorithm, and then it was redrawn.

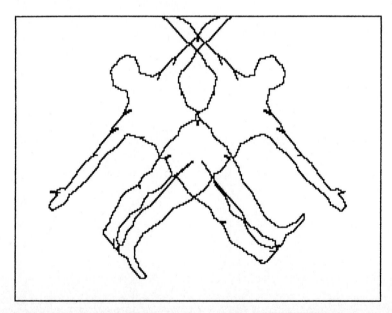

Figure 3.3: Rotation example using da Vinci man. *(Courtesy of The Waite Group.)*

A mathematical entity called a matrix can be used to assemble several transforms into one neat package. Using a matrix, it is possible to have a single mathematical operation that performs a rotation, a scaling, and a translation in one compact form. Some of the really sophisticated graphics processors perform such matrix operations in hardware!

3.3. CLIPPING AND WINDOWING

Often you see graphics programs that zoom in on some small object in a particular scene, magnifying it until it consumes the entire screen. This zooming is accomplished with the transforms of scaling and translation. But while watching a single object envelope a screen, did you ever wonder what happens to the parts of the scene that are now out of the picture? Are they being drawn on an invisible part of the display? No, they are dealt with by a process known as clipping, which means to eliminate that portion of the scene that will not appear on the display.

The purpose of clipping is to cut off portions of the object that are invisible. This is surprisingly not an entirely trivial task; in fact it is the subject of much scholarly research. In most cases it is not enough to simply determine all points that are not within the screen area and then not plot them. This would be extremely slow, as even in a magnified image there may be millions of pixels that are not displayed. We must attempt to clip larger elements or sections of the picture. This involves the use of clipping algorithms that can determine portions of the picture that are visible and invisible, such as vectors, text characters, and polygons.

To appreciate the problem, consider clipping the triangle that is partly shown on the screen in the figure on page 88. Imagine this as part of a rocket ship, or missile that is moving into the display area. It is no problem to clip lines that are *entirely* off the screen. It is done by simply throwing them away!

Assume you have line-drawing commands at your disposal. In order to clip the triangle, you must examine all the points that make it up. As you examine these points you look for ones that are off the screen edge. Assume also that your object starts at point A. You immediately discover that point B is off the screen edge. So you must draw a line from point A to a point at the edge of the screen where the line *would have* intersected the screen edge if it had extended all the way to point B. This requires your software to calculate where the line intersects the screen edge. (A simple algebraic formula exists to do this.) Next you ignore the rest of the shape that is off the screen edge (i.e., from the edge to point B, from B to C, and from C to the edge). You must then draw a second line from the edge of the screen at the point where the line would have intersected had it been drawn from point C to point A.

The problems here are finding the points outside the screen and determining where the intersection points are on the screen edge. Such clipping is usually done with algorithms that involve rejection tests to find parts that lie off the screen and subdivision calculations, which break the line into new parts that lie within the screen boundary.

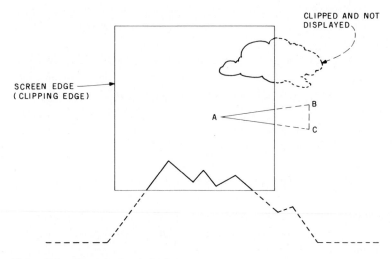

Figure 3.4: An example of clipping.

Applesoft Transformation Example

In case you are interested, here is a partial listing of a larger Applesoft BASIC program that can be studied (it can also be modified for other computers). It will help you to understand how the drawing of the rotated figure of the da Vinci Man was produced. The lengthly DATA statements for the program are not included. You can create your own if you wish (use two arrays, one for all the X values and one for all the Y values). Besides demonstrating how to do the rotation, this program also illustrates brute force clipping and scaling transform. To produce more images of the man at different angles on the screen, simply increase the size of the FOR/NEXT loop in line 2020 and change the initial angle in line 2015 and the incremental angle in line 2040.

Main Program:

```
2000 REM 'Hall of Mirrors' Da Vinci Man
     rotation example
2005 A = 140: B = 95: GOSUB 21 : REM set
     clipping limits
2006 PI = 3.14159            : REM good
     ol Pi
2007 GOSUB 45               : REM clear
     the screen, draw border
2008 GOSUB 30               : REM read
     the man's data statements
     into the array
2010 J=2: K=2: GOSUB 40     : REM
     double his size with stretch
     transform
2015 ANG = -PI/4            : REM sets
     the first angle to -45 degrees
2020 FOR P = 1 TO 2         : REM draw
     first and second man
2030   C = COS (ANG) : S = SIN (ANG)
2040   ANG = PI/2           : REM sets
     the incremental angle
     at 90 degrees
2100   GOSUB 60             : REM
     rotate the man (he's at zero
     degrees start)
2200   FX = X(0): FY = Y(0): GOSUB 10
     : REM do clipping (simple)
2205   HPLOT A + FX,B + FY
2210   FOR I = 1 TO N:
       FX = X(I): FY = Y(I): GOSUB 10
                           : REM clip
     this point first and then....
2220   HPLOT TO A + FX,B + FY : REM
     finally draw line between
     Points
2230   NEXT I
2235 NEXT P
```

Subroutines:

```
10 REM     do the clipping
11 IF FX > XH THEN FX = XH
12 IF FX < XL THEN FX = XL
13 IF FY > YH THEN FY = YH
14 IF FY < YL THEN FY = YL
15 RETURN
21 REM       set X and Y clipping limits
22 XL = -A: XH = 278 - A:
   YL = -B : YH = 191 - B:
   RETURN
```

(continued)

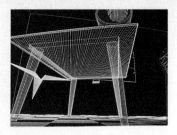

```
30 REM       read in the data
             (N=# of points, F=aspect
             correction
31 RESTORE:
   FOR I = 0 TO N:
     READ X(I):
   NEXT I
32 FOR I = 0 TO N:
     READ Y(I):
     Y(I) = -Y(I)/F:
   NEXT I:
   RETURN
40 REM       stretch or shrink transform
41 FOR I = 0 TO N:
     X(I) = J * X(I):
     Y(I) = K * Y(I):
   NEXT I :
   RETURN
45 REM       clear screen draw border
46 CALL -936: HGR: POKE -16302,0:
   HCOLOR = 3:
   GOSUB 50:
   RETURN
50 HPLOT 0,0 TO 279,0 TO 279,191
   TO 0,191 TO 0,0:
   RETURN

60 REM       actual rotation transform
61 FOR I = 0 TO N
62   X1 = C * X(I) + S * Y(I)
63   Y1 = -S * X(I)  C * Y(I)
64   X(I) = X1: Y(I) = Y1
65 NEXT I:
   RETURN
```

Figure 3.5: Applesoft Transformation Example.

Viewing and Windowing Transform

You now know about clipping a picture to remove the invisible parts and transforming a picture to change the scale and orientation of it. One of the immediate advantages we gain from the use of transformations is the ability to define pictures in the coordinate system of our choice. So far we have just used the screen's limited coordinate system, and in practice this may be quite awkward. For example, what happens when the picture's coordinates are expressed in floating point (decimal) numbers between ± 999,999.999 and the screen coordinates are integers between

0 and 1023 or 0 and 279 (as in personal computers)? We can avoid these problems if we can define our picture in its own coordinate system and then use a transformation to convert it to the screen coordinate system when we are ready to display it. Such a transformation is referred to as a viewing transform.

A viewing transform is simply a combination of clipping, scaling, translation, and rotation that converts all the picture's coordinates to screen coordinates. (Actually rotation is rare in the viewing transform.) It can be adjusted to allow us to view the picture through a viewing window, a rectangle that surrounds some portion of the picture. In computer graphics, the coordinates for the object or picture we are going to transform are called world coordinates. The world coordinates are the database of points for the picture itself (our large decimal numbers in the above example). These values may be large or small numbers with decimal points, arrays such as game boards, graphs with dates, and so on. Our screen's coordinates, on the other hand, are usually in integer form (i.e., whole numbers), and are called screen coordinates. It is the purpose of the viewing transform to convert the world coordinates from the picture's original database of points to fit into the screen coordinates. The viewing transform is particularly useful when we cannot always predict the range of numbers our application will produce. This might be the case, for example, when the data is coming from an experiment or mathematical model.

The window, a rectangular section of the world coordinate system, can specify the viewing transform to be operated on. A window can float around the picture's database of points and select out just the part we wish to zoom in on, expand, etc. The main use of defining a window is that we can lessen the work that the transform has to perform. It also makes it easy for us to examine other parts of our graph, picture scene, or whatever by simply readjusting the window's corner limits.

A viewport, in contrast, is a rectangular section of the screen coordinate system to which we can have the output of the viewing transform directed. Often the viewport is smaller than the screen, thereby allowing text menus and system messages to be placed under the picture. There may, in fact, be several viewports on a screen.

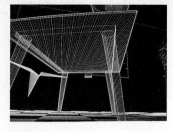

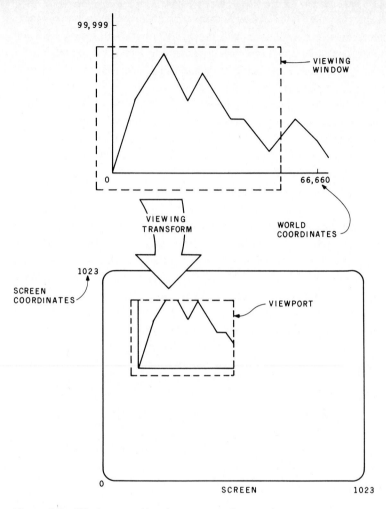

Figure 3.6: Windows, world and screen coordinates, viewports.

3.4. FILLS AND SCAN CONVERSION

We have discussed objects with wire frame construction, i.e., where the shapes are comprised of lines, like the superstructure of a building before the walls are put up. Unfortunately for the graphics designer, the real world is not made up of wire frame models, but rather contains solid areas that give a shape its substance. How does one go about filling in the wire frame outlines that make up a graphics shape? This whole process is an interesting area of study that is just now being pursued with relish in the personal computer field.

Three properties are required to fill in an area. First a mask, which defines the pixels that lie inside and outside the area to be filled, is generated. For example, a binary 0 may mean pixels outside and a binary 1 may mean pixels inside. The mask may consist of a list of the corners (vertices) of the geometric object to be filled. Computing the mask from the geometric image of the object as it exists on the screen is called scan converting. Second, there is usually a shading rule that defines what the intensity of each pixel inside the mask shall be. Different intensities inside the mask lead to different shading, shadows, colorations, textures, etc. Third, there is usually a priority assigned to the sides to be filled. Priority is the property that defines what parts of overlapping areas are obscured and which are shown. Thus when we do an actual fill we will know what areas are to cover which.

The process of converting from the geometric representation of an object (its corner coordinates) to one that can be filled on the screen is usually not complex when simple shapes are involved. A rectangle, for example, can be scan converted (filled) with a very simple algorithm that only plots pixels (or draws lines) between the left and right sides, starting at the top and finishing at the bottom. But since unadorned rectangles are uncommon in most graphics scenes, some way must be developed for scan converting a more general shape such as the polygon. The real problem of the scan conversion filling is in handling a polygon with holes, corners, and convoluted nooks and crannies.

Advanced Fills

One of the most popular scan conversion approaches for polygons involves extending an imaginary line from some point outside the polygon to the opposite side of the polygon and counting the number of boundaries (an edge of the polygon's perimeter) crossed. If an odd number of intersections is encountered, the point in question must lie inside the shape, otherwise it lies outside.

Using this algorithm, we can plot points on the line while we are inside the polygon and cease plotting when we are outside the area. This is a rather slow algorithm, as every point must be tested and compared with each edge of the polygon. This approach can be improved, however, by using the concept of coherence, which states that "if a given pixel is inside the polygon, then adjacent pixels are likely to be inside as well." This property suggests that a number of pixels should be tested together, and the most convenient group to test is the entire scan line. This leads to the famous YX Algorithm in which all intersections of scan lines are first found and put in a list. The list is then sorted so that the various intersections are grouped by increasing X values. By using the values in this list, we can quickly plot the entire line between two boundaries, without ever having to test every point.

Another popular approach to filling involves using the computer's stack. The stack is an area in the computer's memory where

we can temporarily place information and quickly retrieve it. It works like the pop-up trays or plates in a cafeteria. With this method, we scan from top to bottom and left to right filling in pixels as the scan proceeds. When the algorithm discovers that a left or right boundary changes (due to a corner, for example), it saves the current boundary coordinates (pushes them onto the stack) so it can later retrieve them and continue. The algorithm then begins filling in the new area until it finds the new right boundary and continues until it hits bottom. Upon finding the bottom, it will restore the old boundary coordinates (pop them off the stack) and continue the fill from where it left off. In essence, this algorithm searches for edges until the entire shape is filled. Such algorithms have been implemented on personal computers such as the Apple and IBM. Microsoft's BASIC for the IBM fills using the stack approach.

3.5.   THREE-DIMENSIONAL REPRESENTATION

Perhaps the most remarkable achievement of computer graphics is the modeling and displaying of three-dimensional images. Whereas two dimensions involve X and Y coordinates of width and height, the third dimension takes us into the realm of depth (the Z coordinate) and perspective realism. In two dimensions, our pictures do not require the subtle qualities of an image seriously attempting to represent reality. Realism puts an incredible burden on the graphics computer and its software. For example, since the screen is set up to display two dimensions, how is the third dimension of depth to be displayed? And how are parts of the object that are hidden by the frontal parts to be identified and removed? In addition, how will lighting, color, shadows, and texture be added to the display? All of these questions must be answered by those who employ three-dimensional computer graphics. Lets take a look at some of the concepts involved.

Achieving Realism

The degree of desired realism in computer graphics images depends on the application. Perfect realism comes at a high price in terms of the cost of hardware and software, the amount of information stored for the model, and the time required for computing different views of the display. Since a three-dimensional scene must be projected onto a two-dimensional screen, the major stumbling block is depth perception, sometimes called depth cuing. Many techniques have evolved for providing depth cues on computer graphics display, as described in the following paragraphs.

Parallel Projection   Although many different types of projection exist, all are designed to ease the task of generating three-dimensional views of images. Parallel projection is a method by which three views of an object are projected (see Figure 3.7). One application is when an architect draws three parallel projections to illustrate a house, e.g., a front view, a side view and a top view. The viewer must then infer the final shape from the three views. Most people, however, have difficulty inferring the three-dimensional view from parallel projections.

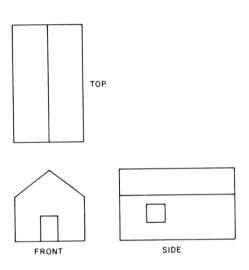

TOP

FRONT   SIDE

Figure 3.7:   Parallel projection.

Perspective Projection   This is the most common projection and involves showing the object in three dimensions on the screen, with distant objects smaller than nearer ones (see Figure 3.8). There is a potential problem here if objects are limited in depth, as there may be front/back ambiguity. For example, everyone is familiar with the wire frame cube illusion where the front and the back can change places depending on how you view it or imagine it to be. If we view the image through a wide angle lens and exaggerate the perspective depth, the front/back ambiguity disappears, but undesirable distortion effects take its place.

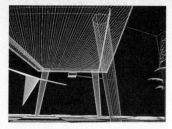 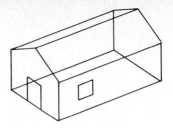

Figure 3.8: Perspective projection.

Intensity Cues   If we use intensity modulation to brighten lines that are in the foreground, we can give the illusion that they are closer to the viewer. When foreground lines are widened, the same effect is achieved. This is a simple way to create depth cues, which requires a gray scale capability in the computer (we covered gray scale in Chapter 2). If the object is very complex, however, or the depth is small, this technique may not work well.

Stereoscopic Views   If separate images are created for the left and right eyes and presented so each eye can only see the image intended for it, a powerful illusion of depth can result. Several methods have been developed for implementing this technique, including flashing shutters, polarized glasses, color filters, and so on.

Kinetic Depth Effect   Watching the movement of an object can help the viewer experience the depth effect. Motion around a vertical axis, for example, can resolve the ambiguity of a simple wire frame object because lines near the viewer move more rapidly than those at a distance. The rotation must be rapid for the effect to work, and this may require special graphics hardware.

Hidden Line Elimination   By removing lines that would not be visible to a viewer, considerable depth cues and realism can be achieved. This is a powerful and much studied technique in computer graphics. For all but the most simple of wire frame objects, it requires large amounts of computing time.

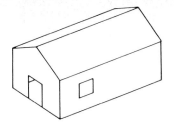

Figure 3.9: Perspective projection with hidden lines removed.

Shading, Surfacing, Texturing   By adding shading, surface texture, and shadow, computer images can achieve a degree of realism that makes them indistinguishable from photographs of real objects. The realism of many of the computer graphics photographs in this book are due to high quality shading, texturing, and surfacing.

Three-Dimensional Coordinate Systems

When dealing with three dimensions, a new axis is added to the standard two-dimensional X-Y coordinate system with which we are familiar. We use the letter Z to represent the new axis which takes on the quantity of depth. The three numbers (X, Y, Z) specify a point in this coordinate space. The choice of the directions of the three axes depends on the application. For computer graphics, it is standard to have the Y axis point up, the X axis to the right and the Z axis point either out from or in to the screen. If the Z axis points out from the screen, we have a right-handed system. If it points in to the screen, we have a left-handed system. (In computer graphics, the most popular orientation is a left-handed system so that as objects get farther away, their Z values increase.) "Handedness" answers the question "Which hand must you wrap around the Z axis so when the thumb points outward along that axis, the fingers on that hand wrap around it in a counterclockwise direction?" You can prove this to yourself on the coordinate system below. (Note in mathematics the Z axis is usually drawn facing upward.)

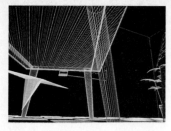

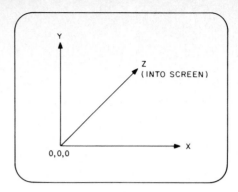

Figure 3.10: Three-dimensional coordinate system (left-handed).

To generate the view of a three-dimensional scene, three parameters must first be specified. They are viewpoint, viewing direction, and aperture (see Figure 3.11). These parameters are similar to the adjustments a photographer must make when photographing a scene. The viewpoint is the location where the camera must be physically set to take the picture, the viewing direction is the direction in which the camera points, and the aperture is the lens that determines how much of the scene will be included in the picture. These parameters are similar to the window parameters we used for two-dimensional viewing. Note that in this figure the Z axis points upward.

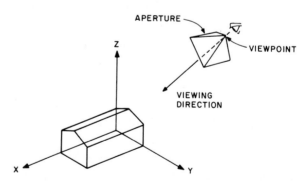

Figure 3.11: Three kinds of viewing parameters.

Modeling in Three Dimensions

Before we discuss how curves and surfaces of three dimensions are created, it is important to understand how a three-dimensional object is modeled in the computer. As shown in Figure 3.12, in two dimensions we use polygons, two-dimensional n-sided figures, like rectangles, trapezoids, pentagons, and hexagons, to model our shapes. In three dimensions we use polyhedrons (as well as polygons) to model objects. Polyhedrons are three-dimensional volumes whose sides are comprised of polygon faces. Some typical polyhedrons are cubes, parallelepipeds, wedges, prisms, etc. (see Figure 3.12).

The polygon face is specified by its vertices and its edges. A vertex is a corner of the polygon. An edge of a polygon is the line connecting two vertices. A polyhedron is also specified by its faces, which in turn are polygons that can be specified by a list of its vertices or edges. This list, referred to as the geometric description, is usually presented in a certain order so we know what vertices connect to what edges.

a) POLYGONS

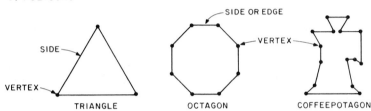

b) POLYHEDRONS

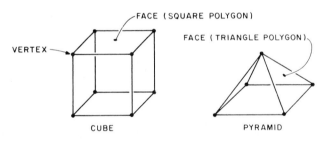

Figure 3.12: Polygons and polyhedrons defined.

Since a face has two sides (one inside the object and one facing out), some convention must be chosen for representing these faces to the computer. One way is to list the vertices of the edges in counterclockwise order when the face is viewed from outside.

Table 3.1 shows how a simple cube in the figure is represented mathematically so the computer graphics software can operate on it. Another property of the cube is its topological attributes. Whereas the geometric values give the locations of points in the image (i.e., the coordinate values for each point), the topology gives the underlying structure of the shape. This is done by listing the faces (i.e., F1, F2, etc.)

of the shape. The table may also include auxiliary information about the cube, such as the colors of the various faces, their texture, etc.

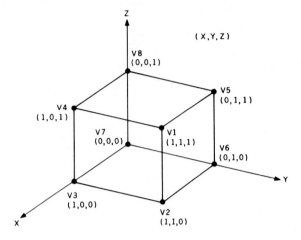

Figure 3.13: The three-dimensional cube with vertices indicated.

GEOMETRY

Vertices

V1	(1,1,1)
V2	(1,1,0)
V3	(1,0,0)
V4	(1,0,1)
V5	(0,1,1)
V6	(0,1,0)
V7	(0,0,0)
V8	(0,0,1)

(continued)

TOPOLOGY

Faces	Edges	
(list of vertices counterclockwise when viewed from outside)	(can be derived from faces but duplicates are removed)	
F1 V1,V5,V8,V4	V1,V4	V7,V8
F2 V5,V6,V7,V8	V4,V3	V8,V5
F3 V6,V2,V3,V7	V3,V2	V5,V1
F4 V1,V4,V3,V2	V2,V1	V8,V4
F5 V8,V7,V3,V4	V5,V6	V6,V2
F6 V6,V5,V1,V2	V6,V7	V7,V3

AUXILIARY DATA

Colors

(red, green, blue components)
F1   (0.4, 0, 0.3)
F2   (0.3, 0.6, 0.1)
remaining faces repeat F2

Table 3.1: Representing the cube with a data list.

Almost any shape may be created by assembling a group of polyhedrons. As the number of faces of each polyhedron in the shape is increased, very complex objects can be represented. It is beyond the scope of this book to discuss modeling in detail, but it is sufficient to understand that the object to be modeled will be represented as an ordered list of vertices or faces. It is on this list that the transformation, clipping, windowing, and upcoming hidden line removal and surfacing algorithms must operate.

Constructing three-dimensional models is extremely difficult as vast quantities of data must somehow be entered into the computer. The usual method is to make a complex object from more primitive shapes. For example, we might create a three-dimensional ant by making the body from previously defined spheres which were constructed, in turn, from many-sided polyhedrons. We would then only need to add legs which could be made of cylinders, and so on.

3.6. CURVES AND SURFACES

One of the most intriguing aspects of three-dimensional graphics is how a curve is made and how surfaces are produced. We have already learned how to represent a three-dimensional object by using many-sided

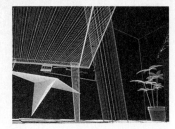

polyhedrons. Although it would be logical to assume that complex curved surfaces could be modeled by simply increasing the number of polyhedrons and making them smaller, it is often very difficult to modify such shapes because of the number of faces involved. A simple bottle, for example, might be approximated by a single polyhedron with 1000 faces. Changing its diameter would then involve thousands of coordinate points, all of which would have to be altered by the designer.

The need for smooth curves and surfaces is dependent on the actual application. In some applications, such as the design of a simple mechanical part for an engine, for example, constructing the shape from plane face polyhedra may be completely adequate. On the other hand, designing car bodies, where smooth graceful curves are required, calls for more complex shapes and very smooth surfaces. Such shapes are too cumbersome to represent with a finite number of polyhedrons. There must be other ways to modify curves that involve changing only a few parameters thus affecting the curve in some predictable manner.

There are basically two different methods for describing and creating curves and surfaces: analytic and synthetic. Analytic methods are used to describe shapes that can be measured, i.e., data points exist, and we wish to come up with the curve that is described by these points. Analytic methods are employed when we are trying to achieve a precise fit, to represent a shape in some compact form, and so on. Examples are fitting a curve to a set of data points, fitting a surface to the measured properties of some real object, etc. Synthetic methods, on the other hand, are more often encountered when curves are being created from scratch in the design process. With synthetic methods a designer interacts with a program to create or modify a model of a shape, changing and improving the design until it meets the desired criteria. That model may then be used to create an image of the shape which can be examined.

With synthetic methods we are more concerned with the design process and the exploration of the appearance of new curves and surfaces. Once a curve is created with synthetic methods, the data which describes it can then be used in the analytic methods, allowing measurement of the curve. In this section we will concentrate on the synthetic approach, i.e., interactive shape modeling, and the techniques that we describe for curves can be extrapolated for use with surfaces.

Ordinarily, when a designer is modeling a shape based on curves, there is an interactive program involved. The designer first makes a rough approximation of the shape, then improves it with the program until it more closely resembles the desired shape. A very common way to control the shape of a curve is to locate points through which the curve must pass. These points, called the curve's control points, can be connected by straight lines to make the curve's open polygon. Since the creation of curves is conceptually simple but mathematically complex, we will stick with a visual explanation. (See Figure 3.14.)

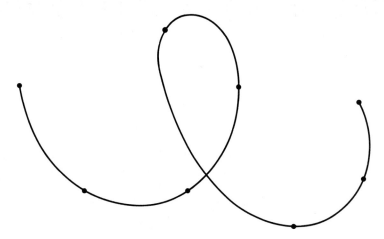

Figure 3.14: Control points for a curve.

By manipulating and moving these control points, it is possible to control the shape of the curve in a predictable way. A complex curve is made up of several curves pieced together end to end. As a designer alters a control point, the curve may change shape only in the region of the control point, or throughout the entire curve. This capability allows the designer to fine tune the curve as desired and is respectively referred to as local and global control.

Control points for a curve or surface may actually be off the curve. One such type of control point altered curve is called Bezier curves (pronounced bay-zee-YAY). A simple Bezier curve with four control points is shown in Figure 3.15. Bezier, a Frenchman who worked for Renault, created a computer modeling program for designing auto body surfaces. The key to his work is special blending functions. These are mathematical functions that represent the *influence* that each of the control points exerts on the curve. By controlling these blending functions, the designer can change the Bezier curve in very predictable and uniform ways.

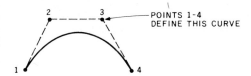

Figure 3.15: Bezier curve and four control points.

Modeling three-dimensional surfaces is merely an extension of control points. Using Bezier curves we can produce a three-dimensional surface by multiplying two curves! Usually a surface is pieced together

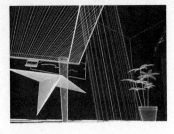

from several patches and continuity between them (the places where they connect) is formed with special mathematics. Figure 3.16 shows a Bezier surface and its control points.

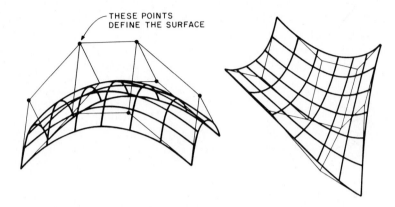

THESE POINTS
DEFINE THE SURFACE

Figure 3.16: Bezier surface and its control points.

One problem with Bezier curves is that changing the control point can affect more of the curve than the designer wishes. Points that are far from the altered control point, for example, can be affected. Another technique for generating curves that doesn't suffer from this problem is called the B-spline curve. B-splines allow multiple control points at the same location (i.e., the control points can overlap). This in turn allows good local control of the curve without affecting distant points.

Displaying curves and surfaces on a CRT is more difficult than displaying shapes constructed from straight lines. The simplest technique for displaying curves is using wire frame techniques. In this process, the curve is evaluated using the techniques described above and the points are then connected by many short, straight line segments. Getting depth cues for the display of curves can be tricky too. Often the method of intensity modulation is used for providing a depth impression, but this is not always adequate for complex shapes. Revolving the shape about an axis can help in visualization.

Another approach to visualizing subtle curves in surfaces is by using the hedgehog method. Here small vectors which are normal (perpendicular) to the surface are displayed (see Figure 3.17). Although this technique makes the display look like grass shoots projecting from the surface, its orientation gives the eye a better idea of the general changes the surface will undergo.

Although all of these are valid techniques, shading, which we will discuss soon, is perhaps the best way to visualize curves.

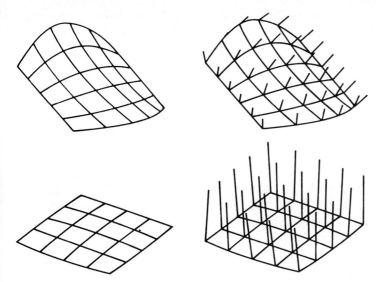

Figure 3.17: Hedgehog method for visualizing subtle curves.

3.7. HIDDEN LINE AND SURFACE REMOVAL

Perhaps the greatest challenge facing the computer graphics user is the removal of hidden parts of images from solid objects. In real life we don't concern ourselves with hidden lines because an object's solidity automatically blocks light from unviewed parts. (Perhaps there is a survival value for not having X-ray vision like Superman, for had we such an ability we would probably have a difficult time figuring out the front of objects from the back, not to mention the privacy problem.) Given our "limited" visual abilities, we are seldom conscious of what the back side, or inside, or hidden parts of an object look like. When objects are projected on the screen in computer graphics, however, there is no such automatic hidden line removal, and every single part of the object is displayed. To rectify this, special hidden line and hidden surface algorithms have been developed.

In the early 1960s most algorithms centered on hidden *line* removal because raster displays and surface fills were still in their infancy. We have certainly come a long way since then. Today hidden surface algorithms that utilize hardware can generate views of objects at rates of up to 30 images per second. Although there are many algorithms for hidden line and surface elimination, there is no one best algorithm. Each is ideal for a certain type of scene model or a certain degree of image complexity.

Hidden line and hidden surface algorithms basically work much like the scan converting we discussed earlier. They all use geometric sorting to determine which parts of the shape are visible and which are invisible. Geometric sorting involves finding the objects which are closest to the viewer. Once the near objects are determined, the parts far from the

viewer can be tossed in the proverbial garbage can. Geometric sorting is, in reality, much more difficult than it may sound because complex objects do not always fall into simple order. Many algorithms rely on the property of coherence (lines in close proximity are similar) to simplify the determination of lines or surfaces that are hidden.

The most popular form of hidden surface removal is the depth-buffer algorithm. In this method we scan through the object by looking at each of its points in the database. Imagine peering into each pixel with X-ray vision. You would be able to see every surface of every object which falls directly behind that pixel. The Z value of each of these surfaces is checked, and only the one with the lowest value (the closest one in relation to the viewer) is saved. A record is then made of the depth (Z) of this closest surface in a separate array which has the same resolution as the screen. The intensity of this closest surface at that pixel is recorded in another array.

Thus two arrays are used, one for the depth and one for the intensity. When the depth-scanning algorithm is finished, the intensity array contains the image with the hidden surfaces removed. Note that the algorithm only works on objects that have been converted into screen coordinates. Thus if the object is magnified, the entire process will need to be repeated.

The depth-buffer algorithm is not always practical because of the huge size of the depth and intensity arrays. A 400×400 coordinate system would require two arrays with 160,000 elements each! One way around this is to use smaller arrays and work on individual sections of the picture. This is a good solution since we can throw out the depth array after each pixel is done. The 400×400 system can be divided into 100 rasters of 40×40, so only 1600 elements are needed per array.

The process of computing the arrays is still very time consuming and eats up memory like a starving elephant. The way to solve the problem of excessive processing time is to use coherence techniques, as were described earlier, for the scan conversion methods. The need to cut down on processing time has given rise to a class of removal techniques called scan line algorithms that solve the hidden surface problem one scan line at a time. These capitalize on the fact that for each single scan line, short spans of pixels will lie within the same polygon.

Another approach to hidden surface removal involves comparing two polygons to determine which obscures the other. We can compute each polygon's plane equation, which precisely defines the surface of that polygon. This equation allows us to then determine if a particular point in the display scene lies inside or outside the polygon plane. We can also locate all the polygons with back faces (those which cannot be viewed by the observer because they lie on the side of the object facing *away* from the viewpoint).

Many more advanced algorithms exist for removing hidden surfaces, each having characteristics that make it better for one type of object than another. The more available the tools, the better, because as scene complexity grows, hidden surface elimination limits the ability of a computer to process pictures in real time.

3.8. SHADING

Now we come to shading, the one component of graphics processing that does more to help create realism than any other factor. After we have identified the visible surfaces with our hidden surface algorithms, a shading model is used to compute the colors and intensities for the surface. The shading model has two main aspects: properties of the surface and properties of the illumination falling on it. This model attempts to simulate the behavior of light on an object as it would appear in the real world to the eye. To do this, it must simulate the surface properties of the object, such as its reflectance, texture, color, and transparency. Reflectance tells us how much incident light returns to the eye. If the surface is textured, the reflected light will vary with the position of the texture on the surface. If the surface reflection changes for different wavelengths of light, it will appear to be colored. If some light passes through the object then it has transparency.

In addition, the model must simulate the illumination on the object. If the illumination is uniform from all directions it is called diffuse illumination. If the illumination comes from one location it is called a point source. Point source lighting causes highlights to appear on the surface. If the object moves, as it will in animation, the model must change the lighting accordingly. This is a difficult task indeed.

Photo 3.1, below and on the next page, shows a good example of curved objects, hidden surface removal, and shading.

a)

(continued)

b)

c)

Photo 3.1: Hidden line removal and shading: a) Artist's Table (wireframe) represents one way of previewing an image without incurring the overhead of a full rendering. The color of the wireframe components approximates the colors of the final image. Once the wireframe image is constructed and situated to satisfaction, a solid image with hidden surfaces removed is rendered. b) Artist's Table (with stand-ins) shows the next step in establishing a shot, which is a hidden-surface rendering with "stand-ins," i.e., simpler, less detailed substitutes for the objects to be used in the final image. These stand-ins allow decisions about placement, coloring and lighting to be made and changed more quickly than would be possible with a fully detailed image. c) Artist's Table shows the final still-life, with all the fully detailed parts included in the scene. Spline-based primitive objects, as well as simpler geometric primitive shapes make up the objects in this scene. Light is from two light sources: a white light from over the viewer's left shoulder and a yellow one from the rear left of the scene. These pictures are antialiased, full color, 512 X 512 images (see color insert). They were produced on a PDP 11/44 computer using the UNIX operating system, C programming language, and a DeAnza 6400 frame-buffer. Software and images were produced by Richard Chuang, Glenn Entis, and Carl Rosendahl. *(Courtesy of Pacific Data Images.)*

Here is how it's done. A mathematical model that takes all the above parameters into account is developed for each pixel of the object in the scene. The model determines the amount of light energy coming from a point on the display. The model can be broken down into three parts, the contribution from diffuse illumination, contributions from one or more light sources, and a transparency effect. The actual mathematics must utilize the rays of light arriving from different parts of the scene. Each of these effects contributes to the final shading of the object.

An example of a shading formula would be

$$E(pd) = R(p) * I(d)$$

where E(pd) is the energy coming from the point P due to diffuse illumination, I(d) is the diffuse illumination falling on the entire scene, and R(p) is the reflectance coefficient at point P, which ranges from 0 to 1. The actual formulas used for modeling shading use this one as a starting point and expand to be much more complex. Such things as reduction in intensity due to changing angles of incidence (Lambert's Law), single point source contributions, and transparency must also be included in the formula.

The actual calculations must be performed many times (for each point on the object) to produce a properly shaded image. Thus much of the work in shading involves finding ways to reduce the amount of effort required to evaluate the model. A 1024 × 1024 raster, for example, will require that the calculation be performed on over one million pixels. Once again, the concept of coherence is utilized to reduce the amount of calculation required. (Shading coherence relies on the fact that the intensity of adjacent pixels is very nearly identical.)

Two popular algorithms for improving the shading of an object are the Gouraud (pronounced goor-ROE) shading technique and the Phong technique. The Gouraud algorithm involves computing the normal vectors (the perpendiculars) of the numerous surfaces, vertices, and intensities of the shape, and then averaging them. The main advantage to this approach is that it partially eliminates Mach bands, i.e., unwanted intensity ridges that arise from simple shading of the object. On the other hand, the effectiveness of the algorithm is lessened when motion is induced. While the Phong technique eliminates the problems of Gouraud shading, it requires much longer to calculate.

One real problem facing those who use shading is the limitations of the hardware. If the spot size of the electronic beam changes (i.e., the diameter of the beam when it strikes the CRT), the sharpness of the image suffers. If the spot is too small, an array of dots will appear where smooth shading was supposed to show through.

Some of today's most sophisticated special effects utilize shading techniques. The use of transparency, surface detail, shadows, texture, and reflections are more of an art than a science. Although it is difficult to imagine how these techniques will one day be simiplified, it is almost certain that they will. Perhaps LSI chips (large scale integration — the technique used to make microprocessors) will be developed that apply shading algorithms to user-generated scenes.

3.9. ANTIALIASING LINES

Antialiasing (pronounced anti-AY-lee-es-sing) is a technique used to remove the jagged staircase effect that occurs on a computer screen when lines are drawn. Since the distance between pixels is not infinitesimal, a staircase effect occurs as the line bounds towards its endpoint. Also known as dejagging, antialiasing involves using intensity modulation to make the line appear a smooth entity, thus minimizing the staircase effect. (See Figure 3.18.)

Ideally, a line on a computer screen would be drawn from one point to another, turning on only that portion of a pixel necessary to represent the line (a). This is not possible since pixels must be either on or off. So the software or hardware that draws the line must take a staircase path from one pixel to the next, approximating the straight line (b). The higher the resolution, the less the staircase (aliasing) effect will be noticed. There is, however, another method besides more resolution to get rid of the "jaggies."

With antialiasing, we can control the *intensity* of each pixel that the line goes through rather than just turning it on or off. The importance of this capability is apparent when we draw a straight line through the pixels from the start point to the endpoint (c). The line will cut the boxes (pixels) into sections. The antialiasing routine determines what percentage of the box is intersected by the line and uses this to figure the *shade* of that pixel. For example, if the area above the line is black and the screen is white, then the pixel (1,0) would be a color which was a mixture of 50 percent black and 50 percent white (because half of it is crossed by the line). On the other hand, the pixel (0,0) in the figure would be 85 percent black and 15 percent white (only 15 percent is below the line), and pixel (0,1) would be completely black (none of it is below the line).

If this intersecting line represented the outline of a color filled object, then we would use the same figures to compute the percentages of each color that the pixel should receive. If the color above the line was 100 percent green and the color below the line was 100 percent yellow, then a pixel (1,0) which has the line cutting it exactly in half would be 50 percent green and 50 percent yellow.

Some of the more prominent graphics effects houses, such as Lucasfilm, are staunch supporters of antialiasing and even wear T-shirts with "jaggies forbidden" symbols on them. Personal computer owners must learn to live with jaggies for the time being, given the limited resolution of their machines.

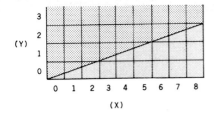

a) IDEAL BUT IMPOSSIBLE.
CANNOT DIVIDE A PIXEL IN HALF

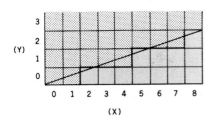

b) JAGGIES
PIXEL IS EITHER ON OR OFF.

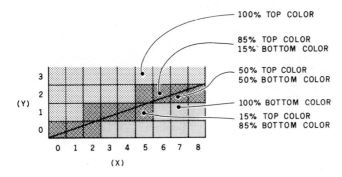

c) ANTIALIASING
USING MIXTURES OF COLORS

Figure 3.18: Antialiasing example.

a)

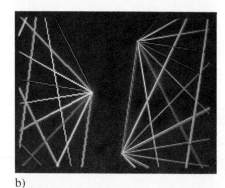

b)

c)

Photo 3.2: Antialiasing on a CRT: a) Two graphic objects — the one on the left a) is antialiased, the one on the right b) is regular. Note how a) seems smoother. b) Closeup of both objects shows how antialiased a) is made smoother by shading edges of the line. c) Extreme closeup of antialiased object reveals details of shading effect on jaggies. *(Courtesy of Advanced Electronic Design, Inc.)*

3.10. PERSONAL COMPUTER ANIMATION SOFTWARE

The state of software techniques for personal computers is not nearly as advanced as those used for high-tech machines. The main reason for this is that memory for these machines has purposely been kept below 64K to keep the price realistically within the consumer's range. Although this is changing with new, large-memory 16-bit personal computers like the IBM PC and Apple's Lisa, the software for taking advantage of the larger memory of these machines is still not available. This is not to say, however, that the graphics software on the personal computer has not matured. As we point out in detail in the next chapter, personal computer graphics software offers a large array of new ideas and techniques, especially in the area of real-time animation. You won't find built-in transformation algorithms, texturing and shading techniques, or shadow mechanisms (at least right now). But you will find automatic movement of simple graphics objects in real time, built-in color fill, special programmable graphics definition languages, circle generation routines, neat graphics languages, numerous text and color modes, page-flipping animation, image array plotting, players, sprites, hardware background scrolling, and more.

We will cover all these concepts in Chapter 4. For now you should be aware that the personal computer is hot on the tail of the high-tech machines, and, as memory capacity grows and programs mature, personal computers will eventually have special software for doing the same complex three-dimensional effects that are seen on the higher memory devices.

3.11. HIGH-TECH DIGITAL PAINT SYSTEMS

To many artists the computerization of painting is nothing less than a mortal sin. This is understandable since the majority of artists eke out a meager existence expressing the more subtle emotions of the heart, delving into rarer forms of meaning, and in general are humanists rather than technocrats. To most of them, digital and all its ramifications is the antithesis of true art. You would be lucky to get one to even consider that a computer could outmaneuver the stroke of a paint brush. The day has come, however, when artists must begin to wake up and see the graphics computer as an entirely new form of artistic expression rather than a device that should be shunned. A graphics computer equipped with good software for drawing can offer extraordinary artistic control. (Using such a system can even save on oil and canvas expenses.)

a)

(continued)

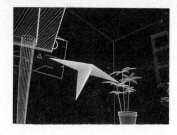

b)

c)

Photo 3.3: These examples were created on high-tech paint systems. In a) "Mt. Fuji," a very high resolution image shows reflectance of the snow-covered mountain, with a small boat crossing the water in front of it. Note the delicate light blue tones. b) Shows a hand-drawn Santa Claus: note the exquisite shading. *(Courtesy of Aurora Systems, Damon Rarey-artist.)* In c), the city skyline was created on a Video Palette 3 paint system as part of the film *Subway,* nicely demonstrating the level of creativity an artist can achieve on a paint system. (See color insert.) *(Courtesy of Digital Effects Inc.; Mark Lindquist — artist.)*

What Are Paint Systems?

To allow artists to utilize the power of computer graphics, special "paint" software has been developed. These paint systems are programs that can work in conjunction with digital tablets and light pens (described in Chapter 2). They allow the artist to draw on the computer screen by moving the stylus on the tablet, or the light pen on the CRT itself, as if it were a paint brush. The artist usually has a menu presented on part of the computer screen in a viewport (out of the way of the picture) that contains instructions for using the system. (These might include selection boxes for choosing color, brush width, and other parameters.) By using the keyboard along with the menu and the pen, an artist can, for example, select the brush width that draws anything from a very fine line only one pixel wide to a very wide line comprised of many pixels. Some advanced systems even allow the brush to simulate a paint sprayer, sputtering and feathering the edges of the painted line as if there were an aerosol can behind the stylus!

In addition to allowing the selection of paint brush sizes, the paint system that is implemented on a high-tech computer allows the artist to choose from a fabulous array of colors. On some systems there may actually be a maximum of 16 million colors to choose from.

With a paint system, an artist can also superimpose multiple images. For example, the artist can create a background scene and then merge it with previously created foreground images. The foreground images can be moved around on the background until they are in the perfect position. Other effects possible for the artist are color cycling (causing certain colors on the screen to change simultaneously to new colors), zooming (magnifying any particular section in a scene so it fills the entire screen), and adding patterns and textures. This last feature, sometimes called rubber stamping, is truly an example of something that computers can easily do that painters cannot. For example, suppose the artist uses the computer paint system to create a brick pattern to be used for a wall. Once a small patch of brick has been made, it can be attached to a brush. Then every time the brush is pressed down on the tablet, the pattern is placed on the screen. In this way the entire wall is rubber stamped on the screen.

Technical Details

Technically, such sophisticated paint systems require large frame buffers, powerful computers, and very large hard disks. The software for these systems is very expensive (over $10,000 on the average), and the hardware can easily exceed $50,000. Digitizing tablets with very high resolution are needed. To use this system for video production, a video tape recorder is attached. For film quality images, an expensive film recorder is required for capturing the output onto film.

Main Applications

Some of the main uses of paint systems today are in television news, weather reporting, and creating textures for high-tech three-dimensional texture mapping (e.g., the Genesis planet in *Star Trek II*). It is relatively easy, for example, for an artist at the TV station to quickly draw up maps and pictorials on the computer, alter them to fit the news situation and finally capture them on video tape.

Another important use of the paint system is in filling cartoon ''cels'' with color (we'll say more about that later). A scan conversion algorithm can evenly fill an enclosed boundary faster and far more accurately than a human artist. The animation field is also utilizing paint systems for creating special effects not possible or not easily made by conventional techniques.

One popular software paint system was AVA. It was based on NYIT's paint program (written by Alvy Ray Smith) and modified by Tom Porter (who went on to write Lucasfilm's amazing paint program). AVA ran on a DEC PDP-11 and was designed to be simple to use. However, because it was too sophisticated for its time (it had *too many* functions for the average user), it was pulled off the market by its owners,

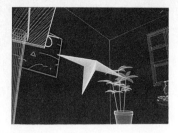

Ampex. The CBS network, however, still uses AVA for many of its news graphics.

Big names in paint systems include Dick Shoup's Aurora system in San Francisco, Digital Effects in New York, and NYIT's "Images" system. Microprocessors used frequently in these systems are the DEC LSI 11/23 and the Z80. Popular minicomputers (more expensive but also more powerful) used with paint systems include the HP 1000 and General Nova among others. The principal computer language for paint systems is C. As described at the end of Chapter 2, C is a compiled language that is fast in execution, fairly easy to maintain, and becoming more popular among computer users. Most paint systems require at least 192K of RAM. Most of them store images on disk using the same run-length encoding techniques for compression that were described in Chapter 2.

An excellent survey of digital paint systems appeared in the April 1982 issue of *Computer Graphics World*, volume 5, number 4, page 61.

Personal Computer Paint Systems

Today there are several low-cost paint systems designed for personal computers like the Apple and ATARI. (These might actually replace the need for high-tech systems when low-resolution with only a few colors is all that is required.) One particularly fine piece of software can help your Apple emulate a $250,000 graphics system for just $39.95! The package is called Special Effects. It was written by Mark Pelczarski of Penguin Software (830 4th Ave, Geneva, IL 60134) and requires DOS 3.3, 48K of RAM, and a joystick, paddle, or graphics tablet. Special Effects provides 96 different paint brushes that can be moved about the screen. You can load your brush with any of 107 colors or color patterns and move the brush anywhere on the screen. Borders are not required for filling with patterns and colors! Even shading is possible. Brushes and color palette is displayed on screen 2 of the Apple, so it is easy to switch back and forth between your picture and your menu. The package includes a magnify mode which lets you magnify the area around the cursor two or four times so you can see individual pixels. In addition, there is software for taking fonts created with a font generator and merging it into your scene. Mirror image flips and negative image tricks can also be performed (reversing the color of all pixels).

The most impressive aspect of this software is that you can take a rectangular portion of your picture and move it to any other portion of the display. This allows the production of some terrific animation effects. There is also a picture-packing routine for crunching pictures to use less storage space on the disk (just like in the high-tech machines). You can even string several pictures together so they can be quickly and automatically loaded into the display RAM by a BASIC program statement.

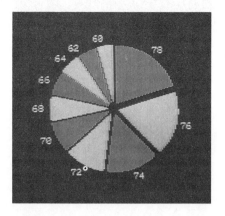

Photo 3.4: This pie chart, created on the screen of the Apple III personal computer, has a resolution of 280 × 192. This photo shows the jaggies very clearly. Although few people know it, the Apple has a higher 560 × 192 resolution, but it is only black and white. *(Courtesy of Apple Computer Company, Inc.)*

Photo 3.5: Scene created on Apple II using "Special Effects" paint system by David Lubar (see color insert). *(Courtesy of Penguin Software.)*

Of course, the Apple and the Special Effects software lack the high resolution and color capability of the high-tech paint systems. But consider a $3,000, 280 × 192 resolution, six-primary color computer, and $39.95 paint software package versus a $150,000, 1024 × 1024 resolution, 16 million color computer, and $10,000 paint software package. It is easy to see why these low-cost systems are extremely attractive — and it surely won't be long before their resolution and color capabilities increase to a point where they are rivaling the high-tech machines.

3.12. COMPUTER-ASSISTED AND COMPUTER-GENERATED ANIMATION

Now that you know the basics of graphics software, you are probably anxious to discover how computers are used in professional film animation today. There are two very broad categories of computer animation: computer-assisted animation (also called computer-aided animation) and computer-generated animation, which can be further subdivided into real-time and non-real-time computer-generated animation. Computer-assisted animation is used to aid artists in the production of two-dimensional animation (with paint systems, cel opaquing, etc.) whereas computer-generated animation is the process by which the computer generates a realistic three-dimensional image under the direction of a human-designed database and animation controls. We will explain these in more detail.

A third area outside the realm of computer animation in which computers are being used today in film is called motion control photography. Motion control photography involves using a computer to control the movement of the motion picture camera. The camera has several "stepper" motors that can change its position in almost any direction by very small increments. By doing this, the computer has taken over a laborious task which has previously been relegated to the animator. The camera may be snapping pictures of a spaceship model, for example, while revolving around the model, giving the illusion that the ship is moving. Or it may simply be passing over a long landscape. The computer simplifies the calculations for pans (left to right movement), tilts, rotations, and accelerations.

The movie *Dragonslayer* used these techniques extensively in addition to a new technique called Go-Motion. The models of the dragon were also provided with stepper motors and connected to an Apple II. Rather than moving the dragon and *then* taking a picture, as is usually done with stop motion photography, the movie's creators moved the dragon by the computer *while* the frame was being exposed. This caused each frame to be slightly blurred (as is the case with normally photographed scenes using live actors), resulting in extremely smooth motion. Industrial Light and Magic (a division of Lucasfilm) is a pioneer of such exciting effects.

Computer-Generated Animation

This book primarily focuses on computer-generated animation. As we learned in previous sections, the generation of the original artwork in such animation usually comes from the initial generation of a database of coordinate points that describe the fundamental shape of an object. The method used to enter these points into the computer depends on the object to be animated.

A simple cube that will fly and twist across the screen can be completely generated by mathematics, since its mathematical description is fairly simple and the number of points describing it is minimal. It can thus be entered by a formula, through the digitizing tablet, or with a simple sketch and a digitizing camera. (A digitizing camera is a camera connected to the computer in such a way that anything that appears in front of its lens is scanned and converted to a bit image and stored in the frame buffer.) A three-dimensional image as complex as a person juggling geometric objects might take so long to describe mathematically (given the complex and subtle motions involved) that methods for entering the datapoints which involve shortcuts might be required.

Once the initial coordinates for the image have been entered into the computer, there are several steps that may occur for the production of the final image. In general, they will involve mathematically affecting the image, transforming it, including rotation and scaling, removing hidden lines and surfaces, shading, coloring, texturing, and shadowing. A paint system may be employed for several of the coloring functions.

As always, the actual steps involved are dependent on the particular image and application. In order to get a feel for how an application of computer-generated animation might proceed, we will describe the making of the Juggler film (see Chapter 1). The processes used to produce the Juggler cover the gamut of animation technique, but remember that other animations may take a different approach. The end product is what is important; how it is accomplished is secondary. This sequence is renowned as an excellent example of the realism that can be achieved with computer animation today.

Making of the Juggler   If you forgot our description of the Juggler film, now would be a good time to reread it at the beginning of Chapter 1.

The film shows a juggler in a black tuxedo juggling three geometric shapes. Incredible camera angles, smooth realistic body movements, vivid color, and an eerie manikin face, make this film an outstanding example of computer animation. The film was produced by Information International, Inc. (Triple I), a California company which excelled in animation and computer graphics effects. As we explained above, the first step in the production of any computer animation is obtaining the database for the objects.

Triple I had two choices for getting the initial image inside the computer. They could either synthesize the juggler inside the computer using pure mathematics or they could somehow get the coordinate points of a real juggler's movements inside the computer. Synthesizing their own was almost impossible because there are so many subtle movements of the human body that it would have taken years to describe it mathe-

matically. So they hired a professional juggler named Ken Rosenthal (the computerized juggler is called Adam Powers).

The first step in getting the datapoints into the system was to have Ken dress up in a white leotard and stand on a stage. One camera was placed above him and one directly in front of him. The cameras were synchronized so each frame picked up the exact same movement. The people at Triple I then painted black dots at each joint of Ken's body and connected them with black lines.

With Ken on stage and the camera rolling, they had him juggle three objects for five minutes. The film was then viewed and edited down to one minute of exceptional juggling. After studying the film very carefully, its creators found a simple three second sequence of juggling that could be used for cyclical animation. In other words, this three-second piece of film could be played over and over and it would appear as if Ken (Adam Powers now) were continuously juggling the shapes.

The next step was to rotoscope Ken. Triple I mounted one of the projectors on a device called an animation stand and advanced the three seconds of film one frame at a time, projecting each frame onto a large piece of engineering paper. As each frame was illuminated on the paper, they ignored the other parts of his body and carefully traced onto the paper all the dots at the joints and the black lines connecting them. This process was repeated for the top and front camera views. When they were done, they ended up with 144 frames of data (pieces of paper). This number of frames comes from the fact that the cameras run at 24 frames per second; 24×3 seconds $= 72$ frames, and since there were two views, 72×2 gives 144.

Their next task was to get all this data into the computer, so they took their paper frames to a digitizing table and entered the captured points and lines into the computer. (Recall that a digitizing table is a tablet with a special pen. A piece of paper with an image on it is placed flat on the table and is traced over with the pen. The computer is able to follow the pen's motion and record the X and Y coordinates of each pen position.)

They pressed the pen down at a joint to tell the computer it was an endpoint. The two camera views allowed them to track each joint in three dimensions, thereby giving 19 points per frame, for each of the 72 frames. The result was that all the frame information from Ken's juggling was entered into the computer. From this information they formed a database of points for each frame. The precise movements of the juggler were now captured inside of the computer.

The next step was to create the juggler's body parts and make him appear three-dimensional. For this they used a geometric wire frame cylinder for each limb, modeling it mathematically inside the computer, and then attaching it around the limb and joint data already stored in the computer. (See Photo 3.6.) Much experimenting was needed with the

cylinders to get them to correspond properly to the database. Each cylinder was merged with its neighbor in the final filming. The shoes and details of the tuxedo were also added later. Because each cylinder penetrated its neighbor, they decided to make the tux black. This would make the connection points less noticeable.

Photo 3.6: This is the wire frame substructure of the Juggler model, which was created from a digitization of a live model. *(Courtesy of Information International, Inc.)*

Once the wire frame image was perfected, the difficult part was completed. At that point a hidden line removal method called Bouknight's algorithm (a special mathematical method) was used to make the hidden lines disappear. Color was then added by using a cubic patch program and polygon coloring. Shading was accomplished with Lambert's Cosine Law.

Creating the face presented a unique problem. Two views of a face (front and side) were sketched on four-foot square engineering grid paper. Then they approximated the face using 400 polygons. It was done this way because it is extremely difficult to enter curves into a computer. Triple I wanted the face to be as natural as possible and therefore needed many polygons, because people react negatively to a face with distortions in it.

The next step was to take the engineering paper with the polygons on it and lay it on the digitizing table. The data for the polygon's locations

was entered in the computer's database by tracing the polygons of the face on the table — thus it "knew" how the face was shaped. Triple I only digitized half the face and then mirrored the image into two pieces and joined them in the computer. Since it looked too perfect, they had to add some imperfections, and did this by moving some of the datapoints around. Finally, they mathematically smoothed the polygons of the face by using the special Gouraud's algorithm we described earlier in this chapter. By the time the entire face was completed, they had used more than 1000 polygons.

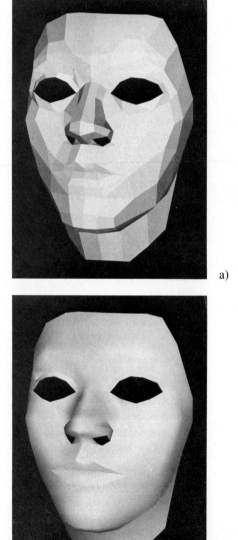

a)

b)

Figure 3.19: Human face simulated with polygons. *(Courtesy of Henri Gouraud, University of Utah.)*

If you're wondering about the computer that Triple I used, it was not an ATARI or an Apple II. Rather, it was a custom-made computer prototype called a Foonly, designed to be faster than many minicomputers. The resolution at which the Juggler was photographed on 35 mm film was 3000 points by 2400 lines, and that's 130 times finer than the Apple. On 4 × 5 transparencies, Triple I records at a resolution of 6000 points by 4000 lines. When recording on film, the company uses an incredible 9 bits per color, which amounts to over 134 million color levels.

Real-Time High-Tech Animation

For real-time animation, the same concepts described throughout this book are used. The only difference is that the speed at which the software processes the images must be much faster. This is usually accomplished by using very high-speed computers that cost in the millions of dollars. (The CRAY X-MP is an example.) These are called vector processors because they deal with real-time computation of vectors. The use of many microprocessors, each representing a certain object or portion of the object in the scene, all running in parallel as they compute, is being considered as an antidote to the cost of the high-speed computer.

Now that you understand a little about the process behind computer-generated animation, let's investigate computer-assisted animation as it is used in the cartoon industry.

Computer-Assisted Animation

To appreciate how much time and effort the computer has saved the cartoonist, consider the six manual steps to creating a cartoon.

Initial Design   The artist creates a storyboard which is a quick sketch of the main pieces of the entire cartoon from beginning to end, somewhat like a comic strip. It shows all the significant frames of the cartoon, i.e., the important ones that specify a major change in characters or environment.

Key Frames   The key frames are then drawn in more detail to create significant character positions. Key frames are the frames that hold the peak positions of the figures in the cartoon. They tell the cartoonist the path of the cartoon and where the figures in each motion sequence start and end.

In-betweening   Many frames *between* peaks of movement in the storyboard are drawn to produce movement. Frames must be eased (also called faired), i.e., properly accelerated from start to rest or jerky movements will result. Usually 24 frames are needed for each second of movement in the final film! Thus just one quarter hour of viewing time of the cartoon requires 21,600 drawings! This is one of the most time-consuming aspects of making an animated cartoon.

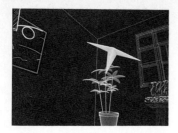

Pencil (Line) Testing   The drawings are now photocopied on acetate (called cels) and then filmed on an animation stand to test quality of movements. The animation stand (also called an animation rostrum) is a camera and a platform-like device that allows the drawings to be accurately transferred to film for viewing. If an error is found at this point, then the animator must go back to the drawing and in-betweening and fix it, and the line test is repeated.

Opaquing   Once modifications from the line test are completed, the cels are actually painted in (opaqued) by hand to add color, so characters stand out from backgrounds. This is another expensive, time-consuming step.

Filming   Finally the backgrounds and characters are brought together on the animation stand and filmed by the camera to make the cartoon. Sound is joined with the film at this stage. (Sound is always recorded before the key frame stage since it is easier to make the drawings match the sound than vice versa.)

Computerization of Cartoons

In making cartoons, the computer can help solve many of the time-consuming manual techniques we described above. The following methods are utilized at Hanna Barbera, a company famous for *Fred Flintstone* and *Superfriends*.

After the pencil sketch has been created by the artist and cleaned up, it is entered into the computer via a digitizing camera. Because the pencil sketch has gray shades in its outlines, the picture gets automatically antialiased and no special software techniques are needed to obtain smooth non-jaggy edges. Once the picture is inside the computer, a paint system is used to do the opaquing and fill the image with color. With the use of a paint system, the opaquing step only requires the artist to place the cursor in the center of the object, choose the fill color and press the respective button. In a fraction of a second, the interior of the entire shape will be flooded with color.

In such cartoon applications, there are usually 16 shades of 16 colors, allowing a total of 256 different hues. With the various shades the flooding (filling) algorithm blends the colors as they approach the outline of the figure for a smooth, antialiased border.

Of course, once we have the database of points for the figure in the computer, it is relatively simple to rotate and scale the figure in two dimensions. We can make our figures spin, expand, shrink, flip over, mirror, and so on.

Another major contribution of the computer in cartoon applications is in the area of in-betweening. With proper software, the computer can mathematically estimate the in-between positions of two-dimensional objects given their starting and ending drawings. This process is only beginning to be used and needs much work before it can easily handle all two-dimensional situations, but it is certainly on the way to becoming very effective. The in-betweening of three-dimensional animation is actually much easier than two-dimensional because the notion of ''behind'' exists in a three-dimensional database.

The computer is making cartoon generation much easier due to its ability to solve the overlapping cel problem. In the old, manual approach when several painted acetate sheets were superimposed on each other, the color of the figure would change because of the increased density of the many cels. For example, each cel is usually devoted to each of the figure's different body parts. The torso will be on one, the eyes on another, lips on still another, and so on. This saves having to redraw all the parts when only one feature changes (for example, if an eye blinks, just the eye cel needs to be altered). However, the change in color due to the overlapping of the cels meant the colors of each cel had to be carefully selected to compensate. With the computer, we can completely eliminate this problem. The color is of a hue exactly determined by the software. There is no density effects from underlying cels.

Manipulation of the graphic image that is stored in the computer is a very difficult process that requires intense mathematical knowledge of the algorithms described earlier in this chapter. Special software is available to help the animator. Checking the accuracy of the animation may also be difficult because of the non-real time aspect. The images must be loaded into the frame buffer and filmed (or videotaped) one at a time before the entire sequence can be viewed. Some new systems, like those at Hanna Barbera, can store the images of the animation on disk and then call them up quickly enough to see the cartoon in real time.

You shouldn't think that making cartoons using manual techniques, computer assistance, and computer-generated imagery are totally independent or mutually exclusive. Actually all techniques blend together in many new ways. The next section explains how manual techniques are combined with computer-generated animations and gives a glimpse of what is on the horizon in computer animation.

3.13. THE MAKING OF *TRON*

Our book would not be complete without mentioning how a high-tech computer is used today in a modern motion picture. *TRON,* a feature-length film from Disney Studios, is about a programmer whose great computer games are ripped off by the ultimate computer pirate — another computer program. Through the magic of artistic license and computer imagery, our hero gets laser digitized into a patch of pixels and swallowed up by the computer. In his new RAM-based consciousness, he wanders about the frame buffer searching for the villains who stole his best program (called Space Paranoids). When he finds them, a fantastic

battle erupts in the frame buffer. The effectiveness of the film is the result of brilliantly blending computer graphics and old-fashioned animation.

With *TRON*'s release came a new awareness on the part of the public regarding computer animation. Never before have special computer effects been so pronounced. Playing a major role in the making of *TRON* was Richard Taylor of Triple I and formerly with Robert Abel and Associates (equally famous for candy apple neon 7-Up and Levis Jeans commercials).

The process of making *TRON* required artist-designers to interact with programmer-technicians, and this presented some interesting problems. The artists were at one end of the country and the programmers at another, further complicating matters. The *TRON* artists were at Disney studios in Los Angeles, and the programmers were at Mathematics Applications Group, Inc. (MAGI) in New York. When Chromatics terminals were installed at each end, work settled down. Modems were used to send low-resolution motion tests to the director at Disney before committing the images to film.

For example, after MAGI received the storyboards for the vehicular animation from Disney, they took these crude images and plotted them in three views using combinatorial geometry on a 40 × 60 inch Talos digitizing tablet. They then made up flowcharts of the speed and angles of the moving objects for the camera path. The results then went back to Disney for corrections in pacing, staging, and animation. MAGI incorporated these corrections and committed them to film using a high-speed raster system and film recorder.

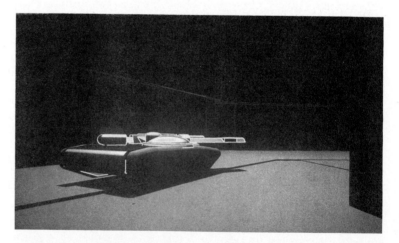

Photo 3.7 From *TRON*, a video game tank patrols a dark alleyway. Note the incredible effects of color shading (see color insert). The image is by MAGI. *(Courtesy of Walt Disney Production, World Rights Reserved.)*

Photo 3.8: This is the computer-simulated master control I/O tower of *TRON*. The image is by Information International, Inc. *(Courtesy of Walt Disney Production, World Rights Reserved.)*

The characters in *TRON* had to be candy apple neon in appearance (i.e., glowing tubes using bright colors, so that they looked like electronic images inside a computer memory). They were done by having the actors wear white costumes and perform in front of a set with just a black backdrop. They were filmed in 70 mm black and white. Then each frame (and that's thousands of frames) was enlarged for the production of four cels for each frame. Cel painters then came in and applied holdout mattes, masking out unwanted sections, one for the face, another for the costume, one for the eyes and teeth, and a fourth for the glowing circuitry on the front of the costume. A roto-scoping process (combining the four cels into one continuous tone positive film) was then used.

The back-lighting for the film came from the techniques Abel used in the 7-Up commercials. No reflected light is used in the microworld of *TRON*; all light comes from the creatures and objects themselves. Everything glows dimly from within, giving a forbidding and oppressive end effect.

Computer graphics were used throughout the film, often in places that weren't obvious. Even the scene showing a nighttime landing of a helicopter used computer graphics (the city lights were computer-generated, not the helicopter).

After the computer animation in *TRON* was so well received, we can expect to see its expanded use in future films.

3.14. AN ANIMATION HOUSE — EXAMPLES

The figures below are from one of the most prolific animation houses in the United States, Robert Abel and Associates. This company is responsible for many television commercials that use computer animation and is perhaps most famous for their Levis commercials, which strangely enough used the computer only to help figure out camera angles (even though it looks very computer-like). The Philips Radio commercial is completely synthetic except for the background, which was airbrushed in. This shows how other media can be mixed in with computer animation.

a)

b)

c)

(continued)

d)

Photo 3.9: These are examples of animation from Robert Abel and Associates. *(Courtesy of Robert Abel and Associates.)*

a) Levi's Commercial — this commercial won a Cleo Award and great acclaim for Abel. Millions of people loved this when it first appeared on television in 1974. To help plan the commercial, an Evans and Sutherland Picture System 2 was used to calculate the camera moves. The final commercial, however, contains no computer graphics, just live actors and standard animation. (Directed by Robert Abel.)

b) Philips Radio Commercial — the entire scene is synthetic (created with a three-dimensional vector-shading routine) except for the cloud background, which was conventionally painted with an airbrush and then matted in. An Evans and Sutherland Picture System II is used for all of their computer animation work. (Directed by Bill Kovacs.)

c) CBS Evening News Opening — for those of you who watched the evening news on CBS during 1981-1982, you'll recognize this spinning globe with the CBS "eye" symbol indicating the cities. (Directed by Clark Anderson.)

d) AT&T Energy Commercial — this was entirely computer generated. (Directed by Rod Davis.)

3.15. AN APPLE FOR ANIMATION — JAMES LEATHAM

Can a low-cost twentieth century personal computer simulate a high-tech graphics machine from the twenty-first century? Are personal computer users destined to play Space Invaders and Pac Man because they just don't have enough pixels to do anything more significant? Or is there a fantastic animation potential inside your personal computer that's dying to "worm" its way to the surface and do something wonderful?

One person who has answered all these questions with a resounding YES is James Leatham, located in Chester, New York. James is a multitalented programmer and filmmaker who, using a standard Apple II, a SubLogic A2-3D1 Graphics Package (SubLogic Communications Corp, 713 Edgebrook Dr., Champaign, IL 61820), and a special homemade equipment bench, has created fantastic animation scenes for an 8 mm film called *Asteroid*. The movie concerns space age asteroid belt miners. In the scene that Jim worked on, the ship's computer detects and analyzes a particularly valuable asteroid. The ship's computer creates a simulation of the asteroid and rotates it in three

dimensions. A jagged magnetic field appears to float around the asteroid, rotating with it. The photo below shows another one of James' creations. This is from the flip movie of a mathematical function. In the movie the two functions appear like colorful wire frame mountains that grow and shrink.

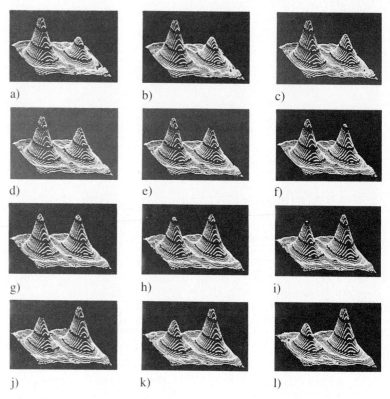

Photo 3.10: Frames from James Leatham's Calculus Mountains, a good example of how a microcomputer can be used for computer animation. James used a Super-8 camera under the direct control of an Apple II computer. The computer draws a high-resolution picture on the screen, positions a filter from the filter wheel in front of the lens, takes the picture, and draws the next frame with a new color or advances the film as appropriate a) through e): a short sequence of film using three exposures per frame (r-g-b); f): black and white version; g) through i): red, green and blue exposures. *(Courtesy of James Leatham.)*

a)

b)

c)

(continued)

d)

Photo 3.11: Four slides taken from a CT5 continuous-tone, real-time visual simulation system. CT5 was designed by Evans & Sutherland in collaboration with Rediffusion Simulation, Inc., for flight simulation applications. CT5 generates these high quality, high complexity scenes in real-time, 50 times per second. *(Courtesy: Evans & Sutherland/Rediffusion Simulation.)*

James used the SubLogic A2-3D1 package to define a three-dimensional database for the asteroid. It was simple to enter rough coordinates that resembled a round object. Next a control program was written in BASIC to rotate the object in single degree increments on the Apple screen. James devised a special bench for holding the camera and a rotating filter. The control program could move the proper filter in front of the camera and snap the shutter of the camera for each different filter color. The control program and camera mechanism took almost all the labor out of the filming of the animation sequence.

The film was later projected onto the spaceship's CRT at 18 frames per second, which was a speed-up of 180 times over the original rate. Figure 3.20 and Photo 3.12 show James' set up. He uses an Apple II with a Eumig 881 PMA Super-8 movie camera. A black and white monitor is used for maximum resolution, and that explains the reason for all the color filters. The computer can open the camera's shutter and hold it open for as long as required. The computer can also capture the display modes from the text to either of the two high-resolution pages. Each new image is drawn on an alternate graphics page. When it's done, the new page is switched on by the computer program, and the old page (now out of view) is erased. The proper filter is then rotated into place by the stepper motors and the camera shutter is opened for the required time.

James Leatham is one of the first pioneers in the amazing field of home computer animation. His example shows that one can achieve incredible effects on a very small budget. He may be at the forefront of a new phase in computer movies where stick figures and clay models are replaced with data statements and programmed logic.

Photo 3.12: James Leatham's Apple II budget 16 mm animation equipment. This equipment produced the frames in Photo 3.10 as well as animation sequences for a science fiction movie.

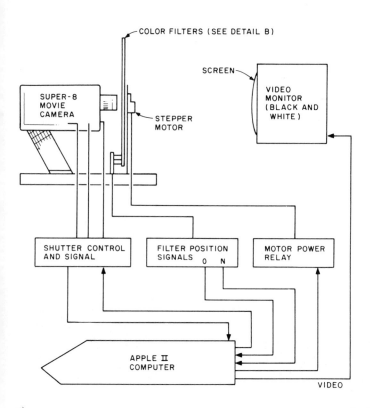

a)

(continued)

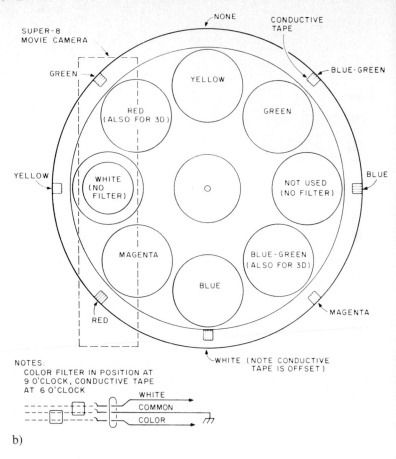

b)

Figure 3.20: Using an Apple for film animation. a) equipment set up and b) color filter details.

Now that you have had a good introduction to computer graphics software, you are in a good position to solve a particular problem using a graphics-oriented computer. You may also be asking yourself, "What is available for a low budget in the way of graphics machines?" Anticipating this, we have prepared the next chapter. It is a survey and analysis of the graphics-oriented personal computers you can purchase today. Although the survey doesn't cover everything on the market, we think our particular sample will whet your appetite. We have not covered the expensive, non-microcomputer-based graphics machines, the S-100 boards, or the most super high-tech computers; we'll leave those for another book.

Chapter 4

Personal Computer Animation Features

Now that you know enough about the million dollar, high-technology animation computers to want to own one, it's time to draw up plans for "borrowing" a few bars of gold from Fort Knox. If this isn't quite your style, don't worry, there's another way out. Consider, instead, the more reasonably priced color personal computer.

Given the rapid advances in technology, today's personal computers, once the poor relatives of high-tech machines, are quickly catching up in performance. And even though this is the case, the prices for these marvels (with a single built-in programming language) start at a nominal $99, average $1500, and peak at $3500.

In addition to their attractive low cost, color personal computers offer the animator some other pulses which are lacking in the high-tech machines. To begin with, the personal computer owner will find many books (like this one), which make learning about the machines' capabilities a pleasant task. Likewise, the abundance of add-on hardware products facilitates expanding the system as your needs change. Also, personal computers have a sufficiently large base of owners to support the creation of a wide selection of animation programming tools. A case in point is the easy-to-use machine language animation routines developed as part of this book for use on the ATARI Home Computers; these enable you to design your own animation programs that perform in real time. Due to the projected number of sales for these kinds of programs, their cost is likely to be very reasonable. Therefore, after you've mastered your system and created your own programs, you might wish to sell them to a ready-made market that is eager for all the software it can get.

Because color personal computers offer so much for the money, they are extremely attractive to the consumer on a low budget. As a consumer, the first thing you'll want to know is "What can they do (in terms of graphics and animation), and how can I make them do it?" Answering these questions is the basis of this chapter.

4.1 FORMAT OF THIS CHAPTER

We have identified 13 key features you should be aware of when evaluating a personal computer for graphics animation. These features are:

- BASIC Graphics Statements
- Special Hardware Features
- Graphics and Text Modes
- Graphics Language Statements
    Mode Selection
    Color Selection
    Plotting
    Line Drawing
    Shapes, Graphics Definition Language
    Paint, Fill, Flood
    Defined Object Statements
    Image Array Plotting
    Miscellaneous Statements
- Players/Sprites
- Hardware Scrolling
- Graphics Characters
- Custom Characters
- Color Registers
- Vertical Blank Interrupts
- Display List and Display List Interrupts
- Page Flipping
- Speed of Plotting

The bulk of this chapter will examine each of these features, defining each and explaining its importance to the animator. We will also occasionally make reference to actual personal computers, languages, and products. Our main goal is to expose you to what is important, rather than to endorse a particular machine.

4.2 BASIC GRAPHICS STATEMENTS

BASIC is by far the most popular language for executing graphics on personal computers today. To better understand the things your personal computer can do in the area of graphics, you should examine those BASIC statements that pertain specifically to graphics on the machine(s) in question. In some cases, as in the Apple III, BASIC offers primitives rather than regular statements. Primitives are graphic functions performed when certain character sequences are sent to a special graphics program called a driver. You should understand, however, before getting involved with graphics primitives, that they are definitely more difficult to use than BASIC statements.

What Language?

Although BASIC is the most common language in use on personal computers and its merits are simplicity of use and immediate feedback, it is not accurate to conclude that it is the only or even the best language for graphics. Another popular language for microcomputer graphics is Pascal, particularly Apple Pascal. Since Pascal is a compiled language,[1] its graphics programs usually execute faster than those written in BASIC. The major drawback with Pascal is that it is a structured language. This means a front-end or preamble of instructions must be first created for your program before you can try an idea. This kind of programming demands much preplanning and is good for long and involved projects but difficult for the ''just try it and see'' approach.

Another graphics language which is growing in popularity is Logo. Logo is built around a concept called turtle graphics. Turtle graphics allows the user to see a turtle (with an imaginary drawing pen in its mouth) on the screen. The turtle can be moved with simple commands like TURN and MOVE, and in so doing it leaves a line of color behind it. Children have an easy time drawing with the turtle because its movements are obvious to them and intuitively understood. A simple box, for example, can be drawn in Logo with very few statements (see box on the next page).

---

[1]Pascal for the Apple compiles into what is called P-code. This is an intermediate set of instructions that must be interpreted before they can be understood by the processor. Other Pascals (called native compilers) produce pure native machine code, or N-code. that can be run immediately. Each has its advantages. For more details on Pascal see *Pascal Primer* by David Fox and Mitchell Waite, Howard W. Sams and Company, Indianapolis, IN.

Making a Box in Logo and BASIC

```
TO BOX :SIDE
HOME
REPEAT 4 [FORWARD :SIDE LEFT 90]
END
```

Figure 4.1: Logo Box Program.

In this program we have previously typed TELL TURTLE to activate the drawing turtle. FORWARD sends the turtle ahead a distance set by the variable SIDE and in any direction on the compass. The turtle starts point straight up (due north). The instruction LEFT 90 turns the turtle 90 degrees. We started the program by typing BOX 10, which made the value of SIDE equal to 10 and then executed the program.

Compare this to the same box done with Applesoft BASIC and decide which is easier to understand. One of the authors was once a devotee of BASIC and worshipped it at every turn. Now after playing with Logo he no longer finds BASIC as friendly as it once was.

```
100 HGR :REM clear the hi-res screen
110 HCOLOR = 3 :REM set the color
     to white
120 XC = 140 : YC = 80 :REM set
     the center coordinates
130 INPUT "Enter length of side "; SI:
     REM enter side
140  HPLOT XC,YC TO XC,YC-SI TO
     XC-SI,YC-SI TO XC-SI,YC TO XC,YC
     :REM and draw it
150 END
```

Figure 4.2: Applesoft BASIC Box Program.

In this program, we must first clear the screen to black, set the drawing color to white, set the center coordinates XC and YC, and request the user to input the length of the sides. Then the HPLOT statement draws the actual box.

Some versions of Logo may, however, hold back the programmer of complex objects because its number crunching ability is more limited than BASIC or Pascal. For example, Apple LOGO has floating point while TI Logo has only integers.

The language C is often used in larger computers for doing graphics. C is similar to Pascal but is easier for creating programs that must manipulate the byte and bits of the microprocessor. It executes faster than Pascal and is just beginning to appear on low-cost personal computers like the ATARI Home Computer (it has been available on CP/M-based computers for some time). With C and the addition of an S-100 graphics board with a high-resolution bit map, you would have a very powerful, low-cost graphics machine.

You may also want to investigate Forth as a graphics language. Although it is rather difficult to learn, it is a somewhat elegant language and your own graphics instructions are easily added to it. Its advantages include high speed, immediate execution of programs (no compilation like in Pascal and C), ability to define your own commands, and very compact code.

Assembly language is another way to go if you have lots of patience and perseverance. Graphics written in assembly (8080 and 6502 are among the most popular codes) will execute very quickly, allowing the rapid and fluid movement of objects on the screen. One of the authors has created a set of graphics extension routines in 6502 assembly language that enhances Applesoft so you can draw circles, polygons, and fill shapes with color. These routines, however, were very difficult to create, requiring hundreds of programming hours. Rather than attempting to create your own assembly language routines, first check animation aids and products currently available on the market by looking through magazines such as *Popular Computing* and *Byte*.

4.3. SPECIAL HARDWARE FEATURES

As a graphics programmer, it may be important to understand how your personal computer works on a hardware level. It all depends on the degree of control you want to have over the graphics effects produced. In the Apple, for example, it doesn't really matter how the hardware for graphics works if you're using only BASIC or Pascal. If you want to program your Apple in assembly language though, the hardware is extremely important because you must access bits and bytes in screen memory with a rather complex algorithm. If you are using an ATARI Home Computer with its custom graphics chips and want to have absolute control over the pictures that the machine is capable of creating, then you'll need an intimate understanding of the built-in hardware.

4.4. GRAPHICS AND TEXT MODES

Every manufacturer has its own way of defining the numerous modes in which a computer can function. A graphics mode (sometimes referred to as a map or pixel mode) sets up the screen for responding to the graphics instructions that are in the language, whereas a text mode screen is set up for displaying words, programs, etc. Usually the text mode is used for program development, and the graphics mode is used for running graphics programs. Text and graphics can often be mixed, but the precise method of doing this varies from machine to machine. For example, when the Apple is in a graphics mode, text can appear only in a window of four lines at the bottom of the graphics screen. On the IBM, on

the other hand, text can be displayed anywhere on the graphics screen. (As a rule, such mixing is more restricted on other computers.) Mixing modes is very important in business graphics where graphs and charts need to be labeled but less critical in animation where objects are simply moved about. Often, as in the case of the Apple, special programs can be purchased that allow the creation of text characters that will appear on the graphics screen. Use of these programs, however, may be a bit complex for the beginner.

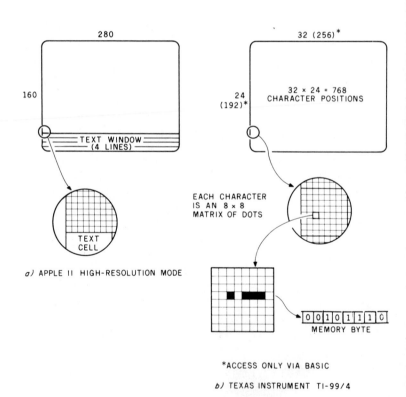

Figure 4.3: A typical graphics mode.

Resolution Selection

Mode selection also allows you to choose which resolution you desire. The IBM PC, for example, has a medium- and a high-resolution mode, the difference between the two being the number of pixels and amount of color allowed.

When considering a personal computer for animation, you should not simply assume higher resolution is better. Some lower resolutions offer more color, and careful use of this color can result in brilliant effects.

How High Is HI Resolution?

There is an interesting phenomenon about the various resolution modes which is that the terms high, medium, and low resolution have entirely different meanings on different computers. High resolution on the VIC-20, for example, is more like the low resolution of the ATARI Home Computer, and high resolution on the ATARI Home Computer is like medium resolution on the IBM PC. And high resolution on the IBM would be considered low resolution on the large high-tech computers. The ultimate truth in the use of any of these terms lies in the number of horizontal and vertical elements that can be accessed on the screen. For a long time the highest resolution in personal computer graphics was the Apple II's 280 × 192 mode. Then the IBM came out with a 640 × 200 mode which they also called high resolution (which it certainly is), even though it does not have color. This gives you an idea of the kinds of problems that consumers face when choosing a computer.

Mode Color Capability

Another important item to consider when examining graphics modes is the color capability of each. Here things can get very confusing. There are foreground, background, and border colors. Background colors refer to the color taken on by the entire screen when it is cleared. Foreground colors (called playfield colors on the ATARI computers) are the colors that can be plotted on top of the background color. Border colors are those which can surround the perimeter of the active screen area. In computers that offer these three choices there are usually a certain number of colors that can be used in each area. For example, the IBM PC's medium resolution mode allows 16 background colors and 3 foreground colors to be chosen from one of two sets. Some computers (Apple) have no user-selectable background colors (although the screen can be filled or plotted with color).

Maximum Color

The maximum number of colors allowed in any mode is usually a function of the resolution of the mode. As resolution increases, color capability decreases. This is a consequence of the fact that display pixels are encoded in an area of memory. If memory size is fixed and resolution is increased, then the feature that must suffer is color. This is clearly illustrated with ATARI's medium-resolution mode (80 × 192), which offers a maximum of 16 colors, and the highest mode which offers only two colors.

Disappearing Colors

As someone interested in computer graphics, you should be aware of the "case of the disappearing colors on a television" problem. A television set has a limited band width, meaning it can respond only to a limited number of changes in electric current per second. Because a computer encodes color information via these changes, there is an upper limit at which the TV cannot recognize a change in color. (If you just use white on a black and white TV, this is not a problem. Also, color RGB monitors have a higher band width than regular televisions so they permit greater color changes on a line.) All this means that there is a limit to the number of color changes that can occur on a horizontal line on the TV. The result is that certain columns are restricted from having certain colors. On the Apple II the problem is further complicated by the way the screen colors are encoded in memory. A drawback like this has not kept people from developing Apple programs, but moving color objects about without having sections of them disappear complicates the programming techniques.

Text Modes

In the text mode we are concerned with several things, including the number of dots per character, the number of characters on a line, and the number of lines on the screen. (These numbers correspond to the degree of resolution in graphics modes.) In reference to the matrix of dots which comprises each character, the more dots the finer the character's detail and the easier it is on the eye. A minimum dot matrix is 5×7; a maximum on the computers we are covering is about 8×8. The actual number of characters on a line varies from as low as 20 to as high as 80, with 40 as standard for television sets. The final factor in text mode displays is the number of lines on a screen, which varies from 16 to 25, with 24 being the most popular. In most cases the general rule of thumb is "the more characters per line the better"; however, 80 characters per line is very difficult to read due to the television's limited band width problem which we mentioned above. On a black and white monitor and on color RGB monitors, however, 80 characters is very readable.

Many text modes allow you to use color as well. This can be a marvelous benefit in word processing applications or in any application where you want text to stand out. In some computers, such as the IBM PC, there are two horizontal dots for every vertical position in the 40-column text mode. This feature is called double dot and gives the impression of a 16×8 matrix, which results in text characters that appear to have serifs! Serifs are the curly ends of characters that give them a certain distinction.

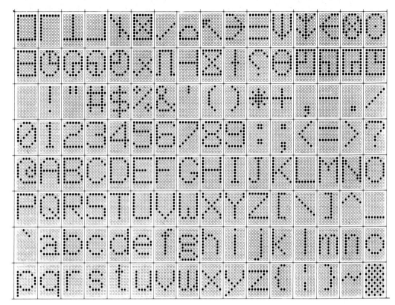

Figure 4.4: A text dot matrix.

4.5. GRAPHICS LANGUAGE STATEMENTS

Here we present the various features for selecting modes, selecting colors, plotting, drawing lines, creating shapes, filling, defining objects, plotting image arrays, and miscellaneous other uses.

Mode Selection

Computers vary from having no mode selection to having several modes to choose from. A machine might offer mode selection through the use of a single statement (such as Apple's HGR or TEXT) or, as in IBM's SCREEN, through the use of a complex statement containing four parameters which the user can set. Some computers, such as the TRS-80 color, have two statements for setting the mode (PMODE and SCREEN).

Pages

The mode statement will usually select the screen's text or graphics modes. In addition, it may select the page that will be used for display as well as the page that will receive the results of output statements. Pages are sections of memory that can be used for the screen's contents. Often there exist several of these pages but only one is active at a given time. For example, when the IBM is used in the text mode, it has eight pages, one of which can be made the active page and one the output page. The output page will receive the results of any PRINT statements. The TRS-80 Color Computer allows graphics images to be drawn on the various pages and then flipped into view instantly. The Apple has two pages for high-resolution graphics. The idea behind pages is to allow

generation of graphics on an output page while the user is viewing an active page. This permits the new picture to be instantly switched on, *before* the old picture is erased. If we were to erase the old picture and then redraw the new one, the delay in time to draw the new picture would result in an annoying flicker effect. However, because a page can be enabled almost instantly, no flicker effects occur (however there may still be some jerky motion). This method permits the programmer to create animation by letting each page contain one of several frames of, for example, a figure in different positions. The program could then flash through sequential screens to give the effect of movement.

The mode statement may also be used for instantly activating color (color burst) or disabling color in a particular scene. Some computers, such as the ATARI Home Computer, allow changing modes with a very simple statement like GRAPHICS *n*, where *n* is the graphics mode number. (By making *n* equal to 0 the machine will operate in a text mode.)

Color Selection

Colors may be automatically selected by the mode statement or specifically selected with a special color statement. In some computers the color selection statement allows choosing colors for the foreground, background, and border. Computers that feature color registers usually have one statement for selecting which color register will be used to paint a pixel, and a second statement that sets each register's color value. In the ATARI Home Computer the two statements are COLOR and SETCOLOR. When color registers are used, the statement may select the luminance as well as the hue of the color. There may also be a statement for setting the color of any special programmable objects, such as TI's sprites.

Colors Available

The choice of colors on personal computers is very limited compared to the selection available on expensive high-technology computers. In some computers, like the IBM, there are eight colors with two intensities of each (high and low) for a total of sixteen (this is just in the text mode). Most manufacturers include black and white when specifying the number of available colors. In some computers, like the Apple, there are only six colors available. On the other hand, the ATARI user can choose from 128 colors (16 hues, 8 intensities) in most modes and 256 colors in two special modes, but this is the exception rather than the rule.

The names chosen for computer colors follow no standard; one company's aqua may be another's blue-green. Further complicating matters is the fact that the colors that actually appear on the TV depend greatly on the setting of the television color control and the fine tuning.

Some computers thoughtfully present a band of each color next to its name so you can perform this adjustment before using any programs.

Plotting

Plotting is the most fundamental graphics function. It consists of using horizontal and vertical coordinates to illuminate a point on the screen. Sometimes the plotting command is referred to as PSET, and sometimes it is simply referred to as PLOT, POINT, or HPLOT. The plot statement is analogous to a needlepoint stitch done with a certain color yarn. In some cases you may be able to specify the color within the plot statement itself, while in other cases you must first set the color with a color statement. Erasing of plotted points is much simpler than removing a needlepoint stitch. It is done by setting the point color to the background color and replotting. Some computers, like the IBM PC, offer a special erasing command called PRESET X,Y.

Some systems may allow the X,Y coordinates to be relative by use of the word STEP in the plot statement. This means that the new point is plotted X,Y locations away from the last plotted point. Relative coordinates are good for simplifying the coordinate values for a complex object. Although plotting is probably the simplest graphics function to perform on a computer, it is usually too slow for real-time animation in BASIC. With C and Forth, however, point plotting may provide sufficient plotting speed for the animator.

Line Drawing

Line drawing is an important graphics instruction, because it allows complex multi-sided objects to be drawn quickly and simply. It eliminates the need to do a repeated PLOT in a loop of some sort. Line-drawing statements can be as simple as Apple's HPLOT x1,y1 TO x2,y2 or IBM's LINE (x1,y1)-(x2,y2),color,B. The IBM and TRS-80 Color Computer line-drawing statement is unique in that it has a special option that allows a rectangle to be drawn. When the letter B (for BOX) is included in the statement, the x1,y1 and x2,y2 coordinates are taken as diagonal corners of a box. If BF is included, the rectangle gets filled with color (when color is also set in the line statement). Line-drawing statements are often used to put fixed objects on the screen, with DATA statements holding the coordinates of the shape's numerous corners. Line drawing for real-time animation, unfortunately, is usually too slow from BASIC.

Shapes and Graphics Definition Language

Shapes are a feature originated by Apple Computer as part of its famous Apple II's graphics software. Shapes are ingenious graphics objects composed of tiny vectors, which are small line segments that can be drawn in one of four directions (up, down, right, or left). The

programmer uses simple rules to string these vectors together like tiny arrows connected end to end. A shape can be made from a few vectors or hundreds of them. Once these shapes have been created, they can be drawn on the screen with one very simple statement, like DRAW 1 AT X,Y. There also exists an entire set of additional statements for manipulating these shapes, including ones that scale them in size from 0 to 255, and ones that rotate them from 0 to 360 degrees! These statements make shapes incredibly useful for games and programs where objects fly, sail, spin, or otherwise bounce across the screen. They may be limited for real-time animation however, because the BASIC statements that move them are slow. For non-real-time animation (i.e., when you use film or the disk to store the frames of the picture), they are ideal.

Graphics Definition Language (GDL) is a feature currently found only on the IBM Personal Computer and the TRS-80 Color Computer. GDL is a set of drawing commands that are placed in a string variable (as opposed to being inserted into memory with POKE or BLOAD as needed with Apple's shapes). These drawing commands specify the way the line segments are to be drawn on the screen. There is a very complete set of commands including ones that draw up, down, right, left, and diagonal segments, repeat these patterns, move without drawing, rotate, and draw relative to a point. The GDL is too slow for animation when the number of vectors comprising the shape is greater than ten (when this is the case an unacceptable screen flicker occurs). However, for slow moving shapes, complex objects that don't move at all, or non-real-time animation, it is an excellent feature. One problem with the GDL shapes is that there can be vectors in only one of eight directions. This means smooth curves are impossible to draw.

Paint, Fill, Flood

These terms all refer to the same thing — filling an enclosed boundary with a particular color. There are different types of fills, the main difference among them being the ability to circumvent corners and fill every nook and cranny of the enclosed area. A fill, or paint, works by the user specifying an x,y location inside an enclosed area and a particular color with which to flood it. Fills are usually slow and do their filling in a method that resembles many bizarre window shades closing at the same time. Because of the way some computer screens are set up (with rules specifying which colors can be positioned next to each other), fills have a tendency to distort the color of adjacent objects.

Defined Object Statements

Often it is desirable to draw certain geometric shapes (squares, triangles, polygons) on the screen. This is fairly easy to accomplish using the LINE statement. The procedure, however, is somewhat more complex when curved surfaces are involved. Drawing a simple circle can be very demanding for the non-mathematically oriented user because we usually need to use complex BASIC programs involving trigonometric functions such as SIN and TAN. One way out of this dilemma is to use the defined object statements that make graphics programming much easier. One such statement is the CIRCLE command (available on the IBM, TRS-80 Color, and VIC-20 Personal Computers), which allows you to draw a circle, ellipse, or arc at any x,y location on the screen. The circle you draw can be of any radius with distortion in either axis and can be used for anything from the petals of a flower to the wheels of a bicycle to complex mandala patterns. CIRCLE permits the drawing of elaborately curved shapes using very little programming code; unfortunately, it is too slow for fast animation, but may work well for slow moving objects.

Image-Array Plotting

Image-array plotting is another way to plot complex objects on the screen, and it is a terrific graphics feature. There are two statements involved here: GET and PUT. The GET statement is used to store an object that has already been drawn on the screen in a two-dimensional array (as a matrix of on and off bits/pixels). A pair of x,y coordinates in the GET statement specifies the area on the screen to be stored in the array. These coordinates define the diagonal corners of a rectangle that surround the object on the screen. A corresponding statement, PUT, is then used to draw the object now stored in the array at any x,y (upper left corner of the rectangle) screen location. Since the object is drawn using the bit map stored in the array, an optional action statement can be used to control the way each of the object's ON bits interacts with the image already on the screen. The action command allows you to AND, OR, or XOR the array contents onto the screen background. In essence, this means you can draw the object on a background without having to erase it! After storing an object with GET, you can use PUT as a specially created paint brush to dab on the screen wherever you wish.

As might be expected, not all BASICs offer GET and PUT. You'll find it on the IBM and TRS-80 Color Computer. Image-array plotting is too slow for complex animation but can be used effectively when slow movement is desired or when objects are very small or very simple. Apple III's drawblock command, although cruder, is another example of image-array plotting. It is a graphics primitive and not easily used from within BASIC because up to 20 arguments for it are stored in memory. Even so, it is probably faster in operation than regular array plotting and might work well in animation.

Miscellaneous Graphics Statements

Other graphic statements that you will find useful are those designated for clearing the entire screen to a certain color, a width statement

for controlling the number of text columns that can be displayed, and a screen function that returns the ASCII value of a character at a particular row and column. Also useful are the point function for returning the color at a specified location on the screen, a locate statement for positioning the text cursor, a command for setting the viewport (a rectangular window on the screen that graphics drawing is restricted to), and a page copy statement for moving graphics information from one page to another.

4.6. PLAYERS AND SPRITES

Players and sprites are graphics objects that can be moved by custom hardware. ATARI calls them players while Texas Instruments refers to them as sprites, but their function is similar in nature. Players solve a major graphics problem — namely, they are separate from the background and don't require complex erasing to be moved on the screen. They are somewhat easier to update than the normal plotting methods, and they don't interfere with other objects made from players.

With normal software, the program must keep track of the position of an object, erasing and redrawing it as it moves across the screen. With players, however, you only have to POKE a register with the horizontal value of the object's screen destination, and the hardware does all the moving for you. For vertical movement, bytes representing the object in a special area of memory must be moved. There are techniques to accomplish this from within BASIC, but a machine language routine makes it simpler. ATARI's Players have their own color register so they can be a different color than anything else on the screen. You can even combine Players to create larger objects or objects of more than one color.

Sprites function differently from players. A sprite is twice as large as a regular character (16 × 16), whereas the players are 8 bits wide with a maximum height of 256 bits. Sprites are more powerful than players when it comes to moving them on the screen. Once a sprite is put into motion, it keeps moving as directed until told otherwise. The sprite has a large number of special commands for moving it, including a MOTION command for specifying velocity and direction, COINC for detecting sprites coincidence (collision), DISTANCE for telling the distance between two sprites, and MAGNIFY for changing the size of sprites on the screen. You can tell all the sprites to FREEZE and to THAW; you can change colors of any of them at any time, and you can redefine which ones appear on the screen. For some time sprites were available only on the TI 99/4. However, because sprites are generated by a special TI chip that is on the open market, you can now buy a board for the Apple that gives it sprite ability.

It should also be noted that some of the sprite's manipulation commands are available with ATARI's players through a direct POKE or

PEEK to the hardware registers. The collision of a player with another player or specific screen color can be detected, the width of a player can be changed, and the Player's priority in relation to the screen Playfield colors (non-background screen color) can be controlled. (By priority we mean whether the player passes in front or in back of a screen color.) Each player is also associated with a two-bit wide missile, which can be moved about the screen.

Players and sprites are perfect for animation — they were designed for this purpose. Using them in a program eliminates flicker, update overhead and superfluous, convoluted programming code!

4.7. HARDWARE SCROLLING

Hardware scrolling causes the display screen to move over a screen memory area which is actually larger than the screen. Conventional brute force scrolling, where bytes must be moved one at a time into the display area of memory, results in a visual effect which is slow, wavy, and choppy. With hardware scrolling, the software only needs to change single two-byte pointers to cause the entire screen image to move up or down, right or left, or diagonally, resulting in a very fast and smooth scroll.

There are two distinct kinds of hardware scrolling — coarse and fine. Coarse scrolling moves the screen window many bytes at a time (entire characters), whereas fine scrolling moves the screen on a pixel (dot) basis, allowing a smooth gliding effect. This technique is used in Chapter 9 for moving our program backgrounds.

Although hardware scrolling is perfect for animation background, it is a rare feature usually found only in the most sophisticated computers. The only personal computers currently possessing this feature are the ATARI Home Computers.

4.8. GRAPHICS CHARACTERS

Many personal computers have, in addition to the normal built-in text characters, a set of graphics characters. These are usually tiny shapes such as boxes, line segments, circles, card symbols, smiling faces, Greek characters, and corners. In some quick and dirty types of animations, these graphics characters may be very useful.

4.9. CUSTOM CHARACTERS SETS

A most important feature for animation is the ability to create and manipulate objects which are made from your own custom characters set.

This feature is available on most of today's personal computers. A single custom character usually consists of an 8 × 8 matrix of dots. With careful planning, you can create a custom character set that satisfies a variety of purposes. You can create a complex object that can be made up of several of these adjacent custom characters. The Walking Man program (Chapter 5), as well as the trees and houses in Chapter 9, were created using a custom character set.

Some computers, like the Apple, feature special programs that facilitate the creation and use of custom characters. Therefore, if the system lacks the ability to mix text and graphics, as the Apple II does, it is possible to actually create your own character set, as well as graphics characters, and mix them on the screen.

4.10. COLOR REGISTERS

Color registers (see Chapter 2 for more details on these) are a feature just beginning to appear on personal computers. First implemented on the ATARI Home Computer and now found on the VIC-20 color computer as well, color registers provide an indirect way to specify pixel color while giving more power and flexible graphics control. Personal computers use color registers in a manner similar to that of high-tech animation computers, with the exception that they are not as wide, bit-wise (and thus hold fewer colors), nor are they as numerous (nine in the ATARI Home Computer, four in the VIC-20). With enough color registers you can perform animation colors through them. Areas on the screen that reference these registers then change color accordingly. Chapter 6 shows, through program examples, how to use color registers in animation on the ATARI Home Computer.

4.11. VERTICAL BLANK INTERRUPTS

Every 1/60 of a second the entire screen is redrawn. From the time when one screen has been completed and the next one is begun, there is a short period called the vertical blank. If the computer allows it, the microprocessor can be interrupted at this point, and a custom machine language program can be executed. This routine can be used to process animations in a background mode, which means you can have certain graphics events occur unattended and almost automatically, such as moving an object, playing music, or reading the joystick. The ability to interrupt the microprocessor during the vertical blank period is called a vertical blank interrupt and is another rare feature which is available on the ATARI Home Computer. Vertical blank interrupts are an advanced concept which we thoroughly cover in Chapter 8.

4.12. DISPLAY LISTS AND DISPLAY LIST INTERRUPTS

Display lists are popular in high-technology animation computers but rare in personal computers. A display list is a section of memory that contains a set of graphics instructions for a graphics processor. So far, only available on the ATARI Home Computers, the display list controls into which graphics modes the screen is divided. The ATARI screen can be horizontally divided into as many different modes as you wish. Display list interrupts are display list instructions that actually interrupt the microprocessor after a mode line has been drawn on the screen and make it possible to change aspects of the display, such as screen color. Chapter 9 features display list interrupt programming examples.

4.13. SPEED OF PLOTTING

A good general test of the speed of your graphics processor is to use the BASIC plotting statement to place a certain number of pixels on the screen using a FOR/NEXT loop and see how long it takes to do this. (If you subtract the time to do the loop and divide the number of pixels by the number of seconds, you have the number of pixels plotted per second — a good measure of graphics speed.) We created the program below to perform this test. The starting and ending values are adjustable to take into account each computer's particular display format. Here is the benchmark program we used for the IBM. You can modify this program to work with other computers' unique statements.

```
100 REM test pixels per second for ibm
110 CLS
120 SCREEN 1: REM sets 320 x 200 mode
130 COLOR 0,1: REM selects background,
    palette
140 XMIN=1: XMAX=320: REM start and end x
150 NROWS=10: REM enough rows to time it
160 YMIN=1: REM starting y
170 FOR Y=YMIN TO NROWS
180   FOR X=XMIN TO XMAX
190     PSET (X,Y),1
200 NEXT X,Y
210 END
```

Figure 4.5: Benchmark Program for testing plotting speed.

Run the above program, and time it with a stopwatch. Calculate the total number of pixels plotted by multiplying XMAX by NROWS. (XMAX

varies for each computer screen resolution.) After this number is obtained, put a REM statement in front of the plotting command on line 190 (here PSET for the IBM), run the program, and time it again. (In other words line 190 would look like 190 REM PSET (X,Y),1.) Subtract the difference between the two times and divide the total number of pixels by this difference. The final answer is the number of pixels plotted per second.

As an example of how fast a personal computer can plot, we found that in IBM's medium- and high-resolution color modes, 320 pixels per second could be PSET to a color.

Part II

Introduction

Earlier you saw what can be done with million dollar computers. Now let's look at the kind of animation that can be created with a personal computer costing only a few hundred dollars. In this half of the book, we will show you how to bring the exciting world of animation into your own home. If you have an ATARI microcomputer (a 400, 800, XL, or equivalent) with ATARI BASIC, you will be able to turn your computer into a fabulous animation machine. If you own something different, read on anyway — some of our examples can be modified for other microcomputers.

This second half of the book is organized differently from the first. This is the hands-on section, and we will be presenting animation program examples that you can type into your computer. We will start out with very simple examples and conclude with a sophisticated demonstration program which uses most of the ATARI's special graphics features.

We assume that you already have some experience with the BASIC programming language. Although we explain the logic behind our animation demonstration programs, we don't cover the meaning of the BASIC keywords (e.g., PRINT, GOTO, GOSUB, etc.). Therefore, if you are new to programming in BASIC, reading a beginning book like *BASIC Programming Primer* (by Waite and Pardee, Howard W. Sams & Co., Indianapolis, IN) or *Armchair BASIC* (by Fox and Fox, Osborne/McGraw-Hill, Berkeley, CA) will help you better understand our examples.

You *do not* need to understand assembly language to use the examples in this book. We have provided you with several *black box* machine language routines which will give you control over the ATARI features such as Player-Missile graphics, Fine Scrolling, and Display List Interrupts. By black box we mean that you can use these routines without knowing what's inside them — you POKE something into them and the desired result comes out. We have designed them so they are easy to use from within BASIC.

If you have thumbed through this section of the book already, you probably noticed many pages of program listings. To save you the time and trouble of entering all this code, a diskette is available through

Adventure International which contains our major demo programs and all the assembly language routines.

Many of our programming examples are expansions of previous examples. This means that instead of typing an entire program, you will often need only to add new sections to an existing program. Therefore, *do not* erase the programs you type in — save them on cassette or diskette, you may need them later on. Also, as you enter the examples, it is important to copy them exactly as they are, without changing any line numbers or omitting any lines. Otherwise, when it is time to expand the programs or merge some of them together, you will have quite a bit of difficulty.

Chapter 5

Character Set Animation

I n this chapter, we will show you how to use ATARI's built-in and user-defined character sets to create animated pictures. These techniques can be employed with any computer which allows you to redefine the character set. There are four demonstration programs in this chapter. The first one will produce a flying bird, the next a walking man, the third a screenful of galloping horses, and the last a bomb exploding in brilliant colors.

5.1.   BUILT-IN CHARACTER SETS —
MAKING DO WITH WHAT YOU HAVE

As we have mentioned earlier, animation is created simply by rapidly displaying a series of pictures which differ only slightly from each other. The brain is fooled into thinking that it is seeing continuous motion rather than individual pictures. The most basic method of implementing animation on a computer is by using PRINT statements to draw a figure on the screen and then using PRINT to go over the figure with a different picture. When these figures are PRINTed in rapid succession, we perceive motion.

To draw our figures, we can use the computer's built-in characters — the letters of the alphabet, numbers, punctuation, and special graphics characters. (See your ATARI BASIC Manual for the complete ATARI character set.) A graphics character set is made up of straight lines, diagonal lines, corners, squares, and circles. When the imaginative programmer puts these elements together, he or she can create a crude picture. Computers such as the IBM Personal Computer and the Commodore computers (PET, VIC, CBM, Commodore 64) all have built-in graphics character sets. The greater the variety of characters, the more flexibility a budding animator has in creating ''living'' figures. In our first example, we will use the ATARI's graphics character set to create a bird in flight on the screen.

Creating the Frames

To produce the effect of animation, you need to create a series of individual pictures that can be rapidly flashed on the screen. Each picture is called a *frame*. In conventional cel animation, the animator usually draws the *key frames* first. These are the ones which show the figure in extreme or key positions. With a very short animated motion, there might be two frames: the initial position of the figure (before the action begins) and the final position of the figure. For example, a person waving good-bye could be animated with two key frames. Longer actions, on the other hand, might contain many key frames, each one occurring at every directional shift in the action. An example of this might be a battle between two figures. The key positions are created as the fight is choreographed. This is done by breaking the extended, complicated action into short, simple actions. (In Example 1, our flying bird, we use two key frames, one with the bird's wings fully raised and one with the wings pointing downwards at the bottom of the flapping cycle.)

The next step is to create the *in-between frames,* i.e., the ones used between the key frames. The number of in-between frames determines the smoothness of the animation. In Example 1, if we had used only our two key frames, without any in-between frames, the animation would have looked jerky and unnatural. (This jerkiness is called *judder* and is an indication of lazy animators or tight production budgets.) On the other hand, since the computer can only PRINT a limited number of frames per second, too many in-between frames would result in slow motion. This is because the computer would not be able to flip through the frames fast enough to make the bird flap its wings at the proper speed.

In film animation, frames are flashed on the screen at the rate of 24 per second. The cartoons produced during the golden age of animation used full animation in which each of those 24 frames required a separate drawing. Today's low-budget cartoons necessitate the reuse of each drawing in consecutive frames. A drawing is placed under the animation camera and photographed two, three, four, or even six times before the next drawing in the sequence is used. This yields a respective animation rate of twelve, eight, six, or four frames per second. Twelve frames per second is tolerable, but anything slower looks painfully crude in comparison to the classics.

In character set animation, the problem of how many frames to display is approached from a different angle. With built-in character sets, we are restricted to the number of in-between frames which can be created with the limited set of characters. In the flying bird example, we could only draw two in-between frames with the available graphics characters, resulting in a total of four unique frames. Even without the restriction of built-in character sets, there is another limiting factor — the computer's processing speed. How many frames can the computer draw in one second without becoming bogged down? The answer is dependent

upon the complexity (size) of each frame, the number of different objects which must be animated at one time, and the other programmed functions (sound effects, calculations, or joystick inputs) that must be taken care of during the animation cycle.

How do you decide how many frames to use in your animated sequence? After months of creating animation programs we will now pass on our foolproof technique for creating realistic looking animations — it is called "Trial and Error."

The Art of Trial and Error?   Most of the development time for this program was spent deciding which characters to PRINT on the screen to create something that looked like a flying bird. Writing the actual program logic took very little time, which is often the case in creating computer animation. Much time is spent in trial and error, trying to get the figure on the screen to look just right. We had certain prerequisites. Not only must our figure resemble a bird, but when it moved, it had to reflect the image of a bird in flight. If the wings moved too fast, the viewers would see only a blur. If the wings moved too slowly, the effect of motion would be lost.

As you begin to create your own animated figures, you'll begin observing the motion of living things. Another excellent source for learning about animation is by watching cartoons. Notice how simple and limited the animation can be while still conveying the effect of movement. At first you may become frustrated with your results, especially after looking at the video games created by the masters. Don't give up! In time, you'll develop an intuitive feeling for animation and will find that your trials are shorter and the errors farther apart. After all, even masters spend much time throwing away earlier attempts that don't look just right.

One nice thing about computer animation is that the results are visible immediately. You don't have to wait for the film to come back from the lab before discovering that your bird looks like a boomerang with arthritis! With a computer, if you don't like what you see, you can adjust the graphics accordingly.

The Flying Bird Frames

Four individual frames were used to create our flying bird, as shown in Figure 5.1. Notice that only four different graphics characters are used throughout the frames.

CHARACTERS USED:

CTRL F   CTRL G   CTRL M   CTRL T

(continued)

FRAME 1

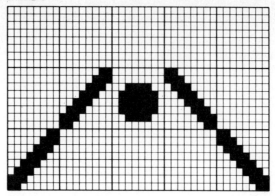

FRAME 2

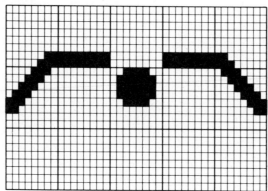

FRAME 3

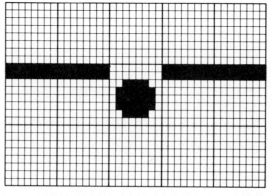

(continued)

FRAME 4

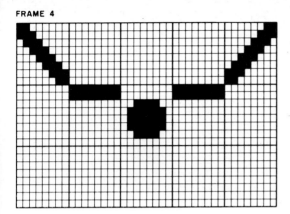

Figure 5.1: Frames of the flying bird.

Each frame is five characters across and three high. To make the job of animating the bird easier, each frame should be identical in size and shape. To accomplish this, many of the character positions in the frame are filled with spaces.

By taking these four frames and cycling through them in a specific order, the bird flaps its wings. Here is the order of the sequence:

Frame 1   beginning of cycle
Frame 2
Frame 3
Frame 4   midpoint of cycle
Frame 3
Frame 2
Frame 1   end of cycle and beginning of next cycle
Frame 2
Frame 3
Frame 4   midpoint of cycle
Frame 3
etc...

For obvious reasons, this is called *cyclic animation*. It is relatively easy to implement because the object can be animated for many seconds or minutes by using only a few different frames. In conventional cel animation, each frame would be photographed in order, over and over again. This can be very time consuming. But with a computer, we can use a simple GOTO loop to repeat the cycle. In the upcoming program, Example 1, six frames are displayed before the cycle repeats.

Listing Conventions — How We Represent Those Invisible ATARI Characters

Throughout the listings in this section of the book are many characters which either cannot be printed by our printer or are difficult to find on the ATARI keyboard (e.g., inverse video, cursor control, and graphics characters). To make it easier to enter the programs, we modified the listings so that all special characters are indicated. Inverse video characters are underlined, and all other special characters are surrounded with curly brackets { }. This includes all graphics characters (entered with the **CTRL** key) and all cursor control characters. When spaces are critical, they are represented as a "b" with a slash through it (ƀ).

You may have noticed that our printed listings look different from programs listed on your screen. We used a special program to print them in a manner which emphasizes their structure, thus making them more easily read and understood. All F O R / N E X T loops are indented so it's easy to see where the loop starts and ends. I F / T H E N statements are also indented — you can see exactly what will be executed if the condition is TRUE. Also, the multiple parts of all statements (separated by colons) are printed on a separate line. Of course, when you enter the programs, the structure will disappear; therefore, *don't* try to maintain it by entering each statement on a separate line!

Although our formatted listings are easier to read, the formatting makes the programs appear to be longer than they really are. Don't let the number of pages it takes to display each program discourage you from entering it. Of course, if you don't want to spend your time typing programs in, you can always purchase them on a disk (see the order card in the back of this book).

Before you try entering the programs, read the complete information in Appendix C, "Listing Conventions."

The listings in this book are in a special format and use special codes. Before you try to enter any of our programs, read the above box *and* Appendix C, "Listing Conventions."

Some of the listings in Chapters 5 through 9 are rather small and difficult to read. However, the complete listings are printed again, larger, in Appendix A for your reference.

Example 1

Exercise Using the built-in ATARI graphics character set, write a program that draws a flying bird with flapping wings on the screen.

a)

b)

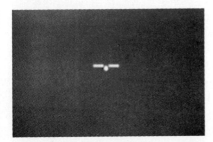

c)

d)

Photo 5.1: Screen photos of the Flying Bird program.

Here is the listing of the Flying Bird program. Look at the lines where the B I R D strings are initialized (lines 120–150). We are using a special convention here to tell you which keys to press to get the appropriate graphics characters. When you see a word or character which is surrounded by curly brackets { }, you must do something special to get the appropriate character into the string. The box called ''Listing Conventions'' and Appendix C explain how this is done.

```
10 REM     *** FLYING BIRD ***
20 REM          Example 1
30 REM
40 REM Demonstration of Character Set Animation using Atari's built-in graphics characters
50 REM Copyright (C) 1982 by David Fox and Mitchell Waite
60 REM
100 REM Initialize
110 DIM BIRD1$(17),BIRD2$(17),BIRD3$(16),BIRD4$(16)
120 BIRD1$="{DOWN}{F}{T}{G}{DOWN}{5 LEFT}{F}bbb{G}"
130 BIRD2$="{DOWN}{F}{M}{T}{M}{G}{DOWN}{5 LEFT}bbbbb"
140 BIRD3$="bbbb{DOWN}{5 LEFT}{2 M}{T}{2 M}"
150 BIRD4$="{G}bbb{F}{DOWN}{5 LEFT}b{M}{T}{M}b"
160 POKE 752,1
170 PRINT "{CLEAR}"
180 REM
200 REM Animation Loop
210 FOR I=1 TO 6
220    POSITION 17,10
230    ON I GOSUB 310,320,330,340,330,320
240    FOR W=1 TO 25:
       NEXT W: REM Pause
250 NEXT I
260 GOTO 210
270 REM
300 REM Draw Frame
310 PRINT BIRD1$;:
    RETURN
320 PRINT BIRD2$;:
    RETURN
330 PRINT BIRD3$;:
    RETURN
340 PRINT BIRD4$;:
    RETURN
```

Figure 5.2: Listing of the Flying Bird program.

How it Works   In line 110, we D I Mension the string variables we will be using in this program. The number within the parentheses tells BASIC the maximum number of characters each string may hold. In ATARI BASIC, all strings must be declared in this manner.

The four frame strings, B I R D 1 $, B I R D 2 $, B I R D 3 $, and B I R D 4 $ (initialized in lines 120–150), contain three different types of characters. They contain:

1. The graphics characters which make up the bird (see Figure 5.1).
2. The cursor control characters which move the cursor before printing a graphics character.
3. Spaces which are used to erase sections of previous frames.

Whenever something is being printed (with P R I N T) on the screen, you will see the little white box, called the cursor, following each printed character. The P O K E in line 160 turns off the cursor (makes it invisible),

so we don't see little white boxes swarming around like a bunch of hornets while each frame is drawn.

The Animation loop (lines 200–270) contains the logic to print each frame in the correct order. This section is simple and straightforward. We just have to place the cursor in the middle of the screen with ATARI's cursor positioning command (line 220) and print the appropriate frame. The entire wing-flapping cycle consists of six frames (two of which are repeated). To accomplish this we use a FOR/NEXT loop from 1 to 6 to step through the frames. An ON GOSUB (line 230) uses the current FOR/NEXT value (I) to control which frame is printed. When I equals 1, line 310 is executed and BIRD1$ gets printed. When I equals 2, line 320 is executed, and so on.

Line 240's FOR/NEXT loop is used to slow down the rate at which the frames are printed. Try changing the value on this line to see what happens to the bird. You may like the bird better at a different frame rate.

Modifications   Here are a few modifications you can try on Example 1:

1. Change the program so that more than one bird is flapping its wings on the screen. This could easily be done by repeating lines 220 and 230 within the main Animation loop and changing the X,Y coordinates of the POSITION statement. You will also have to change the value in the Pause loop (line 240) to adjust the frame rate of the birds. (You may be able to gain some animation speed by using separate PRINT statements for each of the three horizontal rows of bird characters per frame. This will save you from having to use the cursor control characters — the fewer characters printed, the faster the program will run.)
2. Make the bird move around the screen. To do this, just control the values in line 220's POSITION statement. Be sure to erase the bird each time you move it or the screen will become wallpapered in birds! Another point to remember is this: anytime you erase and redraw a figure, it will appear to *flicker* on the screen (the light from the image is interrupted by blankness during the instant the image is erased, thus the flicker). To minimize the flicker, erase the bird immediately before drawing the next frame — avoid inserting any program logic or calculations while the bird is erased.
3. Add sound effects. As we will see in later programs, sound effects can add a great deal of realism to a program.
4. Make the bird look like it is flying away from or closer to you. Add new frames of the bird which are smaller and frames of a larger bird which have greater detail. As you display each set of frames in order, it will look as though the bird is flying towards or away from you.

Summary

Now you have seen how a simple animation program can be put together from start to finish. The result is a crude beginning, but the next technique allows us to produce animated figures with far greater sophistication.

5.2. USER-DEFINED CHARACTER SETS — A BOUNCY WALKING MAN

We must admit that after all that talk about making the bird look like a bird, it takes some imagination on the part of the observer to look at a dot and a bunch of lines and see a flying bird. Using the built-in character set of your computer is very limiting! In this section, we will see how to make use of the ATARI's capability to *redefine* the character set. Using the same animation technique as in the first program, we can now sculpture the individual characters into any shapes we wish. In other words, you can create individual characters which can be printed together to make up a larger, perfectly designed shape. Many other computers, such as the IBM Personal Computer,[1] the Apple II,[2] and the Apple III also have this capability. Now our animated figures can be created with a high degree of detail rather than being limited to the coarseness offered by the built-in character set.

The Character Set

When you first turn on your ATARI computer, you will see a word or words printed on the screen (i.e., READY if you are using your BASIC cartridge). What happens inside your computer to display those words? A series of number codes are placed in an area of RAM called screen memory, one code for each character. These codes are then interpreted in a predetermined way (depending on which graphics mode you are in). In the standard text mode, GRAPHICS 0, the numbers in screen memory are translated as addresses which are used to look up some permanently stored information. This information, stored in ROM (read-only memory) is called a *character set*.[3] Each character in the set is composed of

---

[1]The IBM PC allows you to define characters only in its two graphics modes. Only the top 128 character codes can be redefined.

[2]The Apple II's character set is not really redefinable. However, a number of software products now on the market allow you to define a character set that is displayed on the high-resolution graphics screen rather than the standard text screen.

[3]See *Computer Graphics Primer* by Mitchell Waite, Howard W. Sams & Co., Indianapolis, IN for more details.

dots in an array that is 8 dots wide and 8 dots high. Each of these 64 dots can be turned on or off, thus defining a character. The information which describes which dots to turn on or off for a character is called the *character definition*. Figure 5.4 shows the dot array, or character definition, for the letter A.

APPEARANCE OF LETTER ON THE SCREEN	THE EIGHT BYTES DEFINING THE CHARACTER	
	BINARY REPRESENTATION	DECIMAL REPRESENTATION
	00000000	0
	00011000	24
	00111100	60
	01100110	102
	01100110	102
	01111110	126
	01100110	102
	00000000	0

Figure 5.3: Character definition for the letter "A."

Try typing some letters on your screen and see if you can make out the individual dots. If your television set is sharp enough, you will be able to see them.

Photo 5.2: Screen photo — close-up of the letter "A."

The information in each character definition is stored as a series of 8 bytes, with each byte representing one horizontal row of 8 dots.[4] Since

---

[4]This is the same as the IBM Personal Computer's graphics mode.

there are 8 bits in a byte, whether a bit is on will determine whether the corresponding dot on the screen will be turned on. Each character in the character set is defined in this manner.

There are 128 distinct characters in the ATARI character set. If we multiply this number of characters (128) by the number of bytes needed to define each character in the character set (8), we get 1024, or 1K (128 * 8 = 1024 bytes). This is the amount of ROM space needed to store the ATARI built-in character set. Since each character can also be represented in reverse video, there are a possible 128 * 2 = 256 codes (from 0 to 255) which can appear in screen memory and be interpreted as characters. The codes from 0 to 127 represent normal video characters and the codes from 128 to 255 are reserved for inverse video characters.[5]

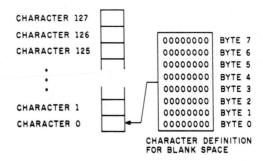

Figure 5.4: Map of ROM character set.

In many personal computers, the built-in character set is all you get. But the ATARI Home Computer has the capability to display user-defined character sets! As we said, the ROM character set is permanent. You can't change any of the character definitions in this ROM. However, what if we were to create our own set of character definitions and POKE them into RAM? How would we let the computer know where to find this customized set of character definitions? The answer is simple — ATARI has memory location 756 (decimal) reserved for this purpose. This RAM location always contains the page address of the current character set. (A page of memory is 256 bytes, therefore to convert a page address to an actual address, multiply by 256.) When you turn on your computer, press the **SYSTEM RESET** button, or change GRAPHICS modes, the value in 756 is automatically initialized to 224 (the page address of the ROM

---

[5]The IBM PC has a separate byte for each character position to control attributes!

character set; thus we say that 756 *points* to the character set in ROM). But you can change the value in 756 so it points instead to an address in the computer's RAM. If you POKE the page address of your customized character set into 756, you ''turn on'' the new character set. As we shall soon see, the results are instantaneously visible.[6]

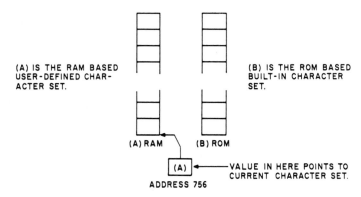

Figure 5.5: Switching between RAM and ROM character sets.

Turning On Character Sets

Let's try a simple program to see what happens if we change the value in 756. Try typing in the following short program:

```
10 GRAPHICS Ø
20 FOR I=Ø TO 255 STEP 4
30    POKE 756,I: REM Switch character sets
40 NEXT I
50 GOTO 2Ø
```

Now run this program. Don't worry, your computer isn't broken! What you will see on your screen is a rapidly changing, finely drawn display which fills the entire screen. Exactly what is happening? Let's see. When line 10 is executed, the screen is cleared. The ATARI clears its screen by filling screen memory with 0s. These 0s are used to look up the *0th character* in the current character set. In the ROM character set,

---

[6]On the IBM PC, changing the location of the character definition table affects only *future* characters to be written, not characters already printed on the screen.

this 0th character is the space. A character set must always begin on a "1 K boundary." This means it can begin at any address which is evenly divisible by 1024. In converting to pages, the value in 756 must be evenly divisible by 4 (there are 4 pages in 1 K). So in line 20, we increment I by four. As we POKE the different values of I into 756, the current character set is changed. Of course, we really aren't switching to different character sets, just to whatever random information happens to be at that memory location. What we see on the screen is the current character definition for the 0th character (the space character). Whatever happens to occupy the first 8 bytes in each character set (i.e., the character definition for the 0th character) determines how the space character will be displayed. When the first 8 bytes are 0s, the screen goes blank.

Now press **RESET**, and POKE 756 with 200. The screen immediately becomes a mass of swirling, ever-changing interference patterns. But how could this be — there's no program running! Ah, but there is. We have discovered an address which is being used by the ATARI operating system. It is changing the contents of the first 8 bytes at machine-language speed.

Reserving Character Set Memory

After we have designed a character set, we must find a safe place in memory for it. A good location is immediately below screen memory. Where is screen memory? In most computers, screen memory is always located at the same address. However, the ATARI Home Computer automatically reserves space at the very end of RAM for screen memory. This means you'll find the screen memory at different addresses, depending on how much memory your computer contains and which graphics mode you are using. In GRAPHICS 0, 1 K of memory is used to display the screen.[7]

The ATARI uses memory location 106 to store the number of pages of memory it thinks it currently has. By taking the value in 106 and subtracting 4 from it for screen memory and another 4 for the size of the character set, we can obtain the page address for our character set (see Figure 5.6).

---

[7]Actually GRAPHICS 0 uses 960 bytes of screen RAM and 32 bytes for the display list (covered later in this chapter) for a total of 992 bytes.

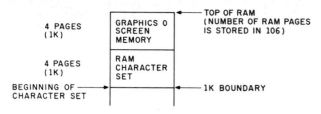

Figure 5.6: Memory map of upper RAM.

Creating a Character Set

Now that we know the why and wherefore of user-defined character sets, we can create one of our own. There is a difficult and a not-so-difficult way to create user-defined character sets. The difficult way is to:

1. Photocopy the grid of squares in Figure 5.8 or obtain a sheet of graph paper, preferably 8 squares per inch. (Our grid has been prepared to accurately reflect the true proportions, 7:8, of each character — the vertical side is longer than the horizontal side.)
2. Decide on the size of the character matrix you want your figure to occupy and draw it on your grid of squares.
3. Draw the outline of the figure you wish to represent within the character matrix.
4. Fill in all the little squares which lie more than halfway inside the boundaries of your outline. Use your judgement to improve the appearance of the figure for borderline squares.
5. Calculate the decimal value for each row of each character cell.
6. Enter these byte values into your program.

This method is difficult in that it involves the manual transfer of information from paper to a program. If you only needed to do this once it wouldn't be so bad. But, as we mentioned earlier, creating an effective animation requires a large degree of trial and error — it's exceedingly rare to get it right the first time. So once you've done all your work, tried the program and discovered that your animated figure looks as if it's critically ill, you must go through the entire process again.

A more efficient approach is to use one of the commercial font editing programs currently available to consumers.[8] A product like this will allow you to work with your characters in an interactive environment: you can see the characters on the screen as you create and edit

---

[8]The word "font" refers to the style of the characters on the screen. You can design an Olde English font, a computer-like font, a script font, or even a walking-man font.

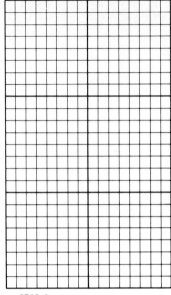

STEP 2:
2 × 3 MATRIX OF CHARACTERS

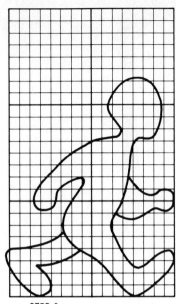

STEP 3:
DRAW OUTLINE OF FIGURE

STEP 4:
FILL IN THE SQUARES

STEP 5:
CALCULATE BYTE VALUES
FOR CHARACTER DEFINITIONS

0		0
0		0
0		0
0		0
0		0
0		0
0		28
0		62
0		62
0		62
0		28
0		240
3		240
15		240
29		240
59		251
51		255
7		220
7		192
7		192
15		227
252		118
112		60
48		24

a)

(continued)

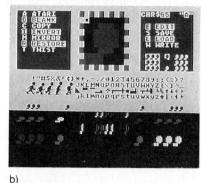

b)

Figure 5.7: a) Steps to create a character set frame b) using a font editor "IN-STEDIT" by Sheldon Leemon, ATARI Program Exchange, Apx 20060.

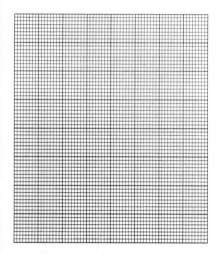

Figure 5.8: Grid for creating character set figures. A full-size grid appropriate for photocopying can be found in Appendix B.

them. The computer can also take care of the laborious calculations necessary to determine the byte values for each character. You will still spend much time trying and erring, but the computer will handle much of the tedium.

The digitizing tablet is another labor-saving device which facilitates the creation of character sets. As we mentioned in Chapter 2, it consists of a large, flat drawing surface and an electronic pen or pointer. By placing your artwork on the tablet's surface, you can enter information directly into the computer by pressing down on the pen. When you outline the sections you want to transfer, the computer creates an image of your drawing on the screen. Before you rush out and buy a digitizing tablet, though, make sure you can also buy an accompanying program (for your computer) designed to help you create character sets.

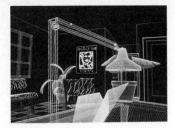

Color Artifacts   One thing you should be aware of when creating your character sets is the problem with or capability of (depending on how you look at it) color "artifacts." You may have noticed that every vertical line in the ATARI built-in character set is at least two dots wide. This is done to make sure the line shows up on a color television screen in the desired color. If a vertical line is only one dot wide, or if every other dot in a row (byte) is turned on, you'll see a color artifact. For example, instead of appearing white, the character may be blue or some other color. The dictionary defines artifact as *an artificially produced changed appearance*. In this case, it is a color that is produced by the nature of the color television screen rather than intentionally by the computer. Artifacts can be used to add color to a screen, but these colors may look different on someone else's ATARI (depending on whether it has a GTIA or a CTIA chip — see Chapter 6). Harry Brown, an ATARI programmer, used artifacts to add extra color to the playing cards of his poker game (see Photo 5.3). The green background was created by filling the screen with quadruple-wide Players and Missiles with holes cut in them for the text and cards (see color insert; see also Chapters 7 and 8 for more on Player-Missile Graphics).

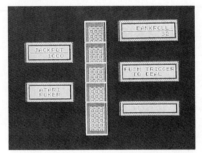

Photo 5.3: Poker game using color artifacts (see color insert). *(Courtesy of Harry Brown.)*

We will introduce a much better technique for producing extra colors in a character set in Example 4. For more on artifacts, see the box on "Pixels, Dots, and Color Clocks" later in this chapter.

The Walking Man Program

Our next program demonstrates the power of user-defined character sets. We will define a character set that we can use to draw a picture of a little man walking across the screen. Below are the character definitions for our Walking Man character set. Each frame is made up of six characters arranged in a 2 × 3 array (see Figure 5.9). We are using five frames for the walking cycle, and each frame is displayed only once during each of his steps. This means that we need only 30 characters (6 characters per frame * 5 frames) to animate the man. Actually, we need only 26 characters since 4 of the characters that appear within the frames are blank. To the right of each frame are the byte values we need to POKE into the character set RAM.

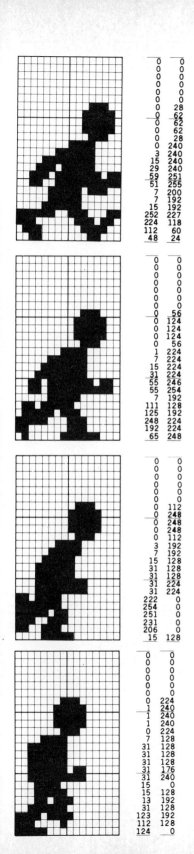

0	0
0	0
0	0
0	0
0	0
0	28
0	62
0	62
0	62
0	28
0	240
3	240
15	240
29	240
59	251
51	255
7	200
7	192
15	192
252	227
224	118
112	60
48	24

0	0
0	0
0	0
0	0
0	0
0	0
0	56
0	124
0	124
0	56
1	224
7	224
15	224
31	224
55	246
55	254
7	192
111	128
125	192
248	224
192	224
65	248

0	0
0	0
0	0
0	0
0	0
0	112
0	248
0	248
0	112
3	192
7	192
15	128
31	128
31	128
31	224
31	224
222	0
254	0
251	0
231	0
206	0
15	128

0	0
0	0
0	0
0	0
0	0
0	224
1	240
1	240
1	240
0	224
7	128
31	128
31	128
31	128
31	176
31	240
15	0
15	128
13	192
31	128
123	192
112	128
124	0

(continued)

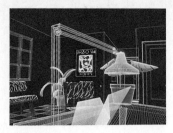

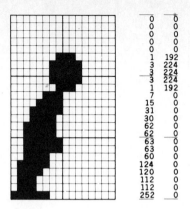

0	0
0	0
0	0
0	0
0	0
1	192
3	224
3	224
3	224
1	192
7	0
15	0
31	0
30	0
62	0
62	0
63	0
63	0
60	0
124	0
120	0
112	0
112	0
252	0

Figure 5.9: Walking Man character set.

Animation implemented on microcomputers is often considered crude. This is most often because the programmer is usually not an animator or an artist, *not* because the computer isn't capable of handling the job. Attention to detail makes animation come alive. Take a look at the position of the man's head in these five frames. As he walks, his entire body bounces up and down. This is much more realistic than a walking man with moving feet and a stationary head!

To create this character set, *Animation*, by Preston Blair (published by Walter Foster Art Books, Tustin, CA), a book on conventional animation, was used. This is an excellent yet simple book showing how to draw your own animated characters. We placed graph paper over a set of drawings from the book of a walking man and filled in the appropriate squares. A font editing program (*FONTEDIT*, from the software package IRIDIS 2 by The Code Works, Goleta, CA) was used to help convert the filled-in squares to character set data. One technique you can try (if you can't find the figure you wish to animate in an animation book) is to cut out a drawing of your animated character from paper. At each of your figure's joints (i.e., knees, elbows), use paper clasps or string to create a hinge. Then position your figure for each frame and outline its shape onto graph paper. It will still take some practice to create smooth, realistic motion, but the proportions of each body part will be correct.

Example 2

Exercise   Using a user-defined character set, write a program that displays a man walking across the screen. Use the joystick button to control his forward movement. Give him life with a bounce in his step. Include the sounds of his footsteps.

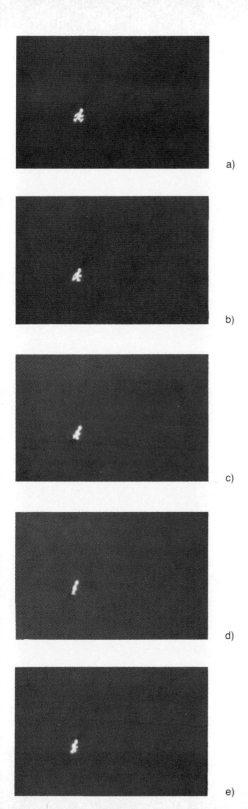

a)

b)

c)

d)

e)

Photo 5.4: Walking Man.

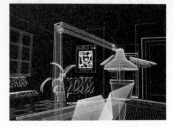

Here is the Walking Man program. There are four main sections: the initialization section, the section which reads in the new character set, the actual character set data, and the animation loop. The complete listing can be found in Appendix A.

```
10   REM    WALKING MAN CHARACTER SET
20   REM              Example 2
30   REM
40   REM Demonstration of user-defined character set
50   REM Copyright (C) 1982 by David Fox and Mitchell Waite
60   REM
100  REM Initialize
110  FRAMES=5: REM Number of frames
120  FRMSZE=12: REM Characters in frame (including cursor control chars)
130  DIM MAN$(FRAMES*FRMSZE),FRAME$(FRMSZE),ERASE$(7)
140  MAN$="ﬔa(DOWN)(2 LEFT)bc(DOWN)(2 LEFT)deﬔf(DOWN)(2 LEFT)gh(DOWN)(2 LEFT)ij"
150  MAN$(25)="ﬔk(DOWN)(2 LEFT)lm(DOWN)(2 LEFT)nopq(DOWN)(2 LEFT)rs(DOWN)(2 LEFT)tﬔ"
160  MAN$(49)="uv(DOWN)(2 LEFT)wx(DOWN)(2 LEFT)yz"
170  ERASE$="ﬔ(LEFT)(UP)ﬔ(LEFT)(UP)ﬔ"
180  GRAPHICS 0
190  POKE 752,1: REM Turn off cursor
200  PRINT "One moment please..."
210  GOSUB 8000: REM Read in Character Set
220  PRINT "(CLEAR)"
230  SETCOLOR 1,0,14:
     SETCOLOR 2,1,2
240  POKE 756,HICHRB: REM Switch to new Char Set
250  REM
```

Figure 5.10: Listing of Example 2 — lines 10–250.

Initialization   Each of the five man frames is made up of six graphics characters and six cursor control characters for a total of twelve characters. The variable FRMSZE (line 120) is set to this value. On line 130 we reserve string space for our frames with the DIMension statement. All of our frames are stored in one string variable, called MAN$, rather than in a series of strings as we did in the Flying Bird program (Example 1). This reduces the size of the program code needed to access a specific frame and makes the program more flexible if we want to use a different set of frame data. We could have initialized MAN$ in one statement, but it would have been much more difficult to understand and enter. The variable FRAME$ will temporarily hold the current frame to make it easier to manipulate.

Make sure you enter lines 140–160 *exactly* as they appear, including the four spaces. Even though you are entering letters of the alphabet now, when you switch over to the new character set, these will be printed as sections of the man.

ERASE$ (line 170) is used to erase the man every time he moves one character position to the right. If this wasn't used, our friend would leave behind a trail of old body parts as he moved across the screen.

In line 230, the color of the screen background and foreground is changed with the SETCOLOR command. For now, a brief description of it should be enough. The syntax of the command is

SETCOLOR *n,hue,lum*

where *n* selects the *color register* which will receive the new color, *hue* is the hue of the color (a value from 0 to 15; see Table 6.2), and *lum* is the

luminance or brightness of the color (an even value from 0 to 14). The use of color registers is a very important ATARI feature, requiring all of Chapter 6 to cover. The hue we are choosing is gold with the brightness of the man turned to maximum (the 14 in SETCOLOR 1 ,0 ,14) and the background set to dark brown (SETCOLOR 2 ,1 ,2). We will be covering the SETCOLOR command in depth in Chapter 6.

In line 240, we POKE the address of the new character set into memory location 756. (This is done to turn on the user-defined character set and turn off the built-in ATARI character set).

```
8000  REM Set Up Alternate Character Set
8010  HICHRB=PEEK(106)-8: REM Reserve memory space (1024 bytes) below screen
8020  CHRBAS=HICHRB*256: REM Find start of Character Set
8030  REM Read in data, skip first 97 characters
8040  OFFSET=97*8:
      CHARS=26
8060  READ TOTAL:
      TEMP=0
8070  FOR I=CHRBAS+OFFSET TO CHRBAS+OFFSET+CHARS*8-1
8080    READ BYTE:
        POKE I,BYTE:
        TEMP=TEMP+BYTE
8090  NEXT I
8100  IF TOTAL<>TEMP THEN
        GRAPHICS 0:
        PRINT "ERROR In Character Set Data":
        END
8110  REM Clear out first char (background)
8120  FOR I=CHRBAS TO CHRBAS+7
8130    POKE I,0
8140  NEXT I
8150  RETURN
8160  REM
```

Figure 5.11: Listing of Example 2 — lines 8000–8160.

Set Up Alternate Character Set   Here we POKE the new character set into RAM. First, on line 8010, some memory is set aside for our character set. Recall that address 106 is where the ATARI stores the number of pages of memory it thinks are in the computer. We've set the variable HICHRB (HIgh byte of CHaRacter set Base) to the total number of RAM pages in the computer minus eight pages (2 K), four pages for screen memory and four pages for the character set.

In line 8020, the RAM page number in HICHRB is converted to an actual RAM address by multiplying it by 256 (number of bytes in a page) and then stored in CHRBAS.

The next step is to read in the character set data. The first letter of the character set will replace the lowercase ''a,'' the second letter, lowercase ''b,'' etc. In some programs, you may need to copy all or part of the ATARI ROM character set into our RAM character set. You may want to retain the uppercase and numeric characters for use in your screen display. By redefining only the lowercase letters, you would still be able to print text on the screen or read your program when it was listed with the new character set still installed. You could copy the ROM character set into your RAM character set with the statements

```
100 ROMSET=224*256: REM Calculate address
    of ROM character set
110 FOR I=0 TO 1023:
    POKE CHRBAS+I, PEEK(ROMSET+I):
    NEXT I
```

where `CHRBAS` is the RAM address of your new character set. In our Running Man program, we didn't need to do this, so it really doesn't make any difference whether we redefined the lowercase letters or any other sequence of characters.

In line 8040, the `OFFSET` for the lower case ''a'' (number of bytes from the beginning of the character set) is calculated, and the number of characters we are redefining is stored in `CHARS`.

To assure that the character set data is entered accurately, a checksum value is used. All of the bytes in our data statements were added together to obtain this value. Then this value, which came to 16845, was placed in a `DATA` statement on line 20020. This checksum value is `READ` into the variable `TOTAL` (line 8060), and all the bytes in our `DATA` statements are added together and stored in `TEMP` as the character set is `READ` and `POKE`d into RAM (lines 8070–8090). If the checksum value in `TOTAL` doesn't equal the calculated sum in `TEMP`, an error message is printed out. If this happens, recheck the values typed into the character set data statements.

On lines 8120 through 8140 the first character in the character set is filled with 0's. As stated before, this is the character definition for the space character. You already know what kind of designs can appear on the screen if the space character isn't a blank!

```
20000  REM Character Set Data        20320  REM , Frame 5
20010  REM , Checksum                 20330  DATA 0,0,0,0,0,0,0,1
20020  DATA 16845                     20340  DATA 0,0,0,0,0,0,224,240
20030  REM                            20350  DATA 1,1,0,7,31,31,31,31
20040  REM , Frame 1                  20360  DATA 240,240,224,128,128,128,128,176
20050  DATA 0,0,0,0,0,0,28,62         20370  DATA 31,15,15,13,31,123,112,124
20060  DATA 0,0,0,0,3,15,29,59        20380  DATA 240,0,128,192,128,192,128,0
20070  DATA 62,62,28,240,240,240,240,251
20080  DATA 51,7,7,15,252,224,112,48
20090  DATA 255,220,192,192,227,118,60,24
20100  REM
20110  REM , Frame 2
20120  DATA 0,0,0,0,0,0,0,56
20130  DATA 0,0,0,0,1,7,15,31
20140  DATA 124,124,124,56,224,224,224,224
20150  DATA 55,55,7,111,125,248,192,65
20160  DATA 246,254,192,128,192,224,224,248
20170  REM
20180  REM , Frame 3
20190  DATA 0,0,0,0,0,0,112,248
20200  DATA 0,0,0,3,7,15,31,31
20210  DATA 248,248,112,192,192,128,128,128
20220  DATA 31,31,222,254,251,231,206,15
20230  DATA 224,224,0,0,0,0,0,128
20240  REM
20250  REM , Frame 4
20260  DATA 0,0,0,0,0,1,3,3
20270  DATA 0,0,0,0,0,192,224,224
20280  DATA 3,1,7,15,31,30,62,62
20290  DATA 224,192,0,0,0,0,0,0
20300  DATA 63,63,60,124,120,112,112,252
20310  REM
```

Figure 5.12: Listing of Example 2 — lines 20000–20380.

Character Set Data   This is where the data for our Walking Man is stored. As previously mentioned, the first value (16845) is the sum of the rest of data. Each line, starting with 20050, contains one character definition — the 8 bytes which define a single character.

```
300  REM Animation Loop
310  X=3: REM Set starting horizontal position of Man
320  FOR I=1 TO FRAMES
330     FRAME$=MAN$(I*FRMSZE-(FRMSZE-1),I*FRMSZE)
340     POSITION X,14:
        PRINT ERASE$;FRAME$:
350     IF I=1 THEN
           SOUND 1,0,0,14: REM Footsteps
360     IF I=2 THEN
           SOUND 1,24,0,14
370     SOUND 1,0,0,0: REM Turn off sound
380     FOR W=1 TO 10:
        NEXT W: REM Slow him down a little
390  NEXT I
400  REM Walk man across screen if Joystick button is down
410  IF STRIG(0)=0 THEN
        X=X+1:
        IF X=36 THEN
           PRINT "(CLEAR)":
           GOTO 310
420  GOTO 320
430  REM
```

Figure 5.13:   Listing of Example 2 — lines 300–430.

Animation Loop   The logic behind this section is similar to the animation loop in the Flying Bird program with the addition of a few new techniques. Since all the frames are stored in one long string, the desired frame can be pointed to directly with the formula in line 330. In ATARI BASIC, a substring (section of a string) can be accessed by indicating the first and last characters:

STRING$(*first,last*)

The formula in line 330 allows access to the I th substring of MAN$ which is FRMSZE characters long. When I equals 1, the first 12 characters of MAN$ are stored in FRAME$ (Frame 1). When I equals 4, the fourth set of 12 characters is stored in FRAME$ (Frame 4).

On line 340, the cursor (now invisible) is positioned on the screen. ERASE$ is used to clear away any of the previously drawn man, and then the current frame is drawn.

On lines 350 to 370, the sounds of a footstep are added. The syntax of the SOUND command is

SOUND *voice, frequency, distortion, volume*

There are four separate sound registers or *voices* in the computer, num-bered 0 to 3. The *frequency* can be any number from 0 to 255. It determines how low or high in pitch the sound will be. By changing the

value of the sound's *distortion* (even numbers from 0 to 14), anything from a pure tone to a roar can be created. The *volume* can be any number from 0 (no sound) to 15 (loud sound). By using two different frequency settings in our program, one sound is made when the man's heel hits the ground and another when the rest of his foot makes contact.

Finally, on line 410 the man's horizontal position on the screen is incremented if the joystick button is pressed. The screen is cleared when he reaches the right edge of it, and the starting horizontal position (X) in line 310 is reinitialized.

Running the Program   Before you run the program, plug a joystick into the first joystick port (on the left). Now type RUN, and you'll see the man walking in place on the left side of the screen. No mistaking him for a bunch of wobbly pick-up sticks — he really looks like a walking man! Adjust the volume on your television set so you can hear the footsteps. When you press the joystick button, the man will begin walking eastward.

Modification   Make a modification which prints more than one man on the screen at the same time. This could easily be done by adding a few more lines like 340, but changing the vertical position to other values. How many men can you have walking across the screen before they look like they're walking through a vat of cold molasses? Don't forget to delete line 380 to gain some speed.

Notice how the walking men seem to be stepping slightly out of sync. This is due to the time it takes for BASIC to move the cursor to the next man's position and draw a new frame. This modification really shows BASIC's limitations in animating character set graphics with multiple figures — BASIC just doesn't PRINT fast enough on the ATARI.

Summary

By making use of the increased resolution and control gained by user-defined character sets over built-in character sets, your animations can look much more lifelike! The next problem to overcome is that of BASIC's slowness when it comes to animating more than one figure at the same time. In the next section we will see how this can be accomplished without the use of machine language.

5.3. FLIPPING CHARACTER SETS —
THE GALLOPING HORSE

The next technique overcomes the problem of animating multiple figures with BASIC. The problem relates to the speed at which BASIC can PRINT something on the screen. BASIC can't maintain adequate animation frame rates for the simultaneous display of more than a few separate figures. It can handle one or two simple figures, but then it becomes overloaded, and the result is sluggish and stilted animations. We could use machine language at this point (called from BASIC) to greatly increase the frame rate, but there is a simpler technique — character set flipping. Using this technique in upcoming Example 3, even though the screen will be completely filled with moving figures, the program actually needs to be *slowed* down to obtain the proper frame rate.

How Does Character Set Flipping Work?

In the last program, *one* alternate character set was created and then switched on. The animation was created by rapidly PRINTing each frame (made up of characters from that one character set) on the screen. Recall our short introductory program which POKEd a series of numbers into RAM location 756. Do you remember how quickly the display changed? By repeatedly changing the value in 756, we were actually flipping through a series of character sets with random characters. The screen looked like a rapidly changing mess. What would happen if we made use of this flipping technique, but gave it *real* character sets to flip through? One character set for *each* frame could be created. Then, rather than redrawing the figure on the screen with PRINT, each of these character sets could be rapidly flipped through! When we PRINT something on the screen, it will be displayed using the character set that is currently being pointed to (by the value in 756). When another character set is pointed to, the image on the screen will *immediately* change.[9] Each value in a screen location will "index" into the current character set. The frame rate will be determined then by how rapidly we can POKE in the addresses of our different character sets as opposed to how rapidly the computer can PRINT something on the screen.

In our next example, we will borrow from the man who made the first live action movie. As we mentioned in Chapter 1, in 1872 the ex-governor of California, Leland Stanford, and another millionaire horse lover, Fred McCrellish, had an argument about whether a galloping horse ever had all its hooves off the ground at any moment. They hired a

---

[9]This technique will not work for the IBM Personal Computer — once a character is printed on the screen, its appearance can't be changed by flipping to a different character set.

famous photographer named Eadweard Muybridge to find out. After his first attempts using only one camera failed to produce convincing results, he tried again six years later with 12 cameras. Each of these cameras, equally spaced along a wall, was connected to a trip wire. As the famous trotter Abe Edgington galloped by, it set off each of the cameras in succession. By examining each of the photographs, it was determined that the horse did indeed have all of its feet off the ground at one point during its galloping cycle. Governor Stanford won the argument and had a famous university named after him.

Perhaps more important for us, when Muybridge rapidly flipped through the photographs, the motion of the galloping horse was recreated! He later built the first movie projector (the Zoopraxiscope) and toured North America and Europe, astounding crowned heads on both sides of the Atlantic with the first feature-length (1–2 seconds) films. Five of the frames from his original horse sequence were used to create the character definitions for the next example.[10]

Figure 5.14 illustrates the character definitions for our galloping horse. Each of the five frames is composed of a 6 × 4 array of characters (24 characters).

FRAME

0	0	0	0	0	0
0	0	0	0	0	0
0	0	0	0	6	0
0	0	0	0	118	0
0	0	0	1	155	128
0	0	0	1	127	192
0	0	0	6	247	32
0	0	0	15	231	136
0	0	0	59	135	196
0	0	0	15	14	204
0	3	255	254	60	48
3	252	31	192	124	0
14	188	0	0	12	0
29	14	24	0	8	0
5	11	31	0	8	0
0	11	157	240	56	0
0	15	207	252	112	0
0	5	223	191	248	0
0	126	243	223	254	0
0	127	224	127	142	0
0	97	192	3	252	0
0	99	192	3	248	0
0	103	128	1	128	0
0	99	128	1	128	0
1	193	192	1	128	0
1	128	224	1	192	0
0	0	112	1	224	0
0	0	24	0	48	0
0	0	28	0	56	0
0	0	0	0	0	0
0	0	0	0	0	0
0	0	0	0	0	0

FRAME

0	0	0	0	0	0
0	0	0	0	8	0
0	0	0	0	12	0
0	0	0	1	190	0
0	0	0	5	121	0
0	0	0	8	248	128
0	0	0	59	252	32
0	0	0	87	191	208
0	0	0	255	187	144
0	7	255	1	184	192
3	252	32	0	48	0
7	208	32	0	16	0
15	151	108	4	16	0
29	31	255	28	16	0
0	31	255	252	48	0
0	15	255	184	240	0
0	15	255	248	28	0
0	15	143	255	254	0
0	62	0	31	6	0
0	60	0	60	12	0
0	56	0	48	56	0
0	236	0	112	48	0
0	204	0	96	0	0
0	198	0	192	0	0
0	220	1	0	0	0
0	216	1	0	0	0
0	192	1	0	0	0
0	96	0	0	0	0
0	112	0	0	0	0
0	0	0	0	0	0
0	0	0	0	0	0
0	0	0	0	0	0

(continued)

FRAME

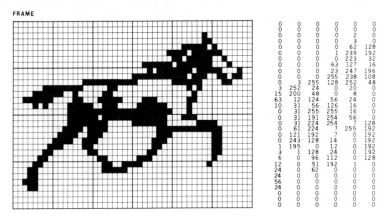

```
0     0     0     0     0     0
0     0     0     0     0     0
0     0     0     0     2     0
0     0     0     0     3     0
0     0     0     0    62   128
0     0     0     1   239   192
0     0     0     0   223    32
0     0     0    63   127    16
0     0     0    23   247   196
0     0     0   255   238   108
0     3   255   128   252    48
3   252    24     0    20     0
15   200    48     0     8     0
63    12   124    56    24     0
10    31    56   126    16     0
0    31   255   255    16     0
0    31   191   254    56     0
0    31   224   254     7   128
0    61   224     7   255   192
0   121   192     7     0   192
0   243   128    14     0   192
1   195     0    12     0   192
3     1   128    24     0   192
6     0    96   112     0   128
12     0    51   192     1     0
24     0    62     0     0     0
24     0     0     0     0     0
56     0     0     0     0     0
24     0     0     0     0     0
0     0     0     0     0     0
0     0     0     0     0     0
```

FRAME

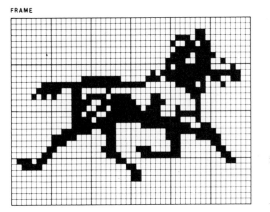

```
0     0     0     0     0     0
0     0     0     0     6     0
0     0     0     0   118     0
0     0     0     0   155     0
0     0     0     0   127     0
0     0     0     0   247   128
0     0     0     1   231    32
0     0     0     1   127     8
0     0     0    11   255   252
0     3   252    29   254   204
3   255   127   224   122    32
7   204    16     0    30     0
10   141   239    12    12     0
0    15    63   142     4     0
0    14   111   220    68     0
0    13   159   252   124     0
0    15   127   255   196     0
0    15   248    63   243     0
0    63    56     1   255   128
0   248    24     1   199   192
0   224    24     0   192   192
1   128    56   112   192    96
3     0    28    63   192    48
118     0     6     0     0    24
60     0     1   128     0     0
0     0     0   192     0     0
0     0     0   192     0     0
0     0     0     0     0     0
0     0     0     0     0     0
0     0     0     0     0     0
0     0     0     0     0     0
```

FRAME

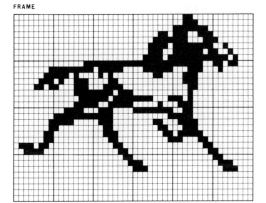

```
0     0     0     0    48     0
0     0     0     0    56     0
0     0     0     0   254     0
0     0     0     6   231     0
0     0     0    15   227   128
0     0     0    30   255    32
0     0     0    28   253   144
0     0     0    61   255   232
0     3   255   255   252   216
1   255   124    63    28    64
3   232    80    12    56     0
7    78    24     0    56     0
13   142    60     0    24     0
0    15   247     0    16     0
0     7   239   241   208     0
0    15   159     4   112     0
0    60   112   255    48     0
0   255   240     1   240     0
1   240   112    12   120     0
1   128    48     6    56     0
3     0    56     3   124     0
3     0    24     1   198     0
118     0    12     0     3     0
60     0     6     0     1   128
0     0     3     0     0   192
0     0     1   192     0   112
0     0     0   224     0    56
0     0     0     0     0     0
0     0     0     0     0     0
0     0     0     0     0     0
0     0     0     0     0     0
```

Figure 5.14: Character definitions of the Galloping Horse.

[10]Our thanks to Eadweard Muybridge for taking the original photos, Leland Stanford for hiring him to do so, Charlie Kellner for first digitizing them on the Apple computer, and Tandy Trower for the ATARI conversion of the Galloping Horse character set.

Even though the same number of frames is used here as was used in our last program, these frames employ a larger character array, thus allowing us to create a figure of much greater detail. The drawback, however, is that we have a lot more bytes to enter into our data statements.

Example 3

Exercise   Using the Galloping Horse character sets, fill the screen with 36 horses, all galloping in unison. Use the technique of character set flipping, and add the sound of hoofbeats. Use paddle 0 to control the animation frame rate.

a)

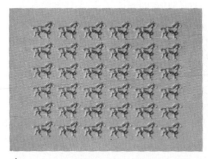

b)

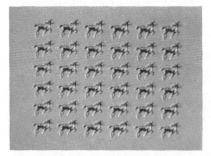

c)

(continued)

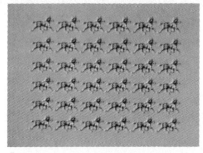

d)

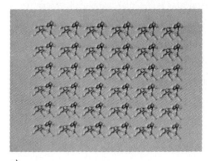

e)

Photo 5.5: Galloping Horses.

Here is the Galloping Horse program. The same four main sections are present in this program as in Example 2: initialize, set up alternate character set, character set data, and animation loop. In this program, however, each section is somewhat different.

```
10   REM        GALLOPING HORSE DEMO
20   REM              Example 3
30   REM
40   REM Example using the technique of flipping through multiple character sets
50   REM Copyright (C) 1982 by David Fox and Mitchell Waite
60   REM
100  REM Initialize
110  FRAMES=5: REM Number of frames
120  DIM HICHRB(FRAMES)
130  GRAPHICS 0
140  POKE 752,1: REM Turn off cursor
150  PRINT "One moment please...";
160  GOSUB 8000: REM Read in Character Set
170  PRINT "(CLEAR)"
180  SETCOLOR 1,0,2:
     SETCOLOR 2,1,10:
     SETCOLOR 4,1,10
190  POKE 756,HICHRB(1): REM Switch to Frame 1 Char Set
200  REM Fill Screen With Horses
210  FOR Y=0 TO 20 STEP 4
220     FOR X=2 TO 32 STEP 6
230        POSITION X,Y:
           PRINT "WWWabc"
240        POSITION X,Y+1:
           PRINT "defghi"
250        POSITION X,Y+2:
           PRINT "jklmno"
260        POSITION X,Y+3:
           PRINT "pqrstu";
270     NEXT X
280  NEXT Y
290  REM
```

Figure 5.15: Listing of Example 3 — lines 10-290.

Initialize   Rather than dimensioning a string to hold our frames (as we did in the last program), we will dimension an array called HICHRB (line 120) to hold the RAM page address of each of the five character sets. HICHRB(1) will hold the address for character set one (Frame 1), HICHRB(2) for character set two (Frame 2), and so on. This will make it very easy to select the appropriate frame.

The border around the active area of the screen[11] is set to the same color as the background in line 180. SETCOLOR 2,1,10 sets the background, and SETCOLOR 4,1,10 sets the border. SETCOLOR 1,0,2 sets the brightness of the horses (to dark).

On line 190, the first character set is switched on so when you PRINT the horses on the screen, you'll see horses and not letters of the alphabet.

Next, on lines 210–280, the screen is filled with horses using two nested FOR/NEXT loops. There will be six horses across and six down for a total of 36 horses — how about that! An instant racing stable!

```
8000  REM Set Up Alternate Character Set
8010  HICHRB=PEEK(106)-24: REM Reserve mem space (5 X 1024 bytes) below screen
8020  OFFSET=97*8:
      CHARS=21
8030  READ TOTAL:
      TEMP=0
8040  FOR J=1 TO FRAMES
8050    HICHRB(J)=HICHRB+4*(J-1): REM Find start of Character Sets
8060    REM Read in data, skip first 97 characters
8070    CHRBAS=HICHRB(J)*256
8080    FOR I=CHRBAS+OFFSET TO CHRBAS+OFFSET+CHARS*8-1
8090      READ BYTE:
        POKE I,BYTE:
        TEMP=TEMP+BYTE
8100    NEXT I
8110    REM Clear out first char (background)
8120    FOR I=CHRBAS TO CHRBAS+7
8130      POKE I,0
8140    NEXT I
8150    PRINT ".";
8160  NEXT J
8170  IF TOTAL<>TEMP THEN
        GRAPHICS 0:
        PRINT "ERROR In Character Set Data":
        END
8180  RETURN
8190  REM
```

Figure 5.16:   Listing of Example 3 — lines 8000–8190.

Set Up Alternate Character Set   This time enough room for *five* character sets plus the screen memory must be reserved. This comes to 24 pages: 4 pages for each of the five character sets (20 pages) plus 4 pages for screen memory. Line 8050 initializes the HICHRB array to point to each of the five character sets. Line 8150 prints out a period after each character set is read, so we have an indicator that the program is still running.

---

[11]This active area is called the Playfield — more on this later.

```
20000  REM Horse Character Set Data
20010  REM . Checksum
20020  DATA 46921
20030  REM
20040  REM Frame 1
20050  DATA 0,0,0,0,1,1,6,15,0,0,6,118,155,127,247,231,0,0,0,0,128,192,32,136
20060  DATA 0,0,0,3,14,29,5,0,0,0,3,252,188,14,11,11,0,0,255,31,0,24,31,157
20070  DATA 59,15,254,192,0,0,0,240,135,14,60,124,12,8,8,56,196,204,48,0,0,0,0,0
20080  DATA 0,0,0,0,0,0,0,0,15,5,126,127,97,99,103,99,207,223,243,224,192,192,128,128
20090  DATA 252,191,223,127,3,3,1,1,112,248,254,142,252,248,128,128,0,0,0,0,0,0,0,0
20100  DATA 1,1,0,0,0,0,0,0,193,128,0,0,0,0,0,0,192,224,112,24,28,0,0,0
20110  DATA 1,1,1,0,0,0,0,0,128,192,224,48,56,0,0,0,0,0,0,0,0,0,0,0
20120  REM
20130  REM Frame 2
20140  DATA 0,0,0,1,5,8,59,87,0,8,12,190,121,248,252,191,0,0,0,0,128,32,208
20150  DATA 0,0,3,7,15,29,0,0,0,7,252,208,151,31,31,15,0,255,32,32,108,255,255,255
20160  DATA 255,1,0,0,4,28,252,184,187,184,48,16,16,16,48,240,144,192,0,0,0,0,0,0
20170  DATA 0,0,0,0,0,0,0,15,15,62,60,56,236,204,198,255,143,0,0,0,0,0,0,0
20180  DATA 248,255,31,60,48,112,96,192,28,254,6,12,56,48,0,0,0,0,0,0,0,0,0,0
20190  DATA 0,0,0,0,0,0,0,0,220,216,192,96,112,0,0,0,1,1,0,0,0,0,0,0
20200  DATA 0,0,0,0,0,0,0,0,0,0,0,0,0,0,0,0,0,0,0,0,0,0,0,0
20210  REM
20220  REM Frame 3
20230  DATA 0,0,0,0,1,0,63,0,0,2,3,62,239,223,127,0,0,0,0,128,192,32,16
20240  DATA 0,0,3,15,63,10,0,0,0,3,252,200,12,31,31,0,0,255,24,48,124,56,255
20250  DATA 23,255,128,0,0,56,126,255,247,238,252,20,8,24,16,16,196,108,48,0,0,0,0,0
20260  DATA 0,0,0,0,1,3,6,31,31,61,121,243,195,1,0,191,224,224,192,128,0,128,96
20270  DATA 254,254,7,7,14,12,24,112,56,7,255,0,0,0,0,0,128,192,192,192,192,192,128
20280  DATA 12,24,24,56,24,0,0,0,0,0,0,0,0,0,51,62,0,0,0,0,0,0
20290  DATA 192,0,0,0,0,0,0,1,0,0,0,0,0,0,0,0,0,0,0,0,0,0,0
20300  REM
20310  REM Frame 4
20320  DATA 0,0,0,0,0,0,1,0,0,6,118,155,127,247,231,0,0,0,0,0,0,128,32
20330  DATA 0,0,0,3,7,10,0,0,0,0,3,255,204,141,15,14,0,0,252,127,16,239,63,111
20340  DATA 1,11,29,224,0,12,142,220,127,255,254,122,30,12,4,68,8,252,204,32,0,0,0
20350  DATA 0,0,0,0,0,1,3,13,15,15,63,248,224,128,0,159,127,248,56,24,24,56,28
20360  DATA 252,255,63,1,1,0,112,63,124,196,243,255,199,192,192,192,0,0,128,192,192,96,48
20370  DATA 118,60,0,0,0,0,0,0,0,0,0,0,0,0,0,6,1,0,0,0,0,0
20380  DATA 0,128,192,192,0,0,0,0,0,0,0,0,0,0,24,0,0,0,0,0,0,0
20390  REM
20400  REM Frame 5
20410  DATA 0,0,0,6,15,30,28,61,48,56,254,231,227,255,253,255,0,0,0,0,128,32,144,232
20420  DATA 0,1,3,7,13,0,0,0,3,255,232,78,142,15,7,15,255,124,80,24,60,247,239,159
20430  DATA 255,63,12,0,0,0,241,4,252,28,56,56,24,16,208,112,216,64,0,0,0,0,0,0
20440  DATA 0,0,1,1,3,3,118,60,60,255,240,128,0,0,0,0,112,240,112,48,56,24,12,6
20450  DATA 255,1,12,6,3,1,0,0,48,240,120,56,124,198,3,1,0,0,0,0,0,0,0,128
20460  DATA 0,0,0,0,0,0,0,0,0,0,0,0,0,0,3,1,0,0,0,0,0,0
20470  DATA 0,192,224,0,0,0,0,0,0,0,0,0,0,0,0,192,112,56,0,0,0,0,0
```

Figure 5.17: Listing of Example 3 — lines 20000–20470.

Horse Character Set Data   Starting with line 20050, each line contains three character definitions or 24 bytes.

```
300  REM Animation Loop
310  FOR I=1 TO FRAMES
320   POKE 756,HICHRB(I)
330   IF I<>3 THEN
        SOUND 0,0,8,10:
        SOUND 0,0,0,0: REM Hoof Beats
340    FOR W=1 TO PADDLE(0):
        NEXT W: REM Use 15 if you don't have paddles
350  NEXT I
360  GOTO 310
370  REM
```

Figure 5.18: Listing of Example 3 — lines 300–370.

Animation Loop   This section is extremely simple. A FOR/NEXT loop is used to flip through the five frames. On line 330 we turn on the sound effect for a hoof beat on every frame but the third one. Line 340 uses an ATARI game paddle to allow the interactive control of the frame rate of the galloping horses. If you don't have a paddle, replace the word PADDLE(Ø) with a numeric value — 15 seems about right.

When you run the program, you'll see all 36 horses galloping in perfect synchronization. If you turn your paddle to the fastest speed (or remove line 340), the horses will be moving so fast that their legs will begin to blur (they'd be a sure thing in the Kentucky Derby!). This means that if we used character set flipping in a game, there would be quite a bit of extra processor power to do other things.

5.4. EXPLODING WITH A THREE-COLOR CHARACTER SET

Up until now, it's only been possible to display animated figures on the screen in one color, even though the choice of color is ours. But not for long! The ATARI Home Computer has a graphics mode which allows the display of a custom character set in *three* colors! We will drop a whistling bomb from the top of the screen and then explode it in a burst of color and sound.

The Display List and Antic Mode 4

Most of today's computers can only operate in two or three different graphics modes. The Apple II, for example, has a text mode, a low-resolution graphics mode, and a high-resolution graphics mode. The ATARI Home Computer is much more flexible than this. In fact, there are *twelve*[12] different graphics modes which are supported by the ATARI 400 or 800's operating system[13] and *sixteen* modes supported by ATARI's XL Home Computers' operating systems.[14] These graphics modes can be easily set up from within BASIC using the GRAPHICS *N* command (where *N* can be a value from 0−11 on the ATARI 400 and 800, or 0−15 on the ATARI XL Home Computers). Some of them are text (or character) modes, and some are plotted point modes (also called bit mapped or map modes). Most of them can be split screen modes (plotted points on the top part of the screen and four lines of GRAPHICS 0 text on the bottom). The exceptions are GRAPHICS 0 (the whole screen is a text window) and modes 9, 10, and 11 (GTIA modes — see Chapter 6). The split screen modes can be changed into full screen modes (no text window) by adding 16 to the value of *N*:

---

[12]There are an additional five graphics modes available, including Antic 4, which are not supported by the ATARI 400 or 800 operating system.

[13]One more mode, Antic 3, isn't supported by the ATARI XL Home Computers' operating system. This mode displays 10 pixel high characters with descenders.

[14]The operating system is contained within the 10K ROM cartridge in your ATARI 800, or inside the computer if you have an ATARI 400 or XL Home Computer.

GRAPHICS 3   split screen mode 3
                  (four lines of mode 0 at bottom of screen)
GRAPHICS 3+16 full screen mode 3

Introducing ANTIC   For you ATARI 400 or 800 owners who are feeling jealous that you can't access the four additional modes the XL Home Computers can access, hold on. Your computer can display anything the XL Home Computer can, it just might be a little more awkward for you to achieve. And for you ATARI XL Home Computer owners who might be feeling a little smug, the following information will help you get the maximum graphics power from your computer.

One of the things which makes the ATARI Home Computers so versatile for creating animation is its custom chip set, the primary thing all ATARI Home Computers have in common. Rather than giving all of the work to the computer's microprocessor, Atari designed three LSI (large scale integration) chips to help share the load. One of the chips, called Antic, has the responsibility of interpreting the bytes in screen memory into a form which can then be displayed on your television screen (by another custom chip, CTIA or GTIA, depending on the age of your computer). Antic is actually another microprocessor. As with any microprocessor, it has a program (called the *display list*), data (screen memory), and output (the television picture). Among other things, the display list specifies the graphics mode or modes to be used on the screen. By altering the display list, you can *horizontally* divide the screen into *many* strips or ribbons of different graphics modes. This gives the programmer who is able to modify the display list a great deal of flexibility when designing the appearance of the computer's video output.

When using the GRAPHICS command in a BASIC program, the ATARI's operating system will automatically set aside the appropriate amount of screen memory for that mode. A low-resolution map mode will take up much less memory than a high-resolution map mode. The OS (operating system) will also create a display list that will tell Antic how to interpret the data (bytes) in screen memory. Should the bytes be interpreted as text characters or as plotted points? How large should each character or *pixel* (the smallest dot you can plot in the current graphics mode — see box) be displayed on the screen, and what color should it have?

Pixels, Dots, and Color Clocks

In many books about computer graphics, there is no distinction between the words pixels, points, and dots. Pixel is derived from the words *picture element*. It refers to the smallest dot you can access

(directly turn on or off) on the screen. Since the physical size of this dot is different for each ATARI graphics mode, this could be confusing. We are modifying the definition of a pixel to be "the smallest point you can plot *in the current graphics mode,"* and we are using the word "dot" to mean the smallest point the screen is capable of displaying (320 × 192 dots). This means that the only time a pixel and a dot will look the same is in GRAPHICS 8 when there are 320 × 192 pixels on the screen.

Any color of the rainbow can be created by combining varying amounts of the three primary colors of light, i.e., red, green and blue. If you look *very* closely at your color television screen, you will see vertical stripes of phosphors in these three colors, first red, then green, and finally blue. (It is hard to see all three phosphors unless you are looking at a white area on the screen.) The width of each group of red, green, and blue phosphors is equal to one *color clock.* A television term rather than a computer term, a color clock is a unit of measurement that is related to the maximum number of color changes possible on one line. There are 227.5 color clocks in each horizontal scan line, 160 of which are within the active area (for plotting or printing) of your screen (playfield). To have full control over the color of a pixel, the pixel must be large enough to have *one of each of the three colored phosphors in it,* which means it is at least one color clock wide. Therefore, in GRAPHICS 8, where each of the 320 pixels in a line is one half of a color clock wide, you can't independently control pixel color. You may have wanted the pixel to look white, but it might appear as blue (only the blue phosphor was turned on) or orange (both the red and green phosphors were partially turned on). This is called a color artifact and can be exaggerated by turning on every other pixel in a horizontal line. Your pixels will only look white if there are at least two of them horizontally adjacent to each other, turning on all three phosphors. This is also true for the pixels that make up each character in GRAPHICS 0 or for any other graphics mode with pixels that are one half of a color clock wide.

Examining the Screen   Look closely at your ATARI's video picture. You will notice that it is made up of many extremely fine horizontal lines. There are 192 of these horizontal scan lines in the active area of your screen (we'll wait if you care to count them). The active area is that portion of the screen on which you can place text or plot points. ATARI calls this area the *playfield.* The playfield is 160 *color clocks* wide (see box) and is made up of 320 dots. Surrounding the playfield is a border which can sometimes be independently colored, depending on the graphics mode in use.

In GRAPHICS 0, each byte is represented as a character which is eight dots wide (four color clocks) and eight scan lines high (remember our character definitions from the last section). This provides us with the previously mentioned 320 × 192 dots, since there can be 40 characters in a line (40 * 8 dots per character = 320 dots) and 24 lines of text to a

screen (24 * scan lines per character = 192 scan lines). In GRAPHICS 5, a low-resolution map mode, each pixel (plotted point) is a square which is four dots across (two color clocks) and four scan lines high. This means there are 80 pixels across a line (80 * 4 dots per pixel = 320 dots) and 48 pixels down (48 * 4 scan lines per pixel = 192 scan lines). Figure 5.19 compares the characters, pixels, and bytes in GRAPHICS Ø and GRAPHICS 5.

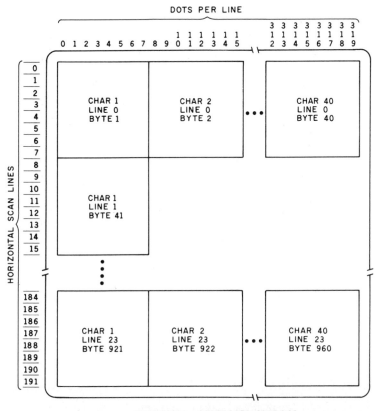

GRAPHICS 0 - CHARACTER GRAPHICS
2 COLORS (ONE HUE W/TWO INTENSITIES)
40 BY 24 CHARACTERS
8 SCAN LINES PER "MODE" LINE
40 BYTES PER LINE
960 BYTES TOTAL

a)

(continued)

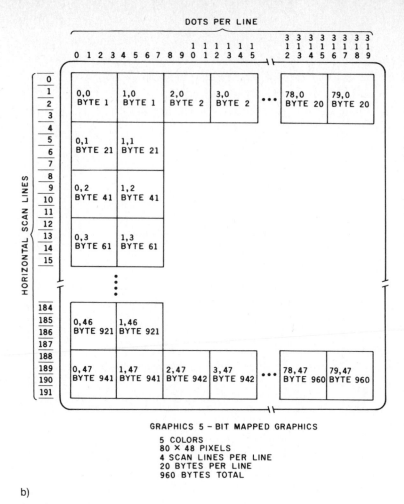

b)

Figure 5.19: a) GRAPHICS 0 and b) GRAPHICS 5 on the screen.

By modifying the display list, you can access some additional graphics modes which are not supported by the OS. The Exploding Bomb program is compatible with any ATARI Home Computer. (Later on we'll tell you about a short cut for the ATARI XL Home Computers.) This program uses something called Antic mode 4 (don't confuse Antic 4 with BASIC's GRAPHICS 4 — they are totally different). This means that we can't use a GRAPHICS statement to set it up on an ATARI 400 or 800; we must do so manually by altering the display list. Table 5.1 indicates all the Antic and OS graphics modes. The pixels/column and bytes/screen are calculated for the full screen modes (GRAPHICS N + 16). As you can see, the number of bytes needed for each mode depends on the resolution (number of pixels) and the available number of colors.

GRAPHIC MODES

Antic Mode	BASIC Mode	Char or Map	Number Colors	Pixels/ Line	Pixels/ Column	Color Clocks Char/ Pixel	Scan Lines Char/ Pixel	Bytes/ Line	Bytes/ Screen*
2	0	Char	2**	40	24	4	8	40	960
3	none	Char	2	40	19	4	10	40	760
4	12•	Char	4	40	24	4	8	40	960
5	13•	Char	4	40	12	4	16	40	480
6	1	Char	5	20	24	8	8	20	480
7	2	Char	5	20	12	8	16	20	240
8	3	Map	4	40	24	4	8	10	240
9	4	Map	2	80	48	2	4	10	480
A	5	Map	4	80	48	2	4	20	960
B	6	Map	2	160	96	1	2	20	1920
C	14•	Map	2	160	192	1	1	20	3840
D	7	Map	4	160	96	1	2	40	3840
E	15•	Map	4	160	192	1	1	40	7680
F	8	Map	2**	320	192	½	1	40	7680
F	9†	Map	16***	80	192	2	1	40	7680
F	10†	Map	9	80	192	2	1	40	7680
F	11†	Map	16‡	80	192	2	1	40	7680

*   Memory is also set aside for the display list in each mode. Most modes also have some unused memory reserved (see Appendix H, "Graphics Memory Map Modes").

**   One hue, two luminance values.

*** 16 luminance values, one hue.

‡   All 16 hues, one luminance value.

†   Note: OS Modes 9–11 are GTIA modes. Bits 6 and 7 of PRIOR (location 623) control which mode will be used. See Table 7.5.

•   Only supported by the ATARI XL Home Computers' operating systems.

Table 5.1:   Antic and operating system graphics modes.

Antic 4 uses the same amount of screen RAM as GRAPHICS 0. In fact, it is very similar to GRAPHICS 0 with one exception. Instead of each bit in the character definition representing a dot on the screen (either on or off), the bits in each row are *paired*. By considering this pair of bits as one pixel, the horizontal resolution is halved so that each character is now *four double-wide* dots across (instead of eight single-wide dots) and eight horizontal scan lines down (as before). But by losing some horizontal resolution, we gain color information! Because each of the character's pixels is now a full color clock wide, it can be displayed in any of three colors depending on its bit pattern. If the bit pattern is 01, you can control that pixel's color with SETCOLOR 0. If the pattern is 11, use SET- COLOR 2. Table 5.2 shows how this works.

SETCOLOR for Antic 4

Bit pair in character definition	Use following SETCOLOR value	Color register name
00	SETCOLOR 4	COLBAK
01	SETCOLOR 0	PF0
10	SETCOLOR 1	PF1
11	SETCOLOR 2	PF2
11 (inv. video)	SETCOLOR 3	PF3

Table 5.2: SETCOLOR table for Antic 4.

As the chart indicates, if the character is printed in inverse video (most significant bit is set in screen memory), only the bit pair "11" will be affected. Its color will now be controlled with a SETCOLOR 3. This can give us another color on the screen, but still only three colors within each character. So, let's create a character definition example for Antic 4, since we will soon use it in our falling bomb example.

	BIT PATTERN	BYTE VALUE	DISPLAYED	INVERSE
ROW 1	01010101	85		
ROW 2	01010101	85		
ROW 3	00000000	0		
ROW 4	10101010	170		
ROW 5	10101010	170		
ROW 6	00000000	0		
ROW 7	11111111	255		
ROW 8	11111111	255		

Figure 5.20: Character definition for striped character.

As you can see, we are filling each of the eight rows with one of the four possible bit patterns. By using the above byte values for our character definition, the above Antic 4 character would be displayed as three horizontal bands of color separated by two thin stripes of the background color.

Now let's set the color registers as follows to color the bands red, blue, and green with a black background:

```
SETCOLOR 4,0,0 : REM Black
SETCOLOR 0,3,6 : REM Red
SETCOLOR 1,7,6 : REM Blue
SETCOLOR 2,12,6 : REM Green
SETCOLOR 3,5,6 : REM Purple
```

We will be covering the SETCOLOR command in greater detail in the next chapter. For now, recall that the syntax of the command is

SETCOLOR *n,hue,lum*

If we printed this character in inverse video, only the bottom band of color will change. It would become purple because its color is now controlled by SETCOLOR 3 instead of SETCOLOR 2 (see Table 5.2).

Explosions and an Antic 4 Character Set

Have you played any games at a video arcade recently? You are flying your spaceship around the universe and suddenly an attacking alien creeps up from behind. Lasers fire and KABRASHH!! Your spaceship vanishes in a brilliant explosion . . . and you lose another quarter. How was that explosion created on the screen? Two basic techniques are used. One shows the exploding object bursting into a mass of dots or debris that rapidly moves outwards towards the corners of the screen. This technique requires a fast machine language algorithm which can directly control each piece of debris. In the other technique, a colorful fireball replaces the destroyed object. Often, you will see flames flick out in different directions as three or four versions of the fireball are rapidly displayed where your spaceship once was. This technique can be easily duplicated using Antic 4 character set animation.

Since you already understand how characters in Antic 4 are displayed, let's look at the character set for our Exploding Bomb program. The actual explosion is created with four frames, each made of a box of four characters arranged in a 2 × 2 array. Each frame shows the explosion getting a little larger and in a different shape. By consecutively executing PRINT for each frame at the same screen position, we will see what looks like an expanding explosion. We also need to define a single character for our falling bomb, as shown in Figure 5.21.

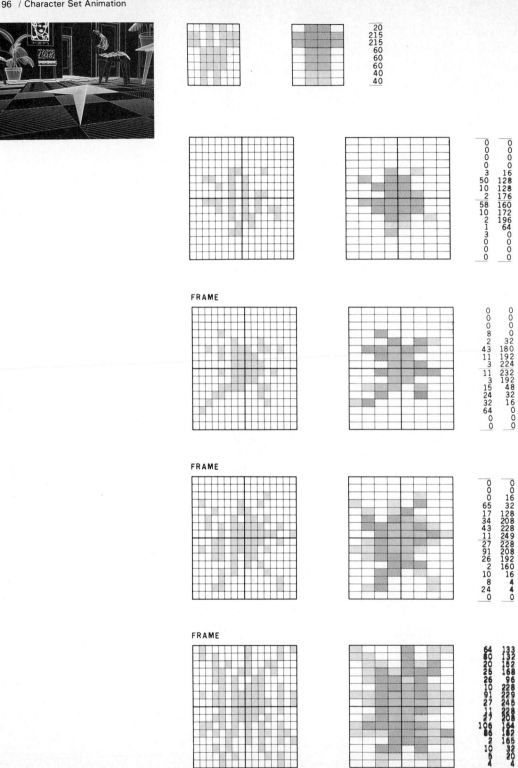

Figure 5.21: Character definitions for Exploding Bomb program.

In the above figure, the bit pattern of each character is shown on the left; in the center are the actual characters as they will appear on the screen; on the right are the decimal values needed to define each character. Notice that the pixels that make up each character are now rectangular instead of square. This decreased resolution makes it a little more difficult to represent a detailed figure.

Example 4

Exercise   Randomly drop a whistling bomb from the top of the screen. When it falls to the bottom half of the screen, make it explode in a burst of color and sound. Modify the display list to Antic 4 so that you can use a three-color character set.

a)

b)

c)

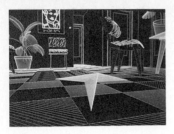

d)

Photo 5.6: Screen photos of Exploding Bomb program.

Here is the Exploding Bomb program. Before you begin entering it, you'll notice that one section is almost identical to a section in the Walking Man program. To save time, instead of typing this section (lines 8000–8160, Set up alternate character set) from scratch, you can copy it over from the other program.

```
10  REM *** EXPLODING BOMB PROGRAM ***
20  REM                 Example 4
30  REM Program to demonstrate the three color text mode – ANTIC 4
40  REM Copyright (C) 1982 by David Fox and Mitchell Waite
50  GOTO 110
60  REM Hi-speed Subroutines
70  SOUND 0,RND(0)*150+30,0,VOL:
    SOUND 1,RND(0)*80+175,2,VOL:
    SOUND 2,RND(0)*150+30,8,VOL:
    RETURN : REM Sound
80  FOR I=1 TO 10:
      POKE 712,RND(0)*255:
    NEXT I:
    POKE 712,0:
    RETURN : REM Flash
90  SETCOLOR 0,4,LUM(0):
    SETCOLOR 1,2,LUM(1):
    SETCOLOR 2,1,LUM(2):
    RETURN : REM Color
```

Figure 5.22: Listing of Example 4—lines 10–90.

Hi-Speed Subroutines   You'll notice that there are three subroutines at the very beginning of the program. These are specifically placed here for a reason. In ATARI BASIC, the closer a section of code is to the *beginning* of the program, the faster its execution speed will be. (This has to do with the time it takes ATARI BASIC to search through *all* the line numbers of a program to find the next one it is supposed to execute. The closer the line is to the beginning of a program, the faster it finds it.) One of the subroutines controls the explosion sound effects, another creates a background flash, and the third sets the colors. All these subroutines need to be executed as rapidly as possible, so we placed them at the beginning. In fact, you'll notice that we place most of the initialization subroutines and data towards the end of the program, and the time-critical animation loops towards the beginning.

Line 70 will turn on three of the sound registers (voices) with random explosion-like sounds. Each voice has a different frequency range/distortion combination. Once the registers are on, this line is executed again to randomly change the sound quality of the explosion.

Line 80 rapidly flashes the screen background ten times with random colors. Memory location 712 is where the background color information is stored for this graphics mode. Using SETCOLOR 4 would achieve the same result, but a direct POKE to this location is quite a bit faster. This is because BASIC doesn't have to take the time to calculate the color value by combining the SETCOLOR hue and lum values together (color value = hue * 16 + lum). The flash is used at the first instant of the explosion.

Line 90 sets the colors of the explosion and is also used to fade out the brightness of the explosion.

```
100  REM Initialize
110  FRAMES=4:  REM Number of Frames
120  FRMSZE=7:  REM Characters in frame (including cursor control chars)
130  DIM EXPL$(FRAMES*FRMSZE),FRAME$(FRMSZE),LUM(2)
140  EXPL$="ab(DOWN)(2 LEFT)cdef(DOWN)(2 LEFT)ghij(DOWN)(2 LEFT)klmn(DOWN)(2 LEFT)op"
160  GRAPHICS 0
170  POKE 752,1:  REM Turn off cursor
180  PRINT "One moment please..."
200  GOSUB 8000:  REM Read in Character Set
210  PRINT "(CLEAR)"
220  GOSUB 6000:  REM Alter Display List
230  POKE 756,HICHRB:  REM Switch to new Char Set
240  REM
```

Figure 5.23: Listing of Example 4—lines 100–240.

Initialization   The only thing new here is the call to the display list modification subroutine in line 220. We'll explain this subroutine in just a second.

```
8000  REM Set Up Alternate Character Set
8010  HICHRB=PEEK(106)-8:  REM Reserve memory space (1024 bytes) below screen
8020  CHRBAS=HICHRB*256:  REM Find start of Character Set
8030  REM Read in data, skip first 97 characters
8040  OFFSET=97*8:
      CHARS=17
8060  READ TOTAL:
      TEMP=0
8070  FOR I=CHRBAS+OFFSET TO CHRBAS+OFFSET+CHARS*8-1
8080      READ BYTE:
          POKE I,BYTE:
          TEMP=TEMP+BYTE
8090  NEXT I
8100  IF TOTAL<>TEMP THEN
          GRAPHICS 0:
          PRINT "ERROR In Character Set Data":
          END
8110  REM Clear out first char (background)
8120  FOR I=CHRBAS TO CHRBAS+7
8130      POKE I,0
8140  NEXT I
8150  RETURN
8160  REM
20000 REM Character Set Data
20010 REM . Checksum
20020 DATA 8264
20030 REM
20040 REM . Frame 1
20050 DATA 0,0,0,0,3,50,10,2
20060 DATA 0,0,0,0,16,128,128,176
20070 DATA 58,10,2,1,3,0,0,0
```

```
20080   DATA 160,172,196,64,0,0,0,0
20090   REM
20100   REM . Frame 2
20110   DATA 0,0,0,8,2,43,11,3
20120   DATA 0,0,0,0,32,180,192,224
20130   DATA 11,3,15,24,32,64,0,0
20140   DATA 232,192,48,32,16,0,0,0
20150   REM
20160   REM . Frame 3
20170   DATA 0,0,0,65,17,34,43,11
20180   DATA 0,0,16,32,128,208,228,249
20190   DATA 27,91,26,2,10,8,24,0
20200   DATA 228,208,192,160,16,4,4,0
20210   REM
20220   REM . Frame 4
20230   DATA 64,80,20,25,26,10,91,27
20240   DATA 133,132,152,168,96,228,229,245
20250   DATA 11,27,106,86,2,10,5,4
20260   DATA 228,208,164,182,165,32,20,4
20270   REM
20280   REM . Bomb
20290   DATA 20,215,215,60,60,60,40,40
```

Figure 5.24: Listing of Example 4—lines 8000–20290.

Set Up Alternate Character Set and Character Set Data

The lines in the first section (8000–8150) are identical to those in the Walking Man program. The only thing you need to change is the value assigned to CHARS in 8040. The character set data (20000–20290) contains the character definitions for the four frames of the explosion and the bomb character.

```
6000   REM Modify Display List
6010   DLIST=PEEK(560)+PEEK(561)*256: REM Find Display List
6020   POKE DLIST+3,68: REM LMS byte plus 4 (line 1)
6030   FOR I=6 TO 28:
          POKE DLIST+I,4:
       NEXT I: REM Lines 2 through 24
6040   RETURN
6050   REM
```

Figure 5.25: Listing of Example 4—lines 6000–6050.

Modify Display List   This is the section where we modify the display list to Antic 4. Since GRAPHICS Ø is so close to Antic 4, we need to change only the values in the already existing DL (display list). In line 6010 we find where in memory the DL is. In line 6020, we change the DL instruction that controls the first text line. Don't worry about this now; we will cover LMS (load memory scan) and display lists in greater depth in Chapter 9.

In line 6030, we change the DL instruction for text lines 2 through 24 when we POKE in a 4 (and that's why it's called Antic 4). When this subroutine is executed, you will see what looks like a black curtain rapidly descending over your screen as each byte of the DL is modified.

If you have an ATARI XL Home Computer, you can modify this program to let your OS set up the new display list with a GRAPHICS 12 + 16. Because cursor control won't work in this mode, you will have to PRINT each line of the frames separately on the screen with the PRINT #6 command.

```
600 REM Falling Bomb
610 SETCOLOR 0,3,8:
    SETCOLOR 1,7,6:
    SETCOLOR 2,5,6
620 X=INT(RND(0)*36+2):
    Y=INT(RND(0)*10+12): REM Select random explosion point
630 FOR I=0 TO Y-1
640     SOUND 0,I*2+16,10,8
650     POSITION X,I:
      PRINT "K(DOWN)(LEFT)q";
660     SOUND 0,I*2+17,10,8
670 NEXT I
680 PRINT "(CLEAR)":
    SOUND 0,0,0,0
690 RETURN
700 REM
```

Figure 5.26: Listing of Example 4—lines 600–700.

Film 3
"The Juggler," Information
International, Inc. Here are three
segments from "The Juggler" film
which we describe in Chapters 1 and 3
(see Photo 1.1 on page 3). *(Courtesy of
Information International Inc.)*

Falling Bomb   This subroutine displays the falling bomb. The
spot on the screen where the bomb will explode is randomly selected (line
620). The vertical coordinate (Y) will always be in the lower half of the
screen (because of the +12). A FOR/NEXT loop (lines 630–670) is
used to move the bomb down the screen. We are drawing the bomb in its
new position and erasing the old bomb with the same PRINT statement.
As it falls, sound register 0 is used to create a whistling sound. The
whistling sound was split onto two lines, 640 and 660, to create a more
even whistle. It smoothly drops two frequency steps for every position of
the bomb. One of the SOUND statements could have been omitted, but
the change in frequency would have been more choppy.

When the bomb reaches its explosion point, line 680, the screen is
cleared and the sound turned off in preparation for the explosion routine
in the animation loop.

```
300 REM Animation Loop
310 LUM(0)=6:
    LUM(1)=8:
    LUM(2)=12:
    VOL=14
320 GOSUB 600: REM Falling Bomb
330 GOSUB 90: REM Set colors
340 GOSUB 70: REM Turn on sound
350 GOSUB 80: REM Flash background
360 FOR I=1 TO FRAMES
370     FRAME$=EXPL$(I*FRMSZE-(FRMSZE-1),I*FRMSZE)
380     POSITION X,Y:
      PRINT FRAME$;
390     GOSUB 70: REM Change sound
400 NEXT I
410 FOR J=0 TO 2: REM Fade out explosion
420     LUM(J)=LUM(J)-2
430     IF LUM(J)<0 THEN
        LUM(J)=0
440 NEXT J
450 GOSUB 90
460 VOL=VOL-1:
    GOSUB 70: REM Fade sound
470 IF LUM(2)>0 THEN 410
480 PRINT "(CLEAR)"
490 IF VOL>0 THEN
        VOL=VOL-1:
        GOSUB 70:
        GOTO 490: REM Fade sound off
500 FOR W=1 TO INT(RND(0)*400+50):
    NEXT W: REM Random pause
510 GOTO 310
520 REM
```

Figure 5.27: Listing of Example 4—lines 300–520.

Animation Loop   This is where the entire explosion is orchestrated. After setting the LUMinance (brightness of the color, used in the subroutine at line 90) and VOLume levels (used in the subroutine at line 70) to their initial values (310), the bomb is dropped (320). The color registers are reset, the explosion sound turned on, and the background flashed. In a real life explosion, you would see the flash before you heard the sound, but when we tried it that way the effect didn't seem quite right. The viewer expects to hear noise as soon as something hits so we took the liberty of changing the laws of physics.

The frame loop, lines 360–400, is identical to those in our earlier programs. We didn't need to erase the explosion after each frame, just write over it. Instead of a pause loop, the sound of the explosion is changed to add the effect of randomness to our pre-dawn graphics.

In lines 410 to 490, the LUMinance values of the last explosion frame as well as the VOLume level of the sound registers fade out. This technique of altering the SETCOLOR values gives the illusion of motion when none is taking place (more on this in the next chapter).

Finally, on line 500 we wait for a random period of time before we drop the next bomb.

Modifications   Here are some modifications to try:

1. Switch the order of the initial sound and flash of light so that the flash comes first. Which do you like better?
2. Use a different set of colors in the explosion. Maybe you can come up with a better or more exciting combination.
3. Run this program with the sound on your television turned off. Notice how much the sound adds to the effect.
4. Try to improve the explosion character set to create a more realistic effect.
5. Program multiple explosions on the screen. What sets the limit to the maximum number?

Commercially Available Software Using Character Sets

The character-set flipping technique is used in a popular ATARI Home Computer game from Automated Simulations, Inc., entitled "Crush, Crumble, and Chomp!" In this game, you control your favorite movie monster on a rampage. The screen can display running people, police cars with flashing lights, helicopters with moving blades, flickering flames, and smoldering ruins all at the same time. The animation uses only two frames and is created by flipping between two character sets. Although the effect is very impressive (especially the flames and ruins), as we have seen, the technique is very simple. Most of the program is written in BASIC, with a number of machine language subroutines to help out (see Chapter 8). To simplify the BASIC portion of the program,

the task of alternating between the character sets is automatically carried out with a Vertical Blank Interrupt routine. (This technique is covered in depth in Chapter 8.) For now, think of it as giving the computer a separate task to do *while* BASIC is running the main part of the program.

Photo 5.7a) and b) is from the game's introduction and shows the two frames which appear on the screen. The two parts [c) and d)] show two consecutive frames from the middle of the game. Notice the position of the flames and the people's legs. The monster (we chose to be ''Mantra'' in this game) is made of two adjacent *Players*. (Players, objects which can be moved anywhere on the screen without changing the background, are covered in Chapter 7.) Even though GRAPHICS Ø is being used, you'll notice some extra colors on the screen (the green of the trees and light blue on the buildings; see color insert). These extra colors are obtained by turning on every other bit in those characters, resulting in color artifacts (see box on artifacts in next section).

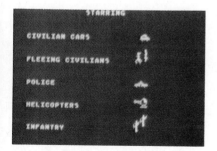

a)

b)

(continued)

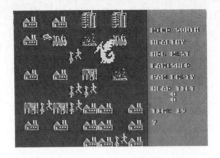

c)

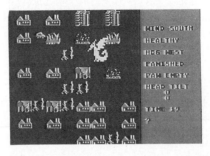

d)

Photo 5.7: Four screen frames from "Crush, Crumble, and Chomp!" (Copyright (c) 1981, Automated Simulations, Inc.)

The ATARI Home Computer version of Space Invaders™ (trademark of Taito America Corp.) is another program which makes use of character set animation. This program, however, uses a different technique than the two we've previously introduced. Each of the invading alien types (there are six) is made of two adjacent characters in graphics mode 1. Rather than flipping through entire character sets, it uses machine language to rapidly change the character definitions of each invader. Since each row is made up of the same type of alien, the entire row is animated at once. This doesn't exhaust much processing power since there are only four different frames for each of the six alien types. Three Players were used in this game, one for the large green spaceship on the left of the screen, one for the gun base at the bottom of the screen, and one for the occasional flying saucer which appears at the top of the screen (not pictured). The projectiles being fired by the invaders and the game player are Missiles. Display list interrupts (Chapter 9) were used to add extra colors for the invaders.

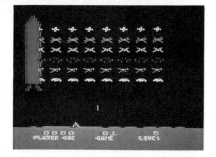

a)

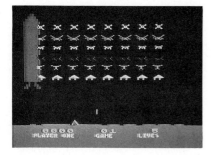

b)

Photo 5.8: Screen photos of Space Invaders™. (Trademark of Taito America Corp.)

Summary

You have learned a powerful and flexible animation technique which can be implemented without any use of machine language. Although defining a new character set can be time consuming, the advantages are well worth the effort in many cases. Using character set animation in GRAPHICS 0 (or the XL Computers' GRAPHICS 12) can provide the same resolution as the ATARI's highest resolution mode (GRAPHICS 8), but with only one-eighth of the memory overhead. By using Antic 4, more colors can be placed on the screen at twice the resolution (and one-fourth the memory overhead) as with GRAPHICS 7. As we will see later, this saving of memory also speeds up the processing speed of the computer for faster animation programs.

Making animated figures roam the screen is exciting, but our programs have been somewhat one dimensional — each character we have animated so far exists in a void, without any background or foreground! In the next chapter, we will explore the advanced graphics feature of color registers and create some beautiful animated backgrounds!

Chapter 6

Color Register Animation

O n most personal computers, after you've selected a color from a limited number of choices, that color is placed on the screen with PLOT or DRAW statements. The only way to change it is to PLOT again in a new color, and this is very time consuming. In addition, your program must "remember" the screen coordinates of each pixel whose color is to be changed. The ATARI Home Computer, as well as many of the high-tech animation computers, has a feature called the *color register*, which we first introduced in Chapter 2 when we talked about our "Magic Paint Store." In this chapter we will see how ATARI's powerful method of drawing graphics using color registers can be put to work in colorful, action-packed animated scenes. Color register animation will be used to draw a beautiful, ever-changing kaleidoscope of colors, create the illusion that you are rapidly flying through a trench (à la *Star Wars*), and display the motion of water in a cascading waterfall.

6.1.　WHY COLOR REGISTERS?

Color registers were first created to provide the users of professional computer paint systems with a relatively inexpensive way to use a polychromatic (many-colored) palette. Suppose the computer artist wanted sixteen million colors (give or take a few) from which to choose. The expensive technique would be to make each pixel capable of displaying *any* of these colors so that all sixteen million could appear on the screen *at once*. Each pixel must then contain 24 bits of information to directly represent any of the sixteen million colors. If the display contained 1024×1024 pixels, it would represent over three million bytes of screen RAM. That's why it costs so much.

The less costly method allows the artist to create a palette from a *subset* of the sixteen million colors, for example, 256 different colors. Instead of storing information at each pixel which *describes* the color, an 8-bit value is stored which points to a palette (or table or colors) entry, eliminating 16 bits per pixel. The table would contain the 256 different 24-bit descriptions of the sixteen million colors (see Figure 6.1). If the

EXPENSIVE METHOD –
ANY ONE OF 16,777,216
COLORS ON THE SCREEN

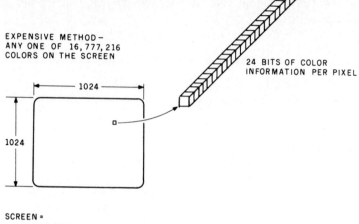

24 BITS OF COLOR
INFORMATION PER PIXEL

1024

1024

SCREEN =
 1,048,576 PIXELS × 24 BITS
 = 3,145,728 BYTES

8 BITS OF
COLOR TABLE INFORMATION
PER PIXEL
 = 43

LESS EXPENSIVE METHOD –
USES A 256 – COLOR PALETTE.
EACH PALETTE COLOR CAN BE
ANY ONE OF 16,777,216 COLORS

1024

1024

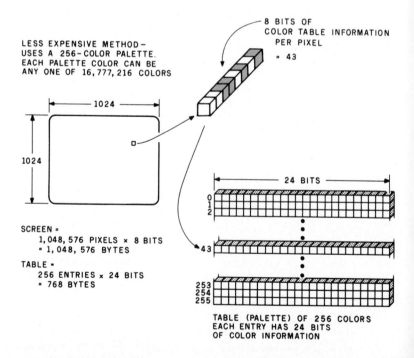

SCREEN =
 1,048,576 PIXELS × 8 BITS
 = 1,048,576 BYTES
TABLE =
 256 ENTRIES × 24 BITS
 = 768 BYTES

24 BITS

TABLE (PALETTE) OF 256 COLORS
EACH ENTRY HAS 24 BITS
OF COLOR INFORMATION

Figure 6.1: Palette of colors.

value in a pixel was 43, then the computer would look into the forty-third entry of the table. The color value that is contained in this table position is then displayed at that pixel. Screen RAM would only take about one million bytes, and a negligible 768 bytes would be used for the table. This represents a computer hardware investment of about one-third of the price of the previous method! Of course, this way the artist could only display 256 unique colors on the screen at the same time, but this is really not as limiting as it sounds. The artist who plans a picture carefully can create striking scenes with much *fewer* than 256 different colors.

This second technique of displaying color is called *color mapping*, and the table of colors is called the *color map*. When color maps became popular, many advantages other than the lower cost were discovered. An artist could alter colors without having to redraw an entire picture. In the field of computer animation, wonderfully animated scenes could be created without plotting a single pixel simply by moving the colors around the color map! In medical applications, in the analysis of a computer image of an X-ray, formerly unnoticed details could be brought out by assigning contrasting colors to areas which had been depicted with only slight shading differences.

Color Maps and the ATARI Home Computer

The ATARI Home Computer is one of the few personal computers that uses this technique to display its colors on the screen. However, there are only 128 possible colors to choose from instead of sixteen million (hope you didn't get your hopes up!) and only nine entries in the color map, rather than 256. These nine entries are called *color registers*. Most ATARI graphics modes don't use all nine color registers. In fact, many use only four or less. Table 6.1 shows most of the different ATARI graphics modes and the color registers which are active for each.

Modes	Default Colors	SETCOLOR	POKE	COLOR	Description
GRAPHICS 0		—	—	(Not	
(text mode and	Lt Blue	1	709	normally	Char. Lum.
all text windows,				used)	(uses bkg color)
1 hue,	Blue	2	710		Background
2 luminances)		—	—		
	Black	4	712		Border
GRAPHICS 12†,					
(Antic 4)*	Orange	0	708	(Not	Character Pixel
GRAPHICS 13†					
(Antic 5)	Lt Green	1	709	normally	Character Pixel
(special text	Blue	2	710	used)	Character Pixel
modes, 5 colors)	Red	3	711		Character Pixel
	Black	4	712		Background, Border

(continued)

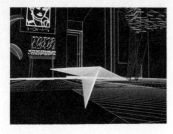

Modes	Default Colors	SETCOLOR	POKE	COLOR	Description
GRAPHICS 1 and GRAPHICS 2 (large text modes, 5 colors)	Orange	0	708	(Not normally used)	Character
	Lt Green	1	709		Character
	Blue	2	710		Character
	Red	3	711		Character
	Black	4	712		Background, Border
GRAPHICS 3, GRAPHICS 5, GRAPHICS 7 and GRAPHICS 15† (Antic E) (4 colors)	Orange	0	708	1	Pixel
	Lt Green	1	709	2	Pixel
	Blue	2	710	3	Pixel
	—	—	—	—	
	Black	4	712	0	Pixel/Background, Border
GRAPHICS 4, GRAPHICS 6 and GRAPHICS 14† (Antic C) (2 colors)	Orange	0	708	1	Pixel
	—	—	—	—	
	—	—	—	—	
	—	—	—	—	
	Black	4	712	0	Pixel/Background, Border
GRAPHICS 8 (1 hue, 2 luminances)	—	—	—	—	
	Lt Blue	1	709	1	Pixel Lum. (uses bkg color)
	Blue	2	710	0	Pixel/Background
	—	—	—	—	
	Black	4	712	—	Border
GRAPHICS 9 (GTIA mode, 1 hue, 16 luminances)	Black	4	712	0	Pixel/Background, Border
	↓	—	—	1	Pixel
		—	—	2	Pixel
		—	—	3	Pixel
	Dk Gray	—	—	4	Pixel
		—	—	5	Pixel
	↓	—	—	6	Pixel
Change hue with SETCOLOR 4,n,0 or POKE 712,n		—	—	7	Pixel
	Gray	—	—	8	Pixel
		—	—	9	Pixel
	↓	—	—	10	Pixel
		—	—	11	Pixel
	Lt Gray	—	—	12	Pixel
	↓	—	—	13	Pixel
		—	—	14	Pixel
	White	—	—	15	Pixel
GRAPHICS 10 (GTIA mode, 9 colors)	Black	—	704	0	Pixel/Background, Border
	Black	—	705	1	Pixel
	Black	—	706	2	Pixel
	Black	—	707	3	Pixel
	Orange	0	708	4	Pixel
	Lt Green	1	709	5	Pixel
	Blue	2	710	6	Pixel
	Red	3	711	7	Pixel
	Black	4	712	8	Pixel

(continued)

Modes	Default Colors	SETCOLOR	POKE	COLOR	Description
GRAPHICS 11 (GTIA mode, 1 luminance, 16 hues)	Black	4	712	0	Pixel/Background, Border
	Lt Orange	—	—	1	Pixel
	Orange	—	—	2	Pixel
	Red-orange	—	—	3	Pixel
	Pink	—	—	4	Pixel
	Purple	—	—	5	Pixel
	Purple-blue	—	—	6	Pixel
Change luminance with SETCOLOR 4,0,n or POKE 712,n	Azure Blue	—	—	7	Pixel
	Sky Blue	—	—	8	Pixel
	Light Blue	—	—	9	Pixel
	Turquoise	—	—	10	Pixel
	Green-blue	—	—	11	Pixel
	Green	—	—	12	Pixel
	Yellow-grn	—	—	13	Pixel
	Orange-grn	—	—	14	Pixel
	Lt Orange	—	—	15	Pixel

†These GRAPHICS commands are only supported by the newer ATARI XL Home Computers.
*See Example 4 in Chapter 5 for more on Antic 4.

Table 6.1: ATARI Color Registers for graphics modes.

The Modes column lists the different ATARI graphics modes and the number of colors they support. The Default Colors are the colors set by the OS when the computer is first turned on or reset. The SETCOLOR column gives the active SETCOLOR commands (used to change the color value in the color registers) for that mode. The POKE column lists the corresponding RAM addresses of the color registers for each mode. When you POKE numbers into these addresses, you can bypass the SETCOLOR command for faster color changing. (This is the only way to change some of the registers in mode 10.) The numbers in the COLOR column are the values of the COLOR command that will choose the current color register with which to draw.

The Description column lists which of the three screen elements each color register controls. First there is the screen background. When the screen is cleared, you are looking at background. It is the ''canvas'' upon which pixels are plotted and text is printed. Next is the border around the background. Although this area sometimes has its own color register, depending on the graphics mode it is really the frame surrounding the canvas and cannot be drawn on. Finally, there are the playfield pixels (any pixel that is plotted with a non-background color register). Each group of plotted pixels using a specific color register is considered to be a *separate* playfield. For example, look in the table for the section on GRAPHICS 3. Registers 0, 1, and 2 (in the SETCOLOR column) each control the color of playfields 0, 1, and 2 respectively. Register 4

controls the background of the screen and the border. Therefore, in this mode, the background's color cannot be controlled separately from the border's color. Notice that register 4 also controls a pixel; however, this is not a playfield pixel. Think of plotting with a background color register as *removing* the playfield pixels so the background color shows through again.

Using the Default Colors   At first glance, this table may seem somewhat overwhelming, so let's look at a few examples. Suppose you want to use GRAPHICS 3. Drawings done in this mode have a very coarse resolution of 40 × 24 pixels. Do you remember the buckets of paint in our Magic Paint Store? The store owner (ATARI operating system) was kind enough to fill some of these buckets when he first opened up the store. These are called the default colors and can be selected for drawing with the COLOR command. If you wanted to use only these default colors, then you can ignore the SETCOLOR and POKE columns, because these colors are automatically placed in the color registers when the computer is first turned on or **SYSTEM RESET** is pressed. To use the table, first choose a color from the default color column — light green, for example. Look across to the COLOR column, and you'll find a 2. Therefore, the command COLOR 2 selects the bucket filled with light green paint.

To place a light green pixel at 10,8, you would execute the following statements:

```
 10 GRAPHICS 3+16  : REM Full screen mode
 20 COLOR 2        : REM Choose your bucket
 30 PLOT 10,8
200 GOTO 200       : REM Stay in GRAPHICS 3
```

In line 10, the full screen version of GRAPHICS 3 is used (16 is added to the mode number). This means that there will be no text window at the bottom of the screen. Try temporarily removing line 200 and see what happens when you run this program. The screen flashes to black, the pixel is plotted, and before you get to look at it, the blue GRAPHICS 0 screen has reappeared. At the end of a program which uses a full screen graphics mode, the OS will automatically switch back to GRAPHICS 0. Line 200 is added to prevent this from happening until you press the **BREAK** button and exit the program.

To draw an orange line across the screen from this light green dot, add the following lines:

```
40 COLOR 1     : REM Choose another bucket
50 DRAWTO 29,8
```

Now use one more color register available in this mode. This one is filled with blue:

```
60 COLOR 3        : REM One more bucket
70 PLOT 30,8
```

To erase a pixel, choose the background color (which always happens to be COLOR 0):

```
80 COLOR 0        : REM Select background
90 PLOT 20,8
```

This screen will now appear as in Photo 6.1.

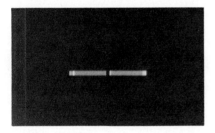

Photo 6.1: Default colors of GRAPHICS 3 (see color insert).

Using SETCOLOR

Now that we understand the use of the default colors, let's see what else is available to us. As we've mentioned before, the ATARI Home Computer has 16 different hues from which to choose, and each one can be displayed in any of eight levels of brightness or luminance. As we mentioned earlier, the BASIC command to *change* a color in a color register is

SETCOLOR *n,hue,lum*

where *n* is the value from the SETCOLOR column in Table 6.1, *hue* is a number from 0 to 15 that controls the hue, and *lum* is an even number from 0 to 14 (0,2,4…14) that controls the luminance of the color (the odd lum values have the same effect as the next lowest even value, e.g., lum = 1 and lum = 0 have the same effect). Table 6.2 shows the different hues available on the ATARI Home Computer.

	SETCOLOR
Hue	Hue Value
Gray	0
Light Orange (gold or yellow)	1
Orange	2
Red-orange	3
Pink (magenta)	4
Purple	5
Purple-blue	6
Azure Blue (cyan)	7
Sky Blue	8
Light Blue	9
Turquoise	10
Green-blue	11
Green	12
Yellow-green	13
Orange-green	14
Light Orange	15

Table 6.2: ATARI hues and SETCOLOR values.

Let's look at a few examples to see how the luminance value combines with the hue to instantly produce a new color. Try the following SETCOLOR commands while in GRAPHICS Ø to change the color of the border (just type them in direct mode):

Command	Hue	Luminance	Color Result
SETCOLOR 4,Ø,14	Gray	14	White
SETCOLOR 4,Ø,Ø	Gray	0	Black
SETCOLOR 4,1,4	Light Orange	4	Brown
SETCOLOR 4,1,12	Light Orange	12	Bright Yellow
SETCOLOR 4,3,4	Red-orange	4	Deep Red
SETCOLOR 4,3,12	Red-orange	12	Flesh

With a little experimentation, you'll be able to produce almost any color you wish.

Adjusting Your Color Television

Now would be a good time to make sure the color on your television is set correctly. This is a two-step process which may require you to adjust a hidden control on your computer. First, while in GRAPHICS 0, enter the following statement:

SETCOLOR 1,0,0

This will change the luminance values of the lettering so it will show up during the next steps. Now enter:

SETCOLOR 2,1,10

ATARI calls this color light orange, but at this luminance level it is actually a bright yellow. If the color is too green or too orange, then adjust the tint control on your television set until it looks yellow to you. Mark the position of your tint control so you can easily find it again if anyone adjusts your television.

Next, enter the following statement:

SETCOLOR 2,14,6

This is a strange color called orange-green (a khaki-gold color). After you execute this command, your screen will be filled with this delightful color. If this color doesn't fall exactly halfway between orange and green, you must make an adjustment on your ATARI Home Computer (trying to fix it with the tint control will just throw off the first color you adjusted). There is a small hole at the back of your computer through which you can insert a tiny screwdriver (see Photo 6.2). Inside this hole is the color adjustment control. Insert your screwdriver and turn it very slightly in both directions. You'll find that a very slight adjustment will produce a significant change on the screen. Swing back and forth from orange to green until you find that elusive point which yields a perfect orange-green.

When you have finished, all the other colors will be correctly adjusted as well. To make sure, change the screen to yellow (SETCOLOR 2,1,10) again. It should still be adjusted properly. If not, then go back to step one and try again. (We noticed that the ATARI color adjustment has no effect on this yellow.)

Photo 6.2: Adjusting the color on an ATARI Home Computer.

Now let's have a little fun! Add the following lines to the last program you entered:

```
 80  COLOR 1              :REM Choose bucket 1
                                again
 90  PLOT 20,5:
     PLOT 20,6
100  PLOT 19,7:
     DRAWTO 21,7
110  PLOT 19,9:
     DRAWTO 21,9
120  SETCOLOR 1,3,6  : REM Change to Red
130  SETCOLOR 2,12,6 : REM Change to Green
140  FOR I=1 TO 50:
     NEXT I          : REM Pause
150  SETCOLOR 1,0,0  : REM Change to Black
160  SETCOLOR 2,0,0  : REM Change to Black
170  FOR I=1 TO 400
180  IF RND(0)*20<1 THEN
        SETCOLOR 4,0,14:
        SETCOLOR 4,0,0: REM Random lightning
                             flash
190  NEXT I
200  GOTO 120
```

When you execute this program, you will see a crude airplane heading towards you with red and green lights blinking at the tips of its wings. Every so often the background will flash as if the plane were flying through a lightning storm.

Lines 120–130 turn on the wing lights, then after a pause, lines 150–160 turn them off. SETCOLOR 1 changes the color of the pixel plotted with COLOR 2, and SETCOLOR 2 changes the pixel plotted with COLOR 3. This may seem a little confusing, so refer back to Table 6.1 to see the relationship between the SETCOLOR and COLOR commands.

If the value of the random number expression on line 180 is less than 1 (one chance in 20, or 5 percent), the lightning is turned on and off by setting the background color register first to white and then immediately back to black. As you can see in Table 6.1, SETCOLOR 4 controls the screen background.

We could have created the blinking wing lights by replotting the tips with the background color. This technique executes much more slowly than one which just changes the color registers. Although we don't need the speed in this case, the effect would be slightly different. Notice that during the lightning flash the darkened wing lights are silhouetted against

the sky. This effect could not be easily duplicated on a computer without color registers!

Using POKE to Change Colors

Referring back to Table 6.1, you'll notice that there is one more column to cover. Each color register has an address in memory associated with it. The value in the color register can be changed by using POKE to put a new value into this address. In GRAPHICS 10, the only way to change the values in the first four color registers is with the use of a POKE. To obtain the value to POKE into a memory location, take the hue value of the color and multiply by 16, then add in the luminance value

POKE *addr, hue*∗16+*luminance*

In GRAPHICS 7, for example, the following two statements would be equivalent:

```
SETCOLOR 0,4,8     POKE 708,72
```

To see why, first find the SETCOLOR 0 entry for GRAPHICS 7 in Table 6.1. Then move one column to the right, and you will see the address 708. Multiply the hue in the above SETCOLOR by 16 (4∗16 = 64), add the luminance value to it (64 + 8 = 72), and you have your POKE value! In many cases you may want to use a POKE instead of SETCOLOR, because POKE will execute more rapidly. This is because it takes time for BASIC to do the necessary conversion from SETCOLOR's hue and luminance values to a single value which it then POKEs into the proper address. You speed up the process by precalculating the value while you are *writing* your program and then have BASIC just POKE it in during execution.

This technique was used in the Exploding Bomb program (Chapter 5, Example 4) to flash the background rapidly at the moment of the explosion. Here is that line again:

```
80 FOR I=1 TO 10:
    POKE 712,RND(0)*255:
  NEXT I:
  POKE 712,0:
  RETURN: REM Flash
```

This line selects 10 random colors to flash on the background and then resets the background color to black.

Film 5
"Times Square," Digital Effects Inc./Rosebush, Kleiser, Leich, Cox, Loen, Prins, Deas and Cohen, 1979. Hold on as we take a brief ride through Times Square as it might have appeared on an evening in the year 1890. *(Courtesy Digital Effects Inc.)*

Now type in the following short program and see what happens:

```
10 GRAPHICS 3+16
20 FOR I=0 TO 254 STEP 2 : REM Step through
                                every color
30 POKE 712,I            : REM Change
                                background
                                color
50 NEXT I
60 GOTO 20
```

When you run it, your screen will flash through all the colors so quickly that you will hardly be able to see them. Add the following line to slow it down to human speeds:

```
40   FOR W=1 TO 50:
        NEXT W
```

Try doing *this* trick without color registers!

Summary

Color registers can be used to rapidly change portions of the screen with a simple `SETCOLOR` or `POKE`. But what purpose do they serve for animation? In the next section, we will explore the real power of color registers in three amazing demonstration programs.

6.2. CREATING MOTION WITH COLOR REGISTERS

In Chapter 5's Exploding Bomb program, we use color registers to flash the background and then to fade out the explosion on the screen. With careful planning, this ability to *instantaneously* change the color of a specific area on the screen can be used to create the effect of high-speed motion without resorting to machine language.

To understand how to create motion using color registers, first consider our paint store analogy again. It had nine paint buckets numbered from 0 to 8, each filled with a different color. Now let's add a temporary paint tray called TEMP. We are going to use the nine buckets and the tray to play "pass the colors" (see Figure 6.2). First, empty the paint contained in Bucket 0 into the TEMPorary tray. Then pour Bucket 1's contents into the now emptied Bucket 0. Next, pour the paint in Bucket 2 into Bucket 1. Continue passing the colors until Bucket 8 is emptied into Bucket 7. There are no more buckets left with which to fill Bucket 8. Aha! Stored in TEMP, we still have the paint that first filled

Figure 6.2: Rotating the colors through the buckets.

Bucket 0! So we take the paint in TEMP and empty it into Bucket 8. Then go back to the very first step and empty the paint now in Bucket 0 into TEMP and so on. (This is called a "bucket brigade" in electronics.) We have just created an endless loop of moving colors, which is seen on the screen as a rapidly changing pattern. Depending on what was drawn and how it was organized on the screen, a hypnotically abstract design or an exciting, realistic scene can be produced.

As animators, we must now form the pattern of moving colors into something interesting to look at.

The Moving-Color Curtain Program

Let's see how color register animation actually looks on the screen. In our first program, the screen is filled with vertical bars that have colors rotating through them. We will use GRAPHICS 10, a mode especially suited to color register animation as it allows you to use the full nine ATARI Color Registers (see box).

The GTIA and the CTIA

When the ATARI Computer first came out, it had a special television interface chip called CTIA. Beginning in early 1982, all ATARI's were manufactured with a new and better chip called GTIA. The GTIA supports three additional BASIC graphics modes, 9, 10, and 11, which were not available on the earlier ATARI computers. The resolution on these modes is 80 × 192, yielding the same vertical resolution as GRAPHICS 8 (as well as the same memory consumption). GRAPHICS 9 allows the selection of one hue which can then be simultaneously displayed on the screen with 16 different luminances (see Photo 6.3).

Photo 6.3: Screen photos of GRAPHICS 9.

GRAPHICS 11 allows the placement of up to 16 different hues on the screen, all set to the same luminance value.

Photo 6.4: Screen photo of GRAPHICS 11.

These two modes won't be covered in this book since they can't be used for color register animation. We will be discussing GRAPHICS 10, however, which allows you to chose any *nine* colors from the ATARI palette of 128 colors!

To tell whether your ATARI Home Computer has the CTIA or the GTIA chip, enter and run the following program:

```
10 GRAPHICS 10
20 GOTO 20
```

If your screen first flashes black and then returns to blue, you have the CTIA. The program will still be running, but the CTIA will not be able to properly display a GRAPHICS 10 screen. If your screen stays black, congratulations! You have the GTIA and may run our GTIA examples. You may get your computer upgraded to the GTIA chip for a small fee. If you haven't already done so, you will be missing out on many new ATARI programs which require this chip.

Using the Amazing GRAPHICS 10

GRAPHICS 10 has a rather strangely shaped pixel. Each pixel is about four times as wide as it is high, with a screen resolution of 80 × 192. This doesn't present a problem in Example 5, but it is awkward to use when drawing curved surfaces. As you can see in the following figure, lines that are almost horizontal show very fine resolution, and those that approach vertical are extremely coarse.

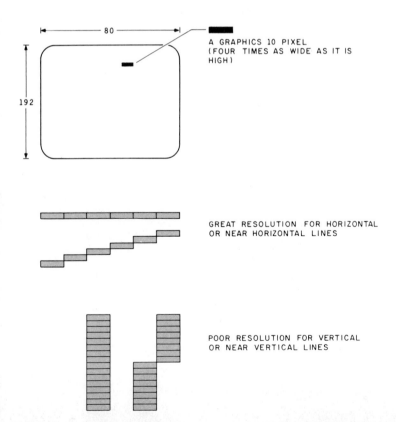

A GRAPHICS 10 PIXEL
(FOUR TIMES AS WIDE AS IT IS HIGH)

GREAT RESOLUTION FOR HORIZONTAL OR NEAR HORIZONTAL LINES

POOR RESOLUTION FOR VERTICAL OR NEAR VERTICAL LINES

Figure 6.3: GRAPHICS 10 pixels.

To change the values in the color registers for the standard CTIA graphics modes (0 through 8), you can use the BASIC SETCOLOR command. However, ATARI BASIC isn't *fully* set up for the GTIA graphics modes. The only way to change the colors in the first four color registers (see Table 6.3) is to POKE them directly into the color register's RAM address. The following table shows the relationship between this RAM address and the SETCOLOR command. Even though BASIC's SETCOLOR isn't adequate in GRAPHICS 10, BASIC's COLOR command *can* be used to choose any of the registers for painting. For example, to draw an orange (hue 2, luminance 8) pixel on the GRAPHICS 10 screen with register 1, use the statements:

```
POKE 705,40    : REM Fill register 1 with
                 orange (hue=2, lum=8)
COLOR 1        : REM Select register 1
                 for drawing
PLOT X,Y       : REM Place an orange pixel
                 at X,Y
```

To draw with register 6, you could use either the SETCOLOR command *or* a direct POKE:

SETCOLOR 2,2,8 or POKE 710,40

Here is the GRAPHICS 10 section of Table 6.1 for easy reference:

Modes	Default Colors	SETCOLOR	POKE	COLOR	Description
GRAPHICS 10 (GTIA mode, nine colors)	Black	—	704	0	Pixel/Background, Border
	Black	—	705	1	Pixel
	Black	—	706	2	Pixel
	Black	—	707	3	Pixel
	Orange	0	708	4	Pixel
	Lt Green	1	709	5	Pixel
	Blue	2	710	6	Pixel
	Red	3	711	7	Pixel
	Black	4	712	8	Pixel

Table 6.3: GRAPHICS 10 — color registers and COLOR command.

Even though we have nine color registers to play with on a GTIA ATARI, we seldom use all of them for color rotations in an animated scene. In the next example, we use the eight color registers that color the

playfields (all colors except the background) and leave the screen background register (register 0) alone.

Example 5

Exercise   Create a beautiful kaleidoscopic pattern by filling the screen with vertical bars drawn with all eight of GRAPHICS 10's playfield color registers. Divide the screen in half so that when you rotate colors through the registers, both the left and right halves of the screen move towards the center. Leave the background black.

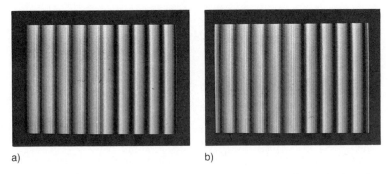

a)   b)

Photo 6.5:   Screen photos of moving color curtain program (see color insert).

There are three sections to this program: the initialization section, the section which draws the bars on the screen, and the section which animates the picture by rotating the colors. You'll notice that this last section was placed at the beginning of the program. It makes use of the previously discussed fact that statements towards the beginning of an ATARI BASIC program execute at a faster rate than those at the end.

```
200  REM Initialize
210  GRAPHICS 10: REM GTIA Mode - 80 X 192 with 9 color registers
220  COL=1:
     LUM=8: REM Set starting COLor Register & LUMinance values
230  REM
240  REM Set initial colors
250  POKE 704,0: REM Background to black
260  FOR I=1 TO 8: REM Other registers to different colors
270     POKE 704+I,I*16+LUM
280  NEXT I
290  REM
```

Figure 6.4:   Listing of Example 5 — lines 200–290.

Initialize   First, GRAPHICS 10 is turned on. Even though the ATARI operating system fully supports GRAPHICS 10, BASIC doesn't. Since the normal SETCOLOR command to control the first four

registers can't be used, we will directly POKE in the initial colors (lines 250–280).

```
300  REM Draw Bars, Increment COLOR
310  FOR I=0 TO 79
320     COLOR COL
330     PLOT I,0:
        DRAWTO I,191
340     IF I<40 THEN
           COL=COL-1:
           IF COL=0 THEN
              COL=8
350     IF I>=40 THEN
           COL=COL+1:
           IF COL=9 THEN
              COL=1
360  NEXT I
370  GOTO 100
```

Figure 6.5: Listing of Example 5 — lines 300–370.

Draw Bars, Increment Color   This is the section of a color register animation program which requires the most work, i.e., drawing the picture on the screen. The color register is set to the value in C, then this color is used to draw a vertical bar. (The values from 0 to 8 can be used in the COLOR command without any problems.) After each bar is drawn, the value in C is changed so the next bar will be drawn using a different color register. On the left half of the screen, we are decrementing through the color registers. On the right half, we are incrementing through them and continue to draw bars until the screen is completely filled. Again, notice that the background register, COLOR 0, is not used.

```
10   REM *** MOVING COLOR CURTAIN ***
20   REM              Example 5
30   REM
40   REM Program to demonstrate Color Register Animation in GRAPHICS 10
50   REM (GTIA chip required)
60   REM Copyright (C) 1982 by David Fox and Mitchell Waite
70   REM
80   GOTO 200
90   REM
100  REM Rotate Color Registers
110  TEMP=PEEK(705)
120  FOR I=705 TO 711:
        POKE I,PEEK(I+1):
     NEXT I:  REM Rotate colors
130  POKE 712,TEMP:
        GOTO 110
140  REM
```

Figure 6.6: Listing of Example 5 — lines 10–140.

Rotate the Color Registers   Now that the scene is drawn, it can be animated. We play our game of ''pass the colors'' with eight of the registers, using a FOR/NEXT loop for simplicity, even though it slows the execution speed a bit. Listing out each POKE in the color rotation sequence (as we do in Example 6) would increase the program's execution speed.

When this program is executed, the colors are seen moving from each half of the screen towards the middle.

Modifications   For variety, try the following changes:

1. Use a different initial set of colors and/or a different luminance value.
2. Change line 110 to the following:

```
110 TEMP=PEEK(705)+16:
    IF TEMP>255 THEN
    TEMP=LUM:   REM Add a new color
```

This will change the color stored in TEMP to the next color in the ATARI rainbow of colors. This will cause the colors displayed on the screen to circulate constantly through the 16 different hues as they move towards the center of the screen.

3. For those who like surprises, change line 110 to the following:

```
110 TEMP=RND(1)*256: REM Pick random color
```

4. Change the program so the background color is rotated.

Summary

Creating kaleidoscopes is fun, but what about some real action! In the next section, we will use the same technique and apply it to the beginnings of a space game.

6.3.   THE TRENCH PROGRAM

Everyone who saw *Star Wars* remembers the flight through the Death Star's trench. In the next program, Example 6, we will use color register animation to create this effect. We will be using GRAPHICS 7 (available on all ATARI Home Computers) which will give us fewer registers to play with (GRAPHICS 7 has a resolution of 160 × 96 and uses four color registers). This program can be the core of an exciting game.

The theory behind the Trench program is the same as that in Example 5. The main difference is that we will rotate colors through only three registers. This will almost triple the speed of the color rotation loop. Also, the size of the sections on the screen that will be animated are much larger than those in Example 5. This will so exaggerate the effect of motion that there will be more than enough processing time left for sound effects and major improvements to the program.

Example 6

Exercise   Draw a trench on the screen in GRAPHICS 7 in such a way that the viewer will have the experience of rapidly traveling through it when color register rotation is used. Make the trench U-shaped, with two vertical sides and a horizontal bottom. Using a game paddle, give the viewer control of speed through the trench and forward/reverse motion. Make the roar of the engines change as the velocity changes.

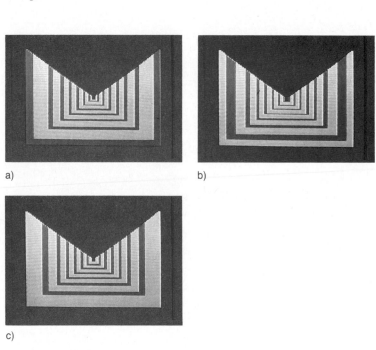

a) b)

c)

Photo 6.6:   Screen photos of the Trench program.

This program has three main sections: the initialization section, the section which draws the trench on the screen, and the section which animates the picture by rotating the colors and reading the game paddle. The drawing section was difficult to write. It took quite a while to create a formula that could simulate the perspective of the trench. We could have drawn the trench on graph paper and just translated the plotting coordinates to the program, but that would have used much more memory (and would have been much more boring).

```
200  REM Initialize
210  COL=1:
     Y1=45:
     Y2=49
220  REM
```

Figure 6.7:   Listing of Example 6 — lines 200–220.

Initialize The initial values are set along with the colors to be drawn. Notice that two of the registers are set to the same color. Even though we are using three color registers in our animation sequence, only two colors will be passed through them. This yields a smoother animation effect (see Figure 6.8). The three boxes, A, B, and C, show the progression of the two colors through the three registers. Even though the width of the moving color is two bars wide, the step size of the movement is only one bar wide.

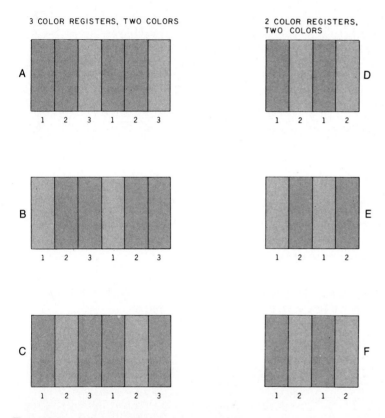

Figure 6.8: Using two colors and three registers.

If only two colors and two registers were used (boxes D, E, F), the viewer would just see the two colors alternating places. There wouldn't be any illusion of movement, just a flickering effect. With three colors and three registers, there would be too many colors in the trench and the effect would be spoiled. (Darth in a candy-striped trench?)

```
300 REM Draw Trench on Screen
310 GRAPHICS 7+16: REM Full screen graphics
320 SETCOLOR 0,3,8: REM Set Color Register values
330 SETCOLOR 1,3,8
340 SETCOLOR 2,3,4
350 FOR X=2 TO 79: REM Increment horizontal coordinates
360    COLOR INT(COL+0.5): REM Choose which Color Register to draw with
370    PLOT X+80,Y1:
       DRAWTO X+80,Y2:
       DRAWTO 79-X,Y2:
       DRAWTO 79-X,Y1
380    Y1=Y1-0.6:
       Y2=Y2+0.6: REM Increase vertical line length
390    IF Y1<0 THEN
          Y1=0: REM Prevent overflow
400    IF Y2>95 THEN
          Y2=95
410    COL=COL+(79-X)/160: REM Increment Color Register
420    IF COL+0.5)=4 THEN
          COL=COL-3
430 NEXT X
440 GOTO 100
```

Figure 6.9: Listing of Example 6 — lines 300–440.

Draw Trench on Screen   This section draws the trench on the screen using the appropriate color register. We start near the horizon, draw the three sides of the trench, then move out towards the edges of the screen. The algorithms used here were all arrived at through the scientific method of trial and error. Line 370 increments the value of C in smaller and smaller steps as X (the horizontal position of our lines) increases. This creates the illusion of perspective — the closer the different colored panels are to the viewer, the wider they appear.

```
10 REM       *** THE TRENCH ***
20 REM           Example 6
30 REM
40 REM Program to create the illusion of flying through a trench by rotating
50 REM the Color Registers in GRAPHICS 7
60 REM Copyright (C) 1982 by David Fox and Mitchell Waite
70 REM
80 GOTO 200
90 REM
100 REM Rotate the Colors
110 SOUND 3,255,0,8: REM Background roar (always on)
120 REM If the trigger on PADDLE 0 is pressed, reverse the direction
130 IF PTRIG(0)=1 THEN
       TEMP=PEEK(710):
       POKE 710,PEEK(709):
       POKE 709,PEEK(708):
       POKE 708,TEMP:
       GOTO 150: REM Not pressed
140 TEMP=PEEK(708):
       POKE 708,PEEK(709):
       POKE 709,PEEK(710):
       POKE 710,TEMP: REM Pressed
150 PDL=PADDLE(0)/5: REM Speed and sound controlled by PADDLE 0
160 SOUND 0,PDL,0,8:
       SOUND 1,PDL+80,0,8:
       SOUND 2,PDL+160,0,8
170 FOR PAUSE=1 TO PDL:
       NEXT PAUSE
180 GOTO 130
190 REM
```

Figure 6.10: Listing of Example 6 — lines 10–190.

Loop to Rotate the Colors This program calls for sound effects and an element of interaction. Sound register 3 is used to give us a constant background roar (line 110). The game paddle is used to control the speed through the trench (line 150) and to reverse the direction we are traveling (line 130). If the paddle button is pressed, we move backwards (line 140). To gain as much execution speed as possible, each POKE in lines 130–140 is written out rather than using FOR/NEXT loops. In line 160, the position of the game paddle is also used to control the pitch of the other three sound registers. To add to the realism, the whine of the engine rises in pitch as velocity increases. Line 170 takes the paddle value and uses it to control a pause loop.

If you don't have game paddles, use a joystick to change the value in PDL — if you push forward, increment PDL; if you pull back, decrement PDL.

Modifications The following are modifications for you to try:
1. You may want to modify this program to use GRAPHICS 10 instead of GRAPHICS 7. This will give you some extra registers for stars and other objects.
2. Turn this program into a game. After reading the next chapter on player-missile graphics, see if you can create the target spacecraft in front of you as well as a movable gunsight.

Summary

Moving from the excitement of outer space, we will visit a sylvan scene of the wilderness. In the next section the same techniques are used to animate only a single portion of a scene.

6.4. AUTUMN WATERFALL PROGRAM

The tranquility of this program is for those of you who don't enjoy roaring through a narrow trench at almost the speed of light. GRAPHICS 10 will be used to draw an autumnal landscape complete with trees casting long shadows from an early morning sun. The scene is brought to life by a foaming waterfall cascading down a steep cliff and across a green valley.

We are not introducing any new animation techniques, just expanding on earlier ones. Because of the complexity of the scene on the screen, this program is quite a bit longer than some of our previous examples. The section which actually animates the scene, however, is only three lines long! This reveals that much of our ATARI animation involves set up while the actual motion code is simple.

Only four color registers will be used for the program's animation. The other five registers will be used to draw the landscape. This takes

some planning, as there is an interdependency between what we want to include in the picture and how many colors can be used. One way to plan the picture is to keep adding details as long as there are colors left. That's the method we used. The background register was used for the sky, another register for the brown cliffs, and a third for the grass covering the top of the cliff and the valley floor. That left two unused registers, so we planted trees across the valley. The brown of the cliffs was recycled for the tree trunks, and the tree tops were painted orange-red to add some color. Finally, a darker shade of green was used in the last register for tree shadows. The foam at the base of the waterfall was drawn with the sky's color rather than one of the waterfall's colors, since we didn't want its color to change at all. There were no more registers left for new colors, so the scene was completed!

Using Fill

To make it easier to color large areas of the screen rapidly, the ATARI operating system's built-in Fill routine is used. Unfortunately, this Fill is not the same as the Fill or Flood used in professional computer paint systems. ATARI's Fill will not seek out all the adjacent nooks and crannies within the area to be filled. Since it's more of a box fill, it just draws a series of horizontal lines towards the right of the screen. Each line is completed when it hits a non-background color. Even worse than its inadequacy is the fact that there doesn't even exist a simple ATARI BASIC statement to implement the OS's Fill (although there is a F I L L in ATARI Microsoft BASIC). Instead, we must use a special call to the OS to activate Fill after setting up the screen in a particular way. This makes it very inconvenient to use, but it's still better than nothing.

Photo 6.7 shows how Fill works. The left boundary of the area being filled is created as Fill is at work. This outline was drawn in a color different from the filled-in area to make it easier to see precisely how Fill operates. The steps are further described in the text that follows.

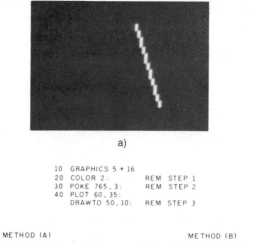

a)

```
10  GRAPHICS 5 + 16
20  COLOR 2:        REM STEP 1
30  POKE 765,3:     REM STEP 2
40  PLOT 60,35:
    DRAWTO 50,10:   REM STEP 3
```

METHOD (A)   METHOD (B)

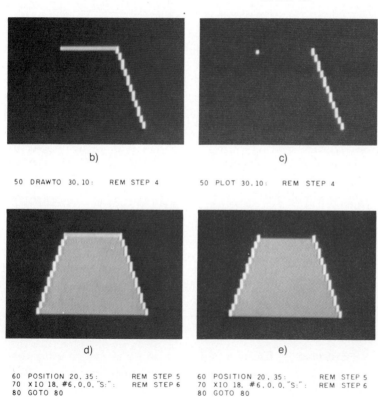

b)   c)

```
50  DRAWTO 30,10:   REM STEP 4     50  PLOT 30,10:    REM STEP 4
```

d)   e)

```
60  POSITION 20,35:      REM STEP 5    60  POSITION 20,35:      REM STEP 5
70  XIO 18,#6,0,0,"S:":  REM STEP 6    70  XIO 18,#6,0,0,"S:":  REM STEP 6
80  GOTO 80                            80  GOTO 80
```

Photo 6.7:   The Fill routine in action.

Since Fill is an OS routine and not directly supported by BASIC, it must be accessed through BASIC's XIO command. This is a general input/output statement used for special operations which, in addition to Fill, can be used to perform special disk operations like Rename, Delete, Lock. (For more information on XIO, see your ATARI BASIC manual.) Here are the steps you need to go through to use Fill:

1. Using the COLOR command, select the outline color of the area to be filled.
2. Select the color for Fill with a POKE of the appropriate COLOR value into RAM location 765.
3. Make sure there is a right edge to the area you want to fill. If there isn't one, then draw it in.
4. There are two ways to mark the starting point of the fill (see Photo 6.7). One, you can draw a horizontal line from step 3's right edge to the starting point of the Fill. Fill doesn't actually begin until the *next line* (up or down) towards the end point (X2, Y2 in step 5). Two, you can indicate the starting point with a PLOT X1, Y1. In this case, the first horizontal line will again begin on the next line towards X2, Y2 and will end when it reaches the right edge of step 3. However, with this method a pixel will be left out in the open at X1, Y1. This is fine when you are filling in an area by sections and this pixel blends into the previous section. We used this second method in our Waterfall Program.
5. Indicate the ending point with a POSITION X2, Y2. This is where the final horizontal line will begin. It too will end when it reaches the right edge of step 3.
6. Call the Fill routine with the XIO function (XIO 18, #6,0,0,"S:"). This will fill in the defined area with the color set in step 2. Note that the borders may be in a different color than the filled area (see above photos).

Example 7

Exercise   Create a practical example of motion using color registers. Draw a peaceful scene on your computer's screen with a waterfall roaring over the edge of a cliff onto a valley floor. Draw some trees using the colors of autumn. Use color register animation to create the motion of the water in the river and the falls. Use four registers for the moving water and the remaining five registers for the scenery.

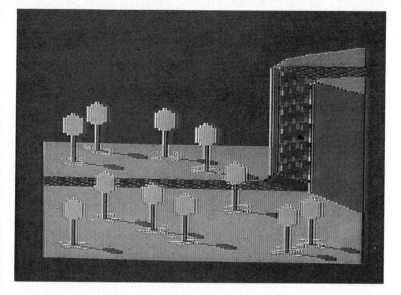

Photo 6.8 Screen photo of Autumn Waterfall Program (see color insert).

There are three main parts to this program: initialize, draw the scene, and animate the scene. However, because the program is longer than the earlier ones, we divided the draw-the-scene portion of the program into several smaller sections.

```
200 REM Initialize
210 FILL=1300
220 GRAPHICS 10
230 POKE 704,9*16+10: REM Sky – COLOR 0
240 POKE 705,8*16+10: REM Water – COLOR 1
250 POKE 706,8*16+8: REM Water – COLOR 2
260 POKE 707,8*16+6: REM Water – COLOR 3
270 SETCOLOR 0,8,4: REM Water – COLOR 4
280 SETCOLOR 1,12,4: REM Tree shadow – COLOR 5
290 SETCOLOR 2,2,4: REM Cliff & tree trunks – COLOR 6
300 SETCOLOR 3,12,6: REM Grass – COLOR 7
310 SETCOLOR 4,3,6: REM Treetops – COLOR 8
320 REM
```

Figure 6.11: Listing of Example 7 — lines 200–320.

Initialize   Set up the palette of colors we will be using.

```
400 REM Draw Grass and Cliff
410 COLOR 7:
    POKE 765,7: REM The grass
420 PLOT 79,10:
    DRAWTO 79,45:
    X1=78:
    Y1=10:
    X2=66:
    Y2=15:
    GOSUB FILL
430 X1=65:
    Y1=15:
    X2=61:
    Y2=18:
    GOSUB FILL:
    X1=60:
    Y1=18:
    X2=56:
    Y2=25:
    GOSUB FILL
440 X1=56:
    Y1=25:
    X2=65:
    Y2=35:
    GOSUB FILL:
    X1=66:
    Y1=35:
    X2=78:
    Y2=45:
    GOSUB FILL
450 COLOR 6:
    POKE 765,6: REM The cliff
460 PLOT 79,46:
    DRAWTO 79,145:
    X1=56:
    Y1=26:
    X2=56:
    Y2=117:
    GOSUB FILL
470 Y1=117:
    X2=68:
    Y2=132:
    GOSUB FILL:
    X1=68:
    Y1=132:
    X2=78:
    Y2=145:
    GOSUB FILL
480 COLOR 7:
    POKE 765,7: REM More grass
490 PLOT 0,191:
    DRAWTO 79,191:      .
    DRAWTO 79,146:
    X1=0:
    Y1=191:
    X2=0:
    Y2=91:
    GOSUB FILL

1300 REM Fill Subroutine
1310 PLOT X1,Y1:
     POSITION X2,Y2:
     XIO 18,#6,0,0,"S:":
     RETURN
1320 REM
```

Figure 6.12: Listing of Example 7 — lines 400–490, 1300–1320.

Draw Grass and Cliff   As in oil painting, we must first paint in the large background areas, then the details. We are using ATARI's built-in Fill routine to rapidly color these large areas. To make this process simpler, a subroutine on lines 1300–1310 is used. It carries out Fill steps 4–6 as described earlier.

```
500 REM Draw the Falls and River
510 FALL=58:
    CFLAG=0: REM Draw the river on top of the cliff
520 FOR Y=25 TO 34
530   GOSUB 1500
540   FOR X=79 TO FALL STEP -1
550     COLOR COL
560     PLOT X,Y
570     COL=COL-1:
        IF COL=0 THEN
          COL=4
580   NEXT X
590   FALL=FALL+1
600 NEXT Y
610 FALL=0:
    CFLAG=-1: REM Draw the falls
620 FOR X=58 TO 66
630   FALL=FALL+1
640   GOSUB 1500
650   PLOT X,25+FALL
660   FOR Y=30 TO 120 STEP 4
670     COLOR COL
680     DRAWTO X,Y+FALL
690     COL=COL-1:
        IF COL=0 THEN
          COL=4
700   NEXT Y:
    NEXT X
710 COLOR 6:
    PLOT 58,28:
    DRAWTO 58,25:
    DRAWTO 59,25:
    PLOT 66,38:
    DRAWTO 66,129: REM Cleanup
720 COLOR 7:
    PLOT 73,33:
    DRAWTO 79,33:
    PLOT 68,34:
    DRAWTO 79,34
730 FALL=57:
    CFLAG=1: REM Draw the river on the valley floor
740 FOR Y=121 TO 128
750   GOSUB 1500
760   FOR X=FALL TO 0 STEP -1
770     COLOR COL
780     PLOT X,Y
790     COL=COL-1:
        IF COL=0 THEN
          COL=4
800   NEXT X
810   FALL=FALL+1
820 NEXT Y
830 REM

1500 REM Choose Color
1510 COL=INT(RND(1)*4)+1:
     IF COL=STARTCOL THEN 1510:REM No two adjacent strips with same color pattern
1520 STARTCOL=COL+CFLAG: REM Calculate next starting color to avoid
1530 IF STARTCOL=0 THEN
       STARTCOL=4
1540 IF STARTCOL=5 THEN
       STARTCOL=1
1550 RETURN
1560 REM
```

Figure 6.13: Listing of Example 7 — lines 500–830, 1500–1560.

Draw the Falls and River In our scene, the water is the only thing which is animated. Four color registers are used to animate the moving water. The water is drawn in three sections: the river on top of the cliff (lines 510–600), the waterfall (lines 610–720), and the river on the valley floor (lines 730–820). The water consists of a series of parallel strips. To give some randomness to these strips, a subroutine (lines 1500–1530) is called which chooses the starting color register for each strip of water, making sure that no two adjacent strips will be identical.

On lines 710–720 some grass and dirt are added around the falls to depict the natural forces of erosion.

```
900  REM Draw the Trees
910  FOR T=1 TO 11
920    READ X,Y
930    COLOR 8: REM Treetop
940    FOR I=0 TO 2:
         PLOT X-I,Y-40+2*I:
         DRAWTO X-I,Y-20-2*I:
       NEXT I
950    FOR I=-2 TO -1:
         PLOT X-I,Y-40-2*I:
         DRAWTO X-I,Y-20+2*I:
       NEXT I
960    COLOR 6: REM Tree trunk
970    PLOT X,Y:
       DRAWTO X,Y-21
980    COLOR 5: REM Shadow of tree
990    PLOT X,Y+1:
       DRAWTO X+7,Y+4:
       PLOT X+8,Y+3:
       DRAWTO X+8,Y+5:
       DRAWTO X+9,Y+6
1000   DRAWTO X+9,Y+3:
       DRAWTO X+10,Y+3:
       DRAWTO X+10,Y+7
1010   PLOT X+11,Y+7:
       DRAWTO X+11,Y+4:
       DRAWTO X+12,Y+5:
       DRAWTO X+12,Y+7
1020   COLOR 8: REM Fallen leaves around tree trunk
1030   FOR I=1 TO 15
1040     RX=X+INT(RND(1)*7)-3:
         IF RX=X THEN 1040
1050     RY=Y+INT(RND(1)*8)-3:
         PLOT RX,RY
1060   NEXT I
1070 NEXT T
1080 REM

2000 REM Data for Location of Trees
2010 DATA 7,106,13,96,30,100,40,112,47,145,7,179,15,155,27,164,35,173,60,181,66,174
```

Figure 6.14: Listing of Example 7 — lines 900–1080, 2000–2010.

Draw the Trees   This section draws 11 identical trees. The X and Y base coordinates for the trees are stored on line 2010. An X,Y coordinates pair is READ and a new tree is drawn at that location. Lines 980–1010 add a great deal of realism by creating a shadow in a darker shade of green. Lines 1020–1060 create some randomness by scattering 15 leaves about the base of each tree.

```
1100 REM Draw the Foam
1110 COLOR 0: REM Same color as the sky
1120 PLOT 57,114:
     DRAWTO 65,122
1130 PLOT 57,115:
     DRAWTO 65,123
1140 PLOT 57,116:
     DRAWTO 65,124
1150 PLOT 56,116:
     DRAWTO 65,125
1160 PLOT 56,117:
     DRAWTO 65,126
1170 PLOT 56,118:
     DRAWTO 65,127
1180 PLOT 56,119:
     DRAWTO 65,128
1190 PLOT 55,119:
     DRAWTO 64,128
1200 PLOT 55,120:
     DRAWTO 63,128
1210 REM
```

Figure 6.15: Listing of Example 7 — lines 1100–1210.

Draw the Foam   As the water hits the base of the falls, white foam is created. Since there are no color registers left for white foam, the sky color is reused.

```
1250 REM Turn on the Sound
1260 FOR I=0 TO 3:
        SOUND I,I*50,0,8:
     NEXT I
1270 GOTO 100
1280 REM
```

Figure 6.16: Listing of Example 7 — lines 1250–1280.

Turn on the Sound   All the sound registers are used to create the roar of the waterfall. The sound is constant and does not need to be changed anywhere else in the program.

```
10  REM *** FALL WATERFALL ***
20  REM             Example 7
30  REM
40  REM Demonstration of animating a scene by rotating the Color Registers
50  REM (Uses GRAPHICS 10 - GTIA is needed)
60  REM Copyright (C) 1982 by David Fox and Mitchell Waite
70  REM
80  GOTO 200
90  REM
100 REM Rotate the Colors
110 TEMP=PEEK(705):
        POKE 705,PEEK(706):
        POKE 706,PEEK(707):
        POKE 707,PEEK(708):
        POKE 708,TEMP
120 FOR WT=1 TO 5:
        NEXT WT
130 GOTO 110
140 REM
```

Figure 6.17: Listing of Example 7 — lines 10–140.

Rotate the Colors   This section is similar to the corresponding sections in the other programs of this chapter. Of course, we only need to rotate the color registers for the four colors of the water.

Modifications   Try the following modifications:
1. Simulate a sunset by gradually changing the sky color to orange, pink, and purple and by decreasing the luminance values of each of the color registers. Then, after a period of time, reverse the process for a sunrise.
2. Change this program into a representation of the different seasons of the year. Simply by changing the colors in the appropriate registers, you can turn this into a summer scene (turn the treetops green). By altering the color of the grass and treetops to white, the sky to grey, and slowing or stopping the flow of the river, you can create a winter scene.

Commercially Available Games Using Color Register Animation

After scouring the marketplace, we could find not a single example of color register animation being used in a current game. What untapped potential!

Summary

Color register animation is a wonderful tool for creating a background scene with some life to it. Very little computer processing power is needed to create fantastic effects. Using color registers, it's a simple matter to create an entrancing picture. It would be somewhat difficult, however, to combine this technique with character set animation for two reasons.

One, color register animation is more suited for map modes than for text modes. In GRAPHICS Ø, there aren't enough registers available to do color register animation. In ANTIC 4, where there are enough registers available, it would be difficult to design the picture to be animated.

Two, GRAPHIC modes can't be mixed at the same location on the screen — only in horizontal bands. It would be possible to carefully lay out your screen so that your animated character set figure only stayed in its own band and the rest of the screen was a beautiful animated scene. Although this technique would be more than adequate for many well thought-out programs, it is somewhat limiting because the figure could only stay in this horizontal band and not move freely about the screen.

Fortunately there is a solution to this problem. It's possible to move animated figures over complex backgrounds without having to worry about erasing anything! This feature is called player-missile graphics, and we will cover it in the next chapter.

Chapter 7

Player-Missile Graphics

In advertisements for many ATARI games you'll see the words ". . . uses ATARI player-missile graphics!" What are player-missile graphics, you may have wondered, especially if the game has nothing to do with war or fighting? In this chapter, you will be introduced to this powerful feature through a Bouncing Ball program. Even though this sounds like a trivial example, it reveals the fundamental method behind animating players on the ATARI Home Computer. You will be able to control the ball's initial velocity and how much "bounce" it has — from a bowling ball dropped into a vat of mud to a ball which *gains* energy every time it hits the ground. To move the ball on the screen, the untapped power of ATARI BASIC string manipulations will be used. All of the upcoming examples from Chapters 8 and 9 build on this program, using much of the same program code, so save each program to avoid endless retyping.

7.1. WHY PLAYER-MISSILE GRAPHICS?

In Chapter 5 some lively animated figures are created, and in Chapter 6 some spellbinding backgrounds are produced. Unfortunately, it is somewhat difficult to combine these two elements because every time a figure is moved from one part of the screen to another, the old figure must be erased before the new one is drawn. This is a simple procedure when the figure is moving across a blank screen. A number of problems arise, however, if our little man were to stroll through a forest or down a city street. The first difficulty results from the computer's inability to mix different graphics modes on the same horizontal line. By altering the display list, the screen *can* contain different graphic modes, but only in horizontal bands stacked one on top of another. A character set walking man can't traverse a map mode screen!

There are several apparent solutions to this first problem. If the man can be restricted to a horizontal band on the screen, and this band can be created in a solid background color, then the technique of altering the display list could work. Even though the rest of the screen contains a

colorful scene, the man could only walk over a solid background, and the techniques of Chapter 5 would apply. This approach takes quite a bit of planning and is still very confining.

Another solution is to make sure the animated figure and the entire background are created in the same graphics mode. This is done either by producing the background out of character sets so it matches the man, or making the man out of plotted points to match the background. This solution, however, presents the second problem. Let's assume you painstakingly construct a beautiful scene using an Antic 4 character set (difficult but not impossible). What happens when you want the man to walk across the scene? As you erase him from the old position, a portion of the background is also erased. By the time the man reaches the other side, he has ripped a long hole in the background scenery and done more damage than an ambitious strip mining operation. In order for this technique to work properly, the man must be erased by precisely redrawing the background over his old position. Although techniques to accomplish this feat are available, they are awkward to implement and require machine language's quick calculation power.

Fortunately, ATARI had a better idea! Rather than relying on complicated software routines to mix animated figures and complex backgrounds, they gave the task to two of their custom chips, Antic and GTIA (or CTIA). Now, you can create an animated figure, move it quickly to any part of a screen consisting of *any* mixture of graphics modes, and not worry about erasing the existing background! This capability is called player-missile (PM) graphics.

What Are Player-Missile Graphics?

A player is actually a section of RAM, totally separate from normal screen memory, which controls a vertical bar on the screen. This bar, consisting of a stack of bytes, can be horizontally positioned anywhere on the screen. Defining a player is very similar to defining a character (see Chapter 5). Just turn on the appropriate bits of the appropriate bytes. On the first screen in Figure 7.1, evey bit in the player has been turned on

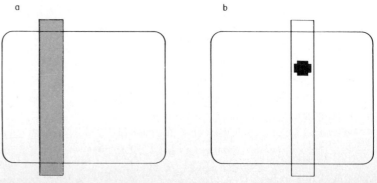

Figure 7.1: Players on the screen.

(each byte in the stack has the value of 255). This results in a solid vertical bar. On the second screen, a round ball has been defined by turning on some of the bits in five adjacent bytes only. The player is invisible where bits are turned off. Moving the object vertically is a simple matter of moving its byte image up and down within the vertical bar.

Since there are 8 bits in a byte, a player has a horizontal resolution of eight pixels. The vertical resolution of a player can either be one or two horizontal scan lines, depending on how you set up PM (player-missile) graphics. There are 128 bytes in the stack of a double-line resolution player and 256 bytes in a single-line resolution player (it takes twice as many bytes to display the increased resolution). All examples in this book use the double-line resolution mode. A player pixel in this mode is one color clock wide and two scan lines high, exactly the same size as a pixel in GRAPHICS 7, and four times as large (twice as wide and twice as high) as a GRAPHICS 0 character set pixel. Figure 7.2 shows how a ball might be represented as both double- and single-line resolution players. Even though these close-ups exaggerate the pixel steps, the single-line resolution ball still looks rounder.

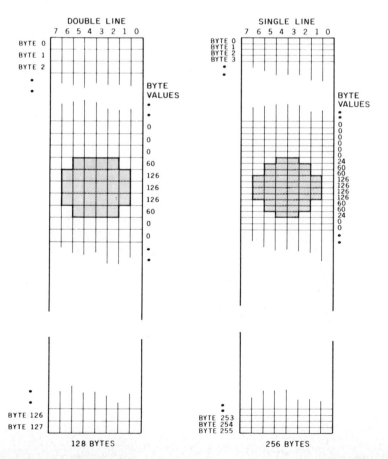

Figure 7.2: Player in double-line resolution.

Even though players are larger than characters, the proportions of their pixels are identical. This means that you can use all the tools for creating user-defined character sets to help make players, including a font-editing program or our character grid (Figure 5.8). Also watch for software tools designed especially for creating players.

A total of four players is available in the ATARI Home Computer, and each one can be independently controlled. Each has it own *color, width,* and *area of RAM* and can be moved separately from the others (see the section in this chapter on player parameters). In addition, each of the four players has a missile. A missile is similar to a player except that it is only 2 bits wide instead of 8. Each player-missile pair shares the same color. It is possible to combine the four missiles into a fifth independent player. (None of our demonstration programs use missiles.)

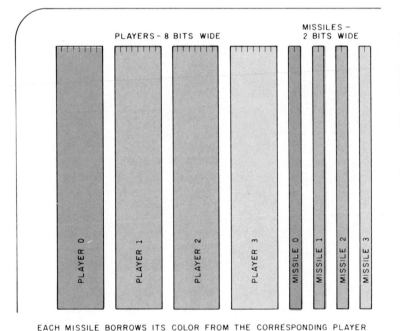

PLAYERS - 8 BITS WIDE

MISSILES – 2 BITS WIDE

PLAYER 0 PLAYER 1 PLAYER 2 PLAYER 3 MISSILE 0 MISSILE 1 MISSILE 2 MISSILE 3

EACH MISSILE BORROWS ITS COLOR FROM THE CORRESPONDING PLAYER

Figure 7.3: The four players and their missiles.

Figure 7.4 is a memory map of PM RAM. PMBASE, the address where PM RAM begins, must be on a 1 K address boundary for double-line resolution (a RAM address which is evenly divisible by 1024) or a 2 K boundary for single line resolution (evenly divisible by 2048). Notice that there is some wasted memory at the beginning of the PM RAM area. This RAM can be used for other purposes (e.g., storing frame information).

DOUBLE LINE RESOLUTION   SINGLE LINE RESOLUTION

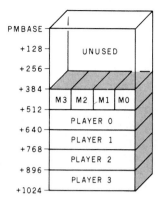

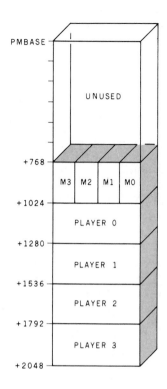

PMBASE MUST BE ON A 1K BOUNDARY
FOR DOUBLE LINE RESOLUTION
AND A 2K BOUNDARY FOR
SINGLE LINE RESOLUTION.

Figure 7.4: Memory map of player-missile RAM.

7.2. PLAYER MOTION

Each player can be moved independently in a horizontal, vertical, or diagonal direction. Horizontal movement is the easiest. How much easier is it to move a player than to move an object using other techniques? Let's find out.

Moving a Player Horizontally

It is *extremely* simple to move a player across the screen from left to right (or from right to left). Each player (and each missile) has its own address called a *horizontal position register*. To move a player to any horizontal position, simply POKE the proper value into the player's horizontal position register and the player immediately appears at its new position! Table 7.1 lists the locations of these registers for each player and missile.

	Addresses		ATARI's
	Decimal	**Hex**	**Name for it**
Player 0	53248	D000	HPOSP0
Player 1	53249	D001	HPOSP1
Player 2	53250	D002	HPOSP2
Player 3	53251	D003	HPOSP3
Missile 0	53252	D004	HPOSM0
Missile 1	53253	D005	HPOSM1
Missile 2	53254	D006	HPOSM2
Missile 3	53255	D007	HPOSM3

Table 7.1: Player-missile horizontal position registers.

The value you POKE into the horizontal position registers is in color clocks (see Chapter 5). Each horizontal scan line is 227.5 color clocks wide, but because of overscan (television manufacturers adjust their sets so that part of the picture overflows the screen and is lost), each end of the scan line is off the screen. So, although you can POKE a value from 0 to 255 into any of these registers, a player positioned with the low and high values will not be visible. Depending on your television set, the values less than 20–60 will be off the left edge and the values greater than 200–245 will be off the right edge. Therefore, to make a player vanish, all you have to do is POKE its horizontal position register with a 0. It will immediately disappear from the screen. Actually, it is hiding off the left edge of the screen, waiting for your next command.

Hardware Registers and Shadow Registers

Try the following experiment — press SYSTEM RESET on your ATARI, POKE a value into 53248 (the horizontal position register for player 0), and then immediately PEEK into this address to see what's there:

```
POKE 53248,50
PRINT PEEK(53248)
```

0   The ATARI printed this.

No there isn't anything wrong with your computer. No matter what value you POKE into 53248, you won't be able to alter the value you find when you PRINT its contents! This is because any address in the ATARI from 53248 to 55295 (D000-D7FF Hex) is

not really a RAM address; it is a *hardware register.* These addresses are mapped to locations in the ATARI special chip set, which gives direct access to the power of the computer (see Figure 7.5). In this case, Antic, which is tied to location 53248, received your value and immediately put it to use. If PM graphics were enabled (turned on), you would see Player 0 move to the indicated position, but you wouldn't be able to verify this by a PEEK into the register. This is called a *write-only register.*

ADDRESSES

DECIMAL	HEX	FUNCTION	SIZE
65535	FFFF	OPERATING SYSTEM AND MATH ROUTINES	10K
55296	D800		
55295 53248	D7FF D000	HARDWARE REGISTERS	2K
53247 49152	CFFF C000	RESERVED FOR FUTURE OPERATING SYSTEM EXPANSION	4K
49151 40960	BFFF A000	BASIC CARTRIDGE OR RAM (IN 48K SYSTEM WITH NO CARTRIDGES)	16K
40959 32768	9FFF 8000	RAM (IN ATARI WITH 40K OR MORE MEMORY)	
32767 16384	7FFF 4000	RAM (IN ATARI WITH 32K OR MORE MEMORY)	16K
16383 0	3FFF 0000	RAM (IN ATARI WITH 16K OR MORE MEMORY)	16K

Figure 7.5: Memory map showing hardware registers and RAM.

There is a limited number of addresses set aside for this purpose, so ATARI has them doing double duty. The address 53248, for example, has a split personality. In addition to its function as the write-only horizontal position register for Player 0, it is also tied to a

read-only GTIA register that is used for collision detection. You can PEEK into this address to find out if Missile 0 has collided with a playfield (see the upcoming section on collision detection). The 0 that you just PRINTed on the screen means that no collisions of this nature have occurred.

What about color registers? They do not follow our description of hardware registers in two ways. They don't fall within the specified hardware register addresses, *and* we were able to PEEK at their contents and POKE them with color information. Certain hardware registers have "scratch pad" RAM locations associated with them called *shadow registers*. A shadow register is a normal RAM location. Every sixtieth of a second, the computer looks into its shadow registers, grabs their values, and places them into the corresponding hardware registers (or, with some registers, the information is transferred from the hardware register to the shadow register). This is necessary when a register controls some aspects of the screen display. For example, if the gathering of color information were not synchronized with the display (which is also being refreshed every sixtieth of a second), you would see the color change on the screen at random horizontal positions resulting in an annoying flicker (see the sections on the vertical blank in the next chapter). So, the color registers we have been using are really *shadow* registers of the *hardware* color registers. The use of shadow registers made the color register animation programs from the last chapter as simple to implement as they are!

When a shadow register is available for a specific hardware register, we will only give you that shadow register address. If you try to POKE information (from within BASIC) into a hardware register that is shadowed, it will be set back to its shadowed value during the next sixtieth of a second. Some amazing things can be accomplished, however, by directly accessing these shadowed hardware registers through machine language as we will see in Chapter 9. (Appendix G furnishes a list of ATARI hardware and shadow registers.)

Moving a Player Vertically with BASIC

Vertical player movement is slightly more difficult to accomplish than its horizontal counterpart. Since there is no vertical position register, the only way to move a player up and down is to actually move its bit pattern through player RAM. To do this effectively, machine language speed is required. There is a technique, however, by which we can trick BASIC into helping us with this problem through the use of string manipulations.

Background on Strings   As you enter a BASIC program line which contains string variables, some information is stored in two tables. One table, called the variable name table, keeps a list of all variable names, and another, called the variable value table, has information as to where in memory each string's data will be stored. (This table also has information about numeric arrays, which we won't be covering here.) The location of the table can be discovered from within BASIC by checking a pair of memory locations called VVTP (variable value table pointer). The value of VVTP is calculated like this:

```
VVTP=PEEK(134) + PEEK(135) * 256
```

Suppose, for example, you had a program which started like this:

```
10 DIM A$(25),B$(256)
20 A$="This is a test"
30 B$="done"
```

Here is how the beginning of the variable table would look if we PEEKed into the contents of RAM starting at VVTP. All of the values are given in decimal:

		Byte Numbers			
	1	2	3&4	5&6	7&8
String (DIMensioned)	129		Offset from	Current	DIMed
(unDIMensioned)	128	Var #	STARP	length	length
Entry for A$	129	0	0 0	14 0	25 0
Entry for B$	129	1	25 0	4 0	0 1

Table 7.2: Variable value table.

Each variable's entry in the table is 8 bytes long. Byte 1 indicates whether the variable has been DIMensioned yet (a 129 is stored here if it has and a 128 if it hasn't). The second byte indicates the variable's position in the variable name table. It is important to note that this number represents the order in which the variables were *entered* (time-wise) into the program, not the order in which they *occur* in the listing. In our example above, another string variable now added at line 5 would be the *third* variable in the program. This order is maintained even when the program is saved on disk (or cassette), and even variables which have been deleted from the program remain in the table. The only way to reorder the variables in the table (or to purge old variables) is to LIST the program to disk (or cassette), type NEW, and then use ENTER to bring the program back into memory. As far as BASIC is concerned, the

program is being entered by hand for the first time. This information is important to remember for Examples 8 and 9 in which the string manipulation is used.

The next 6 bytes in the table are paired as low and high bytes. This means the second byte is multiplied by 256 and added to the first byte to get the proper (16 bit) value. Bytes 3 and 4 in the table give the "offset" from the beginning of the *string/array area* (where the string data and array data are actually stored). This area, located elsewhere in memory, can be pinpointed by a PEEK into a pair of memory locations called STARP (for string/array pointer):

```
STARP =PEEK(140) + PEEK(141) * 256
```

Offset refers to the number of bytes from the beginning of the string/array area to where the string's data is stored. A$'s contents are at the beginning of this area, and B$'s contents have an offset of 25 (which also happens to be the reserved length for A$ when A$ is DIMensioned). This offset value is what will give us vertical control over our players!

Bytes 5 and 6 contain the current length of the string, and bytes 7 and 8 contain the DIMensioned values for the string, or the number of bytes reserved for the string in the string/array area.

By *changing* the offset value in bytes 3 and 4, we can switch the area in RAM where the data for a specific string will be stored. In our next program, this offset value for the first entry in the variable value table is changed so the first string coincides with the RAM for Player 0. This means if something is stored in this relocated string, it will appear on the screen as a player! If we fill the string with zeroes (ATASCII 0), the image in the player will be erased! **By using normal string manipulation techniques, BASIC is forced to move the player image up and down at machine language speeds!** Later, in the next chapter, we will introduce some machine language routines to do the same thing a little more efficiently.

Moving an Object Through a String   Once the string is relocated over the player RAM, how is an object or character moved up and down? The technique used in upcoming Example 8 allows the player to jump from one vertical position to any other in one move. This ability is essential for fast action games. A temporary string buffer (BUFFER$) is used which is the same size (in bytes) as the RAM for one player (128 bytes). Another string of the same length (BLANK$) contains 128 blank characters (ATASCII 0, not space characters). PLR0$ is the string which has been moved to player RAM. There are four steps executed each time the player is moved vertically:

1. Obtain the player's new vertical position in a variable called YPOS.

2. Fill BUFFER$ with blanks:

BUFFER$=BLANK$

3. Move the player image, stored in FRAME$, into the proper vertical position in BUFFER$. FRMSIZE is the number of bytes contained in FRAME$:

BUFFER$(YPOS,YPOS+FRMSIZE-1)=FRAME$

4. Move BUFFER$ to the player RAM area where its contents will be immediately displayed. This step also erases the old player since BUFFER$ is filled with blanks as well as the player image:

PLR0$=BUFFER$

This isn't the only possible method of player movement that uses string manipulation, but it has a number of advantages over the others. By employing the two 128-character strings, BUFFER$ and BLANK$, we give up 256 bytes of memory and gain animation speed. Storing blanks in BLANK$ saves time when erasing the old frame information in BUFFER$ (step 2), and thus a manual clearing of BUFFER$ isn't necessary. Since the old player is automatically erased at the same time the new player is moved to the screen (step 4), there is no screen flicker and the computer doesn't have to remember the player's old position.

This method also makes it very simple to add another step which stores *new* frame information in FRAME$. This provides a rapid means of animating a figure.

If the program you are designing only required the player to be moved up and down in *single steps* rather than in random jumps, it would be possible to eliminate step 2 and combine steps 3 and 4 so FRAME$ is moved directly into PLR0$:

PLR0$(YPOS,YPOS=FRMSIZE-1)=FRAME$

It would be necessary to include one blank space at the beginning of the frame and one at the end so the player would erase itself as it moved. Otherwise, a vertical trail of player pieces would be seen as the frame is moved up and down the screen.

Moving a Player Diagonally

Diagonal motion is simple once horizontal and vertical player motion is understood. It is achieved by combining a number of horizontal

and vertical moves. One horizontal move to the left and one vertical move up results in a diagonal move towards the upper left.

7.3. PLAYER PARAMETERS

Each player has a number of parameters which can be independently controlled. In addition to its motion, the player's color and width can be specified. Also, a player can be given a priority to determine whether it will be displayed in front of or behind a specific playfield. Lastly, there is a way to easily determine when a player has a collision with another player or a playfield!

Selecting Player Color

The color of each player can be independently controlled through the use of its own color register. To change a player's color, just POKE the color value directly into the appropriate RAM location (704–707 — see Table 7.3). Recall from the last chapter that the color is determined by multiplying the selected *hue* by 16 and adding in the *luminance* value:

$$color = hue * 16 + luminance$$

Notice in the following table that each player and its missile share the same color (except when combined to make a fifth player — see upcoming section on Using Five Players).

	Addresses		ATARI's
	Decimal	Hex	Name for it
Player-Missile 0	704	2C0	PCOLR0
Player-Missile 1	705	2C1	PCOLR1
Player-Missile 2	706	2C2	PCOLR2
Player-Missile 3	707	2C3	PCOLR3

Table 7.3: Player-missile color registers (shadow registers.)

These same color registers are also used in GRAPHICS 10 to color the background and three of the playfields. If you use PM graphics in GRAPHICS 10, you will have to be careful that the player doesn't rest on one of these colors, or it will seem to disappear! However, in

GRAPHICS 9 and 11, you will be able to display 20 different colors on the screen at once when using PM graphics.

Unfortunately, unless special machine language routines are used (along with display list interrupts — see Chapter 9), each player can only be shown in one color. Although PM graphics greatly increases animation speed and simplicity, there is a loss of color detail, and this is its major drawback. (See the section on Enabling Multiple Color Players.)

Selecting Player Width

Each player can appear on the screen in one of three sizes: single width, double width, and quadruple width. In double width, for example, each bit in the player definition controls two adjacent pixels instead of one. In the following figure, you can see how our player ball would look in these different sizes.

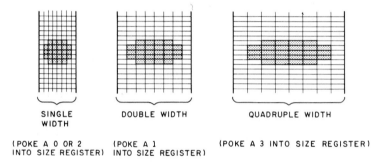

SINGLE WIDTH	DOUBLE WIDTH	QUADRUPLE WIDTH
(POKE A 0 OR 2 INTO SIZE REGISTER)	(POKE A 1 INTO SIZE REGISTER)	(POKE A 3 INTO SIZE REGISTER)

Figure 7.6: Example of different player widths.

Table 7.4 show the addresses of the four player width registers.

	Addresses		ATARI's
	Decimal	Hex	Name for it
Player 0	53256	D008	SIZEP0
Player 1	53257	D009	SIZEP1
Player 2	53258	D00A	SIZEP2
Player 3	53259	D00B	SIZEP3
All Missiles	53260	D00C	SIZEM

Table 7.4: Player-missile width registers.

To change Player 2 to double width, execute the following statement:

```
POKE 53258,1
```

To change Player 3 to quadruple width, execute

```
POKE 53259,3
```

To restore Player 2 to single width (the default when the computer is turned on or **SYSTEM RESET** is pressed), execute *either* of the following statements:

```
POKE 53258,0
POKE 53258,2
```

Priority Control

In most cases, you probably will want your players to appear on top of the background scenery. When this happens, the scenery, which is made up of all the different available playfields[1] and the background color, is always obscured by a passing player. Other effects, however, are possible. For example, the playfields (not the background color) can take precedence over the players. The trees of a dark and dangerous forest could be drawn using playfields. When the walking man then moved across the screen, he would appear to move *behind* the trees. Or you could make a figure enter a house and watch it pass by the windows. For different effects, a combination of the above could be used. The available priority settings are listed in the following table, where a Pn (as in P0) represents Player n and PFn means Playfield n. To change a priority setting, just POKE the indicated value into memory location 623 (26F Hex), which is called GPRIOR.

---

[1]Recall that each color register controls the color of a different playfield, e.g., pixels plotted with Color Register 2 are considered to be Playfield 2. This means that in each graphics mode, the number of playfields available is the same as the number of active color registers for pixel plotting (not counting the background register).

Bit Number:	7	6	5	4	3	2	1	0
Bit Value:	128	64	32	16	8	4	2	1
Priorities								1
Set only one of							1	
these four bits						1		
					1			
Fifth Player Enable				1				
Multiple Color Players			1					
CTIA modes		0	0					
GTIA modes:								
GRAPHICS 9		0	1					
GRAPHICS 10		1	0					
GRAPHICS 11		1	1					

Value in 623	Priorities of Players and Playfields
1	P0 P1 P2 P3 All Playfields
2	P0 P1 All playfields P2 P3
4	All Playfields P0 P1 P2 P3
8	PF0 PF1 P0 P1 P2 P3 PF2 PF3

Table 7.5: Bit values for GPRIOR.

Using Five Players If you don't need any missiles but could use an extra player, add a 16 to the value in 623 (if we don't say Hex, we always mean decimal). This will enable a fifth player by assigning all the missiles the same color, which is obtained from Playfield 3 (SETCOLOR 3 or address 711). Note that this mode affects only the color of the missiles — to move this new player horizontally, you must change *all* the missile registers together (53252 to 53255). Vertical motion can be achieved in the same manner as with the other players.

Enabling Multiple Color Players Although each Player can have only one color, you can create the appearance of players with two colors by creating a single figure made up of two players. For example, a two-tone tree could be created by making the brown trunk out of one player and the leafy green top out of another (see Example 12 in the next chapter).

A third color can be obtained by enabling a special multicolor player mode. This is accomplished by adding a 32 to the chosen priority value

from the above table. Now, where Player 0 overlaps with Player 1, their colors will blend to form a third new color — voilà, a three-color figure! The same blending will occur where Player 2 overlaps Player 3. Also note that the top two bits in GPRIOR enable GTIA modes.

Collision Detection

When using PM graphics in a game, it might be important to know when one player rams into a wall, or when a missile strikes the opponent's player. The ATARI Home Computer provides us with a series of 16 *Collision Registers* that are automatically set when any such collision occurs. These registers are updated every sixtieth of a second, and all collision information remains there until it is cleared by your program.

	Addresses		ATARI's
Function	Decimal	Hex	Name for it
Player 0 to Playfield	53252	D004	P0PF
Player 0 to Player	53260	D00C	P0PL
Player 1 to Playfield	53253	D005	P1PF
Player 1 to Player	53261	D00D	P1PL
Player 2 to Playfield	53254	D006	P2PF
Player 2 to Player	53262	D00E	P2PL
Player 3 to Playfield	53255	D007	P3PF
Player 3 to Player	53263	D00F	P3PL
Missile 0 to Playfield	53248	D000	M0PF
Missile 0 to Player	53256	D008	M0PL
Missile 1 to Playfield	53249	D001	M1PF
Missile 1 to Player	53257	D009	M1PL
Missile 2 to Playfield	53250	D002	M2PF
Missile 2 to Player	53258	D00A	M2PL
Missile 3 to Playfield	53251	D003	M3PF
Missile 3 to Player	53259	D00B	M3PL

Table 7.6: Collision registers for players and missiles.

To determine whether there was a collision, just PEEK into the appropriate collision register. You will have to perform some checks on the value obtained to see what type of collision (if any) occurred. The four right-most bits of the value are used to discover which player or playfield was hit (see Figure 7.7).

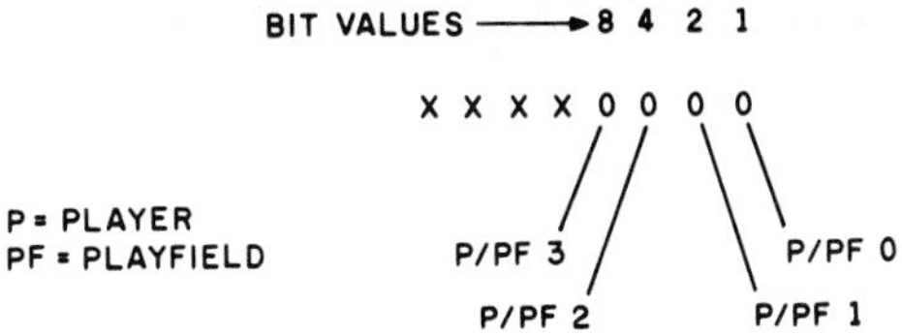

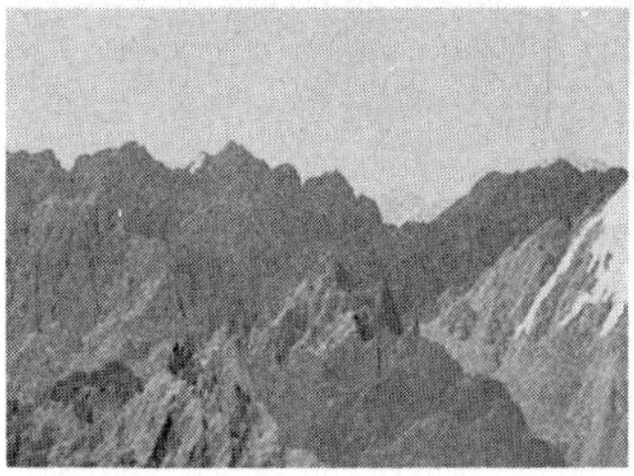

Figure 7.7: Significant bits in collision registers.

Discovering which collisions happened is awkward from within ATARI BASIC since there is no easy way to check selected bits of a byte (no masking of bits). To see if Player 1 collided with Playfield 2, use Table 7.6 to find out which collision register keeps track of all Player 1 collisions with any playfield (it's 53253). Then use the following statement:

```
HIT = PEEK(53253)
```

If the value in HIT is 4, then the anticipated collision occurred. If the value is 5, then there was a collision with Playfield 2 *and* Playfield 0 (bits 4 + 1 = 5). The following short program shows how BASIC can be used to translate the value in HIT to collision information. This program will only give accurate results for values of 15 or less.

```
1Ø PRINT "Enter value in HIT: ";
2Ø INPUT BYTE
3Ø BIT=8
   : REM Start with bit 3
4Ø PRINT "P/PF 3 2 1 Ø" :
   PRINT "ƀƀƀƀ";
5Ø IF BYTE>=BIT THEN
     BYTE=BYTE-BIT:
     PRINT " 1";:
     GOTO 7Ø
     : REM Bit is on, print '1'
6Ø PRINT " Ø";
   : REM Bit is off, print 'Ø'
7Ø BIT=BIT/2
   : REM Next bit
8Ø IF BIT<1 THEN
     PRINT:
     PRINT:
     GOTO 1Ø
9Ø GOTO 5Ø
```

Here is a sample run of this program:

```
Enter value in HIT: ?5
P/PF 3 2 1 0
     0 1 0 1
```

So a value of 5 obtained from a Player-1-to-playfield collision register means that the Player collided with Playfields 2 and 0 since the last time the registers were cleared.

Clearing the Collision Register   Some of the addresses for the Collision Registers might look familiar to you. For example, 53248 (Missile 0 to playfield) is also the horizontal position register for Player 0, as we explained earlier. There is really no RAM at the other end of these addresses, however. The RAM addresses just provide an easy way to pass the information back and forth. The custom ATARI chips are designed so they directly receive the information intended for them and will directly provide requested data. They know when the request was in the form of a POKE or a PEEK and respond accordingly, never allowing information to move in the wrong direction. This means you can read (PEEK) information from the collision registers, but the POKE information is always routed to the horizontal position registers. Likewise, you can't discover the horizontal location of your player by a PEEK into its horizontal position register, or its width by a PEEK into its size register! Furthermore, once a collision value is set, it can't be cleared by a POKE of zero into the register. The only way to clear a collision register is to POKE *any* value into RAM location 53278 (called HITCLR):

```
POKE 53278,0
```

All the collision registers will now be cleared to 0.

Summary

Okay — enough theory and explanation. Let's put this information to use. In the next section we present our Bouncing Ball program, which uses player-missile graphics. With this program as a foundation, you can go on to make dazzling programs using this flexible ATARI feature.

7.4. WATCH THE BOUNCING BALL —
USING PM GRAPHICS

Now that you understand how PM graphics work, let's explore its applications. Example 8 will simulate a bouncing ball. You will be able to enter the initial velocity of the ball and its elasticity coefficient — how

bouncy it will be. The ball (made out of a player) will not only bounce, but will also be displayed using three different frames to give it some added life and allow it to "squash" when it hits.

Graphics Mode and Execution Speed

In many of our player examples, we use GRAPHICS 3 even though PM graphics will work in *any* graphics mode. You may wonder, "Why GRAPHICS 3? It has such a coarse resolution." That is exactly why we chose it — coarse graphics means low memory overhead. In fact, no ATARI graphics mode uses less memory than GRAPHICS 3. Okay, you say, but these programs aren't that long — why conserve memory? Ah . . . do you remember how it's Antic's responsibility to gather display information to update the screen? Well, only one microprocessor can use the address and data buses of the computer at any time. So during this update process Antic halts the 6502 CPU and takes control of the buses for its direct memory access (DMA) *once for each byte of screen memory*. At this time, the 6502 is asleep and can't do *anything*, including BASIC program execution or calculations. The more screen RAM used in a particular graphics mode, the more often Antic halts the CPU, and the longer it takes the CPU to do its chores. This entire update process must happen 60 times a second! So, GRAPHICS 3 (or GRAPHICS 2 which uses the same amount of RAM) yields the fastest execution time for a BASIC program, or a program written in any other language, including assembly language.

The same 6502 slowdown occurs when PM graphics are enabled. Antic must fetch information from PM RAM for display. Once enabled, Antic grabs every byte of PM memory during each update of the screen (60 times a second), even if PM graphics are no longer being used. This amounts to 76,800 wasted machine cycles each second — processing cycles during which the 6502 could be doing something better than sleeping! So, remember to disable PM graphics if you no longer need them in your program but do need the increased CPU speed which this can provide (see the next section).

Initializing Player-Missile Graphics

After setting aside a section of RAM for player-missile memory, there are three POKEs which must be executed to turn on player-missile graphics. The first one tells Antic where to find PM RAM. POKE address 54279 with the memory page where PM RAM begins:

```
POKE 54279, PMPAGE
```

Next, Antic must be told that it should begin grabbing information from PM memory. This is done through address 559 (22F Hex). ATARI

calls this address SDMCTL (Shadow for Direct Memory Access Control). SDMCTL affects not only PM graphics, but the entire screen display as well. Different bits are used for different purposes as shown in Table. 7.7.

SDMCTL

Bit Number:	X	5	4	3	2	1	0	(X = not used)
Bit Value:	X	32	16	8	4	2	1	
Enable Screen DMA		1						
PM Resolution			1					
Enable Player DMA				1				
Enable Missile DMA					1			
Playfield Width						1	1	

Examples							POKE **Value**	
Normal Screen, PM graphics off	1	0	0	0	1	0		= 34
Normal Screen, 2-line PM graphics, Player DMA enabled	1	0	1	0	1	0		= 42
Normal Screen, 2-line PM graphics, Player DMA enabled, Missile DMA enabled	1	0	1	1	1	0		= 46
Normal Screen, 1-line PM graphics, Player DMA enabled, Missile DMA enabled	1	1	1	1	1	0		= 62

Table 7.7: Bit control of SDMCTL.

Bit 5 enables the direct memory access (DMA) using the display list. This bit is normally on (1). But if you turn it off (0), Antic stops fetching display RAM, the screen displays only the background, and the 6502 is no longer halted by Antic for screen updating. This technique can be used if you need to do some extra number crunching and don't mind if the computer looks like it's "out to lunch." Bit 4 controls whether a one- or two-line PM display is to be used: one-line if the bit is on (1); two-line if the bit is off (0). Bit 3 (when on) enables DMA from Player RAM. Bit 2 (when on) enables DMA from Missile RAM. This means that either players *or* missiles *or* both can be used by selecting a combination of bits 2 and 3. Bits 1 and 0 control the width of the Playfield. We will discuss the three playfield widths in Chapter 9. For now, note that bit 1 should be on and bit 0 off for a normal playfield.

Therefore, a POKE of 42 into 559 will leave us with a normal screen, a two-line PM display, and an enabled Player DMA:

POKE 559,42

Since missiles are not being used, this is the value which is used in all PM programs in this book. It would also be all right to enable missile DMA by a POKE of 46 instead of 42, but this would cause Antic to unnecessarily grab an extra 128 bytes of memory every sixtieth of a second, thus slowing the 6502 just a bit more.

The third POKE gives Antic the go ahead to begin sending player-missile information to GTIA so it can be displayed on the screen. Address 53277 (D01D Hex), called GRACTL (Graphics Control) by ATARI, uses the bits as indicated in Table 7.8.

GRACTL

Bit Number:	X	X	X	X	X	2	1	0	(X = not used)
Bit Value:						4	2	1	
Latch Joystick button						1			
Enable Player data transfer							1		
Enable Missile data transfer								1	

Examples				POKE **Value**
Enable Players	0	1	0	= 2
Enable Players, Enable Missiles	0	1	1	= 3

Table 7.8: Bit control of GRACTL.

Bit 2 isn't used for PM graphics. It causes the joystick buttons (TRIG0-TRIG3) to be latched when this bit is on. This means that the button will act as if it is still being pressed even after you have released it. This is useful in interactive programs — normally, if you don't happen to check the button at the instant the operator is pressing it, there is no way to tell if it has been pressed. When latched, the button can be checked later and then released by turning off this bit. Bit 1 is used to enable the transfer of player information to GTIA. Bit 0 is used to enable the transfer of missile information to GTIA. Again, you can choose to use either

players or missiles or both. Since missiles aren't being used in our programs, the value of 2 will be used:

```
POKE 53277,2
```

Player graphics are now enabled and ready to go. Disabling them takes an extra step, however. If there is a player on the screen, setting SDMCTL and GRACTL back to their original values may not make it vanish. (This is because even though no new player information will be sent to GTIA for display, it still has the old player information.) You will need to first move the player off the screen by a POKE of 0 into its horizontal position register, then disabling PM graphics:

```
POKE 53248,0 : REM Move Player 0 to left
                 of screen
POKE 559,34  : REM Disable PM DMA, normal
                 screen display
POKE 53277,0 : REM Disable PM information
                 to GTIA
```

Creating the Frames

Have you ever noticed how cartoons tend to exaggerate life? When a coyote falls off a cliff, he flattens out at the bottom as if he were made of clay. When a rabbit is going to jump over a wall, it will squash down in anticipation of its feat, then stretch out during the jump, and finally flatten when it hits the ground again. These overcompensation techniques add a degree of realism to simple two-dimensional drawings by making them seem more alive. Well, we can do the same thing with a bouncing ball by using three frames: a round ball — for most of the ball's flight; a vertically elongated ball — immediately before and after impact; and a flattened ball — at impact. (See Figure 7.8.) Don't laugh at frames two and three until you have seen this program in action. They look silly but they really work as part of the sequence!

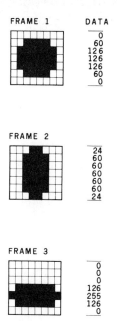

FRAME 1   DATA

```
0
60
126
126
126
60
0
```

FRAME 2

```
24
60
60
60
60
60
24
```

FRAME 3

```
0
0
0
126
255
126
0
```

Figure 7.8: Frames of a bouncing ball.

Example 8

Exercise   Using player-missile graphics and string manipulation, create a simulation of a bouncing rubber ball. Allow the user to enter values from the keyboard for initial velocity and elasticity to see what will happen. Have the program calculate the positions of the ball using the formula for gravity. Use exaggerated animation to create three different frames. Create a sound effect for the bounce of the ball.

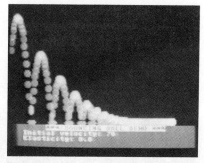

Photo 7.1: The bouncing ball (multiple exposures).

Overview As with some of our previous examples (and all of our subsequent examples), most of the code in this program sets everything up for the relatively short main animation loop. You will notice that we skipped large blocks of line numbers throughout the program; for example, one section is numbered 5000, 5100, 5120, 5130, 5170, 5360. This was intentional, and in later examples every "skipped" line number will be filled in as our programs become more complex. For this reason, it is essential that you *enter every line with its given line number* in the remainder of our example programs. Otherwise, there may be a line numbering conflict and the programs in later chapters may not run correctly. For the same reason, don't add extra lines, even if they are REMarks, into these programs *unless* their line numbers don't end in 0.

```
10 REM *** BOUNCING BALL 1 PROGRAM ***
20 REM                Example 8
30 REM
40 REM Program to demonstrate Player-Missile Graphics using string manipulation
50 REM Copyright (C) 1982 by David Fox and Mitchell Waite
60 REM
70 DIM PLR0$(128):
   GOTO 140: REM This MUST be the first variable in the program
80 REM
100 REM Hi/Lo Byte Calculation
110 HIBYTE=INT(X/256): REM Calculate High Byte
120 LOBYTE=X-HIBYTE*256: REM Calculate Low Byte
130 RETURN
```

Figure 7.9: Listing of Example 8 — lines 10–130.

Heading and High/Low Byte Calculation First look at line 70. This is where the first entry into the variable value table is made with string variable PLR0$. This line must be entered *before* entering any other line containing variables or the program will not work properly. Later, the location of the data for this variable will be moved to coincide with the RAM for Player 0.

The subroutine on lines 100–130 is called when the value of a 16-bit number, X, needs to be separated into high and low bytes. This is necessary when the HIBYTE and/or LOBYTE will be put into memory address by a POKE.

```
140 REM Initialize
150 DIM BLANK$(128),PLR(3),HPLR(3)
160 BLANK$(1)=CHR$(0):
    BLANK$(128)=CHR$(0):
    BLANK$(2)=BLANK$: REM Fill with blanks
170 GRAPHICS 3:
    POKE 752,1:
    PRINT "One moment please...": REM Turn off cursor, print message
190 GOSUB 5000: REM Set up memory locations
220 GOSUB 7000: REM Set up Player area
230 GOSUB 9000: REM Point PLR0$ to Player 0 RAM
240 GOSUB 10000: REM Read frames into RAM
300 PRINT "{CLEAR}bbbbb***bBOUNCINGbBALLbDEMOb***"
310 VEL=70:
    ELASTIC=0.8
320 PRINT "Initial velocity: ";VEL:
    PRINT "Elasticity: ";ELASTIC:
330 REM
```

Figure 7.10: Listing of Example 8 — lines 140–330.

Initialize   This section initializes the program's variables and sends the computer off into four initializing subroutines. On line 150, three variables are D I Mensioned — BLANK$ will be used to clear a temporary player buffer; PLR(*n*) will hold the RAM address of the four players; and HPLR(*n*) will be set to the address of the horizontal position registers for the four players.

On line 160, an ATARI BASIC trick is used to fill BLANK$ with 128 ATASCII 0 (ATARI ASCII) characters. After the first and last characters of BLANK$ are initialized to CHR$(Ø), the magic begins with the statement

BLANK$(2)=BLANK$

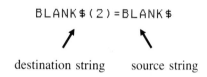

destination string   source string

BASIC copies the first character of the source string into the second character of the destination string, then the second character of the source string into the third character of the destination string, and so on. In this way, each character of the string will be copied from the one before until the string is filled! Try this out — it really works!

Line 170 sets the screen to GRAPHICS 3, turns off the cursor and PRINTs a message on the screen. Lines 180–240 call some special set-up subroutines that we will cover next. Lines 300–320 PRINT information on the screen and set the initial VELocity and ELASTICity values. By elasticity, we mean the percentage of the ball's current velocity which remains when it hits the ground. An elasticity of 0.5 (50 percent) means that the ball maintains half its current velocity and loses the other half every time it bounces. An elasticity of 1.0 (100 percent) is a perfect bouncing ball. It never loses any energy and will bounce forever. The closest to perfect we have seen is about 0.85 (85 percent) for a toy super ball. An elasticity of 0 (0 percent) is a ball that will not bounce at all — it just hits the ground and dies.

```
5000  REM Set Up Memory Locations
5100  READ FRAMES,FRMSIZE,NUMPLRS
5120  PLRFRMMEM=FRAMES*FRMSIZE
5130  FRAMEMEM=PLRFRMMEM*NUMPLRS
5170  DIM BUFFER$(128),FRAME$(FRMSIZE),FRAMEMEM$(FRAMEMEM)
5360  RETURN
5370  REM
20000 REM FRAME DATA
20030 REM
20040 REM Number of Frames, Frame Size, Number of Players
20050 REM . (Bouncing Ball)
20060 DATA 3,7,1
```

Figure 7.11:   Listing of Example 8 — lines 5000–5370, 20000–20060.

Set Up Memory Locations   This subroutine reserves memory space (in the form of strings) for the frame data. Line 5100 reads the number of frames used in the sequence (FRAMES = 3), the size of each frame in bytes (FRMSIZE = 7), and the number of players used in this program (NUMPLRS = 1). The data is located on line 20060. On 5120, the variable PLRFRMMEM (PLayeR FRaMe MEMory) is set to the total number of bytes necessary to store the frames for each player. Line 5130 sets FRAMEMEM (FRAME MEMory) to the total number of frame bytes needed for all players.

On line 5170, string memory is reserved for three variables. BUFFER$ is the temporary buffer used in vertical player movement (see earlier explanation in section on vertical player movement). FRAME$ will hold the current frame to be displayed and FRAMEMEM$ holds all frames for every player.

```
7000  REM Initialize Player-Missile Graphics
7010  TEMP=PEEK(106)-8: REM Set aside Player-Missile area
7020  POKE 54279,TEMP: REM Tell ANTIC where PM RAM is
7030  PMBASE=256*TEMP: REM Find PM Base address
7040  FOR I=0 TO 3
7050     PLR(I)=PMBASE+128*I+512: REM Set addresses of Players
7060     HPLR(I)=53248+I: REM Horizontal Player Position registers
7070  NEXT I
7080  POKE 559,42: REM Set PM 2 line resolution, Players enabled
7090  POKE 704,12*16+8: REM Color ball green
7100  POKE 53277,2: REM Enable Player display
7120  RETURN
7130  REM
```

Figure 7.12:   Listing of Example 8 — lines 7000–7130.

Initialize Player-Missile Graphics   In this section, memory is reserved for the players, and PM graphics are enabled. As we mentioned before, it takes extra work on Antic's part to move the information in player RAM to GTIA for display on the screen. When PM graphics are turned on, the 6502 is slowed down just a bit more.

Line 7010 reserves four pages of memory for the player and four pages for the screen. GRAPHICS 3 only occupies 240 bytes of memory so why use four pages for screen RAM when only one is necessary? Recall that PM RAM must begin on an even 1 K boundary (in double-line mode). If necessary, the wasted memory could be used for storage of frame information or other data.

Line 7020 tells Antic where to find PM RAM by placing the starting memory page number (TEMP) in 54279 (D407 Hex). The actual RAM address of PM RAM is calculated and stored in PMBASE in line 7030.

In lines 7040–7070, two arrays are initialized. PLR(I) holds the RAM address for Players 0 through 3 (see Figure 7.4). HPLR(I) holds the address of the horizonal position register for each player.

In line 7080, SDMCTL, address 559 is initialized and Antic begins DMA (direct memory access) from player RAM. A POKE of 42 into 559 leaves us with a normal screen, a two-line PM display, and enabled player DMA (but no missiles).

In line 7100, Antic starts sending player information to GTIA so it can be displayed on the screen when GRACTL, 53277, is POKEd with a 2.

```
9000  REM Point PLR0$ to Player 0 RAM
9010  STARP=PEEK(140)+PEEK(141)*256: REM Start of String Array area
9020  VVTP=PEEK(134)+PEEK(135)*256: REM Start of Variable Value Table
9030  OFFSET=PLR(0)-STARP: REM Calculate offset from String Array to Player 0
9040  X=OFFSET:
      GOSUB 110
9050  POKE VVTP+2,LOBYTE: REM Poke offset of string into Variable Value Table
9060  POKE VVTP+3,HIBYTE: REM This points the first string (PLR0$) to PLR(0)
9070  RETURN
9080  REM
```

Figure 7.13: Listing of Example 8 — lines 9000–9080.

Point PLR0$ to Player 0 RAM   Here is where BASIC is tricked into moving a string variable to coincide with Player 0 RAM. In lines 9010–9020 the locations of the string/array area and the variable value table are calculated. In 9030 the number of bytes from the beginning of the string/array area to the start of Player 0 RAM is stored in OFFSET. Line 9040 uses the HI/LO byte subroutine on OFFSET so these values can be POKEd into the variable value table and the first variable in the program is now relocated! See the earlier section ''Moving a Player Vertically With BASIC'' for more information on this technique.

```
10000  REM Read in Frame Data
10090  FOR J=1 TO PLRFRMMEM
10100     READ BYTE
10110     FRAMEMEM$(J,J)=CHR$(BYTE)
10120  NEXT J
10130  RETURN
10140  REM

21000  REM Frame Data for Bouncing Ball
21010  REM Frame 1
21020  DATA 0,60,126,126,126,60,0
21030  REM Frame 2
21040  DATA 24,60,60,60,60,60,24
21050  REM Frame 3
21060  DATA 0,0,0,126,255,126,0
```

Figure 7.14: Listing of Example 8 — lines 10000–10140, 21000–21060.

Read in Frame Data   This loop reads the frame data for the bouncing ball into the string FRAMEMEM$. Each BYTE is converted to a character with CHR$.

```
700 REM Move Player 0 to Left of Screen
710 POKE HPLR(0),0
730 RETURN
740 REM
```

Figure 7.15: Listing of Example 8 — lines 700–740.

Move Player 0 to Left of Screen   This subroutine will move Player 0 off the left side of the screen. This routine will be expanded in later programs.

```
400 REM Main Animation Loop
410 BOTTOM=91:
    XPOS=40:
    TIME=0.5:
    HORIZ=0.75
420 GOSUB 700: REM Move Player off screen
430 IF ELASTIC<=0.1 THEN
    SNDFLAG=1
440 YPOS=BOTTOM-(VEL*TIME-16*TIME*TIME):
    FRMNO=1
450 IF YPOS>82 AND VEL>30 THEN
    FRMNO=2
460 IF YPOS>=BOTTOM THEN
    YPOS=BOTTOM:
    VEL=VEL*ELASTIC:
    TIME=0:
    FRMNO=1:
    IF VEL>14 THEN
      FRMNO=3
470 IF XPOS>220 OR YPOS<=1 THEN 600
480 POKE HPLR(0),XPOS
490 FRAME$=FRAMEMEM$((FRMNO-1)*FRMSIZE+1,FRMNO*FRMSIZE): REM Select correct frame
500 BUFFER$=BLANK$: REM Fill Buffer with blanks
510 BUFFER$(YPOS,YPOS+FRMSIZE-1)=FRAME$: REM Move current frame into buffer
520 PLR0$=BUFFER$: REM Move buffer into Player 0 RAM
530 XPOS=XPOS+HORIZ
540 IF YPOS=BOTTOM AND (VEL+SNDFLAG>0.5) THEN
    SOUND 1,250,10,14:
    SNDFLAG=0:
    SOUND 1,0,0,0
550 IF VEL>0.5 THEN
    TIME=TIME+0.15:
    GOTO 440
560 HORIZ=HORIZ-0.01:
    IF HORIZ>0 THEN
      FRMNO=1:
      GOTO 470
570 REM
```

Figure 7.16:   Listing of Example 8 — lines 400–570.

Main Animation Loop   This section controls the movement of the ball on the screen. There is some mathematics involved to calculate the positions of the ball as it is being affected by gravity and its elasticity, but don't worry about them if you aren't a math person. Just skim the parts you don't understand; we promise not to test you later.

On line 410 four constants are initialized. BOTTOM is the lowest vertical screen position to which the ball will go and is analogous to the floor. XPOS is the starting horizontal position of the ball (off the screen to the left). TIME holds the elapsed time from the moment the ball is launched or bounced. HORIZ holds the horizontal velocity. This value is constant until the ball begins to roll.

The ball is moved to the left of the screen in 420, and the value of ELASTIC is checked in 430. Later, when input is accepted from the keyboard, this line makes sure that if the elasticity is very low, there is at least one bouncing noise when the ball hits the ground.

The important loop begins at 440 with the gravity calculation. The effect gravity has on the motion of an object can be represented by the formula

$$-16*TIME^2$$

or

$$-16*TIME*TIME$$

This shows the acceleration of gravity over time. TIME*TIME is used rather than the exponent function ($\char`^$) to increase calculation speed. By subtracting the above value from the current velocity (VEL) multiplied by TIME, the current height of the ball off the ground is obtained:

$$VEL*TIME-16*TIME*TIME$$

This must be subtracted from the value of the ground (BOTTOM) to convert the number to screen coordinates:

$$YPOS=BOTTOM-(VEL*TIME-16*TIME*TIME)$$

FRMNO, the number of the current frame to be displayed, is set to 1 (the round ball).

In line 450 the YPOS and VEL are checked; if the ball is near the ground and the velocity is high enough, the vertically elongated ball frame is chosen to exaggerate the vertical motion.

Line 460 checks for contact with the ground. If the ball has hit (YPOS will be greater than or equal to BOTTOM), the ball's VELocity is recalculated by multiplying the current VELocity by ELASTIC. With the initial ELASTICity of 0.8, 80 percent of the current velocity will be conserved and 20 percent lost. TIME is set to 0 since as far as gravity is concerned, the ball is first starting out and was thrown by the ground. The frame number is set to 1 unless the velocity is high enough to cause the ball to flatten, at which time it is set to 3.

Line 470 checks to see if the ball is still on the screen. If not, the animation loop is exited, and new values can be entered from the routine starting at 600.

Now that all the values are calculated, the ball will be positioned on the screen. The horizontal position of the player is set in line 480. On 490 the correct frame is transferred from FRAMEMEM$ (where all three frames are kept) to FRAME$. This is the same technique used in the Walking Man program (Example 2) from Chapter 5. Lines 500–520 position FRAME$ at the proper vertical position in player RAM as

described in a previous section, "Moving a Player Vertically With BASIC." The ball is now in place.

In line 530 the horizontal position of the ball (XPOS) is incremented. Line 540 turns on the bounce sound if the ball has just struck bottom and the velocity is high enough. If SNDFLAG was set in line 430 (low elasticity), the sound will be heard on the first bounce.

In line 550, TIME is incremented by 0.15 and the loop continues at line 440 if the velocity is greater than 0.5. A different value can be substituted for the 0.15 to simulate the ball bouncing in slow or fast motion. Use a smaller TIME increment to make the ball move in tinier increments (slow motion).

Finally, line 560 will be reached if the velocity of the ball is so slow that it can only roll rather than bounce. HORIZ is decremented to simulate the effect of friction on the ball's horizontal velocity. If the ball is still rolling (HORIZ will be greater than 0), frame 1 is selected, and the program jumps to 470 since the bouncing calculations of 440–460 are no longer needed. If the ball has stopped rolling, the program will fall through to the routine at 600.

```
600  REM Get Parameters for Ball
610  GOSUB 700
620  POKE 752,0: REM Turn on cursor
630  PRINT "(CLEAR)Enter initial velocity: ";
640  TRAP 630:
     INPUT VEL
650  PRINT "Enter the ball's elasticity (a number":
     PRINT " from 0-1 [or more]): ";
660  INPUT ELASTIC
670  POKE 752,1:
     PRINT " ";: REM Turn off cursor
680  TRAP 40000:
     GOTO 400
690  REM
```

Figure 7.17: Listing of Example 8 — lines 600–690.

Get Parameters for Ball   This section of the program is executed after every ball finishes bouncing to allow you to enter your own velocity and elasticity values. The ball is moved off the screen in line 610. The TRAP command is used in line 640 to trap any INPUT errors which may occur. If there are any, the program will jump to line 630 and the values can be reentered. In line 670, after executing the "cursor off" POKE, at least one character must be PRINTed before the cursor vanishes. Line 680 turns off error trapping by setting TRAP to a nonexistent line number, and the animation loop is restarted.

Modifications   Try the following modifications:
1. Experiment with different velocities and elasticities. Try a velocity of 1 and an elasticity greater than 1.0. Did you ever see the Walt Disney movie, *The Absent-Minded Professor*, which is about an amazing

substance called Flubber? This flying rubber *gained* velocity every time it bounced.

2. Change the constant (16) in the gravity equation (line 440) to simulate a ball falling on a different planet with stronger or weaker gravity.

3. Modify the program so there is a ceiling as well as a floor off which the ball can bounce. Will the ball speed up if you use an elasticity greater than or equal to 1.0?

Commercially Available Games and Player-Missile Graphics

Almost every action game now appearing on the market includes the use of player-missile graphics. The only exceptions are those games which are straight conversions from computers which don't have players or sprites (e.g., the Apple II). The use of players usually results in extra color and much smoother action. The game Threshold (by Warren Schwader and Ken Williams of On-Line Systems) is an example of an Apple conversion which doesn't use PM graphics. As do most conversions, it uses GRAPHICS 8, the closest mode to the Apple's 280 × 192 screen. The object of the game is to destroy the endless waves of attacking aliens. The first wave is made up of bird-like creatures. The flapping of their wings is achieved with four different frames, much like our Example 1. The motion of the figures and their animation is done with a technique called byte move (or playfield animation). Rather than plotting individual pixels on the screen, entire bytes (8 pixels wide) are rapidly moved into screen memory to create the effect. All the color on the screen is a result of artifacts. Even though the only special ATARI feature used is sound, the game still plays well with more than enough action.

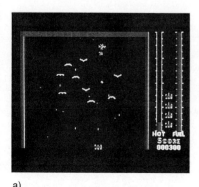

a)

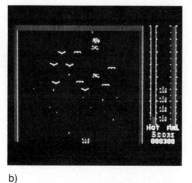

b)

Photo 7.2: These frames are from the game Threshold. (Copyright (c) 1982 by On-Line Systems.)

Another game, Apple Panic (by Olaf Lubeck of Broderbund Software, Inc.), uses a combination of PM graphics and map mode graphics. The object of the game is to avoid and destroy the apples. This is accomplished by pounding holes in the bricks. When an apple walks by, it falls into your trap. Then you must pound the apple on its head with the hammer, driving it into oblivion. The little man is made up of all four players in the single-line resolution mode (thus the different colors). The game uses graphics mode Antic E (also affectionately known as GRAPHICS 7 1/2 by ATARI 400 and 800 programmers). Known as GRAPHICS 15 on the ATARI XL Home Computers, it has the same number of colors (four) and horizontal resolution as GRAPHICS 7 but twice the vertical resolution (160 × 192). The wandering apples were drawn with a technique similar to the one used in Threshold using playfield animation. Each time an apple moves, it is Exclusive ORed (XOR) with the background. When one passes in front of a ladder, rather than temporarily erasing the background, the ladder shows through the apple in the color of the bricks. With this technique, it is not necessary to remember what the background looked like when it needs to be restored.

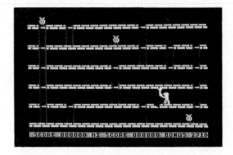

Photo 7.3: A frame from the game Apple Panic. (Copyright (c) 1982 by Broderbund Software, Inc.)

In ATARI's PAC-MAN™, each ghost is the chomping PAC-MAN as well as a player. This was accomplished by combining the four missiles into a fifth player. Notice the two lines of GRAPHICS 0 text at the top of the screen.

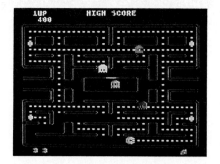

Photo 7.4: A frame from the game PAC-MAN. (Trademark of Bally Midway Mfg. Co., licensed by Namco-America, Inc., Copyright (c) 1982, Atari, Inc.)

Summary

ATARI player-missile graphics can be an extremely powerful animation tool. Although somewhat awkward to set up, once implemented in your program, they are capable of effects that would be much more difficult to achieve by other means.

Up to this point in our examples, everything can be accomplished using BASIC programming. In the next chapter, we introduce you to three of our black box machine language routines which enable us to use the ATARI Home Computer's special features most effectively. Don't let the words "machine language" scare you away from trying out these examples! Remember, you do not need to understand anything about assembly language or machine language to use our routines. Black box means that all you see are the results without seeing the mechanics of production.

Chapter 8

Using Machine Language Routines In BASIC Programs

We have come about as far as we can with pure BASIC programs, so in this chapter a modification is made to the previous program, Example 8, by adding two machine language routines to it. *Wait!* Don't go away! We know we're talking about something that is terrifying to many BASIC programmers, but believe it or not, machine language routines are not monsters waiting to confuse and befuddle you or erase programs from your disks! We will first introduce you to a couple of very friendly machine language routines that are going to change your attitude permanently. For those of you who speak ''assembly,'' complete listings of the assembly language source code for these routines are included in Appendix F. As for the rest of you, don't worry; it's going to be painless because all of our machine language routines are like black box machines — you don't need to understand their inner workings to take advantage of them. We will show you how to coax them into your programs and how to feed them parameters so they will do your bidding. In essence, these machine language routines will expand ATARI BASIC by adding new statements that will allow control over some of the most powerful but elusive ATARI features.

Four separate routines are introduced in this chapter, and another two are introduced in Chapter 9. The simplest routine will rapidly fill any portion of memory with a selected byte value. Then we'll provide you with a routine to move the players to any point on the screen, one to automatically move frame information into the players at a selected rate, and one to assign a horizontal velocity to the players.

8.1. WHAT IS MACHINE LANGUAGE?

Machine language is a series of number codes and memory addresses that the CPU understands as a program. Each code, actually a byte, will cause the CPU to do one tiny task. Because these tasks are so small (it requires a lot of them for anything interesting to happen), machine language is called a low-level language. BASIC, which is really a large machine language program, is called a *high-level* language because each

of its commands causes the CPU to execute a flurry of its tiny tasks. The main advantage of machine language is its speed of execution. This is essential for fast-action game and graphics. Machine language's main disadvantage is the amount of effort the programmer must put forth to produce the finished product.

To make it easier for us humans to produce the byte codes of machine language, assembly language was invented. This allows the programmer to write programs using short words called *mnemonics*, which have more meaning for us than a bunch of numbers would. When the assembly language programmer has completed writing this program, called the *source code*, it is processed by another program called an *assembler*. The assembler checks the mnemonics for errors and produces the final product by assembling all the information in the source code into the numbers which the CPU can understand. These number bytes are called the *object code*, *machine code*, or *machine language* and can be directly executed by the CPU when stored in the computer's memory. Routines, then, are originally a list of letters and numbers that get boiled down to just plain numbers.

Using Our Black Box Machine Language Routines

We keep on stressing how easy it is to use our machine language routines and that they have been designed for programmers who don't necessarily know assembly language. Once they have been entered into memory, most of our routines use a reserved section of RAM for a parameter table. To talk to the routines or check on their progress, use BASIC PEEK and POKE statements to access this table. To make it easier to remember which table locations do what, their memory locations are assigned to BASIC variable names, and in some cases, to arrays (e.g., to control the horizontal position of Players 0 through 3, we POKE values into table locations stored in array variables HPLR(0) through HPLR(3)).

All of our routines are designed to be as flexible as possible rather than specific to our demonstration programs. This means they will be somewhat longer than other less versatile routines designed for a single application. Our routines do, however, have some limitations — there are bound to be some features which we didn't include that would be perfect for your dream program. Just think of our routines as some important programming tools to add to your ATARI workshop.

If you are an assembly language programmer, feel free to either modify our routines or to use them as guides for creating your own. The complete source code listings for our routines are found in Appendix F and are also included on our program diskette.

Entering the Routines Into Memory

There are different methods for getting the machine language program into memory. Programs which are pure machine code can be stored in cartridges, diskettes, or cassettes. They are simply loaded in and executed. We will be using a mixture of BASIC and machine language, so two different types of program information must get into memory. For disk owners, it would be a simple task for the BASIC program to pull the machine language routine off the disk and into a reserved section of memory. But what about those cassette recorder owners who aren't so fortunate? One solution would be to store the machine code bytes as DATA statements in your BASIC program. This way everything is loaded at the same time from disk or cassette. The BASIC program would then POKE each number into consecutive memory locations. There are two disadvantages to this method. If the routine is long, it could take quite a while to POKE each byte into RAM. A more serious problem is that the machine language routine will be occupying precious memory space *two times* — once as DATA statements (where each number actually takes up seven bytes) and once in its reserved RAM.

ATARI BASIC provides a simple solution. The routine bytes can be stored in strings! Each byte has a value from 0 to 255 and can be converted to a character representation using the CHR$ function. By using the ATARI BASIC ADR function (which returns the address of a string's data), the machine language routine can be located and executed. The above problems are solved with this technique. The routines are moved into the strings at machine language speed when the strings are initialized, and a byte stored as a character only takes up one byte of RAM rather than seven. In addition, memory for the routines is automatically reserved by BASIC when the string is DIMensioned.

Now, how do we get those bytes into strings? We have written a String Loader BASIC program for you which will read bytes from DATA statements and then stuff them into strings. These strings, complete with line numbers, can be outputted to disk, cassette, or even the screen. It's a simple task then to merge these saved strings into your BASIC programs. The only real difficulty is that some of the routines are long — the longest two contain about 300 bytes each! There are a few ways to get around entering all these bytes into DATA statements: enter and assemble the source code yourself, talk a quick-typing friend into entering the DATA, or purchase the program diskette from Adventure International.

The listing and explanation of our String Loader program is found in Appendix D. Now would be a good time to enter it so you can convert our first machine language routine, MFILL, into a string. (The data bytes for MFILL are included in the String Loader listing.) MFILL will allow you to rapidly fill a section of RAM of any size with the byte value of your choice. MFILL is used in the rest of our program examples as a utility program, a program designed to make some frequently used function

easier and more efficient. This routine could be replaced with some simple BASIC code, but then it would execute *much* more slowly.

Flashing with Memory Fill

Now for some fun! We will use MFILL in a program called Flash to create some wonderful patterns on your screen. Type NEW and enter the MFILL routine string (created by the String Loader Program, Appendix D) into memory. Use the following commands depending on whether you used the String Loader program to save it on disk or cassette:

```
ENTER "D:MFILL.STR"   (disk)
ENTER "C:"            (cassette)
```

Next, enter the following statements (of course, lines 11610–11620 containing the MFILL string will have just been entered). Since it isn't necessary to represent the routine's string characters (line 11620) in our listings, we will indicate where they belong with the phrase "<<<Routine String goes here >>>" in this and all subsequent programs.

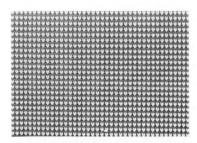

```
10   REM * * * F L A S H * * *
20   REM
30   REM Program to demonstrate the Memory Fill Machine Language Routine
40   REM
50   REM Copyright (C) 1982 by David Fox and Mitchell Waite
60   REM
100  REM Initialize
110  GRAPHICS 0
120  GOSUB 11610: REM Store routine
130  SCREEN=PEEK(88)+PEEK(89)*256: REM Address for start of screen memory
140  REM
200  REM Main Loop
210  FOR I=0 TO 255
220     TEMP=USR(MFILL,SCREEN,960,I): REM Call routine
230  NEXT I
240  GOTO 210
250  REM
11600 REM Routine
11610 DIM MFILL$(41)
11620 MFILL$(1)=" <<<Routine String goes here>>>  "
11630 MFILL=ADR(MFILL$): REM Find address of routine
11640 RETURN
```

Figure 8.1: Listing of FLASH.

Go ahead and run the program. Phew! What's happening? The entire screen immediately begins flashing through all of the characters, first in normal and then in inverse video. The characters fill the screen so rapidly that it's difficult to make out each one. Let's look at the listing and find out why. After the graphics mode in line 110 is chosen, the subroutine at 11600–11640 is called. This initializes the memory fill routine and discovers its location in RAM by using the ADR function. This address is then saved in the variable MFILL (named after guess what).

In line 130, the address of screen RAM is calculated. This address will correspond to the first byte of screen memory or the upper left corner of the screen. To check this, stop your program and clear the screen. Then POKE a value into SCREEN and watch the corner:

POKE SCREEN,33

You'll see an 'A' appear in that corner because 33 is the position in the ROM character set for 'A' (see Chapter 5 on user-defined character sets).

In lines 210–230, a FOR/NEXT loop is used to cycle through all the possible byte values. Line 220 calls the machine language routine and passes it the needed information (parameters). Here is the syntax for using MFILL:

TEMP=USR(MFILL,*start,length,byte*)

The variable TEMP is necessary for proper syntax of the USR function; however, in this case it is a dummy variable (although a value could be passed to BASIC from a routine, we aren't doing so here). USR is the BASIC function which allows the use of machine language routines. The first value within the parentheses is the address of the routine (MFILL). When USR is used, there must always be an address here. The next three parameters tell MFILL where in memory the filling should *start*, how many bytes should be filled (*length*), and what *byte* value should be used to fill memory. Any parameters after the first one have been established by the routine's programmer. Here is line 220 again:

```
220 TEMP=USR(MFILL,SCREEN,960,I)
    : REM Call routine
```

The address of the first byte to be filled is SCREEN, the beginning of screen memory. Since the entire screen is to be filled, the length parameter must equal the number of bytes in screen RAM. By checking Table 5.1, we discover that there are 960 bytes in a GRAPHICS 0 screen. The byte value (I) will be controlled by the FOR/NEXT loop and will cycle through all the possible values. So, this line says "call the machine language routine located at address MFILL and fill the 960 bytes starting at SCREEN with the value in I." Once the FOR/NEXT loop is completed, it starts over again with 0.

Flashing in Other Graphics Modes   Since GRAPHICS Ø is being used, the values which are filling the screen are interpreted as characters. If you use a different GRAPHICS mode (change line 110), some beautiful and colorful patterns will appear. Use Table 5.1 to determine the number of bytes in screen memory for the mode you are using. Notice that with the higher resolution graphics modes, the screen takes much longer to fill — you can actually see a "curtain" of new colors fall from the top of the screen.

Summary

Now that you have successfully implemented a machine language routine in a program, we can proceed to much more useful and powerful applications. Notice that you never had to understand exactly how the machine language routine worked! Our next goal is to make ATARI's player graphics more accessible and controllable from within BASIC.

8.2.   MOVING PLAYERS WITH PMOVER

In this section we will introduce a machine language routine to move a player or players to specific positions on the screen. Since we have already successfully moved players without machine language, you may be wondering, "Why bother?" This routine, the first part of an integrated set of machine language routines, can accomplish certain tasks more rapidly than BASIC and automatically carry them out *while* your program is executing BASIC statements. The power this places at your disposal will soon become apparent.

Synchronizing the Screen

Aside from all this, a number of other advantages are gained with the use of our next routine, called PMOVER. In the Bouncing Ball program (Example 8), a single, very small player was moved on the screen. When a large player (or even worse, several large players) moves horizontally across the screen, a tearing effect is sometimes observed. This is caused by a synchronization problem between the player's movement and the updating of the screen. To understand how this works, let's talk about how the screen is updated. As we mentioned in Chapter 2, the television picture is actually painted by an electronic beam. The beam starts in the upper left corner of the screen and paints one horizontal scan line to the right. Then it's turned off and returned to the left side of the screen where it paints the second horizontal scan line. There are actually 262 horizontal lines on the screen which need to be painted, 192 of which make up the ATARI playfield. After the 262nd line is painted, the electron beam must return to the upper left corner in preparation for painting the next complete screen. This entire process happens 60 times a second, which means it takes one-sixtieth of a second to paint each screen frame! (See Figure 8.2.)

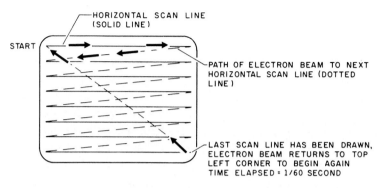

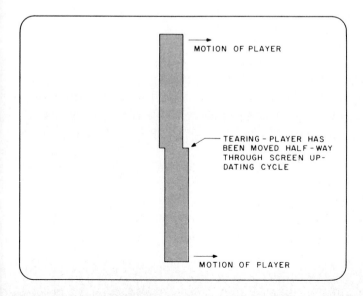

Figure 8.2: Screen updating cycle.

Imagine a very tall player being moved horizontally from left to right across the screen. What would happen if this player was moved *while* the screen was being updated (redrawn by the electron beam)? It is possible that the top half of the player will be in the original position while the bottom half is updated in the new position. Of course, when the beam gets to the top of the screen, the top half of the player will also be updated. But if this happens over and over as the player is moved, it will look like the player is being torn in half (see Figure 8.3).

Figure 8.3: Tearing of a player during horizontal motion.

Vertical Interrupts

The problem intensifies when two or more players have been combined into one larger player for increased color or resolution. The combined player must appear to move as *one* player, or it may risk losing its solidity as some parts try to catch up with others. This will happen if we attempt to use BASIC to move them simultaneously. BASIC just isn't fast enough to allow the perfectly synchronized movement of players. That's the problem, and here comes our machine language routine to the rescue! The first part of the solution is to execute all horizontal player movements during the period of time (about 1400 microseconds) when the electron beam is returning from the bottom of the screen to the upper corner, called the *vertical blank* or *vertical retrace* period. In this way, the players will never move horizontally *during* a screen update, and the problem of tearing is solved. The second part of the solution is to have the machine language routine move all desired players vertically with one call to the routine rather than a separate call for each player. All players will appear to arrive at their new vertical positions together. Since there is no tearing problem with vertical player movement, the VBLANK (vertical blank) isn't needed and vertical movement can be executed immediately.

Fortunately, the people who designed the ATARI Home Computer made the first part to this solution easy to implement through the use of the vertical blank interrupt (VBI). During vertical blank, the 6502 is interrupted with whatever it is doing (e.g., calculating the number of peanuts which will fit in a Volkswagen), and the ATARI OS performs all of its updating of hardware registers by grabbing information from shadow registers, reading joysticks and paddles, incrementing the real-time clock, etc. It is possible to add in our own program, which will be executed after the OS does its updating tasks.

In PMOVER we created eight new shadow registers (see Chapter 7 for an explanation on shadow registers), one for the horizontal and vertical position of each player. By POKEing information into these locations, PMOVER is told where to move the players. These shadow registers, however, are ignored until all POKEs have been completed. At that time, PMOVER is called (activated) and told which player or players are to be moved. There are actually two separate programs in PMOVER. One is a normal machine language routine which vertically moves each player to its new position. The other is a vertical blank interrupt routine which will fetch the horizontal position from our shadow register during the next VBLANK and store it in the appropriate player's horizontal position register. All this happens so rapidly that all the players seem to appear at their new screen locations. In addition to eliminating horizontal tearing, BASIC's inherent lack of speed is bypassed by avoiding a series of consecutive calls to the routine to move each player separately. The call to the routine looks like this:

```
TEMP=USR(PMOVER,FLAG)
```

The value in FLAG determines which player or players will be moved during the next VBLANK. The table below lists the addresses which PMOVER uses and the bit values indicating which players are to be moved.

Variable Name	Offset From PARAMBASE	Address (Decimal)	Description
PARAMBASE		1024	Start of Parameter area
PMBAS	0	1024	Page address of Player 0 (hi byte)
PMBUF	1	1025,1026	Low and High bytes of Player Buffer
HPLR(0)	6	1030	Player 0 Horizontal Shadow Register
HPLR(1)	7	1031	Player 1 Horizontal Shadow Register
HPLR(2)	8	1032	Player 2 Horizontal Shadow Register
HPLR(3)	9	1033	Player 3 Horizontal Shadow Register
VPLR(0)	10	1034	Player 0 Vertical Shadow Register
VPLR(1)	11	1035	Player 1 Vertical Shadow Register
VPLR(2)	12	1036	Player 2 Vertical Shadow Register
VPLR(3)	13	1037	Player 3 Vertical Shadow Register

Bits of FLAG byte										
Bit Number:	*X*	*X*	*X*	*X*	*3*	*2*	*1*	*0*	*(X = not used)*
Bit Value:					*8*	*4*	*2*	*1*	
FLAG for Player #:					3	2	1	0	

Examples — FLAG **Value**

Move Player 1 only					0	0	1	0	= 2
Move Players 0, 2 & 3					1	1	0	1	= 13
Move all Players					1	1	1	1	= 15

Table 8.1: Parameters for PMOVER.

All of our machine language routines will be utilizing a parameter table starting at 1024 for shadow registers and to hold temporary values. This memory is normally used by the OS when reading or writing to a cassette recorder (you can't use your recorder *during* the execution of these programs). The above table shows only the parameter table entries used by PMOVER. The first column contains the variable names we

assigned to each parameter table address. The first three addresses listed in the table are used only during the initialization selection of a program. PARAMBASE is set to the base address of the parameter table (1024), PMBAS will hold the page address (high byte) of Player 0 so PMOVER knows where the players are, and PMBUF will hold the two byte address of the temporary player buffer. This buffer will be used in much the same way as BUFFER$ in the Bouncing Ball program. When a player is to be moved vertically, all 128 bytes of it are copied into this buffer. Then, using the information in its vertical position shadow register, it is copied back into Player RAM with the appropriate vertical offset. This is the fastest method when the player needs to jump around the screen. Each vertical relocation requires moving 256 bytes of RAM (128 into the buffer from player RAM and 128 out of the buffer back into player RAM). See Figure 8.4.

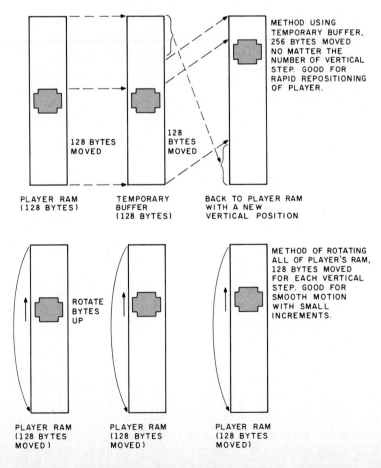

Figure 8.4: Two methods for moving a player.

An alternate method would be to slide or rotate all of the player's RAM up or down a byte at a time directly *within* the player's RAM (no buffer). Each vertical step would require the movement of 128 bytes of RAM as each byte moves one position up or down. As a result, this technique executes more rapidly when the player needs to move up or down only one vertical increment. The farther the player must move, the longer it will take, since the player must occupy every intermediate position between its starting location and its destination. The player will appear to slide smoothly to its new position rather than just materializing there. This technique would not work in our Bouncing Ball program, however, as it would take too long for the player to arrive at each new position, and the sliding effect isn't appropriate.

These two methods are excellent as general-purpose player movers, where the height of the player may not be known. When sliding the player is acceptable and you know exactly how tall the player is, a third technique, mentioned in the last chapter, may be more efficient. This would be to include a blank byte immediately above and below the player object as part of the object. Then, when the object is moved in single steps either up or down, this blank space would erase the object in the original position. We used a similar technique with the falling bomb in Example 4 when the bomb erased itself as it moved down the screen.

The array HPLR(n) holds the addresses of the shadow registers for the horizontal position of Player n and the array VPLR(n) holds the vertical position shadow register for Player n. Here is an example of how PMOVER might be used. If you wanted to move both Players 0 and 1 together, you would add the following to your program (assuming the variables have already been initialized):

```
100 POKE HPLR(0),100
110 POKE HPLR(1),108    : REM Player 1 is
                              adjacent to
                              Player 0
120 POKE VPLR(0),50
130 POKE VPLR(1),50
140 TEMP=USR(PMOVER,3) : REM Move Players 0
                              and 1
```

Notice that the position of Player 1 is eight steps over from Player 0. Since the players in normal width are eight pixels wide, this will place them adjacent to each other. The two players would appear in their new positions on the next updated screen.

Setting Up Vertical Blank Interrupts

After our routine is in memory, its VBI (vertical blank interrupt) section must be connected to the "plumbing" of the existing ATARI VBI routines. The program flow during the vertical blank period is similar to the flow of water through pipes. To connect additional "fixtures" to the existing pipes, a special sequence of steps must be followed to avoid an accident (water on the floor). Figure 8.5 shows the process of installing our VBI routine into the normal path of the operating system's VBI routines.

Normally, once the OS has completed the updating process, the VBI program goes through a vector (direction sign) called VVBLKD (deferred vertical blank vector), which is located at address 548 and 549 (0224 Hex). (This is indicated in part a) of Figure 8.5.) VVBLKD contains the address of XITVBV (exit vertical blank interrupt, E462 Hex), where there is a simple interrupt termination routine. By placing the address of the VBI section of PMOVER into VVBLKD, the program flow gets rerouted through our program (the new plumbing fixture). When PMOVER has finished its job, it returns the flow to XITVBV (part c) of Figure 8.5).

There is one potential problem at this point. Since we must POKE a two-byte address into VVBLKD, it is possible that a VBI may occur *after* the POKE of the first byte but *before* the POKE of the second. This will cause the interrupt routine to shoot off to some unknown part of memory and the computer will crash! As any amateur plumber knows, you must turn off the water or detour it before disconnecting any pipes. ATARI has provided us with a "detour valve" precisely for this purpose. It is called CRITICAL and is found at location 66. Before changing the values in VVBLKD to connect PMOVER, we POKE a l into CRITICAL to open the detour pathway (part b) of Figure 8.5). Then, after the connections (POKEs) are completed, CRITICAL is closed by a POKE of 0:

```
13010 POKE CRITICAL,1: REM Open CRITICAL
      "valve", set up detour
```

(connect PMOVER to the ATARI VBI routine at this point)

```
13170 POKE CRITICAL,0: REM Close CRITICAL
      valve, routine installed
```

Stuffing the PMOVER String

The next step in implementing PMOVER is to enter its byte values into DATA statements, and then run our String Loader program to convert these values into a string. Load the String Loader program into

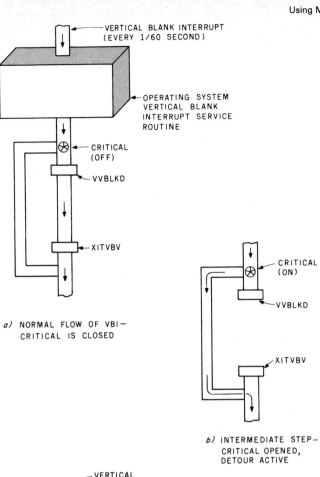

VERTICAL BLANK INTERRUPT
(EVERY 1/60 SECOND)

OPERATING SYSTEM
VERTICAL BLANK
INTERRUPT SERVICE
ROUTINE

CRITICAL
(OFF)

VVBLKD

XITVBV

a) NORMAL FLOW OF VBI—
CRITICAL IS CLOSED

CRITICAL
(ON)

VVBLKD

XITVBV

b) INTERMEDIATE STEP—
CRITICAL OPENED,
DETOUR ACTIVE

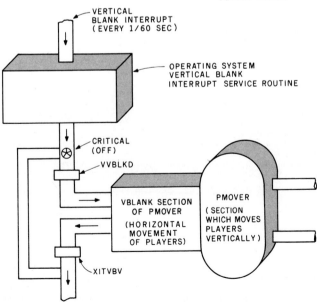

VERTICAL
BLANK INTERRUPT
(EVERY 1/60 SEC)

OPERATING SYSTEM
VERTICAL BLANK
INTERRUPT SERVICE ROUTINE

CRITICAL
(OFF)

VVBLKD

VBLANK SECTION
OF PMOVER

(HORIZONTAL
MOVEMENT
OF PLAYERS)

PMOVER
(SECTION
WHICH MOVES
PLAYERS
VERTICALLY)

XITVBV

c) CONNECTION COMPLETED — CRITICAL IS CLOSED AGAIN

Figure 8.5: Vertical blank interrupt pathway.

memory, making sure that the DATA statements from MFILL are deleted. Then add the lines shown in Figure 8.6.

```
26000  REM Player Move Routine DATA
26010  DATA PMOVER,11310,186,22157
26020  DATA 184,80,16,76,98,228,162,3,189,38,4,157,0,208,202,16,247,48,240,162,6,181,223,157,83
26030  DATA 4,202,208,248,104,104,104,133,227,165,227,133,226,172,4,4,162,0,142,4,4,70,226,144,6
26040  DATA 189,6,4,157,38,4,232,224,4,208,241,140,4,4,162,0,134,224,173,0,4,133,225,173,1
26050  DATA 4,133,228,173,2,4,133,229,173,3,4,133,226,142,3,4,70,227,176,30,165,224,73,128,133
26060  DATA 224,208,2,230,225,232,224,4,208,237,165,226,141,3,4,232,189,84,4,149,224,202,16,248,96
26070  DATA 160,127,177,224,145,228,136,16,249,142,76,4,189,42,4,72,189,10,4,157,42,4,168,104,170
26080  DATA 142,77,4,140,78,4,138,168,177,228,172,78,4,145,224,200,16,2,160,0,232,16,2,162,0
26090  DATA 236,77,4,208,229,174,76,4,184,80,165
```

Figure 8.6: Listing of DATA statements for PMOVER.

Now run the program to create the routine string. We are now ready to use PMOVER in a program.

Example 9

Exercise   Create a version of the previous Bouncing Ball program that uses the machine language routine PMOVER to place the ball at its horizontal and vertical position on the screen. Everything else in this program will remain the same as before.

The Bouncing Ball program, Example 8, will be modified to use PMOVER, so load that program into memory and delete the following lines:

160   500   510   7060

We will now present the sections of this program which have new or modified lines. Just add to your program the lines which are highlighted. Refer to Figure 8.7.

```
 10  REM *** BOUNCING BALL 2 PROGRAM ***
 20  REM                Example 9
 30  REM
 40  REM Program to demonstrate Player-Missile Graphics with Machine Language routine to move players
 50  REM Copyright (C) 1982 by David Fox and Mitchell Waite
 60  REM

140  REM Initialize
150  DIM PLR(3),HPLR(3),VPLR(3)
170  GRAPHICS 3:
     POKE 752,1:
     PRINT "One moment please...": REM Turn off cursor, print message
180  GOSUB 11000: REM Initialize Routine strings
190  GOSUB 5000: REM Set up memory locations
220  GOSUB 7000: REM Set up Player area
230  GOSUB 9000: REM Point PLR0$ to Player 0 RAM
240  GOSUB 10000: REM Read frames into RAM
280  GOSUB 12000: REM Set up parameter addresses
290  GOSUB 13000: REM Turn on interrupts
300  PRINT "(CLEAR) bbbbb***bBOUNCINGbBALLbDEMOb***"
```

Figure 8.7: Listing of Example 9 — lines 10–60, 140–300

Initialize   Line 150 eliminates the D I Mensioning of B L A N K $ (no longer needed) and adds V P L R (3) for the parameter table entry of the players' vertical position. Lines 180, 280, and 290 call the added subroutines to initialize, install, and turn on P M O V E R.

```
470  IF XPOS>220 OR YPOS<=1 THEN 600
480  POKE HPLR(0),XPOS:
     POKE VPLR(0),YPOS:
     TEMP=USR(PMOVER,P0)
490  FRAME$=FRAMEMEM$((FRMNO-1)*FRMSIZE+1,FRMNO*FRMSIZE): REM Select correct frame
520  PLR0$(YPOS)=FRAME$: REM Move new frame into Player 0
530  XPOS=XPOS+HORIZ
540  IF YPOS=BOTTOM AND (VEL+SNDFLAG>0.5) THEN
     SOUND 1,250,10,14:
     SNDFLAG=0:
     SOUND 1,0,0,0
```

Figure 8.8: Listing of Example 9 — lines 470–540.

Main Animation Loop   In line 480, the horizontal and vertical positions for the ball are P O K E d into P M O V E R's shadow registers and then P M O V E R is called. P M O V E R is passed the value in P Ø, which is a 1, to move only Player 0. Since the player has already been positioned by P M O V E R, the current frame can be placed directly over the old frame in line 520 without fear of leaving multiple balls in player RAM.

```
700  REM Move Player 0 to Left of Screen
710  POKE HPLR(0),0
720  TEMP=USR(PMOVER,P0)
730  RETURN
740  REM
```

Figure 8.9: Listing of Example 9 — lines 700–740.

Move Player 0 to Left of Screen   Line 720 calls P M O V E R to move the ball off the screen to the left.

```
5000 REM Set Up Memory Locations
5090 READ FRAMES,FRMSIZE,NUMPLRS
5110 PLRFRMMEM=FRAMES*FRMSIZE
5120 FRAMEMEM=PLRFRMMEM*NUMPLRS
5160 DIM BUFFER$(128),FRAME$(FRMSIZE),FRAMEMEM$(FRAMEMEM)
5270 PMOVER=ADR(PMOVER$)
5300 MFILL=ADR(MFILL$)
5310 BUFFER=ADR(BUFFER$)
5340 RETURN
5350 REM
```

Figure 8.10: Listing of Example 9 — lines 5000–5350.

Set Up Memory Locations   Lines 5270–5310 use A D R to find the address of the two machine language routines and the temporary player buffer.

```
7000  REM Initialize Player-Missile Graphics
7010  TEMP=PEEK(106)-8: REM Set aside Player-Missile area
7020  POKE 54279,TEMP: REM Tell ANTIC where PM RAM is
7030  PMBASE=256*TEMP: REM Find PM Base address
7040  FOR I=0 TO 3
7050    PLR(I)=PMBASE+128*I+512: REM Set addresses of Players
7070  NEXT I
7080  POKE 559,42: REM Set PM 2 line resolution, Players enabled
7090  POKE 704,12*16+8: REM Color ball green
7100  POKE 53277,2: REM Enable Player display
7110  TEMP=USR(MFILL,PLR(0),512,0): REM Use memory fill routine to clear Players
7120  RETURN
7130  REM
```

Figure 8.11: Listing of Example 9 — lines 7000–7130.

Initialize Player-Missile Graphics   Line 7110 is added to clear out Player RAM with zeroes. Notice that 7060, the line which stored the addresses of the horizontal position registers, has been deleted. The equivalent line appears in a later section.

```
11000  REM INITIALIZE ROUTINE STRINGS
11300  REM Set PMOVER routine
11310  DIM PMOVER$(186)
11320  PMOVER$(1)="  <<<Routine String goes here>>>  "
11330  PMOVER$(91)="  <<<Routine String goes here>>>  "
11340  PMOVER$(181)="  <<<Routine String goes here>>>  "
11600  REM Set MFILL routine
11610  DIM MFILL$(41)
11650  MFILL$(1)="  <<<Routine String goes here>>>  "
11650  RETURN
11660  REM
```

Figure 8.12: Listing of Example 9 — lines 11000–11660.

Initialize Routine Strings   The next three sections are all new to this program. This subroutine places the routine strings into RAM. First, ENTER the saved routine strings for PMOVER and MFILL, then add the lines which are highlighted.

```
12000  REM Set Parameters for Routines
12010  PARAMBASE=1024: REM Parameter Base address
12020  PMBAS=PARAMBASE: REM Hi Byte of PLR0 Location goes here
12030  PMBUF=PARAMBASE+1: REM Address of a 128 byte buffer
12070  FOR I=0 TO 3
12080    HPLR(I)=PARAMBASE+6+I: REM Player horizontal "shadow" registers
12090    VPLR(I)=PARAMBASE+10+I: REM Player vertical "shadow" registers
12130  NEXT I
12190  VVBLKD=548: REM Deferred Vertical Blank Interrupt Vector
12200  CRITICAL=66: REM Critical Flag
12210  P0=1:
       P1=2:
       P2=4:
       P3=8: REM Control bits for the four Players
12240  TEMP=USR(MFILL,PARAMBASE,94,0): REM IMPORTANT: Clear out parameter area
12250  X=PLR(0):
       GOSUB 110:
       POKE PMBAS,HIBYTE: REM Poke Hi Byte of Player 0 into PMBAS
12260  X=BUFFER:
       GOSUB 110:
       POKE PMBUF,LOBYTE: REM Poke address of buffer
12270  POKE PMBUF+1,HIBYTE
12530  RETURN
12540  REM
```

Figure 8.13: Listing of Example 9 — lines 12000–12540.

Set Parameters for Routines   This section initializes the values necessary to support our machine language routines. As we said before, PARAMBASE is the starting address of the memory reserved for the shadow registers and other parameters used by all of our routines. The routines look into PMBAS to learn where Player 0 RAM begins and into PMBUF for the address of the temporary player buffer. In lines 12070–12130, the addresses of the horizontal and vertical shadow registers are initialized. In line 12210, a bit value is assigned to variables P0–P3 to make it easier to pass parameters to PMOVER. When PMOVER is called, it is only necessary to include the appropriate P variable:

TEMP=USR(PMOVER,P0+P1)   to move Players 0 and 1
TEMP=USR(PMOVER,P2+P3)   to move Players 2 and 3
TEMP=USR(PMOVER,P0+P1+P2+P3) to move all the players

Line 12240 uses MFILL to clear the entire parameter area to zeroes. If this isn't done, then the random values in the parameter area could cause the computer to crash.

Line 12250 uses the subroutine at 110 to calculate the high byte of Player 0's RAM address and then POKEs it into PMBAS. Lines 12260 and 12270 POKE the high and low bytes of the temporary buffer into PMBUF.

```
13000  REM Install Interrupt Routine
13010  POKE CRITICAL,1: REM Open CRITICAL "valve", set up detour
13080  X=PMOVER+6:
       GOSUB 110
13090  POKE VVBLKD,LOBYTE: REM Set VBLANK vector to PMOVER
13100  POKE VVBLKD+1,HIBYTE
13170  POKE CRITICAL,0: REM Close CRITICAL "valve", routine installed
13200  RETURN
13210  REM
```

Figure 8.14: Listing of Example 9 — lines 13000–13210.

Install Interrupt Routine   This is the section in which the VBI portion of PMOVER gets patched into the operating system's vertical blank routines. Notice that in line 13080 the address which is POKEd into VVBLKD is actually PMOVER+6 and not the starting address of PMOVER. This is to link the VBI portion of PMOVER and not the section which vertically moves the players.

Important: You can stop this program with the BREAK key, but make sure you use the SYSTEM RESET button before you try to rerun it or list it!!! Otherwise, the computer will lock up and will have to be momentarily turned off (thus fully resetting the computer) before it can be used again. The same procedure must be followed for any other program that uses VBIs!

When you run this program, it will look nearly the same as Example 9. Then why all this work if no apparent improvement has been gained? Rather than giving you all of our machine language routines at once, we are allowing you to test each one separately in a program to make sure it works properly! This road testing is a necessary step for the more advanced programs to come.

Modifications   Try these variations:

1. Turn the Trench program (Example 6) into a real game by adding PM graphics to it and using PMOVER to move the players. Create a crosshairs (gunsight) from one player and an enemy ship from another. Use the joystick to move the crosshairs around the screen.

2. Add some players to the Waterfall program (Example 7). How about a bird or two flying across the sky or a deer drinking from the river?

Summary

With the first two machine language routines successfully implemented, we are ready to move on to more exciting applications. In the next section, the power of VBI's will be put to use to *automatically* flip through the different frames of an animation sequence for us — a change from the slow and inefficient BASIC loop.

8.3.   AUTOMATIC ANIMATION WITH ANIMATE

In all of our previous animation programs that included the transfer of frame information from a string to the screen, the current frame had to be calculated and displayed from within BASIC. The frame rates (number of frames per second) that could be achieved with this method are adequate for demonstration programs, but fast-action games might require the rapid transfer of frames for all *four* players in addition to a variety of other computer activities. It would be nice to be able to turn over this frame flipping task to a background machine language routine while more complicated things were being orchestrated by BASIC. (A background routine is one which is executing independently *while* the computer is running another program, e.g., BASIC or another machine language routine.) By patching a routine into the vertical blank interrupt routines, a program can be made to automatically carry out a task (like flipping frames) as fast as every sixtieth of a second. This is exactly what our next machine language routine, ANIMATE, can do!

Revisited by Our Walking Man

Before explaining how to use ANIMATE, let's take a look at our subject matter. In the next example, we will borrow our Walking Man from Example 2 and animate him using players. A two-by-three array of characters was needed to represent the man on the screen. This provided

16 bits of horizontal resolution and 24 bits of vertical resolution. Since a player only has 8 bits of horizontal resolution, two players are placed side by side to give us the required 16 bits. However, only 19 of the 24 bits of vertical resolution are used in the character set man, and the remaining 5 are left blank. This wasted space is avoided when converting to players, which can be any number from 1 to 128 pixels (in double-line mode) high. Recall that each player pixel is twice as wide and twice as high as a character set pixel, so a walking man made of players will be four times as large (and four times as coarse) as a character set man.

Below is the frame data for our Walking Man character set. The numbers are the same, but there are now two long strips rather than six small boxes, so the organization of these numbers in a program will be

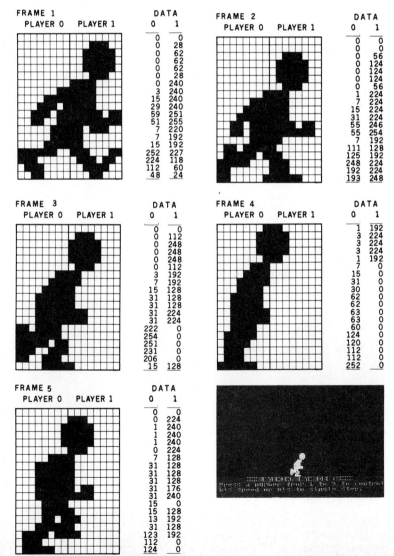

FRAME 1 — PLAYER 0 / PLAYER 1

DATA 0	1
0	0
0	28
0	62
0	62
0	62
0	28
0	240
3	240
15	240
29	240
59	251
51	255
7	220
7	192
15	192
252	227
224	118
112	60
48	24

FRAME 2 — PLAYER 0 / PLAYER 1

DATA 0	1
0	0
0	0
0	56
0	124
0	124
0	124
0	56
1	224
7	224
15	224
31	224
55	246
55	254
7	192
111	128
125	192
248	224
192	224
193	248

FRAME 3 — PLAYER 0 / PLAYER 1

DATA 0	1
0	0
0	112
0	248
0	248
0	248
0	112
3	192
7	192
15	128
31	128
31	128
31	224
31	224
222	0
254	0
251	0
231	0
206	0
15	128

FRAME 4 — PLAYER 0 / PLAYER 1

DATA 0	1
1	192
3	224
3	224
3	224
1	192
7	0
15	0
31	0
30	0
62	0
62	0
63	0
63	0
60	0
124	0
120	0
112	0
112	0
252	0

FRAME 5 — PLAYER 0 / PLAYER 1

DATA 0	1
0	0
0	224
1	240
1	240
1	240
0	224
7	128
31	128
31	128
31	128
31	176
31	240
15	0
15	128
13	192
31	128
123	192
112	0
124	0

Figure 8.15: Frame data for Walking Man players.

different. Unfortunately, this means that you will have to type in this data once again when we reach Example 10.

How ANIMATE Works

ANIMATE was designed for cyclic animation, animation such as in our Walking Man and Galloping Horse programs which repeat a few frames in a specific order. However, the cycle can be much greater than four or five frames long. Very complex sequences can be produced with much longer cycles. For example, an entire dance could be choreographed using only 20–25 unique frames that are put together in an imaginative sequence. An excellent example of this technique is found in Leo Christopherson's TRS-80 program called Dancing Demon. In this program, the user can program the demon's dance to original music by choosing from a selection of 26 tap dance steps. Each of these steps is composed of a few frames from a pool of twenty-two unique frames (see Figure 8.16a). The genius of this program is in the creation of these twenty-two frames — the demon is always unbelievably life-like. Using ANIMATE, the same level of animation can be achieved on the ATARI Home Computer.

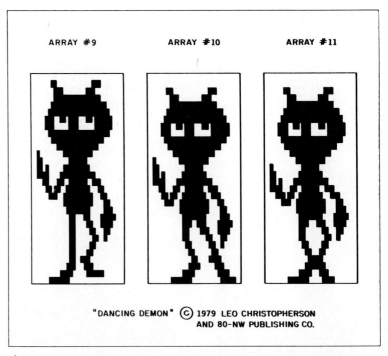

a)

Figure 8.16a: Three of the twenty-two frames for Leo Christopherson's "Dancing Demon" program.(Copyright© 1979 by Leo Christopherson and 80-NW Publishing Co.)

Frame Data ANIMATE requires two types of information. The first is the actual *Frame Data* (the bytes which define the shape of the figure) and is stored in a string. This data is stored in the manner shown in Figure 8.16b.

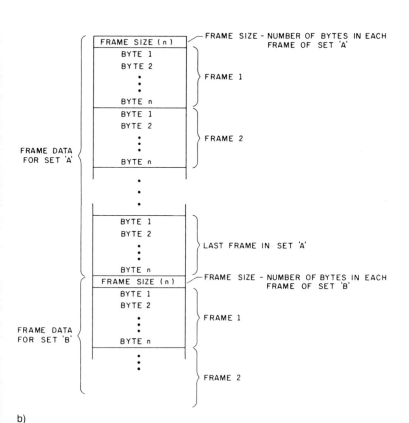

b)

Figure 8.16b: Frame data for ANIMATE.

Two sets of frame data are represented in Figure 8.6b, set A and set B. A set contains data for all the frames of a figure for one player. In reference to the frame data in Figure 8.15, one set would be the entire left vertical column (all five frames) for Player 0, and another set would be the right column for Player 1. At the beginning of each set of data is stored the *frame size* of the following frames in that set (19 for our Walking Man data). Each frame of a set must contain exactly that number of bytes. There can be as many sets of frame data in the string as you wish.

Frame List We call the second type of information a frame list. This is an ordered list of the frames which are to be moved into a player. Figure 8.17 illustrates how frame lists are stored in memory.

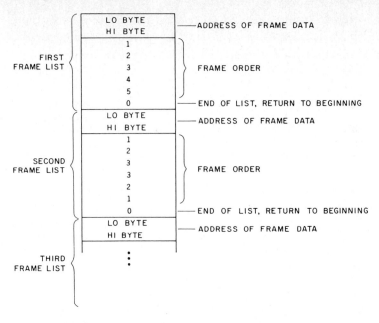

Figure 8.17: Frame list for ANIMATE.

The first two bytes of a frame list contain the address of the frame data that is to be used. Then follows the order in which the frames are to be displayed (their animation cycle). For example, our Walking Man uses five frames numbered 1 through 5. The frame list for the man would look like this:

Lo Byte
Hi Byte
1
2
3
4
5
0   (end of list, return to beginning)

The two-byte address points to the first byte of the frame data that will be used for this player. The numbers from 1 to 5 tell ANIMATE the order of the frames to be grabbed from the frame data. There must always be a 0 at the end of each frame list. This tells ANIMATE to return to the first frame indicated in the list (see Figure 8.18).

Passing Information to ANIMATE

Unlike PMOVER (which accepts parameters through the USER function *and* the parameter table), there is only one road through which

ANIMATE receives its parameters — the parameter table. The ANI-
MATE table entries as well as four read-only addresses are listed in Table
8.2.

Variable Name	Offset From PARAMBASE	Address (Decimal)	Description
INITANIMATE	3	1027	Flag to initialize ANIMATE
RATE(0)	14	1038	Player 0 Animation Rate Shadow Reg.
RATE(1)	15	1039	Player 1 Animation Rate Shadow Reg.
RATE(2)	16	1040	Player 2 Animation Rate Shadow Reg.
RATE(3)	17	1041	Player 3 Animation Rate Shadow Reg.
FRMLSTPTR(0)	18	1042,1043	Player 0 Pointer to Frame List
FRMLSTPTR(1)	20	1044,1045	Player 1 Pointer to Frame List
FRMLSTPTR(2)	22	1046,1047	Player 2 Pointer to Frame List
FRMLSTPTR(3)	24	1048,1049	Player 3 Pointer to Frame List

The following addresses are read-only addresses — don't change their values:

FLPOS0	62	1086	Player 0 Frame List Position
FLPOS1	63	1087	Player 1 Frame List Position
FLPOS2	64	1088	Player 2 Frame List Position
FLPOS3	65	1089	Player 3 Frame List Position

Table 8.2: Parameters for ANIMATE.

The RATE parameters set the duration in "jiffies" or sixtieths of a
second which each frame will remain on the screen. Each player's frame
rate can be changed independently of the others. A POKE of 4 into
RATE(0) means that a new frame will automatically be moved into
Player 0 every four jiffies (4/60 second, or 15 times a second).

The frame list pointer (FRMLSTPTR) contains the RAM address
of the frame list that is to be used for that player. It's possible to have a
large number of frame lists stored in RAM describing various types of
motion. Any one of these can be selected simply by a POKE of its address
into FRMLSTPTR (n).

INITANIMATE is the address which alerts ANIMATE to change
its parameters. The values in RATE(n) and FRMLSTPTR(n) are
ignored until all values have been POKEd in. In the meantime, ANI-
MATE checks the contents of INITANIMATE for your "ready" signal
every jiffy. As soon as ANIMATE sees your signal value in IN-
ITANIMATE, it goes to work.

The value you POKE into INITANIMATE tells ANIMATE what
to do. Table 8.3 contains the bit information for INITANIMATE.

	Bits of FLAG byte								
Bit Number:	7	X	X	4	3	2	1	0	*(X = not used)*
Bit Value:	128			16	8	4	2	1	
Resume Animation	1								
Modify Frame Rate only				1					
FLAG for Player #:					3	2	1	0	

Examples									**FLAG Value**
Begin Animation, Players 0 & 1	0			0	0	0	1	1	= 3
Modify Frame Rate, Players 2 & 3	0			1	1	1	0	0	= 28
Halt All Animation	0			0	0	0	0	0	= 0
Resume All Animation	1			0	0	0	0	0	= 128

Table 8.3 Bit values for INITANIMATE ready signal.

As in PMOVER, the player or players to be affected are indicated by turning on the appropriate bits (0–3). To tell ANIMATE that it must begin animation with a new frame list, these bit values are used by themselves. Once ANIMATE is happily flipping frames, you may want to change only the frame rate. Using the player bit value by itself will not only change the rate but also will begin the frame sequence from the first one on the list. Adding a 16 (bit 4) to the player bit value will change only the rate. To halt animation for all players, POKE INITANIMATE with a 0. To continue the animation where it left off, POKE INITANIMATE with a 128 (bit 7). To stop a *specific* player's animation, POKE its RATE with a 0, then POKE INITANIMATE with 16 plus the player's bit value:

```
POKE RATE(1),0     : REM Halt Player
                     1 only
POKE INITANIMATE,18 : REM Ready Flag - 16+2
```

ANIMATE is a *state machine*, a program which looks at its status (value in INITANIMATE) to find out what its supposed to be doing. By a PEEK into INITANIMATE, we can tell whether it has received our new information yet. When ANIMATE has accepted any non-zero information from INITANIMATE, it changes the value in IN-ITANIMATE to 128. When making rapid changes in the parameter table values (RATE and FRMLSTPTR), you should first check the value of INITANIMATE. Problems can appear in a loop with very little or no code between successive table changes. For example, if after a

POKE of 18 (see above) into INITANIMATE, we still find an 18 there (rather than a 128), ANIMATE has not yet received our new parameter table information (or even the message to retrieve that information). If the values in RATE (*n*) are changed before ANIMATE has a chance to grab them, a synchronization problem could occur between the player's frame rates. (See Example 10, line 710.)

Finally, in most of our programs, we need to discover what frame is currently being displayed in a player. This can be accomplished by a PEEK into FLPOS0 through FLPOS3. Do not POKE information into these locations or ANIMATE will lose track of what frame it's on!

The ANIMATE Chain of Command

Now that you have all of the pieces of ANIMATE, let's pull it all together. Figure 8.18 shows how ANIMATE would operate on the Walking Man.

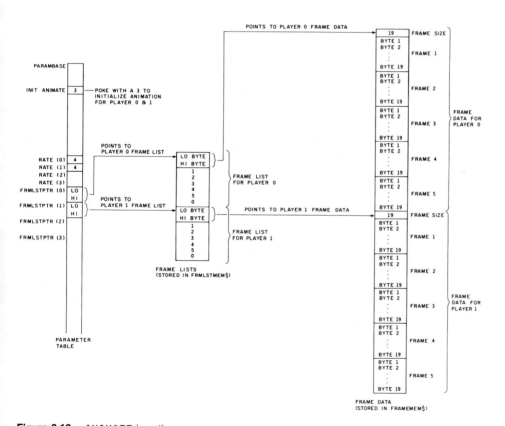

Figure 8.18: ANIMATE in action.

During the initialization process in the program, the frame data is POKEd in, making sure that the first byte of each set of player data is the frame size (19 in this case). Then the frame lists are constructed, setting the address of the appropriate set of frame data into the first two bytes of the list. Now, to turn on the Walking Man, all we need to do is:

```
POKE RATE(0),4              : REM Set
   Frame Rates
POKE RATE(1),4
POKE FRMLSTPTR(0),POINTER(0) : REM Point to
   Frame Lists
POKE FRMLSTPTR(1),POINTER(1)
POKE INITANIMATE,3          : REM Begin
   Animation of Players 0 & 1
```

The initial frame rate is set to four jiffies per frame, and ANIMATE is given the addresses of the two frame lists which will be used — their addresses are stored in POINTER(0) and POINTER(1). Then the ready flag is set with a 3 (INITANIMATE), and the animation begins!

Even though the frame data is stored in the same sequence as the number of the frame lists, this is not at all necessary. For example, by changing the numbers in the frame list to

5
4
3
2
1
0   (end of list, return to beginning)

the man would appear to be walking backwards! It would be a simple matter to maintain this information in an additional frame list that could then be switched on simply by pointing the frame list pointers (FRMLSTPTR) to it and POKEing INITANIMATE with a 3! This flexibility can save a tremendous amount of program development time.

Installing ANIMATE

As with PMOVER, ANIMATE must also be installed into the ATARI vertical blank interrupt routines. Each of our VBI routines can be joined together in any order, very much like a set of Leggo interlocking blocks. Recall that when PMOVER has completed its tasks, it returns control to the exit point of the ATARI VBI routine. This exit address, XITVBV, is stored in the fifth and sixth bytes (starting address + 4, starting address + 5) of each of our VBI routines. All that is necessary to patch in another of our VBI routines is to change this exit value from XITVBV to the entry point of the next routine, which is always the seventh byte (starting address + 6). Figure 8.19 shows how ANIMATE is patched in.

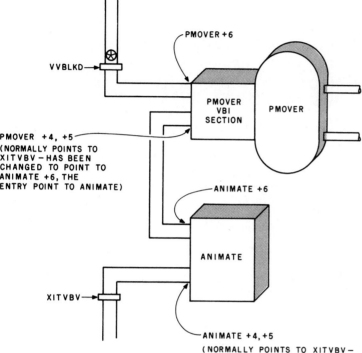

Figure 8.19: Connecting our VBI routines together.

To patch in another routine after ANIMATE simply POKE its address into the fifth and sixth bytes of ANIMATE.

Stuffing the ANIMATE String

Now it's time to enter the bytes of ANIMATE into the String Loader program so a routine string can be created. Before you begin entering this information, it would be a good idea to LIST the DATA statements from PMOVER into a separate file. To do this, use one of the following commands:

```
LIST "D:PMOVER.DAT",26000,26070   (for disk)
LIST "C:",26000,26070             (for cassette)
```

Now delete the PMOVER DATA and enter the lines indicated in Figure 8.20. After you have RUN String Loader, we can go on to the next example!

```
27000  REM Animate Routine DATA
27010  DATA ANIMATE,11410,294,34779
27020  DATA 184,80,3,76,98,228,216,162,3,181,224,157,89,4,202,16,248,173,3,4,240,237,48,72,10
27030  DATA 10,10,141,80,4,162,0,78,3,4,176,16,144,2,240,218,232,224,4,208,242,169,128,141,3
27040  DATA 4,208,43,189,14,4,208,2,169,255,157,46,4,138,10,168,185,18,4,153,50,4,185,19,4
27050  DATA 153,51,4,173,80,4,48,214,189,14,4,157,58,4,169,1,157,62,4,208,201,169,0,133,224
27060  DATA 173,0,4,133,225,162,0,189,46,4,240,9,201,255,240,37,222,58,4,240,25,165,224,73,128
27070  DATA 133,224,208,2,230,225,232,224,4,208,227,189,88,4,149,223,202,208,248,240,149,189,46,4,201
27080  DATA 255,208,2,169,1,157,58,4,138,10,168,185,50,4,133,226,185,51,4,133,227,254,62,4,189
27090  DATA 62,4,168,177,226,208,9,169,2,157,62,4,208,244,80,186,141,80,4,206,80,4,160,0,177
27100  DATA 226,72,200,177,226,133,227,104,133,226,136,177,226,141,81,4,169,0,160,8,78,80,4,144,4
27110  DATA 24,109,81,4,74,110,82,4,136,208,240,168,173,82,4,56,101,226,133,226,152,101,227,133,227
27120  DATA 142,80,4,189,42,4,168,162,0,140,82,4,138,168,177,226,172,82,4,145,224,200,232,236,81
27130  DATA 4,208,237,174,80,4,189,46,4,201,255,208,3,254,46,4,184,80,151
```

Figure 8.20: Listing of DATA statements for ANIMATE.

Example 10

Exercise   Write a program which uses players to animate our Walking Man from Example 2. Use the ANIMATE routine to automatically flip through the five frames. Accept keyboard entry to control his walking speed: pressing a number from 1 through 9 for the number of jiffies per frame. Single step the man when 0 is pressed.

Again, much of this program is the same as the previous program (Example 9), so load it into memory, and away we go. First, all the lines controlling the Bouncing Ball, relocating a string, and miscellaneous others must be deleted. Delete the following lines.

230   310–330   410–740   7090   9000–9080

In the following sections you'll only need to enter the lines that are highlighted.

```
10  REM *** WALKING MAN PLAYER DEMO ***
20  REM            Example 10
30  REM
40  REM Program to introduce the Animate Machine Language routine with the walking man
50  REM Copyright (C) 1982 by David Fox and Mitchell Waite
60  REM
70  GOTO 140
80  REM

140  REM Initialize
150  DIM PLR(3),HPLR(3),VPLR(3),RATE(3),FRMLSTPTR(3),FRMDATA(3)
```

Figure 8.21: Listing of Example 10 — lines 10–80, lines 140–150.

Initialize   The old line 70 has been replaced because the technique to move frame information into player RAM is being taken over by ANIMATE. Some of the new parameters are D I Mensioned in line 150.

```
5000  REM Set Up Memory Locations
5090  READ FRAMES,FRMSIZE,NUMPLRS
5110  PLRFRMMEM=FRAMES*FRMSIZE+1
5120  FRAMEMEM=PLRFRMMEM*NUMPLRS
5130  FRMLSTSIZE=FRAMES+3
5140  TOTFRMLSTSIZE=FRMLSTSIZE*NUMPLRS
5160  DIM BUFFER$(128),FRAMEMEM$(FRAMEMEM),FRMLSTMEM$(TOTFRMLSTSIZE)
5270  PMOVER=ADR(PMOVER$)
5280  ANIMATE=ADR(ANIMATE$)
5300  MFILL=ADR(MFILL$)
5310  BUFFER=ADR(BUFFER$)
5320  PLRFRAMES=ADR(FRAMEMEM$)
5330  FRMLSTMEM=ADR(FRMLSTMEM$)
5340  RETURN
5350  REM
```

Figure 8.22: Listing of Example 10 — lines 5000–5350.

Set Up Memory Locations   In line 5110, 1 is added to the value to create space for the frame size byte. In line 5130, the size of one frame list is calculated. In addition to the number of frames, two bytes are needed for the address of the frame data, and one byte is needed for the terminating 0. Line 5140 calculates the total frame list size by multiplying the size of one frame list by the number of players. The string variables for the temporary player buffer, frame data memory (FRAMEMEM$) and the frame list memory (FRMLSTMEM$) are D I Mensioned in line 5160. In lines 5280, 5320, and 5330, the addresses for the new string variables are determined.

```
7040  FOR I=0 TO 3
7050     PLR(I)=PMBASE+128*I+512: REM Set addresses of Players
7060     POKE 704+I,3*16+10: REM Color him peach
7070  NEXT I
```

Figure 8.23: Listing of Example 10 — lines 7040–7070.

Initialize Player-Missile Graphics   Line 7060 is the only new line here. It sets the players to a peach color. Actually the color of Players 2 and 3 are also being set here — that's fine since they never appear on the screen.

```
10000  REM Read in Frame Data
10010  OFFSET2=0
10030  FRAMELIST=FRMLSTMEM
10050  FOR I=0 TO NUMPLRS-1
10060     FRMDATA(I)=PLRFRAMES+OFFSET2: REM Store addresses of frame data
10070     OFFSET2=OFFSET2+PLRFRMMEM
10080     POKE FRMDATA(I),FRMSIZE: REM Poke Frame size at beginning of each set of frame data
10090     FOR J=1 TO PLRFRMMEM-1
10100        READ BYTE
10110        POKE FRMDATA(I)+J,BYTE
10120     NEXT J:
       NEXT I
10130  RETURN
10140  REM
```

Figure 8.24: Listing of Example 10 — lines 10000–10140.

Read In Frame Data This section has been modified so it begins the frame list set up and POKEs in the frame size at the beginning of each set of frame data. In line 10010, OFFSET2 is a temporary variable, which helps calculate the beginning of the next set of frame data. Line 10030 sets the variable FRAMELIST to the beginning of frame list memory.

The FOR/NEXT loop beginning at 10050 sets up the frame data. FRMDATA(I) in line 10060 points to the beginning of each set of frame data. Later in the program, these values will be used when constructing the frame lists. OFFSET2 is set to point to the beginning of the next set of frame data in line 10070. The frame size is POKEd into the beginning of each set of frame data in line 10080.

Finally, the actual DATA bytes are POKEd into RAM in lines 10090–10110. Notice that in line 10110 a different technique is being implemented than in the last program where the following statement was used:

```
10110 FRAMEMEM$(J,J)=CHR$(BYTE)
```

Both lines accomplish exactly the same thing; only the current version executes almost 50 percent faster.

```
11000 REM INITIALIZE ROUTINE STRINGS
11300 REM Set PMOVER routine
11310 DIM PMOVER$(186)
11320 PMOVER$(1)=" <<<Routine String goes here>>> "
11330 PMOVER$(91)=" <<<Routine String goes here>>> "
11340 PMOVER$(181)=" <<<Routine String goes here>>> "
11400 REM Set ANIMATE routine
11410 DIM ANIMATE$(294)
11420 ANIMATE$(1)=" <<<Routine String goes here>>> "
11430 ANIMATE$(91)=" <<<Routine String goes here>>> "
11440 ANIMATE$(181)=" <<<Routine String goes here>>> "
11450 ANIMATE$(271)=" <<<Routine String goes here>>> "
11600 REM Set MFILL routine
11610 DIM MFILL$(41)
11620 MFILL$(1)=" <<<Routine String goes here>>> "
11650 RETURN
11660 REM
```

Figure 8.25: Listing of Example 10 — lines 11000–11660.

Initialize Routine Strings Now is the time to ENTER the ANIMATE routine strings from your storage device.

```
12000 REM Set Parameters For Routines
12010 PARAMBASE=1024: REM Parameter Base address
12020 PMBAS=PARAMBASE: REM Hi Byte of PLR0 Location goes here
12030 PMBUF=PARAMBASE+1: REM Address of a 128 byte buffer
12040 INITANIMATE=PARAMBASE+3: REM Initialize Frame Animate routine
12070 FOR I=0 TO 3
12080    HPLR(I)=PARAMBASE+6+I: REM Player horizontal "shadow" registers
12090    VPLR(I)=PARAMBASE+10+I: REM Player vertical "shadow" registers
12100    RATE(I)=PARAMBASE+14+I: REM Animate rate "shadow" registers
12110    FRMLSTPTR(I)=PARAMBASE+18+I*2: REM Pointer to Frame Lists
12130 NEXT I
12190 VVBLKD=548: REM Deferred Vertical Blank Interrupt Vector
12200 CRITICAL=66: REM Critical Flag
12210 P0=1:
      P1=2:
      P2=4:
      P3=8: REM Control bits for the four Players
12220 FST2P=P0+P1
```

Figure 8.26: Listing of Example 10 — lines 12000–12220.

Set Parameters For Routines   In this section the new ANI-MATE variables must be initialized (INITANIMATE, RATE(I), FRMLSTPTR(I)). In line 12220, a variable is set to the bit value that will control the first two players (FST2P). This saves having to do this addition in a section where calculation speed is critical.

```
12390  REM
12400  REM Set Up Frame Lists
12410  DIM POINTER(NUMPLRS-1)
12430  FOR I=0 TO NUMPLRS-1
12440     LET POINTER(I)=FRAMELIST+I*FRMLSTSIZE: REM Points to start of each Frame List
12450     X=FRMDATA(I):
          GOSUB 110
12460     POKE POINTER(I),LOBYTE: REM Put in address of Frame Data
12470     POKE POINTER(I)+1,HIBYTE
12480     FOR J=1 TO FRAMES: REM Make up a Frame List (numbers 1 thru FRAMES)
12490        POKE POINTER(I)+J+1,J
12500     NEXT J
12510     POKE POINTER(I)+FRAMES+2,0: REM End of frame list marker
12520  NEXT I
```

Figure 8.27:   Listing of Example 10 — lines 12390–12520.

Set Up Frame Lists   This new section creates the two frame lists needed in this program. In line 12410, the variable that will hold the beginning address of each frame list (POINTER) is DIMensioned. Lines 12430–12520 create a frame list for each player in use. Line 12440 calculates the beginning addresses of each frame list. (Make sure you use the LET in front of the variable POINTER since it contains the ATARI BASIC reserved work POINT.) The high and low bytes of the beginning of each set of the frame data are obtained (12450) and POKEd into the beginning of the appropriate frame list (12460–12470). Lines 12480–12500 POKE in the frame numbers (1 through 5 in this case), and the terminating 0 is POKEd in on line 12510.

```
13000  REM Install Interrupt Routine
13010  POKE CRITICAL,1: REM Open CRITICAL "valve", set up detour
13080  X=PMOVER+6:
       GOSUB 110
13090  POKE VVBLKD,LOBYTE: REM Set VBLANK vector to PMOVER
13100  POKE VVBLKD+1,HIBYTE
13110  X=ANIMATE+6:
       GOSUB 110
13120  POKE PMOVER+4,LOBYTE: REM Points PMOVER to ANIMATE
13130  POKE PMOVER+5,HIBYTE
13170  POKE CRITICAL,0: REM Close CRITICAL "valve", routine installed
13200  RETURN
13210  REM
```

Figure 8.28:   Listing of Example 10 — lines 13000–13210.

Install Interrupt Routines   Lines 13110–13130 have been added to point the exit vector of PMOVER to the entry point to ANI-MATE (see Figure 8.19).

```
20000  REM FRAME DATA
20030  REM
20040  REM Number of Frames, Frame Size, Number of Players
20050  REM . (Walking Man)
20060  DATA 5,19,2
21000  REM Frame Data For Walking Man
21010  REM Frame 1, Player 0
21020  DATA 0,0,0,0,0,0,0,0,3,15,29,59,51,7,7,15,252,224,112,48
21030  REM Frame 2, Player 0
21040  DATA 0,0,0,0,0,0,0,1,7,15,31,55,55,7,111,125,248,192,193
21050  REM Frame 3, Player 0
21060  DATA 0,0,0,0,0,0,3,7,15,31,31,31,31,222,254,251,231,206,15
21070  REM Frame 4, Player 0
21080  DATA 1,3,3,3,1,7,15,31,30,62,62,63,63,60,124,120,112,112,252
21090  REM Frame 5, Player 0
21100  DATA 0,0,1,1,1,0,7,31,31,31,31,31,15,15,13,31,123,112,124
21110  REM Frame 1, Player 1
21120  DATA 0,28,62,62,62,28,240,240,240,240,251,255,220,192,192,227,118,60,24
21130  REM Frame 2, Player 1
21140  DATA 0,0,56,124,124,124,56,224,224,224,224,246,254,192,128,192,224,224,248
21150  REM Frame 3, Player 1
21160  DATA 0,112,248,248,248,112,192,192,128,128,128,224,224,0,0,0,0,0,128
21170  REM Frame 4, Player 1
21180  DATA 192,224,224,224,192,0,0,0,0,0,0,0,0,0,0,0,0,0,0
21190  REM Frame 5, Player 1
21200  DATA 0,224,240,240,240,224,128,128,128,128,176,240,0,128,192,128,192,0,0
```

Figure 8.29: Listing of Example 10 — lines 20000–21200.

Frame `DATA`   This section contains the frame data for the Walking Man. Each `DATA` line contains one 19-byte frame for a single player.

```
1500  REM Put Frame List Address in Param Table
1510  FOR I=0 TO NUMPLRS-1
1520    X=POINTER(I):
        GOSUB 110
1530    POKE FRMLSTPTR(I),LOBYTE
1540    POKE FRMLSTPTR(I)+1,HIBYTE
1550  NEXT I
1560  RETURN
1570  REM
```

Figure 8.30: Listing of Example 10 — lines 1500–1570.

Put Frame List Addresses in Parameter Table   This subroutine transfers the addresses in the `POINTER` array into the appropriate parameter table addresses (`FRMLSTPTR(I)`).

```
1000  REM Parameters For Players
1010  REM Man
1020  GOSUB 1500: REM Point to Frame Lists
1030  FOR I=0 TO NUMPLRS-1
1040    POKE VPLR(I),PY
1050    POKE HPLR(I),PX+I*8
1060  NEXT I
1070  TEMP=USR(PMOVER,FST2P)
1080  RETURN
1090  REM
```

Figure 8.31: Listing of Example 10 — lines 1000–1090.

Parameters For Players   This subroutine positions the man on the screen at coordinates `PX,PY`. First, the subroutine at 1500, which puts the frame list addresses in the parameter table is called. Then the vertical and horizontal coordinates are POKEd in. On line 1050, the players are set next to each other with Player 0 on the left. Line 1070 calls PMOVER to position the players.

```
700  REM Set Frame Rate
710  IF PEEK(INITANIMATE)<>128 THEN 710
720  FOR I=0 TO NUMPLRS-1
740     POKE RATE(I),SPEED
750  NEXT I
760  POKE INITANIMATE,FST2P+16
780  RETURN
790  REM
```

Figure 8.32: Listing of Example 10 — lines 700–790.

Set Frame Rate   This subroutine sets all the frame rates to the value in SPEED. Line 710 checks to make sure ANIMATE has received its last set of information before giving it new information (the value in INITANIMATE is set to 128 when it is finished). Line 760 changes only the frame rate (+16).

```
300  PRINT "(CLEAR)(6 RIGHT)*** WALKING MAN DEMO ***"
310  PRINT "Press a number from 1 to 9 to control his speed or 0's to single step.";
330  PX=120:
     PY=77
340  GOSUB 1000
350  SFLAG=2
360  POKE INITANIMATE,FST2P
370  SPEED=4:
     GOSUB 700
380  OPEN #2,4,0,"K:":
     POKE 754,255
390  REM
```

Figure 8.33: Listing of Example 10 — lines 300–390.

Initialize Revisited   This section prepares the final parameters and variables before entering the main animation loop. The horizontal (PX) and vertical (PY) player coordinates are set in line 330. The subroutine at line 1000 (called in 340) places the man on the screen at this position and calls the 1500 subroutine, which puts the frame list address-es in the parameter table. Line 350 sets a variable (SFLAG, sound flag) to its initial value. This variable is used in the main animation loop to determine during which frames a footstep will be heard. Line 360 initializes ANIMATE, and line 370 sets the frame rates to 4.

In order to accept keyboard information without using an INPUT, the keyboard is opened as a device in 380. Location 754 is an ATARI location used as a key ready flag — if there is anything other than a 255 in it when checked later on, then a key has been pressed.

```
400  REM Main Animation Loop
410  IF PEEK(1086)=SFLAG THEN
        SOUND 0,0,0,10:
        SFLAG=3: REM Footsteps
420  IF PEEK(1086)=SFLAG THEN
        SOUND 0,24,0,10:
        SFLAG=2
430  SOUND 0,0,0,0
480  IF PEEK(754)=255 THEN 410
490  GET #2,BYTE:
        SPEED=BYTE-48:
        POKE 754,255:
        IF SPEED<0 THEN
          SPEED=0
500  IF SPEED>9 THEN
        SPEED=9
510  GOSUB 700
520  GOTO 410
530  REM
```

Figure 8.34: Listing of Example 10 — lines 400–530.

Main Animation Loop   This section keeps track of the frames so the sound of footsteps can be added. It also enables the computer to accept frame rate information from the keyboard. As we mentioned earlier, parameter table locations FLPOS0–FLPOS3 (RAM locations 1086–1089) are scratch pad addresses used by ANIMATE. They contain the current frame number being displayed for each of the players. By checking the value in 1086 (FLPOS0), we can synchronize the man's actions with footstep sounds. When frame 2 is being displayed, a heel sound is created and when frame 3 appears, a sole sound is turned on. The variable SFLAG is used so the sound only occurs *once* during each of the appropriate frames. Otherwise, you would hear a continuous buzz during the slower frame rates (or single stepping) as the sound was constantly being turned on and off. Line 480 checks for a keypress. If the value in 754 is anything other than what we set it to (255), then the following lines are executed. Line 490 accepts the BYTE value of the key which was pressed, converts it to a number from 0 to 9, and location 754 is reset to 255. Then the value in SPEED is checked for low and high errror values and corrected. Line 510 calls the subroutine which implements the new frame rate, and the cycle repeats.

Before you run this program, make sure it has been saved to disk or cassette! Now go ahead and run it. At the fastest frame rate (one frame per jiffy), the man is walking so fast that his feet become a blur! While the man is walking along, stop the BASIC program with the **BREAK** key. Wait a second! The man keeps on chugging away as if nothing happened. This is because our VBI routines are still active and executing. Press **SYSTEM RESET** before typing anything else, or the computer may lock up requiring you to turn it off and on again.

Modifications

1. Play around with the frame lists. Implement one for a backwards walk.
2. Store both the normal and backwards frame lists in RAM. Modify the

program so pressing a special key will alternate from a forwards and backwards walk.

3. Use `PMOVER` to make the man walk across the screen rather than walking in place.

4. Starting with the same BASIC program, create a new set of frame data for a flying bird. After you have successfully gotten the bird to fly in place, use `PMOVER` to make it fly around the screen. Since the frame flipping is now on automatic, this should not be too difficult. You could even increase the flapping rate as the bird flies upwards and decrease it as it soars towards the ground.

Summary

You now have some very powerful animation tools at your disposal. The drudgery of moving the frames into Player RAM is now a thing of the past. In the next section, one final player machine language routine will be added. This will liberate even more BASIC processing power.

8.4. SETTING A HORIZONTAL VELOCITY WITH `AUTOMOVE`

The last machine language routine of this chapter, `AUTOMOVE`, allows us to assign a horizontal velocity to a player. Once this velocity is set, the player will continue to move to the right or left until we stop it or it goes off the screen. To show off this routine, a new *four*-player-wide animated character, Running Boy, will be introduced.

How `AUTOMOVE` Works

`AUTOMOVE` is a fairly simple routine to use. Each player has its own velocity shadow register, `MOVERATE(I)`, and there is a ready flag location called `INITAUTOMOVE` which is similar in purpose to `INITANIMATE`. In addition to these addresses, there are four more locations which can be used to discover the current horizontal position of a player (`PLR0X–PLR3X`), which can also be used for `PMOVER`. Here are the addresses for `AUTOMOVE`:

Variable Name	Offset From PARAMBASE	Address (Decimal)	Description
INITAUTOMOVE	4	1028	Flag to Initialize AUTOMOVE
MOVERATE(0)	32	1056	Player 0 Horizontal Velocity
MOVERATE(1)	33	1057	Player 1 Horizontal Velocity
MOVERATE(2)	34	1058	Player 2 Horizontal Velocity
MOVERATE(3)	35	1059	Player 3 Horizontal Velocity

The following addresses are read-only addresses — don't change their values:

PLR0X	38	1062	Player 0 Horizontal Position
PLR1X	39	1063	Player 1 Horizontal Position
PLR2X	40	1064	Player 2 Horizontal Position
PLR3X	41	1065	Player 3 Horizontal Position

Table 8.4: Parameter table for AUTOMOVE.

The velocity is entered as horizontal steps per jiffy, a step being the minimum horizontal distance which a player can be moved (one color clock). If you want the player to move to the right, use a positive number. Use a negative number for movement to the left, and a 0 for no movement. Because you can't POKE in negative values, add 128 to all velocities (called a bias). This means a value of 127 is 1 horizontal step per jiffy to the left, 128 is stopped, and 129 is 1 horizontal step per jiffy to the right. Here are some more examples:

```
POKE MOVERATE(0),128+3    : REM Player 0
  moves 3 steps/jiffy to the right
POKE MOVERATE(3),128-5    : REM Player 3
  moves 5 steps/jiffy to the left
POKE MOVERATE(1),128      :REM Player 1
  is halted
```

Once the values are POKEd in, tell AUTOMOVE you are ready by POKEing INITAUTOMOVE with the bit numbers of the players you wish to move (see Table 8.5).

Bits of FLAG Byte								
Bit Number:	7	X	X	X	3	2	1	0 (X = not used)
Bit Value:	128				8	4	2	1
Resume Player Motion	1							
FLAG for Player #:					3	2	1	0
Examples								FLAG **Value**
Begin Player Motion								
Players 0 & 1	0				0	0	1	1 = 3
Halt All Motion	0				0	0	0	0 = 0
Resume All Motion	1				0	0	0	0 = 128

Table 8.5: Bit values for INITAUTOMOVE ready signal.

A POKE of 0 into INITAUTOMOVE will halt the horizontal motion of all players; a POKE of 128 will resume player motion at the *last* initialized rates:

```
POKE MOVERATE(2),131  : REM Player 2 moves
   3 steps/jiffy to right
POKE INITAUTOMOVE,1   : REM Begin movement
   with current velocities
POKE INITAUTOMOVE,0   : REM Halt all
   Player movement
POKE INITAUTOMOVE,128 : REM Resume
   movement at old velocity
```

In practice, a POKE of 128 into INITAUTOMOVE is seldom used. The only difference between using a 128 and using the player bit values is that these bit values cause AUTOMOVE to grab new data from the appropriate MOVERATE addresses. The 128 option does not check the MOVERATE addresses but uses the *last* values grabbed by AUTO-MOVE. It is important to always use the player bits the first time AUTOMOVE is used, so some values are transferred from the MOVE-RATE addresses. As with ANIMATE, you can check the value in INITAUTOMOVE to see whether it has received your last read message. If its value is 128, it has; otherwise wait as we did for INITANI-MATE in line 710 of Example 10.

Note that if PMOVER is called while AUTOMOVE is moving a player, the player will continue its travels from its new horizontal and vertical position. Once a player reaches position 255 or position 0, its velocity and its PLRnX value are both set to 0.

IMPORTANT: AUTOMOVE requires PMOVER to be in memory for it to work. AUTOMOVE uses PMOVER to reposition the players on the screen.

Stuffing the AUTOMOVE String

Figure 8.35 shows the DATA statements for AUTOMOVE. Follow the earlier procedure of LISTing the DATA for ANIMATE onto a disk or cassette before deleting it.

```
28000  REM Automove Routine DATA
28010  DATA AUTOMOVE,11510,74,6564
28020  DATA 184,80,3,76,98,228,216,173,4,4,240,247,48,23,162,0,78,4,4,144,6,189,32,4,157
28030  DATA 71,4,232,224,4,208,240,169,128,141,4,4,162,3,189,71,4,73,128,8,24,125,38,4,144
28040  DATA 5,40,48,12,16,3,40,16,7,169,128,157,71,4,169,0,157,38,4,202,16,223,48,185
```

Figure 8.35: Listing of DATA statements for AUTOMOVE.

The Running Boy DATA

Before we go on to the program, here is the player information for the Running Boy. He is 31 bytes high and 32 bits (four players) wide and uses four frames. See Figure 8.36.

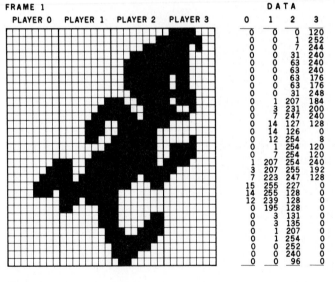

a)

(continued)

FRAME 2

PLAYER 0	PLAYER 1	PLAYER 2	PLAYER 3

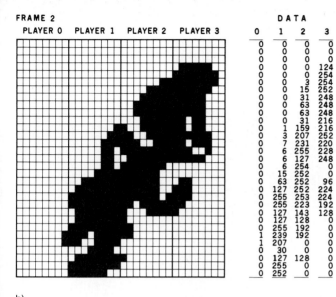

D A T A

0	1	2	3
0	0	0	0
0	0	0	0
0	0	0	0
0	0	0	124
0	0	0	254
0	0	3	254
0	0	15	252
0	0	31	248
0	0	63	248
0	0	63	248
0	0	31	216
0	1	159	216
0	3	207	252
0	7	231	220
0	6	255	228
0	6	127	248
0	6	254	0
0	15	252	0
0	63	252	96
0	127	252	224
0	255	253	224
0	255	223	192
0	127	143	128
0	127	128	0
0	255	192	0
1	239	192	0
1	207	0	0
0	30	0	0
0	127	128	0
0	255	0	0
0	252	0	0

b)

FRAME 3

PLAYER 0	PLAYER 1	PLAYER 2	PLAYER 3

D A T A

0	1	2	3
0	0	0	0
0	0	0	126
0	0	3	255
0	0	7	255
0	0	15	255
0	0	15	252
0	0	15	236
0	0	15	236
0	0	15	254
0	0	7	238
0	0	1	242
0	0	1	252
0	0	7	224
0	0	63	128
0	0	255	0
0	1	255	0
0	1	255	0
0	3	254	0
0	7	255	128
0	15	255	128
0	31	252	0
0	63	255	128
0	255	255	0
1	252	252	0
3	192	62	0
15	0	14	0
30	0	0	0
30	0	0	0
28	0	0	0
30	0	0	0
30	0	0	0

c)

(continued)

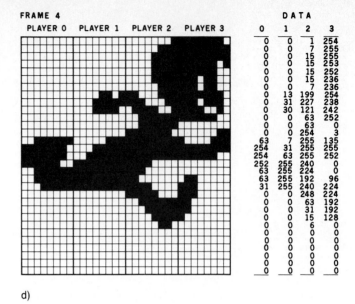

| FRAME 4 | | | | DATA | | | |
PLAYER 0	PLAYER 1	PLAYER 2	PLAYER 3	0	1	2	3
				0	0	1	254
				0	0	7	255
				0	0	15	255
				0	0	15	253
				0	0	15	252
				0	0	15	236
				0	0	7	236
				0	13	199	254
				0	31	227	238
				0	30	121	242
				0	0	63	252
				0	0	63	0
				0	0	254	3
				63	7	255	135
				254	31	255	255
				254	63	255	252
				252	255	240	0
				63	255	224	0
				63	255	192	96
				31	255	240	224
				0	0	248	224
				0	0	63	192
				0	0	31	192
				0	0	15	128
				0	0	6	0
				0	0	0	0
				0	0	0	0
				0	0	0	0
				0	0	0	0
				0	0	0	0

d)

Figure 8.36: Running Boy player frames.

It's difficult to tell from the static pictures, but as the boy runs, his hair bounces up and down. The book *Animation*, by Preston Blair (published by Walter Foster Art Books, Tustin, California), was used again to help create these frames.

Example 11

Exercise Modify the last program, Example 10, to create a four-player-wide Running Boy. Use AUTOMOVE to smoothly move him across the screen. As before, create the sound of his footsteps and accept frame rate information from the keyboard.

This program is very close to Example 10, so there are no lines to delete and not too many new lines to enter.

a)

b)

(continued)

c)

d)

Photo 8.1: Screen photos of Running Boy.

```
10  REM *** RUNNING BOY PLAYER DEMO ***
20  REM           Example 11
30  REM
40  REM Program to introduce the AUTOMOVE Machine Language routine and the running boy
50  REM Copyright (C) 1982 by David Fox and Mitchell Waite
60  REM

150  DIM PLR(3),HPLR(3),VPLR(3),RATE(3),FRMLSTPTR(3),FRMDATA(3),MOVERATE(3),MSPEED(9)
```

Figure 8.37: Listing of Example 11 — lines 10–60, 150.

Initialize Line 150 has some new variables. You already know about MOVERATE, but MSPEED is new. It will contain the proper horizontal velocity for each frame rate that is entered from the keyboard. If the boy's feet are moving too fast or too slow for his horizontal velocity, it will look like he's running on the ice because his feet will be slipping and sliding in relation to the floor. These velocities were determined through trial and error until the boy's running looked as realistic as possible.

```
5000  REM Set Up Memory Locations
5090  READ FRAMES,FRMSIZE,NUMPLRS
5110  PLRFRMMEM=FRAMES*FRMSIZE+1
5120  FRAMEMEM=PLRFRMMEM*NUMPLRS
5130  FRMLSTSIZE=FRAMES+3
5140  TOTFRMLSTSIZE=FRMLSTSIZE*NUMPLRS
5160  DIM BUFFER$(128),FRAMEMEM$(FRAMEMEM),FRMLSTMEM$(TOTFRMLSTSIZE)
5270  PMOVER=ADR(PMOVER$)
5280  ANIMATE=ADR(ANIMATE$)
5290  AUTOMOVE=ADR(AUTOMOVE$)
5300  MFILL=ADR(MFILL$)
```

Figure 8.38: Listing of Example 11 — lines 5000–5300.

Set Up Memory Locations Line 5290 assigns the location of AUTOMOVE to the variable of the same name.

```
11500  REM Set AUTOMOVE routine
11510  DIM AUTOMOVE$(74)
11520  AUTOMOVE$(1)=" <<<Routine String goes here>>> "
```

Figure 8.39: Listing of Example 11 — lines 11500–11520.

Initialize Routine Strings

This is where you can enter the AUTOMOVE string into the program from your disk or cassette.

```
12000  REM Set Parameters For Routines
12010  PARAMBASE=1024: REM Parameter Base address
12020  PMBAS=PARAMBASE: REM Hi Byte of PLR0 Location goes here
12030  PMBUF=PARAMBASE+1: REM Address of a 128 byte buffer
12040  INITANIMATE=PARAMBASE+3: REM Initialize Frame Animate routine
12050  INITAUTOMOVE=PARAMBASE+4: REM Initialize Player Automove routine
12070  FOR I=0 TO 3
12080    HPLR(I)=PARAMBASE+6+I: REM Player horizontal "shadow" registers
12090    VPLR(I)=PARAMBASE+10+I: REM Player vertical "shadow" registers
12100    RATE(I)=PARAMBASE+14+I: REM Animate rate "shadow" registers
12110    FRMLSTPTR(I)=PARAMBASE+18+I*2: REM Pointer to Frame Lists
12120    MOVERATE(I)=PARAMBASE+32+I: REM Horizontal movement for AUTOMOVE
12130  NEXT I
12190  VVBLKD=548: REM Deferred Vertical Blank Interrupt Vector
12200  CRITICAL=66: REM Critical Flag
12210  P0=1:
       P1=2:
       P2=4:
       P3=8: REM Control bits for the four Players
12220  FST2P=P0+P1
12230  ALLP=P0+P1+P2+P3
```

Figure 8.40: Listing of Example 11 — lines 12000–12230.

Set Parameters For Routines

Lines 12050 and 12120 set up the parameter table entries for AUTOMOVE. Line 12230 provides us with a single variable which can be used to represent the bit values of all the players for PMOVER and ANIMATE.

```
13000  REM Install Interrupt Routines
13010  POKE CRITICAL,1: REM Open CRITICAL "valve", set up detour
13080  X=PMOVER+6:
       GOSUB 110
13090  POKE VVBLKD,LOBYTE: REM Set VBLANK vector to PMOVER
13100  POKE VVBLKD+1,HIBYTE
13110  X=ANIMATE+6:
       GOSUB 110
13120  POKE PMOVER+4,LOBYTE: REM Points PMOVER to ANIMATE
13130  POKE PMOVER+5,HIBYTE
13140  X=AUTOMOVE+6:
       GOSUB 110
13150  POKE ANIMATE+4,LOBYTE: REM Points ANIMATE to AUTOMOVE
13160  POKE ANIMATE+5,HIBYTE
13170  POKE CRITICAL,0: REM Close CRITICAL "valve", routines installed
13200  RETURN
```

Figure 8.41: Listing of Example 11 — lines 13000–13200.

Install Interrupt Routines

AUTOMOVE is installed by pointing the exit vector in ANIMATE to AUTOMOVE's entry address (see Figure 8.19).

```
20000 REM FRAME DATA
20030 REM
20040 REM Number of Frames, Frame Size, Number of Players
20050 REM , (Running Boy)
20060 DATA 4,31,4
21000 REM Frame data for Running Boy
21010 REM Frame 1, Player 0
21020 DATA 0,0,0,0,0,0,0,0,0,0,0,0,0,0,0,0
21030 DATA 0,0,1,3,7,15,14,12,0,0,0,0,0,0,0,0
21040 REM Frame 2, Player 0
21050 DATA 0,0,0,0,0,0,0,0,0,0,0,0,0,0,0,0
21060 DATA 0,0,0,0,0,0,0,0,0,1,1,0,0,0,0
21070 REM Frame 3, Player 0
21080 DATA 0,0,0,0,0,0,0,0,0,0,0,0,0,0,0,0
21090 DATA 0,0,0,0,0,0,0,0,1,3,15,30,30,28,30,30
21100 REM Frame 4, Player 0
21110 DATA 0,0,0,0,0,0,0,0,0,0,0,0,0,63,254
21120 DATA 254,252,63,63,31,0,0,0,0,0,0,0,0,0,0
21130 REM Frame 1, Player 1
21140 DATA 0,0,0,0,0,0,0,0,0,1,3,7,14,14,12
21150 DATA 1,7,207,207,223,255,255,239,195,3,3,1,1,0,0,0
21160 REM Frame 2, Player 1
21170 DATA 0,0,0,0,0,0,0,0,0,0,0,1,3,7,6
21180 DATA 6,6,15,63,127,255,255,127,127,255,239,207,30,127,255,252
21190 REM Frame 3, Player 1
21200 DATA 0,0,0,0,0,0,0,0,0,0,0,0,0,0,0
21210 DATA 1,1,3,7,15,31,63,255,252,192,0,0,0,0,0,0
21220 REM Frame 4, Player 1
21230 DATA 0,0,0,0,0,0,0,13,31,30,0,0,0,7,31
21240 DATA 63,255,255,255,255,0,0,0,0,0,0,0,0,0,0
21250 REM Frame 1, Player 2
21260 DATA 0,1,7,31,63,63,63,63,31,207,231,247,127,126,254
21270 DATA 254,254,254,255,247,227,128,128,128,131,135,207,254,252,240,96
21280 REM Frame 2, Player 2
21290 DATA 0,0,0,0,0,3,15,31,63,63,31,159,207,231,255
21300 DATA 127,254,252,252,252,253,223,143,128,192,192,0,0,128,0,0
21310 REM Frame 3, Player 2
21320 DATA 0,0,3,7,15,15,15,15,15,7,1,1,7,63,255
21330 DATA 255,255,254,255,255,252,255,255,252,62,14,0,0,0,0
21340 REM Frame 4, Player 2
21350 DATA 1,7,15,15,15,15,7,199,227,121,63,63,254,255,255
21360 DATA 255,240,224,192,240,248,63,31,15,6,0,0,0,0,0,0
21370 REM Frame 1, Player 3
21380 DATA 120,252,244,240,240,240,176,176,248,184,200,240,128,0,8
21390 DATA 120,120,240,192,128,0,0,0,0,0,0,0,0,0,0,0
21400 REM Frame 2, Player 3
21410 DATA 0,0,0,124,254,254,252,248,248,248,216,216,252,220,228
21420 DATA 248,0,0,96,224,224,192,128,0,0,0,0,0,0,0,0
21430 REM Frame 3, Player 3
21440 DATA 0,126,255,255,255,252,236,236,254,238,242,252,224,128,0
21450 DATA 0,0,0,128,128,0,128,0,0,0,0,0,0,0,0,0
21460 REM Frame 4, Player 3
21470 DATA 254,255,255,253,252,236,236,254,238,242,252,0,3,135,255
21480 DATA 252,0,0,96,224,224,192,192,128,0,0,0,0,0,0,0
21490 REM
```

Figure 8.42: Listing of Example 11 — lines 20000–21490.

Frame Data   Here is the frame data for the Running Boy. Each frame takes up two DATA lines. The first one has 16 bytes and the second has 15.

```
1000 REM PARAMETERS FOR PLAYERS
1010 REM Boy
1020 GOSUB 1500: REM Point to Frame Lists
1030 FOR I=0 TO NUMPLRS-1
1040     POKE VPLR(I),PY
1050     POKE HPLR(I),PX+I*8
1060 NEXT I
1070 TEMP=USR(PMOVER,ALLP)
1080 RETURN
1090 REM
```

Figure 8.43: Listing of Example 11 — lines 1000–1090.

Film 6

"Walking Man," MAGI (Mathematical Applications Group, Inc.). This is an example of cyclic animation — these frames of a walking mechanical man can be endlessly repeated to show a continuous walk. The images, created by artist Chris Wedge, were computed with the MAGI SynthaVision 3-D computer animation system on a Perkin-Elmer 3240 super-minicomputer. The output was filmed on a CELCO CFR 4000 Color Film Recorder. Resolution is 1680 points per line by 1200 lines. Dynamic range is 256 grey levels for each of the red, green, and blue components of the pictures. *(Courtesy of MAGI/SynthaVision.)*

Parameters For Players   This subroutine POKEs the initial parameter table values for PMOVER. Line 1070 moves all the players to their starting position.

```
300   PRINT "(CLEAR)(6 RIGHT)*** RUNNING BOY DEMO ***"
310   PRINT "Press a number from 1 to 9 to control his speed or 0's to single step.";
320   FOR I=9 TO 0 STEP -1:
         READ TEMP:
         MSPEED(I)=TEMP:
      NEXT I
330   PX=10:
      PY=64
340   GOSUB 1000
350   SFLAG=2
360   POKE INITANIMATE,ALLP
370   SPEED=6:
      GOSUB 700
380   OPEN #2,4,0,"K:":
      POKE 754,255
390   REM

30000  REM Data for MSPEED (Automove speeds)
30010  DATA 1,2,2,3,3,4,5,6,9,0
```

Figure 8.44: Listing of Example 11 — lines 300–390, 30000–30010.

More Initialize   Line 320 reads the MSPEED DATA into the array. The intermediate variable, TEMP, is used because in ATARI BASIC you can't directly READ DATA into an array. Line 330 has new PX and PY values because of the boy's large size. In line 360, ANIMATE is initialized for all the players. Line 370 sets a new initial SPEED.

```
700   REM Set Velocities and Frame Rates
710   IF PEEK(INITANIMATE)<>128 THEN 710
720   FOR I=0 TO NUMPLRS-1
730      POKE MOVERATE(I),128+MSPEED(SPEED)
740      POKE RATE(I),SPEED
750   NEXT I
760   POKE INITANIMATE,ALLP+16
770   POKE INITAUTOMOVE,ALLP
780   RETURN
790   REM
```

Figure 8.45: Listing of Example 11 — lines 700–790.

Set Velocities and Frame Rates   This subroutine now sets the new horizontal velocities for each player in addition to their frame rates. Line 730 POKEs the correct value of MSPEED into the MOVERATE addresses. Line 760 resets the frame rate for all the players, and line 770 starts them moving across the screen.

```
400  REM  Main Animation Loop
410  IF PEEK(1086)=SFLAG THEN
        SOUND 0,0,0,10:
        SFLAG=3: REM Footsteps
420  IF PEEK(1086)=SFLAG THEN
        SOUND 0,24,0,10:
        SFLAG=2
430  SOUND 0,0,0,0
460  IF PEEK(1062)<PX THEN
        POKE INITAUTOMOVE,ALLP:
        TEMP=USR(PMOVER,ALLP): REM Reset Boy
480  IF PEEK(754)=255 THEN 410
490  GET #2,BYTE:
        SPEED=BYTE-48:
        POKE 754,255:
        IF SPEED<0 THEN
        SPEED=0
500  IF SPEED>9 THEN
        SPEED=9
510  GOSUB 700
520  GOTO 410
530  REM
```

Figure 8.46: Listing of Example 11 — lines 400–530.

Main Animation Loop   The only change to this section is line 460, which makes sure the boy is still on the screen. If the horizontal position of Player 0 (determined through parameter table address 1062) is less than the value in PX (10, off screen right), then AUTOMOVE is reactivated by POKEing ALLP into INITAUTOMOVE (the values currently in the MOVERATE registers are used again), and the boy is returned to his starting position with PMOVER.

A rather exotic bug would appear if PMOVER were called before AUTOMOVE on this line; it's possible to cause the boy to split in half as a separation appears between the four players. This would happen if a key is pressed to change the speed at the proper instant — for example, after Player 1, 2, and 3 have reached position 255 and been sent to 0, but before Player 0 reaches 255. All the players would be given the new velocity. Then, after Player 0 reaches 255 and its velocity is stopped when it gets sent to 0, the other players will still be moving from the recent speed change. PMOVER would then properly position all the players, but three of them will keep moving while Player 0 waits the fraction of a second for AUTOMOVE to be called on the same line. The solution is to write the line as we did with AUTOMOVE before PMOVER.

Go ahead and run the program now. Entering the frame data for the boy was a lot of work, but now you'll see it was worth it!

If you press the **BREAK** key while the boy is still on the screen, he will continue running but will not reappear. That's because line 460 needs to be executed for him to reappear from the left side, and the BASIC program has been stopped.

Modifications

1. Implement AUTOMOVE using the Walking Man data. You'll have to create a new set of MSPEED values to create realistic motion in relation to his frame rate.

2. Make the boy run backwards. Change the frame lists and the velocity. Don't forget to make his starting position on the right side of the screen.

Summary

You now have all of our tools to make player graphics easier to use. In the final section of this chapter, we will take these tools and create the animated foreground for our climactic program, the Great Movie Cartoon.

8.5. PLAYER FOREGROUND FOR THE GREAT MOVIE CARTOON

Imagine you own an ion-powered train which can cruise at sub-light speeds or stop on a dime. While traveling through the undeveloped outskirts of a major metropolis, you see cars and trucks speeding by, large green trees, and an occasional resident out for a stroll. Sometimes you choose to stop your train to watch everything move by; other times you enjoy matching the velocities of the inhabitants, or "dragging" with the local automobiles.

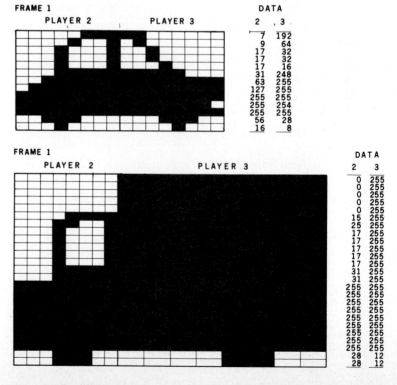

Figure 8.47: Player frame data for cars, trucks, and trees.

In this section we will take everything we know about players and put it together into one program. This program will make use of multi-colored players, double- and quadruple-width players, player priorities, sound effects, keyboard control, and all of the machine language routines introduced so far. This program of foreground objects will later be combined with a background program for the next chapter's Great Movie Cartoon.

The Cast of Players

In addition to the walking man, this program must display cars, trucks, and trees. Each object will use two players: the cars use two adjacent double-wide players of the same randomly selected color, the trucks use one double-wide player for the cab and a quadruple-wide player for the trailer (both in different colors). Finally, the trees use a brown single-wide player for the trunk and a green quadruple-wide player for the leafy top. However, unlike the walking man, each of these objects has only one frame. Their only form of animation will be their motion across the screen. The frame data for these new objects is in Figure 8.47.

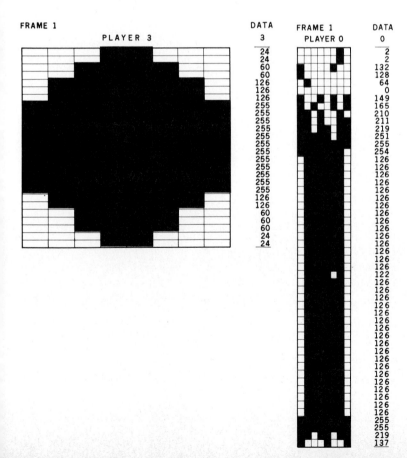

You may be wondering how we can display four objects on the screen, each of which uses two players — don't we really need eight players? That would be nice, but it's not necessary. The trick is: never allow more than two objects on the screen at once.[1] Players 0 and 1 are permanently reserved by the Walking Man. Players 2 and 3 are used for the rest of the objects. When a tree is passing by, the street is suspiciously free of cars and trucks. When a truck hogs the road, not a car or tree is in sight. The little man, however, comes and goes as he pleases, regardless of the traffic or foliage.

Overview of the Player Foreground Demo

To understand this program, take the point of view that we are looking out of a window of a moving vehicle. The only thing we can control is our own velocity in relation to the scene on the screen. From time to time, cars, trucks, and trees appear to pass in front of our window. Our point of view can be moved parallel to these objects at different speeds, but always towards the right (the same direction the man is walking). Each object has its own intrinsic velocity in relation to the ground. To simulate this on the screen, our velocity is subtracted from the object's velocity, and this value is passed to AUTOMOVE for that object. When our velocity is 0, the man (whose velocity is 1) walks past us across the screen. When our velocity is 1, we are moving at the same rate as the man, and he stays framed in our window. This is because our two velocities cancel each other out $(1 - 1 = 0)$. When we increase our velocity beyond 1, the man moves off the screen to the left as we seem to leave him behind.

Trees, on the other hand, have no velocity of their own (of course), so unless our velocity is 0, we pass them by. The velocity of a tree (in relation to our point of view) is calculated by multiplying our velocity by 2 and subtracting the result from the tree's 0 velocity. This won't make much sense until the background is added in the next chapter. For now, just accept that this exaggerated velocity will look realistic in the final program.

When a car occasionally appears on the screen, it is also moving in the same direction as we are, but at a velocity of 4. This means that if we are moving at a velocity less than 4, the car will pass *us* by. Trucks move in the other direction (from right to left) with a velocity of -3. The higher our velocity, the faster the trucks seem to roar across the screen.

Most of the work in this program is handled by our black box

---

[1] By using display list interrupts (see next chapter), it would be possible to cause a player to appear on the screen in more than one incarnation at the same time. Different figures would be stacked within a single player, restricting each to a separate horizontal band on the screen.

machine language routines. BASIC's job is to handle the orchestration of the program — which object should appear next, calculating the object's velocity in relation to our own, watching when an object leaves the screen, accepting keyboard input, and controlling the sound effects. BASIC is also responsible for setting up the frame lists and POKEing the frame data into memory. Much of the program code has been taken from the previous examples to make it easier for you to enter and understand.

Example 12

Exercise   Using your knowledge of players in conjunction with our machine language routines, create a program which simulates a window looking onto a scene that contains a walking man, tall trees, and roaring cars and trucks. We, as observers, can only change our own velocity in relation to the scene by entering numbers from the keyboard.

a)

b)

c)

Photo 8.2:   Screen photos of man, tree, car, and truck.

First, load the Walking Man program, Example 10, into memory. Then save the DATA statements, lines 20050–21200, onto disk or cassette:

```
LIST "D:MAN.DAT",20050,21200   (disk)
LIST "C:",20050,21200           (cassette)
```

You will add this data into the program later on. Next, load the Running Boy program, Example 11, and delete the following lines:

780   21210–30010

Many of the lines in Example 12 are similar but not identical to lines in Example 11. Others are completely new. We will indicate when a line requires only modification, rather than a total retyping, by placing an asterisk (*) before its line number, in addition to highlighting it.

```
  10 REM *** PLAYER FOREGROUND DEMO ***
* 20 REM            Example 12
  30 REM
  40 REM Program using all four Players to create animated foreground
  50 REM Copyright (C) 1982 by David Fox and Mitchell Waite
  60 REM
  70 GOTO 140
  80 REM
 100 REM Hi/Lo Byte Calculation
 110 HIBYTE=INT(X/256): REM Calculate High Byte
 120 LOBYTE=X-HIBYTE*256: REM Calculate Low Byte
 130 RETURN
 140 REM Initialize
*150 DIM PLR(3),HPLR(3),VPLR(3),RATE(3),PMWIDTH(3),FRMLSTPTR(3),MOVERATE(3)
 170 GRAPHICS 3:
     POKE 752,1:
     PRINT "One moment please...": REM Turn off cursor, print message
```

Figure 8.48: Listing of Example 12 — lines 10–170.

Initialize   Some new arrays are introduced in line 150. PMWIDTH contains the addresses of the player width registers. FRMDATA is now DIMensioned in line 5070.

```
5000 REM Set Up Memory Locations
5060 READ OBJS
5070 DIM FRMDATA(OBJS,3):
     DIM FRAMES(OBJS),FRMSIZE(OBJS),NUMPLRS(OBJS),PLRFRMMEM(OBJS),FRMLSTSIZE(OBJS)
5080 FOR I=1 TO OBJS
5090    READ TEMP1,TEMP2,TEMP3
5100    FRAMES(I)=TEMP1:
        FRMSIZE(I)=TEMP2:
        NUMPLRS(I)=TEMP3
*5110   PLRFRMMEM(I)=FRAMES(I)*FRMSIZE(I)+1
*5120   FRAMEMEM=FRAMEMEM+PLRFRMMEM(I)*NUMPLRS(I)
*5130   FRMLSTSIZE(I)=FRAMES(I)+3
5140    TOTFRMLSTSIZE=TOTFRMLSTSIZE+FRMLSTSIZE(I)*NUMPLRS(I)
5150 NEXT I
5160 DIM BUFFER$(128),FRAMEMEM$(FRAMEMEM),FRMLSTMEM$(TOTFRMLSTSIZE)
```

Figure 8.49: Listing of Example 12 — lines 5000–5160.

Set Up Memory Locations   Line 5060 READs the number of objects being displayed in the program (OBJS). (The tree is considered to be two objects, trunk and top, so there will be a total of five objects.) In line 5070, a number of familiar variables has been converted to arrays, so information on each object can be individually maintained. FRMDATA, which contains the addresses of the frame data, is now a two-dimensional array. The first dimension, 5, refers to the number of objects, and the second refers to the player numbers (0 to 3) which make up those objects. This reflects a change from Example 11 where there was only one object to animate (the boy). Now FRMDATA can point to the frame data for each player of each object.

The loop from 5080 to 5150 reserves frame data and frame list memory for each of the objects. The TEMPorary variables in lines 5090 and 5100 are needed because ATARI BASIC can't directly READ data into an array. Lines 5110–5130 have been modified to include the subscripts (I).

```
7000  REM Initialize Player-Missile Graphics
7010  TEMP=PEEK(106)-8: REM Set aside Player-Missile area
7020  POKE 54279,TEMP: REM Tell ANTIC where PM RAM is
7030  PMBASE=256*TEMP: REM Find PM Base address
7040  FOR I=0 TO 3
7050    PLR(I)=PMBASE+128*I+512: REM Set addresses of Players
7060    PMWIDTH(I)=53256+I: REM Set addresses of Player Widths
7070  NEXT I
7080  POKE 559,42: REM Set PM 2 line resolution, Players enabled
7090  POKE 623,1: REM Set priority - Players in front
7100  POKE 53277,2: REM Enable Player display
7110  TEMP=USR(MFILL,PLR(0),512,0): REM Use memory fill routine to clear Players
7120  RETURN
```

Figure 8.50: Listing of Example 12 — lines 7000–7120.

Initialize Player-Missile Graphics   Line 7060 saves the addresses of the player width registers, and 7090 sets the player priority so the players will appear in front of a playfield (see Table 7.5).

```
10000   REM Read in Frame Data
10010   OFFSET=0:
        OFFSET2=0:
        DIM FRAMELIST(OBJS)
10020   FOR K=1 TO OBJS
*10030    FRAMELIST(K)=FRMLSTMEM+OFFSET
10040     OFFSET=OFFSET+(FRAMES(K)+3)*NUMPLRS(K)
*10050    FOR I=0 TO NUMPLRS(K)-1
*10060      FRMDATA(K,I)=PLRFRAMES+OFFSET2: REM Store addresses of frame data
*10070      OFFSET2=OFFSET2+PLRFRMMEM(K)
*10080      POKE FRMDATA(K,I),FRMSIZE(K): REM Poke Frame size at beginning of each set of frame data
*10090      FOR J=1 TO PLRFRMMEM(K)-1
10100        READ BYTE
*10110        POKE FRMDATA(K,I)+J,BYTE
*10120      NEXT J:
          NEXT I:
        NEXT K
10130   RETURN
```

Figure 8.51: Listing of Example 12 — lines 10000–10130.

Read in Frame Data   The main change in this section is the added K FOR / NEXT loop to read in data for all the objects. Line 10010 initializes OFFSET which will be used to calculate the beginning address of the next frame list. FRAMELIST is turned into an array to maintain the beginning address of the frame lists for each object.

Line 10040 calculates the size of the frame list for object K and adds it to OFFSET.

```
12210  P0=1:
       P1=2:
       P2=4:
       P3=8: REM Control bits for the four Players
12220  FST2P=P0+P1
*12230 LST2P=P2+P3:
       ALLP=P0+P1+P2+P3
```

Figure 8.52: Listing of Example 12 — lines 12210–12230.

Set Parameters For Routines

The variable LST2P has been added to make it easier to control the last two players (2 and 3).

```
12400  REM Set Up Frame Lists
12410  DIM POINTER(OBJS,1)
12420  FOR K=1 TO OBJS
*12430   FOR I=0 TO NUMPLRS(K)-1
*12440     LET POINTER(K,I)=FRAMELIST(K)+I*FRMLSTSIZE(K): REM Points to start of each Frame List
*12450     X=FRMDATA(K,I):
           GOSUB 110
*12460     POKE POINTER(K,I),LOBYTE: REM Put in address of Frame Data
*12470     POKE POINTER(K,I)+1,HIBYTE
*12480     FOR J=1 TO FRAMES(K): REM Make up a Frame List (numbers 1 thru FRAMES)
*12490       POKE POINTER(K,I)+J+1,J
12500     NEXT J
*12510     POKE POINTER(K,I)+FRAMES(K)+2,0: REM End of frame list marker
*12520   NEXT I:
         NEXT K
12530  RETURN
```

Figure 8.53: Listing of Example 12 — lines 12400–12530.

Set Up Frame Lists

Again, the main change to this section is the addition of a K FOR/NEXT loop to cover all the objects. In line 12410, POINTER, the variable which holds the addresses of each frame list, is turned into a two-dimensional array. The first dimension is the number of objects, and the second is the number of players. Since none of the objects use more than two players, a 1 is used for the second number (for values 0 and 1).

```
20000  REM FRAME DATA
20010  REM Number of objects
20020  DATA 5
20030  REM
20040  REM Number of Frames, Frame Size, Number of Players
20050  REM . (Walking Man)
20060  DATA 5,19,2
20070  REM . (Tree Trunk)
20080  DATA 1,52,1
20090  REM . (Tree Top)
20100  DATA 1,26,1
20110  REM . (Truck)
20120  DATA 1,25,2
20130  REM . (Car)
20140  DATA 1,13,2
20150  REM
21000  REM Frame data for Walking Man
21010  REM Frame 1, Player 0
21020  DATA 0,0,0,0,0,0,0,3,15,29,59,51,7,7,15,252,224,112,48
21030  REM Frame 2, Player 0
21040  DATA 0,0,0,0,0,0,0,1,7,15,31,55,55,7,111,125,248,192,193
21050  REM Frame 3, Player 0
21060  DATA 0,0,0,0,0,0,3,7,15,31,31,31,31,222,254,251,231,206,15
```

(continued)

```
21070   REM Frame 4, Player 0
21080   DATA 1,3,3,3,1,7,15,31,30,62,62,63,63,60,124,120,112,112,252
21090   REM Frame 5, Player 0
21100   DATA 0,0,1,1,1,0,7,31,31,31,31,15,15,13,31,123,112,124
21110   REM Frame 1, Player 1
21120   DATA 0,28,62,62,62,28,240,240,240,240,251,255,220,192,192,227,118,60,24
21130   REM Frame 2, Player 1
21140   DATA 0,0,56,124,124,124,56,224,224,224,224,246,254,192,128,192,224,224,248
21150   REM Frame 3, Player 1
21160   DATA 0,112,248,248,248,112,192,192,128,128,128,224,224,0,0,0,0,0,128
21170   REM Frame 4, Player 1
21180   DATA 192,224,224,224,192,0,0,0,0,0,0,0,0,0,0,0,0,0
21190   REM Frame 5, Player 1
21200   DATA 0,224,240,240,240,224,128,128,128,128,176,240,0,128,192,128,192,0,0
21210   REM
22000   REM Frame data for Tree
22010   REM Player 2, Tree Trunk
22020   DATA 2,2,132,128,64,0,149,165,210,211,219,251,255,254,126,126,126,126,126,126
22030   DATA 126,126,126,126,126,126,126,126,126,122,126,126,126,126,126,126,126,126,126
22040   DATA 126,126,126,126,126,126,126,126,255,255,219,137
22050   REM Player 3, Tree Top
22060   DATA 24,24,60,60,126,126,126,255,255,255,255,255,255,255,255,255,255,255,255,126
22070   DATA 126,60,60,60,24,24
22080   REM
22100   REM Frame data for Truck
22110   REM Player 2, Truck Cab
22120   DATA 0,0,0,0,0,15,25,17,17,17,17,17,31,31,255,255,255,255,255
22130   DATA 255,255,255,28,28
22140   REM Player 3, Truck Body
22150   DATA 255,255,255,255,255,255,255,255,255,255,255,255,255,255,255,255,255,255,255
22160   DATA 255,255,255,12,12
22170   REM
22200   REM Frame data for Car
22210   REM Player 2, Car back
22220   DATA 7,9,17,17,17,31,63,127,255,255,255,255,56,16
22230   REM Player 3, Car front
22240   DATA 192,64,32,32,16,248,255,255,255,254,255,28,8
```

Figure 8.54: Listing of Example 12 — lines 20000–22240.

Frame Data This section has all the frame data of our objects. Now is the time to ENTER the earlier saved data of the man:

```
ENTER "D:MAN.DAT"   (disk)
ENTER "C:"          (cassette)
```

Then go ahead and enter the rest of the lines (the ones which are highlighted). There are no more than 20 sets of numbers on any of the lines. Look at lines 20070–20100, and you'll see why we separated the tree into two objects. Each player in an object must have the same number of bytes for our routines to work properly. Since the trunk has twice as many bytes (52) as the top (26), it would have been necessary to pad the tree top with an extra 26 zero bytes (bytes with a value of 0) to make them equal.

```
1000   REM PARAMETERS FOR PLAYERS
1010   REM Man
1020   POKE 704,3*16+10:
       POKE 705,3*16+10: REM Set color to peach
1030   FRSTPLR=0:
       OBJECT=1:
       GOSUB 1500: REM Point to proper Frame List
1040   POKE VPLR(0),77:
       POKE VPLR(1),77
1050   IF SPEED=1 THEN 1070
1060   POKE HPLR(0),20:
       POKE HPLR(1),28:
       IF SPEED>1 THEN
          POKE HPLR(0),218:
          POKE HPLR(1),226
1070   WALK=INT(RND(1)*100+20)
```

(continued)

```
1080 RETURN
1090 REM
1100 REM Tree
1110 IF SPEED=0 THEN
       RETURN
1120 POKE 706,14*16+4:
       POKE 707,13*16+6: REM Brown trunk and green leaves
1130 POKE HPLR(2),229:
       POKE HPLR(3),217
1140 POKE VPLR(2),32:
       POKE VPLR(3),18
1150 FRSTPLR=2:
       OBJECT=2:
       GOSUB 1500:
       FRSTPLR=3:
       OBJECT=3:
       GOSUB 1500: REM Point to proper Frame List
1160 POKE PMWIDTH(2),0:
       POKE PMWIDTH(3),3
1170 VF=0
1180 RETURN
1190 REM
1200 REM Truck
1210 POKE 706,3*16+6:
       POKE 707,INT(RND(1)*16)*16+10
1220 POKE HPLR(2),217:
       POKE HPLR(3),233
1230 POKE VPLR(2),57:
       POKE VPLR(3),57
1240 FRSTPLR=2:
       OBJECT=4:
       GOSUB 1500: REM Point to proper Frame List
1250 POKE PMWIDTH(2),1:
       POKE PMWIDTH(3),3
1260 VF=1:
       SCONS=180
1270 RETURN
1280 REM
1300 REM Car
1310 IF SPEED=4 THEN
       RETURN
1320 C=INT(RND(1)*16):
       L=8-INT(RND(1)*2)*4:
       TEMP=C*16+L:
       POKE 706,TEMP:
       POKE 707,TEMP
1330 POKE HPLR(2),0:
       POKE HPLR(3),16
1340 IF SPEED>4 THEN
       POKE HPLR(2),216:
       POKE HPLR(3),232
1350 POKE VPLR(2),76:
       POKE VPLR(3),76
1360 FRSTPLR=2:
       OBJECT=5:
       GOSUB 1500: REM Point to proper Frame List
1370 POKE PMWIDTH(2),1:
       POKE PMWIDTH(3),1
1380 VF=1:
       SCONS=40
1390 RETURN
1400 REM
```

Figure 8.55: Listing of Example 12 — lines 1000–1400.

Parameters For Players   This section consists of four subroutines, one to initialize the player information for the men, trees, trucks, and cars. The color, vertical (VPLR) and horizontal (HPLR) starting position, and player width must be set for each object.

Let's look at the Man subroutine first (lines 1010–1090). After the color is set, another subroutine is called in line 1030, placing the appropriate frame list information into the parameter table. This routine (at 1500) requires two pieces of information: the first player (0 to 3) in which to place the frame data (FRSTPLR) and the number of the OBJECT which is to be used. The first player that the man will occupy is Player 0 (FRSTPLR=0) and the man is object number one (OBJECT=1). Line 1040 sets the vertical position for the man. Line

1050 checks to see if the current velocity (SPEED) is 1. If so, then the horizontal position doesn't need to be set (in line 1060). Since the man also walks at a velocity of one, he will never appear on the screen when we are traveling at this velocity. If he is already on the screen, then line 1060 doesn't need to be executed again. Line 1060 will position the man either off screen left or right, depending on the current value of SPEED. If our SPEED is 0, the man will pass by our window from the left to the right. If we are moving greater than 1, we will seem to pass the man by and he will move from the right edge to the left. In 1070 a flag is set that will keep the man from appearing on the screen for a random period of time.

The tree section (lines 1100–1190) is very similar. In line 1110, the SPEED is checked for a value of 0. If the tree objects are selected to make their appearance while our velocity is 0, this line sends the program back for another selection. This is because if we are stopped when the tree objects are selected, nothing will happen until we begin moving again. Since the tree has no velocity of its own, it would just stand patiently off screen right until we pass by it. As we mentioned before, only one non-man object can be on the screen at a time, so the stationary tree would keep the cars and trucks away.

Line 1150 calls the subroutine at 1500 twice, once for each of the tree's objects. The width of the tree players are set in line 1160 with the tree top set to quadruple width. Line 1170 sets a volume flag (VF) so the main animation section will know whether to make a sound or not. We don't want a roaring tree, so VF is set to 0.

The truck section (line 1200–1280) adds a few variations. In line 1210, the trailer of the truck is assigned a random hue (with a luminance of 10). The cab is always orange to avoid some awful color combinations. In line 1220, notice that the difference between the horizontal position of the two players is 16 rather than 8 as in earlier programs. This is because the cab of the truck will be set to double width (in line 1250). As with the tree, the truck will always emerge from the right side of the screen. In line 1260, the volume flag is turned on (VF = 1), and the pitch of the truck's roar is set by the sound constant (SCONS = 180).

Finally, take a look at the car section (lines 1300–1390). In line 1310, the velocity is checked to see if it matches the car's velocity of 4. If they do match, the two velocities will cancel each other out, and the situation described for the tree with a velocity of 0 will occur. In line 1320, a random color from 0 to 15 is selected along with a random luminosity of either 4 or 8. This is to make sure that in the final program, when the car is traveling over a background with a luminance of 6, the car won't seem to vanish into the street if the luminance and color values happen to match. In lines 1330 and 1340, the initial horizontal position of the car is set based on the current SPEED to make sure the car appears from the correct side of the screen. In line 1380, the volume flag is turned

on and the sound constant value is set to 40. This will create a higher pitched roar than that of the truck.

```
1500  REM Put Frame List Address in Param Table
*1510  FOR I=0 TO NUMPLRS(OBJECT)-1
*1520      X=POINTER(OBJECT,I):
           GOSUB 110
*1530      POKE FRMLSTPTR(I+FRSTPLR),LOBYTE
*1540      POKE FRMLSTPTR(I+FRSTPLR)+1,HIBYTE
1550  NEXT I
1560  RETURN
1570  REM
```

Figure 8.56: Listing of Example 12 — lines 1500–1570.

Put Frame List Address in Parameter Table   This is the subroutine that is called whenever we want to move new objects into the players. As we said before, OBJECT selects which object will be used, and FRSTPLR points to the first player that will be filled. The values in the NUMPLRS array controls how many players the selected object uses.

```
300  PRINT "(CLEAR)(3 RIGHT)*** PLAYER FOREGROUND DEMO ***"
310  FOR I=0 TO 1:
         POKE RATE(I),4:
         NEXT I: REM Frame rate for walking man
320  SPEED=-1: REM Temporary start up condition
330  GOSUB 1000:
         GOSUB 1100
340  SPEED=1
350  TEMP=USR(PMOVER,ALLP)
360  POKE INITANIMATE,ALLP
370  GOSUB 700
380  OPEN #2,4,0,"K:":
         POKE 754,255
390  REM
```

Figure 8.57: Listing of Example 12 — lines 300–390.

More Initializing   This section finishes the initialization process. Line 310 places the frame rate for the man players into the parameter table. Note that the frame rate for Players 2 and 3 are still set to 0, as they will be throughout this program. ANIMATE will therefore be used for two purposes: to automatically animate the man and to move new frame information into the other players. In line 320, SPEED is temporarily set to −1. This will allow us to set the parameters for both the man and the tree (the first object to pass by our window) in line 330 (remember that both the man and tree parameter-setting subroutines check for "legal" values of SPEED). In line 340 the SPEED is set to 1, the starting velocity for the program. Line 350 positions all the players to their starting positions, and 360 moves the frames into player memory and starts the man walking (although he is still off the screen). Then the subroutine (starting at line 700) is called, starting the players across the screen.

```
700  REM Set Horizontal Velocities
710  IF OBJECT=3 THEN
         NSPD=128-SPEED*2:
         GOTO 740: REM Tree
720  IF OBJECT=4 THEN
         NSPD=125-SPEED:
         GOTO 740: REM Truck
730  NSPD=132-SPEED: REM Car
740  POKE MOVERATE(2),NSPD:
         POKE MOVERATE(3),NSPD:
         TEMP=LST2P
750  POKE MOVERATE(0),129-SPEED:
         POKE MOVERATE(1),129-SPEED:
         IF WALK=-1 THEN
           TEMP=ALLP
760  POKE INITAUTOMOVE,TEMP
780  RETURN
```

Figure 8.58: Listing of Example 12 — lines 700–780.

Set Horizontal Velocities This part of the program calculates the proper velocities for each of the objects. This routine is called whenever a new object has been selected or when a key is pressed to change the SPEED. Line 710 calculates the new speed (NSPD) for the trees, line 720 for the trucks, and 730 for the cars. As we mentioned earlier, these velocities are obtained by subtracting our velocity from the object's inherent velocity.

Line 740 places NSPD into the parameter table and sets TEMP to LST2P (last 2 players). The velocity of the man is POKEd into the table in line 750, and then the value of WALK is checked. If it has been set to −1 in the main animation loop, then the man can appear on the screen and TEMP is reset to include the man players. Then, in line 760, AUTOMOVE is started for the players represented in TEMP. An alternate method would be to POKE INITAUTOMOVE once for the man in line 750 and again for the other object in 760. It would then be necessary to add a line 755 to keep checking the value in INITAUTOMOVE until it equalled 128. This would prevent AUTOMOVE from taking the information from line 760 before it was finished with line 750:

```
755  IF PEEK(INITAUTOMOVE)<>128 THEN 755
```

The method we chose insures that the velocity of all players will be changed simultaneously.

```
600  REM Select a New Object
610  IF VOL THEN
         VOL=INT(VOL):
         IF VOL=0 THEN
           VOL=1
620  IF VOL THEN
         VOL=VOL-0.5:
         SOUND 1,SND,8,VOL:
         SOUND 2,SND2,2,VOL:
         GOTO 620
630  TEMP=USR(MFILL,PLR(2),256,0): REM Use memory fill routine to clear Players 2 & 3
640  FLAG=INT(RND(1)*6+1): REM Which object to display (if possible)
650  OBJECT=0: REM No object selected yet
660  ON FLAG GOSUB 1100,1100,1100,1200,1300,1300:
         IF OBJECT=0 THEN
           RETURN
670  TEMP=USR(PMOVER,LST2P)
680  POKE INITANIMATE,LST2P
690  REM
```

Figure 8.59: Listing of Example 12 — lines 600–690.

Select a New Object This routine randomly selects one of the non-man objects to appear on the screen. It is called whenever the main animation loop discovers that one of these objects has exited the screen. In line 610 and 620, the current VOLume level of the last object to zoom across the screen is checked. If a sound is still turned on (VOL > 0), then it will be gradually faded out. Line 630 uses the MFILL routine to clear out Players 2 and 3 before they receive their new objects. Since the ANI-MATE frame rates for these two players is 0, ANIMATE isn't constantly updating them with new information. If the frame rates were non-zero, ANIMATE would refill the players as soon as they were cleared. In line 640, FLAG receives a number from 1 to 6 which will be used to choose the next object. Yes, we know there are only three possible choices, and we'll explain what we're doing in a moment. Line 650 sets OBJECT to 0, so we can use this variable as a flag to indicate whether an object was successfully selected. Line 660 directs the program to the selected subroutine. Notice that the first three line numbers are 1100 (the tree). This means that 3 out of 6 times (50 percent) a tree will be selected. Likewise, the truck will be selected 1 out of 6 times (16.7 percent) and the car 2 out of 6 times (33.3 percent). By changing this line and line 640, a different mix of objects could be created. You could reduce the number of cars and trucks to a very small percentage if you prefer a more rural setting.

If OBJECT is still set to 0 after the selected subroutine has been executed, this subroutine is exited. Otherwise, line 670 moves the new object to its starting position in line 670, and line 680 transfers the appropriate frames into the players. The program then falls through to the routine beginning at line 700 to set the velocities.

```
400 REM Main Animation Loop
410 TEMP=ABS(PEEK(1064)-128):
    SND=TEMP/5:
    SND2=SND+SCONS
420 IF VF THEN
    VOL=(128-TEMP)/9:
    SOUND 1,SND,8,VOL:
    SOUND 2,SND2,2,VOL
430 IF WALK>0 THEN
    WALK=WALK-(SPEED<>1):
    GOTO 470
440 IF WALK=0 THEN
    POKE INITAUTOMOVE,FST2P:
    TEMP=USR(PMOVER,FST2P):
    WALK=-1
450 IF PEEK(1086)=2 THEN
    SOUND 0,10,4,10:
    SOUND 0,0,0,0: REM Footsteps
460 IF PEEK(1062)>218 OR PEEK(1062)<20 THEN
    GOSUB 1050: REM Reset Man
470 IF PEEK(1064)>229 OR PEEK(1065)<16 THEN
    GOSUB 600: REM Reset other players
480 IF PEEK(754)=255 THEN 410
490 GET #2,BYTE:
    SPEED=BYTE-48:
    POKE 754,255:
    IF SPEED<0 THEN
    SPEED=0
510 GOSUB 700
520 GOTO 410
530 REM
```

Figure 8.60: Listing of Example 12 — lines 400–530.

Main Animation Loop   Now we come to the main controlling section of the program. This section creates the sound effects, watches to see when an object leaves the screen, and accepts keyboard input for velocity changes. Line 410 sets the value of two sound variables, SND and SND2, using the horizontal position of Player 2 (location 1063). As an object moves across the screen, the value in TEMP decreases from 128 to 0 (at midpoint) and back to 128. This value can be used to raise the pitch of the passing cars and trucks and then lower it again as they go off the screen. Line 420 controls the VOLume in a similar manner — it increases towards midpoint and fades as the vehicle leaves the screen. Notice that the sound is only turned on if the volume flag (VF) is set to 1.

Line 430 checks the value of WALK, the wait flag which gets set to a random number in line 1070. If WALK is still greater than 0 *and* SPEED is not 1, WALK is decremented and the program jumps to line 470, skipping the selection that creates the footstep sounds for the man. As soon as WALK becomes equal to 0 and the man can appear on the screen (SPEED< >1), line 440 starts the man moving across the screen, making sure he starts from the proper position, and sets WALK to −1 so this line isn't executed again until the next man arrives.

Line 450 checks the current frame number of Player 0 to synchronize a footstep to the man's feet. Line 460 checks the position of the man. If he has moved off the screen on either side, the man is reinitialized starting at line 1050.

If one of the other objects leaves the screen (line 470), a new object is selected in the subroutine beginning at line 600.

Now you may run this program. Have some fun trying to keep up with the man or drag racing with the car. Notice how the truck seems to get shorter as your velocity increases (theory of relativity at work?).

Modifications

1. Animate some of the objects (other than the man) by creating additional frames for them. Try to make the wheels turn, or place a flashing light on top of the car.
2. Add some additional objects — how about a bird, a plane, a differently shaped tree, or a motorcycle?

Commercially Available Software
Using Players and VBI

In addition to player-missile graphics, many commercial games use the vertical blank interrupt to gain more control of the computer. Jaw Breaker, by John Harris of On-Line Systems, uses the VBI to play the game's musical interludes and to redefine the character set. The object of this game is to move your set of teeth around the maze, munching lifesavers and avoiding the bullies who will knock your teeth out if they

catch you. Eating one of the colorful jawbreakers in the corner will turn the bad guys blue — then you can catch them.

John used ATARI's Music Composer cartridge to create the music, then converted the final music file into data for a VBI routine that plays the notes in a background mode while the action is occurring on the screen. GRAPHICS 0 is used for the playfield, with each lifesaver being a redefined character. The constant redefining of the jawbreaker character during VBLANK means that the colors (artifacts) are always changing in perfect unison. The teeth are made of the four missiles combined into a fifth player. If you manage to eat all the lifesavers, a giant toothbrush will appear to clean your teeth for another round. The toothbrush is made of one quadruple-wide player (the red handle) and one single-wide player (the bristles).

One of the features of this game that makes it stand out from the others in the *PAC-MAN* genre is the wonderful animations John added to the four bullies (each made of a player in single-line resolution mode). Each one has its own sequence of frames to go through. One's eyes bounce and mouth changes shape (five frames); one spins like a top (eight frames); one rolls like a coin on its edge (eighteen frames); and one flips upside down (twenty-four frames). The frame changing is not under VBI control, but is part of the main program — every time one of the objects moves, a new frame is placed into the player.

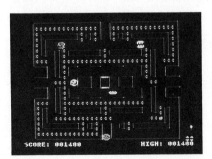

Photo 8.3: Screen photo of Jawbreakers. (Copyright (c) 1981 by On-Line Systems.)

In another game, Mouskattack (On-Line Systems), John Harris uses similar techniques. In this game, you are a plumber who must lay pipes in the dreaded Rat Alley. The rats are constantly trying to destroy you and your work, so you must move fast. In this game, there can be two people playing at the same time. The plumber or plumbers, represented as a hard hat(s), and the rodents are made of players. The inadequate mouse traps that you can lay, the pipes, and your two timid helper cats are made of GRAPHICS 0 redefined characters. The animation isn't quite as clever as in Jawbreakers. The rats stomp their feet up and down as they run after you, and, when a rat gets you, your hat floats to the ground (using five frames). John did, however, do a splendid job with the sound effect of laying the pipes. The clank sound, and all other sounds, are under VBI control.

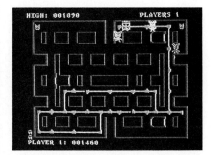

Photo 8.4: Screen photo of Mouskattack. (Copyright (c) 1981 by On-Line Systems.)

Summary

You have now graduated from player-missile graphics class and are ready to tackle some exciting games. However, before you go too far, there are two more special ATARI features we'll be introducing you to in Chapter 9, fine scrolling and display list interrupts. Using these techniques, you'll be able to create a moving background that would be the envy of any cartoon animator! Then, all the techniques discussed in this book will be combined into our grand finale, the Great Movie Cartoon.

Chapter 9

Creating A Scrolling Background

I n the golden years of film animation, companies like Walt Disney Productions perfected the art of fluid and realistic motion for their characters and paid painstaking attention to the quality of the background scenery for their cartoons as well. The results were imaginary worlds which irresistably pulled us in to share in their fantasies. To achieve this level of reality, Disney invented a large machine called a *multiplane*. This enabled artists to create complicated backgrounds consisting of up to six layers, each positioned at a different distance from the camera. As the characters in the foreground moved along, the backgrounds were scrolled behind them, each layer at a different rate, with the furthermost ones moving the most slowly as governed by the laws of perspective. The multiplane produced breathtaking results, but the dozen operators necessary to run it plus the tremendous production costs required to feed it multilevel backgrounds caused this marvel of technology to finally take up residence in the museum.

In today's cartoons, backgrounds usually consist of only one level which is moved behind the characters as they walk or drive along. This succeeds in creating the feeling of movement, but through a very flat, two-dimensional world. In this chapter, we will create a moving background for our foreground players of Example 12, bringing back the feeling of depth to animation. Our background has not one, but *two* levels, and when combined with the three levels of the foreground players in the final program of this book (the Great Movie Cartoon), provides a *five*-level scene with enough realism to bring on motion sickness if you have a weak stomach!

To give motion to our background, the ATARI feature of fine scrolling will be used. To color the screen with more colors than is normally possible, another feature called display list interrupts is utilized. Both features are implemented through our old friend, the ATARI display list.

9.1. THE DISPLAY LIST REVISED

In Chapter 5, we introduced you to the Exploding Bomb program (Example 4), which uses a graphics mode that is only accessible (in the

ATARI 400/800) by modifying the display list (DL). Recall that the DL is actually a program for Antic, the display processor chip. The DL specifies how the screen memory is to be interpreted; what graphics mode is in effect for each horizontal scan line. This enables us to create a screen made up of many different graphics modes. Although that is the primary purpose of the DL, there are some other important features that it can provide.

A GRAPHICS Ø Display List

Besides the specific graphics modes to be used, the display list tells Antic where to find screen RAM and whether to implement fine scrolling or display list interrupts. Different values for each DL instruction specify which functions are in effect. Let's start by taking a look at a normal, no frills display list. Enter and run the following program. It will print out the entire display list for a GRAPHICS Ø screen:

```
10 GRAPHICS Ø
20 DLIST=PEEK(560)+PEEK(561)*256
30 FOR I=Ø TO 31
40    PRINT I,PEEK(DLIST+I)
50 NEXT I
```

In Figure 9.1 are the numbers that will be printed out by this program, plus the description of each display list instruction and a picture of the screen showing which mode lines (horizontal band of scan lines which make up one graphics mode line) are controlled by each instruction.

As we explore the function of each of these bytes, refer to Table 9.1. It shows which bits of a display list instruction are used to control the graphics mode that will be in effect and which bits enable the different display list functions.

Bit Number:			7	6	5	4	3	2	1	0
Bit Value:			128	64	32	16	8	4	2	1
Mode Type								•	•	•
Horizontal Fine Scrolling						•				
Vertical Fine Scrolling					•					
Load Memory Scan				•						
Display List Interrupt			•							

Table 9.1: Display list control bits.

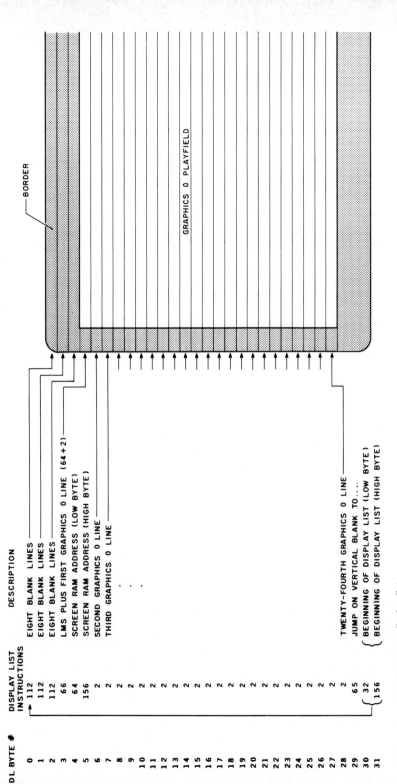

DL BYTE #	DISPLAY LIST INSTRUCTIONS	DESCRIPTION
0	112	EIGHT BLANK LINES
1	112	EIGHT BLANK LINES
2	112	EIGHT BLANK LINES
3	66	LMS PLUS FIRST GRAPHICS 0 LINE (64 + 2)
4	64	SCREEN RAM ADDRESS (LOW BYTE)
5	156	SCREEN RAM ADDRESS (HIGH BYTE)
6	2	SECOND GRAPHICS 0 LINE
7	2	THIRD GRAPHICS 0 LINE
8	2	
9	2	
10	2	
11	2	
12	2	
13	2	
14	2	
15	2	
16	2	
17	2	
18	2	
19	2	
20	2	
21	2	
22	2	
23	2	
24	2	
25	2	
26	2	
27	2	
28	2	TWENTY-FOURTH GRAPHICS 0 LINE
29	65	JUMP ON VERTICAL BLANK TO.....
30	32	BEGINNING OF DISPLAY LIST (LOW BYTE)
31	156	BEGINNING OF DISPLAY LIST (HIGH BYTE)

BORDER

GRAPHICS 0 PLAYFIELD

Figure 9.1: GRAPHICS 0 display list.

Because more than one display list function can be implemented with each instruction, calculating the correct value can be confusing. Table 9.2 can be used to figure out what byte value the display list instruction should have. It gives the decimal byte value for all possible mode/function combinations for creating a custom DL. Don't be overwhelmed by the table's size; it's really very simple to use. Just look in the top section (with all the **X**s) to find the column which has the combination of features you want to implement, then follow that column down to the bottom section until you find the graphics mode you want to use. The number found at that intersection is the value to use in your display list. Note that some DL instructions are always followed by a two-byte address.

Let's use this table to decipher the sample display list in Figure 9.1. Starting at the top of the DL, the first byte is a 112. Now, look at the first number column (on the left) in Table 9.2 (pages 342—343). The eighth entry from the top is also a 112. The table's description says that this instruction creates eight blank horizontal scan lines. Why tell ANTIC to create blank lines? This is to compensate for vertical overscan and to center the playfield on the screen. Look at your GRAPHICS 0 screen, and you'll notice a black border at the top. These blank lines are displayed on the screen in the current border color. Since the next two instructions in the display list are also 112's, this border is made up of a total of 24 blank lines (8 blank lines * 3 instructions = 24), which is the standard followed in all display lists. Notice there is also a bottom border. The size of this border is determined by what screen space is left over after all the mode lines have been displayed.

Try the following experiment:

```
10 GRAPHICS 0
20 DLIST=PEEK(560)+PEEK(561)*256
30 REM Change the number of blank scan
   lines at top of screen
40 FOR I=0 TO 112 STEP 16
50    POKE DLIST,I
60    GOSUB 500
70 NEXT I
80 GOTO 40
90 REM
500 REM Pause loop
510 FOR W=1 TO 10: NEXT W
520 RETURN
```

When this program is RUN, the entire screen will seem to bounce up and down! This is because we are changing the top margin of the screen by changing the value of the first byte of the DL (line 50 in the program). As you can see in Table 9.2, a value of 0 creates one blank scan line, a value of 16 creates two, a value of 32 creates three, etc. Thus a POKE of 0 into this address will decrease the original 24-scan line top border to 17 (1 + 8 + 8). As different numbers are POKEd into the first DL byte, the border will enlarge by one scan line at a time until it is back at 24. Then, the program will loop back to a 17-scan line top border. The remainder of the display list is not changed, so the remainder of the screen that it controls will move up and down in one block. The bottom border will become larger as the top becomes smaller, since the total number of scan lines on the screen always remains constant.

Coarse Scrolling

The next byte (number 3) in the DL of Figure 9.1 serves two purposes. First, it alerts Antic that the *following* two bytes will contain the starting address of screen RAM. This function is called load memory scan (LMS) because it tells Antic to load the address where the scanning of display memory will begin. This byte also tells Antic to display one GRAPHICS 0 mode line. As you can tell from the two tables, a 64 is added to the value of the mode line (a value of 2) to enable LMS. By having more than one LMS instruction in a DL, it is possible to use RAM from totally different parts of memory to make up *one screen*.

Try the following program:

```
10 GRAPHICS 0
20 DLIST=PEEK(560)+PEEK(561)*256
30 LMSLO=DLIST+4       : REM Load Memory
      Scan Low byte
40 LMSHI=DLIST+5       : REM Load Memory
      Scan High byte
50 SCRNLO=0:
   SCRNHI=0
60 REM Take a Scroll Through Memory
70 POKE LMSLO,SCRNLO : REM Point to new
      screen
80 POKE LMSHI,SCRNHI
90 SCRNLO=SCRNLO+40    : REM Increment by
      number of bytes/line
100 IF SCRNLO>255 THEN
      SCRNLO=SCRNLO-256:
      SCRNHI=SCRNHI+1
```

(continued)

```
110 IF SCRNHI=256 THEN
       GRAPHICS 0:
       END
120 GOTO 70
```

When this program is executed, you will see a rapid, vertically scrolling display of numbers and letters. This is called coarse scrolling. When we increment the address of screen memory by 40 (the number of bytes in a line in the current graphics mode), we are constantly changing where in RAM the screen memory is located in increments of one horizontal line of text. You have just taken a visual tour through the entire memory space of your computer! (Use GRAPHICS 7+16 instead of GRAPHICS 0, and the moving patterns will become more apparent.) The visual effect produced by this example will remind you of a LIST of a BASIC program. However, with a LIST, the brute force method of moving 960 bytes of information *through* screen memory is used while coarse scrolling changes two bytes to move the screen window *over* the information.

This ability to redefine the location of screen RAM is a very powerful feature. By only changing two bytes, we were able to move full screens of text or graphics by our "window into memory." Compare this to the microprocessor intensive method of moving *each of thousands of bytes of memory* into a fixed screen area! And with a little more effort, we could scroll horizontally instead of vertically. However, coarse scrolling by itself doesn't compare to the beauty of fine scrolling, which we will look at in the next section.

With a slight modification of the above technique, it is possible to have several different screens set aside at once, each with a different animation frame on it. To flip through the frames, just change the fourth and fifth bytes in your display list, and the new screen instantly appears!

Stereoscopic ATARI

Joe Vierra, a student at California State University, Hayward, decided to undertake the task of creating a stereoscopic view on his ATARI. He wrote a Vertical Blank Interrupt routine which flipped between two pages of screen memory every jiffy. He conserved memory by using GRAPHICS 6, a 160 by 96 mode that only uses one Playfield color, which he also changes from red to blue during VBLANK. To draw the two cubes, he used BASIC, which slowed down the process too much for animation. With assembly language, however, it wouldn't be too difficult to create a *spinning* three dimensional object! Following is a screen photo showing his stereo cube.

Notice that where the red and blue lines meet, it appears to be purple. When viewed with red/blue glasses (left eye red, right eye blue), the image takes on real depth (see color insert).

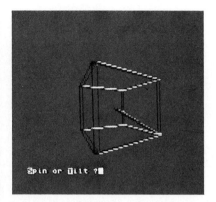

Photo 9.1: Stereoscopic cube by Joe Vierra (see color insert).

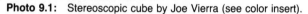

Jump on Vertical Blank   After the two-byte address indicating the beginning of screen memory comes the rest of the mode line instructions. Since there are 24 text lines in a GRAPHICS 0 screen, we need 23 more GRAPHICS 0 mode instructions (2). Remember that the mode instruction for the first screen line was combined with the LMS instruction.

The last three bytes (numbers 29–31) consist of a special jump instruction (similar to the BASIC GOTO command) plus the beginning address of the DL. This is a jump on vertical blank (JVB) instruction. It tells Antic to wait until the vertical blank period, then jump to the beginning of the display list and continue processing display information. This assures that the processing of the DL will be synchronized with the television display. The address following the JVB instruction (which points to the beginning of the DL) is ignored under normal circumstances. This is because during the VBI, the OS takes the address stored in 560,561 and feeds it to Antic as the start of the next display list. By disabling the OS VBI routines, however, it is possible to jump to a completely different DL to create a rapid flipping between two screens. This technique could be used to create a stereo display by showing the left eye view on the first screen in red lines and the right eye on the other in blue lines. The user would see a relatively flicker free three-dimensional

DISPLAY LIST INSTRUCTION CALCULATION AID

H SCROLL (+16)		X		X		X		X	
V SCROLL (+32)			X	X				X	X	
LMS (+64)					X	X	X	X	
DLI (+128)									X
Blank 1 Line	0								128
Blank 2 Lines	16								144
Blank 3 Lines	32								160
Blank 4 Lines	48								176
Blank 5 Lines	64								192
Blank 6 Lines	80								208
Blank 7 Lines	96								224
Blank 8 Lines	112								240
Jump	1								129
Jump Vrt Blnk	65								193
GRAPHICS 0	2	18	34	50	66	82	98	114	130
Antic 3	3	19	35	51	67	83	99	115	131
Antic 4[1]	4	20	36	52	68	84	100	116	132
Antic 5[2]	5	21	37	53	69	85	101	117	133
GRAPHICS 1	6	22	38	54	70	86	102	118	134
GRAPHICS 2	7	23	39	55	71	87	103	119	135
GRAPHICS 3	8	24	40	56	72	88	104	120	136
GRAPHICS 4	9	25	41	57	73	89	105	121	137
GRAPHICS 5	10	26	42	58	74	90	106	122	138
GRAPHICS 6	11	27	43	59	75	91	107	123	139
Antic C[3]	12	28	44	60	76	92	108	124	140
GRAPHICS 7	13	29	45	61	77	93	109	125	141
Antic E[4]	14	30	46	62	78	94	110	126	142
GRAPHICS 8	15	31	47	63	79	95	111	127	143

All values are in decimal.
An **X** means the optional function is turned on.

[1]GRAPHICS 12 on the ATARI XL Computers
[2]GRAPHICS 13 on the ATARI XL Computers
[3]GRAPHICS 14 on the ATARI XL Computers
[4]GRAPHICS 15 on the ATARI XL Computers
NOTE: GTIA makes 9, 10 and 11 use GRAPHICS 12 values as controlled by
GPRIOR (623) — see Table 7.5.

Table 9.2: Display list instruction calculation aid.

X		X		X		X	Horizontal Scrolling
	X	X			X	X	Vertical Scrolling
			X	X	X	X	Load Memory Scan (3-byte instr)
X	X	X	X	X	X	X	Display List Interrupt
							Blank Horizontal Scan Lines for Top Border
							Jump (3-byte instruction) Jump & wait for Vertical Blank (3-byte instruction)
146	162	178	194	210	226	242	
147	163	179	195	211	227	243	
148	164	180	196	212	228	244	Character Mode
149	165	181	197	213	229	245	Instructions
150	166	182	198	214	230	246	
151	167	183	199	215	231	247	
152	168	184	200	216	232	248	
153	169	185	201	217	233	249	
154	170	186	202	218	234	250	
155	171	187	203	219	235	251	Map Mode (Pixel)
156	172	188	204	220	236	252	Instructions
157	173	189	205	221	237	253	
158	174	190	206	222	238	254	
159	175	191	207	223	239	255	

display by viewing the screen with a pair of red/blue glasses (see box). Of course, there's no reason to stop with only two screens — the second DL could jump to a third DL (which could jump to a fourth, etc.) before returning to the beginning of the first one to close the loop.

That's all there is to a GRAPHICS 0 display list! When constructing your own, there are a few rules you must follow. See the following box.

Rules for Creating a Display List

The following three rules must be followed when you create your custom display lists:

1. A display list cannot cross a 1 K boundary, which means they are not fully relocatable. In the rare cases when you must cross a boundary, use the DL JMP instruction (01) and the address of the first byte on the other side of the boundary just before you reach it:

RAM Address		DL
.	.	
.	.	
.	.	
20475	4	
20476	4	
20477	1	JMP over boundary
20478	0	Low byte $\Big\}$ $0 + (80*256) = 20480$
20479	80	High byte
----------------	---------	1 K boundary
20480	4	Resume DL
20481	4	
.	.	
.	.	
.	.	

2. Screen memory cannot cross a 4 K boundary. When using the higher resolution modes, for example GRAPHICS 8 which takes up almost 8 K, this is impossible to avoid. You must include a second LMS instruction in the DL pointing to the second 4 K of screen RAM. Here is an example using GRAPHICS 8:

DL Byte #		DL Instruction
.	.	
.	.	
.	.	
97	15	GRAPHICS 8
98	15	GRAPHICS 8
99	79	GRAPHICS 8 + LMS
100	0	Low byte - Next 4 K of screen RAM
101	144	High byte
102	15	Resume GRAPHICS 8 DL
103	15	
.	.	
.	.	
.	.	

3. No more than 192 horizontal scan lines can be displayed in the playfield (although fewer are okay). When creating a custom DL, you must count the number of scan lines used in all of your mode lines to make sure their total doesn't exceed 192. Otherwise, it may take too much time to display them; Antic will no longer be synchronized with the screen, and the display may roll or break up.

Fine Scrolling

The ATARI feature called fine scrolling allows you to move the mode lines smoothly in any direction. Whereas coarse scrolling moves the image past the screen in whole *byte* or *mode line* increments, fine scrolling vertically moves the image by horizontal scan lines or horizontally moves it by color clocks (see Figure 9.2.).

Horizontal Fine Scrolling   To see what we are talking about, enter and execute the program in Figure 9.3.

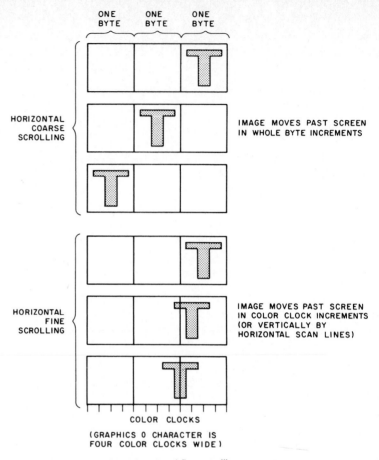

Figure 9.2: Comparing coarse and fine scrolling.

```
10  REM   HORIZONTAL FINE SCROLLING
20  REM
30  GRAPHICS 0
40  HSCROL=54276
60  DLIST=PEEK(560)+PEEK(561)*256: REM Find Display List
70  POKE DLIST+15,18: REM Turn horizontal scroll bit (2+16)
80  POSITION 1,10:
    PRINT "This is a demo of horizontal scrolling! ";
90  FOR I=0 TO 15
100     POKE HSCROL,I
110     GOSUB 500
120 NEXT I
130 FOR I=15 TO 0 STEP -1
140     POKE HSCROL,I
150     GOSUB 500
160 NEXT I
170 GOTO 90
500 FOR W=1 TO 5:
    NEXT W
510 RETURN
```

Figure 9.3: Listing of horizontal fine scrolling demo.

You will see the sentence that was PRINTed by line 80 ("This is a demo of horizontal scrolling!") smoothly sliding back and forth horizontally on the screen. Notice that scrolling is being used to display more information than will fit on one line. When part of the first word ("This") moves off the screen to the left, the cursor will appear on the right. This is one of the major advantages of scrolling — to control a window which peers into a much larger amount of data than will appear on the screen at once.

To use horizontal fine scrolling, just two steps are required. First, enable it by adding 16 to the value of the DL instruction (line 70). Then, all you have to do is POKE a value from 0 to 15 into the special hardware register called HSCROL (54276 Decimal, D404 Hex). The value you POKE determines how many color clocks the line will be moved to the right. Since each GRAPHICS Ø text character is four color clocks wide, this program will slide the sentence four characters over (16 increments/4 color clocks per character = 4 characters).

Now press the **BREAK** key, and LIST the program. What happened?! The screen looks disorganized, but this is only a temporary condition (either press **RESET** or type GRAPHICS Ø). When horizontal fine scrolling is turned on, Antic automatically grabs extra bytes (20 percent more) for that line, throwing off the rest of the display. This is to provide a scrolling buffer. When one character is halfway off the screen on the left, then half of one should be appearing on the right. This means that more than 40 characters will appear on the line at once. The extra characters are taken from the next line down, causing the remainder of the screen to be shifted to the left by eight characters.

Vertical Fine Scrolling   To show off vertical fine scrolling, modify the previous example as follows. The lines with an asterisk in front just need to be altered rather than added.

```
 10  REM   VERTICAL FINE SCROLLING
 20  REM
 30  GRAPHICS 0
 40  HSCROL=54276
 50  VSCROL=54277
 60  DLIST=PEEK(560)+PEEK(561)*256: REM Find Display List
* 70  POKE DLIST+15,34: REM Turn vertical scroll bit (2+32)
* 80  POSITION 1,10:
      PRINT "This is a demo of vertical scrolling! ";
* 90  FOR I=0 TO 7
* 100     POKE VSCROL,I
 110     GOSUB 500
 120  NEXT I
* 130 FOR I=7 TO 0 STEP -1
* 140     POKE VSCROL,I
 150     GOSUB 500
 160  NEXT I
 170  GOTO 90
 500  FOR W=1 TO 5:
      NEXT W
 510  RETURN
```

Figure 9.4: Listing of vertical fine scrolling demo.

Now the line of text slips up and down in horizontal scan line increments. Since the GRAPHICS Ø mode line is only eight scan lines high, we are using values from 0 to 7 to scroll the sentence up one line. Notice that it seems to vanish as it moves up. Add the following line to the program:

```
75 POKE DLIST+14,34
```

Now when you run the program, the entire line remains on the screen as it hops up and down. This is because two adjacent mode lines are now being scrolled rather than one.

Vertical fine scrolling is enabled (activated) by adding a 32 to the DL instruction. Then, values (from 0 to 7) are POKEed into the VSCROL register (54277 Decimal, D405 Hex).

Diagonal Fine Scrolling   Sorry — there is no diagonal fine scrolling register. To achieve diagonal scrolling, just combine horizontal and vertical motion as indicated in the following program. Delete line 75 from the last example and then modify the asterisked lines:

```
  10 REM  DIAGONAL FINE SCROLLING
  20 REM
  30 GRAPHICS 0
  40 HSCROL=54276
  50 VSCROL=54277
  60 DLIST=PEEK(560)+PEEK(561)*256: REM Find Display List
* 70 POKE DLIST+15,50: REM Turn horizontal and vertical scroll bits (2+16+32)
* 80 POSITION 3,10:
     PRINT "This is a demo of diagonal scrolling! ";
  90 FOR I=0 TO 7
*100    POKE HSCROL,I:
        POKE VSCROL,I
 110    GOSUB 500
 120 NEXT I
 130 FOR I=7 TO 0 STEP -1
*140    POKE HSCROL,I:
        POKE VSCROL,I
 150    GOSUB 500
 160 NEXT I
 170 GOTO 90
 500 FOR W=1 TO 5:
     NEXT W
 510 RETURN
```

Figure 9.5: Listing of diagonal fine scrolling demo.

Mixing Coarse and Fine Scrolling

All this smooth motion is nice, but if you ran these programs you may have noticed that fine scrolling can only be implemented over a short distance. What if you want to slide the line *more* than one line up or down (or more than 16 color clocks to the right)? The solution is to combine fine scrolling with coarse scrolling. Look at Figure 9.6 to see how this works.

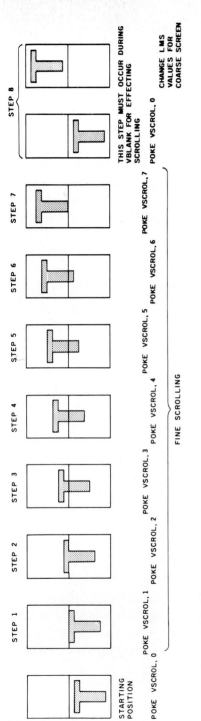

Figure 9.6: Combining fine scrolling and coarse scrolling.

The trick is to use coarse scrolling to move in one-byte increments (in GRAPHICS Ø, each byte represents one character) and use fine scrolling to smooth out the steps between each byte. Using animation terms, think of coarse scrolling as the key positions and fine scrolling as the in-between positions. First, the character (or pixel) is fine scrolled for just enough scan lines or color clocks to reposition it one increment short of the *next* character's original position. Then, it is reset to its starting position, and coarse scrolling takes over to move the display on a byte level by one increment. The process then repeats "forever." The last step must be executed during vertical blank so the jump is never seen on the screen. In fact, a machine language routine should be used for fine scrolling over any distance. (Of course, we will be introducing just such a routine later in this chapter.) You may have noticed some occasional screen glitches (picture "break-ups" that last for a fraction of a second) during our fine scrolling demo programs. This is caused by changing an Antic display register *while* the screen is being drawn. The glitch problem and any jumpiness is totally avoided with a vertical blank interrupt machine language routine.

Applications   Fine scrolling is used in conjunction with coarse scrolling to allow you to access a much larger area of screen memory than is normally available to open a window in RAM. The ATARI game, Eastern Front (1941) by Chris Crawford, uses this technique to present a large map of Russia, which is actually about ten screenfuls large, on the display. With a joystick, the user can fly across the entire terrain at will. For more information on this program and some screen photos, see the end of this chapter.

For another application, imagine a word processing program that allows you to fine scroll through your entire document, either horizontally (for lines wider than the screen width) or vertically. This would be much easier on the eyes than moving around in huge jumps.

Display List Interrupts

The last option which can be implemented with display lists is called the display list interrupt (DLI). We have already talked about vertical blank, the period of time when the television's electron beam has finished painting the screen, turns off, and then moves from the lower right corner of the screen to the top left corner in preparation to turn on and repeat the update process. There is also something called the horizontal blank. This is the period of time after a horizontal scan line is drawn when the beam shuts off and moves from the end of one scan line to the beginning of the next. Vertical blank lasts about 1400 microseconds, and horizontal blank lasts about 14 microseconds. We know that there is not much we humans can do in 14 (or even 1400) microseconds, but the computer is somewhat faster than we are. By setting the DLI bit on a display list instruction (adding 128 to the instruction's value), the 6502 can be interrupted at a specific point in time in relation to the screen updating process (i.e., just before that mode line has been fully displayed). All sorts of interesting things can be accomplished when the CPU is directed to a special DLI routine. For example, the DLI routine could change the hardware color registers to increase the number of colors that are displayed on the screen, move a player horizontally so it appears to be in two or more places at the same time, or change a player's size.

We will not go into much detail on the inner workings of DLI's, as they are beyond the scope of this book. For an excellent discussion on DLI's, see the ATARI publication, *De Re Atari* (product number APX-90008). We will be introducing a black box DLI routine later in this chapter. For now, all you need to know is that the display list instruction gets its DLI bit set for the mode line just preceding the place where the desired change is to go into effect. Again, to set the DLI bit, just add 128 to the display list instruction:

DL Instructions
.
.
.

```
  7  GRAPHICS 2
  7  GRAPHICS 2
135  GRAPHICS 2 with DLI bit set (7 + 128)
  7  GRAPHICS 2 — Color change will be seen on this line
  7  GRAPHICS 2
```
.
.
.

Summary

You now have a fundamental understanding of the power of the display list, coarse and fine scrolling, and DLI's. No other personal computer now on the market can give you the flexibility that the DL provides. By combining all of its features, you can create some exciting effects. In the next section, we will lay the foundation for our scrolling background program using the display list's capabilities.

9.2   THE SCROLLING BACKGROUND PROGRAM

As you look out the window of your ion-powered train, the scene suddenly changes. Gone are the noisy cars and trucks. It's early Sunday morning, and all the people are inside their homes. The sky, a peaceful shade of blue, has cotton clouds in it. "I must have arrived in the

suburbs, you think as row upon row of nicely kept cottages, homes, and large apartment buildings pass by. The lawns are bright green, the shrubs and trees well groomed, the pink and yellow buildings immaculate. "What a nice day for a drive," you decide.

Now that you have glimpsed the world of fine scrolling, we'll show you how to incorporate it into a program by presenting our scrolling street scene example. What we want to create is a long horizontal strip of scenery which can pass across the window of our super train. If the strip is long enough, we won't notice it repeating. One technique would be to use map graphics, for example, GRAPHICS 7, to create the background. However, if we made a long strip in this mode, it would eat up quite a bit of memory. A solution is to create a special character set and use GRAPHICS 2. A full screen in this mode takes up only 240 bytes, whereas a GRAPHICS 7 screen is 3840 bytes long! Furthermore, the working resolution of both modes is identical, and GRAPHICS 2 provides us with one extra color! (By working resolution we are referring to the pixel size within each GRAPHICS 2 character.)

The only major drawbacks to this technique are the development time required to define a new character set and the limitation to the number of characters we can define without resorting to special tricks. Fortunately, for you, we have already solved these problems by creating a custom character set. This set is used to create houses and trees of random shapes, sizes, and colors. Every time the program is executed, a new street scene will be produced out of our characters.

The Street Character Set

To add some originality to the street scene, we designed a series of shapes that fit together to produce a wide variety of houses, cottages, apartment buildings, shrubs, bushes, and trees. The computer is given the task of putting these building blocks together along certain guidelines. Should the house have a fence, a TV antenna, a chimney? How many stories high and how wide should it be? How many windows should the house have, and what color should it be painted? By allowing the program to choose the features for each house, we saved the time it would have taken us to try to think of all the possible combinations, and then lay them out in a random order. Another advantage to our computer-designed street is that the street can be of any length — from two screenfuls wide to twenty. The computer will continue building houses and growing foliage until the allocated space has been filled.

Color Selection In GRAPHICS 2   GRAPHICS 2 allows for four playfield colors and one background color. We are using pink and yellow for the houses, brown for the roofs, fences and tree trunks, and dark green for the tree tops and shrubs. Extra color will be provided with the help of DLI's. We will add white and gray clouds (also made of characters), blue sky, light green grass, sidewalks, and a gray street.

When using either GRAPHICS 1 or GRAPHICS 2, the 128 characters normally available in the ATARI built-in character set are reduced to 64. This is because the upper two bits of each byte in screen memory that were used to help select a character (or activate inverse video) in GRAPHICS Ø have been reassigned for color selection. Try the following experiment. (Notice that the second two *A*'s and the second *123* are in inverse video.)

```
10 GRAPHICS 2
20 PRINT #6;"AaAa123123"
```

When this program is RUN, you will see four capital A's in four different colors and "123" in two different colors. The #6 means PRINT to the graphics screen device that was opened with the GRAPHICS 2 statement. Now type in the following statement:

```
POKE 756,226
```

The four capital A's are now four lowercase a's. The 123's have turned into strange lines, and the background is filled with orange hearts instead of black background. You have switched to the other half of the standard character set (remember from Chapter 5 that location 756 contains the high byte of the current character set's address). The first half contains numbers and uppercase letters, and the second half contains the graphics characters and lowercase letters. To switch back, type the following:

```
POKE 756,224
```

This means that you can't mix uppercase and lowercase letters when using these graphics modes *unless* you resort to redefining the character set.

Displaying the four possible colors for a letter is simple, but what about numbers or graphics characters? There is no such thing as an uppercase or lowercase "2." The first complication is that the byte information stored in screen memory to display a specific character may not match that character's ATASCII code. The screen bytes refer to the order of the character set in ROM (or RAM), not to their ATASCII value. The order of the character set was created so it could easily be divided for GRAPHICS 1 and 2 displays. For example, the ATASCII value of the number 2 is 50. However its screen value is 18, as it occupies the eighteenth position in the character set. Table 9.3 gives the positional value of each character in the ATARI ROM character set.

#	CHR	#	CHR	#	CHR	#	CHR	#	CHR	#	CHR	#	CHR	#	CHR
	Column 1				**Column 2**				**Column 3**				**Column 4**		
0	Space	16	0	32	@	48	P	64	♥	80		96		112	p
1	!	17	1	33	A	49	Q	65		81		97	a	113	q
2	"	18	2	34	B	50	R	66		82		98	b	114	r
3	#	19	3	35	C	51	S	67		83		99	c	115	s
4	$	20	4	36	D	52	T	68		84		100	d	116	t
5	%	21	5	37	E	53	U	69		85		101	e	117	u
6	&	22	6	38	F	54	V	70		86		102	f	118	v
7	'	23	7	39	G	55	W	71		87		103	g	119	w
8	(	24	8	40	H	56	X	72		88		104	h	120	x
9	)	25	9	41	I	57	Y	73		89		105	i	121	y
10	*	26	:	42	J	58	Z	74		90		106	j	122	z
11	+	27	;	43	K	59	[	75		91		107	k	123	
12	,	28	<	44	L	60	\	76		92		108	l	124		
13	−	29	=	45	M	61	]	77		93		109	m	125	
14	−	30	>	46	N	62	^	78		94		110	n	126	
15		31	?	47	O	63	−	79		95		111	o	127	

1. In mode 0 these characters must be preceded with an escape, CHR$(27), to be printed.

Table 9.3: The order of the ATARI character set.[1]

Columns 1 and 2 show the characters available when GRAPHICS 1 and 2 are first initialized. Columns 3 and 4 hold the characters accessible when location 756 is POKEd with a 226. Notice the position of the heart-shaped character (64) in relation to the space character (0). Both occupy the first location in their half of the table. This explains why the background character shows up as hearts when the second half is used.

Try the following experiment:

```
10 GRAPHICS 2
20 SCREEN=PEEK(88)+PEEK(89)*256
30 POKE SCREEN,18
40 POKE SCREEN+1,18+64
50 POKE SCREEN+2,18+128
60 POKE SCREEN+3,18+64+128
```

When you RUN this program, you will see the number 2 displayed in four different colors. In lines 40–60, the upper two bits that control the color are being switched on.

To accomplish the same thing with PRINT statements, you must use the above table. First find 2 on the table. Then, jump over to the other half of the table, and locate the character in the corresponding position. This is the graphics character obtained by typing control-®. Let's try it out by adding the following statement. Remember that the curley brackets mean to hold down the **CTRL** key, and underline means to print in inverse video.

```
70 POSITION 0,1
80 PRINT #6;"2{R}2{R}"
```

You will see a second line of colorful 2's below the first line. The entire process becomes much more difficult when the screen control characters are to be displayed. You can't directly PRINT an "inverse cursor down" by using the inverse key, for example. However, an inverse down arrow can be displayed on the screen by pressing a combination of keys, **ESC** Shift **INSERT** (use the ATASCII table in Appendix B). The semicolon can appear in only three of its color incarnations, because the fourth corresponds to the EOL (RETURN) code and can't be displayed. Our solution is to avoid redefining characters that cannot be displayed in all their incarnations.

Our Street Characters Definitions   Here are the character definitions for the street character set. We are using 35 characters out of the 64. By a change of color, some do double duty as cloud tops and tree tops, others as sections of roofs or walls of houses, and one character is used in clouds, tree tops, houses, and roofs!

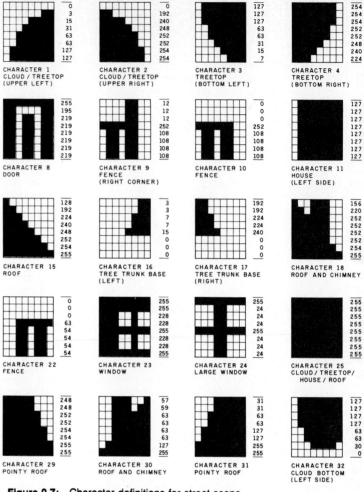

Figure 9.7: Character definitions for street scene.

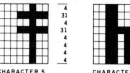

CHARACTER 5
T V ANTENNA

```
4
31
4
31
4
4
4
4
```

CHARACTER 6
FENCE
(LEFT CORNER)

```
48
48
48
63
54
54
54
54
```

CHARACTER 7
TREE TRUNK
(RIGHT SIDE)

```
3
3
3
3
3
3
3
3
```

CHARACTER 12
HOUSE
(RIGHT SIDE)

```
254
254
254
254
254
254
254
254
```

CHARACTER 13
ROOF

```
1
3
7
15
31
63
127
255
```

CHARACTER 14
POINTY ROOF

```
1
1
3
7
7
15
15
```

CHARACTER 19
POINTY ROOF AND
CHIMNEY TOP

```
128
128
192
192
224
224
243
243
```

CHARACTER 20
POINTY ROOF

```
128
128
192
192
224
224
240
240
```

CHARACTER 21
WINDOW

```
255
255
39
39
255
39
39
255
```

CHARACTER 26
POINTY ROOF AND
CHIMNEY

```
251
251
255
252
254
254
255
255
```

CHARACTER 27
TREE TRUNK
(RIGHT SIDE)

```
192
192
192
192
192
192
192
192
```

CHARACTER 28
FENCE

```
0
0
0
255
102
102
102
102
```

CHARACTER 33
CLOUD BOTTOM
(CENTER)

```
255
255
255
255
255
254
124
0
```

CHARACTER 34
CLOUD BOTTOM
(RIGHT SIDE)

```
254
254
254
254
252
252
120
0
```

CHARACTER 35
SIDEWALK

```
255
255
255
0
0
0
0
0
```

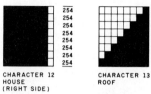

Laying Out the Screen

In the beginning of this chapter we mentioned that our background will consist of two levels. The farthest level is made up of the sky and clouds which are so far away that they will remain stationary no matter how fast we are moving. The second level consists of the houses, trees, and a street. Although the background is in two levels, the screen will actually be split into *three* sections (see Figure 9.8). The center section with the houses and trees is the only section that will be scrolled. The top cloud isn't moved (must be a windless day), and the bottom section, consisting of the grass, sidewalks, and street, doesn't need to be moved, because it doesn't contain any details. There is no way to tell whether it is actually moving or stationary by looking at it. The illusion of movement will be created, since the viewer assumes the foreground must be connected to the center section.

Notice how wide the strip of street is in relation to the screen. To set this up in the display list, eight LMS instructions must be used. There is one for line 1 to establish the beginning of screen memory. Lines 3 through 8 each use one, so coarse scrolling can be used by changing the byte addresses following the LMS instruction. (The horizontal fine scrolling bit is also activated for these lines.) Line 9 also needs one to establish the address for the remainder of the screen.

Creating an Endless Street

Now, how can this long horizontal strip be turned into a loop which endlessly scrolls across the screen? When the end of the strip is reached, it must be reset to the beginning for another pass. Doing this would cause an unpleasant jump, and the entire screen would change. To avoid a potentially jarring experience we copy the first screenful of information onto the area of the strip which contains the last screenful. Then, when that last screen is being displayed, reset all the LMS bytes of the scrolling section back to the starting screen during the vertical blank period (see Figure 9.9). The result is a smooth, invisible transition to the next pass of the strip across the screen window.

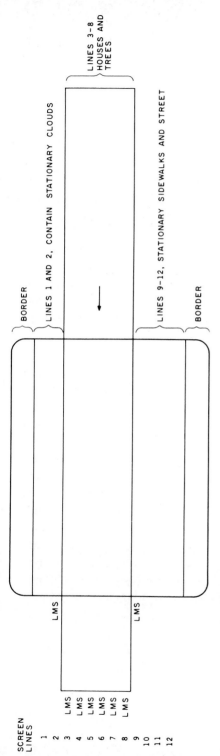

Figure 9.8: Three sections of street scene.

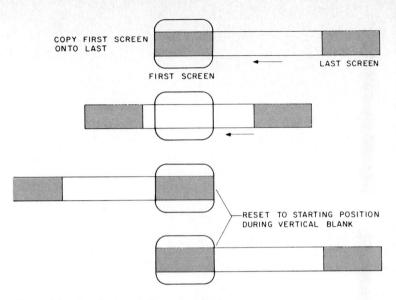

COPY FIRST SCREEN
ONTO LAST

LAST SCREEN

FIRST SCREEN

RESET TO STARTING POSITION
DURING VERTICAL BLANK

Figure 9.9: Creating an endless street loop.

Playfield Width   In Chapter 7, we mentioned that there were three playfield widths from which to choose — wide, normal, and narrow. These widths control the number of bytes of information to be fetched for each line of the screen. The playfield width is controlled by the lower two bits of SDMCTL (559 Decimal, 22F Hex). This register also controls player-missile DMA and display list DMA (see Table 7.7). Try the following POKEs on a GRAPHICS 0 screen. [Bit 5 (+ 32) turns on the DMA for the display list.]

```
POKE 559,33 : REM Narrow Playfield
                  (bits 5 and 0 on)
POKE 559,34 : REM Normal Playfield
                  (bits 5 and 1 on)
POKE 559,35 : REM Wide Playfield
                  (bits 5, 1 and 0 on)
```

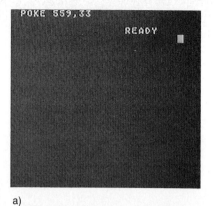

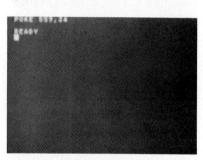

a)

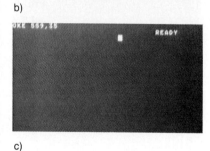

b)

c)

Photo 9.2: Screen photos of each playfield width.

Notice the size of the side borders for each playfield width. The screen is all jumbled up for narrow and wide modes, because the display list is still set up for a normal playfield. Table 9.4 shows the number of bytes fetched for each mode line in GRAPHICS 0 and 2.

Bytes per Mode Line in GRAPHICS 0 and 2

	PLAYFIELD WIDTH		
	Narrow	**Normal**	**Wide**
GRAPHICS 0	32	40	48
GRAPHICS 2	16	20	24

Table 9.4: Bytes per mode line using different playfield widths.

The wide playfield option will be used in our Street Scene program to eliminate the side borders. Using a normal playfield in this program would cause the houses to appear from the void of the border, rather than from the edge of the television screen.

The actual length of the scrolling strip is controllable within the program. It must be at least wide enough to contain two screenfuls — 48 bytes wide (2 screens * 24 bytes per line). This would cause the same screenful of houses to continuously scroll by since the first and last screens are identical.

Adding Extra Color With DLIs   The five colors with which GRAPHICS 2 provides us aren't enough to create a realistic scene. Display list interrupts are used to add additional colors. Figure 9.10 shows where DLIs are set and the colors that they affect.

DLI - CHANGE CLOUD COLORS TO
    HOUSE COLORS (CHARACTERS)

DLI - CHANGE SKY BACKGROUND
    TO GRASS

DLI - CHANGE HOUSECOLOR TO
    SIDEWALK COLOR (CHARACTER)

DLI - CHANGE GRASS COLOR TO
    PAVEMENT COLOR (BACKGROUND)

DLI - CHANGE PAVEMENT COLOR TO
    SIDEWALK COLOR (BACKGROUND)

Figure 9.10: DLIs for extra color.

As you can see from Figure 9.10, five DLIs are used on the screen. During each of these interrupts, our DLI routine is designed to change only three of the five color registers available in GRAPHICS 2 (registers 2, 3 and 4). The brown for the roofs and tree trunks and the green tree tops are left alone. Initially, the background (register 4) is set to the color of the sky, and registers 2 and 3 are set for two different shades of white for the clouds. The DLI set on mode line 2 changes the cloud colors to pink and yellow for the houses. Again, the color change doesn't go into effect until the line *following* the DLI line, line 3 in this case. On line 5, the background register is changed to light green for the grass. This creates a horizon on line 6. On line 8, a house color is changed to the sidewalk color. The background grass color is changed to the gray color for the pavement of the street on line 10. (The light gray distant sidewalk is made from a character, not the screen background.) Finally, on line 12, the background (actually the bottom border) is changed to the near sidewalk.

The SCROLL Routine

The black box machine language routine that horizontally scrolls the strip of street is appropriately called SCROLL. It is extremely easy to use. Once it knows where to find the section of screen memory that is to be scrolled, all you need to do is give it a scroll rate. In Table 9.5 are the parameter table entries used by SCROLL.

Variable Name	Offset From PARAMBASE	Address (Decimal)	Description
SCRLINIT	5	1029	POKE 1 to turn on routine, 0 off
SCRLADR	26	1050,1051	Lo and Hi bytes of scrolling window
SCRLLEN	28	1052,1053	Width of scrolling window in bytes
SCRLCLK	30	1054	Color clocks per mode line byte -1
SCRLSTEP	31	1055	Step size to scroll each jiffy

Table 9.5: Parameters for SCROLL.

To set up for SCROLL, POKE the two-byte address that points to the beginning of the scrolling window into SCRLADR. This is the upper left corner of the section that will be scrolled, not the first byte of screen memory (unless the first mode line is to be scrolled too). In our scrolling street scene program, this is the same two-byte address that follows the LMS instruction for line 3 of the screen. Then POKE the *width* of the scrolling window into SCRLLEN. This is a two-byte value so SCROLL can accept very long window lengths. The next parameter, SCRLCLK, controls the number of fine scrolling steps that will be performed before a coarse scroll. This is based on how wide (in color clocks) the bytes in your mode lines are. GRAPHICS 2 bytes are eight color clocks wide so a 7 will be POKEd into this address. When using a 40-bytes-per-line graphics mode, use the value 3; with a 10-bytes-per-line mode, POKE in a 15.

When all these parameters are POKEd in, SCROLL is turned on by a POKE of 1 into SCRLINIT. (The fifth parameter, SCRLSTEP, need not be set until after SCROLL is activated in this way.) At every sixtieth of a second, the routine will look into SCRLSTEP to determine how quickly to scroll the screen. To begin the movement, just POKE in the rate you want the street to scroll, and the scrolling window will immediately begin to move. The step size is in *color clocks per jiffy* and can be any value from 0 to 255. A step size of 1 yields the slowest rate — the scene moves one color clock every jiffy (1/60 of a second). A POKE of 2 will double the rate to two color clocks per jiffy. To pause the display, POKE SCRLSTEP with a 0, then POKE in a new step size to start it again.

If you wish to reset the display to its starting position, POKE SCRLINIT with a 1. It will immediately begin again from the original starting position at the rate currently in SCRLSTEP. (As with our earlier routines, when SCROLL has received the 1 that was POKEd into SCRLINIT, it replaces it with a 128.)

SCROLL will work in any GRAPHICS mode with any number of *adjacent* scrolling lines. The routine looks for the first display list LMS instruction with the horizontal fine scrolling bit set and defines that mode line as the top of the scrolling window. It continues incrementing all the address bytes following the DL instructions with these two bits set until it reaches the end of the DL. Even if the scrolling lines are not adjacent, they will still be scrolled, but the display will become jumbled.

Note that SCROLL only moves the scrolling window from the right to the left.

Entering SCROLL   Here are the bytes for SCROLL that are entered with the same method as shown in Chapter 8 (with the String Loader program).

```
24000  REM SCROLL Routine DATA
24010  DATA SCROLL,11020,316,29349
24020  DATA 184,80,3,76,98,228,216,173,5,4,240,247,16,72,165,224,141,89,4,165,225,141,90,4,173
24030  DATA 48,2,133,224,173,49,2,133,225,173,30,4,141,80,4,169,192,141,81,4,173,31,4,160,0
24040  DATA 78,80,4,144,7,74,78,81,4,200,208,244,141,80,4,173,31,4,45,30,4,24,109,70,4
24050  DATA 205,30,4,240,14,144,12,176,4,80,173,208,89,238,80,4,45,30,4,141,70,4,77,30,4
24060  DATA 141,4,212,173,80,4,24,109,68,4,141,68,4,144,3,238,69,4,173,68,4,56,109,81,4
24070  DATA 141,68,4,144,3,238,69,4,173,69,4,205,29,4,144,40,208,8,173,68,4,205,28,4,144
24080  DATA 30,169,0,141,68,4,141,69,4,141,80,4,173,26,4,141,66,4,173,27,4,141,67,4,184
24090  DATA 80,19,208,103,80,159,173,68,4,24,237,81,4,141,68,4,176,3,206,69,4,173,66,4,24
24100  DATA 109,80,4,141,66,4,141,82,4,144,3,238,67,4,173,67,4,141,83,4,160,3,177,224,201
24110  DATA 65,240,41,41,80,240,32,41,16,240,26,200,173,82,4,145,224,24,109,28,4,141,82,4,200
24120  DATA 173,83,4,145,224,109,29,4,141,83,4,173,200,200,200,208,211,80,166,173,89,4,133,224,173
24130  DATA 90,4,133,225,184,80,153,169,128,141,5,4,173,30,4,141,70,4,169,0,141,68,4,141,69
24140  DATA 4,173,26,4,141,66,4,173,27,4,141,67,4,184,80,207
```

Figure 9.11: Listing of DATA statements for SCROLL.

The Display List Interrupt Routine (DLIROUT)

We made it! We have finally come to the last machine language program in the book. This routine, called DLIROUT, is used to add the extra colors on the screen as described earlier in this chapter. DLIROUT changes the values in the *hardware* color registers, not the shadow registers that we have been accessing from within BASIC (see Table 9.6). A color value sent to a hardware color register goes into effect *immediately*, whereas a shadow register alteration doesn't take effect until the next vertical blank. This means that all the mode lines *prior* to (and including) the line containing the first DLI instruction take their color values from the shadow color registers. During vertical blank, all the hardware color registers are reset once again to the shadow register values.

COLOR REGISTER #	COLOR REGISTER NAME	HARDWARE ADDRESS		SHADOW ADDRESS	
		Dec	Hex	Dec	Hex
0	COLPF0	53270	D016	708	2C4
1	COLPF1	53271	D017	709	2C5
2	COLPF2	53272*	D018	710	2C6
3	COLPF3	53273*	D019	711	2C7
4	COLBK	53274*	D01A	712	2C8

* The three hardware color registers controlled by DLIROUT

Table 9.6: Hardware and shadow color registers.

DLIROUT uses one parameter table location to store the address of a table of color values. This color table contains the new color values for each DL instruction with the DLI bit set (see Table 9.7).

Variable Name	Offset From PARAMBASE	Address (Decimal)	Description
DLIADR	36	1060,1061	Low and High bytes of DLI color table

Table 9.7: Parameters for DLIROUT.

As we said before, this routine changes the color of registers 2, 3, and 4. The size of its table is determined by the number of display list instructions that have the DLI bit set. For each DLI bit that is set, three table entries are required, one for each of the three color registers to be changed. Since our program uses five DLI instructions, its DLI table is 15 bytes long (5 DLI's * 3 entries per DLI). See Figure 9.12.

DLI TABLE

	BYTES IN TABLE	COLOR REGISTER #'s	
FIRST DLI INSTRUCTION	234	2	YELLOW HOUSES
	90	3	PINK HOUSES
	152	4	SKY
SECOND DLI INSTRUCTION	234	2	YELLOW HOUSES
	90	3	PINK HOUSES
	198	4	GRASS
THIRD DLI INSTRUCTION	10	2	SIDEWALK
	0	3	(NOT USED)
	198	4	GRASS
FOURTH DLI INSTRUCTION	0	2	(NOT USED)
	0	3	(NOT USED)
	6	4	STREET PAVEMENT
FIFTH DLI INSTRUCTION	0	2	(NOT USED)
	0	3	(NOT USED)
	10	4	SIDEWALK

Figure 9.12: DLI color table for DLIROUT.

Look at the color values for the first DLI instruction. Even though we wanted to change the color of only the first two registers (from cloud colors to house colors), the third register had to be reassigned its original sky color. Each of the three registers *must* have a table entry for each DLI instruction, even if there is no color change for that register and even if that register isn't being used. In the last set of table entries, registers 2 and 3 are not used, but a value (any value) still needs to be stored in the table for them.

Using DLIROUT   To use DLIROUT, first create a table and fill it with the desired color values. Turn on the DLI bit (+128) in the appropriate display list instructions. The OS must then be told where the DLI routine is located in memory. This is accomplished by a POKE of the address (low and high bytes) of the routine into locations 512 and 513 (200,201 Hex). DLIROUT must next be told where your table is stored by a POKE of its address into the parameter table:

```
POKE DLIADR,TABLELO
POKE DLIADR+1,TABLEHI
```

As with our previous machine language routines, DLIROUT has a section of code that is executed during vertical blank and must be linked to the VBI vectors (see lines 13000–13210 in upcoming Example 13). Finally, display list interrupts must be turned on by a POKE of 192 into 54286 (NMIEN, non-maskable interrupt enable, D40E Hex). That's all there is to it; the rest is automatically carried out by DLIROUT.

Even though we are using this routine with SCROLL, there is no reason why either of them could not be implemented by themselves. (However, AUTOMOVE requires PMOVER for its execution.)

Entering DLIROUT   The lines containing the DATA statement for DLIROUT follow. Again, use the string loader program to stuff the bytes into strings.

```
25000  REM DLI Routine DATA
25010  DATA DLIROUT,11110,94,12803
25020  DATA 184,80,10,76,98,228,169,0,141,75,4,240,246,72,136,72,152,72,165,224,141,93,4,165,225
25030  DATA 141,94,4,173,36,4,133,224,173,37,4,133,225,172,75,4,177,224,72,200,177,224,170,200,177
25040  DATA 224,200,140,75,4,168,104,234,234,234,234,234,234,234,234,234,141,10,212,141,24,208,142,25,208
25050  DATA 140,26,208,173,93,4,133,224,173,94,4,133,225,104,168,104,170,104,64
```

Figure 9.13: Listing of DATA statements for DLIROUT.

Entering the Scrolling Street Scene Program

You have now been fully briefed on the Scrolling Street Scene program and are ready to enter it into the computer. When you have finished entering this program, it will be combined with the Player Foreground Demo (Example 12) to produce the book's final program.

Most of this program is new and must be entered from the keyboard. For those lazy disk owners who would rather make the poor ATARI do some extra work, we offer the following program to transfer 41 lines from Example 12 to Example 13. To use the Copy program, first load Example 12 into memory, and then LIST the entire program to disk or a cassette:

```
LIST "D:PLAYERS.TXT"        (disk)
LIST "C:"                   (cassette)
```

Then enter and execute the following program. It will copy the common lines to a file called SCROLL.BAS. (Note that there are 15 numbers on each DATA statement but the last.)

```
10  REM  COPY PROGRAM
20  REM Program to transfer duplicate lines from PLAYER program to SCROLL
30  REM
40  DIM LN$(120)
50  OPEN #1,4,0,"D:PLAYERS.TXT"
60  OPEN #2,8,0,"D:SCROLL.BAS"
70  FOR I=1 TO 41
80      READ LNNUM
90      INPUT #1;LN$:
        IF VAL(LN$)<>LNNUM THEN 90
100     PRINT #2;LN$:
        PRINT LN$
110 NEXT I
120 CLOSE #1:
    CLOSE #2
130 REM
200 REM Lines To Copy
220 DATA 30,50,60,70,80,100,110,120,130,140,180,190,280,290,380
230 DATA 390,400,490,530,5000,5300,5340,5350,11000,11600,11610,11620,11650,11660,12000
240 DATA 12010,12190,12200,12240,12530,12540,13000,13010,13170,13200,13210
```

Figure 9.14: Listing of Copy Program.

Now that this program has finished its task, type NEW, and ENTER the newly created file into memory:

ENTER "D:SCROLL.BAS"   (disk)

ENTER "C:"   (cassette)

Example 13

Exercise   Create a scrolling scene filled with houses, trees, and shrubs of different shapes and sizes. Design a custom character set to build these objects, and use GRAPHICS 2 to display them. Use SCROLL to move the scene across the screen and DLIROUT to add extra color. Set up the program so it can later be merged with the Player Foreground Demo.

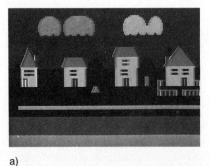

a)

(continued)

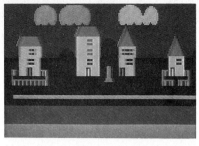

b)

c)

Photo 9.3: Screen photos showing several different types of houses and trees.

Film 2

"Vol Libre," Loren Carpenter. The landscape images from this excerpt are constructed from hundreds of thousands of triangles, created by fractal splitting of only 100 or so original triangles. Fractals are a convenient method for representing natural randomness. The pictures were computed in 15 to 40 minutes each on a DEC VAX 11/780, and are a full 24 bits per pixel, 512 by 512 resolution. No antialiasing was done. *(Courtesy of Loren Carpenter.)*

As before, the lines which are new to this program are highlighted. If you don't use the above Copy Program, just enter all the lines, highlighted or not.

```
10   REM *** SCROLLING STREET SCENE ***
20   REM            Example 13
30   REM
40   REM Program demonstrating Horizontal Fine Scrolling and Display List Interrupts
50   REM Copyright (C) 1982 by David Fox and Mitchell Waite
60   REM
70   GOTO 140
80   REM
100  REM Hi/Lo Byte Calculation
110  HIBYTE=INT(X/256): REM Calculate High Byte
120  LOBYTE=X-HIBYTE*256: REM Calculate Low Byte
130  RETURN
140  REM Initialize
160  DIM CL$(24),SEG$(24),TEMP$(8)
170  CL$(1)=CHR$(0):
     CL$(24)=CHR$(0):
     CL$(2)=CL$: REM Fill with ASCII 0
180  GOSUB 11000: REM Initialize Routine strings
190  GOSUB 5000: REM Set up memory locations
200  GOSUB 6000: REM Set up Display List
210  GOSUB 2600: REM Clear screen
230  GOSUB 8000: REM Load in Character Set
250  POKE 756,HICHRB: REM Switch to Street character set
260  POKE 559,35: REM Turn screen DMA on again, Wide Playfield
270  GOSUB 2800:
     GOSUB 3000: REM Create a street
280  GOSUB 12000: REM Set up parameter addresses
290  GOSUB 13000: REM Turn on interrupts
340  SPEED=1:
     POKE SCRLSTEP,SPEED
380  OPEN #2,4,0,"K:":
     POKE 754,255
390  REM
```

Figure 9.15: Listing of Example 13 — lines 10–390.

Initialize This section of the program calls all the subroutines that set up the screen and machine language routines. To speed up the initialization time, screen DMA has been turned off (line 6020) and must be turned on again so the picture will show. The statement on line 260 turns on the screen and sets the playfield to wide. Line 340 starts the display scrolling.

```
11000 REM INITIALIZE ROUTINE STRINGS
11010 REM Set SCROLL routine
11020 DIM SCROLL$(316)
11030 SCROLL$(1)=" <<<Routine String goes here>>> "
11040 SCROLL$(91)=" <<<Routine String goes here>>> "
11050 SCROLL$(181)=" <<<Routine String goes here>>> "
11060 SCROLL$(271)=" <<<Routine String goes here>>> "
11100 REM Set DLI routine
11110 DIM DLIROUT$(94)
11120 DLIROUT$(1)=" <<<Routine String goes here>>> "
11130 DLIROUT$(91)=" <<<Routine String goes here>>> "
11200 REM Read Color Values Into DLI Table
11210 DLITBLSZE=15:
      RESTORE 25510
11220 DIM DLITABLE$(DLITBLSZE)
11230 DLITABLE=ADR(DLITABLE$)
11240 FOR I=0 TO DLITBLSZE-1
11250   READ BYTE
11260   POKE DLITABLE+I,BYTE
11270 NEXT I
11600 REM Set MFILL routine
11610 DIM MFILL$(41)
11620 MFILL$(1)=" <<<Routine String goes here>>> "
11650 RETURN
11660 REM
25500 REM DLI Color Values
25510 DATA 234,90,152,234,90,198,10,0,198,0,0,6,0,0,10
```

Figure 9.16: Listing of Example 13 — lines 11000–11660, 25500–25510.

Initialize Routine Strings This section initializes the routines and creates the DLI color table for DLIROUT. Enter your SCROLL and DLIROUT strings at this time.

Lines 11200–11270 create the DLI table. Each byte is read in and stored into the string DLITABLE$.

```
5000 REM Set Up Memory Locations
5010 DIF=0
5020 DLSZE=34: REM Display List size
5030 LINELEN=48: REM Horizontal length of scrolling window
5040 SCRNSZE=6*24+LINELEN*6: REM Screen size
5050 MEM=DLSZE+SCRNSZE: REM MEMory to reserve for DL and Screen
5170 DIF=DIF+4:
     IF DIF*256<MEM THEN 5170
5180 HIBASE=PEEK(106)-DIF: REM Find DL Hi and Lo bytes
5190 LOBASE=0
5200 DLBASE=HIBASE*256+LOBASE
5210 SCRN=DLBASE+DLSZE: REM Starting address of Screen RAM
5220 X=SCRN:
     GOSUB 110
5230 SCRNHI=HIBYTE:
     SCRNLO=LOBYTE: REM Find Screen Hi and Lo bytes
5240 SCRLWIN=SCRN+48: REM Beginning of Scroll window
5250 SCROLL=ADR(SCROLL$)
5260 DLIROUT=ADR(DLIROUT$)
5300 MFILL=ADR(MFILL$)
5340 RETURN
5350 REM
```

Figure 9.17: Listing of Example 13 — lines 5000–5350.

Set Up Memory Locations   This section reserves the memory space for the screen and display list. DIF (line 5010) is used to determine the number of memory pages needed to hold the screen. Line 5040 calculates the number of bytes needed for the screen. Note that there are six wide playfield lines of 24 bytes each and six scrolling lines of LINELEN bytes each.

In line 5170, the number of pages of memory needed to hold the screen plus the DL is calculated. The DL will come first, then the screen RAM. Since the DL must not cross a 1 K boundary (four pages), DIF is incremented by 4 each time. When DIF's value is large enough, the high and low bytes of the DL are calculated (lines 5180–5190). The address of the screen (SCRN, line 5210) is determined by adding the length of the DL (DLSZE) to the DL's beginning address (DLBASE).

In line 5240, the address of the scrolling window is found by adding the number of bytes in the first two lines (24*2) to the beginning of screen memory.

```
6000  REM Set Up the Display List
6010  GRAPHICS 2+16: REM Set flags to Graphics mode 2
6020  POKE 559,0: REM Turn off screen DMA
6030  POKE DLBASE,112: REM Set up top border, 24 scan lines
6040  POKE DLBASE+1,112
6050  POKE DLBASE+2,112
6060  POKE DLBASE+3,71: REM LMS for line 1
6070  POKE DLBASE+4,SCRNLO
6080  POKE DLBASE+5,SCRNHI
6090  POKE DLBASE+6,7+128: REM Line 2 (w/ DLI)
6100  FOR I=0 TO 6: REM Loop for lines 3-9
6110    WINDOW=SCRLWIN+I*LINELEN
6120    BYTE=87: REM LMS and HSCRL
6130    IF I=2 OR I=5 THEN
           BYTE=87+128: REM DLI, LMS and HSCRL for lines 5 and 8
6140    IF I=6 THEN
           BYTE=71: REM No scroll for line 9
6150    POKE DLBASE+7+3*I,BYTE: REM LMS and HSCRL
6160    X=WINDOW:
          GOSUB 110
6170    POKE DLBASE+8+3*I,LOBYTE
6180    POKE DLBASE+9+3*I,HIBYTE
6190  NEXT I
6200  POKE DLBASE+28,7+128: REM Last 3 lines
6210  POKE DLBASE+29,7
6220  POKE DLBASE+30,7+128
6230  POKE DLBASE+31,65: REM Jump on VBLANK to beginning of DL
6240  POKE DLBASE+32,LOBYTE
6250  POKE DLBASE+33,HIBASE
6260  X=DLIROUT:
        GOSUB 110
6270  POKE 512,LOBYTE: REM Address of DL for DLI handling routine
6280  POKE 513,HIBYTE
6290  REM Tell ANTIC where the DL is
6300  POKE 560,LOBASE
6310  POKE 561,HIBASE
6320  SETCOLOR 0,15,4:
        SETCOLOR 1,12,4:
        SETCOLOR 2,0,10:
        SETCOLOR 3,0,12:
        SETCOLOR 4,9,8: REM Brn, grn, wht, wht, blue
6330  RETURN
6340  REM
```

Figure 9.18: Listing of Example 13 — lines 6000–6340.

Set Up the Display List   Here is the section that creates the display list. First, line 6010 tells the OS that the computer will be operating a full-screen graphics mode. This is not necessary for the operation of the program since a custom DL has already been created. However, because the OS thinks we're using a full-screen mode, it will immediately return the screen to a normal GRAPHICS Ø mode if an error occurs in the program or if **BREAK** is pressed. On the next line, 6020, screen DMA is turned off to increase the processor speed during the initialization process and to keep the screen from jumping or glitching when we switch over to the new display list. The only drawback is that if the initialization process is too long, the user may think the computer has passed away. It might be a good idea first to display a message stating how long the screen will be blank before turning off the DMA.

Next, the top border of the screen is created by blanking 24 scan lines (6030–6050). The instruction for the first mode line (+7 for GRAPHICS 2) with the LMS bit set (+64) indicates the beginning of screen memory (lines 6060–6080). On line 6090, the second mode line gets its DLI bit set.

Lines 6100–6190 create the DL instructions for mode lines 3 through 9. WINDOW is a temporary variable that holds the beginning memory address for each mode line. The lines get the LMS bit (+64), horizontal fine scroll bit (+16), and mode bits (+7) for a value of 87. Mode lines 5 and 8 (line 6130) also receive a DLI bit. Mode line 9 (line 6140) begins the section of the screen immediately under the scrolling window so its horizontal scroll bit remains unset.

Lines 6230–6250 tell Antic to note that the end of the display list has been reached and to return to the beginning.

The OS receives the address of DLIROUT in lines 6260–6280 so it knows where to send the CPU during a DLI. The new DL is then switched on by a POKE of its location into 560 and 561.

Finally, the color registers are set for the top section of the screen (before the first DLI). Even though the screen DMA is turned off, the background color is still controlled by color register 4 so the screen will turn from black to light blue at this point. This suggests a technique to keep DMA off during program set up but will still show that the computer is alive and functioning — from time to time, just change the color of the screen background.

```
2600 REM Clear the Screen - Fill the Screen With O
2610 TEMP=USR(MFILL,SCRN,SCRNSIZE,0)
2620 RETURN
2630 REM
```

Figure 9.19:   Listing of Example 13 — lines 2600–2630.

Clear the Screen   MFILL is used to clear all of display memory by filling it with 0's.

```
8000  REM Set Up Alternate Character Set
8010  HICHRB=PEEK(106)-DIF-2: REM Reserve space (512 bytes)
8020  CHRBAS=HICHRB*256: REM Find start of Character Set
8030  REM Read in data, skip first 28 characters
8040  OFFSET=28*8:
      CHARS=35
8050  RESTORE 23000
8060  READ TOTAL:
      TEMP=0
8070  FOR I=CHRBAS+OFFSET TO CHRBAS+OFFSET+CHARS*8-1
8080     READ BYTE:
         POKE I,BYTE:
         TEMP=TEMP+BYTE
8090  NEXT I
8100  IF TOTAL<>TEMP THEN
         GRAPHICS 0:
         PRINT "ERROR In Character Set Data":
         END
8110  REM Clear out first char (background)
8120  FOR I=CHRBAS TO CHRBAS+7
8130     POKE I,0
8140  NEXT I
8150  RETURN
8160  REM
```

Figure 9.20:   Listing of Example 13 — lines 8000–8160.

Set Up Alternate Character Set   This subroutine READS in the character definitions for the street character set and POKEs them into memory. This section was stolen from Example 2, the Walking Man Character Set program, with only a few changes (you may want to transfer it over to save some typing). Line 8010 places the beginning of the character set two pages below the display list (remember, only 512 bytes are required for a GRAPHICS 2 character set).

```
23000  REM Character Set Data
23010  DATA 38646
23020  DATA 0,3,15,31,63,63,127,127
23030  DATA 0,192,240,248,252,252,254,254
23040  DATA 127,127,127,63,63,31,15,7
23050  DATA 254,254,254,252,252,248,240,224
23060  DATA 4,31,4,31,4,4,4,4
23070  DATA 48,48,48,63,54,54,54,54
23080  DATA 3,3,3,3,3,3,3,3
23090  DATA 255,195,219,219,219,219,219,219
23100  DATA 12,12,12,252,108,108,108,108
23110  DATA 0,0,0,252,108,108,108,108
23120  DATA 127,127,127,127,127,127,127,127
23130  DATA 254,254,254,254,254,254,254,254
23140  DATA 1,3,7,15,31,63,127,255
23150  DATA 1,1,3,3,7,7,15,15
23160  DATA 128,192,224,240,248,252,254,255
23170  DATA 3,3,7,7,15,0,0,0
23180  DATA 192,192,224,224,240,0,0,0
23190  DATA 156,220,252,252,252,252,254,255
23200  DATA 128,128,192,192,224,224,243,243
23210  DATA 128,128,192,192,224,224,240,240
23220  DATA 255,255,39,39,255,39,39,255
23230  DATA 0,0,0,63,54,54,54,54
23240  DATA 255,255,228,228,255,228,228,255
23250  DATA 255,24,24,24,255,24,24,24
23260  DATA 255,255,255,255,255,255,255,255
23270  DATA 251,251,255,252,254,254,255,255
23280  DATA 192,192,192,192,192,192,192,192
23290  DATA 0,0,0,255,102,102,102,102
23300  DATA 248,248,252,252,254,254,255,255
23310  DATA 57,59,63,63,63,63,127,255
23320  DATA 31,31,63,63,127,127,255,255
23330  DATA 127,127,127,127,63,63,30,0
23340  DATA 255,255,255,255,255,255,124,0
23350  DATA 254,254,254,254,252,252,120,0
23360  DATA 255,255,255,0,0,0,0,0
23370  REM
```

Figure 9.21:   Listing of Example 13 — lines 23000–23370.

Character Set Data   Here are the character definitions for the street scene's houses, trees, etc. Each line contains the eight numbers necessary to define one character. (The first line is the checksum value.)

```
2800 REM Put in Clouds and Sidewalk
2810 SEG$="<T=<TT=[\][\\]";
     CLOUD=1:
     PTR=4:
     HEIGHT=1:
     WIDTH=7:
     GOSUB 2000
2820 SEG$="<T=<=[\\\]";
     CLOUD=2:
     PTR=PTR+3:
     WIDTH=5:
     GOSUB 2000
2830 SEG$="^^^^^^^^^^^^^^^^^^^^^^^^";
     GRND=1:
     HEIGHT=0:
     WIDTH=24:
     GOSUB 2000
2840 RETURN
2850 REM
```

Figure 9.22: Listing of Example 13 — lines 2800–2850.

Put in Clouds and Sidewalk   We have now come to the first part of the program, which fills the screen memory with scenery. This section places the clouds and the sidewalk on the screen. The technique we have chosen places the appropriate characters into a string called SEG$ (for segment). Each object to be displayed is stuffed into SEG$ and then a subroutine at line 2000 is called that POKEs the information into memory. Even though this is a text screen, its unusual dimensions would make it very difficult to PRINT the strings to the screen.

Line 2810 has a number of parameters that instruct the subroutine at 2000 how and where to place the information on the screen. CLOUD is a flag that alerts the subroutine that this is a cloud. PTR gives the string's horizontal screen position as an offset from the left edge of the screen. HEIGHT informs the routine how many mode lines tall (less 1) the shape in the string is. (A height of 1 means 2 mode lines; a height of 0 means 1 mode line.) WIDTH says how many bytes wide the shape is. This means that there will be HEIGHT*WIDTH characters in the string. This line will send two light gray clouds to the screen.

Line 2820 creates another cloud, which will be positioned 3 bytes over from the previous one. Line 2830 then creates the sidewalk string.

```
2000 REM Send Info to Screen
2010 LN=LEN(SEG$):
     IF LN<24 THEN
       SEG$(LN+1)=CL$
2020 IF FENCE THEN
       PTR=PTR+1
2030 FOR I=0 TO HEIGHT
2040   IF FENCE THEN
         GOSUB 2200
2050   FOR J=1 TO WIDTH
2060     P=I*WIDTH+J:
         CHAR=ASC(SEG$(P,P))
```

(continued)

```
2070        GOSUB 1900
2080        IF GRND THEN
              POKE SCRLWIN+6*LINELEN+J+23,CHAR:
              GOTO 2130
2090        IF CLOUD=0 THEN 2120
2100        IF CLOUD=2 THEN
              CHAR=CHAR+64
2110        POKE SCRN+PTR+I*24+J-1,CHAR:
              GOTO 2130
2120        POKE SCRLWIN+PTR+I*LINELEN+J-1,CHAR
2130      NEXT J
2140    NEXT I
2150    PTR=PTR+WIDTH+ABS(FENCE)+SPCFLAG
2160    SPCFLAG=0
2170    ROOMLEFT=LINELEN-25-PTR
2180    RETURN
2190    REM
```

Figure 9.23:   Listing of Example 13 — lines 2000–2190.

Send Information to Screen   After `SEG$` has been filled
with characters defining an object, this subroutine is called. The object's
`HEIGHT`, `WIDTH`, and horizontal placement (`PTR`) are passed to this
routine as well as flags that indicate special objects. `FENCE` means that a
fence is to be placed around the house. `SPCFLAG` is used to increase the
space between objects. `CLOUD` and `GRND` cause the object to be placed
in special locations outside the scrolling window.

Line 2010 makes sure the string is at least 24 characters long by
padding short strings with blanks contained in `CL$`.

Line 2060 obtains the ATASCII value for the individual character to
be transferred to the screen. A subroutine at 1900 converts this value to
the proper byte value so it will be correctly displayed.

After the string has been `POKE`d into memory, line 2150 increments `PTR` for the next object, and line 2170 finds out how much room is
left on the line for more objects.

```
1900   REM Convert to Screen Value
1910   CFLAG=0
1920   IF CHAR>127 THEN
          CHAR=CHAR-128:
          CFLAG=128
1930   IF CHAR<96 THEN
          CHAR=CHAR-32:
          IF CHAR<0 THEN
          CHAR=CHAR+96
1940   IF CFLAG THEN
          CHAR=CHAR+CFLAG+PAINT*64
1950   RETURN
1960   REM
```

Figure 9.24:   Listing of Example 13 — lines 1900–1960.

Convert to Screen Value   As we mentioned earlier, the
ATASCII value of a character doesn't always match its screen value.
This routine makes a conversion which enables the character to be
`POKE`d into the screen. We won't explain lines 1920–1930, but we'll
guarantee they'll work! Line 1940 changes the house color to pink or
yellow, depending on the value of `PAINT`.

```
2200  REM Put In Fence
2210  IF I<4 THEN 2240
2220  IF I=4 THEN
        CHAR=ASC("Q"):
        GOSUB 1900:
        P=-1:
        GOSUB 2250:
        CHAR=ASC("E"):
        GOSUB 1900:
        P=WIDTH:
        GOSUB 2250:
        GOTO 2240
2230  CHAR=ASC("A"):
        GOSUB 1900:
        P=-1:
        GOSUB 2250:
        CHAR=ASC("D"):
        GOSUB 1900:
        P=WIDTH:
        GOSUB 2250
2240  RETURN
2250  REM Poke In Data
2260  POKE SCRLWIN+PTR+I*LINELEN+P,CHAR
2270  RETURN
2280  REM
```

Figure 9.25: Listing of Example 13 — lines 2200–2280.

Put In Fence   This routine is called by line 2040 if a fence is to be placed around the house (a random event). The variable I gives the current mode line being filled (from the loop in the routine at 2000). If I is less than 4, we're too high up so the routine is exited. Otherwise, the side fence pieces are POKEd in. The front bottom section of the fence is contained in SEG$.

```
3000  REM CREATE RANDOM DISPLAY
3010  PTR=0:  REM Initialize Pointer to Scroll Window
3020  HEIGHT=5:  REM How tall is the window
3030  CLOUD=0:
      GRND=0
3040  WIDTH=INT(RND(1)*3+2):  REM From 2-4
3050  IF RND(1)*100<=45 THEN
        STORY=2:
        GOTO 3080:  REM 45% 2 Stories
3060  IF RND(1)*55<=35 THEN
        STORY=3:
        GOTO 3080:  REM 35% 3 Stories
3070  STORY=4:  REM 20% 4 Stories
3080  CHIMNEY=(RND(1)<=0.6):  REM 60% chance
3090  IF SHRUB=0 THEN
        FENCE=(RND(1)<=0.4):  REM 40% chance (only if no shrub)
3100  IF ROOMLEFT<6 THEN
        FENCE=0:  REM Not enough room left for a fence
3110  ANTENNA=(RND(1)<=0.5):  REM 50% chance
3120  PAINT=(RND(1)<=0.5):  REM 50% yellow, 50% pink
3130  SEG$=CL$:
      ON WIDTH-1 GOSUB 3500,3700,3900:
      GOSUB 2000
3140  IF ROOMLEFT<2 THEN
        GOSUB 2400:
        RETURN :  REM No room for tree, exit routine
```

Figure 9.26: Listing of Example 13 — lines 3000–3140.

Create Random Display   This is the master controller section for building the houses and planting the greenery. It makes the random choices that will control many of the features of the street scene. In this city, a tree or shrub is planted between each pair of buildings. The size of the plant depends on the care and feeding provided by a later program section.

Line 3040 selects a random house W I D T H. There is an equal chance for the house to be 2, 3, or 4 bytes wide. Lines 3050–3070 select the number of stories tall the house will be. Given a large enough street, 45 percent will be a two-story house, 35 percent will be a three-story house, and 20 percent will be a four-story house. These percentages could be changed if you want to modify the ambience of your street.

Line 3080 decides whether a chimney can be built on the house. However, since not all houses can receive building permits for chimneys (depending on roof shape), the actual percentage will be lower than 60 percent.

Line 3090 gives a 40 percent chance for a fence around the house only if a shrub wasn't first planted next door.

How many houses have antennas and how many opted for cable? This important decision is made on line 3110. Again, the actual percentage will be different as either a chimney or a flat roof is a prerequisite for "free TV."

Line 3120 chooses the paint color for the house, half yellow and half pink. If you have a preference of one color over the other (or wish a different two-tone town), feel free to make the change.

Line 3130 clears the string and calls the contractor that specializes in building houses of the specified width. After the string is stuffed and transferred to the screen, line 3140 checks for the number of bytes left on the line. If there is no room left for a plant (the next section), then the routine 2400 is called and copies the first screen to the last (see Figure 9.9).

```
3500  REM Width 2
3510  IF STORY>3 THEN
          STORY=3
3520  BT=1
3530  IF STORY=2 THEN
          BT=3
3540  IF CHIMNEY THEN
          SEG$(BT)="INZU":
          GOTO 3560
3550  SEG$(BT)="IOZX"
3560  BT=BT+4:
          FOR I=BT TO BT+(STORY-2)*2 STEP 2
3570     IF RND(1)<=0.5 THEN
             SEG$(I)="TP":
             GOTO 3590
3580     SEG$(I)="RP"
3590  NEXT I
3600  SEG$(9)="CT"
3610  IF FENCE=0 THEN 3640
3620  IF RND(1)<=0.5 THEN
          SEG$(11)="WW":
          GOTO 3640
3630  SEG$(11)="EQ"
3640  RETURN
3650  REM
```

Figure 9.27: Listing of Example 13 — lines 3500–3650.

Width 2   This subroutine builds the small "get away" cottages. To ensure coziness, line 3510 restricts the number of stories to these houses to three. In line 3520, B T, a byte pointer used in the creation of the strings, is set to 1. If there are only two stories (rather than three) for this house, then B T is set to 3 (remember, this is a two-byte wide house). First the roof is built (the contractors we hired are very strange — they believe in a top-down approach). If a chimney has been requested, line 3540 obliges; otherwise 3550 takes over. B T is incremented, and a loop is entered that fills in the third and second stories. Notice the randomness being added. Then line 3600 builds a door, and lines 3620–3630 build a fence, if requested.

```
3700  REM Width 3
3710  BT=(4-STORY)*3+1
3720  IF ANTENNA AND STORY<4 THEN
         SEG$(BT-3)="(,)(,)(,)"
3730  SEG$(BT)="ZTX"
3740  IF RND(1)<=0.5 THEN
         TEMP$="FPG":
         GOTO 3760
3750  TEMP$="FRG"
3760  BT=BT+3:
      FOR I=BT TO BT+(STORY-2)*3 STEP 3
3770     SEG$(I)=TEMP$
3780  NEXT I
3790  SEG$(13)="FCG"
3800  IF FENCE THEN
         SEG$(16)="WWW"
3810  RETURN
3820  REM
```

Figure 9.28: Listing of Example 13 — lines 3700–3820.

Width 3   This section is very similar to the previous one. The main difference, other than the width, is that the antenna is an option and the chimney isn't (those bigger houses just aren't as romantic).

```
3900  REM Width 4
3910  BT=(4-STORY)*4+1
3920  IF STORY=4 THEN
         SEG$(BT)="HTTJ":
         GOTO 4050
3930  IF STORY>2 OR SHRUB OR RND(1)<=0.3333 THEN 4000:REM Which type house?
3940  REM Create Odd House type
3950  ODDHOUSE=1
3960  IF CHIMNEY THEN
         SEG$(1)="(,)IN(2 ,)ZU(,)":
         GOTO 3980
3970  SEG$(1)="(,)IO(2 ,)ZX(,)"
3980  FENCE=0
3990  SEG$(9)="ITTOBRPVBTCV":
         GOTO 4100
4000  REM Create Normal House type
4010  IF ANTENNA AND CHIMNEY THEN
         SEG$(BT-4)="(,)HJ(,)YTTJ":
         GOTO 4050
4020  SEG$(BT-4)="(,)HJ(,)":
      IF CHIMNEY=0 THEN
         SEG$(BT)="HTTJ":
         GOTO 4050
4030  IF RND(1)<=0.5 THEN
         SEG$(BT)="YTTJ":
         GOTO 4050
4040  SEG$(BT)="HTTM"
4050  BT=BT+4:
      FOR I=BT TO BT+(STORY-2)*4 STEP 4
```

(continued)

```
4060    IF RND(1)<=0.25 THEN
            SEG$(I)="FSSG":
            GOTO 4080
4070    SEG$(I)="FPRG"
4080  NEXT I
4090  SEG$(17)="FTCG"
4100  IF FENCE THEN
            SEG$(21)="WEQW"
4110  RETURN
4120  REM
```

Figure 9.29: Listing of Example 13 — lines 3900–4120.

Width 4   The wide body house is assembled in this section. There are actually two different possible versions. If the house has more than two stories, is adjacent to a shrub, or is just lucky (33 percent chance), the house gets normal outer walls (decided in line 3930). Otherwise, it is branded an ODDHOUSE and gets the narrower set of walls. Because of these indented walls, a fence or shrub placed next to it would sit a distance away from the house, so they aren't permitted.

In line 4010, the house can receive both an antenna and a chimney, otherwise, the normal house is not any different than its skinnier cousins.

```
3150  REM Plant Some Foilage
3160  SHRUB=0:
        TREE=0
3170  IF FENCE=0 AND ODDHOUSE=0 AND ROOMLEFT>8 THEN
            SHRUB=(RND(1)<=0.3):
            IF SHRUB THEN 3440
3180  REM Make a tree
3190  WIDTH=2:
        SEG$=CL$
3200  REM Find height of tree
3210  IF RND(1)*10<=1 THEN
            TREE=2:
            GOTO 3260: REM 10%
3220  IF RND(1)*9<=2 THEN
            TREE=3:
            GOTO 3260: REM 20%
3230  IF RND(1)*7<=4 THEN
            TREE=4:
            GOTO 3260: REM 40%
3240  IF RND(1)*3<=2 THEN
            TREE=5:
            GOTO 3260: REM 20%
3250  TREE=6: REM 10%
3260  TRUNK=INT(RND(1)*(TREE-2)+1):
        IF TREE=2 THEN
            TRUNK=0
3270  TREETOP=TREE-TRUNK:
        IF TREETOP>4 THEN
            TRUNK=TREE-4:
            TREETOP=4
3280  BT=(6-TREE)*2+1
3290  SEG$(BT)="(UP)(DOWN)"
3300  IF TREETOP=2 THEN 3340
3310  FOR I=1 TO TREETOP-2
3320      BT=BT+2:
            SEG$(BT)="tt"
3330  NEXT I
3340  BT=BT+2:
        SEG$(BT)="(LEFT)(RIGHT)"
3350  IF TRUNK=1 THEN 3390
3360  FOR I=1 TO TRUNK-1
3370      BT=BT+2:
            SEG$(BT)="BV"
3380  NEXT I
3390  IF RND(1)<=0.5 THEN
            SEG$(BT+2)="KL"
3400  REM Add random spacing on side of tree
3410  TEMP=INT(RND(1)*3+1):
        IF TEMP=3 OR ROOMLEFT<3 THEN 3470
3420  IF TEMP=1 THEN
            PTR=PTR+1:
            GOTO 3470
3430  SPCFLAG=1:
        GOTO 3470
```

```
3440  REM Make a shrub
3450  WIDTH=INT(RND(1)*2+2):
      SEG$=CL$:
      IF WIDTH=2 THEN
        SEG$(9)="(DOWN)(UP)":
        GOTO 3470
3460  SEG$(13)="(DOWN)%(UP)"
3470  ODDHOUSE=0:
      FENCE=0:
      GOSUB 2000
3480  IF ROOMLEFT<4 THEN 3140:REM Add another tree if not enough room for a house
3490  GOTO 3040
```

Figure 9.30: Listing of Example 13 — lines 3150–3490.

Plant Some Foliage   Here is where the gardeners reside. After a house is built, they come in and plant something before the next house is plunked down. There are basically two types of plants: shrubs and trees. A shrub is a quarter of a tree top which rests next to the outer wall of a house. Shrubs only come in pairs, so when one house gets a shrub, its soon-to-be neighbor gets one too. Trees are vertical plants which may or may not have a trunk. By selecting different heights for the tree and deciding how much of that will be leafy green, you can create a wide selection of trees.

First, line 3170 checks whether a shrub is possible. It must be a normal house without a fence with enough room next to it for another house to follow. If a shrub is eligible after these tests, it has a 30 percent chance of appearing; otherwise, a tree is planted. All trees have a width of 2. Their height can range from 2 to 6 bytes (3200–3250). Then, the height of the trunk (3260) and the height of the tree top (3270) are determined. In lines 3280–3340, the tree top is grown first (clever gardeners!), then the trunk (3360–3380), and finally a base is spliced onto half of the trees (3390). Then lines 3400–3430 add random spacing next to either (or neither) side of the tree.

Lines 3440–3460 create the shrubs. They can either have a width of 2 or 3 bytes. If the width is three, then a blank space is inserted between them.

Finally, the amount of room left on the screen is checked. If it isn't enough for a house, line 3140 checks if another plant can be grown instead.

```
2400  REM Copy First Page Onto Last Page
2410  FOR I=0 TO 5
2420    FOR J=0 TO 24
2430      POKE SCRLWIN+I*LINELEN+LINELEN-25+J,PEEK(SCRLWIN+I*LINELEN+J)
2440    NEXT J
2450  NEXT I
2460  RETURN
2470  REM
```

Figure 9.31: Listing of Example 13 — lines 2400–2470.

Copy First Page Onto Last Page   Once the available space
in the scrolling window has been filled with houses and trees, the first
screen page must be copied to the last to allow for a smooth transition
when the screen is reset to its starting position. This loop copies the first
24 bytes of each of the six scrolling lines to the last 24 bytes of each line.

```
12000  REM Set Parameters For Routines
12010  PARAMBASE=1024: REM Parameter Base address
12060  SCRLINIT=PARAMBASE+5: REM Poke a 1 to initialize the scroll routine
12140  SCRLADR=PARAMBASE+26: REM Address of scrolling window
12150  SCRLLEN=PARAMBASE+28: REM Line length of scrolling window
12160  SCRLCLK=PARAMBASE+30: REM Number of Color Clocks per screen byte
12170  SCRLSTEP=PARAMBASE+31: REM Step size of scroll each jiffy
12180  DLIADR=PARAMBASE+36: REM Address of DLI table
12190  VVBLKD=548: REM Deferred Vertical Blank Interrupt Vector
12200  CRITICAL=66: REM Critical Flag
12240  TEMP=USR(MFILL,PARAMBASE,94,0): REM IMPORTANT: Clear out parameter area
12280  X=SCRLWIN:
       GOSUB 110
12290  POKE SCRLADR,LOBYTE
12300  POKE SCRLADR+1,HIBYTE
12320  X=LINELEN:
       GOSUB 110
12330  POKE SCRLLEN,LOBYTE
12340  POKE SCRLLEN+1,HIBYTE
12350  POKE SCRLCLK,7: REM Set to 8 color clocks per byte
12360  X=DLITABLE:
       GOSUB 110
12370  POKE DLIADR,LOBYTE
12380  POKE DLIADR+1,HIBYTE
12530  RETURN
12540  REM
```

Figure 9.32:   Listing of Example 13 — lines 12000–12540.

Set Parameters For Routines   This subroutine sets up the
parameter table for the machine language routines. All the parameters for
SCROLL are POKEd in except SCRLSTEP. SCRLINIT isn't set
until the VBLANK routines are in place.

```
13000  REM Install Interrupt Routines
13010  POKE CRITICAL,1: REM Open CRITICAL "valve", set up detour
13020  X=SCROLL+6:
       GOSUB 110
13030  POKE VVBLKD,LOBYTE: REM Set VBLANK vector to SCROLL
13040  POKE VVBLKD+1,HIBYTE
13050  X=DLIROUT+6:
       GOSUB 110
13060  POKE SCROLL+4,LOBYTE: REM Points SCROLL to DLIROUT
13070  POKE SCROLL+5,HIBYTE
13170  POKE CRITICAL,0: REM Close CRITICAL "valve", routines installed
13180  POKE SCRLINIT,1
13190  POKE 54286,192: REM Enable DLI's
13200  RETURN
13210  REM
```

Figure 9.33:   Listing of Example 13 — lines 13000–13210.

Install Interrupt Routines   SCROLL and DLIROUT are
installed into the vertical blank routines, SCROLL is turned on (line
13180), and the DLI's are enabled (13190).

```
400  REM Main Animation Loop
480  IF PEEK(754)=255 THEN 480
490  GET #2,BYTE:
     SPEED=BYTE-48:
     POKE 754,255:
     IF SPEED<0 THEN
       SPEED=0
500  POKE SCRLSTEP,SPEED
520  GOTO 480
530  REM
```

Figure 9.34: Listing of Example 13 — lines 400–530.

Main Animation Loop   We have reached the last section of this program. All it does is watch the keyboard, accept SPEED values, and POKE them into SCRLSTEP.

Before running this program, make sure you have saved it on disk or cassette! We wouldn't want you to lose all that work! For the first run, set LINELEN (in line 5030) to 48. You won't get much variety in houses, but you won't have to wait as long to see your results. The screen will flash to black for a few seconds, then to light blue for about 15 seconds. Appearing next will be the clouds, the sidewalk, and then the first house and tree, on the far left side of the screen. After the visible screen is covered, it will be copied over to the end of the scrolling window. Don't be alarmed when the houses first appear in gray and white and there is no grass or street — the interrupts aren't turned on until the entire street has been completed. The screen will then spring into full color and start rolling by! Press **RESET** when you have finished admiring your work, and set up a longer scrolling window (160 is a good number to use). Just remember that the wider it is, the longer you'll have to wait for the action to begin.

Try changing the speed. Notice that when you press down on a key, there is sometimes a slight jump at the color border between DLI. This is because the computer's interior speaker interferes with the DLI timing. The only way to avoid it is by not acknowledging keyboard input (don't use the GET command), or avoid using the keyboard as the input device.

Modifications

1. Use the paddles to change the speed rather than the keyboard. This will eliminate the DLI jump upon keypress.
2. To save memory space and set-up time, save the entire screen to disk. Then, replace the street drawing code with a routine to read that disk file back into screen memory.
3. Experiment with creating a scrolling window in a different graphics mode. Be sure to set SCRLCLK to the correct color value.
4. The scrolling background would make a perfect backdrop for many arcade type games (e.g., Defender or racing-type games). Think of the current crop of games, and see if you can come up with any ideas of your own.

Summary

You have now successfully implemented two more very powerful ATARI features into a program. We are about to enter the last stage of this book, combining all the best features into one climactic program, the Great Movie Cartoon.

9.3. THE GREAT MOVIE CARTOON

As you continue your trip through the Sunday morning suburbs you suddenly notice a few very large trees passing by. They are on the curb so they seem to pass faster than the houses in the background. Then the sound of traffic reaches your ears. When you realize that you are going very slowly, you triple your speed. Occasionally, a man appears, walking on the sidewalk. It seems the town has awakened.

Well, this is it — the moment you have been waiting for. It is now time to merge Examples 12 and 13 to create the final program in this book, the Great Movie Cartoon. This process is really very simple. Just delete six lines, modify fourteen lines and add one! That's all!

Example 14

Exercise   Merge the last two program examples, 12 (Player Foreground Demo) and 13 (Scrolling Street Scene) into one program. Use the same keyboard routine to change the speed of the display.

a)

(continued)

b)

c)

d)

Photo 9.4: Screen photos of the Great Movie Cartoon.

There are just ten simple steps you must follow to merge Examples 12 and 13. For everything to work properly, it is essential that all the lines and line numbers were entered exactly as given in the book.

As we mentioned in Chapter 7, every time a variable is entered into a program, it takes up residence in the variable name table. This wouldn't be much of a problem except for two facts: 1) There can be no more than 128 different variable names in an ATARI BASIC program, and 2) the Great Movie Cartoon has exactly 128 different variable names. If there is *one extra* variable name in the table, you will get an error (ERROR 4) while trying to merge Examples 12 and 13. An extra variable may have sneaked its way in while you were entering the programs. If you mistyped any of the variable names and pressed **RETURN**, that name would remain

in the variable table. The method to clear the extra entries from the variable name table is to LIST the program to disk or cassette, type NEW, and ENTER the program back into memory. Here are the steps to follow to create Example 14:

1. Load Example 13 into memory.
2. Delete the following lines:
$$340 \quad 480 \quad 500 \quad 520$$
3. LIST the program into a temporary file:

    LIST "D:TEMP"   for disk
    LIST "C:"   for cassette

4. Load Example 12 into memory.
5. LIST the program onto disk or cassette as in step 3, but use a different file:

    LIST "D:EX12"   for disk
    LIST "C:"   for cassette

6. Type NEW, and ENTER the program back into memory:

    ENTER "D:EX12"   for disk
    ENTER "C:"   for cassette

7. Delete the following lines:
$$300 \quad 7080$$
8. Merge the temporary file into the program in memory:

    ENTER "D:TEMP"   for disk
    ENTER "C:"   for cassette

9. Modify the following highlighted lines:

```
10 REM *** THE GREAT MOVIE CARTOON ***
20 REM           Example 14
30 REM
40 REM Program putting it all together - PM Graphics, Fine Scrolling, & Display List Interrupts
50 REM Copyright (C) 1982 by David Fox and Mitchell Waite
250 POKE 756,HICHRB: REM Switch to Street character set
260 POKE 559,47: REM Turn screen DMA on again, Wide Playfield, PM 2 line resolution, Players enabled
270 GOSUB 2800:
    GOSUB 3000: REM Create a street
```

Figure 9.35: Listing of Example 14 — lines 10–50, 250–270.

Line 260 now enables PM graphics as well as turning the screen DMA back on and setting it to a wide playfield.

```
* 1000  REM PARAMETERS FOR PLAYERS
* 1040  POKE VPLR(0),97:
        POKE VPLR(1),97

* 1140  POKE VPLR(2),42:
        POKE VPLR(3),28

* 1230  POKE VPLR(2),77:
        POKE VPLR(3),77

* 1350  POKE VPLR(2),96:
        POKE VPLR(3),96
```

Figure 9.36: Listing of Example 14 — lines 1000, 1040, 1140, 1230, 1350.

These lines reset the vertical position for the four objects: the man, the trees, the trucks, and the cars. They must now be positioned properly on the sidewalk, the street, or the grass.

```
5000  REM Set Up Memory Locations
5010  DIF=0
5020  DLSZE=34: REM Display List size
5030  LINELEN=160: REM Horizontal length of scrolling window
5040  SCRNSZE=6*24+LINELEN*6: REM Screen size
5050  MEM=DLSZE+SCRNSZE: REM MEMory to reserve for DL and Screen
5060  RESTORE :
      READ OBJS
```

Figure 9.37: Listing of Example 14 — lines 5000–5060.

The RESTORE must be added to line 5060 to READ information on the players.

```
  7000  REM Initialize Player-Missile Graphics
* 7010  TEMP=PEEK(106)-DIF-4: REM Set aside Player-Missile area
  8000  REM Set Up Alternate Character Set
* 8010  HICHRB=PEEK(106)-DIF-4: REM Reserve space (512 bytes)
```

Figure 9.38: Listing of Example 14 — lines 7000–7010, 8000–8010.

Line 7010 is changed so player RAM resides in the 1 K section of memory directly below screen memory. Recall that the players use the upper two pages (512 bytes) of this 1 K section and that the missiles use part of the second page. Since we are not using missiles, the first two pages can be used to store the character set (line 8010), which also requires only 512 bytes.

```
10000  REM Read in Frame Data
10010  OFFSET=0:
       OFFSET2=0:
       DIM FRAMELIST(OBJS):
       RESTORE 21000
```

Figure 9.39: Listing of Example 14 — lines 10000–10010.

The RESTORE 21000 statement is added to line 10010 to again reset the READ pointers.

```
13000  REM Install Interrupt Routines
13010  POKE CRITICAL,1: REM Open CRITICAL "valve", set up detour
13020  X=SCROLL+6:
       GOSUB 110
13030  POKE VVBLKD,LOBYTE: REM Set VBLANK vector to SCROLL
13040  POKE VVBLKD+1,HIBYTE
13050  X=DLIROUT+6:
       GOSUB 110
13060  POKE SCROLL+4,LOBYTE: REM Points SCROLL to DLIROUT
13070  POKE SCROLL+5,HIBYTE
13080  X=PMOVER+6:
       GOSUB 110
13090  POKE DLIROUT+4,LOBYTE: REM Points DLIROUT to PMOVER
13100  POKE DLIROUT+5,HIBYTE
13110  X=ANIMATE+6:
       GOSUB 110
13120  POKE PMOVER+4,LOBYTE: REM Points PMOVER to ANIMATE
13130  POKE PMOVER+5,HIBYTE
13140  X=AUTOMOVE+6:
       GOSUB 110
13150  POKE ANIMATE+4,LOBYTE: REM Points ANIMATE to AUTOMOVE
13160  POKE ANIMATE+5,HIBYTE
13170  POKE CRITICAL,0: REM Close CRITICAL "valve", routines installed
13180  POKE SCRLINIT,1
13190  POKE 54286,192: REM Enable DLI's
13200  RETURN
```

Figure 9.40: Listing of Example 14 — lines 13000–13200.

PMOVER must now be connected to the previous routine, DLIROUT, rather than VVBLKD. Now all the routines are chained together.

10. Add the following new line:

```
700  REM Set Horizontal Velocities
710  IF OBJECT=3 THEN
       NSPD=128-SPEED*2:
       GOTO 740: REM Tree
720  IF OBJECT=4 THEN
       NSPD=125-SPEED:
       GOTO 740: REM Truck
730  NSPD=132-SPEED: REM Car
740  POKE MOVERATE(2),NSPD:
       POKE MOVERATE(3),NSPD:
       TEMP=LST2P
750  POKE MOVERATE(0),129-SPEED:
       POKE MOVERATE(1),129-SPEED:
       IF WALK=-1 THEN
       TEMP=ALLP
760  POKE INITAUTOMOVE,TEMP
770  POKE SCRLSTEP,SPEED
780  RETURN
790  REM
```

Figure 9.41: Listing of Example 14 — lines 700–790.

In line 770, SCROLL receives the new SPEED by POKEing it into SCRLSTEP.

Are you ready to run the culmination of all that code entry? Make sure you have saved the program first and that LINELEN is a small

value to start. Then RUN the program and sit back and enjoy. Remember that there is quite a bit more initialization than before, so don't panic. The screen will remain light blue for about 40 seconds before the first cloud appears on the horizon. May it be a cloud of joy.

Commercially Available Software — Scrolling and DLIs

There are currently two main uses for scrolling in games. One is to create a playing area or map that is much larger than the screen. Then the television screen becomes a moving window into this larger universe. The games Match Racer, The Adventures of Farnsworth, Caverns of Mars, and Eastern Front use scrolling in this manner. The second technique is to move a band of figures across the screen (usually in a horizontal direction). This method is used in Embargo, Chicken, and all the Frogger look alikes.

In Match Racer (by Bill Hooper, Solitaire Group, distributed by Gebelli Software, Inc.), the background consists of a race track with a number of obstacles. There are a total of eight different track sections that are randomly combined to make a continuous race track. A GRAPHICS 2 redefined character set is used for these backgrounds. Racing on the tracks are two cars (when two people are playing the game), each of which is made of two players. The priority control (GPRIOR) is set to allow multi-colored players (see Chapter 7 on priority control), so each car has three colors (the third being a result of the combination of each player's color). The odometer numbers at the bottom of the screen are created with redefined GRAPHICS 0 characters. Also at the bottom of the screen, all four missiles are used to display the current speed. The collision registers are used to determine when a race car collides with a wall or other object.

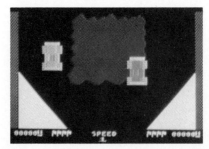

a)

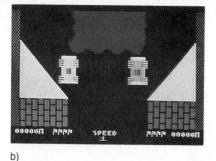

b)

Photo 9.5: Screen photos of Match Racer. (Copyright (c) 1981 by Gebelli Software, Inc.)

A perfect application for scrolling is in an adventure game. The entire game universe fits into memory, and the explorer can view only a portion of it at any time. This is the technique used in The Adventures of Farnsworth (by Doctor Goodcode, Gebelli Software, Inc.). You get to control Farnsworth, the little man with the red hat, moving him around the castle and adjoining maze as he fights off evil characters and bats, while searching for treasures. The background is made of a GRAPHICS 2 character set. All the figures are made of players.

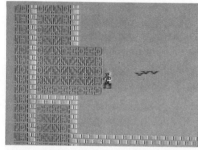

a)

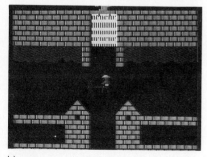

b)

Photo 9.6: Screen photos of The Adventures of Farnsworth. (Copyright (c) 1982 by Gebelli Software, Inc.)

In Caverns of Mars (by Greg Christensen, ATARI, Inc., CX8130), the scrolling background was created in GRAPHICS 7. The object of this game is to make it through a number of levels of the Martian cavern defense system to activate a fusion bomb, leveling Martian Headquarters. Your fighter ship is a player and your laser torpedoes are missiles.

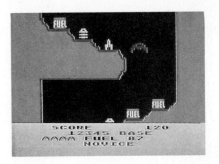

Photo 9.7: Screen photo of Caverns of Mars. (Copyright (c) 1982 by ATARI, Inc.).

We mentioned the game Eastern Front (1941) (by Chris Crawford, ATARI cartridge RX8039) earlier in this chapter. It was one of the first games to make use of fine scrolling on the ATARI Home Computer. (Chris probably knows more about how to push the ATARI Home Computer to its limits than any other programmer.) This game is a simulation of Operation Barbarossa, the German invasion of Russia towards the beginning of World War II. You control the German troops and the computer controls the Russians. The map of Russia (about ten screens large) was created entirely in GRAPHICS 2 with two separate character sets. The second character set (as well as some new colors) is enabled during a DLI. This was rather difficult, since the mode line on which to make this switch changes as the map is scrolled up and down. Players are used for the cursor (the large pink square), the cross, and pointers (arrows, not pictured here). As you move the cursor to one of the edges of the screen, the entire map scrolls to reveal other portions. As the seasons change, so does the background — from brown (summer) to gray (muddy fall) to white (winter). Chris used vertical blank interrupts in a most ingenious way — to have the computer calculate its next move. The computer starts off with a rough guess and then refines it during each successive VBI until the human finally presses the **START** key. The longer the human takes to make a decision, the more time the computer gets to perfect its strategy!

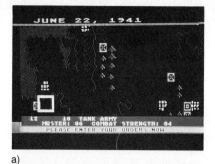

a)

b)

Photo 9.8: Screen photos of Eastern Front (1941). (Copyright (c) 1981 by Chris Crawford.)

The second use of fine scrolling makes a number of playfield objects fly across the screen. The game Embargo (by Bill Hooper, Solitaire Group, distributed by Gebelli Software, Inc.) has a beautifully laid out screen with four bands of Antic 4 ships that move horizontally across the screen. The object of the game is to fly your light blue ship (a player) past the blockade, pick up supplies (a player) on the ground, and then transport them to your mother ship (upper left of screen, Antic 4). To make things more difficult, a small brown enemy ship (another player) flies around trying to shoot you. The ships at the very bottom of the screen that show how many turns are left are also players. As many as nine players can appear on the screen simultaneously using DLI's to move them to a new position. All the objects on the ground are made from map mode Antic E. DLI's are also used to obtain the extra colors on the screen.

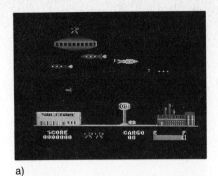

a)

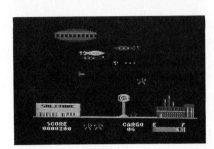

b)

Photo 9.9: Screen photos of Embargo. (Copyright (c) 1981 by Gebelli Software, Inc.)

Finally, there is the delightful game called Chicken (by Mike Potter, Synapse Software). The object of the game is to catch in your wheelbarrow all the eggs that the fox is throwing down at you (the chicken). If you miss an egg, it breaks open and a chick pops out. Then, if you are clumsy enough to step on a chick, the farmer runs out and kicks you off the screen. The sifter is made of three bars of GRAPHICS 0 characters using artifacts for the color. Each bar randomly scrolls back and forth, sifting the eggs down. The fox (standing on top of the sifter), the chicken, the red of the wheelbarrow, the blue of the wheelbarrow, and the farmer are all players. The eggs and chicks are redefined GRAPHICS 0 characters.

Photo 9.10: Screen photo of Chicken. (Copyright (c) 1982 by Synapse Software.)

Film 1
This is the Running Boy from our ATARI program, Example 11.

Summary

Congratulations! You are now a graduate of our course on Personal Computer Animation. The programs in this book are intended as a jumping off place, and we would be thrilled if you will take what you have learned and apply it in some heretofore unseen examples of extraordinary animation. Part of our reason for doing this book was indeed selfish. As more of you can implement animation on a personal computer, two things will happen: 1) Fabulous new games will begin emerging on the computers that exist today, and 2) there will be a demand on the manufacturers of microcomputers to continue making rapid technological advances in their products until they match the power of today's ten million dollar real-time simulation computers. In the meantime, enjoy your personal animation machine!

Appendix A / 395

Appendix A

Complete Listings of BASIC Program Examples

The following is a compilation of all listings from Chapters 5 through 9, reproduced in larger detail for easier reference.

```
10  REM      *** FLYING BIRD ***
20  REM            Example 1
30  REM
40  REM Demonstration of Character Set Animation using Atari's built-in graphics characters
50  REM Copyright (C) 1982 by David Fox and Mitchell Waite
60  REM
100 REM Initialize
110 DIM BIRD1$(17),BIRD2$(17),BIRD3$(16),BIRD4$(16)
120 BIRD1$="{DOWN}B{F}{T}{G}B{DOWN}{5 LEFT}{F}BBB{G}"
130 BIRD2$="{DOWN}{F}{M}{T}{M}{G}{DOWN}{5 LEFT}BBBBB"
140 BIRD3$="BBBBB{DOWN}{5 LEFT}{2 M}{T}{2 M}"
150 BIRD4$="{G}BBB{F}{DOWN}{5 LEFT}B{M}{T}{M}B"
160 POKE 752,1
170 PRINT "{CLEAR}"
180 REM
200 REM Animation Loop
210 FOR I=1 TO 6
220    POSITION 17,10
230    ON I GOSUB 310,320,330,340,330,320
240    FOR W=1 TO 25:
       NEXT W: REM Pause
250 NEXT I
260 GOTO 210
270 REM
300 REM Draw Frame
310 PRINT BIRD1$;:
    RETURN
320 PRINT BIRD2$;:
    RETURN
330 PRINT BIRD3$;:
    RETURN
340 PRINT BIRD4$;:
    RETURN


10  REM      WALKING MAN CHARACTER SET
20  REM            Example 2
30  REM
40  REM Demonstration of user-defined character set
50  REM Copyright (C) 1982 by David Fox and Mitchell Waite
60  REM
```

```
100  REM Initialize
110  FRAMES=5: REM Number of frames
120  FRMSZE=12: REM Characters in frame (including cursor control chars)
130  DIM MAN$(FRAMES*FRMSZE),FRAME$(FRMSZE),ERASE$(7)
140  MAN$="Ma{DOWN}{2 LEFT}bc{DOWN}{2 LEFT}deMf{DOWN}{2 LEFT}gh{DOWN}{2 LEFT}ij"
150  MAN$(25)="Mk{DOWN}{2 LEFT}lm{DOWN}{2 LEFT}nopq{DOWN}{2 LEFT}rs{DOWN}{2 LEFT}tM"
160  MAN$(49)="uv{DOWN}{2 LEFT}wx{DOWN}{2 LEFT}yz"
170  ERASE$="M{LEFT}{UP}M{LEFT}{UP}M"
180  GRAPHICS 0
190  POKE 752,1: REM Turn off cursor
200  PRINT "One moment please..."
210  GOSUB 8000: REM Read in Character Set
220  PRINT "{CLEAR}"
230  SETCOLOR 1,0,14:
     SETCOLOR 2,1,2
240  POKE 756,HICHRB: REM Switch to new Char Set
250  REM
300  REM Animation Loop
310  X=3: REM Set starting horizontal position of Man
320  FOR I=1 TO FRAMES
330      FRAME$=MAN$(I*FRMSZE-(FRMSZE-1),I*FRMSZE)
340      POSITION X,14:
         PRINT ERASE$;FRAME$;
350      IF I=1 THEN
             SOUND 1,0,0,14: REM Footsteps
360      IF I=2 THEN
             SOUND 1,24,0,14
370      SOUND 1,0,0,0: REM Turn off sound
380      FOR W=1 TO 10:
         NEXT W: REM Slow him down a little
390  NEXT I
400  REM Walk man across screen if Joystick button is down
410  IF STRIG(0)=0 THEN
         X=X+1:
         IF X=36 THEN
             PRINT "{CLEAR}":
             GOTO 310
420  GOTO 320
430  REM
8000 REM Set Up Alternate Character Set
8010 HICHRB=PEEK(106)-8: REM Reserve memory space (1024 bytes) below screen
8020 CHRBAS=HICHRB*256: REM Find start of Character Set
8030 REM Read in data, skip first 97 characters
8040 OFFSET=97*8:
     CHARS=26
8060 READ TOTAL:
     TEMP=0
8070 FOR I=CHRBAS+OFFSET TO CHRBAS+OFFSET+CHARS*8-1
8080     READ BYTE:
         POKE I,BYTE:
         TEMP=TEMP+BYTE
8090 NEXT I
8100 IF TOTAL<>TEMP THEN
         GRAPHICS 0:
         PRINT "ERROR In Character Set Data":
         END
8110 REM Clear out first char (background)
8120 FOR I=CHRBAS TO CHRBAS+7
8130     POKE I,0
8140 NEXT I
8150 RETURN
8160 REM
20000 REM Character Set Data
```

Photo 1.1, page 3. (Courtesy of Information International, Inc. [Triple I], Culver City, CA.)

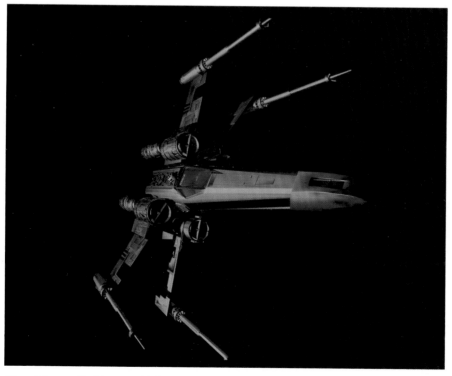

Photo 1.3, page 17. (Courtesy of Information International, Inc.)

Photo 1.4, page 18. (Courtesy of Walt Disney Production,© MCMLXXXII Walt Disney Production. World Rights Reserved.)

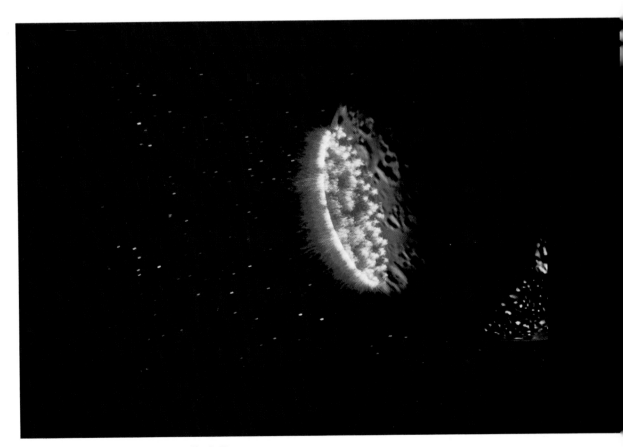

Photo 1.5a, page 18. (Courtesy of Lucasfilm Ltd.)

Photo 1.5b, page 18. (Courtesy of Lucasfilm Ltd.)

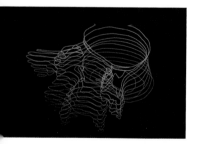

Photo 1.7, page 20. (Courtesy of Digital Effects Inc. — Rutgers Medical School, "Spine," 1981.)

Photo 1.8, page 21. (Courtesy of Advanced Electronics Design, Inc. [AED].)

Photo 1.9, page 22. (Courtesy of Atari, Inc. and The Learning Company.)

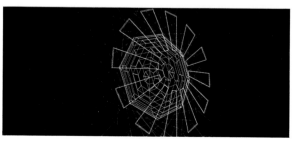

Photo 1.11, page 24. (Courtesy of Digital Effects Inc.)

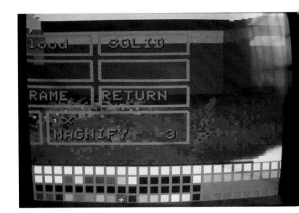

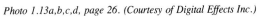
Photo 1.13a,b,c,d, page 26. (Courtesy of Digital Effects Inc.)

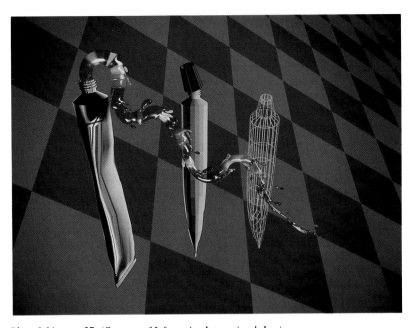

Photo 1.14, page 27. (Courtesy of Information International, Inc.)

Photo 1.15a, page 28. (Courtesy of Nelson Max, Lawrence Livermore National Laboratory.)

Photo 1.15b, page 28. (Courtesy of Nelson Max, Lawrence Livermore National Laboratory.)

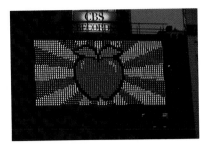

Photo 1.17a,b,c, page 30. (Times Square display courtesy of Spectacolor, Inc.)

Photo 1.18, page 31. (Courtesy of New York Institute of Technology, Computer Graphics Lab. Graphics by David Geshwind.)

Photo 1.19, page 31. (Computer graphics by Colin Cantwell. Courtesy of Marks & Marks.)

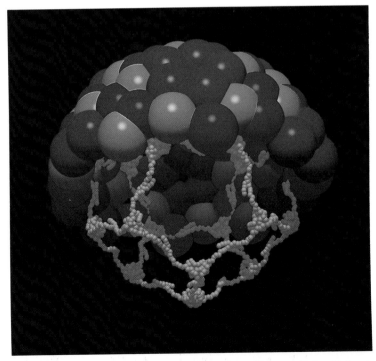

Photo 1.20a, page 33. (Courtesy of Nelson Max, Lawrence Livermore National Laboratory.)

Photo 1.20b, page 33. (Courtesy of Nelson Max, Lawrence Livermore National Laboratory.)

Photo 1.21, page 36. (Courtesy of Information International, Inc.)

Frame from "Vol Libre," Loren Carpenter. (Flip through the book to see this film in motion.) (Courtesy of Lucasfilm Ltd.)

Frame from "Panasonic Commercial — Paper Airplane." (Flip through the book to see this film in motion.)
(Courtesy of Robert Abel and Associates.)

Frame from "Times Square," Digital Effects Inc./Rosebush, Kleiser, Leich, Cox, Loen, Prins, Deas, and Cohen, 1979. (Flip through the book to see the film in motion.) (Courtesy of Digital Effects Inc.)

Frame from "Walking Man," Mathematical Applications Group, Inc. (Flip through the book to see the film in motion.) (Courtesy of MAGI/SynthaVision.)

"Pt. Reyes" — Lucasfilm Ltd., April 1983. This landscape was defined using patches, polygons, fractals, particle systems, and a variety of procedural models. The various elements were rendered separately and later composited. The piece is very much a team effort, a one-frame movie, produced by Loren Carpenter, Rob Cook, Tom Porter, Bill Reeves, David Salesin, and Alvy Ray Smith.

"Maxfield" — Lucasfilm Ltd., December 1983. The upper half of the picture contains computer-generated aspen and spruce trees by Bill Reeves. They are 3-dimensional and fully antialiased. The color scheme is inspired by Maxfield Parrish paintings. The lower half is handpainted using a computer painting program. The picture composition and painting are by John Lasseter; the paint program is by Tom Porter.

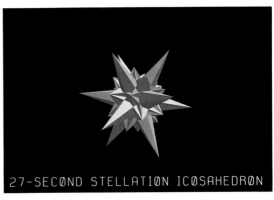

Digital Effects Inc./Hoffman, Green, "Great Northwest Talent,"
1982.

Digital Effects Inc./Walt Disney Production, "The Bit-TRON,"
1982.

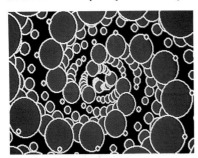

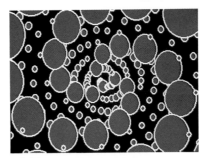

Pacific Data Images, Inc. "Test Flight — Approach." This
spaceship is modelled from various superquadrics. The green
terrain under the ship is a fractal landscape.

Pacific Data Images, Inc. "Test Flight — Orbit." Another
superquadric spaceship. It is in orbit around a planet made by
texture mapping an image of Jupiter's surface onto a sphere.

Photo 2.3a,b, page 63.
(Courtesy of Jane Veeder.)

Photo 2.4a,b,c, page 66. (Courtesy of Digital Effects Inc., R. Greenberg Associates-Lincoln Bank, 1981.)

Photo 2.5, page 71.
(Courtesy of Information International Inc.)

Photo 3.1a, page 107.
(Courtesy of Pacific Data Images.)

Photo 3.1b,c, page 108.
(Courtesy of Pacific Data Images.)

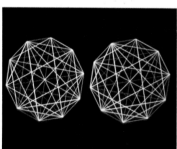

Photo 3.2a,b,c, page 112. (Courtesy of Advanced Electronics Design, Inc.)

Photo 3.3a,b,pages 113-114. (Courtesy of Aurora Systems; Damon Rarey — artist.)

Photo 3.3c,page 114. (Courtesy of Digital
Effects Inc., Mark Lindquist — artist.)

Photo 3.7, page 126. (Image by MAGI. Courtesy of Walt Disney Production. World Rights Reserved.)

Photo 3.8, page 127. (Image by Information International, Inc.(Courtesy of Walt Disney Production. World Rights Reserved.)

Photo 3.9b,d, pages 128, 129. (Courtesy of Robert Abel and Associates.)

Photo 3.11a,b,c,d, pages 131-132. (Courtesy of Evans & Sutherland Rediffusion Simulation.)

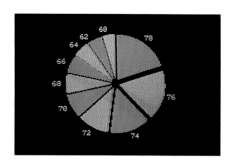

(Left) Photo 3.4, page 117. (Courtesy of Apple Computer Company, Inc.)

(Right) Photo 3.5, page 117. (Courtesy of Penguin Software.)

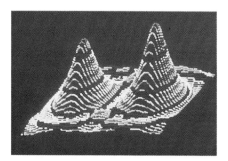
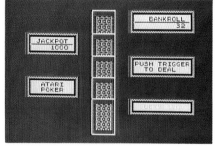

(Left) Photo 3.10e, page 130. (Courtesy of James Leatham.)

(Right) Photo 5.3, page 172. (Courtesy of Harry Brown.)

	BIT PATTERN	BYTE VALUE	DISPLAYED	INVERSE
ROW 1	01010101	85		
ROW 2	01010101	85		
ROW 3	00000000	0		
ROW 4	10101010	170		
ROW 5	10101010	170		
ROW 6	00000000	0		
ROW 7	11111111	255		
ROW 8	11111111	255		

Figure 5.20, page 194.

Photo 5.7c, "Crash, Crumble, and Chomp!" page 204. (Copyright© 1981 Automated Simulations, Inc.)

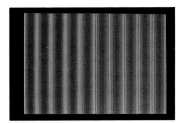

Figure 5.21, page 196.

Photo 5.8b, Space Invaders™, page 205. (Trademark of Taito America Corp.)

Photo 6.1, page 213.

Photo 6.2, page 215.

Photo 6.4, page 220.

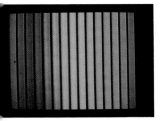

Photo 6.5a, page 223.

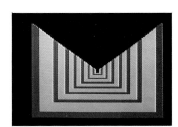

Photo 6.6a, page 226.

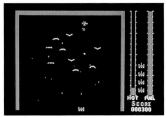

Photo 7.2a, Threshold, page 269. (Copyright© 1982 by On-Line Systems.)

Photo 6.8, page 233.

Photo 7.3, Apple Panic, page 270. (Copyright© 1982 by Broderbund Software, Inc.)

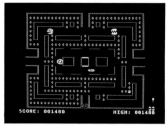

Photo 8.3, Jawbreakers, page 332.
(Copyright© 1981 by On-Line Systems.)

Photo 9.1, page 341. (Courtesy of
Joe Vierra.)

Photo 9.4a, page 383.

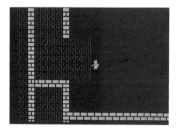

Photo 9.4b,c,d, page 384.

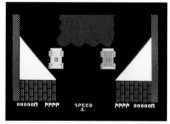

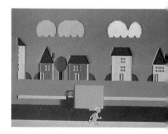

Photo 9.6a, The Adventures of
Farnsworth, page 389. (Copyright©
1982 by Gebelli Software, Inc.)

Photo 9.5b, Match Racer, page 389.
(Copyright© 1981 by Gebelli Software,
Inc.)

Photo 9.7, Caverns of Mars, page 39
(Copyright© 1982 by Atari, Inc.)

Photo 9.8b, Eastern Front (1941), page
391.
(Copyright © 1981 by Chris Crawford.)

Photo 9.9b, Embargo, page 392.
(Copyright© 1981 by Gebelli Software,
Inc.)

Photo 9.10, Chicken, page 393.
(Copyright© 1982 by Synapse Softwar

```
20010  REM . Checksum
20020  DATA 16845
20030  REM
20040  REM . Frame 1
20050  DATA 0,0,0,0,0,0,28,62
20060  DATA 0,0,0,0,3,15,29,59
20070  DATA 62,62,28,240,240,240,240,251
20080  DATA 51,7,7,15,252,224,112,48
20090  DATA 255,220,192,192,227,118,60,24
20100  REM
20110  REM . Frame 2
20120  DATA 0,0,0,0,0,0,0,56
20130  DATA 0,0,0,0,1,7,15,31
20140  DATA 124,124,124,56,224,224,224,224
20150  DATA 55,55,7,111,125,248,192,65
20160  DATA 246,254,192,128,192,224,224,248
20170  REM
20180  REM . Frame 3
20190  DATA 0,0,0,0,0,0,112,248
20200  DATA 0,0,0,3,7,15,31,31
20210  DATA 248,248,112,192,192,128,128,128
20220  DATA 31,31,222,254,251,231,206,15
20230  DATA 224,224,0,0,0,0,0,128
20240  REM
20250  REM . Frame 4
20260  DATA 0,0,0,0,0,1,3,3
20270  DATA 0,0,0,0,0,192,224,224
20280  DATA 3,1,7,15,31,30,62,62
20290  DATA 224,192,0,0,0,0,0,0
20300  DATA 63,63,60,124,120,112,112,252
20310  REM
20320  REM . Frame 5
20330  DATA 0,0,0,0,0,0,0,1
20340  DATA 0,0,0,0,0,0,224,240
20350  DATA 1,1,0,7,31,31,31,31
20360  DATA 240,240,224,128,128,128,128,176
20370  DATA 31,15,15,13,31,123,112,124
20380  DATA 240,0,128,192,128,192,128,0
```

```
 10  REM        GALLOPING HORSE DEMO
 20  REM              Example 3
 30  REM
 40  REM Example using the technique of flipping through multiple character sets
 50  REM Copyright (C) 1982 by David Fox and Mitchell Waite
 60  REM
100  REM Initialize
110  FRAMES=5: REM Number of frames
120  DIM HICHRB(FRAMES)
130  GRAPHICS 0
140  POKE 752,1: REM Turn off cursor
150  PRINT "One moment please...";
160  GOSUB 8000: REM Read in Character Set
170  PRINT "{CLEAR}"
180  SETCOLOR 1,0,2:
     SETCOLOR 2,1,10:
     SETCOLOR 4,1,10
190  POKE 756,HICHRB(1): REM Switch to Frame 1 Char Set
200  REM Fill Screen With Horses
210  FOR Y=0 TO 20 STEP 4
220    FOR X=2 TO 32 STEP 6
230      POSITION X,Y:
         PRINT "▓▓▓abc"
```

```
240      POSITION X,Y+1:
         PRINT "defghi"
250      POSITION X,Y+2:
         PRINT "jklmno"
260      POSITION X,Y+3:
         PRINT "pqrstu";
270    NEXT X
280  NEXT Y
290  REM
300  REM Animation Loop
310  FOR I=1 TO FRAMES
320    POKE 756,HICHRB(I)
330    IF I<>3 THEN
           SOUND 0,0,8,10:
           SOUND 0,0,0,0: REM Hoof Beats
340    FOR W=1 TO PADDLE(0):
           NEXT W: REM Use 15 if you don't have paddles
350    NEXT I
360    GOTO 310
370    REM
8000 REM Set Up Alternate Character Set
8010 HICHRB=PEEK(106)-24: REM Reserve mem space (5 X 1024 bytes) below screen
8020 OFFSET=97*8:
     CHARS=21
8030 READ TOTAL:
     TEMP=0
8040 FOR J=1 TO FRAMES
8050   HICHRB(J)=HICHRB+4*(J-1): REM Find start of Character Sets
8060   REM Read in data, skip first 97 characters
8070   CHRBAS=HICHRB(J)*256
8080   FOR I=CHRBAS+OFFSET TO CHRBAS+OFFSET+CHARS*8-1
8090     READ BYTE:
         POKE I,BYTE:
         TEMP=TEMP+BYTE
8100   NEXT I
8110   REM Clear out first char (background)
8120   FOR I=CHRBAS TO CHRBAS+7
8130     POKE I,0
8140   NEXT I
8150   PRINT ".";
8160 NEXT J
8170 IF TOTAL<>TEMP THEN
       GRAPHICS 0:
       PRINT "ERROR In Character Set Data":
       END
8180 RETURN
8190 REM
20000 REM Horse Character Set Data
20010 REM . Checksum
20020 DATA 46921
20030 REM
20040 REM Frame 1
20050 DATA 0,0,0,0,1,1,6,15,0,0,6,118,155,127,247,231,0,0,0,0,128,192,32,136
20060 DATA 0,0,0,3,14,29,5,0,0,0,3,252,188,14,11,11,0,0,255,31,0,24,31,157
20070 DATA 59,15,254,192,0,0,0,240,135,14,60,124,12,8,8,56,196,204,48,0,0,0,0,0
20080 DATA 0,0,0,0,0,0,0,0,15,5,126,127,97,99,103,99,207,223,243,224,192,192,128,128
20090 DATA 252,191,223,127,3,3,1,1,112,248,254,142,252,248,128,128,0,0,0,0,0,0,0,0
20100 DATA 1,1,0,0,0,0,0,0,193,128,0,0,0,0,0,0,192,224,112,24,28,0,0,0
20110 DATA 1,1,1,0,0,0,0,0,128,192,224,48,56,0,0,0,0,0,0,0,0,0,0,0
20120 REM
20130 REM Frame 2
20140 DATA 0,0,0,1,5,8,59,87,0,8,12,190,121,248,252,191,0,0,0,0,0,128,32,208
20150 DATA 0,0,3,7,15,29,0,0,0,7,252,208,151,31,31,15,0,255,32,32,108,255,255,255
```

```
20160    DATA 255,1,0,0,4,28,252,184,187,184,48,16,16,16,48,240,144,192,0,0,0,0,0,0
20170    DATA 0,0,0,0,0,0,0,0,15,15,62,60,56,236,204,198,255,143,0,0,0,0,0,0
20180    DATA 248,255,31,60,48,112,96,192,28,254,6,12,56,48,0,0,0,0,0,0,0,0,0,0
20190    DATA 0,0,0,0,0,0,0,0,220,216,192,96,112,0,0,0,1,1,1,0,0,0,0,0
20200    DATA 0,0,0,0,0,0,0,0,0,0,0,0,0,0,0,0,0,0,0,0,0,0,0,0
20210    REM
20220    REM Frame 3
20230    DATA 0,0,0,0,0,1,0,63,0,0,2,3,62,239,223,127,0,0,0,0,128,192,32,16
20240    DATA 0,0,0,3,15,63,10,0,0,0,3,252,200,12,31,31,0,0,255,24,48,124,56,255
20250    DATA 23,255,128,0,0,56,126,255,247,238,252,20,8,24,16,16,196,108,48,0,0,0,0,0
20260    DATA 0,0,0,0,0,1,3,6,31,31,61,121,243,195,1,0,191,224,224,192,128,0,128,96
20270    DATA 254,254,7,7,14,12,24,112,56,7,255,0,0,0,0,0,128,192,192,192,192,192,192,128
20280    DATA 12,24,24,56,24,0,0,0,0,0,0,0,0,0,51,62,0,0,0,0,0,0
20290    DATA 192,0,0,0,0,0,0,0,1,0,0,0,0,0,0,0,0,0,0,0,0,0,0,0
20300    REM
20310    REM Frame 4
20320    DATA 0,0,0,0,0,0,1,0,0,6,118,155,127,247,231,0,0,0,0,0,0,128,32
20330    DATA 0,0,0,3,7,10,0,0,0,0,3,255,204,141,15,14,0,0,252,127,16,239,63,111
20340    DATA 1,11,29,224,0,12,142,220,127,255,254,122,30,12,4,68,8,252,204,32,0,0,0,0
20350    DATA 0,0,0,0,0,0,1,3,13,15,15,63,248,224,128,0,159,127,248,56,24,24,56,28
20360    DATA 252,255,63,1,1,0,112,63,124,196,243,255,199,192,192,192,0,0,128,192,192,96,48
20370    DATA 118,60,0,0,0,0,0,0,0,0,0,0,0,0,0,6,1,0,0,0,0,0
20380    DATA 0,128,192,192,0,0,0,0,0,0,0,0,0,0,0,24,0,0,0,0,0,0
20390    REM
20400    REM Frame 5
20410    DATA 0,0,6,15,30,28,61,48,56,254,231,227,255,253,255,0,0,0,0,128,32,144,232
20420    DATA 0,1,3,7,13,0,0,0,3,255,232,78,142,15,7,15,255,124,80,24,60,247,239,159
20430    DATA 255,63,12,0,0,0,241,4,252,28,56,56,24,16,208,112,216,64,0,0,0,0,0,0
20440    DATA 0,0,1,1,3,3,118,60,60,255,240,128,0,0,0,0,112,240,112,48,56,24,12,6
20450    DATA 255,1,12,6,3,1,0,0,48,240,120,56,124,198,3,1,0,0,0,0,0,0,0,128
20460    DATA 0,0,0,0,0,0,0,0,0,0,0,0,0,3,1,0,0,0,0,0,0
20470    DATA 0,192,224,0,0,0,0,0,0,0,0,0,0,0,0,0,192,112,56,0,0,0,0,0



10    REM *** EXPLODING BOMB PROGRAM ***
20    REM                Example 4
30    REM Program to demonstrate the three color text mode - ANTIC 4
40    REM Copyright (C) 1982 by David Fox and Mitchell Waite
50    GOTO 110
60    REM Hi-speed Subroutines
70    SOUND 0,RND(0)*150+30,0,VOL:
      SOUND 1,RND(0)*80+175,2,VOL:
      SOUND 2,RND(0)*150+30,8,VOL:
      RETURN : REM Sound
80    FOR I=1 TO 10:
         POKE 712,RND(0)*255:
      NEXT I:
      POKE 712,0:
      RETURN : REM Flash
90    SETCOLOR 0,4,LUM(0):
      SETCOLOR 1,2,LUM(1):
      SETCOLOR 2,1,LUM(2):
      RETURN : REM Color
100   REM Initialize
110   FRAMES=4: REM Number of frames
120   FRMSZE=7: REM Characters in frame (including cursor control chars)
130   DIM EXPL$(FRAMES*FRMSZE),FRAME$(FRMSZE),LUM(2)
140   EXPL$="ab{DOWN}{2 LEFT}cdef{DOWN}{2 LEFT}ghij{DOWN}{2 LEFT}klmn{DOWN}{2 LEFT}op"
160   GRAPHICS 0
170   POKE 752,1: REM Turn off cursor
180   PRINT "One moment please..."
200   GOSUB 8000: REM Read in Character Set
210   PRINT "{CLEAR}"
```

```
220   GOSUB 6000: REM Alter Display List
230   POKE 756,HICHRB: REM Switch to new Char Set
240   REM
300   REM Animation Loop
310   LUM(0)=6:
      LUM(1)=8:
      LUM(2)=12:
      VOL=14
320   GOSUB 600: REM Falling Bomb
330   GOSUB 90: REM Set colors
340   GOSUB 70: REM Turn on sound
350   GOSUB 80: REM Flash background
360   FOR I=1 TO FRAMES
370      FRAME$=EXPL$(I*FRMSZE-(FRMSZE-1),I*FRMSZE)
380      POSITION X,Y:
         PRINT FRAME$;
390      GOSUB 70: REM Change sound
400   NEXT I
410   FOR J=0 TO 2: REM Fade out explosion
420      LUM(J)=LUM(J)-2
430      IF LUM(J)<0 THEN
            LUM(J)=0
440   NEXT J
450   GOSUB 90
460   VOL=VOL-1:
      GOSUB 70: REM Fade sound
470   IF LUM(2)>0 THEN 410
480   PRINT "<CLEAR>"
490   IF VOL>0 THEN
         VOL=VOL-1:
         GOSUB 70:
         GOTO 490: REM Fade sound off
500   FOR W=1 TO INT(RND(0)*400+50):
      NEXT W: REM Random pause
510   GOTO 310
520   REM
600   REM Falling Bomb
610   SETCOLOR 0,3,8:
      SETCOLOR 1,7,6:
      SETCOLOR 2,5,6
620   X=INT(RND(0)*36+2):
      Y=INT(RND(0)*10+12): REM Select random explosion point
630   FOR I=0 TO Y-1
640      SOUND 0,I*2+16,10,8
650      POSITION X,I:
         PRINT "<K><DOWN><LEFT>q";
660      SOUND 0,I*2+17,10,8
670   NEXT I
680   PRINT "<CLEAR>":
      SOUND 0,0,0,0
690   RETURN
700   REM
6000  REM Modify Display List
6010  DLIST=PEEK(560)+PEEK(561)*256: REM Find Display List
6020  POKE DLIST+3,68: REM LMS byte plus 4 (line 1)
6030  FOR I=6 TO 28:
         POKE DLIST+I,4:
      NEXT I: REM Lines 2 through 24
6040  RETURN
6050  REM
8000  REM Set Up Alternate Character Set
8010  HICHRB=PEEK(106)-8: REM Reserve memory space (1024 bytes) below screen
8020  CHRBAS=HICHRB*256: REM Find start of Character Set
```

```
8030   REM Read in data, skip first 97 characters
8040   OFFSET=97*8:
       CHARS=17
8060   READ TOTAL:
       TEMP=0
8070   FOR I=CHRBAS+OFFSET TO CHRBAS+OFFSET+CHARS*8-1
8080     READ BYTE:
         POKE I,BYTE:
         TEMP=TEMP+BYTE
8090   NEXT I
8100   IF TOTAL<>TEMP THEN
         GRAPHICS 0:
         PRINT "ERROR In Character Set Data":
         END
8110   REM Clear out first char (background)
8120   FOR I=CHRBAS TO CHRBAS+7
8130     POKE I,0
8140   NEXT I
8150   RETURN
8160   REM
20000  REM Character Set Data
20010  REM . Checksum
20020  DATA 8264
20030  REM
20040  REM . Frame 1
20050  DATA 0,0,0,0,3,50,10,2
20060  DATA 0,0,0,0,16,128,128,176
20070  DATA 58,10,2,1,3,0,0,0
20080  DATA 160,172,196,64,0,0,0,0
20090  REM
20100  REM . Frame 2
20110  DATA 0,0,0,8,2,43,11,3
20120  DATA 0,0,0,0,32,180,192,224
20130  DATA 11,3,15,24,32,64,0,0
20140  DATA 232,192,48,32,16,0,0,0
20150  REM
20160  REM . Frame 3
20170  DATA 0,0,0,65,17,34,43,11
20180  DATA 0,0,16,32,128,208,228,249
20190  DATA 27,91,26,2,10,8,24,0
20200  DATA 228,208,192,160,16,4,4,0
20210  REM
20220  REM . Frame 4
20230  DATA 64,80,20,25,26,10,91,27
20240  DATA 133,132,152,168,96,228,229,245
20250  DATA 11,27,106,86,2,10,5,4
20260  DATA 228,208,164,182,165,32,20,4
20270  REM
20280  REM . Bomb
20290  DATA 20,215,215,60,60,60,40,40


10   REM *** MOVING COLOR CURTAIN ***
20   REM              Example 5
30   REM
40   REM Program to demonstrate Color Register Animation in GRAPHICS 10
50   REM (GTIA chip required)
60   REM Copyright (C) 1982 by David Fox and Mitchell Waite
70   REM
80   GOTO 200
90   REM
100  REM Rotate Color Registers
110  TEMP=PEEK(705)
```

```
120  FOR I=705 TO 711:
        POKE I,PEEK(I+1):
     NEXT I: REM Rotate colors
130  POKE 712,TEMP:
     GOTO 110
140  REM
200  REM Initialize
210  GRAPHICS 10: REM GTIA Mode - 80 X 192 with 9 color registers
220  COL=1:
     LUM=8: REM Set starting COLor Register & LUMinance values
230  REM
240  REM Set initial colors
250  POKE 704,0: REM Background to black
260  FOR I=1 TO 8: REM Other registers to different colors
270     POKE 704+I,I*16+LUM
280  NEXT I
290  REM
300  REM Draw Bars, Increment COLOR
310  FOR I=0 TO 79
320     COLOR COL
330     PLOT I,0:
        DRAWTO I,191
340     IF I<40 THEN
           COL=COL-1:
           IF COL=0 THEN
              COL=8
350     IF I>=40 THEN
           COL=COL+1:
           IF COL=9 THEN
              COL=1
360  NEXT I
370  GOTO 100


 10  REM          *** THE TRENCH ***
 20  REM                  Example 6
 30  REM
 40  REM Program to create the illusion of flying through a trench by rotating
 50  REM the Color Registers in GRAPHICS 7
 60  REM Copyright (C) 1982 by David Fox and Mitchell Waite
 70  REM
 80  GOTO 200
 90  REM
100  REM Rotate the Colors
110  SOUND 3,255,0,8: REM Background roar (always on)
120  REM If the trigger on PADDLE 0 is pressed, reverse the direction
130  IF PTRIG(0)=1 THEN
        TEMP=PEEK(710):
        POKE 710,PEEK(709):
        POKE 709,PEEK(708):
        POKE 708,TEMP:
        GOTO 150: REM Not pressed
140  TEMP=PEEK(708):
     POKE 708,PEEK(709):
     POKE 709,PEEK(710):
     POKE 710,TEMP: REM Pressed
150  PDL=PADDLE(0)/5: REM Speed and sound controlled by PADDLE 0
160  SOUND 0,PDL,0,8:
     SOUND 1,PDL+80,0,8:
     SOUND 2,PDL+160,0,8
170  FOR PAUSE=1 TO PDL:
     NEXT PAUSE
180  GOTO 130
```

```
190  REM
200  REM Initialize
210  COL=1:
     Y1=45:
     Y2=49
220  REM
300  REM Draw Trench on Screen
310  GRAPHICS 7+16: REM Full screen graphics
320  SETCOLOR 0,3,8: REM Set Color Register values
330  SETCOLOR 1,3,8
340  SETCOLOR 2,3,4
350  FOR X=2 TO 79: REM Increment horizontal coordinates
360     COLOR INT(COL+0.5): REM Choose which Color Register to draw with
370     PLOT X+80,Y1:
        DRAWTO X+80,Y2:
        DRAWTO 79-X,Y2:
        DRAWTO 79-X,Y1
380     Y1=Y1-0.6:
        Y2=Y2+0.6: REM Increase vertical line length
390     IF Y1<0 THEN
           Y1=0: REM Prevent overflow
400     IF Y2>95 THEN
           Y2=95
410     COL=COL+(79-X)/160: REM Increment Color Register
420     IF COL+0.5>=4 THEN
           COL=COL-3
430  NEXT X
440  GOTO 100


10   REM *** FALL WATERFALL ***
20   REM            Example 7
30   REM
40   REM Demonstration of animating a scene by rotating the Color Registers
50   REM (Uses GRAPHICS 10 - GTIA is needed)
60   REM Copyright (C) 1982 by David Fox and Mitchell Waite
70   REM
80   GOTO 200
90   REM
100  REM Rotate the Colors
110  TEMP=PEEK(705):
     POKE 705,PEEK(706):
     POKE 706,PEEK(707):
     POKE 707,PEEK(708):
     POKE 708,TEMP
120  FOR WT=1 TO 5:
     NEXT WT
130  GOTO 110
140  REM
200  REM Initialize
210  FILL=1300
220  GRAPHICS 10
230  POKE 704,9*16+10: REM Sky - COLOR 0
240  POKE 705,8*16+10: REM Water - COLOR 1
250  POKE 706,8*16+8: REM Water - COLOR 2
260  POKE 707,8*16+6: REM Water - COLOR 3
270  SETCOLOR 0,8,4: REM Water - COLOR 4
280  SETCOLOR 1,12,4: REM Tree shadow - COLOR 5
290  SETCOLOR 2,2,4: REM Cliff & tree trunks - COLOR 6
300  SETCOLOR 3,12,6: REM Grass - COLOR 7
310  SETCOLOR 4,3,6: REM Treetops - COLOR 8
320  REM
400  REM Draw Grass and Cliff
```

```
410   COLOR 7:
      POKE 765,7: REM The grass
420   PLOT 79,10:
      DRAWTO 79,45:
      X1=78:
      Y1=10:
      X2=66:
      Y2=15:
      GOSUB FILL
430   X1=65:
      Y1=15:
      X2=61:
      Y2=18:
      GOSUB FILL:
      X1=60:
      Y1=18:
      X2=56:
      Y2=25:
      GOSUB FILL
440   X1=56:
      Y1=25:
      X2=65:
      Y2=35:
      GOSUB FILL:
      X1=66:
      Y1=35:
      X2=78:
      Y2=45:
      GOSUB FILL
450   COLOR 6:
      POKE 765,6: REM The cliff
460   PLOT 79,46:
      DRAWTO 79,145:
      X1=56:
      Y1=26:
      X2=56:
      Y2=117:
      GOSUB FILL
470   Y1=117:
      X2=68:
      Y2=132:
      GOSUB FILL:
      X1=68:
      Y1=132:
      X2=78:
      Y2=145:
      GOSUB FILL
480   COLOR 7:
      POKE 765,7: REM More grass
490   PLOT 0,191:
      DRAWTO 79,191:
      DRAWTO 79,146:
      X1=0:
      Y1=191:
      X2=0:
      Y2=91:
      GOSUB FILL
500   REM Draw the Falls and River
510   FALL=58:
      CFLAG=0: REM Draw the river on top of the cliff
520   FOR Y=25 TO 34
530     GOSUB 1500
540     FOR X=79 TO FALL STEP -1
```

```
550     COLOR COL
560     PLOT X,Y
570     COL=COL-1:
        IF COL=0 THEN
           COL=4
580   NEXT X
590   FALL=FALL+1
600 NEXT Y
610 FALL=0:
    CFLAG=-1: REM Draw the falls
620 FOR X=58 TO 66
630    FALL=FALL+1
640    GOSUB 1500
650    PLOT X,25+FALL
660    FOR Y=30 TO 120 STEP 4
670       COLOR COL
680       DRAWTO X,Y+FALL
690       COL=COL-1:
          IF COL=0 THEN
             COL=4
700    NEXT Y:
    NEXT X
710 COLOR 6:
    PLOT 58,28:
    DRAWTO 58,25:
    DRAWTO 59,25:
    PLOT 66,38:
    DRAWTO 66,129: REM Cleanup
720 COLOR 7:
    PLOT 73,33:
    DRAWTO 79,33:
    PLOT 68,34:
    DRAWTO 79,34
730 FALL=57:
    CFLAG=1: REM Draw the river on the valley floor
740 FOR Y=121 TO 128
750    GOSUB 1500
760    FOR X=FALL TO 0 STEP -1
770       COLOR COL
780       PLOT X,Y
790       COL=COL-1:
          IF COL=0 THEN
             COL=4
800    NEXT X
810    FALL=FALL+1
820 NEXT Y
830 REM
900 REM Draw the Trees
910 FOR T=1 TO 11
920    READ X,Y
930    COLOR 8: REM Treetop
940    FOR I=0 TO 2:
          PLOT X-I,Y-40+2*I:
          DRAWTO X-I,Y-20-2*I:
       NEXT I
950    FOR I=-2 TO -1:
          PLOT X-I,Y-40-2*I:
          DRAWTO X-I,Y-20+2*I:
       NEXT I
960    COLOR 6: REM Tree trunk
970    PLOT X,Y:
       DRAWTO X,Y-21
980    COLOR 5: REM Shadow of tree
```

```
990     PLOT X,Y+1:
        DRAWTO X+7,Y+4:
        PLOT X+8,Y+3:
        DRAWTO X+8,Y+5:
        DRAWTO X+9,Y+6
1000    DRAWTO X+9,Y+3:
        DRAWTO X+10,Y+3:
        DRAWTO X+10,Y+7
1010    PLOT X+11,Y+7:
        DRAWTO X+11,Y+4:
        DRAWTO X+12,Y+5:
        DRAWTO X+12,Y+7
1020    COLOR 8: REM Fallen leaves around tree trunk
1030    FOR I=1 TO 15
1040      RX=X+INT(RND(1)*7)-3:
          IF RX=X THEN 1040
1050      RY=Y+INT(RND(1)*8)-3:
          PLOT RX,RY
1060    NEXT I
1070 NEXT T
1080 REM
1100 REM Draw the Foam
1110 COLOR 0: REM Same color as the sky
1120 PLOT 57,114:
     DRAWTO 65,122
1130 PLOT 57,115:
     DRAWTO 65,123
1140 PLOT 57,116:
     DRAWTO 65,124
1150 PLOT 56,116:
     DRAWTO 65,125
1160 PLOT 56,117:
     DRAWTO 65,126
1170 PLOT 56,118:
     DRAWTO 65,127
1180 PLOT 56,119:
     DRAWTO 65,128
1190 PLOT 55,119:
     DRAWTO 64,128
1200 PLOT 55,120:
     DRAWTO 63,128
1210 REM
1250 REM Turn on the Sound
1260 FOR I=0 TO 3:
       SOUND I,I*50,0,8:
     NEXT I
1270 GOTO 100
1280 REM
1300 REM Fill Subroutine
1310 PLOT X1,Y1:
     POSITION X2,Y2:
     XIO 18,#6,0,0,"S:":
     RETURN
1320 REM
1500 REM Choose Color
1510 COL=INT(RND(1)*4)+1:
     IF COL=STARTCOL THEN 1510:REM No two adjacent strips with same color pattern
1520 STARTCOL=COL+CFLAG: REM Calculate next starting color to avoid
1530 IF STARTCOL=0 THEN
       STARTCOL=4
1540 IF STARTCOL=5 THEN
       STARTCOL=1
1550 RETURN
```

```
1560  REM
2000  REM Data for Location of Trees
2010  DATA 7,106,13,96,30,100,40,112,47,145,7,179,15,155,27,164,35,173,60,181,66,174


10    REM *** BOUNCING BALL 1 PROGRAM ***
20    REM               Example 8
30    REM
40    REM Program to demonstrate Player-Missile Graphics using string manipulation
50    REM Copyright (C) 1982 by David Fox and Mitchell Waite
60    REM
70    DIM PLR0$(128):
      GOTO 140: REM This MUST be the first variable in the program
80    REM
100   REM Hi/Lo Byte Calculation
110   HIBYTE=INT(X/256): REM Calculate High Byte
120   LOBYTE=X-HIBYTE*256: REM Calculate Low Byte
130   RETURN
140   REM Initialize
150   DIM BLANK$(128),PLR(3),HPLR(3)
160   BLANK$(1)=CHR$(0):
      BLANK$(128)=CHR$(0):
      BLANK$(2)=BLANK$: REM Fill with blanks
170   GRAPHICS 3:
      POKE 752,1:
      PRINT "One moment please...": REM Turn off cursor, print message
190   GOSUB 5000: REM Set up memory locations
220   GOSUB 7000: REM Set up Player area
230   GOSUB 9000: REM Point PLR0$ to Player 0 RAM
240   GOSUB 10000: REM Read frames into RAM
300   PRINT "<CLEAR>bbbbb***bBOUNCINGbBALLbDEMOb***"
310   VEL=70:
      ELASTIC=0.8
320   PRINT "Initial velocity: ";VEL:
      PRINT "Elasticity: ";ELASTIC:
330   REM
400   REM Main Animation Loop
410   BOTTOM=91:
      XPOS=40:
      TIME=0.5:
      HORIZ=0.75
420   GOSUB 700: REM Move Player off screen
430   IF ELASTIC<=0.1 THEN
        SNDFLAG=1
440   YPOS=BOTTOM-(VEL*TIME-16*TIME*TIME):
      FRMNO=1
450   IF YPOS>82 AND VEL>30 THEN
        FRMNO=2
460   IF YPOS>=BOTTOM THEN
        YPOS=BOTTOM:
        VEL=VEL*ELASTIC:
        TIME=0:
        FRMNO=1:
        IF VEL>14 THEN
          FRMNO=3
470   IF XPOS>220 OR YPOS<=1 THEN 600
480   POKE HPLR(0),XPOS
490   FRAME$=FRAMEMEM$((FRMNO-1)*FRMSIZE+1,FRMNO*FRMSIZE): REM Select correct frame
500   BUFFER$=BLANK$: REM Fill Buffer with blanks
510   BUFFER$(YPOS,YPOS+FRMSIZE-1)=FRAME$: REM Move current frame into buffer
520   PLR0$=BUFFER$: REM Move buffer into Player 0 RAM
530   XPOS=XPOS+HORIZ
```

```
540  IF YPOS=BOTTOM AND (VEL+SNDFLAG>0.5) THEN
        SOUND 1,250,10,14:
         SNDFLAG=0:
         SOUND 1,0,0,0
550  IF VEL>0.5 THEN
        TIME=TIME+0.15:
        GOTO 440
560  HORIZ=HORIZ-0.01:
        IF HORIZ>0 THEN
        FRMNO=1:
        GOTO 470
570  REM
600  REM Get Parameters for Ball
610  GOSUB 700
620  POKE 752,0: REM Turn on cursor
630  PRINT "<CLEAR>Enter initial velocity: ";
640  TRAP 630:
        INPUT VEL
650  PRINT "Enter the ball's elasticity (a number":
        PRINT " from 0-1 [or more]): ";
660  INPUT ELASTIC
670  POKE 752,1:
        PRINT " ";: REM Turn off cursor
680  TRAP 40000:
        GOTO 400
690  REM
700  REM Move Player 0 to Left of Screen
710  POKE HPLR(0),0
730  RETURN
740  REM
5000 REM Set Up Memory Locations
5100 READ FRAMES,FRMSIZE,NUMPLRS
5120 PLRFRMMEM=FRAMES*FRMSIZE
5130 FRAMEMEM=PLRFRMMEM*NUMPLRS
5170 DIM BUFFER$(128),FRAME$(FRMSIZE),FRAMEMEM$(FRAMEMEM)
5360 RETURN
5370 REM
7000 REM Initialize Player-Missile Graphics
7010 TEMP=PEEK(106)-8: REM Set aside Player-Missile area
7020 POKE 54279,TEMP: REM Tell ANTIC where PM RAM is
7030 PMBASE=256*TEMP: REM Find PM Base address
7040 FOR I=0 TO 3
7050    PLR(I)=PMBASE+128*I+512: REM Set addresses of Players
7060    HPLR(I)=53248+I: REM Horizontal Player Position registers
7070 NEXT I
7080 POKE 559,42: REM Set PM 2 line resolution, Players enabled
7090 POKE 704,12*16+8: REM Color ball green
7100 POKE 53277,2: REM Enable Player display
7120 RETURN
7130 REM
9000 REM Point PLR0$ to Player 0 RAM
9010 STARP=PEEK(140)+PEEK(141)*256: REM Start of String Array area
9020 VVTP=PEEK(134)+PEEK(135)*256: REM Start of Variable Value Table
9030 OFFSET=PLR(0)-STARP: REM Calculate offset from String Array to Player 0
9040 X=OFFSET:
        GOSUB 110
9050 POKE VVTP+2,LOBYTE: REM Poke offset of string into Variable Value Table
9060 POKE VVTP+3,HIBYTE: REM This points the first string (PLR0$) to PLR(0)
9070 RETURN
9080 REM
10000 REM Read in Frame Data
10090 FOR J=1 TO PLRFRMMEM
10100    READ BYTE
```

```
10110    FRAMEMEM$(J,J)=CHR$(BYTE)
10120  NEXT J
10130  RETURN
10140  REM
20000  REM  FRAME DATA
20030  REM
20040  REM Number of Frames, Frame Size, Number of Players
20050  REM . (Bouncing Ball)
20060  DATA 3,7,1
21000  REM  Frame Data for Bouncing Ball
21010  REM Frame 1
21020  DATA 0,60,126,126,126,60,0
21030  REM Frame 2
21040  DATA 24,60,60,60,60,60,24
21050  REM Frame 3
21060  DATA 0,0,0,126,255,126,0


   10  REM * * *  F L A S H  * * *
   20  REM
   30  REM Program to demonstrate the Memory Fill Machine Language Routine
   40  REM
   50  REM Copyright (C) 1982 by David Fox and Mitchell Waite
   60  REM
  100  REM  Initialize
  110  GRAPHICS 0
  120  GOSUB 11610: REM Store routine
  130  SCREEN=PEEK(88)+PEEK(89)*256: REM Address for start of screen memory
  140  REM
  200  REM  Main Loop
  210  FOR I=0 TO 255
  220     TEMP=USR(MFILL,SCREEN,960,I): REM Call routine
  230  NEXT I
  240  GOTO 210
  250  REM
11600  REM  Routine
11610  DIM MFILL$(41)
11620  MFILL$(1)=" <<<Routine String goes here>>>  "
11630  MFILL=ADR(MFILL$): REM Find address of routine
11640  RETURN
26000  REM  Player Move Routine DATA
26010  DATA PMOVER,11310,186,22157
26020  DATA 184,80,16,76,98,228,162,3,189,38,4,157,0,208,202,16,247,48,240,162,6,181,223,157,83
26030  DATA 4,202,208,248,104,104,133,227,165,227,133,226,172,4,4,162,0,142,4,4,70,226,144,6
26040  DATA 189,6,4,157,38,4,232,224,4,208,241,140,4,4,162,0,134,224,173,0,4,133,225,173,1
26050  DATA 4,133,228,173,2,4,133,229,173,3,4,133,226,142,3,4,70,227,176,30,165,224,73,128,133
26060  DATA 224,208,2,230,225,232,224,4,208,237,165,226,141,3,4,232,189,84,4,149,224,202,16,248,96
26070  DATA 160,127,177,224,145,228,136,16,249,142,76,4,189,42,4,72,189,10,4,157,42,4,168,104,170
26080  DATA 142,77,4,140,78,4,138,168,177,228,172,78,4,145,224,200,16,2,160,0,232,16,2,162,0
26090  DATA 236,77,4,208,229,174,76,4,184,80,165


   10  REM *** BOUNCING BALL 2 PROGRAM ***
   20  REM                 Example 9
   30  REM
   40  REM Program to demonstrate Player-Missile Graphics with Machine Language routine to move players
   50  REM Copyright (C) 1982 by David Fox and Mitchell Waite
   60  REM
   70  DIM PLR0$(128):
       GOTO 140: REM This MUST be the first variable in the program
   80  REM
  100  REM  Hi/Lo Byte Calculation
  110  HIBYTE=INT(X/256): REM Calculate High Byte
```

```
120   LOBYTE=X-HIBYTE*256: REM Calculate Low Byte
130   RETURN
140   REM Initialize
150   DIM PLR(3),HPLR(3),VPLR(3)
170   GRAPHICS 3:
      POKE 752,1:
      PRINT "One moment please...": REM Turn off cursor, print message
180   GOSUB 11000: REM Initialize Routine strings
190   GOSUB 5000: REM Set up memory locations
220   GOSUB 7000: REM Set up Player area
230   GOSUB 9000: REM Point PLR0$ to Player 0 RAM
240   GOSUB 10000: REM Read frames into RAM
280   GOSUB 12000: REM Set up parameter addresses
290   GOSUB 13000: REM Turn on interrupts
300   PRINT "<CLEAR>ษษษษ***ษBOUNCINGษBALLษDEMOษ***"
310   VEL=70:
      ELASTIC=0.8
320   PRINT "Initial velocity: ";VEL:
      PRINT "Elasticity: ";ELASTIC:
330   REM
400   REM Main Animation Loop
410   BOTTOM=91:
      XPOS=40:
      TIME=0.5:
      HORIZ=0.75
420   GOSUB 700: REM Move Player off screen
430   IF ELASTIC<=0.1 THEN
         SNDFLAG=1
440   YPOS=BOTTOM-(VEL*TIME-16*TIME*TIME):
      FRMNO=1
450   IF YPOS>82 AND VEL>30 THEN
         FRMNO=2
460   IF YPOS>=BOTTOM THEN
         YPOS=BOTTOM:
         VEL=VEL*ELASTIC:
         TIME=0:
         FRMNO=1:
         IF VEL>14 THEN
            FRMNO=3
470   IF XPOS>220 OR YPOS<=1 THEN 600
480   POKE HPLR(0),XPOS:
      POKE VPLR(0),YPOS:
      TEMP=USR(PMOVER,P0)
490   FRAME$=FRAMEMEM$((FRMNO-1)*FRMSIZE+1,FRMNO*FRMSIZE): REM Select correct frame
520   PLR0$(YPOS)=FRAME$: REM Move new frame into Player 0
530   XPOS=XPOS+HORIZ
540   IF YPOS=BOTTOM AND (VEL+SNDFLAG>0.5) THEN
         SOUND 1,250,10,14:
         SNDFLAG=0:
         SOUND 1,0,0,0
550   IF VEL>0.5 THEN
         TIME=TIME+0.15:
         GOTO 440
560   HORIZ=HORIZ-0.01:
      IF HORIZ>0 THEN
         FRMNO=1:
         GOTO 470
570   REM
600   REM Get Parameters for Ball
610   GOSUB 700
620   POKE 752,0: REM Turn on cursor
630   PRINT "<CLEAR>Enter initial velocity: ";
```

```
640   TRAP 630:
      INPUT VEL
650   PRINT "Enter the ball's elasticity (a number)":
      PRINT " from 0-1 [or more]): ";
660   INPUT ELASTIC
670   POKE 752,1:
      PRINT " ";: REM Turn off cursor
680   TRAP 40000:
      GOTO 400
690   REM
700   REM Move Player 0 to Left of Screen
710   POKE HPLR(0),0
720   TEMP=USR(PMOVER,P0)
730   RETURN
740   REM
5000  REM Set Up Memory Locations
5090  READ FRAMES,FRMSIZE,NUMPLRS
5110  PLRFRMMEM=FRAMES*FRMSIZE
5120  FRAMEMEM=PLRFRMMEM*NUMPLRS
5160  DIM BUFFER$(128),FRAME$(FRMSIZE),FRAMEMEM$(FRAMEMEM)
5270  PMOVER=ADR(PMOVER$)
5300  MFILL=ADR(MFILL$)
5310  BUFFER=ADR(BUFFER$)
5340  RETURN
5350  REM
7000  REM Initialize Player-Missile Graphics
7010  TEMP=PEEK(106)-8: REM Set aside Player-Missile area
7020  POKE 54279,TEMP: REM Tell ANTIC where PM RAM is
7030  PMBASE=256*TEMP: REM Find PM Base address
7040  FOR I=0 TO 3
7050     PLR(I)=PMBASE+128*I+512: REM Set addresses of Players
7070  NEXT I
7080  POKE 559,42: REM Set PM 2 line resolution, Players enabled
7090  POKE 704,12*16+8: REM Color ball green
7100  POKE 53277,2: REM Enable Player display
7110  TEMP=USR(MFILL,PLR(0),512,0): REM Use memory fill routine to clear Players
7120  RETURN
7130  REM
9000  REM Point PLR0$ to Player 0 RAM
9010  STARP=PEEK(140)+PEEK(141)*256: REM Start of String Array area
9020  VVTP=PEEK(134)+PEEK(135)*256: REM Start of Variable Value Table
9030  OFFSET=PLR(0)-STARP: REM Calculate offset from String Array to Player 0
9040  X=OFFSET:
      GOSUB 110
9050  POKE VVTP+2,LOBYTE: REM Poke offset of string into Variable Value Table
9060  POKE VVTP+3,HIBYTE: REM This points the first string (PLR0$) to PLR(0)
9070  RETURN
9080  REM
10000 REM Read In Frame Data
10090 FOR J=1 TO PLRFRMMEM
10100    READ BYTE
10110    FRAMEMEM$(J,J)=CHR$(BYTE)
10120 NEXT J
10130 RETURN
10140 REM
11000 REM INITIALIZE ROUTINE STRINGS
11300 REM Set PMOVER routine
11310 DIM PMOVER$(186)
11320 PMOVER$(1)="  <<<Routine String goes here>>>  "
11330 PMOVER$(91)="  <<<Routine String goes here>>>  "
11340 PMOVER$(181)="  <<<Routine String goes here>>>  "
11600 REM Set MFILL routine
11610 DIM MFILL$(41)
```

```
11620   MFILL$(1)="  <<<Routine String goes here>>>  "
11650   RETURN
11660   REM
12000   REM Set Parameters for Routines
12010   PARAMBASE=1024: REM Parameter Base address
12020   PMBAS=PARAMBASE: REM Hi Byte of PLR0 Location goes here
12030   PMBUF=PARAMBASE+1: REM Address of a 128 byte buffer
12070   FOR I=0 TO 3
12080      HPLR(I)=PARAMBASE+6+I: REM Player horizontal "shadow" registers
12090      VPLR(I)=PARAMBASE+10+I: REM Player vertical "shadow" registers
12130   NEXT I
12190   VVBLKD=548: REM Deferred Vertical Blank Interrupt Vector
12200   CRITICAL=66: REM Critical Flag
12210   P0=1:
        P1=2:
        P2=4:
        P3=8: REM Control bits for the four Players
12240   TEMP=USR(MFILL,PARAMBASE,94,0): REM IMPORTANT: Clear out parameter area
12250   X=PLR(0):
        GOSUB 110:
        POKE PMBAS,HIBYTE: REM Poke Hi Byte of Player 0 into PMBAS
12260   X=BUFFER:
        GOSUB 110:
        POKE PMBUF,LOBYTE: REM Poke address of buffer
12270   POKE PMBUF+1,HIBYTE
12530   RETURN
12540   REM
13000   REM Install Interrupt Routine
13010   POKE CRITICAL,1: REM Open CRITICAL "valve", set up detour
13080   X=PMOVER+6:
        GOSUB 110
13090   POKE VVBLKD,LOBYTE: REM Set VBLANK vector to PMOVER
13100   POKE VVBLKD+1,HIBYTE
13170   POKE CRITICAL,0: REM Close CRITICAL "valve", routine installed
13200   RETURN
13210   REM
20000   REM FRAME DATA
20030   REM
20040   REM Number of Frames, Frame Size, Number of Players
20050   REM . (Bouncing Ball)
20060   DATA 3,7,1
21000   REM Frame data for Bouncing Ball
21010   REM Frame 1
21020   DATA 0,60,126,126,126,60,0
21030   REM Frame 2
21040   DATA 24,60,60,60,60,60,24
21050   REM Frame 3
21060   DATA 0,0,0,126,255,126,0
27000   REM Animate Routine DATA
27010   DATA ANIMATE,11410,294,34779
27020   DATA 184,80,3,76,98,228,216,162,3,181,224,157,89,4,202,16,248,173,3,4,240,237,48,72,10
27030   DATA 10,10,141,80,4,162,0,78,3,4,176,16,144,2,240,218,232,224,4,208,242,169,128,141,3
27040   DATA 4,208,43,189,14,4,208,2,169,255,157,46,4,138,10,168,185,18,4,153,50,4,185,19,4
27050   DATA 153,51,4,173,80,4,48,214,189,14,4,157,58,4,169,1,157,62,4,208,201,169,0,133,224
27060   DATA 173,0,4,133,225,162,0,189,46,4,240,9,201,255,240,37,222,58,4,240,25,165,224,73,128
27070   DATA 133,224,208,2,230,225,232,224,4,208,227,189,88,4,149,223,202,208,248,240,149,189,46,4,201
27080   DATA 255,208,2,169,1,157,58,4,138,10,168,185,50,4,133,226,185,51,4,133,227,254,62,4,189
27090   DATA 62,4,168,177,226,208,9,169,2,157,62,4,208,244,80,186,141,80,4,206,80,4,160,0,177
27100   DATA 226,72,200,177,226,133,227,104,133,226,136,177,226,141,81,4,169,0,160,8,78,80,4,144,4
27110   DATA 24,109,81,4,74,110,82,4,136,208,240,168,173,82,4,56,101,226,133,226,152,101,227,133,227
27120   DATA 142,80,4,189,42,4,168,162,0,140,82,4,138,168,177,226,172,82,4,145,224,200,232,236,81
27130   DATA 4,208,237,174,80,4,189,46,4,201,255,208,3,254,46,4,184,80,151
```

```
10  REM *** WALKING MAN PLAYER DEMO ***
20  REM            Example 10
30  REM
40  REM Program to introduce the Animate Machine Language routine with the walking man
50  REM Copyright (C) 1982 by David Fox and Mitchell Waite
60  REM
70  GOTO 140
80  REM
100 REM Hi/Lo Byte Calculation
110 HIBYTE=INT(X/256): REM Calculate High Byte
120 LOBYTE=X-HIBYTE*256: REM Calculate Low Byte
130 RETURN
140 REM Initialize
150 DIM PLR(3),HPLR(3),VPLR(3),RATE(3),FRMLSTPTR(3),FRMDATA(3)
170 GRAPHICS 3:
    POKE 752,1:
    PRINT "One moment please...": REM Turn off cursor, print message
180 GOSUB 11000: REM Initialize Routine strings
190 GOSUB 5000: REM Set up memory locations
220 GOSUB 7000: REM Set up Player area
240 GOSUB 10000: REM Read frames into RAM
280 GOSUB 12000: REM Set up parameter addresses
290 GOSUB 13000: REM Turn on interrupts
300 PRINT "<CLEAR><6 RIGHT>*** WALKING MAN DEMO ***"
310 PRINT "Press a number from 1 to 9 to control his speed or 0's to single step.";
330 PX=120:
    PY=77
340 GOSUB 1000
350 SFLAG=2
360 POKE INITANIMATE,FST2P
370 SPEED=4:
    GOSUB 700
380 OPEN #2,4,0,"K:":
    POKE 754,255
390 REM
400 REM Main Animation Loop
410 IF PEEK(1086)=SFLAG THEN
      SOUND 0,0,0,10:
      SFLAG=3: REM Footsteps
420 IF PEEK(1086)=SFLAG THEN
      SOUND 0,24,0,10:
      SFLAG=2
430 SOUND 0,0,0,0
480 IF PEEK(754)=255 THEN 410
490 GET #2,BYTE:
    SPEED=BYTE-48:
    POKE 754,255:
    IF SPEED<0 THEN
      SPEED=0
500 IF SPEED>9 THEN
      SPEED=9
510 GOSUB 700
520 GOTO 410
530 REM
700 REM Set Frame Rate
710 IF PEEK(INITANIMATE)<>128 THEN 710
720 FOR I=0 TO NUMPLRS-1
740   POKE RATE(I),SPEED
750 NEXT I
760 POKE INITANIMATE,FST2P+16
780 RETURN
790 REM
1000 REM Parameters For Players
```

```
1010  REM Man
1020  GOSUB 1500: REM Point to Frame Lists
1030  FOR I=0 TO NUMPLRS-1
1040     POKE VPLR(I),PY
1050     POKE HPLR(I),PX+I*8
1060  NEXT I
1070  TEMP=USR(PMOVER,FST2P)
1080  RETURN
1090  REM
1500  REM Put Frame List Address in Param Table
1510  FOR I=0 TO NUMPLRS-1
1520     X=POINTER(I):
         GOSUB 110
1530     POKE FRMLSTPTR(I),LOBYTE
1540     POKE FRMLSTPTR(I)+1,HIBYTE
1550  NEXT I
1560  RETURN
1570  REM
5000  REM Set Up Memory Locations
5090  READ FRAMES,FRMSIZE,NUMPLRS
5110  PLRFRMMEM=FRAMES*FRMSIZE+1
5120  FRAMEMEM=PLRFRMMEM*NUMPLRS
5130  FRMLSTSIZE=FRAMES+3
5140  TOTFRMLSTSIZE=FRMLSTSIZE*NUMPLRS
5160  DIM BUFFER$(128),FRAMEMEM$(FRAMEMEM),FRMLSTMEM$(TOTFRMLSTSIZE)
5270  PMOVER=ADR(PMOVER$)
5280  ANIMATE=ADR(ANIMATE$)
5300  MFILL=ADR(MFILL$)
5310  BUFFER=ADR(BUFFER$)
5320  PLRFRAMES=ADR(FRAMEMEM$)
5330  FRMLSTMEM=ADR(FRMLSTMEM$)
5340  RETURN
5350  REM
7000  REM Initialize Player-Missile Graphics
7010  TEMP=PEEK(106)-8: REM Set aside Player-Missile area
7020  POKE 54279,TEMP: REM Tell ANTIC where PM RAM is
7030  PMBASE=256*TEMP: REM Find PM Base address
7040  FOR I=0 TO 3
7050     PLR(I)=PMBASE+128*I+512: REM Set addresses of Players
7060     POKE 704+I,3*16+10: REM Color him peach
7070  NEXT I
7080  POKE 559,42: REM Set PM 2 line resolution, Players enabled
7090  REM
7100  POKE 53277,2: REM Enable Player display
7110  TEMP=USR(MFILL,PLR(0),512,0): REM Use memory fill routine to clear Players
7120  RETURN
7140  RETURN
10000 REM Read in Frame Data
10010 OFFSET2=0
10030 FRAMELIST=FRMLSTMEM
10050 FOR I=0 TO NUMPLRS-1
10060    FRMDATA(I)=PLRFRAMES+OFFSET2: REM Store addresses of frame data
10070    OFFSET2=OFFSET2+PLRFRMMEM
10080    POKE FRMDATA(I),FRMSIZE: REM Poke Frame size at beginning of each set of frame data
10090    FOR J=1 TO PLRFRMMEM-1
10100       READ BYTE
10110       POKE FRMDATA(I)+J,BYTE
10120    NEXT J:
      NEXT I
10130 RETURN
10140 REM
11000 REM INITIALIZE ROUTINE STRINGS
11300 REM Set PMOVER routine
```

```
11310  DIM PMOVER$(186)
11320  PMOVER$(1)="  <<<Routine String goes here>>>   "
11330  PMOVER$(91)="  <<<Routine String goes here>>>   "
11340  PMOVER$(181)="  <<<Routine String goes here>>>   "
11400  REM Set ANIMATE routine
11410  DIM ANIMATE$(294)
11420  ANIMATE$(1)="  <<<Routine String goes here>>>   "
11430  ANIMATE$(91)="  <<<Routine String goes here>>>   "
11440  ANIMATE$(181)="  <<<Routine String goes here>>>   "
11450  ANIMATE$(271)="  <<<Routine String goes here>>>   "
11600  REM Set MFILL routine
11610  DIM MFILL$(41)
11620  MFILL$(1)="  <<<Routine String goes here>>>   "
11650  RETURN
11660  REM
12000  REM Set Parameters For Routines
12010  PARAMBASE=1024: REM Parameter Base address
12020  PMBAS=PARAMBASE: REM Hi Byte of PLR0 Location goes here
12030  PMBUF=PARAMBASE+1: REM Address of a 128 byte buffer
12040  INITANIMATE=PARAMBASE+3: REM Initialize Frame Animate routine
12070  FOR I=0 TO 3
12080    HPLR(I)=PARAMBASE+6+I: REM Player horizontal "shadow" registers
12090    VPLR(I)=PARAMBASE+10+I: REM Player vertical "shadow" registers
12100    RATE(I)=PARAMBASE+14+I: REM Animate rate "shadow" registers
12110    FRMLSTPTR(I)=PARAMBASE+18+I*2: REM Pointer to Frame Lists
12130  NEXT I
12190  VVBLKD=548: REM Deferred Vertical Blank Interrupt Vector
12200  CRITICAL=66: REM Critical Flag
12210  P0=1:
       P1=2:
       P2=4:
       P3=8: REM Control bits for the four Players
12220  FST2P=P0+P1
12240  TEMP=USR(MFILL,PARAMBASE,94,0): REM IMPORTANT! Clear out parameter area
12250  X=PLR(0):
       GOSUB 110:
       POKE PMBAS,HIBYTE: REM Poke Hi Byte of Player 0 into PMBAS
12260  X=BUFFER:
       GOSUB 110:
       POKE PMBUF,LOBYTE: REM Poke address of buffer
12270  POKE PMBUF+1,HIBYTE
12390  REM
12400  REM Set Up Frame Lists
12410  DIM POINTER(NUMPLRS-1)
12430  FOR I=0 TO NUMPLRS-1
12440    LET POINTER(I)=FRAMELIST+I*FRMLSTSIZE: REM Points to start of each Frame List
12450    X=FRMDATA(I):
         GOSUB 110
12460    POKE POINTER(I),LOBYTE: REM Put in address of Frame Data
12470    POKE POINTER(I)+1,HIBYTE
12480    FOR J=1 TO FRAMES: REM Make up a Frame List (numbers 1 thru FRAMES)
12490      POKE POINTER(I)+J+1,J
12500    NEXT J
12510    POKE POINTER(I)+FRAMES+2,0: REM End of frame list marker
12520  NEXT I
12530  RETURN
12540  REM
13000  REM Install Interrupt Routine
13010  POKE CRITICAL,1: REM Open CRITICAL "valve", set up detour
13080  X=PMOVER+6:
       GOSUB 110
13090  POKE VVBLKD,LOBYTE: REM Set VBLANK vector to PMOVER
13100  POKE VVBLKD+1,HIBYTE
```

```
13110  X=ANIMATE+6:
       GOSUB 110
13120  POKE PMOVER+4,LOBYTE:  REM Points PMOVER to ANIMATE
13130  POKE PMOVER+5,HIBYTE
13170  POKE CRITICAL,0:  REM Close CRITICAL "valve", routine installed
13200  RETURN
13210  REM
20000  REM FRAME DATA
20030  REM
20040  REM Number of Frames, Frame Size, Number of Players
20050  REM . (Walking Man)
20060  DATA 5,19,2
21000  REM Frame Data For Walking Man
21010  REM Frame 1, Player 0
21020  DATA 0,0,0,0,0,0,0,3,15,29,59,51,7,7,15,252,224,112,48
21030  REM Frame 2, Player 0
21040  DATA 0,0,0,0,0,0,0,1,7,15,31,55,55,7,111,125,248,192,193
21050  REM Frame 3, Player 0
21060  DATA 0,0,0,0,0,0,3,7,15,31,31,31,31,222,254,251,231,206,15
21070  REM Frame 4, Player 0
21080  DATA 1,3,3,3,1,7,15,31,30,62,62,63,63,60,124,120,112,112,252
21090  REM Frame 5, Player 0
21100  DATA 0,0,1,1,1,0,7,31,31,31,31,31,15,15,13,31,123,112,124
21110  REM Frame 1, Player 1
21120  DATA 0,28,62,62,62,28,240,240,240,240,251,255,220,192,192,227,118,60,24
21130  REM Frame 2, Player 1
21140  DATA 0,0,56,124,124,124,56,224,224,224,224,246,254,192,128,192,224,224,248
21150  REM Frame 3, Player 1
21160  DATA 0,112,248,248,248,112,192,192,128,128,128,224,224,0,0,0,0,0,128
21170  REM Frame 4, Player 1
21180  DATA 192,224,224,224,192,0,0,0,0,0,0,0,0,0,0,0,0,0,0
21190  REM Frame 5, Player 1
21200  DATA 0,224,240,240,240,224,128,128,128,128,176,240,0,128,192,128,192,0,0
28000  REM Automove Routine DATA
28010  DATA AUTOMOVE,11510,74,6564
28020  DATA 184,80,3,76,98,228,216,173,4,4,240,247,48,23,162,0,78,4,4,144,6,189,32,4,157
28030  DATA 71,4,232,224,4,208,240,169,128,141,4,4,162,3,189,71,4,73,128,8,24,125,38,4,144
28040  DATA 5,40,48,12,16,3,40,16,7,169,128,157,71,4,169,0,157,38,4,202,16,223,48,185


10   REM *** RUNNING BOY PLAYER DEMO ***
20   REM            Example 11
30   REM
40   REM Program to introduce the AUTOMOVE Machine Language routine and the running boy
50   REM Copyright (C) 1982 by David Fox and Mitchell Waite
60   REM
70   GOTO 140
80   REM
100  REM Hi/Lo Byte Calculation
110  HIBYTE=INT(X/256):  REM Calculate High Byte
120  LOBYTE=X-HIBYTE*256:  REM Calculate Low Byte
130  RETURN
140  REM Initialize
150  DIM PLR(3),HPLR(3),VPLR(3),RATE(3),FRMLSTPTR(3),FRMDATA(3),MOVERATE(3),MSPEED(9)
170  GRAPHICS 3:
     POKE 752,1:
     PRINT "One moment please...": REM Turn off cursor, print message
180  GOSUB 11000:  REM Initialize Routine strings
190  GOSUB 5000:  REM Set up memory locations
220  GOSUB 7000:  REM Set up Player area
240  GOSUB 10000:  REM Read frames into RAM
280  GOSUB 12000:  REM Set up parameter addresses
290  GOSUB 13000:  REM Turn on interrupts
```

```
300   PRINT "{CLEAR}{6 RIGHT}*** RUNNING BOY DEMO ***"
310   PRINT "Press a number from 1 to 9 to control his speed or 0's to single step.";
320   FOR I=9 TO 0 STEP -1:
         READ TEMP:
         MSPEED(I)=TEMP:
      NEXT I
330   PX=10:
      PY=64
340   GOSUB 1000
350   SFLAG=2
360   POKE INITANIMATE,ALLP
370   SPEED=6:
      GOSUB 700
380   OPEN #2,4,0,"K:":
      POKE 754,255
390   REM
400   REM Main Animation Loop
410   IF PEEK(1086)=SFLAG THEN
         SOUND 0,0,0,10:
         SFLAG=3: REM Footsteps
420   IF PEEK(1086)=SFLAG THEN
         SOUND 0,24,0,10:
         SFLAG=2
430   SOUND 0,0,0,0
460   IF PEEK(1062)<PX THEN
         POKE INITAUTOMOVE,ALLP:
         TEMP=USR(PMOVER,ALLP): REM Reset Boy
480   IF PEEK(754)=255 THEN 410
490   GET #2,BYTE:
      SPEED=BYTE-48:
      POKE 754,255:
      IF SPEED<0 THEN
         SPEED=0
500   IF SPEED>9 THEN
         SPEED=9
510   GOSUB 700
520   GOTO 410
530   REM
700   REM Set Velocities and Frame Rates
710   IF PEEK(INITANIMATE)<>128 THEN 710
720   FOR I=0 TO NUMPLRS-1
730      POKE MOVERATE(I),128+MSPEED(SPEED)
740      POKE RATE(I),SPEED
750   NEXT I
760   POKE INITANIMATE,ALLP+16
770   POKE INITAUTOMOVE,ALLP
780   RETURN
790   REM
1000  REM PARAMETERS FOR PLAYERS
1010  REM Boy
1020  GOSUB 1500: REM Point to Frame Lists
1030  FOR I=0 TO NUMPLRS-1
1040     POKE VPLR(I),PY
1050     POKE HPLR(I),PX+I*8
1060  NEXT I
1070  TEMP=USR(PMOVER,ALLP)
1080  RETURN
1090  REM
1500  REM Put Frame List Address in Param Table
1510  FOR I=0 TO NUMPLRS-1
1520     X=POINTER(I):
         GOSUB 110
1530     POKE FRMLSTPTR(I),LOBYTE
```

```
1540     POKE FRMLSTPTR(I)+1,HIBYTE
1550  NEXT I
1560  RETURN
1570  REM
5000  REM Set Up Memory Locations
5090  READ FRAMES,FRMSIZE,NUMPLRS
5110  PLRFRMMEM=FRAMES*FRMSIZE+1
5120  FRAMEMEM=PLRFRMMEM*NUMPLRS
5130  FRMLSTSIZE=FRAMES+3
5140  TOTFRMLSTSIZE=FRMLSTSIZE*NUMPLRS
5160  DIM BUFFER$(128),FRAMEMEM$(FRAMEMEM),FRMLSTMEM$(TOTFRMLSTSIZE)
5270  PMOVER=ADR(PMOVER$)
5280  ANIMATE=ADR(ANIMATE$)
5290  AUTOMOVE=ADR(AUTOMOVE$)
5300  MFILL=ADR(MFILL$)
5310  BUFFER=ADR(BUFFER$)
5320  PLRFRAMES=ADR(FRAMEMEM$)
5330  FRMLSTMEM=ADR(FRMLSTMEM$)
5340  RETURN
5350  REM
7000  REM Initialize Player-Missile Graphics
7010  TEMP=PEEK(106)-8: REM Set aside Player-Missile area
7020  POKE 54279,TEMP: REM Tell ANTIC where PM RAM is
7030  PMBASE=256*TEMP: REM Find PM Base address
7040  FOR I=0 TO 3
7050     PLR(I)=PMBASE+128*I+512: REM Set addresses of Players
7060     POKE 704+I,3*16+10: REM Color him peach
7070  NEXT I
7080  POKE 559,42: REM Set PM 2 line resolution, Players enabled
7100  POKE 53277,2: REM Enable Player display
7110  TEMP=USR(MFILL,PLR(0),512,0): REM Use memory fill routine to clear Players
7120  RETURN
7130  REM
10000 REM Read In Frame Data
10010 OFFSET2=0
10030 FRAMELIST=FRMLSTMEM
10050 FOR I=0 TO NUMPLRS-1
10060    FRMDATA(I)=PLRFRAMES+OFFSET2: REM Store addresses of frame data
10070    OFFSET2=OFFSET2+PLRFRMMEM
10080    POKE FRMDATA(I),FRMSIZE: REM Poke Frame size at beginning of each set of frame data
10090    FOR J=1 TO PLRFRMMEM-1
10100       READ BYTE
10110       POKE FRMDATA(I)+J,BYTE
10120    NEXT J:
      NEXT I
10130 RETURN
10140 REM
11000 REM INITIALIZE ROUTINE STRINGS
11300 REM Set PMOVER routine
11310 DIM PMOVER$(186)
11320 PMOVER$(1)="  <<<Routine String goes here>>>  "
11330 PMOVER$(91)="  <<<Routine String goes here>>>  "
11340 PMOVER$(181)="  <<<Routine String goes here>>>  "
11400 REM Set ANIMATE routine
11410 DIM ANIMATE$(294)
11420 ANIMATE$(1)="  <<<Routine String goes here>>>  "
11430 ANIMATE$(91)="  <<<Routine String goes here>>>  "
11440 ANIMATE$(181)="  <<<Routine String goes here>>>  "
11450 ANIMATE$(271)="  <<<Routine String goes here>>>  "
11500 REM Set AUTOMOVE routine
11510 DIM AUTOMOVE$(74)
11520 AUTOMOVE$(1)="  <<<Routine String goes here>>>  "
11600 REM Set MFILL routine
```

```
11610  DIM MFILL$(41)
11620  MFILL$(1)="  <<<Routine String goes here>>>  "
11650  RETURN
11660  REM
12000  REM Set Parameters For Routines
12010  PARAMBASE=1024: REM Parameter Base address
12020  PMBAS=PARAMBASE: REM Hi Byte of PLR0 Location goes here
12030  PMBUF=PARAMBASE+1: REM Address of a 128 byte buffer
12040  INITANIMATE=PARAMBASE+3: REM Initialize Frame Animate routine
12050  INITAUTOMOVE=PARAMBASE+4: REM Initialize Player Automove routine
12070  FOR I=0 TO 3
12080     HPLR(I)=PARAMBASE+6+I: REM Player horizontal "shadow" registers
12090     VPLR(I)=PARAMBASE+10+I: REM Player vertical "shadow" registers
12100     RATE(I)=PARAMBASE+14+I: REM Animate rate "shadow" registers
12110     FRMLSTPTR(I)=PARAMBASE+18+I*2: REM Pointer to Frame Lists
12120     MOVERATE(I)=PARAMBASE+32+I: REM Horizontal movement for AUTOMOVE
12130  NEXT I
12190  VVBLKD=548: REM Deferred Vertical Blank Interrupt Vector
12200  CRITICAL=66: REM Critical Flag
12210  P0=1:
       P1=2:
       P2=4:
       P3=8: REM Control bits for the four Players
12220  FST2P=P0+P1
12230  ALLP=P0+P1+P2+P3
12240  TEMP=USR(MFILL,PARAMBASE,94,0): REM IMPORTANT: Clear out parameter area
12250  X=PLR(0):
       GOSUB 110:
       POKE PMBAS,HIBYTE: REM Poke Hi Byte of Player 0 into PMBAS
12260  X=BUFFER:
       GOSUB 110:
       POKE PMBUF,LOBYTE: REM Poke address of buffer
12270  POKE PMBUF+1,HIBYTE
12390  REM
12400  REM Set Up Frame Lists
12410  DIM POINTER(NUMPLRS-1)
12430  FOR I=0 TO NUMPLRS-1
12440     LET POINTER(I)=FRAMELIST+I*FRMLSTSIZE: REM Points to start of each Frame List
12450     X=FRMDATA(I):
          GOSUB 110
12460     POKE POINTER(I),LOBYTE: REM Put in address of Frame Data
12470     POKE POINTER(I)+1,HIBYTE
12480     FOR J=1 TO FRAMES: REM Make up a Frame List (numbers 1 thru FRAMES)
12490        POKE POINTER(I)+J+1,J
12500     NEXT J
12510     POKE POINTER(I)+FRAMES+2,0: REM End of frame list marker
12520  NEXT I
12530  RETURN
12540  REM
13000  REM Install Interrupt Routines
13010  POKE CRITICAL,1: REM Open CRITICAL "valve", set up detour
13080  X=PMOVER+6:
       GOSUB 110
13090  POKE VVBLKD,LOBYTE: REM Set VBLANK vector to PMOVER
13100  POKE VVBLKD+1,HIBYTE
13110  X=ANIMATE+6:
       GOSUB 110
13120  POKE PMOVER+4,LOBYTE: REM Points PMOVER to ANIMATE
13130  POKE PMOVER+5,HIBYTE
13140  X=AUTOMOVE+6:
       GOSUB 110
13150  POKE ANIMATE+4,LOBYTE: REM Points ANIMATE to AUTOMOVE
13160  POKE ANIMATE+5,HIBYTE
```

```
13170  POKE CRITICAL,0: REM Close CRITICAL "valve", routines installed
13200  RETURN
13210  REM
20000  REM FRAME DATA
20030  REM
20040  REM Number of Frames, Frame Size, Number of Players
20050  REM . (Running Boy)
20060  DATA 4,31,4
21000  REM Frame data for Running Boy
21010  REM Frame 1, Player 0
21020  DATA 0,0,0,0,0,0,0,0,0,0,0,0,0,0,0,0
21030  DATA 0,0,1,3,7,15,14,12,0,0,0,0,0,0,0,0
21040  REM Frame 2, Player 0
21050  DATA 0,0,0,0,0,0,0,0,0,0,0,0,0,0,0,0
21060  DATA 0,0,0,0,0,0,0,0,0,0,1,1,0,0,0,0
21070  REM Frame 3, Player 0
21080  DATA 0,0,0,0,0,0,0,0,0,0,0,0,0,0,0,0
21090  DATA 0,0,0,0,0,0,0,0,1,3,15,30,30,28,30,30
21100  REM Frame 4, Player 0
21110  DATA 0,0,0,0,0,0,0,0,0,0,0,0,0,0,63,254
21120  DATA 254,252,63,63,31,0,0,0,0,0,0,0,0,0,0,0
21130  REM Frame 1, Player 1
21140  DATA 0,0,0,0,0,0,0,0,0,1,3,7,14,14,12
21150  DATA 1,7,207,207,223,255,255,239,195,3,3,1,1,0,0,0
21160  REM Frame 2, Player 1
21170  DATA 0,0,0,0,0,0,0,0,0,0,0,0,1,3,7,6
21180  DATA 6,6,15,63,127,255,255,127,127,255,239,207,30,127,255,252
21190  REM Frame 3, Player 1
21200  DATA 0,0,0,0,0,0,0,0,0,0,0,0,0,0,0,0
21210  DATA 1,1,3,7,15,31,63,255,252,192,0,0,0,0,0,0
21220  REM Frame 4, Player 1
21230  DATA 0,0,0,0,0,0,0,13,31,30,0,0,0,7,31
21240  DATA 63,255,255,255,255,0,0,0,0,0,0,0,0,0,0
21250  REM Frame 1, Player 2
21260  DATA 0,1,7,31,63,63,63,63,31,207,231,247,127,126,254
21270  DATA 254,254,254,255,247,227,128,128,128,131,135,207,254,252,240,96
21280  REM Frame 2, Player 2
21290  DATA 0,0,0,0,0,3,15,31,63,63,31,159,207,231,255
21300  DATA 127,254,252,252,252,253,223,143,128,192,192,0,0,128,0,0
21310  REM Frame 3, Player 2
21320  DATA 0,0,3,7,15,15,15,15,15,7,1,1,7,63,255
21330  DATA 255,255,254,255,255,252,255,255,252,62,14,0,0,0,0,0
21340  REM Frame 4, Player 2
21350  DATA 1,7,15,15,15,15,7,199,227,121,63,63,254,255,255
21360  DATA 255,240,224,192,240,248,63,31,15,6,0,0,0,0,0,0
21370  REM Frame 1, Player 3
21380  DATA 120,252,244,240,240,240,176,176,248,184,200,240,128,0,8
21390  DATA 120,120,240,192,128,0,0,0,0,0,0,0,0,0,0,0
21400  REM Frame 2, Player 3
21410  DATA 0,0,0,124,254,254,252,248,248,248,216,216,252,220,228
21420  DATA 248,0,0,96,224,224,192,128,0,0,0,0,0,0,0,0
21430  REM Frame 3, Player 3
21440  DATA 0,126,255,255,255,252,236,236,254,238,242,252,224,128,0
21450  DATA 0,0,0,128,128,0,128,0,0,0,0,0,0,0,0,0
21460  REM Frame 4, Player 3
21470  DATA 254,255,255,253,252,236,236,254,238,242,252,0,3,135,255
21480  DATA 252,0,0,96,224,224,192,192,128,0,0,0,0,0,0,0
21490  REM
30000  REM Data for MSPEED (Automove speeds)
30010  DATA 1,2,2,3,3,4,5,6,9,0
```

```
10   REM *** PLAYER FOREGROUND DEMO ***
20   REM             Example 12
30   REM
40   REM Program using all four Players to create animated foreground
50   REM Copyright (C) 1982 by David Fox and Mitchell Waite
60   REM
70   GOTO 140
80   REM
100  REM Hi/Lo Byte Calculation
110  HIBYTE=INT(X/256): REM Calculate High Byte
120  LOBYTE=X-HIBYTE*256: REM Calculate Low Byte
130  RETURN
140  REM Initialize
150  DIM PLR(3),HPLR(3),VPLR(3),RATE(3),PMWIDTH(3),FRMLSTPTR(3),MOVERATE(3)
170  GRAPHICS 3:
     POKE 752,1:
     PRINT "One moment please...": REM Turn off cursor, print message
180  GOSUB 11000: REM Initialize Routine strings
190  GOSUB 5000: REM Set up memory locations
220  GOSUB 7000: REM Set up Player area
240  GOSUB 10000: REM Read frames into RAM
280  GOSUB 12000: REM Set up parameter addresses
290  GOSUB 13000: REM Turn on interrupts
300  PRINT "<CLEAR><3 RIGHT>*** PLAYER FOREGROUND DEMO ***"
310  FOR I=0 TO 1:
        POKE RATE(I),4:
     NEXT I: REM Frame rate for walking man
320  SPEED=-1: REM Temporary start up condition
330  GOSUB 1000:
     GOSUB 1100
340  SPEED=1
350  TEMP=USR(PMOVER,ALLP)
360  POKE INITANIMATE,ALLP
370  GOSUB 700
380  OPEN #2,4,0,"K:":
     POKE 754,255
390  REM
400  REM Main Animation Loop
410  TEMP=ABS(PEEK(1064)-128):
     SND=TEMP/5:
     SND2=SND+SCONS
420  IF VF THEN
        VOL=(128-TEMP)/9:
        SOUND 1,SND,8,VOL:
        SOUND 2,SND2,2,VOL
430  IF WALK>0 THEN
        WALK=WALK-(SPEED<>1):
        GOTO 470
440  IF WALK=0 THEN
        POKE INITAUTOMOVE,FST2P:
        TEMP=USR(PMOVER,FST2P):
        WALK=-1
450  IF PEEK(1086)=2 THEN
        SOUND 0,10,4,10:
        SOUND 0,0,0,0: REM Footsteps
460  IF PEEK(1062)>218 OR PEEK(1062)<20 THEN
        GOSUB 1050: REM Reset Man
470  IF PEEK(1064)>229 OR PEEK(1065)<16 THEN
        GOSUB 600: REM Reset other players
480  IF PEEK(754)=255 THEN 410
```

```
490   GET #2,BYTE:
      SPEED=BYTE-48:
      POKE 754,255:
      IF SPEED<0 THEN
        SPEED=0
510   GOSUB 700
520   GOTO 410
530   REM
600   REM Select a New Object
610   IF VOL THEN
        VOL=INT(VOL):
        IF VOL=0 THEN
          VOL=1
620   IF VOL THEN
        VOL=VOL-0.5:
        SOUND 1,SND,8,VOL:
        SOUND 2,SND2,2,VOL:
        GOTO 620
630   TEMP=USR(MFILL,PLR(2),256,0): REM Use memory fill routine to clear Players 2 & 3
640   FLAG=INT(RND(1)*6+1): REM Which object to display (if possible)
650   OBJECT=0: REM No object selected yet
660   ON FLAG GOSUB 1100,1100,1100,1200,1300,1300:
      IF OBJECT=0 THEN
        RETURN
670   TEMP=USR(PMOVER,LST2P)
680   POKE INITANIMATE,LST2P
690   REM
700   REM Set Horizontal Velocities
710   IF OBJECT=3 THEN
        NSPD=128-SPEED*2:
        GOTO 740: REM Tree
720   IF OBJECT=4 THEN
        NSPD=125-SPEED:
        GOTO 740: REM Truck
730   NSPD=132-SPEED: REM Car
740   POKE MOVERATE(2),NSPD:
      POKE MOVERATE(3),NSPD:
      TEMP=LST2P
750   POKE MOVERATE(0),129-SPEED:
      POKE MOVERATE(1),129-SPEED:
      IF WALK=-1 THEN
        TEMP=ALLP
760   POKE INITAUTOMOVE,TEMP
780   RETURN
790   REM
1000  REM PARAMETERS FOR PLAYERS
1010  REM Man
1020  POKE 704,3*16+10:
      POKE 705,3*16+10: REM Set color to peach
1030  FRSTPLR=0:
      OBJECT=1:
      GOSUB 1500: REM Point to proper Frame List
1040  POKE VPLR(0),77:
      POKE VPLR(1),77
1050  IF SPEED=1 THEN 1070
1060  POKE HPLR(0),20:
      POKE HPLR(1),28:
      IF SPEED>1 THEN
        POKE HPLR(0),218:
        POKE HPLR(1),226
1070  WALK=INT(RND(1)*100+20)
1080  RETURN
1090  REM
```

```
1100  REM Tree
1110  IF SPEED=0 THEN
         RETURN
1120  POKE 706,14*16+4:
      POKE 707,13*16+6: REM Brown trunk and green leaves
1130  POKE HPLR(2),229:
      POKE HPLR(3),217
1140  POKE VPLR(2),32:
      POKE VPLR(3),18
1150  FRSTPLR=2:
      OBJECT=2:
      GOSUB 1500:
      FRSTPLR=3:
      OBJECT=3:
      GOSUB 1500: REM Point to proper Frame List
1160  POKE PMWIDTH(2),0:
      POKE PMWIDTH(3),3
1170  VF=0
1180  RETURN
1190  REM
1200  REM Truck
1210  POKE 706,3*16+6:
      POKE 707,INT(RND(1)*16)*16+10
1220  POKE HPLR(2),217:
      POKE HPLR(3),233
1230  POKE VPLR(2),57:
      POKE VPLR(3),57
1240  FRSTPLR=2:
      OBJECT=4:
      GOSUB 1500: REM Point to proper Frame List
1250  POKE PMWIDTH(2),1:
      POKE PMWIDTH(3),3
1260  VF=1:
      SCONS=180
1270  RETURN
1280  REM
1300  REM Car
1310  IF SPEED=4 THEN
         RETURN
1320  C=INT(RND(1)*16):
      L=8-INT(RND(1)*2)*4:
      TEMP=C*16+L:
      POKE 706,TEMP:
      POKE 707,TEMP
1330  POKE HPLR(2),0:
      POKE HPLR(3),16
1340  IF SPEED>4 THEN
         POKE HPLR(2),216:
         POKE HPLR(3),232
1350  POKE VPLR(2),76:
      POKE VPLR(3),76
1360  FRSTPLR=2:
      OBJECT=5:
      GOSUB 1500: REM Point to proper Frame List
1370  POKE PMWIDTH(2),1:
      POKE PMWIDTH(3),1
1380  VF=1:
      SCONS=40
1390  RETURN
1400  REM
1500  REM Put Frame List Address in Param Table
1510  FOR I=0 TO NUMPLRS(OBJECT)-1
```

```
1520    X=POINTER(OBJECT,I):
        GOSUB 110
1530    POKE FRMLSTPTR(I+FRSTPLR),LOBYTE
1540    POKE FRMLSTPTR(I+FRSTPLR)+1,HIBYTE
1550    NEXT I
1560    RETURN
1570    REM
5000    REM Set Up Memory Locations
5060    READ OBJS
5070    DIM FRMDATA(OBJS,3):
        DIM FRAMES(OBJS),FRMSIZE(OBJS),NUMPLRS(OBJS),PLRFRMMEM(OBJS),FRMLSTSIZE(OBJS)
5080    FOR I=1 TO OBJS
5090      READ TEMP1,TEMP2,TEMP3
5100      FRAMES(I)=TEMP1:
          FRMSIZE(I)=TEMP2:
          NUMPLRS(I)=TEMP3
5110      PLRFRMMEM(I)=FRAMES(I)*FRMSIZE(I)+1
5120      FRAMEMEM=FRAMEMEM+PLRFRMMEM(I)*NUMPLRS(I)
5130      FRMLSTSIZE(I)=FRAMES(I)+3
5140      TOTFRMLSTSIZE=TOTFRMLSTSIZE+FRMLSTSIZE(I)*NUMPLRS(I)
5150    NEXT I
5160    DIM BUFFER$(128),FRAMEMEM$(FRAMEMEM),FRMLSTMEM$(TOTFRMLSTSIZE)
5270    PMOVER=ADR(PMOVER$)
5280    ANIMATE=ADR(ANIMATE$)
5290    AUTOMOVE=ADR(AUTOMOVE$)
5300    MFILL=ADR(MFILL$)
5310    BUFFER=ADR(BUFFER$)
5320    PLRFRAMES=ADR(FRAMEMEM$)
5330    FRMLSTMEM=ADR(FRMLSTMEM$)
5340    RETURN
5350    REM
7000    REM Initialize Player-Missile Graphics
7010    TEMP=PEEK(106)-8: REM Set aside Player-Missile area
7020    POKE 54279,TEMP: REM Tell ANTIC where PM RAM is
7030    PMBASE=256*TEMP: REM Find PM Base address
7040    FOR I=0 TO 3
7050      PLR(I)=PMBASE+128*I+512: REM Set addresses of Players
7060      PMWIDTH(I)=53256+I: REM Set addresses of Player Widths
7070    NEXT I
7080    POKE 559,42: REM Set PM 2 line resolution, Players enabled
7090    POKE 623,1: REM Set priority - Players in front
7100    POKE 53277,2: REM Enable Player display
7110    TEMP=USR(MFILL,PLR(0),512,0): REM Use memory fill routine to clear Players
7120    RETURN
7130    REM
10000   REM Read in Frame Data
10010   OFFSET=0:
        OFFSET2=0:
        DIM FRAMELIST(OBJS)
10020   FOR K=1 TO OBJS
10030     FRAMELIST(K)=FRMLSTMEM+OFFSET
10040     OFFSET=OFFSET+(FRAMES(K)+3)*NUMPLRS(K)
10050     FOR I=0 TO NUMPLRS(K)-1
10060       FRMDATA(K,I)=PLRFRAMES+OFFSET2: REM Store addresses of frame data
10070       OFFSET2=OFFSET2+PLRFRMMEM(K)
10080       POKE FRMDATA(K,I),FRMSIZE(K): REM Poke Frame size at beginning of each set of frame data
10090       FOR J=1 TO PLRFRMMEM(K)-1
10100         READ BYTE
10110         POKE FRMDATA(K,I)+J,BYTE
10120       NEXT J:
        NEXT I:
      NEXT K
10130   RETURN
```

```
10140  REM
11000  REM INITIALIZE ROUTINE STRINGS
11300  REM Set PMOVER routine
11310  DIM PMOVER$(186)
11320  PMOVER$(1)="  <<<Routine String goes here>>>  "
11330  PMOVER$(91)="  <<<Routine String goes here>>>  "
11340  PMOVER$(181)="  <<<Routine String goes here>>>  "
11400  REM Set ANIMATE routine
11410  DIM ANIMATE$(294)
11420  ANIMATE$(1)="  <<<Routine String goes here>>>  "
11430  ANIMATE$(91)="  <<<Routine String goes here>>>  "
11440  ANIMATE$(181)="  <<<Routine String goes here>>>  "
11450  ANIMATE$(271)="  <<<Routine String goes here>>>  "
11500  REM Set AUTOMOVE routine
11510  DIM AUTOMOVE$(74)
11520  AUTOMOVE$(1)="  <<<Routine String goes here>>>  "
11600  REM Set MFILL routine
11610  DIM MFILL$(41)
11620  MFILL$(1)="  <<<Routine String goes here>>>  "
11650  RETURN
11660  REM
12000  REM Set Parameters For Routines
12010  PARAMBASE=1024: REM Parameter Base address
12020  PMBAS=PARAMBASE: REM Hi Byte of PLR0 Location goes here
12030  PMBUF=PARAMBASE+1: REM Address of a 128 byte buffer
12040  INITANIMATE=PARAMBASE+3: REM Initialize Frame Animate routine
12050  INITAUTOMOVE=PARAMBASE+4: REM Initialize Player Automove routine
12070  FOR I=0 TO 3
12080    HPLR(I)=PARAMBASE+6+I: REM Player horizontal "shadow" registers
12090    VPLR(I)=PARAMBASE+10+I: REM Player vertical "shadow" registers
12100    RATE(I)=PARAMBASE+14+I: REM Animate rate "shadow" registers
12110    FRMLSTPTR(I)=PARAMBASE+18+I*2: REM Pointer to Frame Lists
12120    MOVERATE(I)=PARAMBASE+32+I: REM Horizontal movement for AUTOMOVE
12130  NEXT I
12190  VVBLKD=548: REM Deferred Vertical Blank Interrupt Vector
12200  CRITICAL=66: REM Critical Flag
12210  P0=1:
       P1=2:
       P2=4:
       P3=8: REM Control bits for the four Players
12220  FST2P=P0+P1
12230  LST2P=P2+P3:
       ALLP=P0+P1+P2+P3
12240  TEMP=USR(MFILL,PARAMBASE,94,0): REM IMPORTANT: Clear out parameter area
12250  X=PLR(0):
       GOSUB 110:
       POKE PMBAS,HIBYTE: REM Poke Hi Byte of Player 0 into PMBAS
12260  X=BUFFER:
       GOSUB 110:
       POKE PMBUF,LOBYTE: REM Poke address of buffer
12270  POKE PMBUF+1,HIBYTE
12390  REM
12400  REM Set Up Frame Lists
12410  DIM POINTER(OBJS,1)
12420  FOR K=1 TO OBJS
12430    FOR I=0 TO NUMPLRS(K)-1
12440      LET POINTER(K,I)=FRAMELIST(K)+I*FRMLSTSIZE(K): REM Points to start of each Frame List
12450      X=FRMDATA(K,I):
           GOSUB 110
12460      POKE POINTER(K,I),LOBYTE: REM Put in address of Frame Data
12470      POKE POINTER(K,I)+1,HIBYTE
12480      FOR J=1 TO FRAMES(K): REM Make up a Frame List (numbers 1 thru FRAMES)
12490        POKE POINTER(K,I)+J+1,J
```

```
12500     NEXT J
12510     POKE POINTER(K,I)+FRAMES(K)+2,0: REM End of frame list marker
12520    NEXT I:
       NEXT K
12530 RETURN
12540 REM
13000 REM Install Interrupt Routines
13010 POKE CRITICAL,1: REM Open CRITICAL "valve", set up detour
13080 X=PMOVER+6:
       GOSUB 110
13090 POKE VVBLKD,LOBYTE:  REM Set VBLANK vector to PMOVER
13100 POKE VVBLKD+1,HIBYTE
13110 X=ANIMATE+6:
       GOSUB 110
13120 POKE PMOVER+4,LOBYTE: REM Points PMOVER to ANIMATE
13130 POKE PMOVER+5,HIBYTE
13140 X=AUTOMOVE+6:
       GOSUB 110
13150 POKE ANIMATE+4,LOBYTE: REM Points ANIMATE to AUTOMOVE
13160 POKE ANIMATE+5,HIBYTE
13170 POKE CRITICAL,0: REM Close CRITICAL "valve", routines installed
13200 RETURN
13210 REM
20000 REM FRAME DATA
20010 REM Number of objects
20020 DATA 5
20030 REM
20040 REM Number of Frames, Frame Size, Number of Players
20050 REM . (Walking Man)
20060 DATA 5,19,2
20070 REM . (Tree Trunk)
20080 DATA 1,52,1
20090 REM . (Tree Top)
20100 DATA 1,26,1
20110 REM . (Truck)
20120 DATA 1,25,2
20130 REM . (Car)
20140 DATA 1,13,2
20150 REM
21000 REM Frame data for Walking Man
21010 REM Frame 1, Player 0
21020 DATA 0,0,0,0,0,0,0,3,15,29,59,51,7,7,15,252,224,112,48
21030 REM Frame 2, Player 0
21040 DATA 0,0,0,0,0,0,0,1,7,15,31,55,55,7,111,125,248,192,193
21050 REM Frame 3, Player 0
21060 DATA 0,0,0,0,0,0,3,7,15,31,31,31,31,222,254,251,231,206,15
21070 REM Frame 4, Player 0
21080 DATA 1,3,3,3,1,7,15,31,30,62,62,63,63,60,124,120,112,112,252
21090 REM Frame 5, Player 0
21100 DATA 0,0,1,1,1,0,7,31,31,31,31,31,15,15,13,31,123,112,124
21110 REM Frame 1, Player 1
21120 DATA 0,28,62,62,62,28,240,240,240,240,251,255,220,192,192,227,118,60,24
21130 REM Frame 2, Player 1
21140 DATA 0,0,56,124,124,124,56,224,224,224,224,246,254,192,128,192,224,224,248
21150 REM Frame 3, Player 1
21160 DATA 0,112,248,248,248,112,192,192,128,128,128,224,224,0,0,0,0,0,128
21170 REM Frame 4, Player 1
21180 DATA 192,224,224,224,192,0,0,0,0,0,0,0,0,0,0,0,0,0,0
21190 REM Frame 5, Player 1
21200 DATA 0,224,240,240,240,224,128,128,128,128,176,240,0,128,192,128,192,0,0
21210 REM
22000 REM Frame data for Tree
22010 REM Player 2, Tree Trunk
```

```
22020  DATA 2,2,132,128,64,0,149,165,210,211,219,251,255,254,126,126,126,126,126,126
22030  DATA 126,126,126,126,126,126,126,126,126,122,126,126,126,126,126,126,126,126,126
22040  DATA 126,126,126,126,126,126,126,126,255,255,219,137
22050  REM Player 3, Tree Top
22060  DATA 24,24,60,60,126,126,126,255,255,255,255,255,255,255,255,255,255,255,255,126
22070  DATA 126,60,60,60,24,24
22080  REM
22100  REM Frame data for Truck
22110  REM Player 2, Truck Cab
22120  DATA 0,0,0,0,0,15,25,17,17,17,17,17,31,31,255,255,255,255,255,255
22130  DATA 255,255,255,28,28
22140  REM Player 3, Truck Body
22150  DATA 255,255,255,255,255,255,255,255,255,255,255,255,255,255,255,255,255,255,255,255
22160  DATA 255,255,255,12,12
22170  REM
22200  REM Frame data for Car
22210  REM Player 2, Car back
22220  DATA 7,9,17,17,17,31,63,127,255,255,255,56,16
22230  REM Player 3, Car front
22240  DATA 192,64,32,32,16,248,255,255,255,254,255,28,8



10   REM *** SCROLLING STREET SCENE ***
20   REM                 Example 13
30   REM
40   REM Program demonstrating Horizontal Fine Scrolling and Display List Interrupts
50   REM Copyright (C) 1982 by David Fox and Mitchell Waite
60   REM
70   GOTO 140
80   REM
100  REM Hi/Lo Byte Calculation
110  HIBYTE=INT(X/256): REM Calculate High Byte
120  LOBYTE=X-HIBYTE*256: REM Calculate Low Byte
130  RETURN
140  REM Initialize
160  DIM CL$(24),SEG$(24),TEMP$(8)
170  CL$(1)=CHR$(0):
     CL$(24)=CHR$(0):
     CL$(2)=CL$: REM Fill with ASCII 0
180  GOSUB 11000: REM Initialize Routine strings
190  GOSUB 5000: REM Set up memory locations
200  GOSUB 6000: REM Set up Display List
210  GOSUB 2600: REM Clear screen
230  GOSUB 8000: REM Load in Character Set
250  POKE 756,HICHRB: REM Switch to Street character set
260  POKE 559,35: REM Turn screen DMA on again, Wide Playfield
270  GOSUB 2800:
     GOSUB 3000: REM Create a street
280  GOSUB 12000: REM Set up parameter addresses
290  GOSUB 13000: REM Turn on interrupts
340  SPEED=1:
     POKE SCRLSTEP,SPEED
380  OPEN #2,4,0,"K:":
     POKE 754,255
390  REM
400  REM Main Animation Loop
480  IF PEEK(754)=255 THEN 480
490  GET #2,BYTE:
     SPEED=BYTE-48:
     POKE 754,255:
     IF SPEED<0 THEN
       SPEED=0
500  POKE SCRLSTEP,SPEED
```

```
520  GOTO 480
530  REM
1900 REM Convert to Screen Value
1910 CFLAG=0
1920 IF CHAR>127 THEN
        CHAR=CHAR-128:
        CFLAG=128
1930 IF CHAR<96 THEN
        CHAR=CHAR-32:
        IF CHAR<0 THEN
          CHAR=CHAR+96
1940 IF CFLAG THEN
        CHAR=CHAR+CFLAG+PAINT*64
1950 RETURN
1960 REM
2000 REM Send Info to Screen
2010 LN=LEN(SEG$):
        IF LN<24 THEN
          SEG$(LN+1)=CL$
2020 IF FENCE THEN
        PTR=PTR+1
2030 FOR I=0 TO HEIGHT
2040    IF FENCE THEN
          GOSUB 2200
2050    FOR J=1 TO WIDTH
2060      P=I*WIDTH+J:
          CHAR=ASC(SEG$(P,P))
2070      GOSUB 1900
2080      IF GRND THEN
            POKE SCRLWIN+6*LINELEN+J+23,CHAR:
            GOTO 2130
2090      IF CLOUD=0 THEN 2120
2100      IF CLOUD=2 THEN
            CHAR=CHAR+64
2110      POKE SCRN+PTR+I*24+J-1,CHAR:
          GOTO 2130
2120      POKE SCRLWIN+PTR+I*LINELEN+J-1,CHAR
2130    NEXT J
2140 NEXT I
2150 PTR=PTR+WIDTH+ABS(FENCE)+SPCFLAG
2160 SPCFLAG=0
2170 ROOMLEFT=LINELEN-25-PTR
2180 RETURN
2190 REM
2200 REM Put In Fence
2210 IF I<4 THEN 2240
2220 IF I=4 THEN
        CHAR=ASC("Q"):
        GOSUB 1900:
        P=-1:
        GOSUB 2250:
        CHAR=ASC("E"):
        GOSUB 1900:
        P=WIDTH:
        GOSUB 2250:
        GOTO 2240
2230 CHAR=ASC("A"):
     GOSUB 1900:
     P=-1:
     GOSUB 2250:
     CHAR=ASC("D"):
     GOSUB 1900:
     P=WIDTH:
```

```
        GOSUB 2250
2240    RETURN
2250    REM Poke In Data
2260    POKE SCRLWIN+PTR+I*LINELEN+P,CHAR
2270    RETURN
2280    REM
2400    REM Copy First Page Onto Last Page
2410    FOR I=0 TO 5
2420      FOR J=0 TO 24
2430        POKE SCRLWIN+I*LINELEN+LINELEN-25+J,PEEK(SCRLWIN+I*LINELEN+J)
2440      NEXT J
2450    NEXT I
2460    RETURN
2470    REM
2600    REM Clear the Screen — Fill the Screen With 0
2610    TEMP=USR(MFILL,SCRN,SCRNSZE,0)
2620    RETURN
2630    REM
2800    REM Put in Clouds and Sidewalk
2810    SEG$="<T=<TT=[\][\\]":
        CLOUD=1:
        PTR=4:
        HEIGHT=1:
        WIDTH=7:
        GOSUB 2000
2820    SEG$="<T=<=[\\\]":
        CLOUD=2:
        PTR=PTR+3:
        WIDTH=5:
        GOSUB 2000
2830    SEG$="^^^^^^^^^^^^^^^^^^^^^^^^":
        GRND=1:
        HEIGHT=0:
        WIDTH=24:
        GOSUB 2000
2840    RETURN
2850    REM
3000    REM CREATE RANDOM DISPLAY
3010    PTR=0:  REM Initialize Pointer to Scroll Window
3020    HEIGHT=5:  REM How tall is the window
3030    CLOUD=0:
        GRND=0
3040    WIDTH=INT(RND(1)*3+2):  REM From 2-4
3050    IF RND(1)*100<=45 THEN
          STORY=2:
          GOTO 3080:  REM 45% 2 Stories
3060    IF RND(1)*55<=35 THEN
          STORY=3:
          GOTO 3080:  REM 35% 3 Stories
3070    STORY=4:  REM 20% 4 Stories
3080    CHIMNEY=(RND(1)<=0.6):  REM 60% chance
3090    IF SHRUB=0 THEN
          FENCE=(RND(1)<=0.4):  REM 40% chance (only if no shrub)
3100    IF ROOMLEFT<6 THEN
          FENCE=0:  REM Not enough room left for a fence
3110    ANTENNA=(RND(1)<=0.5):  REM 50% chance
3120    PAINT=(RND(1)<=0.5):  REM 50% yellow, 50% pink
3130    SEG$=CL$:
        ON WIDTH-1 GOSUB 3500,3700,3900:
        GOSUB 2000
3140    IF ROOMLEFT<2 THEN
          GOSUB 2400:
          RETURN :  REM No room for tree, exit routine
```

```
3150   REM Plant Some Foilage
3160   SHRUB=0:
       TREE=0
3170   IF FENCE=0 AND ODDHOUSE=0 AND ROOMLEFT>8 THEN
           SHRUB=(RND(1)<=0.3):
           IF SHRUB THEN 3440
3180   REM Make a tree
3190   WIDTH=2:
       SEG$=CL$
3200   REM Find height of tree
3210   IF RND(1)*10<=1 THEN
           TREE=2:
           GOTO 3260: REM 10%
3220   IF RND(1)*9<=2 THEN
           TREE=3:
           GOTO 3260: REM 20%
3230   IF RND(1)*7<=4 THEN
           TREE=4:
           GOTO 3260: REM 40%
3240   IF RND(1)*3<=2 THEN
           TREE=5:
           GOTO 3260: REM 20%
3250   TREE=6: REM 10%
3260   TRUNK=INT(RND(1)*(TREE-2)+1):
       IF TREE=2 THEN
           TRUNK=0
3270   TREETOP=TREE-TRUNK:
       IF TREETOP>4 THEN
           TRUNK=TREE-4:
           TREETOP=4
3280   BT=(6-TREE)*2+1
3290   SEG$(BT)="<UP><DOWN>"
3300   IF TREETOP=2 THEN 3340
3310   FOR I=1 TO TREETOP-2
3320       BT=BT+2:
           SEG$(BT)="tt"
3330   NEXT I
3340   BT=BT+2:
       SEG$(BT)="<LEFT><RIGHT>"
3350   IF TRUNK=1 THEN 3390
3360   FOR I=1 TO TRUNK-1
3370       BT=BT+2:
           SEG$(BT)="BV"
3380   NEXT I
3390   IF RND(1)<=0.5 THEN
           SEG$(BT+2)="KL"
3400   REM Add random spacing on side of tree
3410   TEMP=INT(RND(1)*3+1):
       IF TEMP=3 OR ROOMLEFT<3 THEN 3470
3420   IF TEMP=1 THEN
           PTR=PTR+1:
           GOTO 3470
3430   SPCFLAG=1:
       GOTO 3470
3440   REM Make a shrub
3450   WIDTH=INT(RND(1)*2+2):
       SEG$=CL$:
       IF WIDTH=2 THEN
       SEG$(9)="<DOWN><UP>":
       GOTO 3470
3460   SEG$(13)="<DOWN>B<UP>"
```

```
3470   ODDHOUSE=0:
       FENCE=0:
       GOSUB 2000
3480   IF ROOMLEFT<4 THEN 3140:REM Add another tree if not enough room for a house
3490   GOTO 3040
3500   REM Width 2
3510   IF STORY>3 THEN
           STORY=3
3520   BT=1
3530   IF STORY=2 THEN
           BT=3
3540   IF CHIMNEY THEN
           SEG$(BT)="INZU":
           GOTO 3560
3550   SEG$(BT)="IOZX"
3560   BT=BT+4:
       FOR I=BT TO BT+(STORY-2)*2 STEP 2
3570     IF RND(1)<=0.5 THEN
             SEG$(I)="TP":
             GOTO 3590
3580     SEG$(I)="RP"
3590   NEXT I
3600   SEG$(9)="CT"
3610   IF FENCE=0 THEN 3640
3620   IF RND(1)<=0.5 THEN
           SEG$(11)="WW":
           GOTO 3640
3630   SEG$(11)="EQ"
3640   RETURN
3650   REM
3700   REM Width 3
3710   BT=(4-STORY)*3+1
3720   IF ANTENNA AND STORY<4 THEN
           SEG$(BT-3)="(,)(,)(,)"
3730   SEG$(BT)="ZTX"
3740   IF RND(1)<=0.5 THEN
           TEMP$="FPG":
           GOTO 3760
3750   TEMP$="FRG"
3760   BT=BT+3:
       FOR I=BT TO BT+(STORY-2)*3 STEP 3
3770     SEG$(I)=TEMP$
3780   NEXT I
3790   SEG$(13)="FCG"
3800   IF FENCE THEN
           SEG$(16)="WWW"
3810   RETURN
3820   REM
3900   REM Width 4
3910   BT=(4-STORY)*4+1
3920   IF STORY=4 THEN
           SEG$(BT)="HTTJ":
           GOTO 4050
3930   IF STORY>2 OR SHRUB OR RND(1)<=0.3333 THEN 4000:REM Which type house?
3940   REM Create Odd House type
3950   ODDHOUSE=1
3960   IF CHIMNEY THEN
           SEG$(1)="(,)IN(2 ,)ZU(,)":
           GOTO 3980
3970   SEG$(1)="(,)IO(2 ,)ZX(,)"
3980   FENCE=0
3990   SEG$(9)="ITTOBRPVBTCV":
       GOTO 4100
```

```
4000   REM Create Normal House type
4010   IF ANTENNA AND CHIMNEY THEN
           SEG$(BT-4)="(.)HJ(.)YTTJ":
           GOTO 4050
4020   SEG$(BT-4)="(.)HJ(.)":
       IF CHIMNEY=0 THEN
           SEG$(BT)="HTTJ":
           GOTO 4050
4030   IF RND(1)<=0.5 THEN
           SEG$(BT)="YTTJ":
           GOTO 4050
4040   SEG$(BT)="HTTM"
4050   BT=BT+4:
       FOR I=BT TO BT+(STORY-2)*4 STEP 4
4060     IF RND(1)<=0.25 THEN
             SEG$(I)="FSSG":
             GOTO 4080
4070     SEG$(I)="FPRG"
4080   NEXT I
4090   SEG$(17)="FTCG"
4100   IF FENCE THEN
           SEG$(21)="WEQW"
4110   RETURN
4120   REM
5000   REM Set Up Memory Locations
5010   DIF=0
5020   DLSZE=34: REM Display List size
5030   LINELEN=48: REM Horizontal length of scrolling window
5040   SCRNSZE=6*24+LINELEN*6: REM Screen size
5050   MEM=DLSZE+SCRNSZE: REM MEMory to reserve for DL and Screen
5170   DIF=DIF+4:
       IF DIF*256<MEM THEN 5170
5180   HIBASE=PEEK(106)-DIF: REM Find DL Hi and Lo bytes
5190   LOBASE=0
5200   DLBASE=HIBASE*256+LOBASE
5210   SCRN=DLBASE+DLSZE: REM Starting address of Screen RAM
5220   X=SCRN:
       GOSUB 110
5230   SCRNHI=HIBYTE:
       SCRNLO=LOBYTE: REM Find Screen Hi and Lo bytes
5240   SCRLWIN=SCRN+48: REM Beginning of Scroll window
5250   SCROLL=ADR(SCROLL$)
5260   DLIROUT=ADR(DLIROUT$)
5300   MFILL=ADR(MFILL$)
5340   RETURN
5350   REM
6000   REM Set Up the Display List
6010   GRAPHICS 2+16: REM Set flags to Graphics mode 2
6020   POKE 559,0: REM Turn off screen DMA
6030   POKE DLBASE,112: REM Set up top border, 24 scan lines
6040   POKE DLBASE+1,112
6050   POKE DLBASE+2,112
6060   POKE DLBASE+3,71: REM LMS for line 1
6070   POKE DLBASE+4,SCRNLO
6080   POKE DLBASE+5,SCRNHI
6090   POKE DLBASE+6,7+128: REM Line 2 (w/ DLI)
6100   FOR I=0 TO 6: REM Loop for lines 3-9
6110     WINDOW=SCRLWIN+I*LINELEN
6120     BYTE=87: REM LMS and HSCRL
6130     IF I=2 OR I=5 THEN
             BYTE=87+128: REM DLI, LMS and HSCRL for lines 5 and 8
6140     IF I=6 THEN
             BYTE=71: REM No scroll for line 9
```

```
6150    POKE DLBASE+7+3*I,BYTE: REM LMS and HSCRL
6160    X=WINDOW:
        GOSUB 110
6170    POKE DLBASE+8+3*I,LOBYTE
6180    POKE DLBASE+9+3*I,HIBYTE
6190  NEXT I
6200  POKE DLBASE+28,7+128: REM Last 3 lines
6210  POKE DLBASE+29,7
6220  POKE DLBASE+30,7+128
6230  POKE DLBASE+31,65: REM Jump on VBLANK to beginning of DL
6240  POKE DLBASE+32,LOBASE
6250  POKE DLBASE+33,HIBASE
6260  X=DLIROUT:
        GOSUB 110
6270  POKE 512,LOBYTE: REM Address of DL for DLI handling routine
6280  POKE 513,HIBYTE
6290  REM Tell ANTIC where the DL is
6300  POKE 560,LOBASE
6310  POKE 561,HIBASE
6320  SETCOLOR 0,15,4:
        SETCOLOR 1,12,4:
        SETCOLOR 2,0,10:
        SETCOLOR 3,0,12:
        SETCOLOR 4,9,8: REM Brn, grn, wht, wht, blue
6330  RETURN
6340  REM
8000  REM Set Up Alternate Character Set
8010  HICHRB=PEEK(106)-DIF-2: REM Reserve space (512 bytes)
8020  CHRBAS=HICHRB*256: REM Find start of Character Set
8030  REM Read in data, skip first 28 characters
8040  OFFSET=28*8:
        CHARS=35
8050  RESTORE 23000
8060  READ TOTAL:
        TEMP=0
8070  FOR I=CHRBAS+OFFSET TO CHRBAS+OFFSET+CHARS*8-1
8080    READ BYTE:
        POKE I,BYTE:
        TEMP=TEMP+BYTE
8090  NEXT I
8100  IF TOTAL<>TEMP THEN
        GRAPHICS 0:
        PRINT "ERROR In Character Set Data":
        END
8110  REM Clear out first char (background)
8120  FOR I=CHRBAS TO CHRBAS+7
8130    POKE I,0
8140  NEXT I
8150  RETURN
8160  REM
11000 REM INITIALIZE ROUTINE STRINGS
11010 REM Set SCROLL routine
11020 DIM SCROLL$(316)
11030 SCROLL$(1)="  <<<Routine String goes here>>>  "
11040 SCROLL$(91)="  <<<Routine String goes here>>>  "
11050 SCROLL$(181)="  <<<Routine String goes here>>>  "
11060 SCROLL$(271)="  <<<Routine String goes here>>>  "
11100 REM Set DLI routine
11110 DIM DLIROUT$(94)
11120 DLIROUT$(1)="  <<<Routine String goes here>>>  "
11130 DLIROUT$(91)="  <<<Routine String goes here>>>  "
11200 REM Read Color Values Into DLI Table
```

```
11210   DLITBLSZE=15:
        RESTORE 25510
11220   DIM DLITABLE$(DLITBLSZE)
11230   DLITABLE=ADR(DLITABLE$)
11240   FOR I=0 TO DLITBLSZE-1
11250      READ BYTE
11260      POKE DLITABLE+I,BYTE
11270   NEXT I
11600   REM Set MFILL routine
11610   DIM MFILL$(41)
11620   MFILL$(1)="  <<<Routine String goes here>>>  "
11650   RETURN
11660   REM
12000   REM Set Parameters For Routines
12010   PARAMBASE=1024: REM Parameter Base address
12060   SCRLINIT=PARAMBASE+5: REM Poke a 1 to initialize the scroll routine
12140   SCRLADR=PARAMBASE+26: REM Address of scrolling window
12150   SCRLLEN=PARAMBASE+28: REM Line length of scrolling window
12160   SCRLCLK=PARAMBASE+30: REM Number of Color Clocks per screen byte
12170   SCRLSTEP=PARAMBASE+31: REM Step size of scroll each jiffy
12180   DLIADR=PARAMBASE+36: REM Address of DLI table
12190   VVBLKD=548: REM Deferred Vertical Blank Interrupt Vector
12200   CRITICAL=66: REM Critical Flag
12240   TEMP=USR(MFILL,PARAMBASE,94,0): REM IMPORTANT: Clear out parameter area
12280   X=SCRLWIN:
        GOSUB 110
12290   POKE SCRLADR,LOBYTE
12300   POKE SCRLADR+1,HIBYTE
12320   X=LINELEN:
        GOSUB 110
12330   POKE SCRLLEN,LOBYTE
12340   POKE SCRLLEN+1,HIBYTE
12350   POKE SCRLCLK,7: REM Set to 8 color clocks per byte
12360   X=DLITABLE:
        GOSUB 110
12370   POKE DLIADR,LOBYTE
12380   POKE DLIADR+1,HIBYTE
12530   RETURN
12540   REM
13000   REM Install Interrupt Routines
13010   POKE CRITICAL,1: REM Open CRITICAL "valve", set up detour
13020   X=SCROLL+6:
        GOSUB 110
13030   POKE VVBLKD,LOBYTE: REM Set VBLANK vector to SCROLL
13040   POKE VVBLKD+1,HIBYTE
13050   X=DLIROUT+6:
        GOSUB 110
13060   POKE SCROLL+4,LOBYTE: REM Points SCROLL to DLIROUT
13070   POKE SCROLL+5,HIBYTE
13170   POKE CRITICAL,0: REM Close CRITICAL "valve", routines installed
13180   POKE SCRLINIT,1
13190   POKE 54286,192: REM Enable DLI's
13200   RETURN
13210   REM
23000   REM Character Set Data
23010   DATA 38646
23020   DATA 0,3,15,31,63,63,127,127
23030   DATA 0,192,240,248,252,252,254,254
23040   DATA 127,127,127,63,63,31,15,7
23050   DATA 254,254,254,252,252,248,240,224
23060   DATA 4,31,4,31,4,4,4,4
23070   DATA 48,48,48,63,54,54,54,54
23080   DATA 3,3,3,3,3,3,3,3
```

```
23090   DATA 255,195,219,219,219,219,219,219
23100   DATA 12,12,12,252,108,108,108,108
23110   DATA 0,0,0,252,108,108,108,108
23120   DATA 127,127,127,127,127,127,127,127
23130   DATA 254,254,254,254,254,254,254,254
23140   DATA 1,3,7,15,31,63,127,255
23150   DATA 1,1,3,3,7,7,15,15
23160   DATA 128,192,224,240,248,252,254,255
23170   DATA 3,3,7,7,15,0,0,0
23180   DATA 192,192,224,224,240,0,0,0
23190   DATA 156,220,252,252,252,252,254,255
23200   DATA 128,128,192,192,224,224,243,243
23210   DATA 128,128,192,192,224,224,240,240
23220   DATA 255,255,39,39,255,39,39,255
23230   DATA 0,0,0,63,54,54,54,54
23240   DATA 255,255,228,228,255,228,228,255
23250   DATA 255,24,24,24,255,24,24,24
23260   DATA 255,255,255,255,255,255,255,255
23270   DATA 251,251,255,252,254,254,255,255
23280   DATA 192,192,192,192,192,192,192,192
23290   DATA 0,0,0,255,102,102,102,102
23300   DATA 248,248,252,252,254,254,255,255
23310   DATA 57,59,63,63,63,63,127,255
23320   DATA 31,31,63,63,127,127,255,255
23330   DATA 127,127,127,127,63,63,30,0
23340   DATA 255,255,255,255,255,254,124,0
23350   DATA 254,254,254,254,252,252,120,0
23360   DATA 255,255,255,0,0,0,0,0
23370   REM
25500   REM DLI Color Values
25510   DATA 234,90,152,234,90,198,10,0,198,0,0,6,0,0,10


10    REM *** THE GREAT MOVIE CARTOON ***
20    REM               Example 14
30    REM
40    REM Program putting it all together - PM Graphics, Fine Scrolling, & Display List Interrupts
50    REM Copyright (C) 1982 by David Fox and Mitchell Waite
60    REM
70    GOTO 140
80    REM
100   REM Hi/Lo Byte Calculation
110   HIBYTE=INT(X/256): REM Calculate High Byte
120   LOBYTE=X-HIBYTE*256: REM Calculate Low Byte
130   RETURN
140   REM Initialize
150   DIM PLR(3),HPLR(3),VPLR(3),RATE(3),PMWIDTH(3),FRMLSTPTR(3),MOVERATE(3)
160   DIM CL$(24),SEG$(24),TEMP$(8)
170   CL$(1)=CHR$(0):
      CL$(24)=CHR$(0):
      CL$(2)=CL$: REM Fill with ASCII 0
180   GOSUB 11000: REM Initialize Routine strings
190   GOSUB 5000: REM Set up memory locations
200   GOSUB 6000: REM Set up Display List
210   GOSUB 2600: REM Clear screen
220   GOSUB 7000: REM Set up Player area
230   GOSUB 8000: REM Load in Character Set
240   GOSUB 10000: REM Read frames into RAM
250   POKE 756,HICHRB: REM Switch to Street character set
260   POKE 559,47: REM Turn screen DMA on again, Wide Playfield, PM 2 line resolution, Players enabled
270   GOSUB 2800:
      GOSUB 3000: REM Create a street
280   GOSUB 12000: REM Set up parameter addresses
```

```
290   GOSUB 13000: REM Turn on interrupts
310   FOR I=0 TO 1:
        POKE RATE(I),4:
      NEXT I: REM Frame rate for walking man
320   SPEED=-1: REM Temporary start up condition
330   GOSUB 1000:
      GOSUB 1100
340   SPEED=1
350   TEMP=USR(PMOVER,ALLP)
360   POKE INITANIMATE,ALLP
370   GOSUB 700
380   OPEN #2,4,0,"K:":
      POKE 754,255
390   REM
400   REM Main Animation Loop
410   TEMP=ABS(PEEK(1064)-128):
      SND=TEMP/5:
      SND2=SND+SCONS
420   IF VF THEN
        VOL=(128-TEMP)/9:
        SOUND 1,SND,8,VOL:
        SOUND 2,SND2,2,VOL
430   IF WALK>0 THEN
        WALK=WALK-(SPEED<>1):
        GOTO 470
440   IF WALK=0 THEN
        POKE INITAUTOMOVE,FST2P:
        TEMP=USR(PMOVER,FST2P):
        WALK=-1
450   IF PEEK(1086)=2 THEN
        SOUND 0,10,4,10:
        SOUND 0,0,0,0: REM Footsteps
460   IF PEEK(1062)>218 OR PEEK(1062)<20 THEN
        GOSUB 1050: REM Reset Man
470   IF PEEK(1064)>229 OR PEEK(1063)<16 THEN
        GOSUB 600: REM Reset other players
480   IF PEEK(754)=255 THEN 410
490   GET #2,BYTE:
      SPEED=BYTE-48:
      POKE 754,255:
      IF SPEED<0 THEN
        SPEED=0
510   GOSUB 700
520   GOTO 410
530   REM
600   REM Select a New Object
610   IF VOL THEN
        VOL=INT(VOL):
        IF VOL=0 THEN
          VOL=1
620   IF VOL THEN
        VOL=VOL-0.5:
        SOUND 1,SND,8,VOL:
        SOUND 2,SND2,2,VOL:
        GOTO 620
630   TEMP=USR(MFILL,PLR(2),256,0): REM Use memory fill routine to clear Players 2 & 3
640   FLAG=INT(RND(1)*6+1): REM Which object to display (if possible)
650   OBJECT=0: REM No object selected yet
660   ON FLAG GOSUB 1100,1100,1100,1200,1300,1300:
      IF OBJECT=0 THEN
        RETURN
670   TEMP=USR(PMOVER,LST2P)
680   POKE INITANIMATE,LST2P
690   REM
```

```
700  REM Set Horizontal Velocities
710  IF OBJECT=3 THEN
        NSPD=128-SPEED*2:
        GOTO 740:  REM Tree
720  IF OBJECT=4 THEN
        NSPD=125-SPEED:
        GOTO 740:  REM Truck
730  NSPD=132-SPEED:  REM Car
740  POKE MOVERATE(2),NSPD:
     POKE MOVERATE(3),NSPD:
     TEMP=LST2P
750  POKE MOVERATE(0),129-SPEED:
     POKE MOVERATE(1),129-SPEED:
     IF WALK=-1 THEN
        TEMP=ALLP
760  POKE INITAUTOMOVE,TEMP
770  POKE SCRLSTEP,SPEED
780  RETURN
790  REM
1000 REM PARAMETERS FOR PLAYERS
1010 REM Man
1020 POKE 704,3*16+10:
     POKE 705,3*16+10:  REM Set color to peach
1030 FRSTPLR=0:
     OBJECT=1:
     GOSUB 1500:  REM Point to proper Frame List
1040 POKE VPLR(0),97:
     POKE VPLR(1),97
1050 IF SPEED=1 THEN 1070
1060 POKE HPLR(0),20:
     POKE HPLR(1),28:
     IF SPEED>1 THEN
        POKE HPLR(0),218:
        POKE HPLR(1),226
1070 WALK=INT(RND(1)*100+20)
1080 RETURN
1090 REM
1100 REM Tree
1110 IF SPEED=0 THEN
        RETURN
1120 POKE 706,14*16+4:
     POKE 707,13*16+6:  REM Brown trunk and green leaves
1130 POKE HPLR(2),229:
     POKE HPLR(3),217
1140 POKE VPLR(2),42:
     POKE VPLR(3),28
1150 FRSTPLR=2:
     OBJECT=2:
     GOSUB 1500:
     FRSTPLR=3:
     OBJECT=3:
     GOSUB 1500:  REM Point to proper Frame List
1160 POKE PMWIDTH(2),0:
     POKE PMWIDTH(3),3
1170 VF=0
1180 RETURN
1190 REM
1200 REM Truck
1210 POKE 706,3*16+6:
     POKE 707,INT(RND(1)*16)*16+10
1220 POKE HPLR(2),217:
     POKE HPLR(3),233
1230 POKE VPLR(2),77:
     POKE VPLR(3),77
```

```
1240   FRSTPLR=2:
       OBJECT=4:
       GOSUB 1500: REM Point to proper Frame List
1250   POKE PMWIDTH(2),1:
       POKE PMWIDTH(3),3
1260   VF=1:
       SCONS=180
1270   RETURN
1280   REM
1300   REM Car
1310   IF SPEED=4 THEN
         RETURN
1320   C=INT(RND(1)*16):
       L=8-INT(RND(1)*2)*4:
       TEMP=C*16+L:
       POKE 706,TEMP:
       POKE 707,TEMP
1330   POKE HPLR(2),0:
       POKE HPLR(3),16
1340   IF SPEED>4 THEN
         POKE HPLR(2),216:
         POKE HPLR(3),232
1350   POKE VPLR(2),96:
       POKE VPLR(3),96
1360   FRSTPLR=2:
       OBJECT=5:
       GOSUB 1500: REM Point to proper Frame List
1370   POKE PMWIDTH(2),1:
       POKE PMWIDTH(3),1
1380   VF=1:
       SCONS=40
1390   RETURN
1400   REM
1500   REM Put Frame List Address in Param Table
1510   FOR I=0 TO NUMPLRS(OBJECT)-1
1520     X=POINTER(OBJECT,I):
         GOSUB 110
1530     POKE FRMLSTPTR(I+FRSTPLR),LOBYTE
1540     POKE FRMLSTPTR(I+FRSTPLR)+1,HIBYTE
1550   NEXT I
1560   RETURN
1570   REM
1900   REM Convert to Screen Value
1910   CFLAG=0
1920   IF CHAR>127 THEN
         CHAR=CHAR-128:
         CFLAG=128
1930   IF CHAR<96 THEN
         CHAR=CHAR-32:
         IF CHAR<0 THEN
           CHAR=CHAR+96
1940   IF CFLAG THEN
         CHAR=CHAR+CFLAG+PAINT*64
1950   RETURN
1960   REM
2000   REM Send Info to Screen
2010   LN=LEN(SEG$):
       IF LN<24 THEN
         SEG$(LN+1)=CL$
2020   IF FENCE THEN
         PTR=PTR+1
2030   FOR I=0 TO HEIGHT
```

```
2040    IF FENCE THEN
           GOSUB 2200
2050    FOR J=1 TO WIDTH
2060       P=I*WIDTH+J:
           CHAR=ASC(SEG$(P,P))
2070       GOSUB 1900
2080       IF GRND THEN
              POKE SCRLWIN+6*LINELEN+J+23,CHAR:
              GOTO 2130
2090       IF CLOUD=0 THEN 2120
2100       IF CLOUD=2 THEN
              CHAR=CHAR+64
2110       POKE SCRN+PTR+I*24+J-1,CHAR:
           GOTO 2130
2120       POKE SCRLWIN+PTR+I*LINELEN+J-1,CHAR
2130    NEXT J
2140 NEXT I
2150 PTR=PTR+WIDTH+ABS(FENCE)+SPCFLAG
2160 SPCFLAG=0
2170 ROOMLEFT=LINELEN-25-PTR
2180 RETURN
2190 REM
2200 REM Put In Fence
2210 IF I<4 THEN 2240
2220 IF I=4 THEN
        CHAR=ASC("Q"):
        GOSUB 1900:
        P=-1:
        GOSUB 2250:
        CHAR=ASC("E"):
        GOSUB 1900:
        P=WIDTH:
        GOSUB 2250:
        GOTO 2240
2230 CHAR=ASC("A"):
     GOSUB 1900:
     P=-1:
     GOSUB 2250:
     CHAR=ASC("D"):
     GOSUB 1900:
     P=WIDTH:
     GOSUB 2250
2240 RETURN
2250 REM Poke In Data
2260 POKE SCRLWIN+PTR+I*LINELEN+P,CHAR
2270 RETURN
2280 REM
2400 REM Copy First Page Onto Last Page
2410 FOR I=0 TO 5
2420    FOR J=0 TO 24
2430       POKE SCRLWIN+I*LINELEN+LINELEN-25+J,PEEK(SCRLWIN+I*LINELEN+J)
2440    NEXT J
2450 NEXT I
2460 RETURN
2470 REM
2600 REM Clear the Screen — Fill the Screen With 0
2610 TEMP=USR(MFILL,SCRN,SCRNSZE,0)
2620 RETURN
2630 REM
2800 REM Put in Clouds and Sidewalk
```

```
2810   SEG$="<T=<TT=[\][\\]";
       CLOUD=1;
       PTR=4;
       HEIGHT=1;
       WIDTH=7;
       GOSUB 2000
2820   SEG$="<T=<=[\\\]";
       CLOUD=2;
       PTR=PTR+3;
       WIDTH=5;
       GOSUB 2000
2830   SEG$="^^^^^^^^^^^^^^^^^^^^^^^^";
       GRND=1;
       HEIGHT=0;
       WIDTH=24;
       GOSUB 2000
2840   RETURN
2850   REM
3000   REM CREATE RANDOM DISPLAY
3010   PTR=0;  REM Initialize Pointer to Scroll Window
3020   HEIGHT=5;  REM How tall is the window
3030   CLOUD=0;
       GRND=0
3040   WIDTH=INT(RND(1)*3+2);  REM From 2-4
3050   IF RND(1)*100<=45 THEN
          STORY=2;
          GOTO 3080;  REM 45% 2 Stories
3060   IF RND(1)*55<=35 THEN
          STORY=3;
          GOTO 3080;  REM 35% 3 Stories
3070   STORY=4;  REM 20% 4 Stories
3080   CHIMNEY=(RND(1)<=0.6);  REM 60% chance
3090   IF SHRUB=0 THEN
          FENCE=(RND(1)<=0.4);  REM 40% chance (only if no shrub)
3100   IF ROOMLEFT<6 THEN
          FENCE=0;  REM Not enough room left for a fence
3110   ANTENNA=(RND(1)<=0.5);  REM 50% chance
3120   PAINT=(RND(1)<=0.5);  REM 50% yellow, 50% pink
3130   SEG$=CL$;
       ON WIDTH-1 GOSUB 3500,3700,3900;
       GOSUB 2000
3140   IF ROOMLEFT<2 THEN
          GOSUB 2400;
          RETURN ;  REM No room for tree, exit routine
3150   REM Plant Some Foilage
3160   SHRUB=0;
       TREE=0
3170   IF FENCE=0 AND ODDHOUSE=0 AND ROOMLEFT>8 THEN
          SHRUB=(RND(1)<=0.3);
          IF SHRUB THEN 3440
3180   REM Make a tree
3190   WIDTH=2;
       SEG$=CL$
3200   REM Find height of tree
3210   IF RND(1)*10<=1 THEN
          TREE=2;
          GOTO 3260;  REM 10%
3220   IF RND(1)*9<=2 THEN
          TREE=3;
          GOTO 3260;  REM 20%
3230   IF RND(1)*7<=4 THEN
          TREE=4;
          GOTO 3260;  REM 40%
```

```
3240   IF RND(1)*3<=2 THEN
          TREE=5:
          GOTO 3260: REM 20%
3250   TREE=6: REM 10%
3260   TRUNK=INT(RND(1)*(TREE-2)+1):
          IF TREE=2 THEN
          TRUNK=0
3270   TREETOP=TREE-TRUNK:
          IF TREETOP>4 THEN
          TRUNK=TREE-4:
          TREETOP=4
3280   BT=(6-TREE)*2+1
3290   SEG$(BT)="<UP><DOWN>"
3300   IF TREETOP=2 THEN 3340
3310   FOR I=1 TO TREETOP-2
3320      BT=BT+2:
          SEG$(BT)="tt"
3330   NEXT I
3340   BT=BT+2:
          SEG$(BT)="<LEFT><RIGHT>"
3350   IF TRUNK=1 THEN 3390
3360   FOR I=1 TO TRUNK-1
3370      BT=BT+2:
          SEG$(BT)="BV"
3380   NEXT I
3390   IF RND(1)<=0.5 THEN
          SEG$(BT+2)="KL"
3400   REM Add random spacing on side of tree
3410   TEMP=INT(RND(1)*3+1):
          IF TEMP=3 OR ROOMLEFT<3 THEN 3470
3420   IF TEMP=1 THEN
          PTR=PTR+1:
          GOTO 3470
3430   SPCFLAG=1:
          GOTO 3470
3440   REM Make a shrub
3450   WIDTH=INT(RND(1)*2+2):
          SEG$=CL$:
          IF WIDTH=2 THEN
          SEG$(9)="<DOWN><UP>":
          GOTO 3470
3460   SEG$(13)="<DOWN>K<UP>"
3470   ODDHOUSE=0:
          FENCE=0:
          GOSUB 2000
3480   IF ROOMLEFT<4 THEN 3140:REM Add another tree if not enough room for a house
3490   GOTO 3040
3500   REM Width 2
3510   IF STORY>3 THEN
          STORY=3
3520   BT=1
3530   IF STORY=2 THEN
          BT=3
3540   IF CHIMNEY THEN
          SEG$(BT)="INZU":
          GOTO 3560
3550   SEG$(BT)="IOZX"
3560   BT=BT+4:
       FOR I=BT TO BT+(STORY-2)*2 STEP 2
3570      IF RND(1)<=0.5 THEN
             SEG$(I)="TP":
             GOTO 3590
3580      SEG$(I)="RP"
```

```
3590   NEXT I
3600   SEG$(9)="CT"
3610   IF FENCE=0 THEN 3640
3620   IF RND(1)<=0.5 THEN
           SEG$(11)="WW";
           GOTO 3640
3630   SEG$(11)="EQ"
3640   RETURN
3650   REM
3700   REM Width 3
3710   BT=(4-STORY)*3+1
3720   IF ANTENNA AND STORY<4 THEN
           SEG$(BT-3)="(,)(,)(,)"
3730   SEG$(BT)="ZTX"
3740   IF RND(1)<=0.5 THEN
           TEMP$="FPG";
           GOTO 3760
3750   TEMP$="FRG"
3760   BT=BT+3;
           FOR I=BT TO BT+(STORY-2)*3 STEP 3
3770     SEG$(I)=TEMP$
3780   NEXT I
3790   SEG$(13)="FCG"
3800   IF FENCE THEN
           SEG$(16)="WWW"
3810   RETURN
3820   REM
3900   REM Width 4
3910   BT=(4-STORY)*4+1
3920   IF STORY=4 THEN
           SEG$(BT)="HTTJ";
           GOTO 4050
3930   IF STORY>2 OR SHRUB OR RND(1)<=0.3333 THEN 4000:REM Which type house?
3940   REM Create Odd House type
3950   ODDHOUSE=1
3960   IF CHIMNEY THEN
           SEG$(1)="(,)IN(2 ,)ZU(,)";
           GOTO 3980
3970   SEG$(1)="(,)IO(2 ,)ZX(,)"
3980   FENCE=0
3990   SEG$(9)="ITTOBRPVBTCV";
           GOTO 4100
4000   REM Create Normal House type
4010   IF ANTENNA AND CHIMNEY THEN
           SEG$(BT-4)="(,)HJ(,)YTTJ";
           GOTO 4050
4020   SEG$(BT-4)="(,)HJ(,)";
           IF CHIMNEY=0 THEN
           SEG$(BT)="HTTJ";
           GOTO 4050
4030   IF RND(1)<=0.5 THEN
           SEG$(BT)="YTTJ";
           GOTO 4050
4040   SEG$(BT)="HTTM"
4050   BT=BT+4;
           FOR I=BT TO BT+(STORY-2)*4 STEP 4
4060     IF RND(1)<=0.25 THEN
               SEG$(I)="FSSG";
               GOTO 4080
4070     SEG$(I)="FPRG"
4080   NEXT I
4090   SEG$(17)="FTCG"
```

```
4100  IF FENCE THEN
         SEG$(21)="WEQW"
4110  RETURN
4120  REM
5000  REM Set Up Memory Locations
5010  DIF=0
5020  DLSZE=34: REM Display List size
5030  LINELEN=160: REM Horizontal length of scrolling window
5040  SCRNSZE=6*24+LINELEN*6: REM Screen size
5050  MEM=DLSZE+SCRNSZE: REM MEMory to reserve for DL and Screen
5060  RESTORE :
      READ OBJS
5070  DIM FRMDATA(OBJS,3):
      DIM FRAMES(OBJS),FRMSIZE(OBJS),NUMPLRS(OBJS),PLRFRMMEM(OBJS),FRMLSTSIZE(OBJS)
5080  FOR I=1 TO OBJS
5090     READ TEMP1,TEMP2,TEMP3
5100     FRAMES(I)=TEMP1:
         FRMSIZE(I)=TEMP2:
         NUMPLRS(I)=TEMP3
5110     PLRFRMMEM(I)=FRAMES(I)*FRMSIZE(I)+1
5120     FRAMEMEM=FRAMEMEM+PLRFRMMEM(I)*NUMPLRS(I)
5130     FRMLSTSIZE(I)=FRAMES(I)+3
5140     TOTFRMLSTSIZE=TOTFRMLSTSIZE+FRMLSTSIZE(I)*NUMPLRS(I)
5150  NEXT I
5160  DIM BUFFER$(128),FRAMEMEM$(FRAMEMEM),FRMLSTMEM$(TOTFRMLSTSIZE)
5170  DIF=DIF+4:
      IF DIF*256<MEM THEN 5170
5180  HIBASE=PEEK(106)-DIF: REM Find DL Hi and Lo bytes
5190  LOBASE=0
5200  DLBASE=HIBASE*256+LOBASE
5210  SCRN=DLBASE+DLSZE: REM Starting address of Screen RAM
5220  X=SCRN:
      GOSUB 110
5230  SCRNHI=HIBYTE:
      SCRNLO=LOBYTE: REM Find Screen Hi and Lo bytes
5240  SCRLWIN=SCRN+48: REM Beginning of Scroll window
5250  SCROLL=ADR(SCROLL$)
5260  DLIROUT=ADR(DLIROUT$)
5270  PMOVER=ADR(PMOVER$)
5280  ANIMATE=ADR(ANIMATE$)
5290  AUTOMOVE=ADR(AUTOMOVE$)
5300  MFILL=ADR(MFILL$)
5310  BUFFER=ADR(BUFFER$)
5320  PLRFRAMES=ADR(FRAMEMEM$)
5330  FRMLSTMEM=ADR(FRMLSTMEM$)
5340  RETURN
5350  REM
6000  REM Set Up the Display List
6010  GRAPHICS 2+16: REM Set flags to Graphics mode 2
6020  POKE 559,0: REM Turn off screen DMA
6030  POKE DLBASE,112: REM Set up top border, 24 scan lines
6040  POKE DLBASE+1,112
6050  POKE DLBASE+2,112
6060  POKE DLBASE+3,71: REM LMS for line 1
6070  POKE DLBASE+4,SCRNLO
6080  POKE DLBASE+5,SCRNHI
6090  POKE DLBASE+6,7+128: REM Line 2 (w/ DLI)
6100  FOR I=0 TO 6: REM Loop for lines 3-9
6110     WINDOW=SCRLWIN+I*LINELEN
6120     BYTE=87: REM LMS and HSCRL
6130     IF I=2 OR I=5 THEN
            BYTE=87+128: REM DLI, LMS and HSCRL for lines 5 and 8
6140     IF I=6 THEN
```

```
            BYTE=71: REM No scroll for line 9
6150    POKE DLBASE+7+3*I,BYTE: REM LMS and HSCRL
6160    X=WINDOW:
        GOSUB 110
6170    POKE DLBASE+8+3*I,LOBYTE
6180    POKE DLBASE+9+3*I,HIBYTE
6190  NEXT I
6200  POKE DLBASE+28,7+128: REM Last 3 lines
6210  POKE DLBASE+29,7
6220  POKE DLBASE+30,7+128
6230  POKE DLBASE+31,65: REM Jump on VBLANK to beginning of DL
6240  POKE DLBASE+32,LOBASE
6250  POKE DLBASE+33,HIBASE
6260  X=DLIROUT:
        GOSUB 110
6270  POKE 512,LOBYTE: REM Address of DL for DLI handling routine
6280  POKE 513,HIBYTE
6290  REM Tell ANTIC where the DL is
6300  POKE 560,LOBASE
6310  POKE 561,HIBASE
6320  SETCOLOR 0,15,4:
        SETCOLOR 1,12,4:
        SETCOLOR 2,0,10:
        SETCOLOR 3,0,12:
        SETCOLOR 4,9,8: REM Brn, grn, wht, wht, blue
6330  RETURN
6340  REM
7000  REM Initialize Player-Missile Graphics
7010  TEMP=PEEK(106)-DIF-4: REM Set aside Player-Missile area
7020  POKE 54279,TEMP: REM Tell ANTIC where PM RAM is
7030  PMBASE=256*TEMP: REM Find PM Base address
7040  FOR I=0 TO 3
7050    PLR(I)=PMBASE+128*I+512: REM Set addresses of Players
7060    PMWIDTH(I)=53256+I: REM Set addresses of Player Widths
7070  NEXT I
7090  POKE 623,1: REM Set priority - Players in front
7100  POKE 53277,2: REM Enable Player display
7110  TEMP=USR(MFILL,PLR(0),512,0): REM Use memory fill routine to clear Players
7120  RETURN
7130  REM
8000  REM Set Up Alternate Character Set
8010  HICHRB=PEEK(106)-DIF-4: REM Reserve space (512 bytes)
8020  CHRBAS=HICHRB*256: REM Find start of Character Set
8030  REM Read in data, skip first 28 characters
8040  OFFSET=28*8:
        CHARS=35
8050  RESTORE 23000
8060  READ TOTAL:
        TEMP=0
8070  FOR I=CHRBAS+OFFSET TO CHRBAS+OFFSET+CHARS*8-1
8080    READ BYTE:
        POKE I,BYTE:
        TEMP=TEMP+BYTE
8090  NEXT I
8100  IF TOTAL<>TEMP THEN
        GRAPHICS 0:
        PRINT "ERROR In Character Set Data":
        END
8110  REM Clear out first char (background)
8120  FOR I=CHRBAS TO CHRBAS+7
8130    POKE I,0
8140  NEXT I
8150  RETURN
```

```
 8160   REM
10000   REM Read in Frame Data
10010   OFFSET=0:
        OFFSET2=0:
        DIM FRAMELIST(OBJS):
        RESTORE 21000
10020   FOR K=1 TO OBJS
10030     FRAMELIST(K)=FRMLSTMEM+OFFSET
10040     OFFSET=OFFSET+(FRAMES(K)+3)*NUMPLRS(K)
10050     FOR I=0 TO NUMPLRS(K)-1
10060       FRMDATA(K,I)=PLRFRAMES+OFFSET2: REM Store addresses of frame data
10070       OFFSET2=OFFSET2+PLRFRMMEM(K)
10080       POKE FRMDATA(K,I),FRMSIZE(K): REM Poke Frame size at beginning of each set of frame data
10090       FOR J=1 TO PLRFRMMEM(K)-1
10100         READ BYTE
10110         POKE FRMDATA(K,I)+J,BYTE
10120       NEXT J:
        NEXT I:
        NEXT K
10130   RETURN
10140   REM
11000   REM INITIALIZE ROUTINE STRINGS
11010   REM Set SCROLL routine
11020   DIM SCROLL$(316)
11030   SCROLL$(1)=" <<<Routine String goes here>>>  "
11040   SCROLL$(91)="  <<<Routine String goes here>>>  "
11050   SCROLL$(181)="  <<<Routine String goes here>>>  "
11060   SCROLL$(271)="  <<<Routine String goes here>>>  "
11100   REM Set DLI routine
11110   DIM DLIROUT$(94)
11120   DLIROUT$(1)="  <<<Routine String goes here>>>  "
11130   DLIROUT$(91)="  <<<Routine String goes here>>>  "
11200   REM Read Color Values Into DLI Table
11210   DLITBLSZE=15:
        RESTORE 25510
11220   DIM DLITABLE$(DLITBLSZE)
11230   DLITABLE=ADR(DLITABLE$)
11240   FOR I=0 TO DLITBLSZE-1
11250     READ BYTE
11260     POKE DLITABLE+I,BYTE
11270   NEXT I
11300   REM Set PMOVER routine
11310   DIM PMOVER$(186)
11320   PMOVER$(1)=" <<<Routine String goes here>>>  "
11330   PMOVER$(91)="  <<<Routine String goes here>>>  "
11340   PMOVER$(181)="  <<<Routine String goes here>>>  "
11400   REM Set ANIMATE routine
11410   DIM ANIMATE$(294)
11420   ANIMATE$(1)="  <<<Routine String goes here>>>  "
11430   ANIMATE$(91)="  <<<Routine String goes here>>>  "
11440   ANIMATE$(181)="  <<<Routine String goes here>>>  "
11450   ANIMATE$(271)="  <<<Routine String goes here>>>  "
11500   REM Set AUTOMOVE routine
11510   DIM AUTOMOVE$(74)
11520   AUTOMOVE$(1)="  <<<Routine String goes here>>>  "
11600   REM Set MFILL routine
11610   DIM MFILL$(41)
11620   MFILL$(1)="  <<<Routine String goes here>>>  "
11650   RETURN
11660   REM
12000   REM Set Parameters For Routines
12010   PARAMBASE=1024: REM Parameter Base address
12020   PMBAS=PARAMBASE: REM Hi Byte of PLR0 Location goes here
```

```
12030   PMBUF=PARAMBASE+1: REM Address of a 128 byte buffer
12040   INITANIMATE=PARAMBASE+3: REM Initialize Frame Animate routine
12050   INITAUTOMOVE=PARAMBASE+4: REM Initialize Player Automove routine
12060   SCRLINIT=PARAMBASE+5: REM Poke a 1 to initialize the scroll routine
12070   FOR I=0 TO 3
12080     HPLR(I)=PARAMBASE+6+I: REM Player horizontal "shadow" registers
12090     VPLR(I)=PARAMBASE+10+I: REM Player vertical "shadow" registers
12100     RATE(I)=PARAMBASE+14+I: REM Animate rate "shadow" registers
12110     FRMLSTPTR(I)=PARAMBASE+18+I*2: REM Pointer to Frame Lists
12120     MOVERATE(I)=PARAMBASE+32+I: REM Horizontal movement for AUTOMOVE
12130   NEXT I
12140   SCRLADR=PARAMBASE+26: REM Address of scrolling window
12150   SCRLLEN=PARAMBASE+28: REM Line length of scrolling window
12160   SCRLCLK=PARAMBASE+30: REM Number of Color Clocks per screen byte
12170   SCRLSTEP=PARAMBASE+31: REM Step size of scroll each jiffy
12180   DLIADR=PARAMBASE+36: REM Address of DLI table
12190   VVBLKD=548: REM Deferred Vertical Blank Interrupt Vector
12200   CRITICAL=66: REM Critical Flag
12210   P0=1:
        P1=2:
        P2=4:
        P3=8: REM Control bits for the four Players
12220   FST2P=P0+P1
12230   LST2P=P2+P3:
        ALLP=P0+P1+P2+P3
12240   TEMP=USR(MFILL,PARAMBASE,94,0): REM IMPORTANT: Clear out parameter area
12250   X=PLR(0):
        GOSUB 110:
        POKE PMBAS,HIBYTE: REM Poke Hi Byte of Player 0 into PMBAS
12260   X=BUFFER:
        GOSUB 110:
        POKE PMBUF,LOBYTE: REM Poke address of buffer
12270   POKE PMBUF+1,HIBYTE
12280   X=SCRLWIN:
        GOSUB 110
12290   POKE SCRLADR,LOBYTE
12300   POKE SCRLADR+1,HIBYTE
12320   X=LINELEN:
        GOSUB 110
12330   POKE SCRLLEN,LOBYTE
12340   POKE SCRLLEN+1,HIBYTE
12350   POKE SCRLCLK,7: REM Set to 8 color clocks per byte
12360   X=DLITABLE:
        GOSUB 110
12370   POKE DLIADR,LOBYTE
12380   POKE DLIADR+1,HIBYTE
12390   REM
12400   REM Set Up Frame Lists
12410   DIM POINTER(OBJS,1)
12420   FOR K=1 TO OBJS
12430     FOR I=0 TO NUMPLRS(K)-1
12440       LET POINTER(K,I)=FRAMELIST(K)+I*FRMLSTSIZE(K): REM Points to start of each Frame List
12450       X=FRMDATA(K,I):
            GOSUB 110
12460       POKE POINTER(K,I),LOBYTE: REM Put in address of Frame Data
12470       POKE POINTER(K,I)+1,HIBYTE
12480       FOR J=1 TO FRAMES(K): REM Make up a Frame List (numbers 1 thru FRAMES)
12490         POKE POINTER(K,I)+J+1,J
12500       NEXT J
12510       POKE POINTER(K,I)+FRAMES(K)+2,0: REM End of frame list marker
12520     NEXT I:
        NEXT K
12530   RETURN
```

```
12540  REM
13000  REM Install Interrupt Routines
13010  POKE CRITICAL,1: REM Open CRITICAL "valve", set up detour
13020  X=SCROLL+6:
       GOSUB 110
13030  POKE VVBLKD,LOBYTE: REM Set VBLANK vector to SCROLL
13040  POKE VVBLKD+1,HIBYTE
13050  X=DLIROUT+6:
       GOSUB 110
13060  POKE SCROLL+4,LOBYTE:  REM Points SCROLL to DLIROUT
13070  POKE SCROLL+5,HIBYTE
13080  X=PMOVER+6:
       GOSUB 110
13090  POKE DLIROUT+4,LOBYTE:  REM Points DLIROUT to PMOVER
13100  POKE DLIROUT+5,HIBYTE
13110  X=ANIMATE+6:
       GOSUB 110
13120  POKE PMOVER+4,LOBYTE:  REM Points PMOVER to ANIMATE
13130  POKE PMOVER+5,HIBYTE
13140  X=AUTOMOVE+6:
       GOSUB 110
13150  POKE ANIMATE+4,LOBYTE:  REM Points ANIMATE to AUTOMOVE
13160  POKE ANIMATE+5,HIBYTE
13170  POKE CRITICAL,0: REM Close CRITICAL "valve", routines installed
13180  POKE SCRLINIT,1
13190  POKE 54286,192: REM Enable DLI's
13200  RETURN
13210  REM
20000  REM FRAME DATA
20010  REM Number of objects
20020  DATA 5
20030  REM
20040  REM Number of Frames, Frame Size, Number of Players
20050  REM . (Walking Man)
20060  DATA 5,19,2
20070  REM . (Tree Trunk)
20080  DATA 1,52,1
20090  REM . (Tree Top)
20100  DATA 1,26,1
20110  REM . (Truck)
20120  DATA 1,25,2
20130  REM . (Car)
20140  DATA 1,13,2
20150  REM
21000  REM Frame data for Walking Man
21010  REM Frame 1, Player 0
21020  DATA 0,0,0,0,0,0,0,3,15,29,59,51,7,7,15,252,224,112,48
21030  REM Frame 2, Player 0
21040  DATA 0,0,0,0,0,0,0,1,7,15,31,55,55,7,111,125,248,192,193
21050  REM Frame 3, Player 0
21060  DATA 0,0,0,0,0,0,3,7,15,31,31,31,31,222,254,251,231,206,15
21070  REM Frame 4, Player 0
21080  DATA 1,3,3,3,1,7,15,31,30,62,62,63,63,60,124,120,112,112,252
21090  REM Frame 5, Player 0
21100  DATA 0,0,1,1,1,0,7,31,31,31,31,31,15,15,13,31,123,112,124
21110  REM Frame 1, Player 1
21120  DATA 0,28,62,62,62,28,240,240,240,240,251,255,220,192,192,227,118,60,24
21130  REM Frame 2, Player 1
21140  DATA 0,0,56,124,124,124,56,224,224,224,224,246,254,192,128,192,224,224,248
21150  REM Frame 3, Player 1
21160  DATA 0,112,248,248,248,112,192,192,128,128,128,224,224,0,0,0,0,0,128
21170  REM Frame 4, Player 1
21180  DATA 192,224,224,224,192,0,0,0,0,0,0,0,0,0,0,0,0,0,0
```

```
21190   REM Frame 5, Player 1
21200   DATA 0,224,240,240,240,224,128,128,128,128,176,240,0,128,192,128,192,0,0
21210   REM
22000   REM Frame data for Tree
22010   REM Player 2, Tree Trunk
22020   DATA 2,2,132,128,64,0,149,165,210,211,219,251,255,254,126,126,126,126,126,126
22030   DATA 126,126,126,126,126,126,126,126,126,122,126,126,126,126,126,126,126,126,126,126
22040   DATA 126,126,126,126,126,126,126,255,255,219,137
22050   REM Player 3, Tree Top
22060   DATA 24,24,60,60,126,126,126,255,255,255,255,255,255,255,255,255,255,255,255,126
22070   DATA 126,60,60,60,24,24
22080   REM
22100   REM Frame data for Truck
22110   REM Player 2, Truck Cab
22120   DATA 0,0,0,0,0,15,25,17,17,17,17,31,31,255,255,255,255,255,255
22130   DATA 255,255,255,28,28
22140   REM Player 3, Truck Body
22150   DATA 255,255,255,255,255,255,255,255,255,255,255,255,255,255,255,255,255,255,255,255
22160   DATA 255,255,255,12,12
22170   REM
22200   REM Frame data for Car
22210   REM Player 2, Car back
22220   DATA 7,9,17,17,17,31,63,127,255,255,255,56,16
22230   REM Player 3, Car front
22240   DATA 192,64,32,32,16,248,255,255,255,254,255,28,8
23000   REM Character Set Data
23010   DATA 38646
23020   DATA 0,3,15,31,63,63,127,127
23030   DATA 0,192,240,248,252,252,254,254
23040   DATA 127,127,127,63,63,31,15,7
23050   DATA 254,254,254,252,252,248,240,224
23060   DATA 4,31,4,31,4,4,4,4
23070   DATA 48,48,48,63,54,54,54
23080   DATA 3,3,3,3,3,3,3
23090   DATA 255,195,219,219,219,219,219,219
23100   DATA 12,12,12,252,108,108,108,108
23110   DATA 0,0,0,252,108,108,108,108
23120   DATA 127,127,127,127,127,127,127,127
23130   DATA 254,254,254,254,254,254,254,254
23140   DATA 1,3,7,15,31,63,127,255
23150   DATA 1,1,3,3,7,7,15,15
23160   DATA 128,192,224,240,248,252,254,255
23170   DATA 3,3,7,7,15,0,0,0
23180   DATA 192,192,224,224,240,0,0,0
23190   DATA 156,220,252,252,252,252,254,255
23200   DATA 128,128,192,192,224,224,243,243
23210   DATA 128,128,192,192,224,224,240,240
23220   DATA 255,255,39,39,255,39,39,255
23230   DATA 0,0,0,63,54,54,54,54
23240   DATA 255,255,228,228,255,228,228,255
23250   DATA 255,24,24,24,255,24,24,24
23260   DATA 255,255,255,255,255,255,255,255
23270   DATA 251,251,255,252,254,254,255,255
23280   DATA 192,192,192,192,192,192,192,192
23290   DATA 0,0,0,255,102,102,102,102
23300   DATA 248,248,252,252,254,254,255,255
23310   DATA 57,59,63,63,63,63,127,255
23320   DATA 31,31,63,63,127,127,255,255
23330   DATA 127,127,127,127,63,63,30,0
23340   DATA 255,255,255,255,255,254,124,0
23350   DATA 254,254,254,254,252,252,120,0
23360   DATA 255,255,255,0,0,0,0,0
23370   REM
```

```
25500  REM DLI Color Values
25510  DATA 234,90,152,234,90,198,10,0,198,0,0,6,0,0,10
```

```
10  REM   HORIZONTAL FINE SCROLLING
20  REM
30  GRAPHICS 0
40  HSCROL=54276
60  DLIST=PEEK(560)+PEEK(561)*256: REM Find Display List
70  POKE DLIST+15,18: REM Turn horizontal scroll bit (2+16)
80  POSITION 1,10:
    PRINT "This is a demo of horizontal scrolling! ";
90  FOR I=0 TO 15
100    POKE HSCROL,I
110    GOSUB 500
120  NEXT I
130  FOR I=15 TO 0 STEP -1
140    POKE HSCROL,I
150    GOSUB 500
160  NEXT I
170  GOTO 90
500  FOR W=1 TO 5:
     NEXT W
510  RETURN
```

```
10  REM   VERTICAL FINE SCROLLING
20  REM
30  GRAPHICS 0
40  HSCROL=54276
50  VSCROL=54277
60  DLIST=PEEK(560)+PEEK(561)*256: REM Find Display List
70  POKE DLIST+15,34: REM Turn vertical scroll bit (2+32)
80  POSITION 1,10:
    PRINT "This is a demo of vertical scrolling! ";
90  FOR I=0 TO 7
100    POKE VSCROL,I
110    GOSUB 500
120  NEXT I
130  FOR I=7 TO 0 STEP -1
140    POKE VSCROL,I
150    GOSUB 500
160  NEXT I
170  GOTO 90
500  FOR W=1 TO 5:
     NEXT W
510  RETURN
```

```
10  REM   DIAGONAL FINE SCROLLING
20  REM
30  GRAPHICS 0
40  HSCROL=54276
50  VSCROL=54277
60  DLIST=PEEK(560)+PEEK(561)*256: REM Find Display List
70  POKE DLIST+15,50: REM Turn horizontal and vertical scroll bits (2+16+32)
80  POSITION 3,10:
    PRINT "This is a demo of diagonal scrolling! ";
90  FOR I=0 TO 7
100    POKE HSCROL,I:
       POKE VSCROL,I
110    GOSUB 500
```

```
120    NEXT I
130.   FOR I=7 TO 0 STEP -1
140       POKE HSCROL,I:
          POKE VSCROL,I
150       GOSUB 500
160    NEXT I
170    GOTO 90
500    FOR W=1 TO 5:
       NEXT W
510    RETURN
24000  REM SCROLL Routine DATA
24010  DATA SCROLL,11020,316,29349
24020  DATA 184,80,3,76,98,228,216,173,5,4,240,247,16,72,165,224,141,89,4,165,225,141,90,4,173
24030  DATA 48,2,133,224,173,49,2,133,225,173,30,4,141,80,4,169,192,141,81,4,173,31,4,160,0
24040  DATA 78,80,4,144,7,74,78,81,4,200,208,244,141,80,4,173,31,4,45,30,4,24,109,70,4
24050  DATA 205,30,4,240,14,144,12,176,4,80,173,208,89,238,80,4,45,30,4,141,70,4,77,30,4
24060  DATA 141,4,212,173,80,4,24,109,68,4,141,68,4,144,3,238,69,4,173,68,4,56,109,81,4
24070  DATA 141,68,4,144,3,238,69,4,173,69,4,205,29,4,144,40,208,8,173,68,4,205,28,4,144
24080  DATA 30,169,0,141,68,4,141,69,4,141,80,4,173,26,4,141,66,4,173,27,4,141,67,4,184
24090  DATA 80,19,208,103,80,159,173,68,4,24,237,81,4,141,68,4,176,3,206,69,4,173,66,4,24
24100  DATA 109,80,4,141,66,4,141,82,4,144,3,238,67,4,173,67,4,141,83,4,160,3,177,224,201
24110  DATA 65,240,41,41,80,240,32,41,16,240,26,200,173,82,4,145,224,24,109,28,4,141,82,4,200
24120  DATA 173,83,4,145,224,109,29,4,141,83,4,173,200,200,200,208,211,80,166,173,89,4,133,224,173
24130  DATA 90,4,133,225,184,80,153,169,128,141,5,4,173,30,4,141,70,4,169,0,141,68,4,141,69
24140  DATA 4,173,26,4,141,66,4,173,27,4,141,67,4,184,80,207
25000  REM DLI Routine DATA
25010  DATA DLIROUT,11110,94,12803
25020  DATA 184,80,10,76,98,228,169,0,141,75,4,240,246,72,138,72,152,72,165,224,141,93,4,165,225
25030  DATA 141,94,4,173,36,4,133,224,173,37,4,133,225,172,75,4,177,224,72,200,177,224,170,200,177
25040  DATA 224,200,140,75,4,168,104,234,234,234,234,234,234,234,234,234,141,10,212,141,24,208,142,25,208
25050  DATA 140,26,208,173,93,4,133,224,173,94,4,133,225,104,168,104,170,104,64
```

```
10     REM   COPY PROGRAM
20     REM Program to transfer duplicate lines from PLAYER program to SCROLL
30     REM
40     DIM LN$(120)
50     OPEN #1,4,0,"D:PLAYERS.TXT"
60     OPEN #2,8,0,"D:SCROLL.BAS"
70     FOR I=1 TO 41
80        READ LNNUM
90        INPUT #1;LN$:
          IF VAL(LN$)<>LNNUM THEN 90
100       PRINT #2;LN$:
          PRINT LN$
110    NEXT I
120    CLOSE #1:
       CLOSE #2
130    REM
200    REM Lines To Copy
220    DATA 30,50,60,70,80,100,110,120,130,140,180,190,280,290,380
230    DATA 390,400,490,530,5000,5300,5340,5350,11000,11600,11610,11620,11650,11660,12000
240    DATA 12010,12190,12200,12240,12530,12540,13000,13010,13170,13200,13210
```

Appendix B

Character Set Grid/
ATARI ROM Character Set

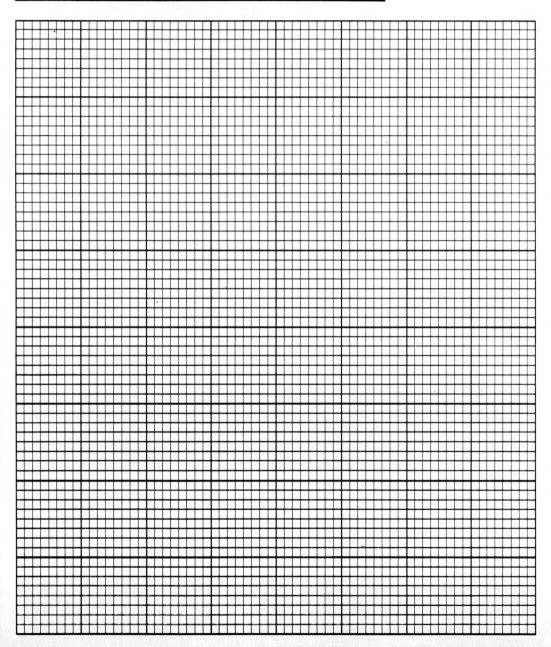

Figure B.1: Grid for creating character set figures. See also Chapter 5.

Column 1				Column 2				Column 3				Column 4			
#	CHR	#	CHR	#	CHR	#	CHR	#	CHR	#	CHR	#	CHR	#	CHR
0	Space	16	0	32	@	48	P	64	 ▦	80	 ▦	96	▦	112	p
1	!	17	1	33	A	49	Q	65	 ▦	81	▦	97	a	113	q
2	``	18	2	34	B	50	R	66	 ▦	82	 ▦	98	b	114	r
3	#	19	3	35	C	51	S	67	 ▦	83	▦	99	c	115	s
4	$	20	4	36	D	52	T	68	 ▦	84	 ▦	100	d	116	t
5	%	21	5	37	E	53	U	69	 ▦	85	 ▦	101	e	117	u
6	&	22	6	38	F	54	V	70	 ▦	86	 ▦	102	f	118	v
7	'	23	7	39	G	55	W	71	 ▦	87	 ▦	103	g	119	w
8	(	24	8	40	H	56	X	72	 ▦	88	 ▦	104	h	120	x
9	)	25	9	41	I	57	Y	73	 ▦	89	 ▦	105	i	121	y
10	*	26	:	42	J	58	Z	74	▦	90	▦	106	j	122	z
11	+	27	;	43	K	59	[	75	▦	91	▦ [1]	107	k	123	▦
12	,	28	<	44	L	60	\	76	▦	92	▦ [1]	108	l	124		
13	—	29	=	45	M	61	]	77	 ▦	93	▦ [1]	109	m	125	▦ [1]
14	—	30	>	46	N	62	∧	78	 ▦	94	▦ [1]	110	n	126	▦ [1]
15		31	?	47	O	63	—	79	 ▦	95	▦ [1]	111	o	127	▦ [1]

1. In mode 0 these characters must be preceded with an escape, CHR$(27), to be printed.

Figure B.2: The order of the ATARI character set in ROM. (Reproduced with permission of ATARI, Inc.)

Appendix C

Listing Conventions

HOW WE REPRESENT THOSE INVISIBLE ATARI CHARACTERS

Throughout the listings in this section are many characters that either can't be printed by our printer or are hard to find on the ATARI keyboard (because they're not obviously indicated). To make it easier to enter the programs, we will use the following conventions:

1. All inverse video characters (characters entered after pressing the "ATARI Key" — light background and dark letters instead of dark background and light letters) will be underlined. In the following example, the letters C, E, and F should be entered in inverse video:

```
S$="ABCDEFGHI"
```

2. Control characters (those entered while the control button is depressed) will be surrounded by curly brackets { }. All of the ATARI's graphics characters are accessed while depressing the control (CTRL on the keyboard) button. In the following example, the letters B, G, and H are control characters:

```
C$="A{B}CDEF{G}{H}IJ"
```

3. Special cursor and screen keys will be represented by printing the name or description of the key within curly brackets { }. To enter these special keys into a string, you will need to press the ESC key first. This puts the code for the key into the string instead of actually carrying out the action. In the following example, we want to clear the screen on line 100. To do this, first tap the ESC key, then hold the shift key down and press the key with the word CLEAR on it (it has ⟨ on it). When the line is executed, the screen will clear:

```
100 PRINT "{CLEAR}"
```

In the next example, the cursor key with the arrow pointing down is used. When this line is executed, the computer will print the word HI, move the cursor down one line, and then print BYE. To enter this character, first press the **ESC** key, then hold the **CTRL** key down and press the key with the down arrow and = on it:

```
110 PRINT "HI{DOWN}BYE"
```

When executed, you will see the following on your screen:

```
HI
  BYE
```

4. When a number appears before a curly bracketed word, it means we want you to enter that character the indicated number of times. In the following example, we want you to enter the letters ''ABCDE,'' then one cursor down, then five cursors left, and finally the letters ''FGHIJ'':

```
120 PRINT "ABCDE{DOWN}{5 LEFT}FGHIJ"
```

When this line is executed, you will see the following on the screen:

```
ABCDE
FGHIJ
```

This technique of embedding the cursor characters enables us to create a block of characters which can be PRINTed with one statement.

5. When spaces are important to an animation, as they are in the programs in Chapter 5, we will represent a space with a lowercase b that has a slash through it:

ƀ

This will enable you to enter the correct number of spaces. As before, if the ƀ character is underlined, enter the space as an inverse video character.

6. In Chapters 8 and 9, our black box machine language routines are presented. Since it would be too confusing to present the actual representations for the routines in the listings, the lines containing the routines will contain the message:

```
<<<Routine String goes here>>>
```

MORE ABOUT THE LISTINGS — HOW THEY WERE CREATED

You may have noticed that our printed listings are formatted differently from programs listed on your screen. We used a special program[1] to print them in a manner which emphasizes their structure, thus making them more readable and easier to understand. All FOR/NEXT loops are indented so that it's easy to see where the loop starts and ends. IF/THEN statements are indented so that you can see exactly what will be executed if the condition is TRUE. Also, the multiple parts of all statements (separated by colons) are printed on a separate line. Of course, when you enter the programs, the structure will disappear — *don't* try to enter each statement on a separate line!

One disadvantage to this method is that our stretched-out listings make the programs appear to be longer than they really are. Don't let the number of pages it takes to display each program discourage you from entering them!

---

[1]Our listing program was based on the ATARI Program Exchange product called *BLIS—BASIC Program Lister* by Image Marketing, Inc. (APX-20049). We modified the program so it would print the special codes for spaces and cursor and screen control keys, and also so it would use the ATARI 825 Printer's proportionally spaced font.

Appendix D

The String Loader Program

HOW TO STORE MACHINE LANGUAGE ROUTINES IN STRINGS

As mentioned in Chapter 8 when we first introduced programs containing machine language routines, loading the bytes of the routine into a string is an excellent storage method when using ATARI BASIC. Here is the String Loader program along with the DATA for MFILL, the first machine language routine we introduced.

```
10   REM *** STRING LOADER ***
20   REM Program to convert data to strings
30   REM Copyright (C) 1982 by David Fox and Mitchell Waite
40   GOTO 110
50   REM Prepare Control Characters for Screen
60   IF (BYTE>26 AND BYTE<32) OR (BYTE>124 AND BYTE<128) OR (BYTE>155 AND BYTE<160) OR
       (BYTE>252) THEN 80
70   RETURN
80   CHAR$(1,1)="<ESC>";
     CHAR$(2,2)=CHR$(BYTE);
     RETURN
90   REM
100  REM Initialize
110  DIM DEV$(15),STRNAME$(8),QUOTE(10),EOL(10),QUOTE$(1),CHAR$(2)
120  QUOTE$=CHR$(34)
130  QTECNTR=0;
     EOLCNTR=0;
     STRPNTR=1;
     START=0;
     BYTETOT=0
140  READ STRNAME$,LINE,SIZE,ERRCHECK
150  GOSUB 800; REM Open Output Device
160  REM Begin Printout
170  PRINT #1;LINE;" DIM ";STRNAME$;"$(";SIZE;")"
180  STRSTART=STRPNTR;
     STREND=STRPNTR+89;
     IF STRSTART>SIZE THEN 400
190  LINE=LINE+10
200  PRINT #1;LINE;" ";STRNAME$;"$(";STRPNTR;")=";QUOTE$;
210  FOR I=STRSTART TO STREND
220    START=START+1;
       IF START>SIZE THEN 300
```

```
230    READ BYTE:
       BYTETOT=BYTETOT+BYTE:
       IF BYTE=34 OR BYTE=155 THEN 260
240    CHAR$=CHR$(BYTE):
       IF DEV$(1,1)="E" THEN
         GOSUB 60
250    PRINT #1;CHAR$;:
       GOTO 280
260    PRINT #1;" ";:
       IF BYTE=34 THEN
         QUOTE(QTECNTR)=I:
         QTECNTR=QTECNTR+1:
         GOTO 280
270    EOL(EOLCNTR)=I:
       EOLCNTR=EOLCNTR+1
280  NEXT I
290  PRINT #1;QUOTE$:
     STRPNTR=STRPNTR+90:
     GOTO 180
300  PRINT #1;QUOTE$
310  REM
400  REM Verify Accuracy of Data
410  IF BYTETOT<>ERRCHECK THEN
       PRINT "{CLEAR}ERROR - Please recheck your data.";
       PRINT " I get ";BYTETOT:
       GOTO 700
420  REM
500  REM Insert Quotes
510  IF QTECNTR=0 THEN 610
520  FOR I=0 TO QTECNTR-1
530    LINE=LINE+10
540    PRINT #1;LINE;" ";STRNAME$;"$(";QUOTE(I);",";QUOTE(I);")=CHR$(34)"
550  NEXT I
560  REM
600  REM Insert End of Line Character
610  IF EOLCNTR=0 THEN 700
620  FOR I=0 TO EOLCNTR-1
630    LINE=LINE+10
640    PRINT #1;LINE;" ";STRNAME$;"$(";EOL(I);",";EOL(I);")=CHR$(155)"
650  NEXT I
700  END
800  REM Choose and Open Output Device
810  PRINT "{CLEAR}   * * * STRING MAKER * * *"
820  PRINT "{4 DOWN}Please the enter storage device:{DOWN}"
830  PRINT "  E = Screen Editor"
840  PRINT "  D = Disk (D, D2)"
850  PRINT "  C = Cassette"
860  POSITION 4,11:
     PRINT "{SHIFT-DELETE}(E,D,C): ";:
     INPUT DEV$
870  TRAP 860
880  LN=LEN(DEV$)
890  DEV$(LN+1)=":"
900  DEV$(LN+2)=STRNAME$
910  DEV$(LEN(DEV$)+1)=".STR"
920  OPEN #1,8,0,DEV$
930  TRAP 40000
```

```
 940   IF DEV$(1,1)="D" THEN
         PRINT "{DOWN}Writing to ";DEV$
 950   RETURN
 960   REM
29000  REM Memory Fill Routine Data
29010  DATA MFILL,11610,41,6244
29020  DATA 104,104,133,204,104,133,203,104,133,206,104,133,205,104,104,160,0,170,138,145,203,200,
         208,2,230
29030  DATA 204,165,205,208,2,198,206,198,205,165,205,5,206,208,234,96
```

Figure D.1: Listing of String Loader program.

Once you have entered this program, you may re-use it for all our subsequent machine language routines just by deleting the old DATA statements for MFILL and entering the new ones for the next routine you want to use. The program will read the name of the routine, its starting line number, how long it is, check whether it was entered correctly, and then save the finished "routine string" on the storage device of your choice. All this is taken care of automatically.

Initialize (lines 100–150) This section sets all the variables to their initial values. In line 110, the string and array variables are DIMensioned. DEV$ will contain the name of the device on which you will store your routine strings (disk, cassette, or screen editor), and STRNAME$ will hold the name of the routine string. There are two byte values which cannot be represented in a string and must be handled separately: quotation marks (ATASCII 34), which would prematurely end a string, and the end-of-line character (ATASCII 155), which would end the statement line. These characters are singled out and their positions in the string are stored respectively in the arrays QUOTE and EOL. QUOTE$ is set to the quotation mark character and CHAR$ temporarily holds the character representation of the current byte.

In line 140, the name of the string, the routine's starting line number and size, and a checksum value (ERRCHECK, to make sure the DATA was accurately entered) are read in from the DATA statements.

Choose and Open Output Device (lines 800–960) This section asks you on which storage device you want to store your routine strings. Once stored on either disk or cassette, they can be merged into any program with the ENTER command. If you have a disk drive, type D (or D2 if you want to use your second drive), and type C if you want to use your cassette recorder. If the E option is selected, the screen will clear and the routine will be printed on the screen. If you enter a non-existent device, you will have another chance to input a valid response.

Begin Printout (lines 160–310)   This is where all the work is done. On line 170, the first line which contains the DIM statement for the string is printed out. In line 180, STRSTART (String Start) is set to the position of the next open string character as saved in STRPNTR (String Pointer). STREND (String End) points to the last string character on the next line which is 89 characters later (there are a maximum of 90 characters per line). A check is made to see whether STRSTART is larger than the number of bytes in the routine (SIZE). Then the LINE number is incremented by 10 (line 190) and the heading for the first string line is printed (line 200).

Next, the loop is started. START keeps track of the number of bytes read. BYTETOT keeps a running total of all bytes read to make sure that the final sum matches the value stored in ERRCHECK. If the user wants to display the strings on the screen, a subroutine at lines 50–80 is called. It checks for cursor or screen control characters and, if any are found, causes the ESCape character to be printed on the screen first (delayed mode). (Note: to enter the ESC character into the string in line 80, you must press the **ESC** key twice.)

Lines 260–270 set the position of quotes and end-of-line characters for later printout. If one of these characters has been discovered, a space is temporarily stored in the proper position of the string. Line 290 sends the program back for the next line of characters.

Verify Accuracy of Data (lines 400–410)   These lines check for any errors which may have been made during entry. If you receive an error message here, all DATA must be rechecked. First count the number of bytes in each DATA statement to make sure it's correct. If you get an ERROR6, then you left out some bytes.

Insert Quotes and End-Of-Line Character (lines 500–650)   These lines will print out any special characters found using the CHR$ function. For example, if the thirty-first byte was a 34 (quotation mark) then the following line might be printed to the output device:

```
11730 ROUTINE$(31,31)=CHR$(34)
```

As it turned out, none of our routines contain either a 34 or a 155.

Memory Fill Routine Data (lines 29000–29030)   This is where we placed the byte data for the MFILL routine. Line 29010 contains the name of the routine, its starting line number, the number of bytes the routine contains, and the checksum value. Each line which follows receives 25 byte values until there are no bytes left. If the program tells you that you have made a mistake in entering this data, this makes it easier to check that each line contains the correct number of bytes.

Using the Program   The operation of this program is very simple. If you have a disk drive, type D (or D2 if you want to use your second drive). The section of program code will be written to your disk and automatically named (with the routine's name). When you are ready to merge the routine into a BASIC program, first load your program into memory (or type NEW if starting from scratch), and then type:

ENTER "D:name.STR"

where *name* is the string name of your routine, MFILL in this case. The ENTER command tells the computer that information will be coming into memory from the following device instead of from the keyboard.

To use with a cassette recorder, press C when prompted. You will hear two beeps from the computer. This means you are to press the PLAY and RECORD buttons on your recorder and then press RETURN. You will hear a high pitched tone from your television speaker, then some distorted sounds (the routine). To merge the routine into a program, use the command:

ENTER "C:"

Programs aren't stored with names on cassette so you must keep track of their location with the tape counter.

If you want to use the screen option, either to watch the routine being written out or because you don't want to use a disk or cassette, choose option E. The screen will clear and you will see the lines being formed. By positioning your cursor over the first line, and pressing RETURN for each statement, you can enter each line into a BASIC program. If you haven't first typed NEW, these lines will be merged into the String Loader program currently in memory.

Here are screen photos of a sample run of this program using the E option for screen output.

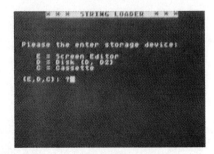

a)

(continued)

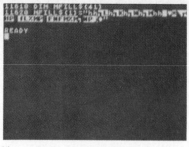

b)

Figure D.2: Screen photos of String Loader program sample run.

Appendix E

Complete List of Parameter Table Entries for Black Box Routines

VARIABLE NAME	OFFSET FROM PARAMBASE	ADDRESS (DECIMAL)	DESCRIPTION
PARAMBASE		1024	Start of Parameter area
PMBAS	0	1024	Page address of Player 0 (hi byte)
PMBUF	1	1025,1026	Low and High bytes of Player Buffer
INITANIMATE	3	1027	Flag to initialize ANIMATE
INITAUTOMOVE	4	1028	Flag to Initialize AUTOMOVE
SCRLINIT	5	1029	POKE 1 to turn on routine, 0 off
HPLR(0)	6	1030	Player 0 Horizontal Shadow Register
HPLR(1)	7	1031	Player 1 Horizontal Shadow Register
HPLR(2)	8	1032	Player 2 Horizontal Shadow Register
HPLR(3)	9	1033	Player 3 Horizontal Shadow Register
VPLR(0)	10	1034	Player 0 Vertical Shadow Register
VPLR(1)	11	1035	Player 1 Vertical Shadow Register
VPLR(2)	12	1036	Player 2 Vertical Shadow Register
VPLR(3)	13	1037	Player 3 Vertical Shadow Register
RATE(0)	14	1038	Player 0 Animation Rate Shadow Reg.
RATE(1)	15	1039	Player 1 Animation Rate Shadow Reg.
RATE(2)	16	1040	Player 2 Animation Rate Shadow Reg.
RATE(3)	17	1041	Player 3 Animation Rate Shadow Reg.
FRMLSTPTR(0)	18	1042,1043	Player 0 Pointer to Frame List
FRMLSTPTR(1)	20	1044,1045	Player 1 Pointer to Frame List
FRMLSTPTR(2)	22	1046,1047	Player 2 Pointer to Frame List
FRMLSTPTR(3)	24	1048,1049	Player 3 Pointer to Frame List
SCRLADR	26	1050,1051	Low and High bytes of scrolling window
SCRLLEN	28	1052,1053	Widths of scrolling window in bytes
SCRLCLK	30	1054	Color clocks per mode line byte -1
SCRLSTEP	31	1055	Step size to scroll each jiffy
MOVERATE(0)	32	1056	Player 0 Horizontal Velocity
MOVERATE(1)	33	1057	Player 1 Horizontal Velocity
MOVERATE(2)	34	1058	Player 2 Horizontal Velocity
MOVERATE(3)	35	1059	Player 3 Horizontal Velocity
DLIADR	36	1060,1061	Low and High bytes of DLI color table

The following addresses are read-only addresses — don't change their values:

PLR0X	38	1062	Player 0 Horizontal Position
PLR1X	39	1063	Player 1 Horizontal Position
PLR2X	40	1064	Player 2 Horizontal Position
PLR3X	41	1065	Player 3 Horizontal Position
FLPOS0	62	1086	Player 0 Frame List Position
FLPOS1	63	1087	Player 1 Frame List Position
FLPOS2	64	1088	Player 2 Frame List Position
FLPOS3	65	1089	Player 3 Frame List Position

CONTROL BITS FOR ROUTINES

In the following tables, X means that bit is not used.

PMOVER

Used when routine is called: TEMP=USR(PMOVER,FLAG)

					Bits of FLAG *byte*				
Bit Number	*X*	*X*	*X*	*X*	*3*	*2*	*1*	*0*	
Bit Value:					*8*	*4*	*2*	*1*	
FLAG for Player #:					3	2	1	0	

EXAMPLES

					FLAG **VALUE**
Move Player 1 only	0	0	1	0	= 2
Move Players 0, 2 & 3	1	1	0	1	= 13
Move all Players	1	1	1	1	= 15

ANIMATE

Used to POKE into INITANIMATE for "Ready" signal

				Bits of FLAG *byte*					
Bit Number:	*7*	*X*	*X*	*4*	*3*	*2*	*1*	*0*	
Bit Value:	*128*			*16*	*8*	*4*	*2*	*1*	
Resume Animation	1								
Modify Frame Rate only				1					
FLAG for Player #:					3	2	1	0	

EXAMPLES

							FLAG **VALUE**
Begin Animation, Players 0 & 1	0		0	0	0	1	1	= 3
Modify Frame Rate, Players 2 & 3	0		1	1	1	0	0	= 28
Halt All Animation	0		0	0	0	0	0	= 0
Resume All Animation	1		0	0	0	0	0	= 128

AUTOMOVE

Used to POKE into INITAUTOMOVE for ''Ready'' signal

				Bits of FLAG *byte*				
Bit Number:	7	X	X	X	3	2	1	0
Bit Value:	128				8	4	2	1
Resume Player Motion	1							
FLAG for Player #:					3	2	1	0

EXAMPLES

							FLAG **VALUE**
Begin Player Motion							
Players 0 & 1	0	0	0	1	1		= 3
Halt All Motion	0	0	0	0	0		= 0
Resume All Motion	1	0	0	0	0		= 128

Appendix F

Source Code Listings of Assembly Language Routines

For those Assembly Language programmers among our readers, we have included the complete source listings of our ''black box'' routines. They contain enough comments to make them fairly clear. Feel free to use all or part of them in your own Assembly Language programs.

Notice that there are two versions of MFILL. Version 1 was written for ATARI BASIC and is the one included in all of our programs. Version 2 will work for either ATARI BASIC or ATARI Microsoft BASIC. To use with Microsoft BASIC, just change the value in line 280 from 1 to 0.

All the other routines will work with *either* BASIC. In PMOVER, change the value in line 670 from 1 to 0 for Microsoft BASIC. The rest will run in Microsoft without any changes.

```
            10 ;   MFILL     ver. 1
            20 ;
            30 ; COPYRIGHT (C) 1982 BY DAVID FOX AND MITCHELL WAITE
            40 ;
0000        0100            .TITLE "CLK-MFILL1.ASM;v01.00,810907-820407"
0000        0110            .PAGE "Memory Fill Routine"
            0120 ;
            0130 ; BY COREY L. KOSAK
            0140 ;
            0150 ; Called from BASIC with TEMP=USR(MFILL,START,LEN,BYTE)
            0160 ;
            0170 ; THIS IS THE ATARI BASIC VERSION (USE ver.2 WITH MBASIC)
0000        0180        *=     $600
00CB        0190 LO     =     $CB        ;POINTER TO DATA
00CC        0200 HI     =     $CC
00CD        0210 LENLO  =     $CD        ;LENGTH IN BYTES
00CE        0220 LENHI  =     $CE
0600 68     0230 MFILL  PLA              ;REMOVE STACK BIAS
0601 68     0240        PLA              ;ADDRESS...
0602 85CC   0250        STA   HI         ;HI
0604 68     0260        PLA
0605 85CB   0270        STA   LO         ;LO
0607 68     0280        PLA              ;LENGTH...
0608 85CE   0290        STA   LENHI      ;HI
```

```
060A 68      0300           PLA
060B 85CD    0310           STA  LENLO       ;LO
060D 68      0320           PLA              ;BYTE TO FILL HI (SHOULD BE ZERO - SO IGNORE IT)
060E 68      0330           PLA              ;DATA
060F A000    0340           LDY  #$00
0611 AA      0350           TAX              ;SAVE FILL BYTE IN X-REG
0612 8A      0360 LOOP      TXA              ;AND TRANSFER IT BACK
0613 91CB    0370           STA  (LO),Y      ;STORE BYTE
0615 C8      0380           INY              ;BUMP POINTER
0616 D002    0390           BNE  OK          ;DID IT ROLL OVER?
0618 E6CC    0400           INC  HI          ;YES, INC HI BYTE
061A A5CD    0410 OK        LDA  LENLO       ;DECREMENT LENGTH BYTES
061C D002    0420           BNE  OK2
061E C6CE    0430           DEC  LENHI
0620 C6CD    0440 OK2       DEC  LENLO
0622 A5CD    0450           LDA  LENLO       ;DOES LENGTH=0?
0624 05CE    0460           ORA  LENHI       ;......?
0626 D0EA    0470           BNE  LOOP        ;NO, GO BACK FOR MORE
0628 60      0480 DONE      RTS              ;LEAVE.


             10 ;  MFILL    ver. 2
             20 ;
             30 ; COPYRIGHT (C) 1982 BY DAVID FOX AND MITCHELL WAITE
             40 ;
0000         0100           .TITLE "CLK-MFILL.ASM;v02.00,810907-810907"
0000         0110           .PAGE "Memory Fill Routine"
             0120 ;
             0130 ; BY COREY L. KOSAK
             0140 ;
             0150 ; This version will work in both MBASIC and Atari BASIC.  To use,
             0160 ; execute the following lines from within BASIC where START is
             0170 ; the first address to fill:
             0180 ;   POKE START,LENLO   ;REM Low byte of length (number of bytes to fill)
             0190 ;   POKE START+1,LENHI ;REM High byte of length
             0200 ;   POKE START+2,BYTE  ;REM Byte value to fill
             0210 ;   TEMP=USR(MFILL,START);REM Call routine
             0220 ;
             0230 ;
             0240 ; B=$4000,FREL
             0250 ;
4000         0260 BASE      =    $4000
             0270 ;
0001         0280 ABASIC    =    1           ;0=MBASIC, 1=ATARI BASIC
             0290 ;
0000         0300 MEQU      .IF  ABASIC @AEQU
             0310 ;
             0320 ARG=$E3
             0330 LEN=$E0
             0340 ;
0000         0350 AEQU      .IF  1-ABASIC @PROG
             0360 ;
00CB         0370 ARG       =    $CB         ; TEMP
```

```
06FE        0380 LEN      =     $6FE
            0390 ;
0000        0400 PROG     *=    BASE
            0410 ;
            0420 START
4000        0430          .IF   1-ABASIC @NOSAVE
4000 68     0440          PLA
4001 68     0450          PLA
4002 85CC   0460          STA   ARG+1
4004 68     0470          PLA
4005 85CB   0480          STA   ARG
            0490 ;
            0500 NOSAVE
4007 A002   0510          LDY   #$02
            0520 LOOP2
4009 B1CB   0530          LDA   (ARG),Y
400B 99FD06 0540          STA   LEN-1,Y
400E 88     0550          DEY
400F D0F8   0560          BNE   LOOP2
4011 B1CB   0570          LDA   (ARG),Y
            0580 ;
            0590 LOOP
4013 91CB   0600          STA   (ARG),Y
4015 AA     0610          TAX
```
CLK-MFILL.ASM;v02.00,810907-810907
Memory Fill Routine

```
4016 ADFE06 0620          LDA   LEN
4019 D003   0630          BNE   OK
401B CEFF06 0640          DEC   LEN+1
            0650 OK
401E CEFE06 0660          DEC   LEN
4021 ADFE06 0670          LDA   LEN
4024 0DFF06 0680          ORA   LEN+1
4027 F008   0690          BEQ   DONE
4029 8A     0700          TXA
402A C8     0710          INY
402B D0E6   0720          BNE   LOOP
402D E6CC   0730          INC   ARG+1
402F D0E2   0740          BNE   LOOP
            0750 ;
            0760 DONE
4031 60     0770          RTS
            0780 ;
4032        0790          .END


            10 ;   PMOVER
            20 ;
            30 ; COPYRIGHT (C) 1982 BY DAVID FOX AND MITCHELL WAITE
            40 ;
0000        0100          .TITLE "CLK-PMOVER.ASM;v02.10-810713,820620"
0000        0110          .PAGE "Player Mover Routine"
            0120 ;
```

```
                0130 ;BY COREY L. KOSAK
                3140 ;
                0150 ;B=$4000,FREL
                0160 ;
4000            0170 BASE      =     $4000
                0180 ;
0000            0190            *=    $400
                0200 ;
                0210 ;CASBUF DATABASE EQUATES
                0220 ;
0400            0230 PMBAS     *=    *+1        ;HIBYTE OF PLAYER MISSILE AREA (LOBYTE EQUALS 0)
0401            0240 PMBUF     *=    *+2        ;ADDRESS OF 128 BYTE BUFFER (FOR PMOVER)
0403            0250 ANIMINIT  *=    *+1        ;INIT LOCATION FOR ANIMATE
0404            0260 AUTOINIT  *=    *+1        ;INIT LOCATION FOR AUTOMOVE
0405            0270 SCRLINIT  *=    *+1        ;INIT LOCATION FOR SCROLLER
0406            0280 HPLR      *=    *+4        ;PLAYERS 0-3 X COORDINATE (FOR PMOVER)
040A            0290 VPLR      *=    *+4        ;PLRS 0-3 Y COORD (FOR PMOVER)
040E            0300 RATE      *=    *+4        ;PLRS 0-3 RATE (FOR ANIMATE)
0412            0310 FLSTPTR   *=    *+8        ;PLRS 0-3 FRAME LIST POINTERS (FOR ANIMATE)
041A            0320 SCRLADR   *=    *+2        ;SCREEN ADDRESS (FOR SCROLL)
041C            0330 SCRLLEN   *=    *+2        ;LINE LENGTH OF SCROLLED AREA (FOR SCROLL)
041E            0340 SCRLCLK   *=    *+1        ;COLOR CLOCKS IN SCREEN BYTE (FOR SCROLL)
041F            0350 SCRLSTEP  *=    *+1        ;SCROLL STEP (FOR SCROLL)
0420            0360 MOVERATE  *=    *+4        ;PLRS 0-3 HORIZONTAL STEP (FOR AUTOMOVE)
0424            0370 DLIADR    *=    *+2        ;ADDRESS OF COLOR TABLE
                0380 ;
                0390 ;*LOCAL* DATABASE EQUATES
                0400 ; THESE LOCATIONS ARE *LOCAL* TO THE ROUTINES
                0410 ; AND SHOULD *NOT* BE MODIFIED BY THE HOST PROGRAM
                0420 ;
0426            0430 O0X       *=    *+4        ;PLRS 0-3 X COORDINATE
042A            0440 O0Y       *=    *+4        ;PLRS 0-3 Y COORD
042E            0450 ORATE0    *=    *+4        ;PLRS 0-3 FRAME CHANGE RATE
0432            0460 OADR0     *=    *+8        ;PLRS 0-3 FRAME LIST ADDRESS
043A            0470 TIMR0     *=    *+4        ;PLRS 0-3 COUNTDOWN TIMERS (HOW MANY JIFFIES UNTIL FRAME CHANGE)
043E            0480 POS0      *=    *+4        ;PLRS 0-3 FRAME LIST POSITION
0442            0490 OSADR     *=    *+2        ;SCREEN ADDRESS FOR SCROLLER
0444            0500 CPOS      *=    *+2        ;COARSE SCROLL POSITION FOR SCROLLER (0-LINELEN)
0446            0510 FPOS      *=    *+1        ;FINE SCROLL POSITION (0-7)
0447            0520 OXSTEP0   *=    *+4        ;PLRS 0-3 HORIZONTAL STEP
044B            0530 DLIPOS    *=    *+1        ;CURRENT POSITION IN COLOR TABLE
044C            0540 PM1       *=    *+1        ;4 LOCATIONS RESERVED FOR PMOVER
044D            0550 PM2       *=    *+1
044E            0560 PM3       *=    *+1
044F            0570 PM4       *=    *+1
0450            0580 EX1       *=    *+1        ;4 LOCATIONS RESERVED FOR ANIMATE, AUTOMOVE, SCROLL, AND MFILL
0451            0590 EX2       *=    *+1
0452            0600 EX3       *=    *+1
0453            0610 EX4       *=    *+1
```

CLK-PMOVER.ASM;v02.10-810713,820620
Player Mover Routine

```
0454            0620 PMSAVE    *=    *+5        ;ZERO PAGE SAVE AREA FOR PMOVER
0459            0630 ZSAVE     *=    *+4        ;ZERO PAGE SAVE AREA FOR ALL OTHER ROUTINES
```

```
            0640 ;
D000        0650 HPOSP0   =    $D000
E462        0660 XITVBV   =    $E462
0001        0670 ABASIC   =    1                ;1=ATARI BASIC, 0=MBASIC
            0680 ;
00E0        0690 ZERO     =    $E0
00E4        0700 ONE      =    $E4
00E3        0710 ARG      =    $E3
00E2        0720 TEMP     =    $E2
            0730 ;
045D        0740          *=   BASE
            0750 ;
            0760 START
4000 B8     0770          CLV
4001 5010   0780          BVC  START1           ;SKIP OVER VBLNK EXIT ROUTINE
            0790 ;
            0800 EXIT
4003 4C62E4 0810          JMP  XITVBV           ;RETURN FROM INTERRUPT
            0820 ;
            0830 VBINT
4006 A203   0840          LDX  #$03             ;MOVE PLAYER X COORDINATES
            0850 LOOP4
4008 BD2604 0860          LDA  00X,X            ;INTO
400B 9D00D0 0870          STA  HPOSP0,X         ;HARDWARE REGISTERS
400E CA     0880          DEX
400F 10F7   0890          BPL  LOOP4
4011 30F0   0900          BMI  EXIT             ;LEAVE.
            0910 ;
            0920 START1
4013        0930          .IF  1-ABASIC @NOSAVE
4013 A206   0940          LDX  #$06             ;SAVE ZERO PAGE LOCATIONS (NOT NECESSARY FOR MBASIC)
            0950 LOOP6
4015 B5DF   0960          LDA  ZERO-1,X
4017 9D5304 0970          STA  PMSAVE-1,X
401A CA     0980          DEX
401B D0F8   0990          BNE  LOOP6
401D 68     1000          PLA                   ;NUMBER OF PARAMS (MUST BE 1)
401E 68     1010          PLA                   ;HI BYTE - DISCARD
401F 68     1020          PLA                   ;LO BYTE
4020 85E3   1030          STA  ARG              ;PUT IN 'ARG'
            1040 NOSAVE
            1050 ;
4022 A5E3   1060          LDA  ARG
4024 85E2   1070          STA  TEMP
4026 AC0404 1080          LDY  AUTOINIT         ;SAVE OLD PARAMETER
4029 A200   1090          LDX  #$00
402B 8E0404 1100          STX  AUTOINIT         ;DISABLE AUTOMOVE SO PLAYERS AREN'T MOVED OUT OF SYNC
402E 46E2   1110 LOOP7    LSR  TEMP
4030 9006   1120          BCC  NOMOVE
4032 BD0604 1130          LDA  HPLR,X
```

CLK-PMOVER.ASM;v02.10-810713,820620

Player Mover Routine

```
4035 9D2604 1140          STA  00X,X
```

```
              1150 NOMOVE
4038 E8       1160          INX
4039 E004     1170          CPX   #$04
403B D0F1     1180          BNE   LOOP7
403D 8C0404   1190          STY   AUTOINIT    ;RE-ENABLE AUTOMOVE
              1200 ;
4040 A200     1210          LDX   #$00
4042 86E0     1220          STX   ZERO        ;'ZERO' IS A POINTER TO
4044 AD0004   1230          LDA   PMBAS       ;PLAYER 0
4047 85E1     1240          STA   ZERO+1
4049 AD0104   1250          LDA   PMBUF       ;'ONE' IS A POINTER
404C 85E4     1260          STA   ONE         ;TO HOST PROGRAM'S
404E AD0204   1270          LDA   PMBUF+1     ;TEMPORARY BUFFER
4051 85E5     1280          STA   ONE+1
              1290 ;
              1300 ; HERE WE DISABLE ANIMATE SO IT DOESN'T DO BIZARRE
              1310 ; THINGS TO OUR PLAYERS WHILE WE'RE MOVING THEM
              1320 ;
4053 AD0304   1330          LDA   ANIMINIT    ;REMEMBER ANIMATE'S STATUS
4056 85E2     1340          STA   TEMP        ;STORE IN TEMP
4058 8E0304   1350          STX   ANIMINIT    ;TELL ANIMATE TO HALT (X STILL EQUALS 0)
              1360 ;
              1370 LOOP
405B 46E3     1380          LSR   ARG         ;GET NEXT PLAYER'S BIT INTO CARRY
405D B01E     1390          BCS   DOIT        ;IF IT'S A ONE, MOVE PLAYER
              1400 NEXT
405F A5E0     1410          LDA   ZERO        ;ADD $80 TO 'ZERO' TO
4061 4980     1420          EOR   #$80        ;MOVE TO NEXT PLAYER
4063 85E0     1430          STA   ZERO
4065 D002     1440          BNE   INC
4067 E6E1     1450          INC   ZERO+1
              1460 INC
4069 E8       1470          INX               ;INCREMENT PLAYER NUMBER
406A E004     1480          CPX   #$04        ;DONE WITH ALL 4 PLAYERS?
406C D0ED     1490          BNE   LOOP        ;NO, LOOP
406E A5E2     1500          LDA   TEMP        ;RESTORE ANIMINIT BYTE TO
4070 8D0304   1510          STA   ANIMINIT    ;WHAT IT WAS ORIGINALLY
4073 E8       1520          INX               ;SET X TO 5
              1530 LOOP5
4074          1540          .IF   1-ABASIC @NOREST
4074 BD5404   1550          LDA   PMSAVE,X    ;RESTORE ZERO PAGE TEMPORARIES
4077 95E0     1560          STA   ZERO,X
4079 CA       1570          DEX
407A 10F8     1580          BPL   LOOP5
              1590 NOREST
407C 60       1600          RTS               ;BACK TO BASIC
              1610 ;
              1620 DOIT
407D A07F     1630          LDY   #$7F        ;MOVE PLAYER INTO TEMPORARY BUFFER
              1640 LOOP2
407F B1E0     1650          LDA   (ZERO),Y
```

CLK-PMOVER.ASM;v02.10-810713,820620
Player Mover Routine

```
4081 91E4  1660          STA   (ONE),Y
4083 88    1670          DEY               ;NEXT BYTE, ARE WE DONE?
4084 10F9  1680          BPL   LOOP2       ;NO, LOOP,
4086 8E4C04 1690         STX   PM1         ;SAVE X-REG
4089 BD2A04 1700         LDA   OOY,X       ;THIS GNARLED MESS OF CODE ENDS UP WITH
408C 48    1710          PHA               ;THE "DESTINATION" COORDINATE IN THE
408D BD0A04 1720         LDA   VPLR,X      ;X-REG, THE "SOURCE" Y COORDINATE IN
4090 9D2A04 1730         STA   OOY,X       ;THE Y-REG, AND MOVES THE DESTINATION
4093 A8    1740          TAY               ;Y COORDINATE INTO THE SOURCE Y
4094 68    1750          PLA               ;COORDINATE LOCATION
4095 AA    1760          TAX
4096 8E4D04 1770         STX   PM2
           1780 LOOP3
4099 8C4E04 1790         STY   PM3         ;SAVE Y-REG
409C 8A    1800          TXA               ;TRANSFER X-REG TO Y-REG
409D A8    1810          TAY
409E B1E4  1820          LDA   (ONE),Y     ;GET DATA BACK FROM BUFFER
40A0 AC4E04 1830         LDY   PM3         ;RESTORE Y-REG
40A3 91E0  1840          STA   (ZERO),Y    ;STORE DATA IN PLAYER IN NEW SPOT
40A5 C8    1850          INY               ;NEXT BYTE
40A6 1002  1860          BPL   OK          ;DID THE Y-REG HIT $80?
40A8 A000  1870          LDY   #$00        ;SET IT BACK TO 0.
           1880 OK
40AA E8    1890          INX
40AB 1002  1900          BPL   OK2         ;DID THE X-REG HIT $80?
40AD A200  1910          LDX   #$00        ;SET IT BACK TO 0
           1920 OK2
40AF EC4D04 1930         CPX   PM2         ;HAVE WE COPIED ALL 128 BYTES?
40B2 D0E5  1940          BNE   LOOP3       ;NO, COPY MORE
40B4 AE4C04 1950         LDX   PM1         ;RESTORE X-REG
40B7 B8    1960          CLV               ;BRANCH BACK TO 'NEXT' TO
40B8 50A5  1970          BVC   NEXT        ;MOVE ANOTHER PLAYER
           1980 ;
40BA       1990          .END
```

```
           10 ;   ANIMATE
           20 ;
           30 ; COPYRIGHT (C) 1982 BY DAVID FOX AND MITCHELL WAITE
           40 ;
0000       0100          .TITLE "CLK-ANIMATE.ASM;v01.05-810714,820619"
0000       0110          .PAGE "Interrupt-driven Player Animater"
           0120 ;
           0130 ; BY COREY L. KOSAK
           0140 ;
           0150 ; B=$4000,FREL
           0160 ;
4000       0170 BASE     =     $4000
           0180 ;
0000       0190          x=    $400
           0200 ;
```

```
              0210 ;CASBUF DATABASE EQUATES
              0220 ;
0400          0230 PMBAS     x=    x+1       ;HIBYTE OF PLAYER MISSILE AREA (LOBYTE EQUALS 0)
0401          0240 PMBUF     x=    x+2       ;ADDRESS OF 128 BYTE BUFFER (FOR PMOVER)
0403          0250 ANIMINIT  x=    x+1       ;INIT LOCATION FOR ANIMATE
0404          0260 AUTOINIT  x=    x+1       ;INIT LOCATION FOR AUTOMOVE
0405          0270 SCRLINIT  x=    x+1       ;INIT LOCATION FOR SCROLLER
0406          0280 HPLR      x=    x+4       ;PLAYERS 0-3 X COORDINATE (FOR PMOVER)
040A          0290 VPLR      x=    x+4       ;PLRS 0-3 Y COORD (FOR PMOVER)
040E          0300 RATE      x=    x+4       ;PLRS 0-3 RATE (FOR ANIMATE)
0412          0310 FLSTPTR   x=    x+8       ;PLRS 0-3 FRAME LIST POINTERS (FOR ANIMATE)
041A          0320 SCRLADR   x=    x+2       ;SCREEN ADDRESS (FOR SCROLL)
041C          0330 SCRLLEN   x=    x+2       ;LINE LENGTH OF SCROLLED AREA (FOR SCROLL)
041E          0340 SCRLCLK   x=    x+1       ;COLOR CLOCKS IN SCREEN BYTE (FOR SCROLL)
041F          0350 SCRLSTEP  x=    x+1       ;SCROLL STEP (FOR SCROLL)
0420          0360 MOVERATE  x=    x+4       ;PLRS 0-3 HORIZONTAL STEP (FOR AUTOMOVE)
0424          0370 DLIADR    x=    x+2       ;ADDRESS OF COLOR TABLE
              0380 ;
              0390 ;xLOCALx DATABASE EQUATES
              0400 ; THESE LOCATIONS ARE xLOCALx TO THE ROUTINES
              0410 ; AND SHOULD xNOTx BE MODIFIED BY THE HOST PROGRAM
              0420 ;
0426          0430 OOX       x=    x+4       ;PLRS 0-3 X COORDINATE
042A          0440 OOY       x=    x+4       ;PLRS 0-3 Y COORD
042E          0450 ORATE0    x=    x+4       ;PLRS 0-3 FRAME CHANGE RATE
0432          0460 OADR0     x=    x+8       ;PLRS 0-3 FRAME LIST ADDRESS
043A          0470 TIMR0     x=    x+4       ;PLRS 0-3 COUNTDOWN TIMERS (HOW MANY JIFFIES UNTIL FRAME CHANGE
043E          0480 POS0      x=    x+4       ;PLRS 0-3 FRAME LIST POSITION
0442          0490 OSADR     x=    x+2       ;SCREEN ADDRESS FOR SCROLLER
0444          0500 CPOS      x=    x+2       ;COARSE SCROLL POSITION FOR SCROLLER (0-LINELEN)
0446          0510 FPOS      x=    x+1       ;FINE SCROLL POSITION (0-7)
0447          0520 OXSTEP0   x=    x+4       ;PLRS 0-3 HORIZONTAL STEP
044B          0530 DLIPOS    x=    x+1       ;CURRENT POSITION IN COLOR TABLE
044C          0540 PM1       x=    x+1       ;4 LOCATIONS RESERVED FOR PMOVER
044D          0550 PM2       x=    x+1
044E          0560 PM3       x=    x+1
044F          0570 PM4       x=    x+1
0450          0580 EX1       x=    x+1       ;4 LOCATIONS RESERVED FOR ANIMATE, AUTOMOVE, SCROLL, AND MFILL
0451          0590 EX2       x=    x+1
0452          0600 EX3       x=    x+1
0453          0610 EX4       x=    x+1
CLK-ANIMATE.ASM;v01.05-810714,820619
Interrupt-driven Player Animater

0454          0620 PMSAVE    x=    x+5       ;ZERO PAGE SAVE AREA FOR PMOVER
0459          0630 ZSAVE     x=    x+4       ;ZERO PAGE SAVE AREA FOR ALL OTHER ROUTINES
              0640 ;
D000          0650 HPOSP0    =     $D000
E462          0660 XITVBV    =     $E462
              0670 ;
00E0          0680 ZERO      =     $E0
00E2          0690 ONE       =     $E2
              0700 ;
045D          0710           x=    BASE
```

```
                0720 ;
                0730 START
4000 B8         0740            CLV
4001 5003       0750            BVC   START1       ;SKIP OVER VBLANK EXIT ROUTINE.
                0760 ;
                0770 EXIT
4003 4C62E4     0780            JMP   XITVBV
                0790 ;
                0800 START1
4006 D8         0810            CLD                ;CLEAR DEC MODE FOR ATARI BASIC!
4007 A203       0820            LDX   #$03         ;SAVE ZERO PAGE TEMPS
                0830 LOOP4
4009 B5E0       0840            LDA   ZERO,X
400B 9D5904     0850            STA   ZSAVE,X
400E CA         0860            DEX
400F 10F8       0870            BPL   LOOP4
                0880 ;
4011 AD0304     0890            LDA   ANIMINIT     ;READ INIT BYTE
4014 F0ED       0900            BEQ   EXIT         ;IF IT'S ZERO, LEAVE.
4016 3048       0910            BMI   DOIT         ;IF > 127, OPERATE NORMALLY
                0920 ;
4018 0A         0930            ASL   A            ;GET '+16' BIT INTO '+128' BIT
4019 0A         0940            ASL   A
401A 0A         0950            ASL   A
401B 8D5004     0960            STA   EX1
                0970 ;
401E A200       0980            LDX   #$00         ;X=CURRENT PLAYER #
                0990 ;
                1000 LOOP
4020 4E0304     1010            LSR   ANIMINIT     ;PLAYER BIT SET?
4023 B010       1020            BCS   MOVE         ;YES, INITIALIZE PLAYER
4025 9002       1030            BCC   NEXT         ;SKIP OVER BUCKET-BRIGADE
                1040 ;
                1050 BBEXIT
4027 F0DA       1060            BEQ   EXIT
                1070 ;
                1080 NEXT
4029 E8         1090            INX                ;NEXT PLAYER
402A E004       1100            CPX   #$04         ;DONE?
402C D0F2       1110            BNE   LOOP         ;NO, LOOP
402E A980       1120            LDA   #$80         ;SET INIT BYTE TO
4030 8D0304     1130            STA   ANIMINIT     ;"ON"
```
CLK-ANIMATE.ASM;v01.05-810714,820619
Interrupt-driven Player Animater

```
                1140 ;
4033 D02B       1150            BNE   DOIT         ;UNCONDITIONAL BRANCH TO DOIT
                1160 ;
                1170 MOVE
4035 BD0E04     1180            LDA   RATE,X       ;DOES RATE=0?
4038 D002       1190            BNE   STORE        ;NO, STORE IT
403A A9FF       1200            LDA   #$FF         ;YES, CHANGE IT TO $FF
                1210 STORE
403C 9D2E04     1220            STA   ORATE0,X     ;MOVE PARAMS INTO LOCAL AREA
```

```
                 1230 ;
403F 8A          1240        TXA              ;MULTIPLY X BY 2
4040 0A          1250        ASL  A
4041 A8          1260        TAY              ;AND PUT INTO Y
4042 B91204 1270            LDA  FLSTPTR,Y    ;MOVE ADR INTO LOCAL AREA
4045 993204 1280            STA  OADR0,Y
4048 B91304 1290            LDA  FLSTPTR+1,Y
404B 993304 1300            STA  OADR0+1,Y
404E AD5004 1310            LDA  EX1          ;WAS '+16' BIT SET?
4051 30D6   1320            BMI  NEXT         ;YES, DON'T INITIALIZE FRAME #
4053 BD0E04 1330            LDA  RATE,X
4056 9D3A04 1340            STA  TIMR0,X
4059 A901   1350            LDA  #$01
405B 9D3E04 1360            STA  POS0,X
405E D0C9   1370            BNE  NEXT         ;UNCOND. BRANCH
                 1380 ;
                 1390 DOIT
4060 A900   1400            LDA  #$00         ;'ZERO' POINTS TO CURRENT
4062 85E0   1410            STA  ZERO         ;PLAYER
4064 AD0004 1420            LDA  PMBAS
4067 85E1   1430            STA  ZERO+1
                 1440 ;
4069 A200   1450            LDX  #$00         ;START WITH PLAYER #0
                 1460 LOOP2
406B BD2E04 1470            LDA  ORATE0,X     ;IS THIS A SPECIAL
406E F009   1480            BEQ  NEXT2
4070 C9FF   1490            CMP  #$FF         ;"RATE=0" PLAYER?
4072 F025   1500            BEQ  CHANGE2      ;YES, FILL PLAYER,
                 1510 ;
                 1520 NOTZERO
4074 DE3A04 1530            DEC  TIMR0,X      ;HAS TIME RUN OUT FOR THIS PLAYER?
4077 F019   1540            BEQ  CHANGEIT     ;YES, CHANGE FRAME
                 1550 ;
                 1560 NEXT2
4079 A5E0   1570            LDA  ZERO         ;POINT TO NEXT PLAYER
407B 4980   1580            EOR  #$80
407D 85E0   1590            STA  ZERO
407F D002   1600            BNE  INC
4081 E6E1   1610            INC  ZERO+1
                 1620 ;
                 1630 INC
4083 E8     1640            INX               ;MOVE TO NEXT PLAYER
4084 E004   1650            CPX  #$04         ;LAST PLAYER?
```

CLK-ANIMATE.ASM;v01.05-810714,820619
Interrupt-driven Player Animater

```
4086 D0E3   1660            BNE  LOOP2        ;NO, LOOP
                 1670 ;
                 1680 LOOP5
4088 BD5804 1690            LDA  ZSAVE-1,X    ;RESTORE ZERO PAGE LOCS
408B 95DF   1700            STA  ZERO-1,X
408D CA     1710            DEX
408E D0F8   1720            BNE  LOOP5
4090 F095   1730            BEQ  BBEXIT       ;UNCOND. BRANCH TO EXIT
```

```
              1740 ;
              1750 CHANGEIT
4092 BD2E04 1760          LDA   ORATE0,X    ;RESET TIMER
4095 C9FF   1770          CMP   #$FF
4097 D002   1780          BNE   NOTSPECIAL
              1790 CHANGE2
4099 A901   1800          LDA   #$01
              1810 NOTSPECIAL
409B 9D3A04 1820          STA   TIMR0,X
409E 8A     1830          TXA               ;SET Y=X*2
409F 0A     1840          ASL   A
40A0 A8     1850          TAY
40A1 B93204 1860          LDA   OADR0,Y     ;MOVE PLR ADDRESS
40A4 85E2   1870          STA   ONE         ;INTO 'ONE'
40A6 B93304 1880          LDA   OADR0+1,Y
40A9 85E3   1890          STA   ONE+1
              1900 ;
40AB FE3E04 1910          INC   POS0,X      ;INCREMENT POSITION IN TABLE
40AE BD3E04 1920          LDA   POS0,X
              1930 ZAPPO
40B1 A8     1940          TAY
40B2 B1E2   1950          LDA   (ONE),Y     ;GET FRAME #
40B4 D009   1960          BNE   OK          ;IF IT'S NON-ZERO, JUMP T 'OK'
40B6 A902   1970          LDA   #$02        ;RESET FRAME POSITION
40B8 9D3E04 1980          STA   POS0,X
40BB D0F4   1990          BNE   ZAPPO       ;UNCOND, BRANCH TO ZAPPO
              2000 BBNEXT2
40BD 50BA   2010          BVC   NEXT2       ;BUCKET-BRIGADE
              2020 ;
              2030 OK
40BF 8D5004 2040          STA   EX1         ;STORE FRAME # MINUS ONE.
40C2 CE5004 2050          DEC   EX1
40C5 A000   2060          LDY   #$00
40C7 B1E2   2070          LDA   (ONE),Y     ;PUT ADDRESS OF
40C9 48     2080          PHA               ;FRAME DATA
40CA C8     2090          INY               ;INTO 'ONE'
40CB B1E2   2100          LDA   (ONE),Y
40CD 85E3   2110          STA   ONE+1       ;STORE IT
40CF 68     2120          PLA
40D0 85E2   2130          STA   ONE
40D2 88     2140          DEY               ;SET Y TO ZERO
40D3 B1E2   2150          LDA   (ONE),Y     ;STORE FRAME HEIGHT
40D5 8D5104 2160          STA   EX2         ;FRAME HEIGHT
              2170 ;
```

CLK-ANIMATE.ASM;v01.05-810714,820619
Interrupt-driven Player Animater

```
              2180 ;PERFORM:
              2190 ;FRAMENUMBER TIMES HEIGHT + FRAME ADDRESS + 1
              2200 ;
40D8 A900   2210          LDA   #$00        ;THIS MULTIPLIES (FRAMENUMBER-1)xHEIGHT
40DA A008   2220          LDY   #$08
              2230 NEXTBIT
40DC 4E5004 2240          LSR   EX1         ;FRAMENUMBER
```

```
40DF 9004   2250           BCC  ALIGN
40E1 18     2260           CLC
40E2 6D5104 2270           ADC  EX2
            2280 ;
            2290 ALIGN
40E5 4A     2300           LSR  A
40E6 6E5204 2310           ROR  EX3
40E9 88     2320           DEY
40EA D0F0   2330           BNE  NEXTBIT
40EC A8     2340           TAY           ;HIBYTE OF RESULT INTO Y
            2350 ;
40ED AD5204 2360           LDA  EX3      ;LOBYTE OF RESULT IN A-REG
40F0 38     2370           SEC           ;+ 1
40F1 65E2   2380           ADC  ONE      ;+ FRAME ADDRESS
40F3 85E2   2390           STA  ONE
40F5 98     2400           TYA           ;NOW ADD THE HIBYTES
40F6 65E3   2410           ADC  ONE+1
40F8 85E3   2420           STA  ONE+1
40FA 8E5004 2430           STX  EX1      ;SAVE X
40FD BD2A04 2440           LDA  00Y,X    ;GET PLAYER Y COORD
4100 A8     2450           TAY           ;PUT IN Y-REG
4101 A200   2460           LDX  #$00
            2470 ;
            2480 LOOP3
4103 8C5204 2490           STY  EX3      ;SAVE Y
4106 8A     2500           TXA           ;MOVE X INTO Y
4107 A8     2510           TAY
4108 B1E2   2520           LDA  (ONE),Y  ;MOVE FRAME INTO PLAYER
410A AC5204 2530           LDY  EX3      ;RESTORE Y
410D 91E0   2540           STA  (ZERO),Y
410F C8     2550           INY
4110 E8     2560           INX
4111 EC5104 2570           CPX  EX2      ;HAVE WE COPIED ALL BYTES?
4114 D0ED   2580           BNE  LOOP3    ;NO, LOOP
            2590 ;
4116 AE5004 2600           LDX  EX1      ;RESTORE X
4119 BD2E04 2610           LDA  ORATE0,X
411C C9FF   2620           CMP  #$FF     ;IS RATE=$FF?
411E D003   2630           BNE  NOTFF
4120 FE2E04 2640           INC  ORATE0,X ;YES, SET RATE=0
            2650 NOTFF
4123 B8     2660           CLV
4124 5097   2670           BVC  BBNEXT2
            2680 ;
4126        2690           .END


            10 ;   AUTOMOVE
            20 ;
            30 ; COPYRIGHT (C) 1982 BY DAVID FOX AND MITCHELL WAITE
            40 ;
0000        0100           .TITLE "CLK-AUTOMOVE.ASM;v01.04-810724,820619"
0000        0110           .PAGE "Automatic Player Mover"
            0120 ;
```

```
             0130 ;BY COREY L. KOSAK
             0140 ;
             0150 ;B=$4000,FREL
             0160 ;
4000         0170 BASE      =     $4000
             0180 ;
0000         0190           x=    $400
             0200 ;
             0210 ;CASBUF DATABASE EQUATES
             0220 ;
0400         0230 PMBAS     x=    x+1          ;HIBYTE OF PLAYER MISSILE AREA (LOBYTE EQUALS 0)
0401         0240 PMBUF     x=    x+2          ;ADDRESS OF 128 BYTE BUFFER (FOR PMOVER)
0403         0250 ANIMINIT  x=    x+1          ;INIT LOCATION FOR ANIMATE
0404         0260 AUTOINIT  x=    x+1          ;INIT LOCATION FOR AUTOMOVE
0405         0270 SCRLINIT  x=    x+1          ;INIT LOCATION FOR SCROLLER
0406         0280 HPLR      x=    x+4          ;PLAYERS 0-3 X COORDINATE (FOR PMOVER)
040A         0290 VPLR      x=    x+4          ;PLRS 0-3 Y COORD (FOR PMOVER)
040E         0300 RATE      x=    x+4          ;PLRS 0-3 RATE (FOR ANIMATE)
0412         0310 FLSTPTR   x=    x+8          ;PLRS 0-3 FRAME LIST POINTERS (FOR ANIMATE)
041A         0320 SCRLADR   x=    x+2          ;SCREEN ADDRESS (FOR SCROLL)
041C         0330 SCRLLEN   x=    x+2          ;LINE LENGTH OF SCROLLED AREA (FOR SCROLL)
041E         0340 SCRLCLK   x=    x+1          ;COLOR CLOCKS IN SCREEN BYTE (FOR SCROLL)
041F         0350 SCRLSTEP  x=    x+1          ;SCROLL STEP (FOR SCROLL)
0420         0360 MOVERATE  x=    x+4          ;PLRS 0-3 HORIZONTAL STEP (FOR AUTOMOVE)
0424         0370 DLIADR    x=    x+2          ;ADDRESS OF COLOR TABLE
             0380 ;
             0390 ;xLOCALx DATABASE EQUATES
             0400 ; THESE LOCATIONS ARE xLOCALx TO THE ROUTINES
             0410 ; AND SHOULD xNOTx BE MODIFIED BY THE HOST PROGRAM
             0420 ;
0426         0430 OOX       x=    x+4          ;PLRS 0-3 X COORDINATE
042A         0440 OOY       x=    x+4          ;PLRS 0-3 Y COORD
042E         0450 ORATE0    x=    x+4          ;PLRS 0-3 FRAME CHANGE RATE
0432         0460 OADR0     x=    x+8          ;PLRS 0-3 FRAME LIST ADDRESS
043A         0470 TIMR0     x=    x+4          ;PLRS 0-3 COUNTDOWN TIMERS (HOW MANY JIFFIES UNTIL FRAME CHANGE)
043E         0480 POS0      x=    x+4          ;PLRS 0-3 FRAME LIST POSITION
0442         0490 OSADR     x=    x+2          ;SCREEN ADDRESS FOR SCROLLER
0444         0500 CPOS      x=    x+2          ;COARSE SCROLL POSITION FOR SCROLLER (0-LINELEN)
0446         0510 FPOS      x=    x+1          ;FINE SCROLL POSITION (0-7)
0447         0520 OXSTEP0   x=    x+4          ;PLRS 0-3 HORIZONTAL STEP
044B         0530 DLIPOS    x=    x+1          ;CURRENT POSITION IN COLOR TABLE
044C         0540 PM1       x=    x+1          ;4 LOCATIONS RESERVED FOR PMOVER
044D         0550 PM2       x=    x+1
044E         0560 PM3       x=    x+1
044F         0570 PM4       x=    x+1
0450         0580 EX1       x=    x+1          ;4 LOCATIONS RESERVED FOR ANIMATE, AUTOMOVE, SCROLL, AND MFILL
0451         0590 EX2       x=    x+1
0452         0600 EX3       x=    x+1
0453         0610 EX4       x=    x+1
CLK-AUTOMOVE.ASM;v01.04-810724,820619
Automatic Player Mover


0454         0620 PMSAVE    x=    x+5          ;ZERO PAGE SAVE AREA FOR PMOVER
0459         0630 ZSAVE     x=    x+4          ;ZERO PAGE SAVE AREA FOR ALL OTHER ROUTINES
```

```
            0640 ;
E462        0650 XITVBV    =     $E462
            0660 ;
00E0        0670 ZERO      =     $E0
00E2        0680 ONE       =     $E2
            0690 ;
045D        0700           *=    BASE
            0710 ;
            0720 START
4000 B8     0730           CLV
4001 5003   0740           BVC   START1
            0750 ;
            0760 EXIT
4003 4C62E4 0770           JMP   XITVBV
            0780 ;
            0790 START1
4006 D8     0800           CLD               ;CLEAR DECIMAL MODE!!!
4007 AD0404 0810           LDA   AUTOINIT    ;INIT BYTE SET?
400A F0F7   0820           BEQ   EXIT        ;NO, LEAVE
400C 3017   0830           BMI   MOVETHEM    ;NORMAL OPERATION IF >127
            0840 ;
400E A200   0850           LDX   #$00        ;START WITH PLAYER #0
            0860 LOOP
4010 4E0404 0870           LSR   AUTOINIT    ;IS THE BIT FOR THIS PLAYER SET?
4013 9006   0880           BCC   NEXT        ;NO, SKIP OVER UPDATE
4015 BD2004 0890           LDA   MOVERATE,X  ;MOVE PARAMS INTO LOCAL LOCATIONS
4018 9D4704 0900           STA   OXSTEP0,X
            0910 NEXT
401B E8     0920           INX
401C E004   0930           CPX   #$04        ;ARE WE ALL DONE?
401E D0F0   0940           BNE   LOOP        ;NO, SO LOOP
4020 A980   0950           LDA   #$80
4022 8D0404 0960           STA   AUTOINIT    ;SET INIT BYTE TO $80
            0970 ;
            0980 MOVETHEM
4025 A203   0990           LDX   #$03        ;START WITH PLAYER #3
            1000 LOOP2
4027 BD4704 1010           LDA   OXSTEP0,X   ;READ STEP
402A 4980   1020           EOR   #$80        ;REVERSE SIGN
402C 08     1030           PHP
402D 18     1040           CLC
402E 7D2604 1050           ADC   O0X,X       ;ADD STEP TO OLD XCOORD
4031 9005   1060           BCC   CCLEAR
            1070 ;
4033 28     1080           PLP
4034 300C   1090           BMI   OK          ;CARRY SET IS OK, IF STEP IS NEGATIVE
4036 1003   1100           BPL   BAD
            1110 ;
            1120 CCLEAR
4038 28     1130           PLP
```

CLK-AUTOMOVE.ASM;v01.04-810724,820619
Automatic Player Mover

```
4039 1007   1140           BPL   OK          ;CARRY CLEAR IS OK, IF STEP IS POSITIVE
```

```
              1150 ;
              1160 BAD
403B A980     1170          LDA  #$80        ;ZERO THE STEP. (STOP MOTION FOR THIS PLAYER)
403D 904704   1180          STA  OXSTEP0,X
4040 A900     1190          LDA  #$00        ;ZERO THE XCOORD OF THIS PLAYER
              1200 ;
              1210 OK
4042 902604   1220          STA  OOX,X       ;STORE XCOORD
4045 CA       1230          DEX              ;DO NEXT PLAYER
4046 10DF     1240          BPL  LOOP2       ;LAST PLAYER? NO, LOOP
4048 30B9     1250          BMI  EXIT        ;YES, LEAVE.
404A          1260          .END


                10 ;    SCROLL
                20 ;
                30 ; COPYRIGHT (C) 1982 BY DAVID FOX AND MITCHELL WAITE
                40 ;
0000          0100          .TITLE "CLK-SCROLL.ASM;v01.09-810719,820619"
0000          0110          .PAGE "Interrupt-driven Screen Scroller"
              0120 ;
              0130 ; BY COREY L. KOSAK
              0140 ;
              0150 ; B=$4000,FREL
              0160 ;
4000          0170 BASE    =       $4000
              0180 ;
0000          0190          x=      $400
              0200 ;
              0210 ; CASBUF DATABASE EQUATES
              0220 ;
0400          0230 PMBAS   x=  x+1            ;HIBYTE OF PLAYER MISSILE AREA (LOBYTE EQUALS 0)
0401          0240 PMBUF   x=  x+2            ;ADDRESS OF 128 BYTE BUFFER (FOR PMOVER)
0403          0250 ANIMINIT x= x+1            ;INIT LOCATION FOR ANIMATE
0404          0260 AUTOINIT x= x+1            ;INIT LOCATION FOR AUTOMOVE
0405          0270 SCRLINIT x= x+1            ;INIT LOCATION FOR SCROLLER
0406          0280 HPLR    x=  x+4            ;PLAYERS 0-3 X COORDINATE (FOR PMOVER)
040A          0290 VPLR    x=  x+4            ;PLRS 0-3 Y COORD (FOR PMOVER)
040E          0300 RATE    x=  x+4            ;PLRS 0-3 RATE (FOR ANIMATE)
0412          0310 FLSTPTR x=  x+8            ;PLRS 0-3 FRAME LIST POINTERS (FOR ANIMATE)
041A          0320 SCRLADR x=  x+2            ;SCREEN ADDRESS (FOR SCROLL)
041C          0330 SCRLLEN x=  x+2            ;LINE LENGTH OF SCROLLED AREA (FOR SCROLL)
041E          0340 SCRLCLK x=  x+1            ;COLOR CLOCKS IN SCREEN BYTE (FOR SCROLL)
041F          0350 SCRLSTEP x= x+1            ;SCROLL STEP (FOR SCROLL)
0420          0360 MOVERATE x= x+4            ;PLRS 0-3 HORIZONTAL STEP (FOR AUTOMOVE)
0424          0370 DLIADR  x=  x+2            ;ADDRESS OF COLOR TABLE
              0380 ;
              0390 ;xLOCALx DATABASE EQUATES
              0400 ; THESE LOCATIONS ARE xLOCALx TO THE ROUTINES
              0410 ; AND SHOULD xNOTx BE MODIFIED BY THE HOST PROGRAM
              0420 ;
0426          0430 OOX     x=  x+4            ;PLRS 0-3 X COORDINATE
042A          0440 OOY     x=  x+4            ;PLRS 0-3 Y COORD
042E          0450 ORATE0  x=  x+4            ;PLRS 0-3 FRAME CHANGE RATE
```

```
0432          0460 OADR0      X=    X+8      ;PLRS 0-3 FRAME LIST ADDRESS
043A          0470 TIMR0      X=    X+4      ;PLRS 0-3 COUNTDOWN TIMERS (HOW MANY JIFFIES UNTIL FRAME CHANGE)
043E          0480 POS0       X=    X+4      ;PLRS 0-3 FRAME LIST POSITION
0442          0490 OSADR      X=    X+2      ;SCREEN ADDRESS FOR SCROLLER
0444          0500 CPOS       X=    X+2      ;COARSE SCROLL POSITION FOR SCROLLER (0-SCRLLEN)
0446          0510 FPOS       X=    X+1      ;FINE SCROLL POSITION (0-7)
0447          0520 OXSTEP0    X=    X+4      ;PLRS 0-3 HORIZONTAL STEP
0448          0530 DLIPOS     X=    X+1      ;CURRENT POSITION IN COLOR TABLE
044C          0540 PM1        X=    X+1      ;4 LOCATIONS RESERVED FOR PMOVER
044D          0550 PM2        X=    X+1
044E          0560 PM3        X=    X+1
044F          0570 PM4        X=    X+1
0450          0580 EX1        X=    X+1      ;4 LOCATIONS RESERVED FOR ANIMATE, AUTOMOVE, SCROLL, AND MFILL
0451          0590 EX2        X=    X+1
0452          0600 EX3        X=    X+1
0453          0610 EX4        X=    X+1
CLK-SCROLL.ASM;v01.09-810719,820619
Interrupt-driven Screen Scroller

0454          0620 PMSAVE     X=    X+5      ;ZERO PAGE SAVE AREA FOR PMOVER
0459          0630 ZSAVE      X=    X+4      ;ZERO PAGE SAVE AREA FOR ALL OTHER ROUTINES
              0640 ;
E462          0650 XITVBV     =     $E462
D404          0660 HSCROLL    =     $D404
0230          0670 SDLSTL     =     $230
              0680 ;
00E0          0690 ZERO       =     $E0
00E2          0700 ONE        =     $E2
              0710 ;
045D          0720            X=    BASE
              0730 ;
              0740 START
4000 B8       0750            CLV
4001 5003     0760            BVC   START1       ;SKIP OVER VBLANK EXIT ROUTINE
              0770 ;
              0780 EXIT
4003 4C62E4   0790            JMP   XITVBV
              0800 ;
              0810 START1
4006 D8       0820            CLD                ;CLEAR DECIMAL MODE FOR ATARI BASIC!
4007 AD0504   0830            LDA   SCRLINIT     ;IS THE INIT BYTE SET?
400A F0F7     0840            BEQ   EXIT         ;NO, LEAVE
400C 1048     0850            BPL   BBINIT2      ;YES, INIT EVERYTHING
              0860 ;
400E A5E0     0870            LDA   ZERO         ;SAVE ZERO PAGE TEMPS
4010 8D5904   0880            STA   ZSAVE
4013 A5E1     0890            LDA   ZERO+1
4015 8D5A04   0900            STA   ZSAVE+1
4018 AD3002   0910            LDA   SDLSTL       ;MOVE DISPLAY LIST POINTER
401B 85E0     0920            STA   ZERO         ;INTO TEMPORARY POINTER
401D AD3102   0930            LDA   SDLSTL+1
4020 85E1     0940            STA   ZERO+1
              0950 ;
              0960 ; NOW WE SPLIT SCRLSTEP INTO A COARSE
```

```
              0970 ; AND FINE STEP, AND ALSO COMPUTE, VIA
              0980 ; SCRLCLK, THE NUMBER OF BYTES PER SCREEN LINE (IN WIDE PLAYFIELD)
              0990 ;
4022 AD1E04 1000        LDA  SCRLCLK   ;MOVE CLOCK VALUE TO EX1
4025 8D5004 1010        STA  EX1
4028 A9C0   1020        LDA  #$C0      ;BYTES PER MODE LINE
402A 8D5104 1030        STA  EX2
402D AD1F04 1040        LDA  SCRLSTEP  ;SHIFT OUT FINE SCROLL
4030 A000   1050        LDY  #$00      ;OFFSET IN SCREEN BYTE TABLE
              1060 CLOOP
4032 4E5004 1070        LSR  EX1       ;SHIFT RIGHT CLOCK VALUE
4035 9007   1080        BCC  CDONE     ;ANY BITS LEFT?
4037 4A     1090        LSR  A         ;YES, SHIFT SCROLL VALUE
4038 4E5104 1100        LSR  EX2       ;DIVIDE MODE LINE LENGTH BY 2
403B C8     1110        INY            ;AND BUMP POINTER
403C D0F4   1120        BNE  CLOOP     ;ALWAYS TAKEN
              1130 CDONE
```

CLK-SCROLL.ASM;v01.09-810719,820619
Interrupt-driven Screen Scroller

```
403E 8D5004 1140        STA  EX1       ;STORE COARSE STEP
              1150 ;
4041 AD1F04 1160        LDA  SCRLSTEP
4044 2D1E04 1170        AND  SCRLCLK   ;GET FINE STEP
              1180 ;
4047 18     1190        CLC
4048 6D4604 1200        ADC  FPOS      ;ADD CURRENT FINESCROLL VALUE
404B CD1E04 1210        CMP  SCRLCLK   ;DID IT GO OVER CLOCK VALUE?
404E F00E   1220        BEQ  OK        ;NOPE.
4050 900C   1230        BCC  OK        ;NOPE.
4052 B004   1240        BCS  INCIT     ;SKIP OVER BUCKET-BRIGADES
              1250 ;
              1260 BBEXIT2
4054 50AD   1270        BVC  EXIT
              1280 BBINIT2
4056 D059   1290        BNE  BBINIT
              1300 ;
              1310 INCIT
4058 EE5004 1320        INC  EX1       ;YES, INCREMENT COARSE STEP
405B 2D1E04 1330        AND  SCRLCLK   ;AND PUT FINE STEP IN RANGE
              1340 ;
              1350 OK
405E 8D4604 1360        STA  FPOS      ;STORE IN CURRENT SCROLL VALUE
4061 4D1E04 1370        EOR  SCRLCLK   ;HSCROLL REGISTER IS
4064 8D04D4 1380        STA  HSCROLL   ;'BACKWARDS'
              1390 ;
4067 AD5004 1400        LDA  EX1       ;GET COARSE SCROLL STEP
406A 18     1410        CLC
406B 6D4404 1420        ADC  CPOS      ;ADD CURRENT SCROLL VALUE
406E 8D4404 1430        STA  CPOS      ;AND STORE BACK
4071 9003   1440        BCC  OK4
4073 EE4504 1450        INC  CPOS+1
              1460 ;
              1470 OK4
```

```
4076 AD4404 1480          LDA  CPOS        ;ADD EX2+1 TO TEST FOR
4079 38   1490            SEC              ;END OF SCREEN
407A 6D5104 1500          ADC  EX2
407D 8D4404 1510          STA  CPOS
4080 9003 1520            BCC  OK5
4082 EE4504 1530          INC  CPOS+1
          1540 OK5
4085 AD4504 1550          LDA  CPOS+1
4088 CD1D04 1560          CMP  SCRLLEN+1   ;HAVE WE SCROLLED TO EDGE OF SCREEN?
408B 9028 1570            BCC  OK2         ;NO, WE'RE OK
408D D008 1580            BNE  RESET       ;YES, SET BACK TO BEGINNING
408F AD4404 1590          LDA  CPOS        ;MAYBE?
4092 CD1C04 1600          CMP  SCRLLEN
4095 901E 1610            BCC  OK2         ;NO, WE'RE OK
          1620 RESET
4097 A900 1630            LDA  #$00        ;SET POINTERS TO BEGINNING OF
4099 8D4404 1640          STA  CPOS        ;SCREEN LINE
409C 8D4504 1650          STA  CPOS+1
CLK-SCROLL.ASM;v01.09-810719,820619
Interrupt-driven Screen Scroller

409F 8D5004 1660          STA  EX1
40A2 AD1A04 1670          LDA  SCRLADR     ;MOVE START ADDRESS
40A5 8D4204 1680          STA  OSADR       ;OF SCROLL WINDOW
40A8 AD1B04 1690          LDA  SCRLADR+1   ;INTO LOCAL AREA
40AB 8D4304 1700          STA  OSADR+1
40AE B8   1710            CLV              ;JUMP OVER BUCKET BRIGADE BRANCHES
40AF 5013 1720            BVC  OK6         ;AND DON'T SUBTRACT EX2
          1730 ;
          1740 BBINIT
40B1 D067 1750            BNE  INIT
          1760 BBEXIT
40B3 509F 1770            BVC  BBEXIT2
          1780 ;
          1790 OK2
40B5 AD4404 1800          LDA  CPOS        ;SUBTRACT THE EX2 WE ADDED EARLIER
40B8 18   1810            CLC
40B9 ED5104 1820          SBC  EX2
40BC 8D4404 1830          STA  CPOS
40BF B003 1840            BCS  OK6
40C1 CE4504 1850          DEC  CPOS+1
          1860 OK6
40C4 AD4204 1870          LDA  OSADR
40C7 18   1880            CLC
40C8 6D5004 1890          ADC  EX1         ;ADD STEP TO SCREEN ADDRESS
40CB 8D4204 1900          STA  OSADR       ;AND MOVE INTO EX3 AND EX4
40CE 8D5204 1910          STA  EX3
40D1 9003 1920            BCC  OK3
40D3 EE4304 1930          INC  OSADR+1
          1940 ;
          1950 OK3
40D6 AD4304 1960          LDA  OSADR+1
40D9 8D5304 1970          STA  EX4
40DC A003 1980            LDY  #$03        ;SKIP OVER FIRST THREE DL INSTRUCTIONS
```

```
            1990 LOOP
40DE B1E0  2000         LDA  (ZERO),Y   ;GET BYTE IN DISPLAY LIST
40E0 C941  2010         CMP  #$41       ;JVB? (END OF DLIST?)
40E2 F029  2020         BEQ  DONE       ;YES, QUIT
           2030 ;
40E4 2950  2040         AND  #$50       ;HSCROLL OR LMS BITS SET?
40E6 F020  2050         BEQ  NOCHANGE   ;NO, FORGET IT
40E8 2910  2060         AND  #$10       ;HSCROLL SET?
40EA F01A  2070         BEQ  NSCROLL    ;NO, SKIP OVER NEXT TWO BYTES
40EC C8    2080         INY             ;NEXT 2 BYTES ARE MEMORY ADDRESS OF CURRENT LINE
40ED AD5204 2090        LDA  EX3        ;MOVE SCREEN ADDRESS
40F0 91E0  2100         STA  (ZERO),Y   ;INTO DISPLAY LIST
40F2 18    2110         CLC
40F3 6D1C04 2120        ADC  SCRLLEN    ;AND ADD SCRLLENGTH
40F6 8D5204 2130        STA  EX3
40F9 C8    2140         INY
40FA AD5304 2150        LDA  EX4        ;DO HIBYTE
40FD 91E0  2160         STA  (ZERO),Y
40FF 6D1D04 2170        ADC  SCRLLEN+1
```
CLK-SCROLL.ASM;v01.09-810719,820619
Interrupt-driven Screen Scroller

```
4102 8D5304 2180        STA  EX4
           2190 ;
4105 AD    2200         .BYTE $AD       ;"LDA ABSOLUTE" OPCODE SKIPS NEXT 2 BYTES
           2210 ;
           2220 NSCROLL
4106 C8    2230         INY
4107 C8    2240         INY
           2250 ;
           2260 NOCHANGE
4108 C8    2270         INY
4109 D0D3  2280         BNE  LOOP       ;ALWAYS (DISPLAY LIST MUSTN'T BE LONGER THAN 256 BYTES)
           2290 ;
           2300 BBEXIT3
410B 50A6  2310         BVC  BBEXIT
           2320 ;
           2330 DONE
410D AD5904 2340        LDA  ZSAVE      ;RESTORE ZERO PAGE TEMPS
4110 85E0  2350         STA  ZERO
4112 AD5A04 2360        LDA  ZSAVE+1
4115 85E1  2370         STA  ZERO+1
4117 B8    2380         CLV
4118 5099  2390         BVC  BBEXIT
           2400 ;
           2410 INIT
411A A980  2420         LDA  #$80
411C 8D0504 2430        STA  SCRLINIT   ;SET INIT BYTE TO "ON"
411F AD1E04 2440        LDA  SCRLCLK    ;SET SCROLL POINTERS TO LEFT OF SCREEN
4122 8D4604 2450        STA  FPOS
4125 A900  2460         LDA  #$00
4127 8D4404 2470        STA  CPOS
412A 8D4504 2480        STA  CPOS+1
412D AD1A04 2490        LDA  SCRLADR    ;MOVE SCREEN ADDRESS TO LOCAL AREA
```

```
4130 8D4204 2500          STA   OSADR
4133 AD1B04 2510          LDA   SCRLADR+1
4136 8D4304 2520          STA   OSADR+1
           2530 LEAVE
4139 B8    2540           CLV
413A 50CF  2550           BVC   BBEXIT3    ;LEAVE.
           2560 ;
413C       2570           .END


           10 ;    DLIROUT
           20 ;
           30 ; COPYRIGHT (C) 1982 BY DAVID FOX AND MITCHELL WAITE
           40 ;
0000       0100           .TITLE "CLK-DLIROUT.ASM;v01.06-810806,820619"
0000       0110           .PAGE "DLI Color Changer"
           0120 ;
           0130 ; BY COREY L. KOSAK
           0140 ;
           0150 ; B=$4000,FREL
           0160 ;
4000       0170 BASE    =      $4000
           0180 ;
0000       0190           x=     $400
           0200 ;
           0210 ; CASBUF DATABASE EQUATES
           0220 ;
0400       0230 PMBAS   x=     x+1       ;HIBYTE OF PLAYER MISSILE AREA (LOBYTE EQUALS 0)
0401       0240 PMBUF   x=     x+2       ;ADDRESS OF 128 BYTE BUFFER (FOR PMOVER)
0403       0250 ANIMINIT x=    x+1       ;INIT LOCATION FOR ANIMATE
0404       0260 AUTOINIT x=    x+1       ;INIT LOCATION FOR AUTOMOVE
0405       0270 SCRLINIT x=    x+1       ;INIT LOCATION FOR SCROLLER
0406       0280 HPLR    x=     x+4       ;PLAYERS 0-3 X COORDINATE (FOR PMOVER)
040A       0290 VPLR    x=     x+4       ;PLRS 0-3 Y COORD (FOR PMOVER)
040E       0300 RATE    x=     x+4       ;PLRS 0-3 RATE (FOR ANIMATE)
0412       0310 FLSTPTR x=     x+8       ;PLRS 0-3 FRAME LIST POINTERS (FOR ANIMATE)
041A       0320 SCRLADR x=     x+2       ;SCREEN ADDRESS (FOR SCROLL)
041C       0330 SCRLLEN x=     x+2       ;LINE LENGTH OF SCROLLED AREA (FOR SCROLL)
041E       0340 SCRLCLK x=     x+1       ;COLOR CLOCKS IN SCREEN BYTE (FOR SCROLL)
041F       0350 SCRLSTEP x=    x+1       ;SCROLL STEP (FOR SCROLL)
0420       0360 MOVERATE x=    x+4       ;PLRS 0-3 HORIZONTAL STEP (FOR AUTOMOVE)
0424       0370 DLIADR  x=     x+2       ;ADDRESS OF COLOR TABLE
           0380 ;
           0390 ;xLOCALx DATABASE EQUATES
           0400 ; THESE LOCATIONS ARE xLOCALx TO THE ROUTINES
           0410 ; AND SHOULD xNOTx BE MODIFIED BY THE HOST PROGRAM
           0420 ;
0426       0430 OOX     x=     x+4       ;PLRS 0-3 X COORDINATE
042A       0440 OOY     x=     x+4       ;PLRS 0-3 Y COORD
042E       0450 ORATEO  x=     x+4       ;PLRS 0-3 FRAME CHANGE RATE
0432       0460 OADRO   x=     x+8       ;PLRS 0-3 FRAME LIST ADDRESS
043A       0470 TIMRO   x=     x+4       ;PLRS 0-3 COUNTDOWN TIMERS (HOW MANY JIFFIES UNTIL FRAME CHANGE)
043E       0480 POSO    x=     x+4       ;PLRS 0-3 FRAME LIST POSITION
0442       0490 OSADR   x=     x+2       ;SCREEN ADDRESS FOR SCROLLER
```

```
0444        0500 CPOS     x=   x+2          ;COARSE SCROLL POSITION FOR SCROLLER (0-LINELEN)
0446        0510 FPOS     x=   x+1          ;FINE SCROLL POSITION (0-7)
0447        0520 OXSTEP0  x=   x+4          ;PLRS 0-3 HORIZONTAL STEP
044B        0530 DLIPOS   x=   x+1          ;CURRENT POSITION IN COLOR TABLE
044C        0540 PM1      x=   x+1          ;4 LOCATIONS RESERVED FOR PMOVER
044D        0550 PM2      x=   x+1
044E        0560 PM3      x=   x+1
044F        0570 PM4      x=   x+1
0450        0580 EX1      x=   x+1          ;4 LOCATIONS RESERVED FOR ANIMATE, AUTOMOVE, SCROLL, AND MFILL
0451        0590 EX2      x=   x+1
0452        0600 EX3      x=   x+1
0453        0610 EX4      x=   x+1
CLK-DLIROUT.ASM;v01.06-810806,820619
DLI Color Changer

0454        0620 PMSAVE   x=   x+5          ;ZERO PAGE SAVE AREA FOR PMOVER
0459        0630 ZSAVE    x=   x+4          ;ZERO PAGE SAVE AREA FOR ALL OTHER ROUTINES
045D        0640 DLI1     x=   x+1
045E        0650 DLI2     x=   x+1
            0660 ;
D018        0670 COLPF2   =    $D018
D019        0680 COLPF3   =    $D019
D01A        0690 COLBAK   =    $D01A
E462        0700 XITVBV   =    $E462
D40A        0710 WSYNC    =    $D40A
            0720 ;
00E0        0730 ZERO     =    $E0
            0740 ;
045F        0750          x=   BASE
            0760 ;
            0770 START
4000 B8     0780          CLV
4001 500A   0790          BVC  DLIDO        ;SKIP OVER VBLANK EXIT ROUTINE
            0800 ;
            0810 EXIT
4003 4C62E4 0820          JMP  XITVBV
            0830 ;
            0840 VBINT
4006 A900   0850          LDA  #$00         ;ON VBLANK, ZERO THE COLOR TABLE POINTER
4008 8D4B04 0860          STA  DLIPOS
400B F0F6   0870          BEQ  EXIT         ;LEAVE
            0880 ;
            0890 DLIDO
400D 48     0900          PHA               ;SAVE A,X, & Y ON STACK
400E 8A     0910          TXA
400F 48     0920          PHA
4010 98     0930          TYA
4011 48     0940          PHA
            0950 ;
4012 A5E0   0960          LDA  ZERO         ;SAVE ZERO PAGE LOCS
4014 8D5D04 0970          STA  DLI1
4017 A5E1   0980          LDA  ZERO+1
4019 8D5E04 0990          STA  DLI2
```

```
401C AD2404 1000          LDA  DLIADR      ;MOVE ADDRESS OF COLOR TABLE
401F 85E0   1010          STA  ZERO        ;INTO POINTER
4021 AD2504 1020          LDA  DLIADR+1
4024 85E1   1030          STA  ZERO+1
            1040 ;
4026 AC4B04 1050          LDY  DLIPOS      ;GET COLOR TABLE POINTER INTO Y-REG
4029 B1E0   1060          LDA  (ZERO),Y    ;GET COLOR
402B 48     1070          PHA              ;A=COLPF2
            1080 ;
402C C8     1090          INY              ;GET THE NEXT COLOR
402D B1E0   1100          LDA  (ZERO),Y
402F AA     1110          TAX              ;X=COLPF3
            1120 ;
4030 C8     1130          INY              ;AND THE NEXT
```

CLK-DLIROUT.ASM;v01.06-810806,820619
DLI Color Changer

```
4031 B1E0   1140          LDA  (ZERO),Y
4033 C8     1150          INY
4034 8C4B04 1160          STY  DLIPOS      ;STORE NEW COLOR TABLE POINTER
4037 A8     1170          TAY              ;Y=COLBAK
4038 68     1180          PLA              ;A=COLPF2
4039 EA     1190          NOP              ;PUT 18 CYCLE DELAY IN FOR
403A EA     1200          NOP              ;TIMING PROBLEM
403B EA     1210          NOP
403C EA     1220          NOP
403D EA     1230          NOP
403E EA     1240          NOP
403F EA     1250          NOP
4040 EA     1260          NOP
4041 EA     1270          NOP
            1280 ;
4042 8D0AD4 1290          STA  WSYNC       ;WAIT FOR HORIZONTAL SYNC
4045 8D18D0 1300          STA  COLPF2      ;QUICK! STORE THOSE COLORS!
4048 8E19D0 1310          STX  COLPF3
404B 8C1AD0 1320          STY  COLBAK
            1330 ;
404E AD5D04 1340          LDA  DLI1        ;RESTORE ZERO PAGE LOCS
4051 85E0   1350          STA  ZERO
4053 AD5E04 1360          LDA  DLI2
4056 85E1   1370          STA  ZERO+1
            1380 ;
4058 68     1390          PLA              ;AND REGISTERS FROM STACK
4059 A8     1400          TAY
405A 68     1410          PLA
405B AA     1420          TAX
405C 68     1430          PLA
405D 40     1440          RTI              ;AND RETURN FROM WHENCE.
            1450 ;
405E        1460          .END
```

Appendix G (Courtesy of ATARI)

ATARI Hardware and Shadow Registers

HARDWARE REGISTER				OS SHADOW		
		Address			**Address**	
Name	**Description**	**Hex**	**Dec**	**Name**	**Hex**	**Dec**
ALLPOT	Read 8 line Pot Port State	D208	53768			
AUDC1	Audio Channel 1 Control	D201	53761			
AUDC2	Audio Channel 2 Control	D203	53763			
AUDC3	Audio Channel 3 Control	D205	53765			
AUDC4	Audio Channel 4 Control	D207	53767			
AUDCTL	Audio Control	D208	53768			
AUDF1	Audio Channel 1 Frequency	D200	53760			
AUDF2	Audio Channel 2 Frequency	D202	53762			
AUDF3	Audio Channel 3 Frequency	D204	53764			
AUDF4	Audio Channel 4 Frequency	D206	53766			
CHACTL	Character Control	D401	54273	CHART	2F3	755
CHBASE	Character Base Address	D409	54281	CHBAS	2F4	756
COLBK	Color Luminance of Background	D01A	53274	COLOR4	2C8	712
COLPF0	Color Luminance of Playfield 0	D016	53270	COLOR0	2C4	708
COLPF1	Color Luminance of Playfield 1	D017	53271	COLOR1	2C5	709
COLPF2	Color Luminance of Playfield 2	D018	53272	COLOR2	2C6	710
COLPF3	Color Luminance of Playfield 3	D019	53273	COLOR3	2C7	711
COLPM0	Color Luminance of Player-Missile 0	D012	53266	PCOLR0	2C0	704
COLPM1	Color Luminance of Player-Missile 1	D013	53267	PCOLR1	2C1	705
COLPM2	Color Luminance of Player-Missile 2	D014	53268	PCOLR2	2C2	706
COLPM3	Color Luminance of Player-Missile 3	D015	53269	PCOLR3	2C3	707
CONSOL	Console Switch Port	D01F	53279	Set to 8 during VBLANK		
DLISTH	Display List Pointer (high byte)	D403	54275	SDLSTH	231	561
DLISTL	Display List Pointer (low byte)	D402	54274	SDLSTL	230	560
DMACTL	Direct Memory Access (DMA) Control	D400	54272	SDMCTL	22F	559
GRACTL	Graphic Control	D01D	53277			
GRAFM	Graphics for all Missiles	D011	53265			
GRAFP0	Graphics for Player 0	D00D	53261			
GRAFP1	Graphics for Player 1	D00E	53262			
GRAFP2	Graphics for Player 2	D00F	53263			
GRAFP3	Graphics for Player 3	D010	53264			
HITCLR	Collision Clear	D01E	53278			
HPOSM0	Horizontal Position of Missile 0	D004	53252			
HPOSM1	Horizontal Position of Missile 1	D005	53253			
HPOSM2	Horizontal Position of Missile 2	D006	53254			

HARDWARE REGISTER				OS SHADOW		
		Address			**Address**	
Name	**Description**	**Hex**	**Dec**	**Name**	**Hex**	**Dec**
HPOSM3	Horizontal Position of Missile 3	D007	53255			
HPOSP0	Horizontal Position of Player 0	D000	53248			
HPOSP1	Horizontal Position of Player 1	D001	53249			
HPOSP2	Horizontal Position of Player 2	D002	53250			
HPOSP3	Horizontal Position of Player 3	D003	53251			
HSCROL	Horizontal Scroll	D404	54276			
IRQEN	Interrupt Request (IRQ) Enable	D20E	53774	POKMSK	10	16
IRQST	IRQ Status	D20E	53774			
KBCODE	Keyboard Code	D209	53769	CH	2FC	764
M0PF	Missile 0 to Playfield Collisions	D000	53248			
M0PL	Missile 0 to Player Collisions	D008	53256			
M1PF	Missile 1 to Playfield Collisions	D001	53249			
M1PL	Missile 1 to Player Collisions	D009	53257			
M2PF	Missile 2 to Playfield Collisions	D002	53250			
M2PL	Missile 2 to Player Collisions	D00A	53258			
M3PF	Missile 3 to Playfield Collisions	D003	53251			
M3PL	Missile 3 to Player Collisions	D00B	53259			
NMIEN	Non-Maskable Interrupt (NMI) Enable	D40E	54286	Set to $40 by IRQ code		
NMIRES	NMI Reset	D40F	54287	written to by NMI code		
NMIST	NMI Status	D40F	54287	read by NMI code		
P0PF	Player 0 to Playfield Collisions	D004	53252			
P0PL	Player 0 to Player Collisions	D00C	53260			
P1PF	Player 1 to Playfield Collisions	D005	53253			
P1PL	Player 1 to Player Collisions	D00D	53261			
P2PF	Player 2 to Playfield Collisions	D006	53254			
P2PL	Player 2 to Player Collisions	D00E	53262			
P3PF	Player 3 to Playfield Collisions	D007	53255			
P3PL	Player 3 to Player Collisions	D00F	53263			
PACTL	Port A Control	D302	54018	Set to $3C by IRQ Code		
PAL	PAL/NTSC indicator	D014	53268			
PBCTL	Port B Control	D303	54019	Set to $3C by IRQ Code		
PENH	Light Pen Horizontal Position	D40C	54284	LPENH	234	564
PENV	Light Pen Vertical Position	D40D	54285	LPENV	235	565
PMBASE	Player Missile Base Address	D407	54279			
PORTA	Port A	D300	54016	STICK0,1	278,279	632,633
PORTB	Port B	D301	54017	STICK2,3	27A,27B	634,635
POT0	Pot 0	D200	53760	PADDL0	270	624
POT1	Pot 1	D201	53761	PADDL1	271	625
POT2	Pot 2	D202	53762	PADDL2	272	626
POT3	Pot 3	D203	53763	PADDL3	273	627

POT4	Pot 4	D204	53764	PADDL4	274	628
POT5	Pot 5	D205	53765	PADDL5	275	629
POT6	Pot 6	D206	53766	PADDL6	276	630
POT7	Pot 7 (right paddle controller)	D207	53767	PADDL7	277	631
POTGO	Start POT Scan Sequence	D20B	53771	Written during VBLANK		
PRIOR	Priority Select	D01B	53275	GPRIOR	26F	623
RANDOM	Random Number Generator	D20A	53770			
SERIN	Serial Port Input	D20E	53774			
SEROUT	Serial Port Output	D20D	53773			
SIZEM	Sizes for all missiles	D00C	53260			
SIZEP0	Size of Player 0	D008	53256			
SIZEP1	Size of Player 1	D009	53257			
SIZEP2	Size of Player 2	D00A	53258			
SIZEP3	Size of Player 3	D00B	53259			
SKCTL	Serial Port Control	D20F	53775	SSKCTL	232	562
SKREST	Reset Serial Port Status (SKSTAT)	D20A	53770			
SKSTAT	Serial Port Status	D20F	53775			
STIMER	Start Timer	D209	53769			
TRIG0	Joystick Controller Trigger 0	D010	53264	STRIG0	284	644
TRIG1	Joystick Controller Trigger 1	D011	53265	STRIG1	285	645
TRIG2	Joystick Controller Trigger 2	D012	53266	STRIG2	286	646
TRIG3	Joystick Controller Trigger 3	D013	53267	STRIG3	287	647
VCOUNT	Vertical Line Counter	D40B	54283			
VDELAY	Vertical Delay	D01C	53276			
VSCROL	Vertical Scroll	D405	54277			
WSYNC	Wait for Horizontal Sync	D40A	54282	Used by keyboard click routine		

Appendix H

Graphics Memory Map Modes

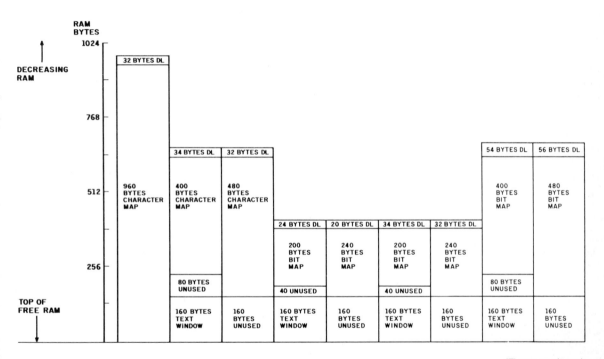

(Figure continues)

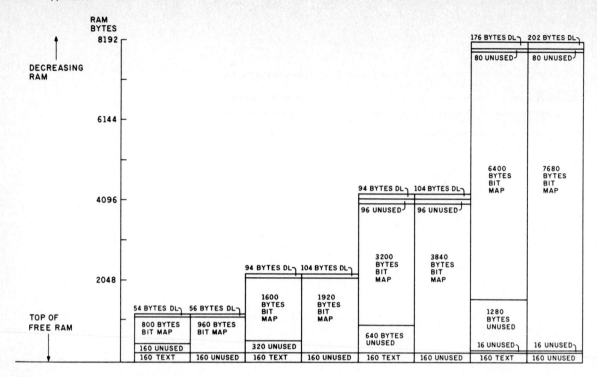

Figure H.1: Graphics memory map modes.

Index

More BYTE Books Coauthored by Mitchell Waite

This is just one of four books coauthored by Mitchell Waite and published by BYTE/McGraw-Hill. You'll find the same friendly, easy-to-follow style and user-centered approach in each of the titles listed below. If you enjoyed and learned from this book, you'll certainly find the others in the Waite series equally helpful.

APPLE BACKPACK: Humanized Programming in BASIC, by Scot Kamins and Mitchell Waite. This book aids all computer users by establishing the "user-friendly" approach to programming in BASIC. The authors present concrete methods for developing programs that are not only easy to use, but also hard to misuse. Specific topics include clear screen formatting, crashproofing programs, developing built-in verifications and validations, presenting directions on the video display, and writing helpful, thorough documentation. Appendices feature an educational game program embodying the authors' user-centered approach and a humanized telephone-message-recording program with model documentation, both with complete Applesoft BASIC listings.

8086/8088 16-bit Microprocessor Primer, by Christopher Morgan and Mitchell Waite. The new, vastly more powerful 16-bit microprocessors are destined to become the basis for the next generation of personal computers, and this book provides the understanding you need to harness this remarkable advance in technology. Using a comfortable, down-to-earth approach, the authors detail the design and capabilities of the Intel 8086/8088 16-bit microprocessor. Also examined are two 16-bit "coprocessors," the 8087 Numeric Data Processor and the 8089 I/O Processor. In addition, the authors survey the current scene in 16-bit technology, reviewing software and products such as the new 8088-based IBM Personal Computer.

Word Processing Primer, by Mitchell Waite and Julie Arca. The first book of its kind, *Word Processing Primer* focuses on the newly available microcomputer-based text-editing programs. The authors begin with a review of the field, giving a working knowledge of the equipment and programs that make text editors work. A section on text formatting shows you how to control the final appearance of your printed copy, and a review of ancillary software, such as programs that check grammar or spelling and those that generate indexes or personalized form letters, shows the potential for customized applications. The book goes on to tell you what to look for when choosing a word processor, and a mini-catalog compares features, capabilities, limitations, and prices of many of the most popular pieces of software and equipment.

ANIMATION MAGIC

Programs From COMPUTER ANIMATION PRIMER

Animation Magic is a two-sided diskette containing all of the animation demonstration programs and Assembly Language Source code from Part Two of this book. The programs are an excellent collection which illustrates the power of the ATARI Home Computer. Included are the examples covering Character Set Animation, Color Register Animation, Player-Missile Graphics, Fine Scrolling, and Display List Interrupts.

Many of the programs make use of special "black box" machine language routines. By black box, we mean that it is not necessary to understand how the routines work. Just plug in the values and call the routine to move Players across the screen, scroll a background scene, or allow the use of many extra colors on the display.

Animation Magic is ideal for the programmer who doesn't have the time or inclination to enter the pages of BASIC listings into the computer. The source code for the black box routines, developed with the ATARI Assembler-Editor cartridge, can be modified for custom applications. Any of the programs or routines can be incorporated into your own programs which can then be marketed. Only an acknowledgment at the beginning of the program and in the documentation is required.

When the programs on the disk are used in conjunction with this book's clear and thorough explanations, they form an excellent tutorial. We think you will find the programs an interesting and efficient way to learn how to maximize the use of your ATARI Home Computer.

To order *Animation Magic,* simply use the form on this page. You may send a check or money order for $19.95 plus $3.00 shipping and handling payable to Adventure International, or you may use your VISA or MasterCard. Mail to:

Adventure International
P.O. Box 3435
Longwood, FL 32750

or you may order directly by calling Adventure International toll free at 1-800-327-7172 (in Florida call 1-862-6917). Ask for *Animation Magic,* catalog number 52-0223.

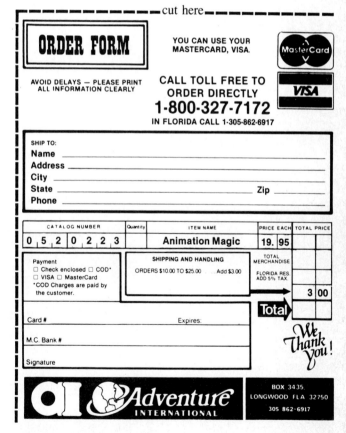